# AMERICA IN OUR TIME

# AMERICA IN OUR TIME

☆ ☆ ☆

## Godfrey Hodgson

VINTAGE BOOKS
A DIVISION OF RANDOM HOUSE
NEW YORK

FIRST VINTAGE BOOKS EDITION, February 1978

Grateful acknowledgment is made for permission to use excerpts from the
following copyrighted material:

Lyrics from "Mother's Little Helper," by Mick Jagger and Keith Richard. Copyright © 1966 ABKCO Music, Inc. All rights reserved. International copyright secured. Reprinted by permission.

Lines from the poem "Howl," which appears in *Howl & Other Poems*,
copyright © 1956, 1959, by Allen Ginsberg; lines from the poem
"Mescaline," which appears in *Kaddish & Other Poems*, copyright ©
1961 by Allen Ginsberg. Reprinted by permission of City Lights.

Lyrics from "The End," words by Jim Morrison. Copyright © 1967
Doors Music Co. Used by permission of the author and publisher.

Lines from the poem "The Second Coming," which appears in COL-
LECTED POEMS, by William Butler Yeats. Copyright 1924 by Mac-
millan Publishing Co., Inc., renewed 1952 by Bertha Georgie Yeats.
Reprinted by permission of Macmillan Publishing Co., Inc., and A. P.
Watt & Son Ltd.

Lyrics from "Mr. Tambourine Man," copyright © 1964 Warner Bros.
Inc., "The Times They Are A-Changin'," copyright © 1963 Warner
Bros. Inc., and "Blowin' in the Wind," copyright © 1962 Warner
Bros. Inc., all three songs by Bob Dylan. Reprinted by permission of
Warner Bros. Music.

*Library of Congress Cataloging in Publication Data*

Hodgson, Godfrey.
America in our time.

Bibliography: p.
Includes index.
1. United States—Social conditions—1960-
2. United States—Civilization—1945-
3. United States—Politics and government—1945-
4. United States—Foreign relations—1945-
I. Title.
[HN59.H59 1978]     309.1′73′092     77-14278
ISBN 0-394-72517-4

*For Pierre, Francis, Jessica and Laura*

# CONTENTS

# PREFACE

"Such an unhappily sensitive community surely never existed in this world," wrote the English actress Fanny Kemble, more than a hundred years ago, of the Americans of her time. "The vengeance with which they visit people for saying they don't admire or like them would be truly terrible," she went on with a little toss of the head, "if the said people were but as mortally afraid of abuse as they seem to be. . . . I live myself in daily expectation of martyrdom."

Fanny Kemble was one of the most remarkable women of the nineteenth century—a great actress, a gifted writer, a courageous crusader against slavery. But she was also something of a termagant. Thackeray, one of the most jovial of men, once confessed that he had learned to "admire, but not to endure" her.

Even so—making all due allowance for Miss Kemble's bloody-mindedness—it is hard to believe she was writing about the same people. Unhappy and sensitive the United States may have been at times over the past twenty years. But surely no society has so systematically; so doggedly; almost, it sometimes seemed, so masochistically; invited the criticism of foreigners.

Unlike Miss Kemble, I do not fear martyrdom: I hope this book makes plain that I admire the United States too much, and like too many individual Americans, for that. But since I have been critical of some beliefs held by most Americans, and of most of the beliefs of some Americans, let me make this defense: that everything I know about the United States has been taught me by Americans and that few of my judgments are not shared by at least some Americans.

Those who have taken part in my education—consciously or unconsciously, through the written word or in conversation—over the twenty-one years since I first arrived, on board the *Queen Mary*, in New York (where, my visa stating that I was a student of history, I was kindly but firmly interrogated on my historical knowledge by an elderly cop), are too numerous to list here, and since it would be tedious to list all even of the essential contributors to my education, I will name none and limit myself to thanking all.

But there are others who have helped me in more concrete ways, and to them I must express my gratitude individually.

My very heartfelt thanks, therefore, are due to the English-Speaking Union of Philadelphia, which enabled me to attend the University of Pennsylvania as a graduate student from 1955 to 1956; to David Astor, editor of *The Observer* of London, for sending me to Washington as his correspondent from 1962 to 1965; to Harold Evans, the editor, and Bruce Page, one of the managing editors, of the London *Sunday Times*, for allowing me to work in the United States so often since 1968, and to Robert Ducas and the rest of the *Sunday Times*'s staff in New York for a thousand generosities; to my friend the late Hal Scharlatt, of E. P. Dutton, who originally commissioned this book; to Benjamin H. Read and the trustees, staff and fellows of the Woodrow Wilson International Center for Scholars, in Washington, for all their help while I was a fellow there in 1972–73; to Professor Howard Higman and Professor John Murphy of the University of Colorado; to Dean Edwin Bayley of the School of Journalism at the University of California at Berkeley; to Robert Manning and Michael Janeway and the other editors at the *Atlantic Monthly*; to Richard Holbrooke of *Foreign Policy* and Thomas L. Hughes of the Carnegie Endowment for International Peace; to Pat Watters and the staff of the Southern Regional Council, in Atlanta; to Al Horne and Bill McPherson and many, many other writers and editors at the Washington *Post*; to my unique research assistant, Mark O'Neill; to my agents, Michael Sissons and Peter Matson, and their colleagues at A. D. Peters in London and at the Harold Matson Company in New York; to George Crile, for helping me find my way around in Gary, Indiana, and to Professor Ed Lurie, of the University of Delaware, for getting me launched in Detroit; and to five friends in particular whose contribution to my education has been so vast, and whose generosity has been so abundant, that I must name them even at the risk of being individious: Frederick G. Dutton, Harry C. McPherson, Daniel Patrick Moynihan, Marcus G. Raskin, and Laurence M. Stern.

Finally, let me express my thanks, in no perfunctory way, to my editors at Doubleday. They found me very much in the condition of the man mentioned in the tenth chapter of the Gospel according to St. Luke, and behaved not just as good editors, but like Good Samaritans: Sam Vaughan, Sandy Richardson, Betty Prashker, Susan Watt, and Mike Ossias.

# PART I

# 1

## Hyperion

"... that was, to this, / Hyperion to a satyr. ..."
William Shakespeare, *Hamlet*

Historical time seems to have accelerated in America.

By the time children graduate from high school, the year in which they went into first grade seems as remote as some prehistoric age of inno-cence: before the Fall. Once, the essential circumstances and assumptions of life changed so slowly that one could speak of many generations living and dying in the same age. Now, events, non-events, fashions, and moods succeed one another so rapidly that an age can be over in half the length of a biological generation. Already, the twelve years from the inauguration of John Kennedy, in January 1961, to Richard Nixon's second inaugura-tion, in 1973, have taken on the shape and unity of an age. And the pace is unrelenting. As the United States celebrates its two-hundredth birthday, in 1976, the hopes that President Nixon expressed in his 1973 inaugural speech have been soaked in bitter irony by constitutional crisis and con-tinuing national disunity.

Looking back at the years from Dallas to Watergate, there can be few Americans who do not agree that the age of Kennedy and Nixon has been a time of lost hopes. Making the comparison not between two men but between the climates of two periods, it is hard not to echo Hamlet's horrified sense of moral retrogression: "Look here, upon this picture, and on this. . . . / . . . that was, to this, / Hyperion to a satyr."

The presidency is so much the master symbol of the public mood and national aspirations that this sense of loss is best measured by one fact and two contrasting images. The fact is that each of the three men who have been elected to the presidency since 1960 has been destroyed by it. The contrasts are those evoked by the words Dallas and Watergate. All nations live by myths. Any nation is the sum of the consciousness of its people: the chaotic infinitude of the experience and perceptions of millions alive and dead. Merely in order to communicate with itself, to function as a conscious organism at all, a nation must distill and simplify this chaos into the ideas and slogans of public debate and politics. One of the essential agents in this crystallization of the national consciousness is myth.

Just as a film director, by optically freezing a single frame, can cause a particular image to etch itself into the viewer's mind, so myth can fix in the national mind a tableau that is instinctively felt to sum up a general truth.

There are old myths which still have the power to express living parts of the American historical experience: Washington at Valley Forge, Lee at Appomattox, John Brown at Harpers Ferry. But in a nation as full of vigor and self-awareness as the United States, new myths are still being created. In a nation that is also deeply divided, not all of these myths, however potent, have universal validity. There are Americans for whom the moon landing epitomizes the essential national qualities: adventure, technological prowess, the drive to go on further than anyone has gone before. There are other Americans for whom the imprisonment and death of George Jackson express a more relevant truth. One man's myth indeed may be, in a society as deeply split as the United States, another man's obscenity.

There is one contemporary American myth, however, that does have an almost universal magic. The force of it is conveyed in two pictures that still have undiminished poignancy.

In the first frame, a youthful President, hatless in the cold air, rededicates a new generation to whom the torch of idealism has been handed.

In the second, the same head is blown to pieces by a bullet.

The Kennedy myth has been so potent because it is a myth of hope shattered by absurd, meaningless death. It thus inverts the redemptive promise of the most universal and powerful of all human myths, in which the blameless king dies so that the people may live.

For contemporary Americans, the assassination was specially charged with tragic meaning. Their culture had come to stress achievement before almost all else. For a people who almost worshiped achievement, to see a leader whose personal and family history were an epic of achievement killed by a loser, a nobody, was peculiarly disturbing.

This was the death of a democratic prince, but still the death of a prince. The President had always been the symbolic as well as the executive head of the nation. In 1963, after thirty years of crisis, the mounting intensity of the people's need for leadership had invested the office with the emotional magic of an elective kingship.

John Kennedy had been elected by a slender margin. But, especially after the Cuban missile crisis of October 1962, his stature in the public mind had risen. Many Americans identified with him as the symbol of their own aspirations both for their country and for themselves. The imagination of some had been caught by the austere vision of national duty and national destiny that was one element in Kennedy's complex personality. More were captivated by his chic, his wit, his glamour. Above all, John F. Kennedy appealed to a sense of upward mobility, individual and national.

A great many Americans had come up in the world by the beginning of the 1960s, and a great many more hoped to do so. Many were not quite sure how the good life should be lived; the Kennedys seemed to know. The United States, too, had come up in the world; and John Kennedy seemed to conduct himself as the leader not just of a very rich and powerful country in a hostile world but of an imperial nation with time on its side, the center and the standard of civilization.

Even those who in no way identified with him could still find him a fitting embodiment of their country. There were plenty of people who didn't particularly like his politics, who doubted whether they would vote for his re-election, yet who still felt, when he died, that something of them died with him.

In life, the President had been only beginning to establish his stature. In death, he became overnight the protomartyr of something akin to a religion of national unity and greatness. The National Opinion Research Center found that, even in the group that was most hostile to him, "anti-Kennedy Southerners," 62 per cent felt his death as "the loss of someone very close and dear." Kennedy had been elected by 49.7 per cent of the popular vote. By June 1963, 59 per cent of those surveyed claimed to have voted for him in 1960. Immediately after the assassination, this posthumous landslide swelled to 65 per cent. In November 1960, one out of every two voters had chosen Kennedy; three years later, two out of every three believed that they had!

Before the assassination, it seemed that the coming years, the age of Kennedy, would be—as Robert Frost put it in lines specially written for the inauguration in 1961—an Augustan age "of poetry and power." The test-ban treaty and the peaceful March on Washington in the summer of 1963 seemed to confirm his promise of imperial splendor in the world, matched by tranquillity and social progress at home.

The circumstances of the crime contributed, as much as the person-

ality of the victim, to the shock; and fear was involved, as well as the loss
of hopes.

There was the fact that it happened in Dallas, a city seething with
the anger of the Right against the Supreme Court's desegregation decision. That aroused all the suspicions of liberals, including the oldest
specter of disunity, the memory of a nation divided between North and
South.

It was generally assumed—for example, even by Chief Justice Earl
Warren—that the murder was somehow caused by this right-wing hatred.
When the Warren Commission later established that Lee Harvey Oswald
had acted alone but that his affiliations had been with Communists rather
than anti-Communists, the opposite suspicions of the Right were
strengthened.

The assassination was like a crack in the earth in volcanic country.
Fumes of suspicion vented to the surface, reminding people of forces they
would have preferred to forget: the irrationality, hatred, and violence that
lay beneath the glittering structure of liberal, imperial America. In retrospect, people looked back to Friday, November 22, 1963, as the end of a
time of hope, the beginning of a time of troubles.

In January 1961, *Camelot* was still a musical.

It was playing at the Majestic, on West Forty-fourth Street, with
Richard Burton and Julie Andrews.

*Time* magazine, that month, chose fifteen American scientists as its
collective men of the year. "Statesmen and savants, builders and even
priests," intoned *Time*, "are their servants. . . . Science is at the apogee of
its power."

Synthetic fabrics were the fashion news that month. Dacron and
Lycra in hot pinks and purples, *The New Yorker*'s fashion pundit reported, were just the thing to wear with the bouffant hair styles that Mr.
Kenneth of Lilly Daché had just invented for Mrs. Kennedy and that
women of all ages were rushing to imitate.

The aerosol sprays with which these ponderous helmets were
lacquered into place, it was said, were a "spin-off" from the space program.
(The crucial patent belonged, in fact, to one Robert Abplanalp, the particular friend in later days of Richard Nixon.) It hardly mattered whether
that was literally true. It expressed something most Americans believed instinctively: that the wonders of the American kitchen and the technological might of America's armed forces were profoundly interconnected;
that Americans lived better because of the strength of American industry
and the inventiveness of American research. Knowledge, it was assumed,
was not only power but happiness as well.

It was a time of faith in science and technology, in technique and artifice, in organized innovation and orderly change. The President-elect talked about the New Frontier, giving popular currency to an earlier coinage of the intellectuals. It was a brilliant slogan, because it combined the promise of restless adventure with reassuring undertones of tried and true American tradition.

That was the paradox. For all its belief in innovation, American society at the beginning of the 1960s was still conservative. People wanted change; they did not want to be changed. Or, rather, they changed their clothes, their cars or their homes more easily than they changed their assumptions, their attitudes or their beliefs.

"What will cars be like in 1980?" a journalist asked the head of Chrysler's product-planning team. He answered, much the same as in 1960, but of course longer, wider, more powerful. Would we really still be groping for the dipstick to check the oil in twenty years' time? the reporter persisted. That would depend on cost: "In our business, the economic barrier is the big thing separating dream from reality."

The most exciting dream of all in January 1961 was the possibility that the economic barrier itself need not be a reality forever.

In 1960, the United States had just enjoyed the most prosperous year in its history, as it had come to expect to do as a matter of course every year. The gross national product had passed $500 billion for the first time. Yet the economic situation was not good. Growth had been sticky and slow. Unemployment stubbornly refused to drop. People were talking about a recession. Balance-of-payments difficulties and foreign competition were beginning to cloud the future prospect. "This is the first time in my lifetime," said William McChesney Martin, chairman of the Federal Reserve Board, "that the credit of the United States has been questioned. A serious shadow lies over the American business picture."

That was the conservative view of the outgoing administration. The professors of the New Economics who were packing up to come down from Cambridge and New Haven, and a few other places, to join the new administration, were more impressed by the opportunity than by the danger. They believed they knew how to guarantee uninterrupted prosperity, unlimited growth. That was the secret they thought they had divined from the theories of John Maynard Keynes.

American scientists might know how to put a man on the moon; American economists might think they had discovered the secret of everlasting prosperity; the papers might be full of new missiles, new drugs, new products and discoveries of every kind; and yet it was a society careering toward the twenty-first century with many of the beliefs and attitudes of the nineteenth.

"With the kind of technology that is likely to be available in 1969," said a young physicist named Herman Kahn, reaching for the most improbable example to make his point, "it may literally turn out that a Hottentot . . . would be able to make bombs."

"These people are the cream of the crop," Dr. Card D. Stewart of the Methodist Committee for Overseas Relief told *Newsweek*, contemplating the Cuban refugees pouring into southern Florida. "It's the poorer people and the ne'er-do-wells who are with Fidel."

Forty-eight million Americans, or more than one in every four, were overweight, according to the Metropolitan Life Insurance Company.

A California state agency calculated that the average working girl still needed to budget to buy dinner and breakfast, for one, every day. But now she could afford to buy twenty-seven pairs of stockings every year, up from a dozen ten years earlier. "She must be a dolt," said a secretary telephoned for comment by a reporter. "Besides," she added, "how is she going to get by with only twenty-seven pairs of stockings?"

An affluent society with growing abundance, and one that was steadily being transformed for the better by science and technology—that was how the great majority of Americans saw their country in January 1961. But that does not mean that the mood was insouciant. On the contrary, the press and television, like the candidates in the presidential election that had just finished, harped ceaselessly on the theme of crisis. On December 29, Ed Murrow was hooked up with CBS correspondents worldwide. *Years of Crisis*, the show was called.

No one needed to be told what the nature of that crisis was.

In mid-January *Time* reported grimly that the United States had survived a week "when the underlying conflict between the West and Communism erupted on three fronts": in Cuba, in Laos, and in the Congo.

On January 23 *Newsweek* celebrated the inauguration with a special section. "Around the restive globe from Berlin to Laos," it began, "the Communist threat seethed, and nowhere more ominously than in Cuba," where Fidel Castro, that month, stood down his mobilization because he believed (wrongly, as it turned out) that no invasion was on the way. There were problems at home, too, *Newsweek* conceded, among them "problems of racial violence, schools and housing." But "the greatest single problem that faces John Kennedy—and the key to most of his other problems—is how to meet the aggressive power of the Communist bloc."

The United States was ready. That same month, *Time* devoted a cover story to CINCPAC, Admiral Harry D. Felt. "To maintain order and build prosperous trade in a free world," the editors explained, "the U.S. must control the seas and be the guardian of the land areas along the shores." From Singapore to the Diomede Islands in the Bering Strait, it was an imperial responsibility. But a double-page spread showed how the gallant admiral was equiped to meet it, with his carriers and his marines and his hundreds of strike aircraft. "He is prepared," wrote *Time* in that peculiar tone of exultation, barely disguised as a stoic sense of duty, that was characteristic of Washington in the early sixties, "to keep the peace if possible, to win a war if necessary."

The journalists who wrote those articles were briefed by the outgoing Eisenhower administration. But their tone, and their assumption that the United States stood on the verge of global war against "the aggressive power of the Communist bloc," were precisely the theme of John Kennedy's inaugural address.

Kennedy struck a Churchillian note of struggle and sacrifice. He offered blood, sweat, toil and tears:

We shall pay any price, bear any burden, meet any hardship. . . . Now the trumpet summons us again . . . to bear the burden of a long twilight struggle, year in and year out, "rejoicing in hope, patient in tribulation"—a struggle against the common enemies of man: tyranny, poverty, disease and war itself.

Only a few generations have been granted the role of defending freedom in its hour of maximum danger. . . .

The energy, the faith and the devotion which we bring to this endeavor will light our country and all who serve it, and the glow from that fire can truly light the world.

Twelve years later, Richard Nixon's second inaugural address echoed that rhetoric. He, too, wanted to kindle a fire:

Let us pledge together to make these four years the best four years in America's history, so that on its 2coth birthday America will be as young and vital as when it began, and as bright a beacon of hope for all the world.

The theme Nixon had chosen for his second inauguration was the Spirit of 1976. By chance, we have an insight into what that meant for him and those about him. One of the casualties of government secrecy in the Nixon years were the files of the American Revolution Bicentennial Commission, a disciplined instrument of the presidential will as interpreted by that most zealous of its agents, John D. Ehrlichman. The commission had been in existence for some years. But now, under White House direction, it made every effort to turn the bicentennial into a partisan promotion. Leaked documents from the commission's offices reveal just how closely the Nixon administration identified patriotism with military glory on the one hand and corporate profit on the other, especially for its friends.

Each state was to celebrate the bicentennial in its own way. The commission looked with favor on Kansas' plans, for example, to build a National Military Museum at a cost of $50 million. This was to be in the shape of a gigantic five-pointed star, visible for miles, and dedicated to commemorating the battles that "helped achieve peace through patriotism." However, as the secretary of the Iowa state bicentennial commission put it, "Principles are nice, but they don't make the cash register ring." The ARBC concentrated most of its efforts on persuading national corporate business how profitable patriotic principles could be. There were plans to tie in the anniversary of the American Revolution with the Orange Bowl parade, the Miss America contest, and the McDonald hamburger chain (run by one of the President's free-spending contributor-friends). Such giant corporations as Ford, AT&T, IBM, and ITT kept in touch. "One of the major efforts of the American Revolution Bicentennial Commission," its chairman wrote in one letter, "is to involve as many Americans as possible in a meaningful observance of our nation's 200th anniversary. With this in mind, I would like to invite approximately twenty principal executives of major corporations of our country to a dinner at Blair House. . . ."

There remained one trifling ideological difficulty before the Spirit of '76 could be finally appropriated for promotional purposes by these corporate marketing men. It was duly disposed of, by the bicentennial commission of the President's own home state, in a way Nixon must have admired if the paper caught his eye. "The American revolution," it formally resolved, "was not a 'revolution.'"

The style of the two speeches is as different as the minds of the two men who made them; and John Kennedy and Richard Nixon were profoundly different men—more different, even, than the ideas and policies they represented. Language was not the only difference between the two speeches. Nixon's vision, however tawdry, was a vision primarily for the United States, a domestic vision. Kennedy's call was to a struggle that, whatever its wisdom, would be played out in the whole world.

Nixon spoke about both foreign and domestic affairs. He spoke proudly and at length about his administration's achievements in international relations, about its "bold initiatives" and its hopes of building "a structure of peace" that would last for generations. But, in one passage, he stated obliquely but unmistakably his sense of priorities. It must be America first.

> Let us accept that high responsibility [to build a structure of peace] not as a burden but gladly—gladly because the chance to build such a peace is the noblest endeavor a people can engage in; gladly also because only if we act greatly in meeting our responsibilities abroad will

we remain a great nation, and only if we remain a great nation will we act greatly in meeting our challenges at home.

For Nixon, the United States must be strong in order to embark upon "a new era of progress" at home. For Kennedy, the argument had been exactly the other way around.

Kennedy did not mention domestic issues at all in his 1961 inaugural. He made a conscious decision to exclude them, according to his chief assistant in drafting the speech, Theodore Sorensen. There were several reasons for that decision, of course, including a simple desire to keep the speech short. None the less, it revealed Kennedy's sense of the national priorities unmistakably.

The change of emphasis should not be put down to the temperament of the two Presidents. Nixon, in 1961, almost certainly shared Kennedy's view of the primacy of foreign policy. Public-opinion poll data show that the priorities of the American people as a whole had changed in exactly the same way.

In 1972 William Watts and Lloyd Free published a book, *State of the Nation*, that reported the results of a survey conducted specially for their project by The Gallup Organization. Their most startling discovery was precisely the fact that the American public, which as recently as 1964 had been far more concerned about foreign affairs, was now overwhelmingly worried about domestic issues.

The evidence for attitudes in 1964 comes from a similar survey carried out in that year by the Institute for International Social Research. These were the issues that most concerned Americans in 1964, in order of urgency:

1. Keeping the country out of war
2. Combating world communism
3. Keeping our military defenses strong
4. Controlling the use of nuclear weapons
5. Maintaining respect for the United States in other countries.

"Only in sixth place," Watts and Free commented, "did a domestic item surface: maintaining law and order." By 1972 they found these priorities exactly reversed. Rising prices, the cost of living, violence in American life, drugs, water and air pollution, health care, misleading advertising, garbage disposal, the problems of the elderly, unemployment, poverty, and education all ranked above any foreign-policy issue, they found, except one: Vietnam.

The Harvard social scientist James Q. Wilson has written, "The decade of the 1960s began in a mood of contentment with domestic affairs and confidence in international ones; it ended in an agony of bitterness and frustration over both." That way of drawing the contrast seems to me wrongly expressed. It underestimates the genuine anxiety with which Americans looked out at the world at the beginning of the 1960s, and forgets the authentic sense of danger and struggle of which Kennedy's inaugural was the classic expression. By the time of Nixon's second inaugural, too, the principle cause of "bitterness and frustration" abroad had been removed. For most Americans, if not for the Vietnamese, the war was over. It would be truer to join the terms of the formula the other way: Americans entered the age of Kennedy and Nixon contented at home and frustrated abroad. They left it relatively confident about the world abroad, but in an agony of bitterness at home.

The shift of emphasis from the problems of the world to the problems of America was only the symptom of a deeper change. The United States entered the 1960s in an Augustan mood: united, confident, conscious of a historic mission, and mobilized for the great task of carrying it out. The Americans of 1960 felt the maturity of their power. They accepted the legitimacy of their institutions. They believed, not in the perfection, but in the perfectibility, of their society. If they were anxious about danger from abroad, it was because they saw their own society as so essentially just and benevolent that danger could come only from elsewhere. If they found international affairs frustrating, it was because they found it infuriating that foreigners could not always believe that their only ambition was a generous desire to share the abundance of American capitalism and the promise of American democracy with those less fortunate than themselves.

Some voted for Kennedy, and some for Nixon. But, except for a small fringe of conservatives and an almost insignificant sprinkling of radicals, political differences were less important in 1960 than the underlying consensus. Most Americans then accepted an ideology of imperial liberalism whose chief tenets were simplicity itself: the American system worked at home, and America must be strong abroad. There was a sense at the beginning of the 1960s that the businessman and the unskilled laborer, the writer and the housewife, Harvard University and the Strategic Air Command, International Business Machines and the labor movement, all had their parts to play in one harmonious political, intellectual, and economic system.

A dozen years later, that system was in ruins. The legitimacy of virtually every institution had been challenged, and the validity of virtually every assumption disputed. Instead of girding themselves for a great mission in the world, Americans seemed increasingly to pray only to be allowed to live peacefully in their habitations.

Two quotations measure the change.

Here is how Professor William L. Langer, holder of a prestigious chair in history at Harvard and former chairman of the Board of National Intelligence Estimates of the CIA, summed up, calmly and in the manner of one stating indisputable fact, the prevailing orthodoxy in 1960:

> The United States has, throughout its history, cherished ideals of independence, freedom and democracy. The energy and ingenuity of its people as well as the extent and resources of its territory have enabled it to attain a level of civil liberty, social equality and general prosperity. . . .
>
> The United States should, at all times, exert its influence and power on behalf of a world order congenial to American ideals, interests and security. It can do this without egotism because of its deep conviction that such a world order will best fulfill the hopes of mankind.

By 1970, it could not be said that there was any prevailing orthodoxy. But here is the concluding passage from a book that was at least well certificated at the time. It was written by Professor Andrew Hacker of Cornell University, a regular contributor to the New York *Times Magazine*. It was respectfully reviewed and went through half a dozen editions in a year.

> America's history as a nation has reached its end. The American people will of course survive; and the majority will continue to exist quite comfortably. . . . But the ties that make them a society will grow more tenuous with each passing year. There will be undercurrents of tension and turmoil, and the only remaining option will be to learn to live with these disorders. For they are not problems that can be solved with the resources we are willing to make available. . . .
>
> The American people will continue to produce new generations and carry on with the business of life. Abroad they will either make peace with a world they cannot master, or they will turn it into a battle ground for yet another century of war. Closer to home, however, Americans will learn to live with danger and discomfort, for this condition is the inevitable accompaniment of democracy in its declining years.

From the world of Langer and Kennedy to the world of Hacker and Nixon, the United States had traveled in just ten years from the vigorous assurance of mid-Victorian England to something like the angry confusion and despair of Weimar Germany.

"America is change."

James Bryce wrote that in his *American Commonwealth*, which was first published in 1888.

More than forty years later, in the month before the Wall Street market break of 1929, an eminent committee of social scientists reported that the country was still suffering from a nasty case of change:

". . . Birth control, race riots, stoppage of immigration . . . governmental corruption, crime and racketeering, the sprawl of great cities . . . imperialism, peace or war, international relations, urbanism . . . shifting moral standards, new leadership in business and government, the status of womankind, labor, child training, mental hygiene, the future of democracy and capitalism . . . all of these grave questions demand attention if we are not to drift into zones of danger."

There never has been a time when the United States has not been changing in ways that a great many Americans found disturbing. This very continuity of change hints at the paradox we have already noted.

America has always been change, yes. But at the beginning of the 1960s it was also still a deeply conservative country. It was the only important state in the world to be operating, essentially unchanged, under an eighteenth-century constitution. It was the only nation where nineteenth-century faith in capitalism and suspicion of socialism were still dominant, and the one among all the major societies of the world to have been the least touched by the twentieth-century experience of war and revolution.

Change and stability seemed in 1961 to be married in America in a fruitful partnership. The pace of technological innovation, the spread of education, and the rise of living standards seemed only to confirm the stability of the American system. The stability of institutions, in turn, seemed to guarantee a continuing flow of beneficent change.

What happened in the age of Kennedy and Nixon was something more than a mere acceleration in the pace of change. There was a real break in the continuity of the American experience.

The country was not invaded. On the contrary, on one pretext or another it invaded or otherwise attacked half a dozen foreign countries, with impunity. Its strategic military strength may or may not now be surpassed by that of the Soviet Union: both are so awesome that the question is academic.

There was civil strife in the United States, but on a scale trivial compared to what has taken place elsewhere: in Chile, in the Indian subcontinent or in Northern Ireland, for example, in the same years, and even compared to earlier periods in American history. When a black sniper killed several policemen in New Orleans in 1973, the mayor said it was the worst crime in the city's history. He had forgotten, or did not know, that two dozen Italians were killed there in a riot in 1893 and four dozen Negroes were massacred by the police in the French Quarter in 1866.

Ten thousand Americans have been put under surveillance by the federal government, and a handful imprisoned for what can only be called political crimes. Yet in general the civil liberties of American citizens are as carefully protected as those of any other state.

The economy has performed well, on the whole. There has been poverty, and even hunger: more of both than people supposed there would be twenty years ago, but less than in the past. And nothing to compare with the widespread destitution of the 1930s. American living standards are no longer as far ahead of those of the rest of the world as they used to be. But the gross national product in 1973 had more than doubled since John F. Kennedy's inauguration.

No: the crisis was in the mind and spirit of the country. That does not mean that it was any less real. It was not a "crisis of confidence," in the foolish sense in which that phrase is sometimes used, meaning that if only everyone had whistled to keep his courage up and drown the voices of doubt, the problems would have gone away. There was too much of that kind of confidence, not too little.

Yet in a more serious sense confidence was involved. The crisis of the sixties went deeper than the sum of "the problems." That is what the older generation of liberals, in particular, found so hard to understand. No period has seen a richer crop of "solutions" spring up to match its problems. Too often, indeed, the solution became the problem.

The real crisis of the sixties was that, for the first time since the Civil War and Reconstruction, a generation of Americans were compelled to ask not, as people asked in the Depression, how to solve their problems, but whether problems could be solved. That is why the great conflicts of the age of Kennedy and Nixon challenged the central promise of American life as it was not challenged by a shortage of jobs in the 1930s, or by war in the 1940s and Cold War in the 1950s.

For many Americans, looking back over the years from Camelot to Watergate, the question is simply: what went wrong?

Many can see as the main theme of that history only a tragic loss, a fall from grace. Not a few have thought of the lines from Yeats's poem *The Second Coming*:

> Things fall apart; the centre cannot hold:
> Mere anarchy is loosed upon the world,
> The blood-dimmed tide is loosed, and everywhere
> The ceremony of innocence is drowned. . . .

That is not my estimate, however, nor the argument of this book. They were terrible years, of course, in many ways. Too many men and women were unnecessarily killed. Too many lives were unnecessarily spoiled. A war was fought, and to no purpose. Peace brought no real honor. Many hopes were disappointed, and some betrayed. Americans turned successively to three ideologies for guidance: the liberal, the radical, the conservative. Each has been discredited for many. Each failed. No one can look forward with easy optimism to the next measure of the dance.

But—to continue the metaphysical metaphor—one can fall from grace only if he has been in a state of grace. The time to which those, who see the past fifteen years as only one of tragic loss, look back was in vital respects a fool's paradise. It was a time of false complacency and of hubristic and dangerous illusions. The promise was flawed from the beginning. America has paid a price, but she has done well to be rid of the assumptions of 1960. It is time to describe those assumptions. But first we must go back even further, to their origins.

## 2

## *The 1940s*

The seeds of the crisis of the 1960s lay in the 1940s. By the end of that decade, four great historical processes were decisively on their way to completion. Between them, they radically modified the structure of American politics and even the direction of American history. They set the foundations for a false consensus in the 1950s, and stored up a tangle of unresolved issues for the angry politics of the 1960s. These processes were so complex, they touched so much of American life, that they inevitably interacted on each other. The four themes can be divided, however, into two pairs, two international and two domestic.

1. Between 1941 and 1945, the United States emerged as the strongest power in the world. At the same time, and partly indeed for this very reason, isolation ceased to be either attractive or even possible as an option for American foreign policy. By the end of the 1940s, the United States had accepted the responsibility of becoming "the leader of the free world"; that is, of influencing the political evolution of as much of the world as its gigantic strength would allow. The effect, though not the intention, was that America became an imperial power; of a new kind, certainly, but nevertheless as committed to intervention as it had been so recently to isolation.

2. Paradoxically, in these same years of victory and supremacy, the safety and even potentially the existence of the United States were threatened, or were widely perceived as being threatened, for the first time since 1814. The rise and hostility of Stalin's Russia, the spread of communism in Eastern Europe and East Asia, the Soviet Union's acquisition of atomic weapons—these defined the threat. The frustration of having so much "power" and then finding that the world refused to be molded by it, brought on the crisis we call after Senator Joseph McCarthy, though in fact it had begun long before he brandished his little list in Wheeling,

West Virginia. The effects were as important inside the United States as they were for foreign policy. The Left was silenced. On the Right, orthodox conservatism was displaced by an obsession with unreal dangers. The nation was committed to an ideology of anti-communism.

3. It was World War II, not the New Deal, that ended the Great Depression. The war unleashed an economic leap forward, which gradually engendered a new social optimism. By 1945, the United States seemed to be the supremely successful society as well as the supremely victorious power. Most Americans benefited from this new prosperity. Large-scale corporate business benefited most of all—not only in profits but in esteem. A few years earlier, capitalism had seemed to be on the defensive. Suddenly it seemed the wave of the future. In the rich humus of the wartime boom, a social ideology sprang up to match anti-communism in international politics. The heart of this new ideology of free enterprise was a faith in the harmony of interests: the promise of American capitalism seemed to be that it could produce abundance on such a scale that social problems would be drowned under a flood of resources. Social conflict would become an anachronism.

4. By a second, deeply ironic historical paradox, the same years saw the origin of new social conflicts that were to haunt the 1960s. The 1940s were the decisive decade in the great migration of both poor white and poor black people from the South. What few foresaw was that the difference between the South and the rest of the country would be eroded, not only by the South becoming more like the North, but also in certain ways by the North (and the West) becoming more like the South; and specifically that the question of race, which had long been the peculiar obsession of southern politics, would move to the center of national concern.

One week after the second atomic bomb was dropped, on Nagasaki, Winston Churchill told the House of Commons: "America stands at this moment at the summit of the world." Three weeks after that, on V-J Day, September 1, 1945, President Truman told his fellow countrymen over the radio that they possessed "the greatest strength and the greatest power which man has ever reached." Neither statement exceeded the bounds of sober and literal truth.

Even without the atomic bomb, the United States was the strongest military power in the world in 1945. The combined strength of U.S. armed forces on V-J Day was 11,913,639; at the same moment, the Soviet Union was estimated to have only 10.6 million men under arms. But if the war had taught any strategic lesson, it was that raw numbers, however brave, could be neutralized by the superior mobility and firepower that came from mechanization, technology, and organization; and those were the very domains in which the United States, in 1945, had no rival. The true measure of American strength was not so much the dozens of aircraft carriers or the dozens of thousands of bombers, but the fact that the United States, alone of the powers, could replace them almost without raising a sweat. At its wartime peak, in late 1944, American industry was working at a rhythm that would have enabled it to equip a power equal to the Soviet Union in a matter of months.

American military strength was grounded in the wealth and productivity of the American economy. In 1945, the United States was bulging with an abundance of every resource that held the key to power in the modern world: with land, food, power, raw materials, industrial plant, monetary reserves, scientific talent, and trained manpower. It was in the war years that the United States shot ahead of all its rivals economically. In four years, national income, national wealth, and industrial production all doubled or more than doubled. In the same period, the Soviet Union's initially much smaller industrial capacity had been cut by more than 40 per cent, and every other industrial nation came out of the war poorer and weaker than when it went in.

A few examples illustrate the margin of American predominance. In 1945, most continental Europeans were living on fewer than fifteen hundred calories a day, and substantial populations averaged one thousand. In Asia, it was estimated, 400 million people faced starvation. The average American consumed close to thirty-five hundred calories. Obesity was beginning to be regarded as a public health problem, and food surpluses were becoming burdensome.

Steel then was regarded as the key indicator of industrial development. The German and Japanese steel industries had been reduced to rubble in 1945, and those of Britain, the Soviet Union, and northwestern Europe had been crippled by years of war damage and capital shortage. The U.S. steel industry, at the same time, had expanded its production from an average of 22 million tons a year in the Depression years 1931–35 to 90 million tons by 1944.

In 1947, with postwar recovery under way everywhere, the United States produced about one half of the world's manufactures: 57 per cent of its steel, 43 per cent of its electricity, 62 per cent of its oil. It owned three quarters of the world's automobiles and was improving on that show by manufacturing well over 80 per cent of the new cars built in the world that year. The American lead was greatest in precisely those industries which contributed to the power to wage modern war: aviation, chemical engineering, electronics. And there was no immediate reason to suppose that this would change. After four years of war boom, American industry, and only American industry, had money to spend on new plant, new processes, higher productivity for the individual worker, larger-scale (and therefore in theory more economical) production facilities, and research and development.

The curve of the gross national product sums up this sudden surge in economic power. In 1929, the last year of boom, it had reached $103 billion, but by 1933 it had slumped to barely more than half that figure: $55 billion. By 1940 it had managed only to climb painfully back to just below the 1929 level, and stood at $99.7 billion. In 1945 it had passed $210 billion, and it has never looked back. In the late 1940s the average American enjoyed an income about fifteen times greater than that of the average foreigner.

No nation in the world, President Truman congratulated his countrymen in his memoirs, had won such a victory and asked nothing for itself in territory and reparations. It was true. But it was also true that no nation in history had ever done so well out of a war.

There had been sacrifices, of course, and casualties, as there must be in any war. But proportionately they were minimal in comparison with those the other warring powers suffered, and with the gains they bought. The United States lost fewer than three hundred thousand dead. The Soviet Union lost 20 million, perhaps more. The United States had gone into the war as one, perhaps the strongest, but still only one, of the world's eight great powers. It had emerged alone. The greater part of the purchase price of that pre-eminence remained to be paid, in various currencies, in the future.

When Robert Oppenheimer saw the "unbelievable light" from the fireball of the first atomic explosion, at Los Alamos, there came into his mind the saying of the God Vishnu from Hindu scripture: "Now I am become death, the destroyer of worlds."

Henry Stimson, the Secretary of War, who was responsible for the building of the bomb and for the choice of its targets, was a more prosaic man. After the Nagasaki explosion he said simply, "The world is changed."

Harry Truman, who took the decision to use the bomb (essentially by taking a decision not to countermand existing orders to drop it), made an even earthier judgment before the Los Alamos test. "If it explodes," he said, "as I think it will, I'll certainly have a hammer on those boys."

The world was indeed changed. Men had become as gods, though in the process mankind itself had become mortal. But the most immediate change those first three atomic explosions brought about was in the power of the United States. For more than four years—at the very least from July 1945 until late August 1949, when U.S. intelligence learned of the first atomic explosion in the Soviet Union, and more realistically until the un-known later date when the Russians achieved the ability to deliver an A-bomb to a hostile target—the United States held the monopoly of a weapon that was without precedent in the dread it inspired.

Of course, President Truman and every other responsible American official were sincere in their frequently expressed hopes that they would never feel obliged to use the bomb. The fact remained that it was they whose feelings on that point had to be reckoned with by every other gov-ernment.

For roughly fifteen years after 1945, American military and diplo-matic planning started from the assumption that there were indeed situa-tions in which an American President might feel obliged to use atomic weapons. This assumption was made long before there was any question of atomic weapons being used by any other power. George Kennan, head of policy planning at the State Department at the time, summarized in 1967 what he understood policy to have been since 1949:

> It was perfectly clear . . . that we were basing our defense posture on such weapons, and were intending to make the first use of them . . . in any major military encounter.

That was indeed quite a hammer to hold on the rest of the world.

The effect of the atomic monopoly on American policy was plain from the start. Winston Churchill had got the message within twenty-four hours of the news from Los Alamos: "We now had something in our hands which would redress the balance with the Russians." It was on this reading of the new situation that Truman acted. He sought to deny the Soviet Union influence in two vital areas of the world, Eastern Europe and Manchuria (the key to both northern China and Japan), where it had been accepted in the wartime talks that its influence would be paramount. Possession of the A-bomb neutralized Stalin's strategic advantage in Europe and emboldened Truman to resist Soviet pressure both there and in the Near East. Everywhere he resisted, he found himself committed to maintaining resistance. The atomic monopoly offered the tempting possi-bility of committing American power where a President would have hesi-tated to commit American troops. It thus made American hegemony pos-sible and perhaps made it inevitable.

Victory in war and at a cost so low that it seemed effortless, an ap-parently invincible military and logistic strength for waging conventional war, an economic base that had more than doubled while every other na-tion was being crippled, and now a monopoly of the most dangerous weapon the world had ever seen—these were formidable advantages. But not even these would have committed the United States to world responsibility if the American people, or at least their leaders, had not wanted to undertake it.

Did entry into World War II irrevocably commit the United States to the burdens of world leadership? Roosevelt thought that it did, though he may have underestimated the burdens. "We have learned," he said in his fourth inaugural, "that we cannot live alone, at peace . . . that we must live as men, and not as ostriches." Senator Arthur Vandenberg, chairman of the Senate Foreign Relations Committee and the most celebrated convert from isolationism, believed this too. "Pearl Harbor," he said, "drove us to the conclusion that peace is indivisible."

Pearl Harbor was perhaps more like the nail for want of which the shoe and the kingdom were lost. Once the United States was at war with Japan and Germany, forces were set in motion that powerfully affected later decisions. The sleeping energies of the American sense of mission were turned outward to the world. American troops went overseas and eventually confronted Soviet power in the middle of Europe. The atomic bomb was built. History was nudging the United States toward a decision.

The decision itself, nevertheless, came later and was consciously taken. In 1917–19, after all, the United States had intervened in Europe in the most activist way, but then had turned back, after only three years of intervention, when the Senate refused to ratify the League of Nations. The United States might have withdrawn again after 1945. Congressional pressure did force Truman to "bring the boys home" faster than either he or his advisers thought wise. "It was no demobilization," said General George C. Marshall, who carried it out; "it was a rout."

Yet, by the end of the decade, the commitment had been made. Isolationism was dead. Its Congressional battalions were the still imposing foliage of a tree whose roots had shriveled up. The first gust of wind would bring it down. It had never been quite what most Europeans took it for. Its strength sprang not from any objection on principle to the United States' pursuing its aims in the world beyond the oceans, but from certain specific ethnic, sectional, and ideological attitudes.

When the isolationists said they were against war, what they often meant was that they thought the United States was being recruited to fight in the wrong war, or on the wrong side. Thus, for example, German-Americans objected to FDR's alliance with Britain because it was against Germany; Irish-Americans disliked it because it was with Britain.

In ideological terms, there had always been an isolationism of the Left and an isolationism of the Right. Many of the leading isolationists of the 1920s were western radicals of one brand or another. At the rational level, they opposed intervention and war as distractions from social reform. But they and their followers had grown up in the bitterness of agrarian poverty and the soured dreams of the frontier. They hated those whom they saw as their oppressors: the railroads, the trusts, Wall Street, the East, and, always shadowy in the background, the British Empire. They believed that America had been dragged into the First World War by a conspiracy of bankers, plutocrats and British lords.

As time went on, however, the ideological center of gravity of the isolationist coalition shifted to the right. Some individual leaders (such as William "Liberty Bell" Lemke and Senator Burton K. Wheeler) moved to the right themselves and began to talk less about the evils of Wall Street and more about the dangers of communism. Europe now seemed, not the homeland of a capitalist conspiracy, but the poisoned source of socialism. The Spanish Civil War reinforced this rightward shift. Many Catholic isolationists saw Franco and his ally Mussolini as the champions of a martyred church against the priest-killing, nun-raping Communists. Many isolationist demagogues, such as Father Coughlin, were openly anti-Semitic. And conservatives of the business class could argue, up to the Nazi-Soviet pact, that a war against Fascism was the wrong war.

World War II knocked the legs from under all these different versions of isolationism. By 1945, every one of these impulses had become either irrelevant or actually an argument against isolationism. Conservatives, Irish-Americans, and midwestern farmers were nothing if not patriotic. Once the U.S.A. was at war with the Axis, sympathy for Germany became un-American. Nazi atrocities disposed of the illusion that Hitler was the champion of Christendom. Anti-Semitism became odious to all but a lunatic fringe. Britain became the courageous ally. Moreover, high wartime food prices doubled farm income. Mortgage and other debt was paid off across the Mid-Western plains where the Sons of the Wild Jackass had once voiced their desperation.

Now that the great question was no longer whether to side with Britain against Germany but whether to resist Soviet Russia, the magnetic polarity of isolationist feeling was reversed. Such ethnic sentiment as continued to be felt, favored intervention. Descendants of immigrants from Eastern Europe hated Russia as the enslaver of their homelands and thought it should be one of the goals of policy to free the "captive nations." Greek-Americans and Italian-Americans wanted the United States to keep Greece and Italy from "going Communist." German-Americans had no objection to an alliance against Russia. And the Catholic Church's considerable weight was thrown in in favor of a strong anti-Communist foreign policy.

Even the suspicion of Europe, and specifically of European colonialism, which had supplied so much of the emotional drive for isolationism, now cut the other way. For a corollary of this feeling had always been the desire to see American interest and concern turn away from Europe toward Asia, and especially toward the Far East. Not all of those who attached themselves to the China Lobby of the 1950s were former isolationists. But some were, and they pressed for intervention in Asia with the same righteous wrath they had spilled against intervention in Europe.

Not only, then, was isolationism after 1945 no longer strong enough to restrain the forces that were moving the United States toward an interventionist foreign policy; it had become irrelevant to the emotional drives and political needs of the former isolationists themselves, who rapidly faced the choice between political oblivion and conversion. Many of them now pressed strongly for intervention. For a while, the architects of the interventionist foreign policy, such men as Stimson and Dean Acheson, would find themselves co-operating with such ex-isolationists as Senators Taft and Vandenberg. But, before long, the reversal of roles had become complete: Acheson and his friends found themselves bitterly attacked from the Right for not being interventionist enough.

Four great facts dominated international politics in the late 1940s. The first was the atomic bomb. The second was the rise of communism, aggressively led by Stalin and armed with the power of the Soviet state. The third was the sheer strength of the United States. And the fourth was the weakness of all the other powers.

American policy was guided by men who had long believed that only an active willingness on the part of the United States to take the lead could avert the danger of a third world war. The Second World War had confirmed their instinct. The disappearance of isolationism freed their hands. But more than that: American public opinion sustained them and pushed them forward. For the next twenty years, it would always be safer for a politician to demand higher defense appropriations than to propose cutting them, and the tougher the stance a President took against the Communists, the more popular he would be. In 1945, a deep sense of the historical mission of the United States came to fruition in the public mind. It was as old as the Republic and had always been as strong as the instinct for isolation, which it only superficially contradicted. Now, in a moment of supreme opportunity and danger, it made the great majority of Americans welcome, as well as fear, the splendid responsibilities of their new power.

The existence of atomic weapons was part of that power, but it was also a source of danger. There was never any doubt in the Administration's mind that the Soviet Union would do its utmost to acquire atom bombs of its own. Truman had been kept in the dark about the atomic bomb as Vice-President. In the very same breath as he told the new President the facts about American atomic monopoly, Secretary of War Stimson added, "It is practically certain that we could not remain in this position indefinitely."

We now know that Soviet nuclear physics had made considerable progress toward knowing how to build a bomb before 1941. By September 1945, U.S. intelligence had evidence that the Soviets had embarked on that quest in earnest, and by the spring of 1946 the Acheson-Lilienthal report of the National Security Council took for granted that "the extremely favored position with regard to atomic devices which the United States enjoys at present is only temporary."

It can be argued that it would have been wise to adopt the policy which Stimson proposed, and the Cabinet debated, in September 1945. The chief lesson he had learned in a long life, Stimson said, was, "The only way you can make a man trustworthy is to trust him." He suggested that Russia's hostility could be allayed by an offer to share the technology of the bomb. The hard-liners blocked the proposal, and the moment passed. But even those who wish that Stimson's worldly generosity had prevailed have to concede that his policy would still have left the Soviet Union on its way to acquiring the bomb, and Stalin in charge of the decision whether to use it. A world in which any foreign nation, let alone a nation as antagonistic to the United States as Stalin's Russia, had acquired atomic weapons, was a world from which the United States dared not remain isolated.

The actual behavior of the Russians had more effect on American policy than the future prospect of a Soviet Union armed with atomic bombs. In 1941, in London, when he heard the news of Pearl Harbor, Charles de Gaulle turned to an aide and made two predictions: the allies would now win the war against Germany, and later, he feared, there would be a war between America and Russia. The probability of friction between the United States and the Soviet Union was inherent in the political systems and the ideologies of the two countries. And indeed the squabbles of victorious allies have always been a consolation to the defeated. "Yee may now sit downe and play," said the aged cavalier general Lord Astley to his captors as he surrendered Charles I's last army, "for you have done all your worke, if you fall not out among yourselves."

Both the Soviet Union and the United States in 1945 were ideologically expansionist powers. The men who controlled the Soviet Union, and the majority of Americans, each held a political philosophy as the Truth. Each believed that in the end their truth must prevail universally. Each believed that history was on their side. It could only be a matter of time before two systems, each justified in its own view by political morality and historical necessity, came into conflict.

At Yalta, in February 1945, Roosevelt, Churchill and Stalin made the last of their wartime attempts to preclude falling out over the shape of the world after the war. Almost immediately, Stalin gave signs that he would not abide by the agreements he had made. Poland was the most vexed of the questions discussed at Yalta and the first on which the underlying intransigence of Stalin's attitude became plain. After much haggling, he had agreed at Yalta to include in the future government of Poland representatives from the democratic governments in exile. But it soon became all too clear that Stalin intended that all power in Warsaw should lie with the "Lublin committee," which he controlled. The Soviet Union's western frontier was to be guarded by obedient hands. Before his death, even President Roosevelt's determination to put the best construction on Stalin's behavior had been shaken.

Before the war in Europe was over, Ambassador Averell Harriman hurried from Moscow to warn President Truman, "Stalin is breaking his agreements." Harriman went further. He predicted a "barbarian invasion" of Europe by America's Soviet ally.

From the start Harry Truman took an altogether less trusting view of Stalin's intentions than Roosevelt had taken. Even before he knew the full power of the atomic card in his hand, Truman made it plain that he meant to take a "firm" line with the Russians: he was tired of "babying" them, he said. If the Russians made good their threat to boycott the United Nations members unless they got their way on Poland, they could "go to hell," he told his advisers.

It would be a mistake to lay too much stress on Truman's personal attitude, however. By the summer of 1945 each significant group of American officials had come to the same conclusion. Acting Secretary of State Joseph C. Grew, the two future secretaries, Byrnes and Acheson, such military men as General Marshall and Admiral Leahy, and especially three men with direct experience of dealing with the Russians in Moscow—Ambassador Harriman, his deputy George Kennan, and the military attaché General John Deane—all agreed that the time had come to stop "pussyfooting." It is far from certain that FDR, if he had lived, would not have shared his closest collaborators' assessment.

Immediately in Austria, and later in Iran, Turkey, Greece, Berlin and Korea, Truman showed that he was willing to resist Soviet encroachment. He moved five divisions to drive Tito—still Stalin's ally—out of Trieste in May 1945. In attempting to pressure Stalin into allowing free elections in Romania and Bulgaria, he went beyond the position Churchill and Roosevelt had taken during the war. They had felt themselves obliged to concede Eastern Europe to Stalin as his sphere of influence. Truman pushed this issue to the point of breakdown at the first meeting of the

Council of Foreign Ministers in London in September 1945. Both James Byrnes, who represented the United States at that meeting, and John Foster Dulles subsequently laid the open rupture between the Soviet Union and the United States to what happened there.

Two incompatible views of the world were put on the table. For Byrnes, and for most Americans, what was at issue was that they were being asked to stand by while Stalin imposed an odious tyranny with the help of the Red Army. A fair-minded French historian of the Cold War has reminded us how the same issue may have looked to the Russians:

> Molotov inferred that the United States wanted to re-establish anti-Soviet governments in those countries "[Romania and Bulgaria, which after all had just stopped fighting alongside Hitler against the Soviet Union and sending their armies to invade it]." . . . He probably thought that his colleagues were going back on their word. . . . For men like the Soviet leaders, obsessed with security, deeply distrustful of the western world, incapable of believing in the existence of disinterested principle in colleagues whose cynicism and inconsistency they had had so many opportunities of observing, Washington's and London's professions of concern for the rights of man in areas where little attention had been paid to them throughout the ages could only mean a new quarrel over the distribution of Hitler's plunder.

There was, in any case, nothing Truman could do about the accomplished fact of Soviet power in Eastern and half of Central Europe. In the crucial April weeks of 1945, the Russian armies had plowed westward, and wherever they had passed, the seeds of Russian domination had been planted. Churchill, inveterately suspicious of the Bolsheviks since 1917, saw what was happening. He beseeched Truman to "come to an understanding with Russia, or see where we are with her, before we weaken our armies." He wanted to use those armies "to open a new front . . . against the onward sweep" of the Russians, or at the very least to push the U. S. Third Army forward to liberate Prague before the Red Army could get there. This, Eisenhower, the Anglo-American supreme commander, refused to do, and Truman backed him up.

By May 12, less than a week after the German surrender, Churchill used what was already a favorite phrase with him in an agonized cable to Washington: AN IRON CURTAIN IS DRAWN DOWN UPON THEIR FRONT FROM STETTIN TO TRIEST. . . .

It is still there.

American leaders differed at the time, just as historians differ today, whether there was anything the United States could safely have done to prevent Stalin's establishing what within little more than two years had become satellite governments all over Eastern Europe. A deeper controversy rages over the meaning of Stalin's policy both in Eastern Europe and in his later, thwarted moves against Iran, Turkey and Greece. Were they, as almost all Americans and most non-Communists in Europe took for granted at the time, the opening moves in a voracious strategy that aimed at putting the whole of Europe and much of the rest of the world under Soviet control? Or was the Soviet Union's aggressivity in those years fundamentally defensive?

This is not the place to try to resolve that argument. What matters here is that by the middle of 1946 virtually every high American official, and the great majority of those in Congress, in the press, and elsewhere who had any influence over the making of American foreign policy, had come to believe the worst of Russia's intentions.

George Kennan first served in Moscow as a diplomat in 1933. His memoirs show that he felt, and still feels, an affection for the Russian people quite different from the sentimental tolerance that is the warmest feeling most diplomats can summon for the countries where they have been *en poste*. In later years, he was to become one of the most astringent critics of the rigidities of Cold War policies. Yet by February 1946 even Kennan, after eighteen months as Harriman's deputy, was so appalled by the stony deceptions of Stalin's government and by the futility of American efforts to "curry favor" with it, that he sat down and dictated, in response to some trivial inquiry from Washington, an eight-thousand-word diatribe about the nature of Soviet policy.

It was true, he began by saying, that the Soviet leadership believed itself to be encircled by the capitalists. "AT THE BOTTOM OF THE KREMLIN'S NEUROTIC VIEW OF WORLD AFFAIRS IS [the] TRADITIONAL AND INSTINCTIVE RUSSIAN SENSE OF INSECURITY." That should not distract attention from this fact:

> WE HAVE HERE A POLITICAL FORCE FANATICALLY COMMITTED TO THE BE-LIEF THAT WITH THE U.S. THERE CAN BE NO PERMANENT MODUS VIVENDI, THAT IT IS DESIRABLE AND NECESSARY THAT THE INTERNAL HARMONY OF OUR SOCIETY BE DISRUPTED, OUR TRADITIONAL WAY OF LIFE BE DESTROYED, THE INTERNATIONAL AUTHORITY OF OUR STATE BE BROKEN, IF SOVIET POWER IS TO BE SECURE. . . .

It was remarkable enough that so coolheaded an observer as Kennan should have arrived at this bleak diagnosis of Soviet aims. What was even more striking was the response in Washington. "Six months earlier," he has written, "this message would probably have been received in the Department of State with raised eyebrows and lips pursed in disapproval. Six months later it would have been preaching to the convinced." As it was, the President read it, and so did everybody in Washington, including, by special order of James Forrestal, soon to become the first Secretary of Defense, some hundreds of officers in the armed forces. Kennan's view of Russian intentions might be bleak, but it is safe to say that thenceforth it was as charitable as any to be met with in official Washington. The Cold War had begun.

About a year after his long telegram, George Kennan developed his analysis of Soviet-American relations in an even more influential paper, published under the signature "X," in *Foreign Affairs*. Kennan has subsequently explained, "What I was talking about when I mentioned the containment of Soviet power was not the containment by military means of a military threat, but the political containment of a political threat." The temper of the time was such that the distinction was brushed aside.

Kennan had defined containment as "the adroit and vigilant application of counterforce at a series of constantly shifting geographical and political points." The speed with which the containment catch phrase caught on shows how accurate this had become as a description of American strategy: what was perceived as a centrally directed, relentlessly aggressive Soviet threat to the liberties of the world must be contained—by political means if possible, by military means if necessary. It remained for this stark view of the world to be translated into specific institutions, pacts, treaties, alliances and commitments.

European weakness decided the precise form that the strategy of containment would take. Not for the last time in the modern world, weakness demonstrated the power it can have over strength.

The Roosevelt administration had clearly understood that Europe would need American help after the Second World War, just as it had after the First. One of President Truman's personal points of departure was his conviction that "the reconstruction of Europe was a matter that directly concerned us, and we could not turn our backs on it without directly jeopardizing our national interest." What came as a surprise to Washington was the seriousness of the economic collapse in Europe.

The second round of that great European civil war which pride and folly unleashed in 1914 had by 1945 completed the transformation of the once lordly economic relationship between Western Europe and the rest of the world.

One aspect of the plight of Europe was that the iron curtain now cut off Western Europe, including the most urbanized and industrial three quarters of the population of Germany, from its traditional supplies of food and raw materials in the East: Romanian oil, Silesian coal, pigs and potatoes from Poland and East Prussia, and Hungarian, Polish and Romanian grain.

But this was only a special case of a general dislocation. Before 1939 Europe had bought roughly one half of the world's exports and supplied in return only two fifths of its imports. The gap was met in part by the income from the investments Europeans had built up around the world since the middle of the nineteenth century not only in their colonies but in American industry, South American railroads and plantations, trade, shipping, insurance and every other kind of business. These investments brought the revenue from "invisible exports" into Hamburg, Paris, Amsterdam and the City of London. The rest of the gap had been comfortably covered in the past by the raw materials exported by the British, French and Dutch colonial empires, especially to the United States.

There were infinite variations and complexities, both over time and from one European country to another. Britain, for example, imported a far higher proportion of her raw materials and staple foods than France. But essentially the pattern of world trade before 1939 was three-cornered. Western Europe earned the income with which it paid for foodstuffs and manufactured goods from North America by exporting its own manufactures to Asia, Africa and South America, which in turn paid for European imports by exporting their own copper, coffee, rubber, tin, chocolate and diamonds to the United States. This structure was now in ruins. The wiser Europeans could see that the time of all colonial empires was running out. All of them could calculate that the cost of defending them against insurgent nationalism would soon make them unprofitable assets. And the terms of trade had turned against Western Europe. It would have to export far more goods to pay for the food, oil and raw materials its industries needed. Yet those industries had been smashed in the war and had not yet recovered.

For two reasons, the Truman administration took the view that economic collapse in Europe would be as disastrous for the United States as Nazi conquest would have been. In the long run, economic collapse in Europe was bound to infect the American economy: even though international trade was proportionately far less important to the United States than to Europe, American industry and farmers need markets; the experience of 1929 had taught the strategists of American business the lesson that the world's economies are interdependent.

More immediately, the risk was that economic crisis meant political chaos and despair. This would provide the opportunity for the Communists, especially the large Communist parties in France and Italy, to seize power from a minority position as they had done in Eastern Europe.

In the spring of 1947, after the most terrible winter in recent European history, a series of reports from Europe brought home to Washington that the danger was more urgent than American officials had realized.

"The recovery of Europe has been far slower than had been expected," General Marshall told the nation over the radio in late April. "It is now obvious," reported Assistant Secretary of State Will Clayton a month later, "that we have grossly underestimated the destruction to the European economy by the war . . . the political situation reflects the economic."

In fifteen breathless weeks in the spring of 1947, the fateful commitment took its twin shape: military in the language of the Truman Doctrine, political and economic in the Marshall Plan. History has dealt more kindly with the plan than with the doctrine. The present prosperity of Western Europe is a monument to the unselfish wisdom of the Marshall Plan, while even those who believe that the Truman Doctrine was responsible for saving Europe and the Near East from Stalin's ambitions concede that its consequences have not all been happy, even for Greece. There is a temptation, in fact, to draw these two great decisions in too heavily contrasting tones. Both plan and doctrine were responses, to the same challenge, at the same moment and of men who shared very much the same view of the world.

The Truman Doctrine was a response to the economic crisis in Europe just as much as the Marshall Plan was. On February 21 the British Government, which had seen a loan of $3.75 billion (intended to tide it over permanently) melt away in the balance-of-payments deficit, announced that it could no longer bear the cost of fighting the Communists in Greece and would have to pull out its rather large forces there by the end of March. Washington was afraid that this would mean the collapse of the anti-Communist governments not only in Greece, but in Turkey and Italy and perhaps in France as well, unless the United States was prepared to move into the breach. Dean Acheson, then under-secretary of state, has described the moment of decision in a memorable passage of his memoirs:

> When we convened the next morning in the White House to open the subject with our congressional masters, I knew we were met at Armageddon. . . . This was my crisis. For a week I had nurtured it. These congressmen had no conception of what challenged them; it was my task to bring it home. Both my superiors, equally perturbed, gave me the floor. Never have I spoken under a more pressing sense that the issue was up to me alone. No time was left for measured appraisal. In the past eighteen months, I said, Soviet pressure on the Straits, on Iran and on northern Greece had brought the Balkans to a point where a highly possible Soviet breakthrough might open three continents to Soviet penetration. Like apples in a barrel infected by one rotten one, the corruption of Greece would infect Iran and all to the East. It would also carry infection to

Africa through Asia Minor and Egypt, and to Europe through Italy and France. . . . The Soviet Union was playing one of the greatest gambles in history at minimal cost. . . . We and we alone were in a position to break up the play.

Acheson's eloquence carried the day. With the help of its principal target, the converted isolationist Senator Arthur Vandenberg, Congress was persuaded to send $250 million to Greece and $150 million to Turkey.

From this modest acorn grew an oak that was to overshadow the world. The specific case of Greece was taken, partly at Vandenberg's insistence, as the test of an unlimited principle. Within three weeks the President had broadened the issue from victory in the Greek Civil War to a universal principle, and committed the United States to a global crusade on behalf of liberty:

> I believe that it must be the policy of the United States to support free peoples who are resisting attempted subjugation by armed minorities or by outside pressures. I believe that we must assist free peoples to work out their destinies in their own way.

It is true that he went on, in the same breath, to say that American support ought primarily to take the form of economic aid, and true, too, that Acheson did his best in the Congressional hearings to dispel the idea that the United States had signed a blank check. The official who actually drafted Truman's speech, under Acheson's supervision, took it to mean that "all barriers to bold action" were now down. The principle that Truman announced in 1947 proved to be the foundation stone of American foreign policy for a quarter of a century.

The Truman Doctrine contained the seeds of American aid, economic or military, to more than one hundred countries; of mutual defense treaties with more than forty of them; of the great regional pacts, alliances and unilateral commitments: to NATO, to the Middle East, to the Western Hemisphere, and to Southeast Asia. It justified fleets of carriers patrolling the Mediterranean and the South China Sea, nuclear submarines under the polar icecap, air bases in the Thai jungle, and police advisers in Uruguay and Bolivia. In support of it, an average of a million soldiers were deployed for twenty-five years in some four thousand bases in thirty countries. It contained the seeds of a habit of intervention: clandestine in Iran, Guatemala, Cuba, the Philippines, Chile and the CIA alone knows where else; overt in Korea, the Lebanon, the Dominican Republic, Laos, Cambodia and Vietnam. "From Korea to Berlin to Cuba to Vietnam," Senator Fulbright has written, "the Truman Doctrine governed America's response to the Communist world. Tactics changed—from 'massive retaliation' to 'limited war' and 'counter-insurgency'—but these were variations on a classic formulation that few questioned."

By the end of the 1940s, then, the United States had set out on the road that led to Vietnam. This fateful commitment to intervene wherever "freedom" was threatened was made at a very exceptional moment in time. It was made, first of all, during the exceedingly brief period when the U.S.A. enjoyed a monopoly of atomic weapons. It was made before the economies of Europe and Japan had recovered and before the U.S.S.R. had reconstructed her shattered industries. It was made when most of the world's gold was safely in Fort Knox, symbolic trophy of victory.

By the 1960s, this exceptional period of dominance was over. American military and economic power continued to be awesome, but they had ceased to be incomparably far ahead of the world in almost every measurable respect, as they had been in the 1940s.

The U.S. gross national product, after lagging in the 1950s, recovered strongly in the 1960s. But the rate of growth lagged well behind that of both Western Europe and Japan. Where, in the late 1940s, many intelligent Europeans sought for some magic secret in the American system, by the late 1960s European incomes lagged little more than a decade behind the American level. In France, for example, GNP per head of population in 1969 was well ahead of the American figure for 1958, and the gap, both in the case of France and generally, was still closing. By the seventies, average income per head was actually higher in some European countries —Sweden, Switzerland, and West Germany—than in the United States. In twenty years, from 1949 to 1969, more than half the gold in Fort Knox had trickled away, and the dollar, instead of being proverbially strong, had become chronically weak. By the late 1960s the average daily intake of calories in Western Europe and in the Soviet Union was virtually identical with that in the United States. In steel production the U.S. share of the world total had fallen to 22.5 per cent by 1969, and in that year both Western and Eastern Europe (counting the Soviet Union in Eastern Europe) separately made more steel than the United States did, with Japan not far behind. By the early 1960s, the United States was building not eight but three out of every ten of the world's automobiles. As early as 1962 the U.S. share of world production had fallen, it has been estimated, not only below its 1937 level but below the 36 per cent it had marked by 1913. And the relative economic position of the United States continued to decline.

American military strength remained terrifyingly great in the 1960s. But it was no longer uniquely terrifying. Just eight years after Hiroshima, the Soviet Union beat the United States to the acquisition of a usable H-bomb, the "dry" lithium bomb, small enough to be carried in an airplane. In every subsequent stage of the strategic arms race, the Soviet Union has managed to stay within range of the United States when it did not have the advantage itself. In terms of raw military power, the United States stayed on the summit Winston Churchill spoke of less than a dozen years previously. The Soviet Union of 1955 was militarily more formidable than the United States of 1945.

The United States became committed indefinitely to world responsibility during the brief halcyon time when its resources seemed not merely great but superhuman. Psychologically, this margin of effortless supremacy came to seem the normal state of affairs both to the makers of American policy and to the electorate whose expectations they first set and then would disappoint at their peril. The first effects of the contrast between expectations and reality had begun to show itself before the 1940s were out.

It was on February 9, 1950, that Senator Joseph McCarthy first told an audience, which happened to be a gathering of the Republican Women's Club of Wheeling, West Virginia, that he had in his hand a list of Communists in the State Department.

That same day, on the floor of the Senate, Senator Homer Capehart, Republican of Indiana, gave vent to his own feelings about the drift of events.

"How much more are we going to have to take? Fuchs and Acheson and Hiss and hydrogen bombs threatening outside and New Dealism eating away at the vitals of the nation! In the name of Heaven, is this the best America can do?"

The sequence of dates bears recalling exactly.

In 1948 the Berlin blockade brought home the danger that war might break out again so soon after victory. The death of Jan Masaryk, in March that year, showed Americans the grim face of Stalin's policy in Europe and seemed to many to reveal the failure of the Democratic administration's policy.

In January 1949 Harry Truman was reinaugurated President. Republicans could reckon that it would be twenty years at the least since FDR took office before the reign of the Democrats in the White House would be ended. There was an edge of desperation about their determination to find an issue that would prove that they were not a permanent minority party. Their success in capturing Congress in 1946 only sharpened the bitterness of the political atmosphere.

In the spring of 1949 it became plain that Chiang's government was tottering. Shanghai fell in May. The end of a dream in which Americans had invested many lives, many billions of dollars, and much hope came at the end of September. Mao Tse-tung became head of the Chinese People's Republic.

By that time, the President had announced that the Soviet Union had successfully exploded an atomic bomb.

It was on January 7, 1950, at a dinner party in Washington, that Senator McCarthy was urged by the Jesuit Father Edmund Walsh, regent of the School of Foreign Service at Georgetown University, to ponder the dangers of Communist infiltration of democratic governments, and also the subject's possibilities as a campaign issue in 1952.

On January 12 Dean Acheson in a speech at the National Press Club, in Washington, appeared to define the American "defensive perimeter" in such a way as to exclude Korea. In point of fact, Korea was protected by treaty. But there was genuine concern that a change of policy was intended, as well as a heaven-sent opportunity for partisan attack.

The next day, at the United Nations, the Soviet ambassador, Jacob Malik, walked out of the Security Council.

On successive days, Senator Bridges asked for a vote of censure on the Administration and Senator Knowland demanded Acheson's resignation. On January 19 the Administration was defeated on Korea in the House by a single vote.

On January 21, in New York, Alger Hiss was convicted of perjury. The charges involved Hiss's denial under oath that he had passed State Department papers to Whittaker Chambers, who swore that they had both been members of a Communist espionage network. The perjury verdict was therefore generally (erroneously but understandably) taken as tantamount to proof that Hiss, a Harvard Law School graduate, New Dealer and State Department official senior enough to have traveled to Yalta with Roosevelt, was a Communist spy.

Hiss was the brother of one of Acheson's law partners. When Acheson was asked for comment, on January 25, he said that he did not intend to turn his back on Alger Hiss.

Two days later, Klaus Fuchs was met by a Scotland Yard inspector at Paddington Station in London, drove with him to the War Office, in Whitehall, and dictated a statement. That same day, Washington learned that Fuchs, who had worked on the Manhattan District Project from the earliest days at Los Alamos, had been passing to the Soviets all the secrets to which he had access.

It was not until January 30 that Fuchs agreed to discuss in detail the technical data he had passed. Since the news of the first Soviet atomic explosion, on August 23, the Administration had been agonizing over the decision whether or not to go ahead building a hydrogen bomb.

The President had referred the decision to a three-man committee of the National Security Council: Acheson, Secretary of Defense Louis Johnson, and Chairman David Lilienthal of the Atomic Energy Commission. The three men had not met since December, but by a sheer fluke they met the day after the full scope of Fuchs's treachery had become known. Dean Acheson's memoirs do not specifically relate the decision to the news about Fuchs. But the committee had been expected to recommend further delay, which might well have proved fatal to the H-bomb. Instead, Lilienthal changed his mind and the committee decided by two votes to Acheson's one to put the matter to the President.

There and then, that same day, January 31, Truman went on the air to announce that he had decided to build the H-bomb. He attributed the necessity for his decision to "the probable fission bomb capability and possible thermonuclear bomb capability of the Soviet Union."

That was what Homer Capehart meant when he spoke of "Fuchs and Acheson and Hiss and hydrogen bombs." There was an almost operatic sense of tragic coincidence, a crescendo of foreboding about the months and weeks before McCarthy's speech at Wheeling.

And the steady drumbeat of bad news did not stop after that.

On June 24 the North Koreans crossed the frontier and within a week they had taken Seoul, and the United States had troops at war again.

The United Nations troops counterattacked successfully. Then, in November, came even worse news. Harry Truman met his staff at his office door early one morning and told them grimly: "The Chinese have come in with both feet."

To a private notebook he confided his fears: "It looks like World War III is near."

The junior senator from Wisconsin was such a thoroughly reprobate demagogue, he talked so wildly and he drank so much in his slide to political and personal self-destruction, that it has been easy, as well as convenient, for both his former victims and his former accomplices to caricature him as little more than a picturesque, blue-jowled badman. In the same way, Hollywood has both magnified and romanticized the legends of Jesse James and Billy the Kid, so that it is easy to forget how dangerous the West really was, how much living flesh was mangled by all those .45 slugs. Certainly McCarthy was so disorganized that it is impossible now to reconstruct from his various statements just how many Communists there were on that list. It is probable that he had not bothered to provide himself with any evidence to support whatever it was that he did say. It hardly matters. The little list was an inspired device for dramatizing the dark imaginings of many millions of his contemporaries. Shame has silenced McCarthy's supporters, and his posthumous portrait has been drawn in the main by his enemies. In their hatred and fear of him they have obscured the uncanny precision with which he put into words what so many Americans incoherently felt.

"The reason why we find ourselves in a position of impotency," he insinuated to the matrons of Wheeling, "is not because our only powerful potential enemy has sent men to invade our shores but, rather, because of the traitorous actions of those who have been treated so well by this nation. . . ."

In that one sentence of saturnine blarney McCarthy succeeded so brilliantly in capturing the essence of a mood that it is not unjust that it should be remembered by his name. As the bad news drummed into their heads—Masaryk, China, Hiss, Fuchs, danger, defeat, treason and conspiracy—what Americans resented above all was the contrast between their country's power and its impotency to make the world conform to their ideals, or even to stop its shocking and frightening them.

Americans were the most powerful people in the history of the world. Then, why couldn't this power be used by their leaders to stop things going to hell in a handcart?

Senator Capehart was not the only one to ask this question. In various idioms and with varying degrees of profanity, it was being asked in the locker rooms of country clubs, in corner saloons, in the editorial conferences of newspapers, and by Catholic intellectuals and fundamentalist Protestants in the lecture rooms of denominational colleges. Joe McCarthy was not the only one to supply the fatally plausible answer: treason must be afoot.

The mood McCarthy seized on can almost be expressed as a syllogism. America is so powerful. Yet things are not going as we want them to. *Ergo*, we are being betrayed.

In an article in *Harper's Magazine* at the end of 1952, Sir Denis Brogan warned Americans against "the illusion of omnipotence."

> This is the illusion, that any situation which distresses or endangers the United States can only exist because some Americans have been fools or knaves. . . .

China, Brogan went on, was the supreme example of this illusion. The Chinese Revolution was one of the great events of history. It had been in the making since before the October Revolution in Russia. It was the fulfillment of yearnings and upheavals in a country so vast and so distant from the United States that there was little Americans either could do or, sensibly, would do to impede them. Yet it was often discussed

> as if it were simply a problem in American foreign and domestic policy and politics . . . simply the result of American action or inaction, the re-

sult of the mistakes, and worse than mistakes, of General Marshall, Secretary Acheson, President Roosevelt and the Institute of Pacific Relations.

Brogan was right in identifying the disappointment of great expectations as one of the causes of McCarthyism. In the late 1940s and early 1950s many Americans, looking out at a recalcitrant world from their thriving, invulnerable island, lacked a sense of what was historically possible. This tempted them to blame their government for problems that it had neither caused nor could reasonably be expected to solve. But McCarthyism was not simply a concomitant of American success; it was also a consequence of American disappointment.

The rapid social and economic progress of the past half century had exacted a harsh price. The experience of the agricultural frontier had been ambiguous. So had the experience of the urban immigrant. White Southerners—and roughly a quarter of the population were white Southerners by birth—had known poverty, quasi-colonial economic exploitation, and the sense of threat that came from the knowledge that they were a minority whose most cherished convictions were viewed with little sympathy by the majority. Millions of Americans had won higher living standards by migrating to the city. But they had paid for them in loss of status, poor housing, tedious work and the various insults laid on them by city officials, employers and labor unions. Economic progress was real enough, but it seemed negated emotionally by a sense of loss and a sense of threat. Perhaps the most threatened group of all was that middle class, of old American stock, that had seen its relatively privileged status successively eroded by almost every social development of the past hundred years: by immigration, urbanization, the eclipse of Protestantism, inflation, depression and now by wartime boom and the high wages it brought to every other group.

The disappointment of great expectations, in fact, is one of the oldest themes in American history, precisely because the expectations have always been so high. From the very earliest period, a certain number of people have reacted to the intolerable contrast between their expectations and their frustrations by blaming foreign conspiracy. "In his spiritual isolation," Max Lerner has written, "the middle-class American seems to suffer from a sense of encirclement and to identify with a 'European' or 'foreign' source whatever ills he feels he is subject to."

A degree of popular xenophobia was to be expected, and was indeed partly rational for the native American working class, given the competition for work and the severe cultural strains imposed on late-nineteenth and early-twentieth century America by the arrival of hundreds of thousands of immigrants each year. Most of them, after all, spoke no English, especially after 1890. Some two thirds of them were not Protestants, and the United States was then very much a Protestant country. And all of them had very different customs, attitudes and experiences. It would have been a miracle if friction had been avoided.

But beneath this natural xenophobia, softened as it was by a strong opposite tradition of welcoming immigrants, there was a recurrent strain of something altogether less rational. There are startling parallels in detail between the anti-Masonic and anti-Catholic literature of the early-nineteenth century, the agitation of the second Ku Klux Klan, in 1915–24, and the anti-Communist hysteria of the 1940s and 1950s. All shared the same readiness to interpret individual acts as evidence of a vast, worldwide conspiracy. Fundamentalist Protestant ministers were prominent in all three. So were informers, often converts or renegades. Above all, each fed on the same instinct to blame American troubles on foreign machinations.

The historian Richard Hofstadter traced this process in a famous essay called *The Paranoid Style in American Politics*, and there are striking similarities between this recurrent conspiracy mania and the clinical indications of paranoia. The paranoid individual begins with a conviction of exceptional gifts and special destiny. When life proves disappointing, and this conviction of special status is threatened, the paranoid is less successful than other personality types in adjusting to reality. It is easier first to find scapegoats, and then to invent them. Thus by degrees all life's hard blows, and in any life there will be plenty of them, are attributed to the machinations of "them." Ultimately, in the fully psychotic paranoiac, this tendency to suspect persecution becomes total delusion. The patient's world becomes wholly manipulated by a conspiracy of tireless malevolence and boundless cunning.

It is possible that Americans are peculiarly prone to the political variety of paranoia (which of course afflicts many persons entirely sane in their personal lives) precisely because of the great expectations of special political destiny that the American ideology has always encouraged. But this is not the point Hofstadter made. He argued that the paranoid right wing was recruited largely from those who were concerned about status politics, and from two groups in particular: members of upwardly mobile immigrant groups (especially German-Americans and Irish-Americans), who were interested in gaining status, and those old-stock, middle-class Americans who were afraid of losing it.

Almost twenty years before Hofstadter wrote this essay, the American Jewish Committee sponsored a massive study by an interdisciplinary team of social scientists to investigate the origins of racial and religious prejudice. Several volumes were published on the relationship between individual psychology and anti-Semitism and other right-wing prejudices.

One volume uncannily anticipated the politics of the 1950s: *The Authoritarian Personality*, by a group of scholars led by T. W. Adorno. The authors started from the assumption that anti-Semitism was not an isolated phenomenon, but part of an ideology of the Right and also related to a particular psychological personality type. Detailed analysis of hundreds of interviews confirmed these assumptions. Adorno and his colleagues also unearthed the prevalence of a particular political/psychological syndrome.

They discovered that a large proportion of their interviewees held views that could not be characterized as genuinely conservative. (They defined conservatives as those who accepted both the capitalist and also the democratic, anti-repressive tenets of traditional Americanism.) On the contrary, they classified many of the interviewees as "pseudoconservatives," whom they regarded as potential fascists. A belief in pseudoconservative politics, they suggested, corresponded with a particular type of personality that seemed to be on the increase in the United States (and perhaps in other industrial societies): conventional, authoritarian and at the same time submissive to authority at the conscious level, but underneath, at the subconscious level, violent, anarchic and destructive. "The pseudoconservative," they concluded, "is a man who, in the name of upholding traditional American values and institutions and defending them against more or less fictitious dangers, consciously or unconsciously aims at their abolition."

There was clay waiting for the potter. Long before McCarthy's speech at Wheeling, suspicion had begun to focus on the danger of Communist subversion. The House Un-American Activities Committee was set up in 1938, and from the start devoted about four fifths of its attention to investigating the Left. The Alien Registration Act of 1940, in practice and intention a sedition act, breached constitutional precedent by embracing guilt by association. The U. S. Chamber of Commerce began publishing, in 1946, a series of reports alleging clandestine Communist influence in various areas of American life. These led on to the HUAC investigation of Hollywood in 1947 and to the accusations of left-wing domination of radio in *Red Channels* (1950). In 1947, President Truman issued an executive order requiring loyalty checks for 2.5 million civil servants, several hundred of whom were dismissed as a result. Union leaders were required by the Taft-Hartley Act, of 1947, to take an oath that they were not Communists, and in 1949 the leaders of the Communist Party themselves were tried and convicted for conspiring to advocate the overthrow of the U. S. Government by force and violence. Well before the end of the 1940s, numerous states and cities had passed statutes and ordinances obliging teachers to take loyalty oaths, though these were subsequently struck down by the Supreme Court.

In the particular case of China, suspicion of a Communist conspiracy to betray American interests was widespread long before Chiang's government fell. In June 1945, the State Department official John Stewart Service was arrested because he had lent some of his reports to Washington to a left-wing periodical. And before the end of the same year—the month before the Administration took that decision to move Chiang's troops to North China which has been called "essentially a decision for counter-revolution"—the American ambassador, General Hurley, called a press conference and announced that he was resigning because "a considerable section of our State Department is endeavoring to support communism generally as well as specifically in China."

By the time McCarthy gave his Wheeling speech, in other words, the suspicions he voiced in it were already deeply embedded in the political culture of the United States. They corresponded with the instinctive fears of a large fraction of the American people. It was not just that McCarthy offered a logical explanation of the frustrations of American foreign policy: he exposed what was already for a significant minority the received explanation. What the mounting frustrations of the period did was to recruit for a while both respectable support and mass support for the suspicions of the paranoid minority.

Perhaps the most important, though not the most obvious, cause of these frustrations was the loss of nuclear monopoly. As any policeman knows, there is no frustration like that of the armed man who has to put up with being pelted with rocks because he has been ordered not to use his gun. It is not in the least surprising that many high-ranking U. S. Air Force officers itched to launch a preventive atomic attack on the U.S.S.R. before the American advantage was dissipated. We now know, too, that General MacArthur did seriously propose that atomic weapons be used on China.

When MacArthur said, "There is no substitute for victory," he meant victory unconditional and merciless. Yet that phrase destroyed him. Once it was known that total victory was MacArthur's strategy, President Truman had no alternative but to fire him. Given the complex equations of political and military reality, there could be no substitute for restraint.

At the end of his life, in October 1947, Henry Stimson had clarified those realities in a wise swan song in *Foreign Affairs*:

> Americans who think they can make common cause with present-day Communism are living in a world that does not exist. . . . An equal and

opposite error is made by those who argue that Americans by strong-arm methods, perhaps even by "preventive war," can and should rid the world of the Communist menace. I cannot believe that this view is widely held. For it is worse than nonsense: it results from a hopeless misunderstanding of the geographical and military situation, and a cynical misunderstanding of what the people of the world will tolerate from any nation. . . .

That was the assessment which guided the foreign policy of the Truman administration. For in spite of a certain arrogance and his sometimes apocalyptic sense of the world struggle, Dean Acheson understood the limits of American power. But it wasn't easy for those with less knowledge of the facts than Stimson or Acheson to understand these limits. Stimson went on to say that those who advocated strong-arm policies revealed "a totally wrong assessment of the basic attitudes and motives of the American people." He may have been right about basic motives. But he underestimated the effect on public attitudes of the contrast between the illusion of omnipotence and the galling frustrations of limited war and limited peace.

It was hard to see billions of dollars that came from the highest taxes Americans had ever paid in peacetime going in foreign aid, and harder still to see so little return and so little gratitude for it. It was hard to swallow the casualties and the humiliations of the Korean War, while knowing all the time that it lay within American power to erase the military strength of both North Korea and China in a single night. It was easier for many, in the end, to reach for simpler explanations than the tangle of technicality and complication which was all the government and the press seemed to offer to assuage their bewilderment. It was tempting to accept the logic of the conspiracy theory as Senator McCarthy offered it, two months after the fall of MacArthur:

> How can we account for our present situation unless we believe that men high in this government are concerting to deliver us to disaster? This must be the product of a great conspiracy, a conspiracy on a scale so immense as to dwarf any previous such venture in the history of men.

The frustration that American foreign policy encountered after 1948, then, gave McCarthyism its opportunity.

McCarthyism was not essentially about foreign policy. It was about America. Its causes lay in American society and American politics. Even at the overt level, it was not concerned with the real actions of the Communist powers in the world nearly as much as it was with the largely mythical danger of Communist conspiracy in the United States. And its principal effect was to transform what ought to have been an issue of foreign policy

—namely, how to deal with Communist power abroad—into the most emotional and dangerous issue in American domestic politics.

The Republican politicians dipped their arrows in bitter juices squeezed out by the pressures of American society: regional rivalry, ethnic hostility, and class feeling. McCarthy drenched his rhetoric in class envy. "The worst of all," he said at Wheeling, "are the young men who were born with silver spoons in their mouths," and worse than all was Dean Acheson. McCarthy got him up as the stage villain of isolationist melodrama: as a "pompous diplomat, with his striped pants and his phony British accent."

The dubious notion that high socioeconomic status and educational privilege predispose the upper class to radical politics is largely peculiar to the United States. It has been held by such varied thinkers as George Wallace, Spiro Agnew and Herman Kahn, and it played a great part in the confusions of the later 1960s. The McCarthyites did not invent that topsy-turvy stereotype. They inherited it from their isolationist, antieastern and Anglophobe antecedents. They handed it down to the 1960s with refinements of their own.

The pseudoconservative frequently conceals his authoritarian support for the *status quo* behind a veil of populism. (It was for this reason that Hitler called his party National Socialist.) This disguise was already to be discerned in the contradictory charges leveled against Franklin Roosevelt: that he was an aristocrat, and also a Red. Adorno's comments on this aspect of Roosevelt-hating help to explain the more general contradictions in the stereotypes of the American Right:

> The conceptions of Communist, internationalist, and warmonger are close to another . . . —that of the snob. Just as the fascist agitator persistently mixes up radicals and bankers, claiming that the latter financed the Revolution and the former seek financial gains, the contradictory ideas of an ultraleftist and an exclusive person alienated from the people are brought together by anti-Roosevelt sentiment. . . .

But Senator Capehart was worried not only by Acheson and Hiss "outside" (!) but also by New Dealism gnawing within. The McCarthy period was an opportunity of revenge for all those who had opposed the New Deal. As such, it attracted and united both pseudoconservatives and conservatives of the classic economic variety. It was no accident that the U. S. Chamber of Commerce was one of the first bodies to demand the hunting down of subversives. Many traditional, business-oriented conservatives did not distinguish between the attack on Communist conspiracy and the fight against "socialism," whether that meant high taxes, strong unions, or government regulation and intervention.

The tenets of McCarthyism boil down to three grand phobias. One was the idea that there was a conspiracy at work in America to undermine capitalism, free business enterprise, and the American way of life. The second was the belief that agents of this conspiracy, Communists or their dupes in education, the churches, and the media, were corrupting the nation's morale, and especially that of the young. And the third was the conviction that high places in government itself had been infiltrated by men who would sell America out.

Such phobias were not new. They had flourished on the extreme Right for years. What was new was that, in 1948–53, such ideas began to be voiced by orthodox politicians, by a considerable fraction, in fact, of the party that controlled Congress and was about to win the White House.

Richard Nixon's account, in *Six Crises*, shows that, to a significant extent, he shared each of these three phobias. The danger of domestic communism could not be brushed off because of the small number of Communist Party members, he wrote. It was "magnified a thousandfold because of its . . . support by the massive power of the world Communist conspiracy centered in Moscow." Point two: Nixon took Hiss as "the symbol of a considerable number of perfectly loyal citizens whose theatres of operation are the nation's mass media and universities, its scholarly foundations, and its government bureaucracies. This group likes to throw the cloak of liberalism around all its beliefs. . . . They are not Communists; they are not even remotely disloyal. . . . But they are of a mindset which makes them singularly vulnerable to the Communist popular front appeal . . . they were 'patsies' for the Communist line." Point three: "No one would question President Truman's anti-Communism," but his behavior was nevertheless "particularly hard to understand." He led "a large segment of the public away from a deeper understanding of the true threat of the Communist conspiracy in America."

In the end, General MacArthur did fade away. So did Joe McCarthy, in the end. The country woke up. But not before the nightmare years had left a legacy of long-term consequences.

The first was in those very places where Richard Nixon was so proud that the Hiss case had alerted the nation to the dangers of communism: in the universities, the scholarly foundations, the mass media and the bureaucracy.

The effect on one small but critically important subsection of the bureaucracy is well known. The investigations of the McCarthy years succeeded in chasing out of the State Department, and out of any positions from which they could have influenced policy, all the men who had understood the nature of the Communist revolution, and that meant all the men with any real expertise on modern China: Owen Lattimore, O. Edmund Clubb, John Stewart Service, John Paton Davies. Those who remained, and those who took their places, with very few exceptions, had learned their lesson.

One of the exceptions was James C. Thomson, who was the White House staff assistant on national security concerned with China policy when I arrived in Washington on my second visit, in 1962. I asked him to explain that policy, and in answer he reached for a pad of scratch paper and drew a recognizable but strangely distorted map of the Far East. A cluster of large blobs represented Japan, sizable ovals Taiwan and the Philippines, and huge, pendulous scribbles South Korea and South Vietnam. Against each he marked in their population: "100 m.," "16 m." and so on. Then, in the center of the map, where the Middle Kingdom should have been, he first inked in the tiniest dot his pen would draw, and scrawled across the page "?700,000,000?"

That was what McCarthyism had done. It had frozen policy into the moronic rigidity of simultaneously trying to pretend that the biggest nation on earth didn't exist, and blowing it up into a bogeyman of implacable Marxist expansionism.

In the next chapter, we will have to look in some detail at certain aspects of the intellectual life of the 1950s. We shall find the same timid conformity and the same dangerous illusions, in one field after another. The nuclear physicists gave up their claim to have a voice in the political decisions affecting their work. Critical reassessment of American history and sociology stagnated. Students of literature shied away from the writers of social and political dissent to pore over the safe obscurity of Pound and Eliot, Yeats and Joyce. The political scientists, for the most part, either fell back to analyzing election statistics or threw themselves into working for the government on nuclear-weapons policy or conflict strategy. Whole schools of area studies arose that did little more than outwork for the intelligence agencies. The effect of McCarthyism has to be measured not only in individual careers destroyed but (more significantly for the nation as a whole) in assumptions unchallenged, in questions unasked, in problems ignored for a decade. The best brief summary of this lamentable hiatus in the intellectual tradition, perhaps, is Ronald Steel's: McCarthyism "debased American intellectual life" and led to the emergence of "a counter-ideology of anti-Communism."

The second great consequence of the disastrous crusade was its effect on the American Right. McCarthyism transformed the issue of Communist subversion into a shibboleth of domestic political alignment. By doing this, it made possible the ultimate fusion of several hitherto separate streams of right-wing sentiment: classic laissez-faire business feeling, the emotional conservatism of small-town America, vestiges of the regional and ethnic prejudices of isolationism, militarism and ultranationalism, fundamentalism in religion, both Catholic and Protestant and the newer cluster of authoritarian attitudes that Adorno called pseudoconservative. Radical anti-communism furnished a respectable ideological stock onto which the new flowering of conservative feeling provoked by the racial convulsions of the 1950s and 1960s could be grafted. This union of conservatives and pseudoconservatives made possible the Goldwater nomination in 1964. A contributing cause of that event was the spread of a subtheory of conspiracy, that the true conservatives in the Republican Party had been robbed of their natural leader, Taft, by eastern internationalists such as Nelson Rockefeller, who was suspiciously soft on the Hisses and Achesons of this world if not on communism itself. The Wallace campaigns of 1964 and 1968 were further false starts in the same direction, similarly based on the merging of conservative (southern) and pseudoconservative (working-class) elements. And the merger finally came to fruition in the victorious Nixon coalition of 1972. Richard Nixon was the living connection between the origins of the new American conservative alliance, in the period 1948–52, and its maturity. The line between the Hiss trial and the Watergate hearings is a direct one.

The country might still never have traveled that line had it not been for the last and most fateful of the consequences of McCarthyism: its effect upon the Democratic Party. The lesson the Democrats drew was that never again could they afford to expose their foreign policy to the charge that it was soft on communism.

In all the years from the Soviet occupation of Eastern Europe to the end of the Truman administration, the one moment when Republican attacks were disarmed was when the President committed American arms to Korea. "Never before" said Joseph Harsh, who had covered Washington for twenty years for the *Christian Science Monitor*, "have I felt such a sense of relief and unity pass through the city." Neither John Kennedy nor Lyndon Johnson was to forget that lesson. They always knew that the one thing a President could do that would push up his standing in the Gallup poll by ten points overnight was to go on television and strike a firm posture of resisting Communist aggression, preferably by restrained but tough military response. President Kennedy, in a moment of revealing frankness, compared the attraction of escalation to the temptation to take just one more "small drink." The basis of that temptation was the plain political fact that the American public could be relied on to approve tough action whenever the expansion of communism was thought to be involved. That public temper was a legacy of the years of frustration after 1945; political sensitivity to it in the Democratic Party was the product of the traumatic experience of McCarthyism.

Until after 1965, when the Vietnam crisis broke in full force, there was no opposition to orthodox anti-communism from the Left in the Democratic Party, or none worth a President's consideration. Opposition from the Right was always a more real concern. Congress consistently pressed for higher military appropriations than the executive, even while protesting against the executive's propensity to spend. The risks of seeming "naïve" or "weak" always far outweighed the danger of seeming too tough. The armature of policy spun between two poles that had been twisted out of true. That, too, was a long-term consequence of the McCarthy trauma.

# 3

## Abundance

When the 1940s began, it was still true that one third of the nation was ill-housed, ill-clothed and ill-fed. The New Deal as an engine of economic recovery had all but run out of steam. Not just for the Appalachian poor whites whom Walker Evans photographed or the country blacks whom Alan Lomax recorded, but for millions of ordinary Americans in every part of the country, the realistic prospect was a dour struggle to keep body and soul together. Unemployment, eviction or bankruptcy were more probable ends to the story than a new car, a new house or the chance to send a child through college. Farmers and industrial workers alike had to fear the possibility that American life would fail to deliver its promise of abundance in their lifetime and in their children's, too.

By the time the decade ended, American society seemed to have discovered the secret of uninterrupted economic progress. Tens of millions looked on as a birthright a standard of economic well-being that had been the privilege of a few only short years before. Persons of a pessimistic temperament stopped worrying about how to achieve prosperity, and began to deplore its supposed consequences: obesity, conformity, materialism and neurosis.

During Franklin Roosevelt's first term, the New Deal saved American capitalism. By restoring confidence and maintaining the legitimacy of institutions, it averted the imminent danger that the Great Depression would lead to political crisis. But the New Deal did not cure the underlying economic problems. It was the war that did that.

The basic problem, and the symptom of all the others, was mass unemployment. Early in 1940 there were still ten million workers unemployed: one American worker out of four. It takes an effort of imagination to understand what that bald statement meant. The price of unemployment was counted not only in individual poverty and lost production but in fear, anger and despair.

Any hope that radical economic policies might have eradicated this social cancer during the second Roosevelt term was scotched by the sharp recession of 1937–38. By March 1938, industrial production was off by a third from the previous July, the stock market had collapsed, and unemployment increased sharply. For the first time, FDR's confidence seemed shaken: he did not know what to do. The very men who provided the intellectual drive for the "second New Deal" recognized with the greatest clarity that they had failed. They also understood that the economic problems that had defeated their best efforts were potentially political problems: that unless mass unemployment and business stagnation could be ended, political upheaval must follow. The only question was what form it would take: revolution, or reaction? Democracy and the constitution had survived one decade of depression. It was not obvious that they could survive another.

"The paramount necessity," Adolf Berle, for example, advised the President in 1938, "is to do some thinking at least one lap ahead of the obvious financial and industrial crisis which is plainly indicated within the next few years."

In 1939, Harry Hopkins, who was even closer to the President, was saying flatly, "With twelve millions unemployed we are socially bankrupt and politically unstable. . . . This country cannot continue as a democracy with ten million or twelve million unemployed. It just can't be done."

As late as 1941, Paul Hoffman of Studebaker, one of the most farsighted of the liberal minority in business leadership, could still say, "After eight years of struggle America has still eight million unemployed. Unemployment is a social disease gnawing at our vitals."

"Old Dr. New Deal has to be replaced by Dr. Win-the-War," said Roosevelt. His cure was miraculously quick. Within a matter of months, six million workers found new jobs. Within a couple of years, mass unemployment had virtually disappeared. Soon the Great Depression itself was becoming an unhappy memory. The Great Boom had begun.

Prosperity gradually seeped back to every corner of the economy. First it filled the main channels, then it filled every crack in the parched soil. War production spilled over from the old industrial heartland in Pennsylvania and the Great Lakes states to California, Texas, and the Piedmont counties of the South.

Farmers had struggled grimly against falling prices through the fat years of the 1920s as well as through the lean years that followed. Suddenly they were reaping bumper crops, and being paid record prices for them as well. Farm income doubled in four years.

The war boom brought record corporate profits, with one third of all war orders going to ten giant corporations. The war brought capital gains and investment opportunities to the people who had money already, but it also meant an end to hard times for most other sections of the population. Even allowing for inflation, real wages jumped by 44 per cent in the four years of war. The proportion of families living on incomes of less than two thousand dollars a year fell from three quarters to one quarter of the population.

To almost everyone's surprise, the boom did not end with the war. Instead, the magic figure of sixty million jobs, the wildest dream of the New Deal optimists, was reached in 1947 and then left far behind. By the end of the 1940s, unemployment had stabilized at around 3 million, or roughly 5 per cent of the work force.

This rapid shrinking of the reserve army of the unemployed radically altered the balance of power between unions and management. The 1930s had been years of pioneering militancy and rapid growth. Union membership grew from under 5 million in 1929 to some 8 million in 1939. Especially after the Supreme Court upheld the Wagner Act in 1937, most workers in the steel, automobile, rubber and textile industries were organized in industrial unions affiliated to the rampant young CIO.

The 1940s, in contrast, were years of consolidation for the unions. Their membership doubled in the decade. In the two years after the war, a series of strikes and tough demands backed by credible threats of strikes brought sharp increases in wages on top of the wartime increases produced by competition for workers. They also brought a conservative reaction in the Taft-Hartley Act of 1947. It did not stop industrial workers' increasingly winning fringe benefits in the form of provision for welfare and economic security written into union contracts. In the ten years from the Wagner Act decision to Taft-Hartley, in short, the unions became less militant, more powerful, more bureaucratic, and less antagonistic toward management. They also became more deeply entrenched in the power structure of the Democratic Party. Their members made a sharp step forward, whether their progress was measured in higher wages, in security, or in status.

High wages created the demand, and high profits created the business confidence necessary for the expansion of construction and the other consumer industries that led the boom. But something more elemental was also at work.

After twelve years of depression and four years of war, people suddenly wanted to have babies again. This was a world-wide phenomenon, but it was more sharply marked in the United States than elsewhere. Americans had more reason for confidence in the postwar world than most other peoples. The birth rate, which had been 30 per thousand in 1910 and still over 25 in 1920, had fallen to 18.7 by 1935, and it was still below 20 in 1940. By 1947, it was over 25 per thousand again, a 25 per cent increase, and it stayed on that plateau until the middle 1950s. That meant that a million extra babies were being born every year above the rate for the depression years: 3.6 million babies, for example, in 1950, as against 2.6 million in 1940. The death rate continued to drift slowly down, but nothing like so fast as the birth rate shot up.

The driving force behind the postwar boom, in fact, was not so much the military-industrial complex, though defense expenditures certainly helped to keep the economy expanding, especially after the Korean War began, in 1950. It was the fusion of demographic trends, government policy and business interests into something like a suburban-industrial complex.

Financed by easy money at low interest rates, by sympathetic federal mortgage policy and often directly by the Veterans Administration, millions of families moved out of city tenements and country shacks into trim little white houses with front lawns and electric kitchens. Construction boomed, of course. So did the domestic-appliance industry. Because people had to get to work and to the new shopping centers, so did the automobile industry and its ancillaries: oil, rubber, machine tools, plastics.

The western frontier had been closed by 1890. Immigration had tailed off in the 1920s, and foreign markets collapsed after 1920. But now, after 1945, it seemed that American society had found a new frontier in the suburbs, and American business had found a way out of the dilemma between war and recession.

The answer to the riddle—or so thoughtful Americans in the late 1940s and 1950s thought with startling unanimity—lay in abundance: not in mere volume of production but in a system that would perpetuate prosperity and at the same time guarantee political harmony by distributing the consumption of goods so lavishly that it would not seem urgent to distribute them equally. In that way, economic privilege could be left undisturbed. Social conflict could be made irrelevant, obsolete. The abundant society could short-circuit the two quintessential questions of politics, the question of justice and the question of priority: Who gets what? What must we do first?

That hope was the master key to the whole elaborate, coherent and, at first glance, persuasive system of social thought which we will have to examine in detail in the next chapter. Here it is relevant to observe that the literal faith in abundance grew naturally out of both faces of the experi-

ences of the 1940s, not only from the economic and social successes of
the affluent society but also from the economic despair which it had so
abruptly replaced.

If American society had always been flowing with a superabundance
of milk and honey, the postwar affluence might not have exercised such a
fascination upon intellectuals, and indeed on most other people. As it was,
the milk and honey appeared suddenly to a people who had been trudging
across an economic Sinai for a decade and a half. And so the miracle was
taken for a sign and a portent. The new philosophy of abundance came
close to being a crude inversion of Harry Hopkins' and Adolf Berle's anguished perception of the connection between economic distress and political crisis. If the United States had been in danger of ceasing to be a
democracy so long as there were ten million unemployed, it was tempting
to jump to the conclusion that there was not much more to democracy
than keeping unemployment under 5 per cent, guaranteeing a swelling
flood of consumer goods to the employed, and increasing the gross national product by a respectable percentage each year.

What occurred to very few of those who celebrated the social revolution implied by this new-found abundance, however, was that—like most
revolutions—it contained its own contradictions. Along with dishwashers,
nylon stockings and automatic transmissions, the new prosperity produced
the antibodies to the strongest ideas that came out of it. The more abundance could be taken for granted, the less it came to seem an adequate or
even a civilized test for political ideas. But the process of contradiction
worked in another, more specific way, too. Whether or not the new prosperity was making Americans more equal, social scientists were almost
unanimous in concluding that it was. Understandably, they drew the inference that production could ultimately make conflict between social and
economic classes obsolete. Yet, at this very moment, the same economic
changes were creating the two new "classes" that were to challenge the
philosophy of abundance in the 1960s: the new students and the new
blacks.

Higher education had always been more widely available in America
than in Europe. This was true even of colonial America. By the 1830s,
when England, for example, with a roughly comparable population, was
acquiring its third and fourth universities (in Durham and London), there
were already more than a score of flourishing colleges of higher education
in the United States. The Land Grant Act of 1862 empowered the federal
government to give the states more than 13 million acres to endow a system of state universities. As a result, even if enrollment rose slowly for a
long time, to go to college was no longer, in the late-nineteenth and early-

twentieth centuries an impossible dream, even for those in modest circumstances. During the 1920s, enrollment continued to grow, largely, according to Christopher Jencks and David Riesman's authoritative account in *The Academic Revolution*, because the colleges had accommodated themselves to the business ethic, so that those intent upon a business career, who would previously have skipped college as a waste of time, now enrolled. The Depression increased the feeling that you needed a college degree to get a safe job in a big organization. College enrollment was one of the few indications of well-being that continued to rise: from 1.1 million students in 1930 to 1.5 million in 1940. By that year, Jencks and Riesman calculated, about one youngster in six was entering college and about one in twelve was graduating.

To graduate from college was still, in 1940, to hurdle one of the more significant class barriers in American life. But it was one that an increasing proportion of the population was intent on clearing if it got the chance.

Only twenty years earlier, even to graduate from high school had been a mark of high achievement, if not indeed a privilege. Fewer than 17 per cent of the age group received high school diplomas in 1920. By 1940, 1.2 million boys and girls, or a fraction over half the age group, graduated from high school. In 1950, the number of high school graduates had fallen by a whisker, because the birth rate had fallen seventeen years earlier, in the depths of the Depression. The proportion of the age group had risen to almost 60 per cent. But the number who graduated from college had leaped ahead to 432,000—substantially more than twice the 1940 figure.

Many factors contributed to this sharp jump in the proportion who went to college and thus obtained the most important single badge of status in American middle-class life. The general rise in prosperity was probably the most important cause. The trend for more people to want to go to college, or to persuade their children to go to college, was long-established. Moreover, from 1945 until the mid '50s the combined cost of tuition and subsistence rose much more slowly than average family income. A substantially increased proportion of young people could afford to pay tuition and living costs, and to forgo earnings, and it was also easier, with full employment, to find part-time jobs.

Another decisive factor was the passage by Congress, in 1944, of the Servicemen's Readjustment Act, better known as the GI Bill of Rights. This was not wholly an educational measure. It also helped veterans with loans to set themselves up in business and in many other ways. One enterprising fellow used it to equip himself with a set of burglar tools. But it did offer to pay for several years' college for all those who were educationally qualified. Several millions of young men took this chance.

The effect was profound, and continuing. Both college enrollment, and the proportion of the age group who went to college, rose even more sharply in the 1950s and 1960s than they had in the 1940s. It was to be twenty-five years before that rising trend reached the point where as much as half the population even started any form of higher education. But, once again, the crucial turning point had been passed in the 1940s. "The returning veterans," Jencks and Riesman comment, "forced many colleges to choose between expansion and exclusion." Some chose exclusion, and started a trend toward greater selectivity in higher education, which was also to leave its mark on the next twenty years. But the system as a whole chose expansion. The GI Bill established the idea that a college education might become not a privilege for the few but a right for the many, just at the moment when falling costs made that idea seem possible.

The GI Bill became law in 1944, and college enrollment began to rise steeply the following year. In the second half of the 1940s, the net increase in the population was exactly twice what it had been in the second half of the 1930s: 1.6 per cent per annum, against 0.8 per cent. Think about those facts, and you have come close to predicting the turbulent youth rebellion of the middle 1960s. The postwar population bulge, swollen by the post-GI-Bill trend for a higher and higher proportion of each age group to go to college, flooded onto campuses between the fall of 1963 and the fall of 1965. By 1968, the climactic year of the troubled 1960s, more than six million students were enrolled. That was more than four times as many as in the 1940s. But not only that. Wholly new categories of young people were going to college. They went there with new attitudes and expectations. And they found a new atmosphere there when they arrived.

The Freedom Riders' bus, aflame like a fiery cross in the warm dusk outside Anniston, Alabama, in May 1961 made an appropriately dramatic symbol of how most people then supposed that relations between blacks and whites in America would be changed. Freedom would come sweeping down from North to South, borne like a torch by a handful of abolitionist martyrs. Their sufferings would be apostolic. They would be reviled, spat upon, thown into cells, beaten with chains. But the photographers and the network cameramen would be there to transform their witness into symbol. The slumbering fervor of the southern black masses would be set alight. Northern opinion would be aroused, and the federal government half-shamed, half-maneuvered into taking a long-overdue stand against the vestiges of segregation. At long last, the Deep South would be dragged into conformity with the American ideal.

But, for more than a generation before 1961, other buses, unpho-tographed and unnoticed, had been rolling routinely in the opposite direction, out of the South. They were Greyhound buses on their scheduled runs up through the Carolinas on U. S. Highway 1 into Washington, D.C., Baltimore, Philadelphia and up the Jersey Turnpike into New York City. Or they were Trailways buses slamming along between washroom stops at the crossroads towns of East Texas on the run from Shreveport into Dallas. Or local buses meandering, always northward, through the pecan groves of southern Georgia toward Atlanta, or out of the Alabama Black Belt, past the statue of Vulcan on the mountain, into Birmingham, or triumphantly across the Ohio river into Cincinnati.

There were trains on the same run, until the 1950s, rocking through the night on the Louisville & Nashville and the Seaboard Line and most of all on the great Illinois Central road, which pulls out of New Orleans along the levee and runs through the ominously quiet county seats in the Mississippi Delta and then carries its exhausted pilgrims, asleep in the coaches, on through the Little Egypt section of southern Illinois into that harsh promised land, Chicago. The narrow concrete highways of the South carried the same exodus, in pickup trucks bumping out of the Appalachian hollows toward Pittsburgh, and jalopies shaking across Arkansas on the rocky road to California with feet stuck out of the windows for some cool air and bedrolls piled on the roof.

No photographers bothered to meet these riders as they stretched their legs at a gas station while some youth who would be taking the same trip himself within the year put another tankful into the Chevy for the last lap north. Certainly no poets thought it worthwhile to romanticize them as they climbed sleepily down from the train, toting their scanty possessions in a cardboard suitcase, or hunted for clean rooms at a dollar fifty a night near the bus station. Yet in their banal way these frowsty travelers were as significant as the wagons that crossed the plains or the huddled masses in quarantine on Ellis Island. They made up a migration comparable in sheer numbers to the movement from Europe to the United States between the Civil War and the First World War, and arguably comparable also in the scope of its implications for American history.

To understand why that is no mere rhetorical exaggeration, it is necessary to remember that in 1940 the South was still, as it had been since colonial times, the great exception in American life. It was so fundamentally different from the rest of the country, so clearly marked off as distinct in its economy, its history, its culture and its population that, seventy-five years after the end of the Civil War, it came closer to being an aborted nation, which had failed to come to its own life inside the body of America, than to being an organic part of the American union.

President Roosevelt had called the South "the nation's number one economic problem." Every one of the thirteen Southern States was poorer than every state outside of the South. Average income there was barely half what it was in the rest of the country: $314 per head per year, as against $604. In industry, southern wages were only a fraction above two thirds of the national average. But the South was still overwhelmingly agricultural. And on the land, more than half the families, white and black, owned no land and received, by sharecropping, *family* incomes that averaged between thirty-eight dollars and eighty-seven dollars a year, which made the sharecroppers of the American South as poor as the poorest peasantry in Europe, and more dependent. Poverty was matched by appallingly low standards of public education and public health. Mississippi, with two separate school systems to support, spent $27.47 a year on each child, against New York State's $141.43. The rate of illiteracy reached 15 per cent in South Carolina. The entire Deep South, the National Emergency Council reported, was a "belt of sickness, misery, and unnecessary death" from syphilis, pellagra, hookworm, malnutrition, typhoid and malaria. By conservative standards, one half of the families in the entire region were in urgent need of rehousing.

Worse still, the South's poverty was avoidable. Potentially the South was rich. It had vast deposits of more than three hundred different minerals, including coal and iron; one quarter of the nation's hydroelectric power; and two thirds of all of the country's oil and natural gas. Part of the trouble was that "a very large share"—99 per cent in the case of some mineral assets—was owned by Yankees and foreigners.

Inside the frontiers of the world's largest and most advanced national economy, in fact, the South in 1940 was suffering from most of the classic evils of colonial underdevelopment: discriminatory freight rates and other commercial practices, absentee ownership, concealed unemployment, shortage of investment, shortage of credit, and overreliance on the export of a few primary products. Absurdest of all, this predominantly agricultural region was a net importer of food. Southern hominy grits were being ground, too often, from Iowa corn. The South had staked everything on cotton, and cotton had been in decline, thanks to the boll weevil, foreign competition and synthetic substitutes, for a generation. Now the employment that the cotton crop did give, however low the price per bale, was threatened by the invention of the cotton-picking machine.

It was not only economics that set the South apart. History had shaped it differently from the beginning, with its plantation system alternating with belts of poor-white farming, its cavalier tradition exercising its agrarian, anti-intellectual pull, its bitter memories of minority status, then defeat, then exploitation. In 1940 the South had essentially missed out on three of the most formative processes of the American experience: immigration, industrialization, and the growth of cities. The 1940 census showed the foreign born as 1.2 per cent for the region as a whole, but even that figure overstated the case. If Texas, with its Mexicans, and Florida, winter playground for the northern cities, are omitted, only one Southerner out of every two hundred was foreign born, as compared with close to one in four in New York State. The overwhelming majority of Southerners, indeed, were not only the children of Southerners; they were either the descendants of Anglo-Saxons of old American stock or they were the descendants of African slaves.

It was this supreme difference, of course, underlying and reinforcing all the others, that more than anything else had historically marked the South off as the great exception. In the South, and only in the South, white American society developed in the presence of a massive subject group too large to annihilate (even if that had been acceptable) and that it resolutely refused to consider assimilating.

Louis Armstrong, taking his horn up the river from New Orleans to Chicago to play at the Savoy ballroom in 1917, was in the vanguard of the first wave of blacks to move out of the South. The depredations of the boll weevil, which ruined hundreds of thousands of black sharecroppers and farmers, and the harsh new reign of Jim Crow, clamped down from the 1890s, a generation after emancipation, pushed some men and women out of the South. Labor shortages in the North after the outbreak of World War I cut off the supply of cheap immigrant workers from Italy and Eastern Europe and sent the labor agents down South to pull others with free railroad tickets and promises of high wages. Close to three quarters of a million blacks had moved to the North by 1920, and another eight hundred thousand followed during the 1920s. Hard times cut the flow to four hundred thousand in the 1930s.

Yet in 1920 it was still true, as it had always been, that only in the South were blacks a massive element in the population. In the North, they were still a rarity outside half a dozen major cities: New York and Chicago, Detroit and Cleveland, Pittsburgh and Philadelphia. Even there, they amounted to no more than 5–10 per cent of the population, roughly the percentage they had always been in the crescent of border states from Maryland to Oklahoma, where the mores had remained essentially southern. In the South proper, as a whole, the 1940 Census reported that Negroes still made up more than a quarter of the population. In Alabama, Georgia and Louisiana they were over 30 per cent, in South Carolina well over 40 per cent, and in Mississippi only a fraction less than half the population. Ten million out of a total of 13 million American Negroes, or 77 per cent, were still Southerners in 1940.

Within a single generation since then, the ethnic peculiarity of the South, one of the great abiding facts of American history since colonial times, has been abolished. The *number* of blacks in the South has continued to rise slightly, and was just under 12 million in 1970. But the proportion that number makes up both of the population of the South as a region and of the total black population of the United States has been steadily dropping. By 1970 blacks had fallen below one fifth of the southern population. And those 12 million southern blacks were only 53 per cent of the total black population. Half the blacks in the United States now live outside the South.

Once again, the 1940s were the decisive years in which this migration reached full spate. In each year of the decade, an average of 160,000 Negroes left the South for good—four times as many as had gone North each year during the Depression. The same rate was almost, though not quite, maintained throughout the 1950s and 1960s: an average of 147,000 black people left the South in each of those twenty years. All told, from 1940 to 1970, more than four and a half million black people moved out of the South to the North and West.

One should not stereotype that flood of humanity, or circumscribe the variety of motives that decided so many individuals to get up and move to a new life. Like the nineteenth-century migration from Europe to the United States, the exodus swept along illiterates and doctors of philosophy, teachers and military personnel, nurses and prostitutes, ministers of religion and hundreds of thousands of young people who had not yet been fitted into any pattern of life when they got on the bus. Among them were the parents of most of the young men and women who were to emerge as the leaders of the black community by the end of the 1960s.

The fundamental precondition for the migration was the slow shift in the southern economy away from colonial, one-crop agriculture. In the rural areas, where plantation slavery had deposited the densest concentrations of black people—in East Texas, in the Delta country of Mississippi, Arkansas and Louisiana, in the Alabama Black Belt and in the long streamer of cotton country that once stretched from South Side Virginia through the Carolinas and Georgia to the Florida Panhandle—mechanization and crop diversification were displacing agricultural labor. But industrialization was not opening up comparable employment for black labor.

As unemployment in the big industrial cities of the Northeast, the Middle West and California was mopped up by the war boom and replaced by labor shortages, jobs did open up there for both black men and black women. To the sharecroppers and cotton choppers, the lumberjacks and maids of the rural South, the wages these new jobs paid were like the end of the rainbow.

But it would be too mechanistic to see the drive behind this epic folk wandering merely in terms of wage differentials and job opportunities. The exodus was the opening of the third act in the historical drama that had begun with emancipation and developed with the failure of Reconstruction. The theme of the story was the ultimate admission of the southern black people into American life. There were few among those caught up in the migration who did not sense this. The first act had been the gift of freedom. The second had been the denial of equality. The third act was to be the pursuit of happiness. Following the oldest of American instincts, black Americans got up and went in search of abundance.

The North now offered good pay and an escape from the known evils of southern life. It might also—the hope lay at the heart of the migration—offer that precious intangible that a black migrant from Texas had gone looking for 'way back in 1917: he was off, he wrote, to "Chicago or Philadelphia. But I don't care where so long as I go where a man is a man."

Of course, black people were escaping from the dehumanizing restrictions of the southern racial code. But it was also a special case of a universal movement. "City air," said a proverb in medieval Germany, "makes free." In all the great migrations from the countryside into the city over the past two centuries—from the green Pennine valleys into sooty Manchester and Liverpool, or from the dusty plains of Bihar into the pestilential bustees of Calcutta—the peasant's son and the landless laborer were lured not just by the promise of high wages but by some dream of a fuller and freer life. Country boys and girls do not always interpret this freedom in any very high-minded way. They simply know that in the city they will be away from the disapproving eyes of parents and neighbors and the unwritten rules that set limits to what you can do with your life. In that sense, in the city you are free to behave, or misbehave, as you please.

It was not only in war plants in Detroit or Los Angeles that black people caught sight of unsuspected possibilities in the middle 1940s. Service in Japan or Europe made hundreds of thousands of black GIs decide that they would never go back to the feudal relations of the South. Many of them found it easier simply not to go back to the South.

Some, then, went North to escape from the South, and some for the money. Some were drawn by families and friends who had already established themselves in Cleveland or Pittsburgh, while others were drawn by the bright lights of 125th Street in Harlem or Sixty-third Street on the South Side of Chicago. People went North to get a job, to get an education, to get on, or to get to be somebody. In each case, it was to the cities that they went.

To some extent, there was a shunting operation. Black people moved out of rural areas and back-country hamlets into southern towns and cities. Other black people moved on North. After 1940, the South began to get its first big cities. By the end of the 1960s, Atlanta, New Orleans, Birmingham and Richmond were all 40 per cent black or more, and smaller but still substantial black minorities had contributed to the startling growth of Houston and Memphis as well.

But the more dramatic and visible migration was the march North. About 90 per cent of all black migrants from the South have moved to six highly industrialized states: California, Illinois, Michigan, Ohio, Pennsylvania and New York. In these states, the migrants were concentrated in the largest cities; and in the cities, they were overwhelmingly concentrated in the center of the inner city—just as it was exploding out of shape as a result of the expansion of the suburbs.

In 1910 almost three quarters of all black Americans were country folk, living in places with fewer than twenty-five hundred inhabitants. Only one black man out of every four had moved beyond the world of William Faulkner's childhood.

By 1970 that proportion had been neatly reversed. Three quarters of all blacks lived in metropolitan areas. The emotional universe of most black Americans was defined not by *Light in August* but by *The Fire Next Time*.

The implications of that change will be one of the main themes of this book. Two of them, however, must be briefly stated here. The first is that the revolution that black Americans have experienced is not only a matter of changed relations with white Americans; the circumstances of black American life have themselves changed profoundly and with jarring suddenness. For the migrants themselves, the difficulties of adjusting from the stultifying certainties of the South to the dangerous uncertainties of the North were superimposed on what must in any case have been a traumatic cultural shock: migration from the country into the industrial, competitive, indifferent, alien city.

The black migration also implied a crisis, both moral and practical, for white society. Between the 1880s and the 1920s, the mass immigration of culturally alien peasants from southern and eastern Europe had severely tested both the tolerance of the old-established groups and the practical capacity of institutions to accommodate the newcomers. Throughout the first third of the twentieth century, that issue had been one of the main themes of American politics. Now, after the mid-point of the century, the same test had to be faced. Only, this time the migrants came from the most deprived and disadvantaged corner of American society. And this time they were black.

For the eighty-odd years since emancipation, the only places where black people were to be found in concentrations dense enough to test the ability of whites to live alongside them had been in the South. Southern society had dealt with the "problem" supposedly caused by the incompatibility of the Negroes (but in fact caused, directly or indirectly, by white racism) in ways that contradicted the central tenets of the American political creed: by segregating them socially, by denying them access in many cases to justice and in most cases to the political process, and by deliberately keeping them in a state of economic and cultural inferiority.

As long as this state of affairs was geographically restricted to one remote region of the country, it could be ignored. As a matter of fact, in the 1910s and 1920s, most middle-class white Americans in the North and West really were ignorant of conditions in the South. Until the 1960s, it was possible to dismiss white supremacy as it was practiced in the South as a vestigial sectional peculiarity that would inevitably be eliminated in time by the pressure of the majority culture.

Suddenly, as a result of the migration, blacks could no longer be ignored. (Other factors contributed to the same result, of course: the upsurge of non-white peoples around the world; the increased inquisitiveness of the news media; even the Cold War, and the need it created to neutralize those aspects of American life that could be exploited by hostile propaganda.) It was no longer only in Sunflower County, Mississippi, or in Lowndes County, Alabama, that massive concentrations of black people were to be found, but in the national capital (71 per cent black by 1970); in the centers of the steel and automobile industries (Gary, Indiana, was 53 per cent black by 1970 and Detroit 44 per cent); and in the capitals of publishing, the news media, television and advertising. There were 1.8 million blacks in New York City by the end of the 1960s (as against 450,000 in 1940), 1.2 million in Chicago, 640,000 in Los Angeles.

The black man was no longer for those white people who had the power to contribute to the American self-image merely a dim, reproachful silhouette, glimpsed in the cottonfields through the heat haze out the window of a train speeding down to Miami or New Orleans. For the industrialist, he was becoming an employee; for the adman, he was an increasingly significant consumer; for the federal bureaucrat, he might be the parent of a child at the bureaucrat's children's school. For the New York TV producer, he might be a neighbor on the subway or at the lunch counter.

Moreover, these new agglomerations of black Northerners were strategically placed at the fulcrum of the political system. For generations, immigrant minorities had enjoyed a disproportionate measure of power in national elections because of the leverage they got by being heavily concentrated in New York City, Philadelphia and Chicago—cities that held the balance of power in three of the four most populous states. By

1970, the vote was 18 per cent black in New York, 28 per cent in Chicago, 39 per cent in Philadelphia. No other ethnic minority came close to possessing the same, strategically sited weight.

The sudden emergence of millions of black citizens in the very center of the national stage confronted American society, in an unexpectedly urgent and concrete shape, with the dilemma that Gunnar Myrdal had foreseen in 1944. It would no longer be possible to qualify the tenets of the American creed with a muttered, *sotto voce* mental reservation: "We hold these truths to be self-evident (except in Mississippi) that all men (except black men) are created equal. . . ." The American ideals of equality, abundance, and constitutional democracy must be extended to black people, or they could be guaranteed to no one. It fell to the 1960s to wrestle with this dilemma. But it had already been posed by those northbound bus passengers in the 1940s.

Any ticket clerk, however, knew something that politicians and social scientists had a tendency to forget. Not all, probably not even a majority, of those one-way, northbound passengers were black. Compared to the steady, unmistakable tramp of the blacks on their way out of the South, white migration has been a swirling, confused phenomenon, hard to measure precisely and hard to describe in broad generalizations. The pressures, ambitions and plain tedium that led white folks to move out of small southern towns were not notably different from the motives that led others to leave, say, western Nebraska or the northern peninsula of Michigan. Another reason why white emigration from the South is hard to quantify is that it has been offset in practice, and concealed in the statistics, by substantial countermovements in the other direction. Some of the areas that have been all but drained of population, such as the hill counties of northwestern Georgia, are within a couple hours' drive of a place such as suburban Atlanta, which has shown spectacular growth.

And yet more than a million white people left the southern Appalachian region in each of the two decades of the 1940s and 1950s. If one adds in the migration of white people from all the other marginal farming areas of the South, as well as the migration of college-educated, middle-class whites to better career opportunities in California and the North, then the net out-migration of white Southerners cannot have been much smaller than that of black. It may have been substantially greater. Perhaps something between 8 and 12 million white people all together left the South in the quarter of a century after 1945.

Some of them have continued to cluster together in identifiable groups after they reached the North. Cities such as Cincinnati, Pittsburgh,

St. Louis, Detroit and Chicago have ghettoes of southern-mountain poor whites as clearly demarcated and almost as wretched as the reception areas for black migrants. But these refugees from the hollows and the worn-out mining towns of Appalachia are no more than a minority of the southern whites who have joined the exodus.

Unlike black Southerners, the great majority of the whites have experienced little external difficulty in adjusting to life in northern cities or suburbs. Helped by some college education or by the skills and drills they have learned in the military service—an incalculably powerful factor in forging a uniform national style for middle-class Americans of differing backgrounds since the draft was introduced, in 1940—these Southerners have been able to get and hold "good" jobs, and to move out to the suburbs. They have become distinguishable from middle-class whites of northern ancestry only by differences scarcely greater than those which separate, say, a Wisconsin German from a Minnesota Swede: the trace of a drawl, membership in a "southern" church such as the Baptists or the Church of Christ, nuances of manner, and attitudes to such matters, important in themselves, as politics, child-rearing, or the relations between the generations.

The significance of the southern white migration, in other words, lies not so much in the experience of the migrants as in its contribution to the general stirring and homogenization that has sharply reduced the special, exceptional character of the South since 1940. The reverse migration of Northerners, who are now to be found in such numbers in the more prosperous suburbs of such a "branch office town" as Atlanta or in rapidly growing industrial centers such as Houston, has contributed to the same effect. So has the increasing industrialization of the South itself, which has been speeded up by southern power in Congress, which ensured that the section would get a disproportionately large share of defense and, later, space appropriations. And of course, since the *Brown* decision in 1954, the dismantling of legal segregation finally reached the point by the early 1970s where the most obvious distinction between the South and the rest of the country had become far less deep.

It was plain enough to any intelligent Southerner in 1940 that the South stood on the eve of revolutionary change of some kind. Most assumed—hopefully, if they belonged to the microscopic liberal minority, and otherwise with deep reluctance—that the change would take the form of making the South more like the North. To the extent that Northerners spared a thought for the South, they made the same assumption with even greater confidence.

Not the least of the many effects of the great migration of the 1940s was to ensure that the difference would be split. The South did become more like the rest of the country. But in certain vital respects, the rest of the country became more like the South.

# PART II

# 4

## The Ideology of the Liberal Consensus

"On the reefs of roast beef and apple pie, socialistic utopias of every society are sent to their doom."
> —Werner Sombart, "Why Is There No
> Socialism in the United States?"

It is always risky to try to draw the portrait of the ideas and beliefs of a society at any point in its evolution. Contradictions and crosscurrents defy generalization. Too much survives from the past, and too much anticipates the future. Usually, perhaps, the attempt is doomed to end either in superficiality or in intellectual dishonesty. But the period from the middle of the 1950s in the United States up to the impact of the crisis of the 1960s was not usual in this respect. It was an age of consensus. Whether you look at the writings of intellectuals or at the positions taken by practicing politicians or at the data on public opinion, it is impossible not to be struck by the degree to which the majority of Americans in those years accepted the same system of assumptions. Official and semiofficial attempts were even made to codify these assumptions in such works as the report of President Eisenhower's Commission on National Goals or in the Rockefeller Brothers Fund panel reports. The crisis of the late 1960s was caused partly by the mistakes and shortcomings of this system of assumptions and partly by a series of attacks upon it.

In the late 1950s Professor Hadley Cantril of Princeton, one of the pioneers of the statistical study of public opinion, conducted a survey of thousands of individuals in ten countries. The results were published in 1965 in a book called *The Pattern of Human Concerns*. Cantril showed that the subject, and the intensity, of human concerns varied widely from one society to another. People in poorer countries, he found, worried more, and about a wider range of possible personal catastrophes, than did people in richer countries.

The American pattern, Cantril discovered on the basis of survey work done in 1959, was the most distinctive of all. Americans were the most confident people in the world:

> The total volume of concerns of the American people was relatively low, especially those related to their hopes and fears for the nation, except for the single overriding concern that war be avoided. On the personal side there was an unusual emphasis on good health. . . . Americans appeared to be chiefly concerned with the two major threats they felt were most beyond their control, war and illness.

Professor Cantril attributed this mood of confidence not to any peculiarity of American culture but to prosperity. As other countries became similarly prosperous, he expected their people also to feel "a general satisfaction with a way of life which promises continued development." And he made an interesting prediction: Confidence and satisfaction would remain the prevailing mood in a prosperous, developed country

> until some major event or crisis transpires which creates major and widespread frustrations. Only then are people likely to become awakened to the inadequacy of the assumptions they have come to take for granted.

All cross bearings confirm the essential accuracy of this picture. At the end of the 1950s, Americans worried about their own personal lives—about health and status. At the other end of the scale of immediacy, they worried about the danger of nuclear war. But few of them doubted the essential goodness and strength of American society.

Four times between 1959 and 1961, the Gallup poll asked its sample what they regarded as the "most important problem" facing the nation. Each time, the most frequent answer (given in each case by at least close to half of the respondents and sometimes by far more than half) was "keeping the peace," sometimes glossed as "dealing with Russia." No domestic issue came anywhere close to challenging that outstanding concern.

In the presidential campaign of 1960, only two types of domestic issues were rated as critical by either candidate or by his advisers: on the one hand, atavistic ethnic issues—the Catholic vote, or Martin Luther King's arrest—and on the other hand, the behavior of the economy. And the latter, to Kennedy, at least, seemed important mainly as a prerequisite of foreign policy.

Kennedy built his appeal around the call to get the country moving again. He left a strong impression that his main reason for doing so was in order to recover lost prestige in the competition with the Soviet Union.

Summing up his campaign, in Hartford, Connecticut, on the eve of polling, Senator Kennedy listed three major differences between his opponent and himself:

> first a different view of the present state of the American economy; secondly a different view of our prestige in the world, and therefore, our ability to lead the free world; and thirdly, whether the balance of power in the world is shifting in our direction or that of our adversaries.

Nixon, too, had three themes. First, that Kennedy was running America down; second, that the Democrats would cause inflation; and third, that he, Richard Nixon, could speak better for America in confrontation with the Soviet leader.

When it came to sensing the issues that had a gut appeal to the electorate as a whole, that is, each candidate chose to stress foreign dangers (and glories) over domestic problems in the proportion of two to one.

The various American elites took more complicated views. A good deal of concern was expressed by intellectuals in the late 1950s about the lack of excellence in American education (especially in the context of an alleged inferiority to Soviet achievements in space science and missile technology), about the (temporarily) lagging growth rate of the economy, and in diffuse and cloudy jeremiads about the materialism of mass culture. But in the most ambitious contemporary analyses, the same dualism was the recurrent major theme: never so much hope in America, never so much danger abroad.

It was in 1956 that the Rockefeller brothers organized their special studies project to "meet and examine the most critical problems facing the nation over the next ten to fifteen years." Never before had such a prestigious team of diagnosticians gathered at the national bedside. Bipartisan and interdisciplinary, it was a roster of those men who had expounded the conventional wisdom since World War II and would remain its champions until the bitter end of the 1960s: Adolf Berle of the New Deal and John Gardner of Common Cause, Chester Bowles and Charles Percy, Edward Teller and David Sarnoff, Lucius Clay and Dean Rusk, Henry Luce and Henry Kissinger.

The reports of the various panels were published separately between January 1958 and September 1960 and as a single volume, *Prospect for America*, in 1961. Together they form a handbook of the shared assumptions of the American governmental and business elite: the two had become hard to distinguish. These were the assumptions that governed the policies of the Kennedy administration, and no one can doubt that they would have guided the Republicans if they had won in 1960.

It would not be fair to call the tone of *Prospect for America* complacent in any vulgar way. It has a muscular Christian strenuousness, rather reminiscent of Kipling's *If*, or of the sermons on the social question preached at expensive boarding schools:

> The number and the depth of the problems we face suggests that the very life of our free society may be at stake, [the report began by saying]. We are concerned that there has not been . . . enough sense of urgency throughout our nation about the mortal struggle in which we are engaged.

Yet all may not yet be lost:

> America has a notable record of responding to challenges and making the most of opportunities. With our growing population, our extraordinary record of rising productivity, the inherent dynamism in our free enterprise economy, there is every reason to face the future with all confidence.

The panel reports contained very able discussion of particular issues such as strategic policy or economic growth. But essentially they saw all the various challenges to America in terms of one big challenge: "the mortal struggle in which we are engaged," the "basic underlying Soviet danger."

The central dualism of the reports' philosophy was baldly, almost naïvely, spelled out right at the beginning in a preface signed by the Rockefellers themselves:

> This project grew out of a belief that the United States in the middle of the twentieth century found itself in a critical situation.
>
> As a nation we had progressed in our domestic development to an extent hardly imaginable a few short decades ago. . . .
>
> Throughout this world alive with hope and change stalks the Communist challenge.

"Stalks" is a nice Manichaean touch. It was this very feeling that the hosts of Midian were on the prowl, that the United States was wrestling with the Evil One, and therefore needed to match the messianic beliefs of the adversary with an equivalent dogma, that made it so fashionable in the late 1950s to define the grand purposes of America. The official report on the national goals produced by the Eisenhower administration in 1960 was strikingly similar in tone and conclusions to that of the Rockefeller brothers and their experts.

The extremely distinguished panel of economists, for example—it included Paul Samuelson and Milton Friedman, Herbert Stein and Charles L. Schultze—drew almost exactly the same picture of a perfectible America threatened from without by the Communist serpent. "The Amer-

ican economy works well," they pronounced; "the system is highly responsive to the demands of the people." Yet, even in a discussion of the economy they felt it appropriate to add, "America and the civilization to
which it belongs stand at an historic turning-point. They confront a critical danger and inspiring opportunities. The danger is indicated by the
phrase 'Cold War.'"

The introduction to the National Goals report gave an official
imprimatur to this same dualism. It was signed by, among others, the head
of DuPont and the head of the AFL/CIO, the head of the University of
California and the head of the First National City Bank of New York. At
home, these Olympians thundered in unison, "We have achieved a
standard of individual realization new to history." Abroad, "The nation is
in grave danger, threatened by the rulers of one third of mankind."

One eminent historian was so carried away by this mood that he even
projected it back into an indefinite past: "In this favored country," wrote
Clinton Rossiter, "we have always found more things on which to agree
than to disagree." Always? In the 1860s? Still, there could be no dissent
from his next proposition: "The early 1960s appear to be a time of broad
consensus on fundamentals." Looking back to the same period, the late
Fred Freed, one of the most thoughtful of television producers, came to
much the same conclusion (it was his habit never to use capital letters):

> when i began doing my documentaries at nbc in 1961 we lived in a con-
> sensus society. those were the days of the' cold war. there was an enemy
> outside, the communists, nikita khrushchev, the red chinese. . . . back
> then there was general agreement in the united states about what was
> right and what was wrong about the country. nobody really questioned
> the system. . . . we had a common set of beliefs and common values.

In political terms, the beginnings of consensus date back to 1954.
That was the pudding time when moderation came back into fashion after
the acerbities of the Korean War and the McCarthy era.

Stalin died in 1953. The Korean War ended four months later, at
Panmunjom.

The Cold War was far from over. One historian considers it reached
its zenith with John Foster Dulles's speech, in January 1954, in which he
called for "the deterrent of massive retaliatory power . . . by means and at
times of our own choosing." Still, the Geneva conference and the Indochina settlement in the summer of 1954 did bring a warmer international climate. The successors of Stalin had problems enough on their
hands. They proclaimed coexistence as their goal, and if they never gave
up on the attempt to turn the new atmosphere to their advantage, they did
show genuine signs of tractability. In the spring of 1955 they unexpectedly

agreed to sign an Austrian peace treaty, and that summer Bulganin and Khrushchev met the American President at the summit. Peace was still a long way off, but war seemed farther away.

It was in June 1954 that a soft-spoken New England lawyer named Joseph Welch destroyed Senator McCarthy by asking him the question no one had dared ask him before: "Have you no sense of decency, sir, at last?" In December, the Senate voted aye to a motion of censure. Intolerance and anti-communist hysteria were not dead, but at least exploiting them was no longer fashionable.

There was a sharp recession over the winter of 1953–54. Industrial production actually declined by 10 per cent. The President had the good sense to turn to the chairman of his Council of Economic Advisers, Dr. Arthur Burns, who prescribed a modest course of Keynesian spending. "It is no longer a matter of serious controversy," Burns was soon saying, "whether the government shall play a positive role in helping to maintain a high level of economic activity." After 1954, traditional Republican orthodoxy as represented by Secretary of the Treasury George M. Humphrey was in retreat.

For some seven years after 1955, few fundamental disagreements, foreign or domestic, were aired in either presidential or Congressional politics. That the United States should in principle seek better relations with the Soviet Union while keeping its guard up and seeking to contain communism—this was common ground. Disagreement was relegated to issues of the second order of importance: the extent to which the United States should support the United Nations, the level of foreign aid, the speed of space development. The main lines of domestic policy were equally beyond controversy. The Eisenhower administration accepted that the federal government must continue social security and such other New Deal programs as had stood the test of public popularity. It was ready to enforce due compliance with the law in civil rights, though reluctantly and with caution. And it was prepared to use fiscal and monetary measures to maintain full employment and economic growth. Not much more, and no less, could be said of the Kennedy administration in its first two years.

The political process, it was taken for granted throughout that period, was a matter of emphasizing one nuance or another of this generally agreed program. A "liberal" congressman, as the word was then used, was one who might be expected to speak up for the particular interests of organized labor; a "conservative" would voice the reservations of corporate business or of the armed services.

Not only in Washington but in the press, on television, and—with few exceptions—in the academic community, to dissent from the broad axioms of consensus was to proclaim oneself irresponsible or ignorant.

That would risk disqualifying the dissenter from being taken seriously, and indeed often from being heard at all.

A strange hybrid, liberal conservatism, blanketed the scene and muffled debate. It stretched from Americans for Democratic Action—which lay at the leftward frontiers of respectability and yet remained safely committed to anti-communism and free enterprise—as far into the board rooms of Wall Street and manufacturing industry as there could be found a realistic willingness to accept the existence of labor unions, the rights of minorities, and some role in economic life for the federal government. Since the consensus had made converts on the Right as well as on the Left, only a handful of dissidents were excluded from the Big Tent: southern diehards, rural reactionaries, the more *farouche* and paranoid fringes of the radical Right, and the divided remnants of the old, Marxist, Left. Together, they hardly added up to a corporal's guard. And they were of course never together.

The lack of clearly opposed alternative policies was revealed, to the point of parody, by the most emotional foreign-policy issue of the time: Cuba.

"For the first and only time" in the presidential campaign of 1960, Richard Nixon wrote in *Six Crises*, he "got mad at Kennedy—personally," when Kennedy advocated support for the anti-Castro rebels. Nixon was not angry because Kennedy's position was a recipe for disaster (though it was). He was angry because Kennedy was saying in public what Nixon had been saying in private but felt bound by the obligations of national security not to reveal. He had reason to believe that Kennedy knew all along that the Eisenhower administration was secretly planning the invasion that Kennedy now, by implication, criticized it for not mounting!

After the venture duly ended in fiasco at the Bay of Pigs, Arthur M. Schlesinger, then a White House aide, was sent a cable by his former Harvard graduate students: "KENNEDY OR NIXON," it read, "DOES IT MAKE A DIFFERENCE?" The question was an unkind reference to a pamphlet with that exact title which Schlesinger had felt moved to dash off during the 1960 campaign.

Schlesinger was right, of course; it did make a difference. But this was hardly because any very distinct issues of basic policy or any sharply divergent visions of the world then lay between John Kennedy and Richard Nixon. They represented the aspirations of different categories of Americans. Their symbolic meaning—vital in the presidency—was almost antithetical. By experience and temperament, they were very different men.

The fact remains that they did share the same basic political assumptions: the primacy of foreign over domestic issues, the paramount importance of containing communism, the reign of consensus in domestic affairs, the need to assert the supremacy of the White House as the command post of a society mobilized to meet external danger. So did their staff and advisers. And so, too, did their running mates and closest rivals: Lyndon Johnson and Henry Cabot Lodge, Hubert Humphrey and Nelson Rockefeller, and everyone else who might conceivably have been nominated as a presidential candidate in that year either by the Democrats or by the Republicans. Kennedy and Nixon, wrote Eric Sevareid, Establishment liberal *par excellence* at the time, were the first two completely packaged products of the managerial revolution in politics. In politics, as in business, it was the era of imperfect competition, with candidates not just for the presidency but for most major offices hardly more different than a Chevy and a Ford, or a Pepsi and a Coke.

In September 1955, at precisely the moment when consensus was settling like snow over U.S. politics, something very similar was happening in American intellectual life. That month, some one hundred fifty intellectuals from many countries foregathered at a conference in Milan to debate "The Future of Freedom." They had been invited there at the initiative of an organization called the Congress for Cultural Freedom, and their proceedings were later reported in the Congress's London monthly review, *Encounter,* by the sociologist Edward Shils. (Both the congress and *Encounter* were later found to have been in receipt of secret funds from the Central Intelligence Agency.) The title the editor put on Shils's article was *The End of Ideology?*

The idea was not new. "Liberal civilization begins when the age of ideology is over," Lewis Feuer had written in an article called "Beyond Ideology," published earlier that same year. Seymour Martin Lipset called one of the chapters in his *Political Man,* published in 1960, "The End of Ideology." But the person with whom the phrase came to be most closely associated was Lipset's close friend the sociologist and journalist Daniel Bell. Originally a product of one of the many fragments of the New York socialist Left, Bell became the labor editor of *Fortune* magazine and was also for a time the director of international seminars for the Congress for Cultural Freedom. His career epitomized, in fact, the intellectual consensus that underpinned its political equivalent during the 1950s. He saw clearly its double foundation: on the fear of communism abroad and on the assumption that American society could solve its problems without irresoluble conflict.

"Politics today," he wrote in 1960, "is not a reflex of any internal class divisions but is shaped by international events. And foreign policy, the expression of politics, is a response to many factors, the most important of which has been the estimate of Russian intentions . . . the need for containment.

What sort of domestic politics did this acceptance of the primacy of anti-Communist foreign policy imply?

> In the West, therefore, there is today a rough consensus among intellectuals on political issues: the acceptance of a Welfare State; the desirability of decentralized power; a system of mixed economy and of political pluralism. In that sense, too, the ideological age has ended.

Both those two highly explicit formulations are taken from the book, published in 1960, which Bell, too, called *The End of Ideology*.

What Bell meant by that was, above all, the end of the ideology of the Left. "By 'the end of ideology,'" even his friend Irving Kristol, the editor who had originally published Shils's article of the same title, was constrained to comment, "Mr. Bell appears to mean, above all, the collapse of the socialist ideal."

Bell and his group, in fact, announced the death of ideology somewhat in the way in which the death of royalty used to be announced. "The King is dead," said the courtiers. "Long live the King!"

At one point in his book, he defined what he called "a total ideology":

> ". . . an all-inclusive system of comprehensive reality, it is a set of beliefs, infused with passion, and seeks to transform the whole of a way of life. This commitment to ideology—the yearning for a "cause," or the satisfaction of deep moral feelings—is not necessarily the reflection of interests in the shape of ideas. Ideology, in this sense . . . is a secular religion.

Consciously or not, Daniel Bell was describing the American ideology of the age of consensus. Cause, commitment, system of beliefs and way of life, it was indeed a secular religion.

Confident to the verge of complacency about the perfectibility of American society, anxious to the point of paranoia about the threat of communism—those were the two faces of the consensus mood. Each grew from one aspect of the experience of the 1940s: confidence from economic success, anxiety from the fear of Stalin and the frustrations of power.

Historical logic made some form of consensus likely. It was natural that the new prosperity should calm the class antipathies of the depression years. It was normal that the sense of an enemy at the gate should strengthen national unity. And a reaction was predictable after the lacerating politics of the McCarthy period. But the basis for the consensus was something more than a vague mood or a reaction to passing events. The assumptions on which it was built had an intellectual life and coherence of their own. In barest outline, they can be summarized in the following set of interrelated maxims:

1. The American free-enterprise system is different from the old capitalism. It is democratic. It creates abundance. It has a revolutionary potential for social justice.
2. The key to this potential is production: specifically, increased production, or economic growth. This makes it possible to meet people's needs out of incremental resources. Social conflict over resources between classes (which Marx called "the locomotive of history") therefore becomes obsolete and unnecessary.
3. Thus there is a natural harmony of interests in society. American society is getting more equal. It is in process of abolishing, may even have abolished, social class. Capitalists are being superseded by managers. The workers are becoming members of the middle class.
4. Social problems can be solved like industrial problems: The problem is first identified; programs are designed to solve it, by government enlightened by social science; money and other resources—such as trained people—are then applied to the problem as "inputs"; the outputs are predictable: the problems will be solved.
5. The main threat to this beneficent system comes from the deluded adherents of Marxism. The United States and its allies, the Free World, must therefore expect a prolonged struggle against communism.
6. Quite apart from the threat of communism, it is the duty and destiny of the United States to bring the good tidings of the free-enterprise system to the rest of the world.

The germ of this intellectual system, which by about 1960 had emerged as the dominant American ideology, was a simple yet startling empirical discovery. Capitalism, after all, seemed to work.

In the early 1940s, the economist Joseph Schumpeter, at work on his last book, *Capitalism, Socialism and Democracy*, reluctantly came to the conclusion that socialism—a system about which he cherished so few illusions that he expected it to resemble fascism when it came—was inevitable. Capitalism was doomed, he feared. Schumpeter was a conservative, though a highly original one, and he had arrived at this conclusion by his own line of argument. The modern corporation would "socialize the bourgeois mind," destroy the entrepreneurial motivation that was the driving force of capitalism, and thus "eventually kill its own roots." He was at pains to distinguish this position from what he saw as the almost universal vulgar anticapitalism of his time. "Every writer or speaker hastens to emphasize . . . his aversion to capitalist and his sympathy with anticapitalist interests."

Well under ten years later, the exact opposite would have been closer to the truth. In the United States (though nowhere else in the world), socialism was utterly discredited. The same transformation could be observed in popular attitudes and in intellectual fashion. In 1942 (the year that Schumpeter's book was published), a poll by Elmo Roper for *Fortune* found that only 40 per cent of respondents opposed socialism, 25 per cent said they were in favor of it, and as many as 35 per cent had an open mind. By 1949, a Gallup poll found that only 15 per cent wanted "to move more in the direction of socialism"; 61 per cent wanted to move in the opposite direction. Making all due allowance for the respondents' possibly vague notion of what socialism means, it was a startling shift, yet not more startling than that of the intellectuals.

As late as the war years, most American economists, led by Alvin Hansen, predicted that capitalism was entering a phase of chronic stagnation. Most other intellectuals took the economists at their word and assumed that the task was to replace capitalism with some more promising system.

Suddenly, in the late 1940s, the moribund system was declared not only alive but healthy. The economic *ancien régime* was acclaimed as the revolutionary harbinger of a brave new world.

In 1949 Daniel Bell wrote an article called "America's Un-Marxist Revolution."

"Keynes, not Marx," wrote Arthur Schlesinger in the same year, "is the prophet of the new radicalism."

"The world revolution of our time is 'made in U.S.A.,'" wrote Peter Drucker, the champion of management, also in 1949. "The true revolutionary principle is the idea of mass production."

And in 1951 the editors of *Fortune* magazine gave to an ambitious, much noticed synthesis of the American Way of Life a title borrowed from Marx and given currency by Trotsky. They called it *U.S.A., the Permanent Revolution:*

> There has occurred a great transformation, of which the world as a whole is yet unaware. . . . No important progress whatever can be made in the understanding of America unless the nature of this transformation is grasped. . . . There has been a vast dispersal of ownership and initiative, so that the capitalist system has become intimately bound in with the political system and takes nourishment from its democratic roots. . . . U.S. capitalism is popular capitalism.

At the root of this optimistic new political philosophy, there lay an appropriately optimistic new economic doctrine. It came to be known as the New Economics, though by the time of its triumph, in the 1960s, when its licensed practitioners monopolized the President's Council of Economic Advisers, many of its leading ideas were going on thirty years old.

There were many strands to the New Economics. But the essence of it was the acceptance in the United States of the ideas of John Maynard Keynes, *not* as first received in the 1930s but as modified by American economists in the light of the success of the American economy in the 1940s.

. The nub of Keynes's teaching was that, contrary to the tenets of classical economics, savings did not necessarily become investment. This was the cause of cyclical depression and of unemployment: left to itself, the capitalist system contained forces that would tend to produce stagnation. To that extent his position was pessimistic. But Keynes was a political economist. He did not think that things should be left to themselves. He believed that governments could cure the kind of deflation that had caused the Great Depression by spending, and if necessary by deficit spending. He actually wrote a long letter to FDR, in early 1938, pleading with him to spend his way out of the recession. The letter was ignored. But after 1945 the university economists succeeded in persuading the more enlightened businessmen, and some politicians, that Keynes was right. Capitalism could be *made* to work. Depression and unemployment were avoidable, and it was up to government to avoid them.

From a conservative standpoint, Schumpeter introduced ideas that matched the new Keynesian orthodoxy better than he would have liked. He stressed the unique character of American capitalism. He emphasized productivity and technological change. He argued that concentration and oligopoly, which most economists had wanted government to destroy by trust busting, actually favored invention and innovation.

Unlike Schumpeter, John Kenneth Galbraith was a Keynesian, and it was he who attempted the inevitable synthesis in *American Capitalism*, published in 1952. Galbraith also started from the observed fact that competition in American corporate capitalism was imperfect. He propounded the theory of what he called "countervailing power." Competition had been supposed to limit private economic power. Well, it didn't. But private power was held in check "by the countervailing power of those who are subject to it." The concentration of industry had brought into existence strong buyers—Sears Roebuck, A & P—to match strong sellers. It had also brought strong unions into existence to match strong employers.

Galbraith and Schumpeter had many disagreements. Their analyses were drawn from different premises and tended toward different conclusions. Yet they shared one common perception: the empirical observation that American capitalism was a success. "It works," said Galbraith shortly on his first page, "and in the years since World War II, quite brilliantly."

> There is another fact about the social situation in the United States that has no analogue anywhere else in the world, said Schumpeter in his second edition, published in 1946, . . . namely the colossal industrial success we are witnessing.

And a few pages later, he italicized a passage that condensed the gist of the new hope and the new pride:

> In the United States alone there need not lurk, behind modern programs of social betterment, that fundamental dilemma that everywhere paralyzes the will of every responsible man, the dilemma between economic progress and immediate increase of the real income of the masses.

In practical terms, the gospel of the New Economics could be translated into exciting propositions. Government can manage the economy by using fiscal and monetary policy. The tyranny of the business cycle, which had brought economic catastrophe and the specter of political upheaval, need no longer be tolerated. Depressions could be a thing of the past.

By changing interest rates and by increasing or decreasing the money supply—technical matters that had the added advantage of being remote from the scrutiny of everyday politics—government could flatten out fluctuations in economic activity.

The economists were emboldened to maintain that these fiscal and monetary controls could be manipulated with such precision—"fine tuning" was the phrase used—that in effect they would be able to fly the economy like an airplane, trimming its speed, course and altitude with tiny movements of the flaps and rudder. That was a later claim. The essential promise of the Keynesian system was that it would allow government to guarantee low and diminishing unemployment without inflation. It could thus banish at a stroke the worst terrors of both liberals and conservatives. At the same time, thus managed, the economy would also be able to deliver growth.

Growth was the second key concept of the new intellectual system, and the link between its strictly economic and its social and political ideas.

We are so accustomed to the idea of economic growth that it comes as a surprise to learn that it was a newer idea than Keynes's discovery of the way to beat the business cycle. Just as modern biology had to wait for the invention of the microscope and modern astronomy for the perfection of the telescope, the idea of economic growth developed only after precise techniques for measuring the gross national product became available. These were perfected only in the late 1930s, by Professor Simon Kuznets, of the University of Pennsylvania.

It is hardly possible to exaggerate the importance that the new concept assumed in the intellectual system of American liberals in the 1950s. It became the test, the aim, even the justification of free enterprise—the race, the runner and the prize.

The economic historian W. W. Rostow offered an interpretation of modern history as a contest in terms of economic growth—and called it an "anti-Communist manifesto."

The political scientist Seymour Martin Lipset came close to making it the chief criterion for judging a political system. "Prolonged effectiveness over a number of years," he suggested in his book *Political Man*, "may give legitimacy to a political system. In the modern world, such effectiveness means primarily constant economic development."

But perhaps the most lyrical description came from Walter Heller, chairman of the Council of Economic Advisers under Presidents Kennedy and Johnson. He called economic growth "the pot of gold and the rainbow."

The liberals did not worship economic growth merely as a golden calf. They saw in it the possibility of solving social problems with the incremental resources created by growth. That will be done, they hoped, without the social conflict that would be inevitable if those resources had to be found by redistributing existing wealth.

This was the hope that both Schumpeter and Galbraith had seen. Brushing aside the pessimists, Schumpeter had dared to predict in 1942 that GNP would reach $200 billion by 1950. (In the event, he was a pessimist himself: GNP in current dollars reached $284 billion by 1950.) "The huge mass of available commodities and services that this figure . . . represents," he wrote, "promises a level of satisfaction of economic needs even of the poorest members of society . . . that would eliminate anything that could possibly be described as suffering or want." And of course Schumpeter was fully aware of the ideological implications. Such a massive creation of new resources could be the key to his central dilemma. It might "annihilate the whole case for socialism so far as it is of a purely economic nature."

What Schumpeter had described as a theoretical possibility in the 1940s had become by the end of the 1950s the "conventional wisdom," and in the 1960s it was to be the foundation of public economic policy.

"Production has eliminated the more acute tensions associated with inequality," Galbraith wrote in *The Affluent Society*, a book whose title was to become a cliché to an extent that did little credit to the subtlety of its argument. "Increasing aggregate output is an alternative to redistribution."

The same idea was spelled out in the stonecutter's prose of the Rockefeller Brothers Fund's drafting committee:

> A healthy and expanding private economy means far more in terms of individual and family well-being than any reasonable expansion of government service and social programs.

"Far greater gains were to be made by fighting to enlarge the size of the economic pie," one of President Johnson's economic advisers wrote, "than by pressing proposals to increase equity and efficiency in sharing the pie." "When firing on all eight cylinders," said another, to an approving audience of bankers, "our economy is a mighty engine of social progress."

In theory, there could be little arguing with that proposition. Its truth in practice would depend on a number of questions: one's definition of social progress, the extent to which social progress could be guaranteed to follow from the application of resources, and the propensity of government to devote incremental resources to other purposes, such as fighting wars. But the relevant point here is that it was a proposition ideally suited to be one of the main props of an ideology of liberal conservatism. It offered to the liberals the hope of progress and a feeling of benevolence, and to the conservatives a vista of business prosperity and an unthreatened *status quo*.

Looking back on the decade, Paul Samuelson touched in a single paragraph all the essential elements of his generation's ideology: the optimism, the confidence that more means better, the faith in the harmony of interests between capitalism and social progress, the cankerous sense that all this must be related to the competition with communism:

"The New Economics really does work," he wrote in November 1968 on the eve of the Democrats' fall from power and of the sharpest fall in the stock market and the severest economic problems for a generation:

> Wall Street knows it. Main Street, which has been enjoying 92 months of advancing sales, knows it. The accountants who have been chalking up record profits know it . . . and so do the school nurses who measure the heights and weights of this generation. . . . You can bet that the statisticians of the Kremlin know it.

No tenet of the consensus was more widely held than the idea that revolutionary American capitalism had abolished the working class, or—as approximately the same thought was sometimes expressed—that everybody in America was middle class now or that American society was rapidly approaching economic equality.

A small encyclopedia of statements to this effect can be garnered from the historians, the social scientists and the journalists of the time.

"The organizing concept of American society," wrote Peter Drucker, "has been that of social mobility . . . which denies the existence of classes."

"The union," said the editors of *Fortune*, "has made the worker, to an amazing degree, a middle class member of a middle class society."

"New Dealism," said historian Eric Goldman, ". . . found that it had created a nation of the middle class."

Yet another historian, Samuel Eliot Morison, boldly dated the abolition of the proletariat rather earlier than some would say the proletariat came into existence. He cited the observations of a Polish Communist visitor to confirm "a fact that has puzzled socialists and communists for a century: the American workman is an expectant capitalist, not a class-conscious proletarian."

Frederick L. Allen, on the other hand, wrote a best seller to prove that "the big change" in American life between 1900 and 1950 was the "democratization of our economic system."

One's first reaction is to yield to the cumulative weight of so many impassioned opinions and to conclude . . . what? For even the most cursory reading of such a miscellany raises questions. Had class stratification never existed in the United States, as Drucker seemed to think? But, then, can one imagine social mobility without class? Mobility between what? Had there never been an American proletariat, as Professor Morison seemed to believe? Or had there been a "big change"? Perhaps the proletariat had ceased to exist. But, then, which agency had earned the credit for this transformation? "Industrial enterprise," as some claimed? *Fortune*'s unions? Or Goldman's "New Dealism"? Corporate business, labor and government may work in harmony. But they are hardly synonyms.

A second reading of this miscellany of texts and of the other evidence suggests two more-modest conclusions:

1) A great many Americans, moved by the ideal of equality but perhaps also by reluctance to admit what was seen as a Marxist analysis of their own society, passionately wanted to believe that the concept of class was alien to the United States.

It suited business to believe this. It suited labor. It suited intellectuals, and it suited the press. It suited liberals, and it suited conservatives. Who was left to argue otherwise?

2) Nevertheless, something *had* happened. In the profound transformations of the 1940s the class structure of American society and its
implications for politics had changed in complex and confusing ways
—though not to the point of making "everybody middle class," still
less of invalidating class analysis.

The abolition of the working class, in fact, was a myth. Like most
myths, it did have a certain basis in fact. But it oversimplified and distorted what had really happened. It transformed a modest and temporary
decline in inequality into a social revolution. At the same time, it confused
the idea that many Americans were far better off than they had been,
which was true, with the claim that poorer Americans had made dramatic
gains at the expense of the better off, which was at best dubious.

Two developments probably explain the strength of this myth. The
real performance of the economy during and after World War II made it
possible to believe it. And the triumph of the liberals over the Left made a
lot of people want to believe it.

The prosperity of the 1940s really was widespread. Mass unemployment ended, after twelve years. Dollar wages, especially for workers in
such strongly unionized (and highly visible) industries as steel, automobiles, and rubber, rose dramatically. But real wages for most workers rose
too.

There was also a highly obvious equalization of *consumption*, which
looked like an equalization of wealth, all the more so because it was concentrated in the most visible forms of consumption: clothes, for example,
and cars. Nylon stockings were a favorite example with economists and
journalists alike. They were introduced in September 1939, the month
Europe went to war. Ten years later, they were still a luxury in Europe.
But in the United States, production in 1949 was 543 million pairs: every
typist could afford to be dressed like a film star from ankle to thigh. The
parking lots full of shiny, late-model automobiles outside factories were
much commented upon; and "everybody" could afford the new electrical
household gadgets.

In other ways, too, it really did look as though the rich were getting
poorer and the poor richer. The rich complained bitterly about the income
tax, and in fact the maximum rate rose from 54 per cent in 1932 to 91 per
cent in the 1950s. Meanwhile, the after-taxes income of families in the
lower income brackets was rising faster than that of the better-off families,
and the income of the wealthiest 5 per cent actually dropped. John Kenneth Galbraith quoted the tax table in *The Affluent Society*, and it certainly conveyed an impression of affluence that was not only growing but
also being more equally distributed.

Between 1941 and 1950, measuring in dollars of 1950 purchasing power, the income of the highest 5 per cent of all families, after income taxes, actually fell. Thereafter, the lower you descended on the income scale, the higher the gains.

| | |
|---|---|
| Highest fifth: | up 8% |
| Second fifth: | up 16% |
| Third fifth: | up 24% |
| Fourth fifth: | up 37% |
| Lowest fifth: | up 42% |

There is a pleasing regularity about that series that would seem to clinch the argument. But, unfortunately, there are several ways of looking at the distribution of income. The whole study of income and wealth, in fact, bristles with treacherous problems for the statistician. He must make up his mind whether different figures from different sources, the only ones available for different periods, are really comparable or not; whether to measure income before or after taxes; what allowance, if any, to make for tax evasion by the rich and for "transfer payments" out of taxes made by government to the poor. And unless he is most unusually naïve, he will be uncomfortably aware that these are not only technical but political decisions.

The best way to measure the distribution of income is to measure what proportion of the total national income has gone at different times to different fractions of the population, ranged in order from the richest to the poorest.

When the historian Gabriel Kolko did this, he came up with a result that shattered the liberal assumption that income had been redistributed to the poor. Here is how he summarized his findings in his book *Wealth and Power in America:*

> Despite the obvious increase in prosperity since the abysmal years of the Great Depression, the basic distribution of income and wealth is essentially the same now as it was in 1939, or even 1910. Most low-income groups live substantially better today, but even though their real wages have mounted, their percentage of the national income has not changed.

Kolko computed the percentage of national personal income received, before taxes, by each tenth of the population by income, over the whole period from 1910 to 1959. He found that while the share of the highest tenth had dropped, it had dropped only from 33.9 per cent in 1910 to 28.9 per cent in 1959. And over the same period, the share of the national income that went to the whole lower half of the population dropped from 27 per cent to 23 per cent. It is certainly hard to talk about the abolition of the proletariat, or even of economic democratization, in reference to a society in which the whole poorer half of the population has been getting relatively poorer.

The same distribution tables also suggest what has actually occurred to give the illusion of social progress. The pattern is best described by comparing the proportions of the national income that went at five different dates to three fractions of the population: the rich, represented by the top tenth of all incomes; the middle class, represented by the next four tenths, taken together; the poor, represented by the lower half. (I should perhaps say that I am not suggesting that the terms "the rich," "the poor" and the "middle class" correspond to those fractions; I am merely using a convenient shorthand for three groups.)

In 1929, before the Depression and the New Deal, the top tenth received 39 per cent of the national income. The middle class got exactly the same share. And the poor got the rest: 22 per cent.

In 1941, after twelve years of massive unemployment, the poor's share had fallen still further, to 19 per cent. The share of the rich had also fallen, by five percentage points, to 34 per cent. The whole gain, at the expense of both rich and poor, had gone to the "middle class."

In 1945, after four decisive years of war, boom and full employment, the poor had . . . recovered to exactly the point where they stood before the Depression: 22 per cent. The rich had lost another five percentage points, to 29 per cent. The middle class took just short of half the national income: 49 per cent.

And in 1949 and 1959, the years of the Permanent Revolution and the Affluent Society? Nothing had changed. That was the remarkable thing. To be precise, the top tenth gained one percentage point in 1949 and had lost it again by 1959. The middle four tenths together dropped a point in 1949, and stayed on 48 per cent in 1959. The poor gained one point, moving to 23 per cent by 1959. That was all.

The fact that the distribution of income in America is not equal, and is not noticeably getting any more equal, is now generally accepted. In a study for the Joint Economic Committee of Congress published in 1972, Lester C. Thurow and Robert E. B. Lucas of M.I.T. showed that the distribution of income from 1947 to 1969 had remained approximately constant: "Everybody's income (male, female, majority, minority, rich and poor) had been rising at approximately the same rate, leaving their ratios unaffected." An analysis of the 1970 census data by Peter Henle, a Library of Congress statistician, reported what he called "a continuing slow trend towards inequality." The commonsense conclusion would seem to be that there has been essentially no change in the distribution of income in the United States since World War II.

There has been only one rather sharp change in the twentieth century. This was the gain made between 1929 and 1945 by the second and third tenths of the population at the expense of the first. Their combined share went up from 22.1 per cent in 1929 to 29 per cent in 1945 and has since remained roughly constant. The redistribution of wealth, then, such as it was, seems to have been over by 1945. And it was a redistribution not from the rich to the poor, but from the very best off to the next best off. The second and third tenths of the income scale at that time would have included some executives, managers, professionals, some higher-paid clerical workers, and the very best-paid craft and industrial workers in the strongest unions. A shift of 10 per cent of the national income in their direction scarcely constituted either the abolition of the proletariat or the coming of the universal middle class. Yet, by a kind of intellectual parallax error, that was how it was seen.

The mood of the country may have been relatively complacent in the late fifties and the early sixties. But this was not, as the liberal analysis assumed, because the condition of the American people left so little to be desired. It was because a number of historical factors had weakened the political unity and consciousness of the working class and deprived it of the means to perceive its own interests and to defend them.

One of these factors was the way the idea of equality had evolved in the United States. Historically, the actual condition of American society—with the two major exceptions of black and red Americans—had probably always more closely approached a condition of equality than European society. The availability of land, the unexploited resources of a "new" country of continental extent, the absence—or near absence—of an established feudal upper class with a vested interest in maintaining inequality, all tended to minimize inequality in practice. Yet in theory Americans had always been less concerned than Europeans with equality of condition. The paradox is only apparent. Because of the relative abundance of their environment, Americans could afford to think equality of condition less important than equality of opportunity. In most other cultures, people knew all too well that there would never be enough opportunities to go round.

The historian David Potter argued powerfully in his 1954 essay *People of Plenty* that almost every distinctive aspect of American life, from child rearing to political institutions, could be traced to the pervasive influence of economic abundance:

> The very meaning of the term "equality" reflects this influence. . . .
> A European, advocating equality, might very well mean that all men
> should occupy positions that are roughly on the same level in wealth,
> power or enviability. But the American, with his emphasis on equality of

opportunity, has never conceived of it in this sense. He has traditionally expected to find a gamut ranging from rags to riches, from tramps to millionaires. . . . In America, "liberty," meaning "freedom to grasp opportunity," and "equality," also meaning "freedom to grasp opportunity," have become almost synonymous.

To a European mind, to equate equality with a freedom to grasp opportunity which guarantees an abundance of tramps and millionaires . . . comes close to equating equality with inequality. It is in any case a habit of mind whose tendency is to inculcate conservative social attitudes. It has tended to make working-class Americans suspicious of appeals to class solidarity. It has enhanced the appeal of the free-enterprise system, which has certainly been a lot more successful at creating opportunities than at creating equality of condition. It explains why people should not be particularly concerned about the failure to redistribute income so long as everyone was getting richer. And it does partially account for the fact that domestic discontent played so small a part in the politics of the fifties.

There was a second group of reasons why American politics failed to reflect class interests or class consciousness. It is true, as Arthur Schlesinger has written, that "in spite of the current myth that class conflicts in America were a fiendish invention of Franklin Roosevelt, classes have, in fact, played a basic part in American political life from the beginning." But the horizontal class lines in American society have always been crosshatched by deep-cut vertical divisions: ethnic, sectional, and racial. Ultimately, these can be traced back to two of the great facts that set American history apart from that of all the other developed Western nations: slavery and immigration. But there were also reasons why their combined impact blurred the reality of class conflict at this particular moment in American history.

One reason was obvious.

The American working class was divided, because the feeling of belonging to a particular ethnic group often took priority over an individual's economic interests or over any sense of class solidarity. In political terms, this frequently meant that the votes of ethnically conscious low-income voters could be recruited to support politicians who, once in office, only fitfully defended the social and economic interests of their constituency. This was notoriously true of the big-city machines, which, in a decadent form, were still one of the typical forms of political organization in the fifties and, for example, played a part in the election of President Kennedy in 1960. But by the fifties the machine no longer fought for the bread-and-butter interests of its immigrant supporters as it had in its classic phase. Instead, traditional ethnic loyalties were played upon at election time to enlist the support of ethnic blocs on behalf of policies that frequently countered the real interests of lower-class voters. Ethnic antics at election time only briefly interrupted the politicians' eager co-operation with the dominant business interests.

The historical fact of immigration had another, less obvious effect. To the extent that Americans are a self-chosen people, their patriotism has always been a more self-conscious emotion than the more visceral tribal feelings of other nations. The immigrant's patriotism has tended to be compounded in roughly equal proportions of status anxiety—the desire to be assimilated as a good American—and of gratitude for his share in the abundance of American life.

Both the abundance and the anxiety were far more visible in the fifties than they had been in the thirties. In the immigrant, this desire to prove oneself a good American had often been in conflict with the impulse to protect the social and economic interests of the lower class. By the fifties, a full generation after the end of mass immigration, the drive for full assimilation was as strong as ever in second- and third-generation Americans; economic needs, as a result of the postwar prosperity, seemed far less urgent. Again, the effect was to increase the conservatism of that considerable proportion of the working class that came of relatively "new" immigrant descent. For this large group, the free-enterprise system was seen as Americanism; social criticism, class solidarity and radical politics were rejected as "un-American."

If ethnic factors dating back to the days of mass immigration, and the preoccupation with equality of opportunity, both helped to obscure the working class's interests from its own members, the sectional and racial basis of the political system derived from the struggle over slavery was responsible for the fact that no great party of the Left was available to represent those interests. In so far as working-class interests were to be effectively represented within the two-party system, they must be represented by the Democrats. But the Democratic Party under Harry Truman and Adlai Stevenson was no party of the Left: It was not only the party of the immigrant, the Negro, the Roman Catholic, the Jew, the city dweller, and the industrial worker; it was also the party of the rural, conservative, nativist South, an element that not only accounted for a third and more of its strength in Congress but held the balance of power in presidential elections.

During the Depression, the New Deal had come closer to being a party of the Left, because the contradiction at the heart of the Democracy was partially concealed by the sheer economic need of the South. Southern Democrats could vote for and work with Roosevelt because they knew the South desperately needed the federal government's economic help. Southerners in Congress might be racial and therefore constitutional conservatives, willing to fight the national Democratic leadership if they must in defense of the South's peculiar social system; but in the New Deal period, that system was not under direct attack. The immediate issues for the South were economic. So long as that remained true, southern "economic liberals"—which often meant men who were not liberals at all except when it came to accepting federal largess—could work happily enough with northern Democrats.

The prosperity of the years after 1941, and in particular the improvement in the economic situation of the southern white working class as a result of industrialization, diminished this incentive for southern Democrats to co-operate with the national party. In spite of much picturesque mythology about their populist fervor and the wool-hats and galluses of their disciples, most of the leading Southerners in Congress in the fifties were essentially responsive to the business elites of the South. While they continued to support some liberal programs, they were not about to allow the Democratic Party to evolve into a national party of the Left. The more racial issues supplanted economic ones in the forefront of their constituents' concern, as they did increasingly after the *Brown* decision in 1954, the more the sectional dilemma made any such evolution of the Democratic Party unlikely.

The Left, in short, had by the late 1950s virtually ceased to count in American political life. But this fateful eclipse was masked by the triumph of the liberals.

To draw a distinction between the Left and the liberals may sound sectarian or obscure. It is not. It is vital to understanding American politics in the age of the consensus, and therefore to understanding what happened after it.

When I say that the Left had almost ceased to exist, I am not thinking of the socialist Left, though that had indeed withered into insignificance long before the collapse of Henry Wallace's Progressive Party, in 1948.

What I mean by the "Left" is any broad, organized political force holding as a principle the need for far-reaching social and institutional change and consistently upholding the interests of the disadvantaged against the most powerful groups in the society. The liberals were never such a force.

What I mean by the liberals is those who subscribed to the ideology I have described: the ideology that held that American capitalism was a revolutionary force for social change, that economic growth was supremely good because it obviated the need for redistribution and social conflict, that class had no place in American politics. Not only are those not the ideas of the Left; at the theoretical level, they provide a sophisticated rationale for avoiding fundamental change. In practice, the liberals were almost always more concerned about distinguishing themselves from the Left than about distinguishing themselves from conservatives.

The confusion between the liberals and the Left arose partly, perhaps, because, in the 1950s, "liberal" was often used as a euphemism for "Left." In the McCarthy era, to call someone a man of the Left carried a whiff of treason with it; to call him a liberal was a graceful alternative.

A deeper reason for the confusion lay in the fact that in the very parts of American society that might have been expected to hold out as the bastions of the Left, the liberals had triumphed. Organized labor, the intelligentsia, and the universities had become the citadels of what was in effect a conservative liberalism.

There were three important developments in the American labor movement in the 1940s, said the editors of *Fortune*: First was the renaissance of the craft-based, politically conservative American Federation of Labor. Fighting back after a period in which it had seemed destined to be swamped by the industrial unions, the AFL doubled its membership in the 1940s and almost recovered parity with the CIO. The second was the "anti-ideological" trend in the CIO, as *Fortune* put it, in the Daniel Bell sense, meaning the trend toward the liberal ideology. And the third was the decline of the left wing in the labor movement generally.

In the forties, the big industrial unions deliberately concentrated on collective bargaining, as opposed to either political activity or drives to increase their membership. They succeeded in winning high wages and fringe packages of social benefits—for their members. But the proportion of union members to the total work force, which had increased sharply in the thirties and the early forties, began a long decline after 1950. By the 1970s, no more than 15 million out of more than 80 million American workers were organized by unions affiliated to the AFL/CIO. Most low-paid workers remain unorganized.

Just as industrial unionism really got going only after the Supreme Court upheld the Wagner Act, in 1937, so two legislative defeats seriously impeded labor's power to organize the unorganized and increased the temptation for the leadership to sit back and enjoy the power and emoluments of its existing strongholds, not to mention the Florida sunshine. Each followed a successful campaign by labor's enemies to capitalize politically on unfavorable news exposure.

The first defeat was the enactment of the Taft-Hartley Law, in 1947, and in particular of its notorious Section 14b, which gave the states the power to pass labor laws that in effect nullified federal law. Taft-Hartley would probably not have passed had the press not given unsympathetic prominence to the series of major postwar strikes, symbolized in the UAW's 113-day strike against General Motors over New Year's 1946. The Republicans recaptured the House of Representatives that fall with the slogan: "Had enough?" Enough had.

"Labor"—that unreal collectivity—had itself more to blame for the second setback: the Landrum-Griffin Act of 1959, which might with equal justice have been called the Kennedy-Griffin Act, since so much of its preparation was done by Senator John F. Kennedy on the Senate Labor Committee.

The background to Landrum-Griffin was the series of exposures of union racketeering that began with the 1952 New York State Crime Commission report on Joe Ryan of the Longshoremen. In 1957, the McClellan Committee, with Robert Kennedy as a young tiger on the staff, began its hearings on the Teamsters. By 1959, George Meany was saying ruefully: "We thought we knew a few things about trade union corruption, but we didn't know the half of it. . . ." Gallup findings show that public approval of labor unions has never subsequently recovered the level (76 per cent) it stood at before the McClellan Committee hearings began. By late 1959, under the influence of this barrage of evidence that some unions were little better than organized crime, Gallup recorded another result that would have been truly astonishing to any European, or to any American in the thirties: almost three times as many Americans (41 per cent) thought Big Labor carried the greatest threat to the economy as thought Big Business did (15 per cent).

When the American Federation of Labor and the Congress of Industrial Organizations finally bit the bullet and merged, in 1955, one of the formal articles of the merger declared:

> the merged federation shall constitutionally affirm its determination to protect the American trade union movement from any and all corrupt influence and from the undermining efforts of Communist agencies and all others who are opposed to the basic principles of our democracy. . . .

It was understandable that the new organization to represent American labor should put itself on record as determined to oppose communism. After all, the vast majority of American workers had always been devoutly anti-Communist. Yet it was unfortunate that in the very years when the American labor movement was losing the battle to organize the general mass of American workers, and so ultimately condemning itself to be no more than a pressure group for one particular fraction of the population, it should have thrown itself so very enthusiastically into the diversion of anti-communism.

In 1946–47, with the help of AFL funds supplied by Meany, the ex-Communist Jay Lovestone was instrumental in breaking strikes called by the French and the Italian Communist unions. By 1948, Lovestone's top agent in Europe, Irving Brown, was paying $1 million in secret U. S. Government money to gangster elements in the French dockers' union in Marseilles. A long and progressively more compromising involvement with the clandestine side of U.S. foreign policy had begun.

By the mid-1960s, the AFL-CIO was showing itself a good deal more adventurous and active in fighting communism abroad than it was in organizing unorganized workers in the U.S.A. But George Meany had always belonged to the more conservative wing of the movement. What is more surprising is that anti-communism became the shibboleth of the originally militant CIO wing to almost the same extent. At the time of the merger, Walter Reuther, the most radical and socially conscious labor leader of his generation, allowed the AFL to take the two top places in the new organization, confident that he would be the ultimate legatee of unity. Reuther had started on the left of the United Auto Workers. He was a socialist, and he spent a year in the Soviet Union in the early thirties. But when he finally emerged as the leader of the union, in the 1947 union elections, it was as the leader of the anti-communist faction, and his victory was generally reported, with approval, as "a swing to the Right." By 1948 Reuther was attacking leftist trade union officials as "colonial agents of a foreign government." At this same time, the future Supreme Court justice and member of the Johnson Cabinet Arthur Goldberg replaced the leftist Lee Pressman as general counsel of the CIO—an archetypal liberal, who was to end up defending the Vietnam War to the United Nations, replacing a man of the Left. It is striking how many of the most prominent liberals of the fifties and sixties—Reuther, Goldberg, Hubert Humphrey—first came to prominence by attacking not the Right but the Left.

"Though intellectuals have not created the labor movement," wrote Joseph Schumpeter, "they have worked it up into something that differs substantially from what it would have been without them." He was right. But in the fifties the role of the intellectual was not so much to radicalize the labor movement, as Schumpeter supposed, as to divert a considerable proportion of its energies and those of what would otherwise have been the American Left, from the feelings and needs of union members and the real though complex problems of American society to a crusade against communism.

Daniel Bell has written of the men who were the intellectual mentors of his generation—he mentions among others Lionel Trilling, Sidney

Hook, Edmund Wilson, Reinhold Niebuhr, James T. Farrell, Richard Wright and Max Lerner—that the reason why there had been no revolt against them was because they had led their own counterrevolt. It was a perceptive remark; conceivably, more so than he realized. He went on:

> They had their Iliad and their Odyssey, were iconistic and icono-clastic. They were intense, horatory [hortatory?], naïve, simplistic and passionate, but after Moscow trials and the Soviet-Nazi pact, disen-chanted and reflective; and from them and their experiences we have inherited the key terms which dominate discourse today: irony, paradox, ambiguity and complexity.

They had their Iliad, too, those heroes of the thirties, "And drunk delight of battle with their peers, / Far on the ringing plains of windy Troy." But now, in the fifties, they had come home and would, "sitting well in order to smite the sounding furrows" of irony, paradox, complexity and other safely non-political abstractions. Soon a younger generation of oarsmen—Bell enumerates himself, Harvey Swados, Hofstadter, Saul Bellow, Leslie Fiedler and Alfred Kazin—would be smiting furrows of ambiguity in a similarly dynamic but well-disciplined manner.

They have had their Iliad and their Odyssey, but unfortunately not yet their Homer. The files of the *Partisan Review, Dissent, Commentary* and the rest over a third of a century are a rich archive, in which one day, perhaps, some intellectual historian may find the materials for a satisfy-ing account of exactly how, and exactly why, a large part of the intelli-gentsia of New York first flirted with revolutionary Marxism and then repented.

Until then, we can keep our suspicions that rather more complex causes were at work than are allowed for in the received version of naïve passion, abruptly turned off by the Moscow trials and the Nazi-Soviet pact. How much did the fragmentation of the Left into what were scarcely more than personal cliques, the Fieldites, the Johnsonites, the Zamites, the Schachtmanites, contribute to its paralysis? How important was the sheer anti-intellectual stupidity of the Communist Party?

Or are we paying too much attention to the factors that may have repelled the intellectuals from the Left and not enough to those that at-tracted them to liberalism? to the reawakened pride in America, *engagé* at last against fascism, prospering and victorious? Didn't Leslie Fiedler, after a visit to Italy in 1952, pronounce to the readers of *Partisan Review*—yes, *Partisan Review*, which had been born to bring a new hope from Europe to the land of the capitalist *Abgang*—that "a hundred years after the Manifesto, the specter that is haunting Europe is—Gary Cooper!" Didn't Lerner end his book with Emerson's proud and boastful hope: "We think our civilization is near its meridian, but we are yet only at the cockcrowing and the morning star"? The last chapter of Kazin's *On Native Ground* opens with a quotation from Abigail Adams: "Do you know that European birds have not half the melody of ours?"

It may be that this optimistic nationalism had a special appeal to intellectuals who were, in such notable proportion, themselves the second- and third-generation children of immigrants, inheritors of the dream. It may be that, like other Americans of the same generation, they felt a need to assimilate under the pressure of the great nativist rebellion that was McCarthyism, to prove themselves good Americans and better than the book burners.

Whatever the exact causes, the intellectual ballast shifted. In 1932 those who endorsed the Communist Party's candidate for President of the United States included Ernest Hemingway, John Dos Passos, James T. Farrell, Langston Hughes, Theodore Dreiser, Erskine Caldwell, Lincoln Steffens, Richard Wright, Katherine Anne Porter, Edmund Wilson, Nathanael West and Malcolm Cowley. Twenty years later, scarcely an intellectual with a shred of reputation could be found even to raise a voice against the outlawing of that same party. The change is measured, too, by the trajectory, in hardly more than a decade, of *Partisan Review*, the most admired highbrow periodical of the time, from dutiful Stalinism through Trotskyite heresy to the bleakest Cold War anti-communist orthodoxy.

Yet it is striking, in retrospect, how central to that supposedly apolitical culture anti-communism became. The formation of Americans for Democratic Action, excluding Communists, Arthur Schlesinger thought, marked "the watershed at which American liberalism began to base itself once again on a solid conception of man and of history." Of American history? No: for Schlesinger, liberalism had virtually been created by anti-communism, apparently. "The growing necessity of checking Communism," he wrote, "by developing some constructive alternative speeded the clarification of liberal ideas in 1947 and 1948."

Long before that, anti-communism had played a key part in defining the specifically American intellectual culture. Sociology was the characteristic discipline of the liberal pundits. And academic sociology had always been more or less explicitly a critique of Marxism. Weber, Durkheim, Pareto, to name only the three greatest masters of the discipline, were all explicit anti-Marxists. Even more interesting, Talcott Parsons, the most admired American sociologist and the *chef d'école* if there was one, consciously turned to Pareto as an alternative to Marx.

> The crisis of the 1930s [Alvin Gouldner has written] led some American academicians to look to European academic sociology as a de-

fense against the Marxism that was recently penetrating American campuses.

. . . A group of Harvard scholars . . . which included Parsons, George Homans and Crane Brinton, formed a seminar on Vilfredo Pareto, which began to meet in the fall of 1932 and continued to meet until 1934. Also attending were R. K. Merton . . . and Clyde Kluckhohn.

The political implications of the circle's interest in Pareto were expressed by George Homans, who candidly acknowledged . . . "I felt during the Thirties I was under personal attack, above all from the Marxists. I was ready to believe Pareto because he provided me with a defense."

After World War II, in almost every department of intellectual life, the doctrine of "American exceptionalism" revived. At the same time, utilitarian doctrines, stressing that morality in politics was an illusion, undercut the moralistic basis of left-wing politics. Sociology, history, economics, political science, even theology in the hands of Reinhold Niebuhr, for example, followed parallel paths, rejecting those who argued for radical change and emphasizing the virtues of "the American way."

What role remains for the men of the Left? Seymour Martin Lipset asked in *Political Man*. Not to advocate change in the society of his own country, if he lived in "the West." Even socialists must agree, Lipset thought, that complete socialism was dangerous and that Marxism was an outmoded doctrine.

Did it follow that the Left was totally obsolete? Lipset thought not. "The leftist intellectual, the trade union leader, and the socialist politician" could still make themselves useful—abroad, where society had not yet evolved to such a fortunate state of perfection as in the United States. Such disaffected persons, no longer required at home, could "communicate and work with non-Communist revolutionaries in the Orient and Africa at the same time that they accept the fact"—it sounds like a polite way of saying "on the condition that they accept the fact"—"that serious ideological controversies have ended at home."

In the culminating chapter, that is, of one of the most admired works of political science that the age of the liberal consensus produced, it was argued as a conclusion of high academic seriousness that the only use for dissenters from the liberal ideology was as its propagandists abroad. It was a proposition that wrapped Irving Brown's transactions with the Corsican *milieu* of Marseilles in *ex post facto* respectability and gave a postdated endorsement to those intellectuals who were to try to win the hearts and minds of Vietnam.

In the great American universities, the twenty years after World War II are beginning to be remembered with nostalgia as a Golden Age. Enrollments were multiplying. Endowments were accumulating. Funds from the federal and state governments and from private foundations were becoming available on a scale undreamed of. The salaries and the social status of professors were rising. They were certainly higher, both absolutely and in relation to those of the business world, than they had been since before World War I, and perhaps higher than they had ever been, at least for men sensible enough to have specialized in some useful subject that would earn them consultancy fees from large corporations, from government, or from the armed services. At a time when the U. S. Air Force was paying (through the RAND Corporation) for a sociological study of the toilet training of the French, even that qualification need not stand in the way of a man of imagination.

Life was still Spartan in the fifties, of course, even in Cambridge, at Berkeley or at Columbia, compared with the splendors to come. But life was also a good deal more soothing and pleasant than it was to be later. Academic affluence had the charm of novelty. Installing the first generation of IBM computers was the most fun. It was pleasant for men whose wives had typed out their dissertations on the kitchen table to become directors of research institutes, commanding generals of armies of researchers. There was a certain temptation to use these logistical resources to attack intellectual problems somewhat as General Eisenhower had overcome the Wehrmacht, by the methodical application of sheer weight. Yet the most influential books of the fifties were, with some exceptions, short, entertainingly written, and the work of individuals.

By the fifties, the academic profession was drawing talent from a wider catchment area. At one end of the income scale, able men of prosperous families who would earlier have gone into business were attracted to the universities in the Depression; at the other, a growing proportion of the population was now graduating from college. Finally, tens of thousands of gifted refugees from Europe leavened American academic life. But the essential reason for the intellectual excitement that blossomed in the best American universities in the late fifties was neither academic influence nor increased competition. It came from the feeling that, for the first time, the academic world seemed thoroughly integrated into the life and purposes of the nation.

To begin with, this may have owed something to the achievement of the atomic scientists. When the mightiest arm of American power was the product of research science, it was hard to dismiss any research as impractical dreaming. Physicists, mathematicians, engineers, were among the first to be accepted by government. But the social scientists were not far behind. (Indeed, one branch of social science, economics, had long moved with assurance in the world of business as well as in Washington.) The earliest big government research contracts dealt with such "nuts-and-bolts" questions as the design of unmanned satellites or the nose cones of missiles. But as early as 1948 Nathan Leites was calling on the academic techniques of textual and literary criticism to describe "The Operational Code of Politburo." It was not long before sociologists, political scientists, even historians, were being called into service by the government—all of the social sciences received from the relationship an injection of adrenalin, as well as of money.

This was the broader context in which the system of thought I have called the liberal ideology was fitted together and came to predominate not only in the universities but in government and to some extent in politics. The interaction, however, was reciprocal. The intellectuals tended to be influential only in proportion as their ideas fitted in with the needs, fears or preconceptions of their new patrons. They tended to be forced into the role of technicians. The "hot" topics of specialization were those most immediately related to the government's most urgent perplexity, or at best to the tactics of its political opponents. Either way, that generally recommended those studies which assumed the permanence and the paramountcy of the Cold War.

"It is remarkable," wrote Henry Kissinger in 1962, "that during a decade of crisis few fundamental criticisms of American policy have been offered. We have not reached an impasse because the wrong alternative was chosen in a 'Great Debate.' The alternatives have rarely been properly defined." It was indeed remarkable. The Pentagon Papers are a sustained commentary on that observation. Yet it is strange that Henry Kissinger, the future virtuoso of the Carrot and the Stick, should find it hard to understand why the alternatives did not get defined. For if the fear of being investigated had shown the intellectuals the stick during the first half of the fifties, the hope of being consulted had shown them the carrot in the second. Alternatives were not what the government wanted. It wanted solutions. It expected to get them from men who displayed a maximum of technical ingenuity with a minimum of dissent.

The liberal ideology equipped the United States with an elaborately interrelated structure of coherent and plausible working assumptions, all poised like an inverted pyramid on two fundamental assumptions, both of which happened to be diametrically wrong.

American capitalism had not, it turned out, eliminated the possibility of serious social conflict at home. Nor was the most urgent danger to the nation from communism abroad. On the contrary, the United States stood on the eve of exceptional social turmoil. Abroad, unified Communist power was breaking up, confronting the world with all the dangers of a period of fragmentation and "*détente.*"

This error was to be pitilessly exposed, and that soon enough. Yet the effect of the liberal consensus was to be even more disastrous than the particular mistaken assumptions on which it was based. It condemned the United States to face the real dangers for too long without any fundamental debate. Thanks to the liberal triumph, the powerful emotions and interests that always work for conservative policies were not balanced by equally powerful forces and principles of the Left. Instead, they were opposed by a liberalism that was in effect hardly to be distinguished from a more sophisticated and less resolute conservatism.

# 5

## The Presidency

". . . the White House, on which an impatient world waited for miracles."

> Theodore H. White, *The Making of the President 1960*, last sentence.

"Somehow we must learn to govern our people from an office that is secular and not from a court that is sanctified."

> George E. Reedy, *The Twilight of the Presidency* (1970), last sentence.

The years of the consensus were also the high summer of the cult of the presidency. And this was natural, for the same forces that had forged the consensus endowed the modern presidency with its prestige and power.

Whatever its deeper origins, in political terms the consensus could be seen as a kind of gigantic deal. The Republicans and all but the most unreconstructed of conservatives accepted the new economics of government intervention, because they understood that government would have to accept responsibility for the well-being of the economy. We are all Keynesians now, said even conservative economists. Democrats and liberals, in return, accepted the new foreign policy of global containment. Indeed, as we have seen, it was to a considerable extent the liberals and the Democrats who framed that policy, or at least who sold it to the country. There was no mystery about the reasons for this drift of policy toward the center. Conservatives had accepted the need for government intervention because in the economic crisis of the 1930s the great majority of the electorate looked to government for help. Liberals had accepted an active, anti-Communist foreign policy because, in the world crisis of the 1940s, the great majority of public opinion took the view that only an interventionist policy could guarantee national security. And it was those very same factors—the need for economic intervention at home and the need for military intervention abroad—that swept away all opposition to the astonishing growth in power and prestige of the presidency.

Indeed, one vital strand in the consensus of the late 1950s and early 1960s was the acceptance, by the Republicans and conservatives generally, of the President's responsibility for the economic well-being of the nation, and in particular of his responsibility for full employment. And another strand in the consensus was the acceptance by the Democrats and liberals of his responsibility for the peace and freedom of a large part of the world.

"The demands of modern life and the unsettled status of the world," wrote President Eisenhower in his economic message to Congress in his very first year in office, "require a more important role for government than it played in earlier and quieter times." By government, Eisenhower clearly meant the executive branch. And his two immediate predecessors, whose times, if earlier, were hardly quieter than his own, took an even more exalted view of the powers and prerogatives of their office, for the simple reason that they, and everyone else, took it for granted that if they didn't act to save the American people first from disaster and then from defeat, no one else would. Congress, certainly, had shown no sign of willingness to shoulder either burden. "The strong presidency," wrote Professor Clinton Rossiter in Eisenhower's time, "is the product of events that cannot be undone and of forces that continue to roll. We have made our decision for the New Economy and the New Internationalism, and in making them we have made this kind of presidency a prerequisite for the effective conduct of our constitutional system."

It is not in the least surprising that the years of the consensus saw the appearance of a spate of books about the presidency. It started in the middle 1950s, reached a climax in the presidential election year 1960, and continued until the onset of disillusion, after 1965.

The study of the presidency, in fact, like the institution itself, lay relatively dormant from Woodrow Wilson's time until FDR's, and then stirred mightily. Harold Laski's *The American Presidency*, based on lectures given at the University of Indiana that came out in 1940, was one early sign of the interest aroused by Roosevelt's bold conception of his office. Another was Professor E. S. Corwin's magisterial treatise on the President's office and powers, which appeared in 1948. There was a marked revival of biographical interest in the strong Presidents of history during the Roosevelt and Truman administrations. Books such as Douglas Southall Freeman's *Washington*, Carl Sandburg's *Linco n*, Marquis

James's *Jackson*, Arthur M. Schlesinger, Jr.'s, *Age of Jackson*, all tended, in differing degrees, to focus attention on the President as hero and savior. But it wasn't until the middle 1950s, or in other words not until the two strong, activist Democratic Presidents had been succeeded by Eisenhower, who was arguably strong but certainly not activist, that books on the presidency as an institution began to jostle one another from the presses.

In 1954 there was Sidney Hyman's *The American President*. In the spring of 1956 Clinton Rossiter gave the series of lectures at the University of Chicago that were then expanded into his *The American Presidency*. The very simplicity of those two titles suggests how relatively little had been written about the presidency as an institution before then. The same year, Richard Neustadt published an essay, *The Presidency at Mid-Century*, that contained the seeds of the ideas developed in his classic *Presidential Power*, which came out in 1960. In the latter year there also appeared Rexford G. Tugwell's *The Enlargement of the Presidency*, Herman Finer's *The Presidency: Crisis and Regeneration*, and at least half a dozen other books most of which shared a general bias in favor of the aggrandizement of the office. Suddenly the academic publishers were scrambling to satisfy the new appetite for books about what was now coming to be called almost ritually, by editorial writers and historians alike, "the most powerful office on earth," a phrase which, if accurate, hardly envisaged a limited view of its power.

And not academic publishers alone. The immensely successful best seller on the 1960 campaign by the reporter-turned-novelist Theodore H. White was not only steeped in the assumptions of the liberal consensus about the country; it was a celebration of the power and aura of the presidency. It drew heavily on the new academic literature of the time, and specifically on Neustadt and Rossiter, especially in its concluding section. White took the new, high doctrines of presidential power, one might say, and stitched them with the threads of his own deference into the ermine of majesty. And he also preached those same doctrines to a far wider market than they had previously reached. His book was perhaps only less responsible than the princely style of its hero for the fascination with the presidency that so many educated Americans seem to have felt in the first half of the sixties. This attitude, bordering on fealty to an elective monarchy, was a striking departure from older traditions and attitudes.

Partly, indeed, because of the success of White's book, the high theory of presidential prerogative later came to be associated in the public mind with Kennedy and his supporters. That is wrong. It first came into fashion under Eisenhower, and it looked back to Truman and Roosevelt. There was a two-way influence, in fact, between the reality of the presi-

dency and the cult of the presidency. Presidents Kennedy, Johnson and ultimately Nixon, and their staffs, were deeply influenced by a conception of
the presidency that they learned, directly and indirectly, from Rossiter,
Neustadt and White. But it is equally true that the model of the presidency that these writers and other intellectuals cherished in the late 1950s
was itself formed by the memory of twenty years of activism in the White
House from 1933 to 1953. One reason why, in the second Eisenhower
term, so many intellectuals stressed not the dangers inherent in the
swollen powers of the presidency but the need for those powers to be used
to the utmost, was that, almost without exception, they felt that
Eisenhower had failed to use them to the full. A President, Woodrow
Wilson had said, "is at liberty, both in law and conscience, to be as big a
man as he can." By that test, the liberal intellectuals felt that Eisenhower
had failed as a President.

"The influence of the Crown," ran Dunning's famous resolution in
the eighteenth-century House of Commons, "has increased, is increasing,
and ought to be diminished." One of the main themes of the literature on
the presidency that accumulated so rapidly during Eisenhower's second
term was almost exactly the opposite. The power of the presidency—so the
liberals maintained—had increased, had temporarily stopped increasing,
and ought to be increased again. There were few who were Whiggish
enough to disagree with Professor Rossiter. "The Presidency," he wrote,
"is a standing reproach to those petty doctrinaries who insist that executive power is inherently undemocratic . . . no less a reproach to those easy
generalizers who think that Lord Acton had the very last word on the corrupting effects of power." Possessing, collectively, more power than any
other group of men in history, the American elite after World War II naturally found it exceptionally difficult to believe that its tendency could be
corrupting.

At a casual reading, the most influential of all these books about the
presidency might perhaps be taken as an exception. Richard Neustadt
took as his text the rueful theme of Harry Truman's table talk as Neustadt
remembered it from his own days in Truman's White House. "He'll sit
here," Truman apparently used to say, contemplating his probable successor, "and he'll say, 'Do this! Do that! *And nothing will happen!* Poor Ike!"
Neustadt's theme was that presidential power, after all, is no more than
the power to persuade. He insisted on the distinction between presidential
powers, which might be imposing enough, and presidential power, which
could turn out in practice to be frustratingly limited. His case studies were
chosen to illustrate this view.

Yet *Presidential Power*, none the less, is only an apparent exception
to the dominant theory of the time about the presidency. Its intention, it

seems to me, was not so much to describe the limitations on the President's power as to exhort Presidents to transcend those limitations, and to show them how they might succeed in doing so. Legend has it that George III's mother used to repeat to him when he was a boy, "George, be a king!" Something not so different was the burden of Neustadt's advice to Presidents. "Neustadt wants to indicate," one critic has written, "how a President can become a powerful leader and what a President must do if he wants to have influence." Whatever the preacher's intention, that certainly was the sense in which the sermon was understood by the most important member of the congregation. For John F. Kennedy read Neustadt's book. He appreciated and enjoyed its Machiavellian realism about the mechanics of power. And if he had no desire to be a king, he certainly meant to be as big a man in the White House as law and conscience allowed.

There was, therefore, no fundamental disagreement between Neustadt's subtle and worldly analysis of effective power and Rossiter's bareheaded glorification of the office. At times, certainly, Rossiter wrote as if there was to be one limitation on the power of the presidency, namely that imposed by the need for it to be compatible with democracy. But nowhere did he feel it necessary to explain how that limitation would make itself felt in practice. He wrote more as if democracy were a mystic ingredient in the American air that would always save the presidency from becoming "a matrix of dictatorship" than as if democracy could ever be threatened by the power of the presidency. "The President is not a Gulliver, immobilized by ten thousand tiny cords," he wrote in a strikingly monarchical image, "nor even a Prometheus, chained to a rock of frustration. He is, rather, a kind of magnificent lion who can roam freely and do great deeds so long as he does not try to break loose from his broad reservation."

The outstanding feature of American constitutional development, for Rossiter and surely for most thoughtful Americans of his generation, had been "the growth of the power and prestige of the Presidency." Few stopped to think deeply about the philosophical traps hidden in the conviction that "there is virtually no limit to what the President can do if he does it for democratic ends and through democratic means."

Who was going to decide which ends, and which means, qualified as "democratic"?

Public opinion? But no force would have more influence over public opinion than the President himself, if he chose to exert it. The formula could be reduced perilously close to the simple statement that there was virtually no limit to what the President could do. Both Lyndon Johnson and Richard Nixon were to teach this lesson in their different ways.

But such a skeptical attitude to the growing power of the presidency simply never occurred to most of the intellectuals of the 1950s, and when it did cross some minds, they generally dismissed it as unworthy, if not un-American. The President, wrote Rossiter, could do great things only if they did not outrage "the accepted dictates of constitutionalism, democracy, personal liberty and Christian morality," a proposition that neither Johnson nor Nixon would have had any difficulty in accepting, but that left distressing problems of interpretation. "The power of the presidency," he believed, "moves as a mighty host only *with* the grain of liberty and morality." As he looked back over his almost completed manuscript, he said, he did detect "a deep note of satisfaction" with the new, aggrandized presidency. It sprang, he supposed, from his own political attitude, which was "more concerned with the world as it is than as it is said to have been by reactionaries and is promised to be by radicals." And this attitude, he thought, he shared with a "staggering majority of Americans." It was another way of saying that the new, imperial presidency matched the ideas of the liberal consensus and was in turn its chosen instrument.

More than a decade later, without Rossiter's "deep note of satisfaction," indeed with a hint of the detachment that comes from disillusion, Professor Marcus Cunliffe summed up what was still the prevailing view:

> Our own thinking on the matter has been shaped by twentieth century experience, which had then been read back into American history by scholars. The lessons presented to us by the dominant "liberal" style may be summed up as follows:
> —"Strong" presidents (Washington, Jefferson, Jackson, Lincoln, Wilson, the two Roosevelts, etc.) have promoted national unity, prosperity, democracy and responsibility.
> —"Weak" presidents (Pierce, Buchanan, Grant, Harding, Coolidge, etc.) have, no doubt unwittingly, countenanced national disunity, economic selfishness, social conservatism and irresponsibility both in domestic and international affairs. . . .
> . . . Historically the legislative branch has sought to weaken executive authority through jealous obstructionism.
> —The executive branch is the hero of the story of American Federal government: Congress the villain.

The identity of interest between the liberals and the presidency, on this view, is not hard to seek. The liberals wanted a strong President because they assumed that strong Presidents would always be on their side. Certainly, as Eisenhower handed over his office to Kennedy, there were few, if any, among those who had made a study of the presidency who would have conceived it possible that within a dozen years a conservative would have become the "strongest" President of all (in terms of his claims for the prerogative of the office), or that the theory of presidential activism should have been put to the service of "social conservatism," "economic selfishness," and even of "national disunity."

The liberals liked the presidency because it was their branch of government. It was the branch that always seemed most likely to do the things they wanted done. As they labored to perfect and extend its power, they little thought it might fall into the hands of those who would use its power to threaten their own political destruction. And yet one of the strong strands that led into the political crisis of the sixties was the identification between the activist, institutionalized presidency and the liberal elite that wanted the President to roam "like a kind of magnificent lion," slaying their enemies for them. It never occurred to them to think of themselves as presidential prey.

There was no arguing with the experts when they said that the power of the presidency had increased. As a matter of fact, it had been growing throughout American history. The founding fathers' original conception of an executive who merely carried out the laws passed by Congress never corresponded to the urgent needs of government. Nor did the original balance between the executive and the legislative as laid down in the Constitution long survive in practice. General Washington was not the man to loiter like the ghost of a lawyer's scruples when there was work to be done; and Washington, Jefferson, Jackson and Lincoln all left the office possessed of more real power than they found it endowed with. None of the occasional periods of presidential retrenchment, in the 1820s, the 1850s and the 1870s, for example, threatened this steady accumulation of power, and for an essentially simple reason. However wise the Founding Fathers' instincts have proved to be about the dangers of excessive power, they did not anticipate the alternative dangers of inadequate political power. The recurrent crises of the nineteenth century showed that the nation needed to be led. And the experience of Congressional government in the generation after the Civil War only confirmed what the greatest Presidents had understood by intuition: that only the President could lead.

With the twentieth century, the aggrandizement of the presidency began to accelerate. Both in its enthusiasm for strong foreign policy and in its willingness to involve the federal government in attempts to solve domestic social problems, the Progressive era anticipated the liberal consensus after World War II. Theodore Roosevelt and Woodrow Wilson held something very close to FDR's active, responsible conception of the office. "I declined to adopt the view," said TR, "that what was imperatively necessary for the nation could not be done by the President unless he could find some specific authorization for it."

It was just this feeling, not only on the part of the President but on the part of most Americans, that transformed the presidency between 1933 and 1953. The 1936 landslide was a measure of how many felt that, faced with economic crisis, vigorous action from the White House was indeed imperatively necessary. And before the Depression was over, the world crisis had begun.

The conduct of American diplomacy in the face of fascism, the decision to enter the war, the conduct of the war and of the alliance, the shaping of the postwar settlement—these were in any case issues in which presidential authority, on the most traditional view, would have been legitimately permanent. But before there was time to grasp the implications of World War II for the presidency, FDR was dead and a neophyte President was confronted by still more urgent challenges. There were nuclear weapons to be tested and used. There was the threat of Stalin's Russia. And there was the sudden proliferation of international responsibilities implied by the global commitment to contain communism. Congress had its part to play in all these great decisions, of course. But it was a subordinate part. Whatever the Constitution might say about the Senate's role in ratifying treaties, for example, only the President could act with the necessary speed and flexibility to forestall economic collapse in Western Europe with Marshall aid, to step into the gap left by British withdrawal from Greece, or to organize United Nations military action in time to prevent South Korea from being overrun. Again, Congress might theoretically retain the power to declare war. But when the President could win a war by using nuclear weapons or lose it by refusing to use them, then Congress' say in the matter came to seem very theoretical indeed, not just to Presidents and to public opinion but to senators and congressmen as well. The invention of atomic weapons made people feel that there might not be time for Congress to play its part in the decision between peace and war. Only the presidency, in general, seemed attuned to the sheer speed of the modern world.

The presidency did not acquire its new powers through Congressional inadvertence, though. In the late 1940s and early 1950s the new responsibilities were formalized in a series of statutes, especially in three pieces of legislation passed within less than eighteen months that together had an incalculably great impact on the presidency. The first was the Employment Act of February 1946. The second was the Atomic Energy Act of July 1946. And the third was the National Security Act of 1947.

Each of these three major acts not only formalized the President's responsibility for a new and important area of national life; it also equipped him with new bureaucratic agencies to carry out his new tasks. Thus, the Employment Act not only laid upon the federal government the duty of promoting "maximum employment, production and purchasing power"; it also created the Council of Economic Advisers, who were charged, among other things, with developing "national economic policies." That was something few would have considered any part of the President's duties before 1933. The Atomic Energy Act not only specified that on matters affecting the "development, manufacture, use and storage of [atomic] bombs," the President's "decision shall be final." It also set up the Atomic Energy Commission to help him with his task. And the National Security Act not only spelled out the President's overriding responsibility for both defense and foreign policy; it furnished him with a whole series of new instruments for the purpose. It erected a new national military establishment headed by a new Secretary of Defense, a new Central Intelligence Agency, and a new National Security Council with its staff. Ultimately, when Dr. Kissinger and General Haig finally persuaded President Nixon to resign, it could be argued that the national security staff had become, in certain extreme circumstances at least, more powerful than the President himself. What has been more generally true under each of the past five Presidents is that, as a result of the creation of the national security bureaucracy, the President has acquired his own general staff. It is small compared with the bureaucracies that serve the Secretary of Defense and the Joint Chiefs of Staff. But it controls those larger bureaucracies as surely as the rudder controls the ship. And it is every bit as much subject to the head of state's personal authority, as secret, and as unchecked by effective constitutional supervision, as were ever the general staffs of nineteenth-century Europe.

The transformation of the personal presidency into a bureaucratic institution had begun even before FDR was inaugurated. By 1936 the President's own personal resources and those of his immediate coterie of secretaries, friends and advisers were obviously inadequate for the effective management of the executive branch's traditional functions, let alone for coping with the growing tide of new business that people expected the President to deal with. In that year President Roosevelt set up the Brownlow Committee to advise on the problem, and early in 1937 the committee produced its report. "The President," it said, "must be helped." In 1939 President Roosevelt was able to carry out most of its recommendations by executive order. From then on, Presidents were provided with a staff of executive assistants and with experts and administrators under them. From this, Executive Order 8248 can be dated—not, as is sometimes said, the "institutionalization of the Presidency," for the office remains to an astonishing extent a personal one, to which different incumbents bring radically different techniques and even conceptions of government—but the development of the presidency as an institution capable of effectively carrying out the will of the President who seeks to intervene actively in foreign and domestic policy.

Two points are worth noticing here about the subsequent growth of the presidency as a bureaucratic institution. The first is that it has been very rapid by any standards. "The White House," in FDR's time, meant fewer than one hundred people. Even late in the Eisenhower administration, "the Executive Office of the President," complete with the Council of Economic Advisers and their staff, with the Office of Defense Mobilization and the NSC staff as well as the Bureau of the Budget and the President's own assistants and helpers, totaled only some twelve hundred. By the second Nixon administration, "the White House" meant well over five thousand people. What had within living memory been the personal power and responsibility of one man, executed by a handful of helpers working in what was still his residence, had become fragmented among a number of officials three times as strong as a marine battle group, and not always as disciplined.

The second point is that "the White House" had become a bureaucracy within the federal bureaucracy of the executive branch. To a considerable extent, therefore, the increased power of the presidency had been gained not only at the expense of Congress but also at the expense of the existing departments of the executive branch.

It is possible that, in time, the departments headed by cabinet officers will wither away in Washington. But, for the time being, this is neither necessary nor possible. For the new White House bureaucracy does not yet duplicate all the functions of the federal bureaucracy. It merely duplicates, and increasingly tends to supersede, the more important ones. Through the Council of Economic Advisers, the White House staff controls long-term economic forecasting and planning and the federal government's impact on economic policy. Through the Office of Management and Budget, it not only controls the federal government's dealings with Congress over financial appropriations and supply; it also supervises the expenditure of all other departments. Through the national security staff, the White House oversees defense and foreign policy. Increasingly, it has tended to go further, and reserve for the President's national security adviser and his office the actual execution of policy in the most important areas. Notoriously this was true when Henry Kissinger held the job, but it was far more true than was generally realized under McGeorge Bundy and Walt W. Rostow as well.

The White House is supreme over war and peace, over economic intelligence and planning, and over the power of the purse. It can, of course, also reach out and take unto itself any other particular issue that it needs to control. For example, it reached out and took control of "civil rights" under Kennedy and more particularly under Johnson. But, in normal times, the four functions that the White House routinely controls—the budget, economics, defense and foreign policy—make it sovereign within the federal government. It has made itself sovereign over existing bureaucracies with established responsibilities. In those four crucial areas, the important decisions are taken not by permanent civil servants or even by presidential appointees at the Treasury, in the Commerce or the Labor Department, in the Pentagon or at State; they are taken by men directly and personally responsible to the President, in the White House.

The presidency, then, by the beginning of the sixties, was already generally perceived as the "modern" element in the federal government, the element whose evolution seemed most to have kept pace with the needs of a period of crisis, and therefore the element with the most expansive future ahead of it.

It was seen as the "efficient" element in the government of a society that still worshiped efficiency.

It was seen as the "national" element. Where senators represented the people of their states and congressmen their districts, where the departments headed by cabinet officers were seen as representing abstract interests such as labor or business or the West, the President was seen as embodying the aspirations and responding to the needs of the nation as a whole. More than that: in a time of nationalism, he was associated with the great national endeavors of which Americans were most proud: with victory in war, with nuclear weapons, with the wonders of space technology, with national power and supremacy. It was the President, not some funny old congressman with ineradicably civilian manners and considerations, who represented America for Americans.

Lastly, only the President was "President of all the people," and so he came to be seen as the most "democratic" element in the American democracy as well.

Modern in a nation whose essential myth was that of its own future, efficient in a nation of efficiency experts, national in a society that was going through a wave of nationalism that was not the less intense for being generous, democratic in a country that remained committed more deeply to democracy—whatever that meant—than to any other value; no wonder the presidency, by the time John Kennedy entered upon it, seemed the key and master institution of American society. And no wonder that the press and especially television intensified the already unfulfillably great expectations with which Americans looked to the President. After all, he was more than their elected representative; he was their chosen symbol. And couldn't the generation of Americans who had won the war and split the atom do anything that they set their minds to?

# 6

## The Establishment

By the spring of 1973, the American foreign policy Establishment had been so divided and demoralized by the Vietnam War that its members disagreed even on whether it existed.

McGeorge Bundy, for example, very much doubted whether there had ever been such a thing as the Establishment. And that was surprising, because a dozen years earlier he would automatically have been mentioned as heir apparent to become the head of it.

When I talked to him in his office in the Ford Foundation's strangely Piranesian headquarters on Forty-second Street in New York, he murmured learnedly about the dangers of misapplying Pareto's theory of the circulation of elites, and then asked somewhat sharply where the Establishment had been during the Eisenhower years. At the head of the State Department and the CIA, for a start, I suggested, in the persons of the Dulles brothers. Surely, he argued, like a very polite tiger moving in for the kill, any definition of the Establishment that included both John Foster Dulles and Adlai Stevenson (whom I had not mentioned) was so wide as to be meaningless. For Bundy, the word Establishment, "like 'intellectual,' is a word that confuses without defining."

Cyrus Vance, in his only slightly smaller office, looking out over the Statue of Liberty from a crisp new skyscraper at the lower tip of Manhattan, disagreed. And there are those who would say that Vance, after a distinguished career in the law, as President Johnson's personal representative from Detroit to Cyprus, as a former deputy secretary of defense, and as a former Vietnam peace negotiator, is poised to succeed Bundy as the next chairman of the Establishment. "I don't think the Establishment is dead," he said. "I think it will continue to function, and usefully."

In his book-lined sanctum in the Littauer Building at Harvard, decorated with some of the exquisite miniatures he brought back from his tour as ambassador in New Delhi, John Kenneth Galbraith disagreed with both Bundy and Vance: "The foreign policy elite was always the world's biggest collection of meatheads."

While in his office in Washington, the one with the view out over the White House that is said to impress clients so much that it has helped him to become the highest-paid lawyer in the country, Clark Clifford recounted gloomily, though perhaps not without a certain lugubrious sense of justice done, how many brilliant reputations in the foreign policy Establishment had been destroyed by the Vietnam War. Take A, he said, naming him: A had something of a reputation as a strategic thinker. He was even, said Clifford, studying his fingertips, something of an oracle. Well, said Clifford, looking up, he has been crucified.

I suggested that it was, above all, the war that had destroyed the influence of the foreign policy elite. He looked at me with the faintly ironic pleasure of a teacher whose pupil has finally seized what to the teacher is a painfully elementary truth. "My friend," he replied, "you are so"—pause—"very"—pause—"right."

Can we afford to beg McGeorge Bundy's question out of hand? Is there, has there ever been, an American foreign policy Establishment?

It was the British journalist Henry Fairlie who coined the phrase "the Establishment" in its modern sense, in an article in the conservative weekly *The Spectator*, in 1955. He did not apply it, as it came to be loosely applied by the New Left in America, to the "upper class," or to the rich, or to conservatives. He coined it to describe a reality of political life in Britain as he saw it at the time: the group of powerful men, who know each other, or at least know someone who knows anyone they may need to know; who share assumptions so deep that they do not need to be articulated; and who contrive to wield power outside the constitutional or political forms: the power to put a stop to things they disapprove of, to promote the men they regard as reliable; the power, in a word, to preserve the *status quo*. Fairlie was explicitly not thinking only of politicians: the editor of *The Times*, the Archbishop of Canterbury, the top civil servants in Whitehall and the most influential bankers in the City of London were members of his Establishment, and not by any means all cabinet members could make the same claim. Again, for Fairlie, membership was emphatically not a question of party politics. The true Establishment man prided himself on his nonpartisanship, on his ability to get along with and work with right-minded fellows of either party or none.

The very existence of such undemocratic and cabalistic influences is shocking to many Americans; it negates the populist mythology of American democracy. No doubt this is one of the reasons why those who display

the purest Establishment reflexes and characteristics are fondest of scoffing
at the very idea that it exists. Back in 1966, for example, Flora Lewis of
the Washington *Post* drew a deft drypoint of John J. McCloy and Dean
Rusk, at a black-tie dinner of the Council on Foreign Relations, rocking
with dignified and apparently not altogether displeased mirth at the notion
that "the Council on Foreign Relations is a member of the Establishment."

And yet when Richard Rovere first imported the term into the
United States, in a famous article in *The American Scholar* in 1961, it was
John J. McCloy and Dean Rusk whom he chose as presidents emeritus and
incumbent, respectively, of his imaginary American Establishment, and it
was the council which he named as "a sort of Presidium for that part of
the Establishment that guides our destiny as a nation."

Rovere's piece was written as a spoof, decked out with fake references.
But since then, the idea that there is indeed an American Establishment,
and that it exercises influence particularly over foreign affairs, has taken
root in earnest and has become part of the common coin of political
debate. Such books as Noam Chomsky's *American Power and the New
Mandarins*, Richard J. Barnet's *The Roots of War*, and David Halberstam's *The Best and the Brightest*, for example, contain elaborate discussions of the proposition that the foreign policy Establishment should bear
a large share of the responsibility for the Vietnam War.

What, then, is the Establishment? It is certainly not identical with
the Council on Foreign Relations, which has become something of a
whipping boy for liberal journalists (as well as for the lunatic Right) and
even the focus of a good deal of conspiracy theory. Its importance, both as
the headquarters and as the test of membership in the Establishment, has
probably been exaggerated.

There has also been a tendency to confuse the Establishment and the
upper class. It may indeed help you to rise in the Establishment if you
have inherited wealth (the Rockefellers, Averell Harriman), or family con-
nections with powerful men in it (the Dulles brothers, the Bundy
brothers), and it certainly helps to have an Ivy League education. But
many representative and influential Establishment figures had none of
these advantages, while many a millionaire alumnus of Harvard or Yale
could not hope for membership. Among the older generation of Establishment leaders—Acheson, the Dulleses, Stimson, Lovett, McCloy—one
does find a high proportion of graduates of the old elite private prepara-
tory schools and of Harvard, Princeton and Yale. Since until recently
those schools charged high fees, gave few scholarships, and reserved a substantial proportion of their places for the children of their own alumni, it
follows that most of those older members of the Establishment came from
what are known in America as "old" or "good" families. By no means all

of them would have been called wealthy families. Both Dean Acheson and the Dulles brothers were the children of clergymen (as was Dean Rusk), and the typical Establishment man of the older generation came from just that kind of background: one that could afford to give its sons the inheritance of a superior education, but had little money to leave after that, and endowed its sons instead with a tradition of service and a certain confidence that the ways to power were open to them. They were American gentlemen, in fact, who approached life with the confidence that came from having inherited all the advantages that their British models had enjoyed in the nineteenth century, without the envy and suspicion that members of that caste have encountered in the twentieth.

To an extent that is quite astonishing to Europeans, who are brought up to think of the United States as a great populist democracy with a strong antiaristocratic bias, the foreign policy of the United States as a great world power over the whole seventy years from 1898 to 1968 was a family affair. John Foster Dulles made his mark at the age of thirty-one at the Versailles peace conference in 1919. He was the grandson of one Secretary of State, John W. Foster, and the nephew of the incumbent Secretary, Robert Lansing. He arrived to join the official family in Paris of a President, Woodrow Wilson, who had been his ethics professor at Princeton; and the other members of that group included, besides his younger brother, Allen (subsequently head of the CIA), Walter Lippmann, Adolf Berle, William Bullitt and Joseph Grew, all of whom were to play leading roles in American foreign policy. The young McGeorge Bundy made his mark at about the same age, in 1947, by editing the memoirs of Henry Stimson, who was Secretary of State under Hoover and Secretary of War under Taft, Roosevelt and Truman, and former law partner of Elihu Root, who in turn was Secretary of War under McKinley and Secretary of State under Theodore Roosevelt. Bundy's father had been Stimson's assistant at the War Department and earlier assistant secretary under Stimson at the State Department; and the father's predecessors at the War Department were John J. McCloy and Robert Lovett. McGeorge Bundy's brother William is married to the daughter of another Secretary of State, Dean Acheson; and when McGeorge Bundy quit teaching his course at Harvard (on "The U.S. in World Affairs," the family business), he passed it on to a young protégé who was also to become Secretary of State, Henry Kissinger.

There are those, of course, who maintain that this feeling of intimacy is to be explained by the unique concentration of intelligence, energy and talent in a handful of families, family law firms and departments of very expensive private universities. This is not a very American instinct, though, and among the younger men, the catchment area in geographic origin and social class has been much wider. If for no other reason, the "GI Bill" after World War II and the Korean War allowed almost any young man of average intelligence who was keen enough to do so to get to a good graduate school, where he could study law—prime avenue to the seats of power in America—or international relations. Even so, the proportion of even the younger men occupying key foreign policy positions who turn out to be graduates of either Harvard or Yale is extremely striking, in relation to the proportion of men from the same two universities whom one would expect to find in the most sought-after jobs in business or in politics. Nevertheless, the foreign policy Establishment, as of the 1960s, was defined not by sociology or education, and still less by genealogy, but by a history, a policy, an aspiration, an instinct, a technique, and a dogma.

The *history* stretches back to Colonel House and the tiny group of businessmen and scholars whom he gathered around him at Versailles for the peace conference in 1919. It continued with the efforts of a handful of Americans, most of them drawn from the international banking community in New York and from its lawyers, to combat the rising tide of isolationism after the Senate defeated American membership in the League of Nations in 1920. Not coincidentally, many of these men, such as Colonel Stimson, had been involved in the triumphs of American imperialism under McKinley and had been followers of Theodore Roosevelt. But, historically speaking, the crucial event was World War II. It was the war that brought together the three groups that make up the armature of the modern foreign policy Establishment: the internationally minded lawyers, bankers and executives of multinational corporations in New York, the government officials in Washington, and the academics, especially in Cambridge.

Government service, especially in the Office of Strategic Services (OSS), the forerunner of the CIA and a freewheeling organization with a marked predilection for the products of the Ivy League, gave a whole generation of intellectuals and academics a lasting taste for power and an orientation toward government service. "We were kids," one of them, Carl Kaysen, later McGeorge Bundy's deputy in the White House and now the head of the Institute for Advanced Study at Princeton, once memorably reminisced: "We were kids, captains and majors, telling the whole world what to do." When they went back to their law offices or their classrooms, they took with them attitudes, and contacts, they had formed with OSS. And they were all to meet again: George Ball, David Bruce, Allen Dulles, Arthur Goldberg, John Kenneth Galbraith, Arthur Schlesinger, Walter Rostow, Paul Nitze, and the rest.

The dangerous complexities of military technology, strategic confrontation and world power in the years after World War II all reinforced this triple alliance. There was a mood of national destiny and, after the Soviet Union acquired nuclear weapons, a sense of national danger. Both were nonpartisan. They were felt equally by largely Republican Wall Street and by the predominantly Democratic intellectuals in the great graduate schools.

Each of the great decisions of American policy in the Truman years tied these same ties tighter. Bankers and professors took time off to work on the administration of the Marshall Plan, on NATO, or on rethinking strategic policy, and found themselves forging a common vocabulary and a common set of policies. A trickle of academics and lawyers began to commute down to Washington as consultants, especially on these international programs, until it was an important auxiliary test of a man's professional standing that he be known to do some work for the federal government. More than a trickle of public money went in the opposite direction, funding centers, institutes, foundations and programs to study communism, or Eastern Europe, or systems analysis, and all the other new subjects that buttressed, and did not challenge, the assumptions of the Establishment's foreign policy.

Given the political weakness of the Democrats in the years 1945-48, their leaders were glad of the bipartisan support that internationalist Republicans in key jobs could bring them. And the eastern Republican internationalists, alarmed by the way the former isolationist wing of their party was turning toward militant anti-Communist interventionism, and beginning to realize that they themselves would remain a permanent minority in their own party, were not unhappy to form a coalition with like-minded Democrats.

Two turning points in the forging of a foreign policy consensus, one well known, the other less so, both illustrate this same process. One was the moment when President Truman, with the help of Dean Acheson, was able to reach out beyond the known internationalists in the Republican ranks and recruit the former isolationist Senator Arthur Vandenberg to the cause of a bipartisan, interventionist foreign policy. The second came three years later, when Vandenberg, then dying of cancer, played the crucial role in persuading Truman (and Acheson, and Rusk, then under-secretary of state) to bring John Foster Dulles to work for his administration, thus incidentally rescuing Dulles' career from what looked like a dead end after his defeat in the previous New York senatorial election. So Dulles was brought within the fold. If for some time subsequently he continued to denounce containment and press for the rolling back of communism instead, after all that was no more than many of the Democrats would have liked to say if they had been out of office, and once confronted with the realities of power, Dulles himself finally enrolled under the banner of containment. If Acheson was the pillar on the Left, Dulles matched him on the Right, and the distance between them was not so great. The grand strategy of the Truman administration was ultimately adopted under Eisenhower, and became the grand design of John F. Kennedy.

The kernel of the bipartisan Establishment's *policy* was simple: to oppose isolationism.

The experience of World War II reinforced that theme, and plaited to it a compatible strand. The American opponents of isolationism, to a man, felt that appeasement had been a disaster and that the lesson to be drawn from the struggle against fascism was that there were those in the world who could be restrained only by force, that the use of force in international affairs might therefore indeed be justified, and that great powers must at all costs maintain the credibility of their willingness to use force. A generation of American leaders, wrote Walter Lippmann later, overlearned the lesson of Munich.

The transformation of the former isolationists, or of many of them, into the nucleus of the China Lobby, described above, added an element that is only superficially confusing. For if, in relation to a Senator Knowland or a General MacArthur, the thinking of the Establishment seemed restrained and even cautious about intervention, that was in part because the Establishment's prime concern had historically been for Europe. The new interventionist emotion of the former isolationists was reserved for Asia and was itself in part a reaction against what seemed to many Westerners an excessive preoccupation on the part of the eastern Establishment with Europe. The confusion is easily explained; yet it was to be the clue to a deep and in the end perhaps fatal division within the ranks of the Establishment.

That was not to become apparent, though, until the strain of the Vietnam War had tested the fabric of consensus. From the start, whatever the suspicions of the radical Right, the policy of the Establishment was vehemently anti-Communist. On that, the capitalist Right and the liberal Left within the coalition could agree. An important qualification must be made, however. Establishment anti-communism was essentially for export. One of the issues that distinguished the Establishment from the Right was the Establishment's far lesser concern with domestic communism—a distinction that had crucial consequences in the McCarthy era, when the conservative, nationalist anti-Communist Acheson found himself attacked as if he had been a man of the Left.

The term the Establishment has preferred to use of its own policy has been "liberal internationalism." What it meant by liberalism was a tend-

ency to advocate restraint, to dislike crude militarism or overbearing
chauvinism, and to show sensitivity to the prickings of conscience.
Galbraith has called this, in tribute to the most prestigious of American
private schools, "the Groton ethic." The motto of Groton, we are told, is
*cui servire est regnare,* a somewhat ambiguous Latin phrase that could
mean, among other things, "whom to serve is to reign," a peculiar injunction to young citizens of a republic. Perhaps a better motto for the American Establishment might be the resonant and terrible lines from the sixth
book of Virgil's *Aeneid* that throbbed in the heads of so many Victorian
Englishmen as a call to spiritual pride and imperial adventure:

> *Tu regere imperio populos, Romane, memento (hae tibi erunt artes),*
> *pacisque imponere morem, parcere subjectis et debellare superbos.*
> [Remember, Roman, to rule the peoples in thy sway (these will be thine
> arts), and to impose the habit of peace, to spare the subject, and to defeat
> the proud.]

For the liberal tendencies in the Establishment's temper were, after
all, relative. Its style was to deprecate chauvinism, while at the same time
pressing for American wishes to be respected, and American strength felt,
around the world; to advocate restraint, and yet to despise softness and to
admire a willingness to use military power; to feel conscience, but by no
means to allow it to paralyze one into inaction; to walk softly with one's
big stick, in fact, but to be ready to crack heads with it.

Opposition to communism, experience of the consequences of appeasement, an intimation of imperial responsibilities and imperial destiny
—all these ingredients went to the making of the Establishment's policy.
Yet there was something else, too, that is unmistakable: a legacy from
half-buried layers of New England Puritanism, spontaneously felt, perhaps, by some, and adopted by others as the badge of membership in an
admired class.

One has only to read the passage I quoted earlier from Dean
Acheson's memoirs, in which he relates the crucial argument with which
he converted Arthur Vandenberg to the cause—surely one of the most
fateful conversations in modern American history—to feel that there was
more than rational calculation and prudent self-protection to the mood in
which such men entered upon the Cold War. There was a real threat to
Greece. But however imminent it was, there remains a disparity between
its potential dimensions and the cosmic, the Miltonian, language in which
Acheson measured it. Stalin was backing General Markos' guerrillas, certainly. He was in fact to drop them sharply enough the next year, partly
indeed as a consequence of Acheson's prompt action. But Acheson was in
no mood to weigh cold probabilities. He said so himself. "There was no

time for measured appraisal," he wrote. *Rien ne dure comme le provisoire,* say the diplomats: nothing lasts like the temporary. Still, given that the policy to which Acheson was committing his country was to last for more than twenty years without fundamental reappraisal, perhaps time was not all that was lacking. Three continents were threatened, said Acheson. Threatened with what? With communism? Worse: with "infection," with "corruption," by the hot breath of the ancient fiend himself. Acheson stood at Armageddon, and as the son of a bishop who had been a British regular officer, he knew that what you did there was to battle for the Lord.

The same sense of religious duty, of a call to take sides in a Manichaean conflict between the forces of light and the forces of darkness, runs through the whole history of American foreign policy since 1947. Harry Truman said that the aim of his foreign policy was to see whether the Sermon on the Mount could be put into effect. Others, too—Lyndon Johnson, Robert McNamara, Dean Rusk, among them—brought to the international arena not only the whole armor of righteousness but the sword of Mr. Standfast as well. And then there was John Foster Dulles. "While it was inherently difficult to separate the elements of conviction, manipulation and self-protection in his posture," his most recent biographer has written, "it seems clear that conviction formed the bedrock." And a contemporary diplomat put the same thought more pithily: "Dulles was a curious cross between a Christer and a shrewd and quite ruthless lawyer." That was the paradoxical combination of temperaments that united Acheson and Dulles and set the tone for the Establishment as a whole: these were Manichaeans who were willing to negotiate with the powers of darkness, Puritans in a post-Christian world.

The Establishment's favorite European, Winston Churchill, called the American commitment to Europe in the Marshall Plan "the most unsordid act in history." Unsordid it certainly was. But it was also characteristic of these men to take on the burdens of world power with a certain avidity. George Ball once penetratingly observed that the Europeans had entered upon colonialism not so much for its economic advantages as for "the satisfactions of power." It is strange that he did not recognize the echo of his own contemporaries' feelings. Power—the unprecedented economic, military and political power of the United States after 1945—was their birthright, and they found it satisfying in the highest degree. Colonialists they were not; they did not need to be. But the Bay of Pigs, as well as the Marshall Plan, illustrated the range of what they meant by internationalism; and so did Vietnam.

For their *aspiration* was quite simply to the moral and political leadership of the world. Once, many years later, after President Kennedy's death, his principal speech writer, Theodore Sorensen, used that very phrase. That was in 1968, and there were those then who found it bombastic. By then, the national mood, the intellectual fashion, had changed. The war had changed them. But Sorensen had expressed precisely the core of the Establishment's aspiration.

Specifically, the Establishment wanted the United States to succeed Britain as the military and economic guarantor and moral leader of an enlightened, liberal, democratic and capitalist world order. "Britain had given up its role as the 'balance wheel,'" Townsend Hoopes put it to me in an interview; "the idea of a single Western coalition holding the world in balance against the infidel is fundamental to this particular Establishment." Walter Lippmann has pointed out, as one specific example, the extent to which "the idea that a Soviet presence in the Mediterranean and the Middle East is something that can't be tolerated was invented by the British as a way of protecting their way to India"; it was, however, taken over by both Acheson and Dulles as a fundamental principle of American policy. In general, the notion of a "power vacuum," into which it was the grim but grand duty of the United States to insert itself, was fundamental to the Establishment's perception of the world. And this idea, in turn, largely sprang from the idea of the U.S.A. as the lineal heir of Britain, and to a lesser extent of the other European powers: of France in the Middle East, France and Belgium in Africa, the Netherlands in Indonesia, and France in Indochina.

The Establishment's *instinct* was for the center. "If American politics have a predilection for the center," McGeorge Bundy has said, "it is a Good Thing." And he went on to list all the "major undertakings of postwar American foreign policy," and to claim that all had "turned upon the capacity of the Executive to take and hold the center." In this context he listed the Marshall Plan, NATO, the Kennedy Round, the Cuban missile crisis, "strategic strength," the test-ban treaty, and even Middle East policy, as the policies of the center. The center is an interesting concept in politics: to some extent, those who want to occupy it must find their positions defined for them by what others are saying. But psychologically it is true, and important, that the characteristic men of the Establishment—Stimson, McCloy, Acheson, Rusk, Bundy—have always seen themselves as the men of judicious, pragmatic wisdom, avoiding ideology and steering the middle course between the ignorant yahoos of the Right and the impractical sentimentality of the Left. That this middle course led one of those five to take the decision to drop the atomic bomb, and three others to play crucial parts in submitting the United States to war (Acheson in Korea, and Rusk and Bundy in Vietnam), would not have caused any of them, I think, to be troubled with doubts as to whether theirs was really the middle road; it would only seem to confirm for them how late the hour was in the world, and how dark the night.

It has been said that one *Leitmotiv* of the Establishment has been the fear of public opinion. That is perhaps too strong. But it is true that its origins did lie in the resistance to isolationist mass opinion. And it is also true that its historical opportunity did not lie in electoral politics, but in what C. P. Snow has called "closed politics." Its "major undertakings," as Bundy noted, were all achievements of the executive branch of government, more or less endorsed by Congress and public opinion, but not initiated there. The power of the foreign-policy Establishment rose step by step with the rise of the executive branch of government at the expense of Congress; and especially with the rise of the White House, and of the new "national security" institutions created since 1945: OSD (the Office of the Secretary of Defense), ISA (the office of the assistant secretary of defense for international security affairs), the CIA, and above all the office of the President's special assistant, or adviser, for national security and the staff of the National Security Council. Its legitimacy has been derived almost wholly not from election but from presidential appointment. It is almost part of the definition of the true Establishment man that he has never run for elective office. Averell Harriman, former governor of New York, is perhaps the exception that proves the rule; politicians might argue that he had little taste for the electoral process and connoisseurs that he was too much of an individualist to be a typical Establishment man.

The fact that the management of American foreign policy has been so largely in the hands of men who were neither elected officials nor professional members of an independent civil service is intimately corrected with the acutely unrepresentative sociological background from which the great majority of them have come. A professional civil service must accept entrants, wherever they come from, who meet fixed criteria or succeed in a competitive examination. A slate of candidates for elective office will generally make up a more or less balanced ticket. Presidents have even traditionally been careful to distribute cabinet posts, which are appointive, with some sensitivity to the need for balance among regions, interests (such as labor and business), and ethnic blocs. But the foreign policy staffs of successive Presidents since 1945, and especially the key foreign policy and national security jobs, have been overloaded, almost to the point of monopoly, with men of the Establishment mold: upper-middle-class Episcopalians or Jews, Ivy League by education, and the great majority of them either lawyers from Wall Street or Washington or professors from Cambridge. The most important job of all, that of special assistant or adviser to the President on national security affairs, was held by three academics from Cambridge (two from Harvard and one from M.I.T.—McGeorge Bundy, Walt W. Rostow and Henry Kissinger—from 1961 to 1975!

Lacking a base of either power or popularity in public opinion, the Establishment therefore developed a characteristic *technique*. It worked out of the public eye and through the executive branch. Its methods were bureaucratic and secretive. If it needed to influence public opinion, it did so by carefully controlled leaking of secret information or authoritative opinion to a hand-picked coterie of Washington journalists, most of whom were chosen for this purpose precisely because they shared the Establishment's background and attitudes, if indeed they didn't, like the Alsops, Rowland Evans, Joseph Kraft and so many others, belong to it.

In particular, its members were generally uneasy with, and often contemptuous of, Congress. "Those who assert that I do not suffer fools gladly," sneered Dean Acheson characteristically, "do me less than justice" for the time he spent as assistant secretary of state for Congressional relations in the Roosevelt administration. In justice it should be said that his generation had confronted a Congress in which the majority did all it could to frustrate the cause they held most dear: that of committing the United States to the fight against the dictators. They were proved right, and Congress was proved wrong. But, twenty years later, when the majority in Congress was vying to excel in enthusiasm for their policies, they still treated the legislative branch with a mixture of condescension and mistrust.

Its members played key roles in all the major presidential decisions to bypass or deceive Congress about foreign affairs, from July 1950, when Acheson persuaded President Truman that he did not need to ask Congress for a joint resolution approving his decision to send American troops to Korea, to May 1964, when Acheson's son-in-law, William Bundy, prepared a cynical scenario for obtaining a joint resolution "authorizing whatever is necessary with respect to Vietnam."

From Roosevelt to Johnson, the Establishment's immense power over American foreign policy was borrowed from the presidency. At the same time, its immense influence was thrown into increasing the power and prerogative of the presidency at the expense of the power of Congress.

One other element was essential: the *dogma* of containment.

The basic source of containment as a policy, Arthur Krock has written, was the famous "long telegram" sent by George Kennan from Moscow on February 22, 1946. This was what "provided the official ground," as Krock put it, "for the reversal of U.S. policy towards the U.S.S.R. from appeasement to containment," a reversal that soon took shape as the Truman Doctrine, the decision to help Greece and Turkey, then as NATO and the Marshall Plan.

There is general agreement that Kennan's telegram was indeed crucial in alerting Washington to the hostility of Stalin's Russia, and also that this message had been accepted in Washington well before Kennan's better-known article appeared in *Foreign Affairs*, the next summer. But it was only in the 1947 article, and not in the 1946 telegram, that Kennan added to his somber warning about the danger from the Soviet Union the word "containment" and the policy prescription it labeled—a policy remarkably similar to that proposed in a long memorandum written for President Truman the previous September by Truman's young assistant Clark Clifford.

That policy was one of patience and restraint. It was also by implication one of relative optimism. The Soviet Union is *farouche*, surly, dangerous, Kennan was saying. But the United States is stronger. If America does not panic, he wrote in the key sentence of his article, "Soviet pressure against the free institutions of the Western world can be contained by the adroit and vigilant application of counterforce." And if it was so contained, then there need be no war with the Soviets.

Containment, in other words, was from the beginning seen as the policy of the center. If it was an alternative to war and to that aggressive strategy aimed at liberating the Soviet gains in Eastern Europe that was known at the time as "rollback," it was also an alternative to appeasement. Dulles called for liberation and rollback in 1950 in his celebrated *Life* article, and Averell Harriman has written that he believed "we should try to check and roll back Stalin's aggressive Communist influence wherever feasible." But Harriman also always advocated, "We should have our guard always up, but the hand for negotiations always extended." And even Dulles showed less enthusiasm for rollback when he was no longer courting ethnic voters in New York but confronting the realities of the world, more or less, as Secretary of State. On the whole, the Establishment, with its instinct for the center, has not wavered in its preference for the doctrine of containment, the middle course between appeasement and rollback. The doctrine has succeeded in the purpose for which the Establishment originally advocated it. On the whole, it has avoided war and discouraged or prevented a Soviet invasion of Western Europe, if indeed one was ever intended.

But what started as a policy admirably adapted to the real dangers and opportunities of a particular situation became elevated to the status of a dogma and was indiscriminately applied.

From the start, the policy of containment, as Kennan advocated it, left two grand ambiguities unresolved:

Should containment be carried out by military power, or could it be done with diplomatic and political means?

Should it apply only to the Soviet Union, or should communism be contained wherever it showed its head?

Within weeks after his "X" article appeared, George Kennan was taken to task by Walter Lippmann on both of these issues. Did he mean containment to be military? Lippmann asked, and was it to be an open-ended policy, to be applied world-wide? Was Congress to be asked, Lippmann wondered, for "a blank check on the Treasury and a blank authorization to use the armed forces"? They were shrewd questions.

Kennan himself has always protested that his article was misunderstood both by Lippmann and by those who made it the basis of a policy of tough, world-wide military containment. ("It must be the policy of the United States to support free peoples who are resisting attempted subjugation by armed minorities or outside pressure": that was the Truman Doctrine, and it certainly implied *armed* support to free peoples *everywhere*.) Kennan went so far as to protest in person to Acheson about this language, which is often considered to have been the first fruits of his doctrine but which he himself considered an unwarranted misinterpretation of it. And years later, in his memoirs, he insisted that he had never meant to advocate "containment by military means or a military threat, but the political containment of a political threat." Both Lippmann and Kennan, in fact, belong not to the main Establishment tradition but to a small and honorable school that, while not wholly dissenting from internationalism, puts its whole emphasis on the need for sobriety and skepticism in the exercise of American power and on the limits to what the United States should undertake.

Sobriety and skepticism have not been the most noticeable characteristics of the Establishment when confronted with the question whether the United States should or should not intervene in a given situation in the world. From Acheson's conviction that victory for General Markos in Greece would "open three continents to Soviet penetration" through John Foster Dulles' conviction that the United States must girdle the world with treaty commitments and the bases to fulfill them, there is a straight line to the commitment to use military force to prevent the fall of governments in South Vietnam, Laos, Cambodia, Thailand. Arthur Schlesinger rightly interprets the State Department's legal brief for intervention in Vietnam in 1966 as implying that "warfare anywhere on earth could, if the President so judged, constitute an attack on the United States and thereby authorize him to wage 'defensive' war without congressional consent."

Schlesinger was reminded, in 1973, of Schumpeter's description of the foreign policy of ancient Rome, for which "the whole world was pervaded by a host of enemies, and it was manifestly Rome's duty to guard against their indubitably aggressive designs." The parallel is striking. Yet Schlesinger seems not to have been reminded of Schumpeter's passage between 1961 and 1963, when the administration of which he was a part was reacting in so classically Roman a fashion to Fidel Castro and to the Viet Cong and even felt that it had a duty to guard against the "indubitably aggressive designs" of such gnatweight enemies as Prince Souphanouvong in Laos and Cyrille Adoula in the Congo.

Lyndon Johnson and Richard Nixon make convenient scapegoats. But the fact is that, before 1964 and even before 1960, the idea of containment had been inflated into a dogma which held that the United States had the right and even perhaps the duty to intervene with whatever means necessary, including military action, covert or avowed, anywhere in the world where such action was needed to restrain the expansion of communism or to frustrate any radical nationalism that seemed either inimical to American interests or unpopular with the American electorate. And that dogma was broadly accepted by the foreign policy Establishment.

To identify the existence of an Establishment, of course, is not to assert that it is monolithic. Any elite will be divided in several directions: by tensions between the leaders and the outer rings of its membership and between the older and younger generations, as well as by genuine intellectual disagreements that are nevertheless within range of being reconciled within the framework of an over-all consensus. It follows that to show that disagreements exist within a given group of men by no means proves that they do not, in terms of their basic beliefs, constitute a group.

Those who are reluctant to admit the historical reality of the American foreign policy Establishment lay heavy stress on the disagreements among its putative members. But these disagreements turn out on examination to have been largely tactical. Should we intervene now, or later? With "advisers," or marines? But on the premises of action, in the underlying assumption that nothing could be worse than letting another country "fall" to the Communists, or to some regime that someone in U.S. politics might conceivably equate with the Communists, the consensus was so nearly absolute that disagreement virtually guaranteed disbarment. Perhaps the most striking single impression one derived from reading the Pentagon Papers is that, through long years of constant, minute-by-minute debate of the immediately available options ("How much pressure should we exert on Diem in return for our support? Should we bomb the North now, or only later? How many American troops, and how fast?"), the most fundamental questions went by default.

From 1956 to 1965, virtually every member of the Establishment endorsed the broad lines of U.S. policy in Southeast Asia. With certain exceptions, there was no serious dissent within Establishment circles from the commitment to extend the containment of communism from Europe to Asia. With certain exceptions, there was no serious dissent within Establishment circles from the commitment to maintain South Vietnam as a separate state from North Vietnam in spite of the 1954 agreements. Nor, indeed, at the level of tactics, was there noticeable dissent from the policy of supporting Diem, or from the initial commitment of military aid and "advisers." And this was because it was a prerequisite for being listened to at all as a foreign policy adviser, either within the bureaucracy or outside it, to genuflect before the dogma of which these were but the specific applications: the dogma of active intervention wherever required to defend "the Free World" against even the slightest possibility of Communist encroachment.

Certain qualifications should be made. The first is that certain individuals with standing in the Establishment did have the foresight to question the wisdom of the commitment in South Vietnam specifically. Both George Ball and John Kenneth Galbraith had done so privately to President Kennedy by the end of 1961, for example.

The second is that, in a larger context, the Establishment had been divided, within the framework of its larger consensus about internationalism and anti-communism, on the specific question of policy toward the Third World. A minority school of thought on the fringes of the Establishment (led, significantly enough, by such men as Adlai Stevenson and Chester Bowles, who *had* held elective office) did constantly question the tendency of the mainstream to relate everything that happened in the Third World to the Cold War; or at least they questioned the military emphasis of the mainstream of thought. Men like Bowles and Stevenson pressed for a more serious commitment to the United Nations (Bundy's "center" was content with mere "adherence" there); for heavier expenditure on development aid; and for priority to be given to those developing countries—such, ironically, as India or Chile—that seemed to promise some hope of evolving their own native forms of democracy, even if this might prove irritating to the United States, as against more militantly anti-Communist regimes such as those in South Korea, Pakistan, "China" —or South Vietnam.

But in truth this Stevenson-Bowles wing was neither very representative nor very effective. And it was decapitated by President Kennedy's appointments in 1960–61. Galbraith was exiled to New Delhi. Stevenson was embalmed alive at the United Nations. And Bowles was soon banished from the State Department and thence to India to replace Galbraith. That was what happened to the "soft-line" men. "Tough-minded" and "hard-nosed" were the epithets in vogue among the lawyers and the bankers, the systems analysts and "defense intellectuals," who congregated in Washington around Rusk, McNamara, Bundy and Paul Nitze.

A third qualification should be made. The Establishment was not in point of fact very interested in Vietnam as such. Harvard, for example, had no program for regional studies of Southeast Asia as it did for Soviet or Western European or Middle Eastern studies. There are still more classes in Tibetan than in Vietnamese there. The Council on Foreign Relations did not sponsor a research project on Vietnam until 1973.

But this perfectly genuine lack of interest in the details of the country to which American power was being committed, with such fatal results, both for the country and American power, did not inhibit the Establishment from supporting, perhaps reluctantly, but in any case almost unanimously, the creeping commitment to Vietnam from the time of the Taylor-Rostow mission of November 1961 until the fall of Diem two years later.

Right up to 1965, the year of decision, the overwhelming consensus of the Establishment accepted without moral or intellectual doubt that the war would have to be escalated—if the only other alternative was losing it. The commitment to "internationalism," the horror of "Munich," the "burdens" of world leadership, the dogma of containment applied with an intellectual rigidity that continued to see the world in terms of a "Communist bloc," and paradoxically even the commitment to the presidency— every element in the Establishment's tradition propelled it in the same direction. By 1965, virtually all Establishment opinion was clustered around a single position: the commitment is inevitable, the war is necessary, escalation is justified—or the dominoes are forfeit. It hardly mattered where Vietnam was, or what the precise circumstances of the case were there. Once a peculiar combination of circumstances had put the unfortunate country forward as a test of the Establishment's will, the war must be supported, and won.

Since the beginning of the Cold War, the political scientist Samuel P. Huntington wrote in an article in *Daedalus* as long ago as the fatal autumn of 1963, the great dividing line in American politics was not between Left and Right but between the Establishment and the Fundamentalists. By the Establishment, Huntington meant roughly what I understand by it, except that he excluded from it the academics and the intellectuals, whereas I think they were an essential component of it. It was, he pointed out, predominantly identified with the East Coast, with the Ivy League, with Wall Street and big business, and it was oriented toward the executive branch. The Fundamentalists, conversely, were rural, midwestern and southern, small-town and small-business people, and they looked toward Congress. The Establishment outlook, Huntington thought, was more international and "sophisticated," the Fundamentalist outlook more nationalistic and "moralistic." In terms of education, he suggested, the military profession belonged to the Establishment. But in feelings and attitudes it was more attuned to the outlook of the Fundamentalists.

There are false antitheses and romantic delusions in that way of stating the case. Just because the Establishment liked to call its policies "internationalist," for example, as opposed to isolationist and as a euphemism for interventionist, that does not mean that its members were not every bit as nationalist as any southern congressman or air-force general: the distinction was between two different styles of nationalism, not two degrees of it. Nor did the Fundamentalist party have much to do with small towns or small business in the Grover's Corners or Gopher Prairie sense. No doubt, top executives in the big defense contractors, and generals and their allies in Congress (such as Carl Vinson, the "Swamp Fox" of Georgia) liked to affect homespun while the Establishment fancied British tweed. Possibly a higher proportion of these men cherished memories of elm-shaded porches west of the Mississippi and south of the Mason-Dixon line than you would have found among their equally ambitious and successful contemporaries on the Council for Foreign Relations. But wherever their executives came from in the first place (and after all even Harvey Bundy came from Grand Rapids, Michigan, in the first place, and Dean Rusk came from Georgia), General Motors, General Electric and American Telephone & Telegraph are not small businesses, nor are Boeing and Lockheed, General Dynamics and McDonnell-Douglas, to take seven names at random from a list of the ten biggest defense contractors in 1968. To the extent that the opposition of view between the Establishment and the Fundamentalists represented the dichotomy between two styles of urban civilization, it was not that between big city and small town, but that between New York and Washington on the one hand, Seattle and St. Louis, Dallas and Los Angeles, on the other. One can call the first pair of cities "sophisticated" if one wants to, and the others "moralistic." But, in practice, to frame one's tactics for a business deal in Dallas or Los Angeles on the assumption that business leaders there are moralistic or unsophisticated would be unwise, to say the least.

The Fundamentalists, in other words, whatever stylistic associations it may have suited them to claim, were none other than the party, in the sense of a loose but nevertheless purposeful coalition, supporting the interests of what President Eisenhower, in his parting speech in 1961, called the "military-industrial complex." And the irreducible element of truth in Huntington's analysis is that the same was true of foreign and military policy from the middle of the 1950s until the crisis of the 1960s as of domestic politics: there was no Left to speak of, and in its absence the battleground lay between the Establishment center and the military-industrial Right.

The "military industrial complex" has often come to be endowed with overtones of naïve economic determinism. Radical critics have often written as if the economic interests of the big defense contractors had simply allowed them to buy the support of the professional military, and the armed services, in turn, had bought political support. The motives of everybody involved were less ignoble than that, and the workings of the system more complicated, though at the end of the day the political clout of the military establishment is hardly less great than even the most alarmist radicals have assumed. What was involved was a spontaneous harmony of interests between conservative politicians, professional military officers, and vast business concerns. The resulting coalition was all the stronger because each of the principal parties to it both benefited materially and fulfilled what they felt were higher aspirations.

Congressmen learned that they could enhance their prospects of re-election by bringing defense bases and defense contracts to their districts. But they also believed that in voting for high defense appropriations they were making the nation strong and doing their duty in the great struggle against the Communist enemy. Adam Yarmolinsky, himself both a former Pentagon official and the political victim of the southern conservatives in the Congress, was surely right, as well as generous, when he insisted that the militaristic views of Congressman Mendel Rivers of South Carolina, chairman of the House Armed Services Committee, were not *caused* by the golden shower of defense expenditure that has been funneled into his Charleston district; Representative Rivers takes the positions he does because he believes in them, and the same was true of all the great champions of maximum defense expenditure—most notably of Senator Richard Russell and Congressman Vinson, conservatives who passionately believed in the need for military strength and who were so invincibly dug in politically that it would be absurd to suggest that winning or losing even the fattest of defense contracts would make any difference to their convictions. Generals and admirals knew that success in persuading Congress to appropriate billions for weapons systems for their services would do no harm to their careers and that there might be jobs waiting for them with the successful contractors. (The growing numbers of former military officers working for defense contractors was the phenomenon that first made President Eisenhower aware of the dangers of the military-industrial complex, according to Malcolm Moos, who wrote the speech for Eisenhower.) But, at the same time, these were military men. Their whole training, their code, taught them that it was their duty to make the defense of the United States as nearly perfect as possible—and was not the United States in those years richer than anyone had dreamed possible, and more threatened than ever before? Industrialists not only saw the prospect of immense profits in defense contracts, and unusually safe profits, at that; they were also attracted by the idea that in "working for the government" they would be rising above mere profit. Defense contractors could offer them the excitement of advanced technology, the distinction of something that seemed to be public service, and the feeling that they were doing their part in the great struggle against communism.

Over the course of time, beginning in the early post-World War II years, an immense network of institutions, habits, associations, loyalties and interests grew up to reinforce this basic harmony of attitudes and interests and to turn it into a supremely effective machine for satisfying all concerned. "The military establishment," Yarmolinsky concluded in a 1971 study for the Twentieth Century Fund, "is the largest single feature in the economic and political landscape." Sheer size alone would have made it powerful enough. Between 1946 and 1967, according to Senator Fulbright, the federal government spent $904 billion on "military power," as against $96 billion on those "social functions," such as education, health and welfare, that were often thought so remarkable that they justified calling the United States a "welfare state." By 1965, 5.75 million Americans owed their employment to the military machine: 2.75 million in the armed services, 1 million in the federal and local governments, and more than 2 million as employees of defense contractors, subcontractors and their suppliers. The indirect impact of this expenditure and employment was not just immense; it was crucial to the postwar prosperity that, in turn, many Americans thought of as the grand justification for their society as a whole.

A labyrinth of mechanisms had been developed to make the impact of this economic power on the political system as flexible and effective as possible. The contract system itself is taken so much for granted that it is worth noting that it grew up only after World War II. Traditionally, the U. S. Army and the U. S. Navy did their own military research, development, and a good deal of their manufacturing in public arsenals and dockyards. The Air Force, a new service with an immense demand for high-technology research and development, in a hurry, developed the contract system. "Our whole philosophy," General Bernard A. Schriever, head of the Air Research and Development Command, once said, "has been one of going to industry and having industry develop and produce for us." The Army and the Navy were obliged to follow suit if they were to compete with the Air Force in developing weapons systems for a strategic role (which was where the big procurement prizes were to be won) in time. "The generosity of Air Force contract practice," H. L. Nieburg commented in 1966 in the *Bulletin of the Atomic Scientists*, "quickly inflated the technical manpower market, depleting the government's in-house pool and demonstrating great political efficacy. In a sense, the Air Force financed through contracting a powerful constituency to advance its interests in Congress." The Navy and the Army were not slow to follow.

But contracting was only the thickest of the links between Congress and the military establishment. By the middle sixties, the Pentagon's "Congressional liaison office" employed senior officers in a ratio not far short of one for every member of Congress, well briefed and ready to go up to the Hill and lobby for any program that seemed in need of help. The budget for these activities, at $3.8 million, was well over ten times that declared by the largest single domestic lobbyist. The various service associations reinforced this effort by the more roundabout method of building up support for the individual services, and of course for their appropriations, at the grass roots. Immense efforts were made in public relations, at all levels, from "helping" with films and television productions that glorified the military and took its world view for granted, through facility trips for reporters to see the good work that was being done, to such imaginative efforts as 999 Air Force Reserve Squadron, an intrepid unit composed entirely of senators, congressmen and their staff, under the command of Major General Barry M. Goldwater, U.S.A.F.R., which guarded the frontiers of freedom in such locations as London and Paris.

Of course the harmony of interests was not unbroken by discord. The Navy and the Air Force feuded over the merits of rival strategic weapons systems. The Army and the Marine Corps disputed the preponderant role in counterinsurgency. Corporations competed for contracts, and congressmen fought for bases and contracts for their districts. Still, the net effect of the over-all harmony and of the conflicts it subsumed was in the same direction: both worked together for higher defense appropriations and to create a political climate in which, when defense or foreign-policy decisions had to be taken, all the danger was from the Right.

It was this lopsided configuration of the political constellations that allowed the Establishment the illusion that its defense policy was a policy of restraint. The strategic thinking forged in the Harvard disarmament seminars of the late 1950s and established as national policy under Kennedy and McNamara, with its emphasis on acquiring the "capabilities" for "flexible response" at any level from guerrilla warfare up a ladder of escalation to all-out nuclear war, was conceived as a more restrained, more rational alternative to the "massive retaliation" strategy of the Air Force and the Eisenhower administration. There was a favorite story in Washington in the days of the Kennedy administration that neatly expressed the Establishment's sense of its own superior rationality and restraint. A young Pentagon official called Alain Enthoven, a graduate of Harvard, Oxford and the RAND Corporation, and a brilliant economist and systems analyst, was being given his first briefing on top-secret war plans by an air-force officer.

"General," said Enthoven when he had finished, "you don't have a plan, you have a *spasm!*"

"In common with many other military men," wrote General Thomas D. White, a former chief of staff of the Air Force, at about the same time, "I am profoundly apprehensive of the pipe-smoking, tree-full-of-owls type of so-called defense intellectuals. I don't believe a lot of these often over-confident, sometimes arrogant young professors, mathematicians and other theorists have sufficient worldliness or motivation to stand up to the kind of enemy we face."

There, in a nutshell, was the political, intellectual and cultural hostility between the Establishment and the Fundamentalists. But in the interaction between two sometimes startlingly different kinds of Americans —and the Pentagon in the early sixties was a place where Daniel Ellsberg and General Curtis LeMay were both to be found at work—it is clear that the influence was not all in one direction. Indignant with the "false and dangerous" image of military power over policy, Professor Huntington has pointed out how much the military had been civilianized between 1945 and 1960. By 1960, few officers were openly advocating either total or pre-emptive war. The great majority of them had come to accept such concepts as deterrence, civilian control and limited war. But Huntington failed to notice the corollary: the extent to which the civilians had been militarized.

This was not just a question of superficial personal style, though it is certainly true that the Ellsbergs and the Enthovens, and even the Bundys and the McNamaras, junior officers at the end of World War II, were far more likely to modify their opinions subconsciously in debate with formidable warriors almost old enough to be their fathers, with chests covered with medals, than the generals were likely to change to please them. It is a matter of the profoundly military assumptions underlying the strategic thinking of the civilian Establishment.

Nationalism; a conviction of the efficacy of force amounting almost to romanticism; a strategic doctrine that, while nominally designed to make nuclear war less likely, had the practical effect of making every other kind of war less unattractive; a boundless program of intervention; and a need, perhaps a desire, to impress the military with their credentials—these were characteristics of the "defense intellectuals" at the beginning of the 1960s at least as apparent as rationality or restraint. Each could be attributed in part to the fact that, in its attempt to hold the center, the Establishment had only to concern itself with the formidable suspicion and competition of the Right, unbalanced by any countervailing power to the Left. And each led straight to involvement in Vietnam.

# The Media

> I shall give up reading newspapers. They are so false and in-
> temperate that they disturb tranquillity without giving informa-
> tion.

Thomas Jefferson

The critic Morris Abrams once wrote a book called *The Mirror and the
Lamp*. It is not a book about journalism, which is a pity, because that
would make a magnificent title for an essay about the two ways of looking
at the journalist's function. Should the news media limit themselves to the
attempt to reflect the world as it is, as accurately, and as neutrally, as possible? Or should they go out and try to illuminate the dark corners of the
world, and so help people to see what they have not seen before?

"This is the man," one of the German philosophers wrote about his
own calling, "who carries the lamp to the back of the cave." That is the
motto for one ancient and honorable school of journalism. But in the
United States, since the decline of muckraking, around the time of the
First World War, the more generally accepted view—until Watergate, at
least—was that the media should simply reflect what is happening out
there in the world, like a mirror.

The mirror metaphor has become almost suspiciously popular with
people in high places in the media. A vice-president of NBC, Robert Kas-
mire, has pronounced, "There is no doubt that television is, to a large degree, a mirror of society." Leonard Goldenson, the president of ABC, told
the National Commission on the Causes and Prevention of Violence, that
"Americans are reluctant to accept the images reflected by the mirror we
have held up to society." "What the media do," Frank Stanton, president
of CBS, has said, "is to hold up a mirror to society and try to report it as
faithfully as possible."

In the early 1970s the presidents of ABC News (Elmer Lower) and NBC News (Reuven Frank) and a former president of CBS News (Sig Mickelson) all published books or articles with the word "mirror" in the title: *The Television Mirror*, "The Ugly Mirror," *The Electric Mirror*.

No doubt this rush by television journalists and executives to adopt the mirror as the emblem of their trade reflected their defensiveness at a time when they were being lambasted by Vice-President Agnew, that ironic custodian of republican virtue, for being "elitist snobs." But it is not only network executives who like the mirror metaphor. At a seminar in Washington in 1973, for example, the columnist Joseph Kraft insisted with some vehemence that all the media could or should claim to do was to hold up a mirror to what happens in the world. All one can say is that for some years, thrice weekly, Joseph Kraft and Joseph Alsop held up two very different mirrors to the world on the op. ed. page of the Washington *Post*.

It is a fact of optics that the shape, composition, location and angle of a mirror affect the image it reflects. So even if we do think of the media as a mirror, we should examine its structure, check its position, and always remember who is holding it, and at what angle.

Even for those who do not want the news media to be a probing, investigating lamp lighting up the back of the cave, the mirror is still an unsatisfactory metaphor. Taken as a whole, the national news media are more like a gigantic stereo system. They have their tuners and their amplifiers, and plenty of feedback. Their Huntleys and their Brinkleys, like the woofer and the tweeter of a good stereo system, are carefully balanced to produce the right texture of sound. The right texture? What does that mean? It means the sound that the men at the controls think the audience wants to hear.

In one crucial respect, the news media are a stereo with a difference. This is a multichannel, two-way system, and two-way is the key word. It is true that the media can report only what is happening. But it is also true that what happens is affected by the impulses and images that the media choose to transmit. Those images are determined by the nation's mood at the time, of course. But that mood, the nation's perception of itself, confident or anguished, internationalist or isolationist, or whatever it may be at any given moment, is in turn to a large extent derived from the news media. The national mood is therefore affected not only by what "happens" but by the way the news media select and present the news—and therefore by internal factors and structural factors within the news industry.

This is not only, or even primarily, a matter of the newspapers, the networks, the stations and the magazines being affected by the need to make profits, though they are affected by that need; more significantly, they are affected by competitive pressures, intellectual fashion, and even by the personalities of key executives.

If it is a mirror we have been looking into, in other words, it is one that has shifted around and shown us very different sides of ourselves over the years. The intriguing thing is that the stages in the internal evolution of the news media between the late fifties and the early seventies fit quite closely with the phases of the history of the period in general.

I have suggested that the first phase, running, roughly speaking, from 1955 to 1963, was a time of consensus. The second period, from 1963 to 1965, was a time of crisis, in which a series of shocks—the assassination of President Kennedy, the breakup of the civil rights movement, and the escalation of the war—dramatically threw doubt on the idea that Americans could make the world conform to their idea of what they wanted it to be like. The third period, from 1965 to 1968, again roughly speaking, was a time of polarization. And the years from 1968 to 1972 were a time of growing doubt, fragmentation, and confusion. Looking at them in a slightly different way, these three periods can be collapsed into three, for Phase II and Phase III, as I have described them, are really two different stages in the evolution of the crisis. Taking this view, the three acts of the drama are 1) the *status quo ante*, the time before the flood; 2) a prolonged national crisis, which began with a series of sudden shocks and continued as the country divided in its response to these troubling events; and 3) a period of adjustment in which, though what the critic Leslie Fiedler called "the Great American Cultural Revolution" was over, nevertheless its effects were still felt and, in many different ways, Americans were driven to accept a lower estimate both of their power to change the world and of the power of political action to change their society.

The question is: what part did the media play in this story?

No one could easily deny that they played a very big part indeed. But how? Did they represent people's unrecognized discontents, or did they distort them? Did they exaggerate the grievances of those groups that knew best how to project them? Did they impose the values of an articulate minority, foisting the ideas of George Wallace's "pointy-heads" or Joseph Alsop's "damfools" on the majority? Or did they act as the bulwark of freedom for a long-suffering people menaced by power-mad elites? Were they a cause of change, or an effect of it?

No doubt, the media were all these things. For the very term "the news media" is an unreal abstraction. It includes newspapers and television, magazines and radio, and, in each of those categories, organizations of every scale from weekly newspapers in Wyoming to the New York *Times*, and from CBS to local radio stations with a broadcasting radius of less than fifty miles. Moreover, the final output of each of these very different media—of some seventeen hundred newspapers, for example, and more than five hundred network-affiliated TV stations, and so on—was the product of the conflicting ideas and interests of publishers, editors, reporters and sources, where newspapers were concerned, and, in TV, of stockholders, management, networks, stations, producers, reporters and those members of the public whom they interviewed, to say nothing of the indirect influence of, for example, advertisers. The sum total of images being transmitted to the American people was therefore affected not only by attitudes and ideologies but also by technological innovation, commercial strategies, competitive pressures and bureaucratic routines. And, finally, these influences were anything but static.

If one does look at the media in this way, something very interesting appears. It is possible to distinguish a succession of stages in the evolution of the news media in relation to public issues—stages that correspond quite closely with the successive phases of the national mood but with this difference: the phases in the history of the media seem in each case to have *preceded* the corresponding phase in the national mood. To conclude that therefore the relationship was one of cause and effect would be too simple. Yet the story hardly bears out the idea that the news media were no more than a passive mirror.

The late fifties were the age of bland in the media. The brief golden age of realistic TV drama was over by the middle of the decade, killed by advertisers and sponsors. Eric Barnouw, in *The Image Empire*, quotes a letter from an advertising agency to the playwright Elmer Rice, who had suggested a TV series based on his play *Street Scene:* "We know of no advertiser or advertising agency in this country who would knowingly allow the products which he is trying to advertise to the public to become associated with the squalor . . . and general 'down' character . . . of *Street Scene*." The most courageous public-affairs program of the golden age, Ed Murrow's "See It Now," was emasculated in 1955, when the sponsor, Alcoa, decided to discontinue supporting it as a regular weekly program after Murrow's interview with J. Robert Oppenheimer and a report on land scandals in Texas, where Alcoa was planning to increase its investments. CBS transformed "See It Now" into an occasional documentary series, and in this guise it limped on until it was finally taken off the air, in 1958; Madison Avenue called it, contemptuously, "See It Now and Then."

But it wasn't only the sponsor who was responsible for the silencing of Murrow's courageous and abrasive voice. Quiz shows made their first appearance on TV in 1954, but it was in 1955 that they really took hold. That was the year when Louis G. Cowan (who for many years now has worn the penitent's white sheet as an advocate of public broadcasting at the Columbia School of Journalism and whose two sons were prominent radicals in the 1960s) introduced "The $64,000 Question" on TV. The show was so successful that it became a fifty-thousand-dollar question every week why CBS should drop that much revenue by running Murrow instead of another quiz show. In the same year, the president of CBS, Frank Stanton, delivered the immortal judgment, "A program in which a large part of the audience is interested is by that very fact . . . in the public interest." For five years, the quiz show dominated the airwaves. Five new ones were introduced on a single day in 1958, and in that year it was estimated that $24 million was being spent on time and talent for all the network quiz shows.

By the end of the fifties, three major trends in the news media, whose origins dated back to the forties and in some cases even earlier, had come to maturity. Together they transformed the news industry in the United States from a brawling, competitive, localized business into an order dominated by a double handful of fiefs of imperial power and wealth. One of these trends was concentration. The second was "corporatization." And the third was the rise of television.

The trend toward concentration was rooted in economics both in newspapers and in television, though it worked rather differently in the two technologies. In newspapers, what happened was a direct and rather rapid concentration of ownership, reinforced by a concentration in the sources from which news and comment originated. The reason for this concentration was not that newspapers were ceasing to be profitable; on the contrary, with the growth of advertising, which accounted for 71 per cent of their revenue in 1958 as against only 63 per cent in 1939, they could be immensely profitable, once competition could be suppressed. As Morris Ernst wrote in 1946, "Many newspapers were consolidated and bought up by chains, not because they were economically unsound, but rather because they were exceedingly valuable properties." William Randolph Hearst, Jr., estimated that if a competitive morning and evening paper each made $100,000 in annual profit, under the same management they would net not $200,000, but $500,000.

Such financial logic was irresistible. According to Professor Raymond Nixon, of the University of Minnesota, 40 per cent of daily circulation in the United States was already noncompetitive in 1945. By 1961, this proportion had risen to almost 60 per cent. The number of American cities with competing daily newspapers went down from 552 in 1920 to fifty-five in 1962. Cities with only one daily newspaper went up from 55 per cent of the total to 84 per cent by 1960.

By January 1962, exactly one third of the total circulation of American newspapers was controlled by just twelve managements. And deals between the Chandler and Hearst, Chandler and Annenberg, and Chandler and Washington *Post* interests, all in the first months of the sixties, illustrated that competition was far from cutthroat even among those twelve giant chains. By that same month, the Chandler family, controlling The Times-Mirror Company in Los Angeles, as well as vast interests in book publishing, agricultural land, oil leases, urban real estate, and many of the most powerful manufacturing and transportation corporations in California, had succeeded in killing the last remaining competition in a circulation area with over eight million population. And in this, as in so many other respects, southern California seemed to be only a little ahead of the rest of the nation.

Even more influential from the point of view of shaping public opinion was the concentration of the sources of news and comment. Growing interest in national and international affairs strengthened the grip of the wire services on news pages. Feature syndicates developed in the 1940s and 1950s to the point where few even of the larger metropolitan dailies, many of them, in any case, now chain-owned, either could afford, or chose to afford, to give their readers comment or analysis with any distinctly local flavor. And gradually, too, a handful of nationally known columnists, most of them based in New York or Washington, began to squeeze out the competition of other syndicated columns. By the mid sixties, the United States had come closer than at any time since the revolutionary period to accepting the lead of an opinion-forming elite.

There was an interesting interaction here between developments in the news industry and a broader national trend. The post-World War II years saw the emergence, for the first time in American history, of something like a national elite in business and politics. Increasingly, younger publishers, editors and columnists shared the style, attitudes and interests of this new elite. This partly explains the "working press's" sympathy for the Kennedy administration: presidential appointees in Washington, and those journalists successful enough to have access to them, more particularly those journalists new enough to such success to be free from the associations of the Eisenhower years, tended to belong to the same elite; that is, either to the upper middle class, or to the meritocracy of middle-class boys who had made good with the help of the great graduate schools.

In television, concentration took a different form: it was built into the technology and therefore into the economics of the medium. Concentration of ownership, indeed, was forbidden by statute: nobody could own more than five stations. But what mattered was concentration of control over broadcast material, and especially control over national-news and current-affairs program making. In this crucial area, the degree of concentration had already been very substantial in the days of radio. (Indeed, it could be argued that the hiving off of NBC's Blue Network, in the forties, to become the kernel of ABC, was one of the few significant steps away from greater concentration.) But as Fred Friendly, formerly of CBS and now of the Ford Foundation, put it to me in an interview:

> There was indeed a decisive concentration in the sources of ideas in the late fifties. And the primary reason is economics. Television is the cheapest way of distributing news. Forget the immediacy, the "I-was-there," the "Now-we'll-take-you-to-the-moon." The fact is that TV can triple the audience and it doesn't cost a penny more. The New York *Times* lost fifty thousand circulation when it put the cost up to fifteen cents. TV can make the viewers pay for its own expansion. That is the primary reason why TV grew.

It was in 1961 that public opinion polls recorded for the first time that a majority of Americans got their information about the world primarily from television. In practice, that meant that they got their information about national and international affairs largely from national network news. Local news was widely watched. As a matter of fact, it is more widely watched now, in raw numbers of viewers, than it was in the early 1960s. But, on the important issues, it was from the networks that Americans increasingly received their signals about the world.

Edward Jay Epstein's book *News from Nowhere* is full of examples of the way the organization and economics of network news have had the effect of concentrating the nation's attention on a limited number of subjects and a limited number of places. He shows, for example, how economic logic dictates that a very high proportion of all stories that find their way onto the nightly news are filmed by camera crews in the cities where the networks have wholly owned stations. Already by the late fifties, purely internal considerations of this kind were centralizing news making in Washington and New York, and to a lesser extent in Los Angeles, Chicago, and a handful of other centers. This, in turn, without anyone willing it, had the effect of tending to impose the attitudes of New York and Washington on the medium from which Americans were increasingly deriving their view of the world.

Network TV was making people think nationally. But TV itself was thinking nationally, in news terms as well as in entertainment terms, because other "nationalizing" forces were at work. National networks wanted to build national audiences, so that they could sell space to national advertisers, through national agencies, who were targeting national markets. The result was clear. On the important issues of the day, whether it was the Cold War or the national issues that were being decided more and more in Washington, what mattered in the late fifties was not what the station did, but what the network did.

By the early 1960s, then, a very substantial proportion of all the sources from which Americans derived their information or their ideas were being controlled by a relatively small number of organizations. There were two wire services; two and a half TV networks (counting ABC, at that time, on the basis of numbers of viewers, as no more than half an NBC or CBS); there were two truly national news magazines; and there were no more than a handful of newspapers with any claim to maintain national and foreign reporting staff of their own, to employ well-informed and influential commentators, and to syndicate their material at all widely to other papers. In a sense, only the New York *Times* and the Washington *Post* fully met these tests. Eight or nine organizations, or at the most generous estimate not more than a couple of dozen, virtually monopolized the supply of news to American minds.

Because they were so few, these oligopolies of the news industry were necessarily very big. Although it was fashionable at the time to talk about the "managerial revolution," a remarkably high proportion of them remained in the control of wealthy individuals or at most families: the Sarnoffs of NBC, William Paley at CBS, Leonard Goldenson at ABC, the Ochses and Sulzbergers of the New York *Times*, the Meyer family at the Washington *Post* and *Newsweek*, the Luces and Chandlers and Hearsts and so on, for all the world like a peerage of greater and lesser nobles, with their feuds and their cousinhoods and their poor relations, down to the country gentry who owned only a couple of papers and a TV station in a single state.

But if ownership was curiously feudal, each of these news organizations was managed by a corporate structure analogous in most respects to that of a steel company or a chain of supermarkets. Their news employees—writers, editors, producers—were far better educated and more "sophisticated"—a favorite word in the business at the time—than the heroes of an earlier generation. The corporate newsman wore horn-rimmed glasses and a Brooks Brothers suit, where the reporter of yore had worn shirtsleeves and a green eyeshade. But if stock options and pension schemes had made the new breed of newsmen prosperous beyond their predecessors' dreams, all their eggs were in the corporate basket, and they tended to have correspondingly bureaucratic, even timid, responses. With few realistic prospects of "crossing the street" to work for a competitor if they didn't like what the management was doing to their work, they were subject to the external discipline of corporate policy. And they were also, more effectively, subject to the internal discipline of a "professionalism" that placed a high premium on such values as "responsibility" and "objectivity."

Once again, we must note the interaction between the world of the media and the world outside. The late fifties were the years of *The Organization Man* (written by an employee of Henry Luce), of *The Man in the Gray Flannel Suit*, and of the "other-directed" corporate executive. Showing all due caution toward the danger of being misled by stereotypes, it was natural enough for the organization men of advertising and business to have their counterparts in the equally corporate world of the new, centralized media; and conversely any tendencies that that generation of middle-class Americans had in the direction of conformity were hardly very violently challenged by the news diet of those years.

Those were also the years of the Cold War. The journalists of the fifties shared with other members of the new national elite a strong sense of the overriding claims of national security. In the U-2 affair of 1960, the New York *Times* reported unquestioningly that the plane that had been shot down was a weather plane on a routine mission.

A year later, the New York *Times*'s posture toward government was still "responsible," or deferential, enough for it to decide not to print advance information of the Bay of Pigs invasion fiasco. It has become conventional to say that the *Times* was wrong to hold the story back. But the reason given for taking this view often misses the point. The *Times* should have published, people now say, because it could have saved the government from getting egg on its face, not because it had a duty to publish whether the government was embarrassed or not. That is an attitude the U.S. press did not have before 1945. To the extent that it still obtains today, it is a survival of the years when the new, national news media thought of themselves as one of the loyal orders of chivalry in the imperial system of liberal America.

By 1959, the quiz shows ruled television. NBC's answer to "The $64,000 Question," "Twenty-One," achieved the ultimate success by nudging "I Love Lucy" out of the top slot in the ratings. Murrow was off the air; news and current-affairs programs had almost completely disappeared from the networks' prime-time schedules.

Then CBS, without explanation, cancelled a quiz show called "Dotto." It transpired that a contestant, waiting in the wings to go on, had picked up a notebook dropped by the woman who was on the air ahead of him. It contained the exact questions that she was then, on stage, in process of answering, for four thousand dollars. CBS investigated, and at first denied all "improper procedures." The Federal Communications Commission, to whom the case was referred, at first agreed not to make public the evidence that the show had been rigged. Then a contestant on "Twenty-One" accused NBC of rigging the show on which Charles Van Doren, an attractive young Columbia instructor, had become something of a national hero by beating him to $129,000. The producers sued for libel, the district attorney moved in, and the cat was out of the bag.

The quiz-show scandals were not merely an unsavory episode. Nor were they important because, as many hand-wringing moralists maintained at the time, they were evidence of widespread dishonesty or of the corruption of affluence. They were a historic turning point because they were the reason for an abrupt change in network policy, from playing news down to emphasizing it. They were therefore in large part responsible for the fact that when, four years later, the crisis broke in Birmingham and Saigon and Dallas, the nation was tuned in. And they also played their part in creating that feverish emphasis on national news, that hypnotic concentration on the psychodrama of the presidency, and that sense of personal involvement, in every American family, with "how we're doing," that set the mood for the crisis.

The connection was direct. The chairman of the FCC, John C. Doerfer, called Robert Kintner of NBC, Frank Stanton of CBS and Leonard Goldenson of ABC down to Washington and ordered them to produce at least one hour of public affairs each week that did not coincide with a similar hour on another network.

The quiz scandals were also responsible for President Kennedy's appointment of Newton Minow as the toughest chairman ever at the FCC. In 1961, Minow made his famous speech denouncing network programing as a "vast wasteland," and when he threatened to hold hearings to discuss direct regulation, the President backed him up. Minow didn't last long. But as long as he was at the FCC, the network managements felt an additional pressure, over and above their own desire to improve their images after the quiz scandals, to make at least some flowers bloom in the wasteland.

Competition between the CBS and NBC news divisions intensified, to the point where people talked about the "Friendly-Kintner War," between CBS's Fred Friendly and NBC's Bob Kintner. CBS, as its response to the FCC's demand, started "CBS Reports," and Friendly, Murrow's old producer, was put in charge of them. Irving Gitlin, an old rival of Friendly's at CBS, had expected the job, and so in October 1960 Kintner was able to persuade Gitlin to move to NBC. There he started his riposte to "CBS Reports," the NBC "White Papers" series, and persuaded a number of CBS's top talents, including the documentary producer Fred Freed, to move across to NBC, too. At the same time, NBC hired a number of top-class reporters from newspapers to improve their news. All together, the number of producers in the NBC news division shot up from four to twenty-one in 1961–62. Kintner's slogan was "CBS plus thirty." That meant that he was ready to stay with live coverage of news events (which is expensive in terms of lost advertising) for thirty minutes longer than CBS would.

Fred Friendly has acknowledged the causal relationship between the quiz scandals and this sudden burst of interest in news and current-affairs programing:

> My job was to create a series of bold documentaries which would help to restore the prestige of CBS and, indirectly, the broadcast industry recently tarred by the quiz scandals.

Documentaries such as Freed's studies of the Cold War and, in 1963, Murrow's classic *Harvest of Shame,* were the first fruits of this public-relations effort. Between October 1958 and January 1959 the three networks had put out only ninety-four hours of public-service broadcasting among them, little of that in prime time. Two years later, in the comparable period, that output had jumped by three fifths, to 151 hours.

But what was to be even more significant for the future than the increased output of documentaries was the new competitive emphasis on hard news. The culmination of this trend came on September 2, 1963, less than three months before the assassination of President Kennedy. That was the day CBS doubled the length of its flagship nightly news program from fifteen minutes to half an hour. Within a couple of weeks, NBC had followed suit.

The corporate decision to double the length of the news may or may not have reflected a judgment that the world had become a more interesting place in that summer of civil rights conflict and the test-ban treaty. What it certainly did reflect was two hard-headed corporate decisions that had nothing whatever to do with the state of the world.

One was simply a matter of making the optimum use of overheads. The big news staffs taken on since 1959 in the news divisions were expensive, and the advertising brought in by the documentaries, specials, and other public-affairs shows that they produced did not begin to cover their costs. Corporate executives had noticed that ratings and sales on the evening news were better than on these specials. Economic logic suggested that if the fifteen-minute format could be doubled, the larger staffs could be more profitably, or rather less unprofitably, employed.

The second calculation involved one of the most important and most delicate formulas in the whole economics of American broadcasting: the share-out of time, and therefore of advertising revenue, between the networks and their affiliates. Networks keep prime time to themselves, and

they also generally have the lion's share of daytime and late-night sched-
ules. The affiliate stations earn their revenue, and justify their FCC
licenses, by the local news and other programs they put out immediately
before and after prime time. In the middle fifties, the networks had made
one advance at the expense of their affiliates, by pushing their own,
nightly, fifteen-minute news programs back out of prime time into affiliate
time. The affiliates had little option but to go along, because the FCC
takes a dim view of affiliates refusing to take network news. Now, in 1963,
the networks saw a chance to take another slice at the salami. By going to
half an hour for the nightly news, they in effect poached from the affiliates
another fifteen minutes of air time, or two and a half minutes of advertising. That was something of the order of thirty thousand dollars a night,
which was not to be sneezed at, even by CBS. . . .

NBC had been planning to go to half an hour with their Huntley-
Brinkley show, partly because of the economic logic just outlined and
partly in obedience to Kintner's strategic perception that news and current
affairs would help NBC to catch up with CBS in the ratings far quicker
than entertainment programs, which take a couple of years' planning and
investment. But CBS beat them to the draw. It announced that the
Cronkite show would go to half an hour on September 2. NBC had heard,
quite incorrectly, as it turned out, that CBS's first half-hour show would
be entirely devoted to civil rights. And so on September 2, 1963, NBC put
out a three-hour news special, which had taken only five weeks or so to
make, about civil rights. It was called *American Revolution 1963*. It was
the first three-hour program ever done on any subject on American television, and its impact on both white and black people who saw it was immense. I did not see it, but I am told that it was a fine piece of work, and
no doubt its effect was in many ways benign. Yet one cannot help observ-
ing that both the decision to put out a three-hour spectacular and the
choice of subject were largely conditioned by internal considerations of a
kind that not one American in a hundred, having just been told that a
new American revolution was taking place, would have suspected. "It was
a political show," one of the men who helped to make it told me, "in the
sense that it was an anti-CBS show. . . . Bob Kintner had to find something that would pre-empt that premiere."

For its own, various reasons, the new, news-conscious television hastened the transition from the confident years of consensus to the anguished years of polarization. Another turning point was television coverage of the assassination that same autumn. The poignant, round-the-clock
coverage of the bereaved Kennedy family, the widow, the orphaned children, the lying-in-state, and the funeral, and perhaps most of all the sudden trauma of the murder of Lee Harvey Oswald by Jack Ruby in the

Dallas police station—the fact that tens of millions of Americans experienced these things in their own homes transformed a public catastrophe into a private wound. It intensified that strong personal identification, on the part of millions of non-political Americans, with the presidency that is one of the most striking characteristics of the period.

Even before the assassination, though, the rise of television had accentuated the dominance of the presidency over all other American political institutions. The President personifies political issues as neither Congress nor the courts can do. Nothing a President does can be entirely dull. And once television networks, having discovered this last fact, allowed Presidents to know that they would always cover their informal journeys as well as their formal speeches, any President found himself enjoying unprecedented opportunities to communicate, directly, with the people through the media.

It was no accident that John Kennedy, the first President to understand the power of television and to make himself a master of it, was also the first President elected after television had achieved primacy among the news media. Ben Bagdikian's study of the clash over the steel companies' price increase in October 1962 documents the immense new power that TV conferred on a President who knew how to use it. Kennedy and his successors could reach over the heads of the established intermediary powers and recruit the people directly to their side.

But if television contributed to the power of the presidency, it also contributed to the emotional demands people made of the office. Lyndon Johnson inherited the power to use television. (All, that is, except that part of Kennedy's power that came from his personal charm and skill at using the medium.) But Johnson also inherited the insatiable demand for the President to solve the "problems" that television itself was revealing to people. Some of those problems could not of their nature be solved. Others could not be solved easily or quickly. And others, again, could hardly be solved by the President. No wonder, then, that, as Fred Freed mused to me shortly before his early death, "one of the things that happened was that from 1960 to 1963 the news that people got from TV was essentially optimistic. From 1963 on, it wasn't."

The first duty of any holder of a television license, in the FCC's official view, is to let the people have the news. In 1949 the commission held it "axiomatic" that the "basic purpose" of broadcasting as a whole was "the development of an informed public opinion through the public dissemination of news and ideas concerning the vital public issues of the day."

There are in theory, and to some extent in the actual practice of TV in other parts of the world, where commercial considerations do not bear as directly on program production as they do in the United States, three main ways in which you can attempt to report and interpret what is happening in the world.

The first is news as we usually know it, whether live on electronic cameras (as at a political convention), or on tape or film, or read out of the studio by a newscaster. There are varying degrees of immediacy from the unedited live event to wire-service copy read off a teleprompter, but that is all hard news.

The second method is live studio discussion by the people who are making the news, or by people who are thought to be qualified to explain it, or by just plain citizens who are going to be affected by it. Here, too, there is a considerable range from the extreme of high access and democratic participation at one end, to the extreme of elitist punditry at the other. Yet it is all discussion of the news, unstructured by the producer.

The third technique, which runs by far the greatest risk of bias but also affords by far the greatest opportunities for truly explanatory presentation of complex issues, is documentary. Only in documentary is it possible for television to apply sustained, analytical intellectual effort to material that is controlled by the program maker in the same way that a writer controls his, so that powerful ideas can not only be transmitted but can also be put in their true context.

Essentially for commercial reasons, the U.S. networks, and local affiliates imitating them, have concentrated on the first of these three possible ways of reporting and interpreting the news, almost to the exclusion of the second and the third.

They have relegated discussion almost entirely to the ossified formula of the panel interviews in the Sunday lunchtime "ghetto"—"Face the Nation," "Meet the Press," and so on—in which extremely deferential labor produces a pompous little mouse of information.

The case of documentary is more complicated. As we have mentioned, fine documentaries have been done since the demise of Ed Murrow's "See It Now": Fred Freed's and Ted Yates's work for NBC, and CBS's *Hunger in America* come to mind. But these were exceptions. Documentaries must be sold to a sponsor, and while there have been gallant exceptions, few sponsors want to be associated with controversial subjects, and almost none with any criticism of their own interests. Moreover, the audience tends to shy away from even mildly controversial subjects. The ABC research department did a survey of the documentaries produced by all three networks from 1963 to 1966—that is, over the height of the crisis, when one might expect that people would have wanted to know what was happening to the country, and that network news executives would have wanted to try to tell them. In that period, 164 documentaries were shown, or roughly one every other week per network, not a particularly high frequency. Only nine of them dealt in any way with the Vietnam War, unquestionably the biggest single issue of that period. Five were about race in one form or another, but of those, three were about the problems of the police! Only sixteen, or under 10 per cent, fell within a broad category of "U.S. social conflicts and problems," and on the whole they were far less successful in terms of ratings than films with such titles as *The World of James Bond*, *The Legend of Marilyn Monroe*, and *The World of Jacqueline Kennedy*.

"What the public seems least likely to watch," Edith Efron commented, "is the 'social problem' documentaries, shows discussing inflation, water and air pollution, disease, poverty, racial oppression and dope addiction." And the networks showed no great enthusiasm for giving people such unpopular medicine. "Television is lacking in excitement these days," David Brinkley told an interviewer in mid 1967, at the height of the Vietnam War and of the urban riots. "In the non-news areas, like documentaries, we lean toward soft, pastel programs—trips through the Louvre, or up the Nile with gun and camera—that seem to me rather irrelevant to the time we live in."

The reason was simple enough. It had not changed since 1959, when it was spelled out with painful clarity at FCC hearings by a certain Robert Foreman, of the advertising agency Batten, Barton, Durstine & Osborn: "A program that displeases any substantial segment of the population is a misuse of the advertising dollar." In the crisis years of the sixties, advertisers remained every bit as reluctant to misuse the advertising dollar as in the age of bland. To take a single but by no means insignificant example, NBC had a contract with Gulf Oil under which the oil company agreed in advance to sponsor news specials and documentaries. But by 1967 Gulf was equally unhappy about sponsoring programs on racial problems in the United States and on politics in the Middle East. And NBC was unhappy, too, at least at the production level, because those were the two big stories it ought to have been reporting that year.

It should in fairness be added that, whatever NBC's arrangements with Gulf were, they did not in the end prevent the network from putting out a fine documentary by Fred Freed about the Detroit riot of 1967, or, for example, Ted Yates's work on the Middle East. The point is, however, that to the extent that American viewers between 1963 and 1968 were getting an alarming picture of the world from their television screens and were coming to see the world in terms of a series of problems threatening them, it was not because of any conscious policy or of liberal bias on the part of the networks, as Vice-President Agnew and his friends were to argue; on the contrary, it was to some extent in spite of conscious network policy.

Because ratings were low for discussion programs and news specials and documentaries, and because of the additional problems of getting sponsorship, the overwhelming majority of the networks' news effort went into their nightly news programs. It was essentially from the nightly network news that Americans got their picture of what was happening in the unpredictable, frightening world of the sixties. And because of the format of the nightly news, that meant that, especially from 1963 to 1968, the American viewer was exposed, in his own living room, to a nightly bombardment of vivid and threatening images that were largely unexplained and out of context. Over that period, the images of danger became more and more confusing. They also crept closer and closer to home, until even the viewer watching in the security of a suburban home began to wonder whether anything was sacred, or any place safe.

First came the civil rights movement. There were the marches and the sit-ins, the freedom songs and the attacks by police on peaceful demonstrators, culminating in the graphic frieze of the Alabama troopers, horse and foot, wreathed in dust and tear gas, pitching into the marchers at the Pettus bridge at Selma in the spring of 1965. But, for most viewers, the Deep South was as remote and exotic as Indochina. After Watts, in the summer of 1965, the urban riots deposited a heavier and more toxic coating of images on the national subconscious: blazing stores and shattered window glass on streets that looked just like ones you drove along to work, and young black faces like those you saw on the street, apparently contorted with anger as they screamed threats to "take care of business by whatever means necessary."

Then, from early 1965 on, but especially after November of that year, when both CBS and NBC beefed up their Saigon bureaus, it was the living-room war. By the end of 1967, with staffs of some two dozen each in Saigon, the three networks were spending around $5 million between them on covering the war. That was a big enough outlay to ensure that Vietnam would be on the nightly news whenever possible. And so, for two years, the average American family sat down and watched infantry search-and-destroy missions, bombardments, and napalm raids, varied by optimistic pronouncements from government officials and generals and by occasional public executions carried out by the democratic ally in Saigon.

It was television's first war, and technically the reporting was often brilliant. But the way the networks covered it had the effect of enhancing the viewers' confusion. At CBS, reporters and camera crews knew what kind of film was likely to get on the air (and the whole purpose of their being in Vietnam, and sometimes under fire, was to get on the air): the kind of film they called "shooting bloody." "Some of the correspondents kept a kind of scorecard as to which pieces were and were not used," Mike Wallace said in an interview later, "and it seemed as though an inordinate number of combat pieces were used, compared with some first-rate pieces in the political area, or the pacification area, or non-bloody stories."

For traditional journalistic reasons, then, with brief news spots to fill, the producers tended to prefer combat footage. For equally under-standable reasons, they chose footage of Americans, as opposed to South Vietnamese, in combat. And of course the footage tended disproportion-ately to be of successful actions. If a patrol makes no contact with the enemy, the film crew with it will bring back dull footage. If it is wiped out in an ambush, no film will come back at all. Lastly, because transmitting all but the most important stories by satellite was too expensive, the producers like "timeless" stories—not of a specific battle, but of "recent fighting."

The net effect of all these factors was to make sure that each night on the news there was film in which American troops seemed to be forever moving forward with the apparently irresistible momentum of logistical strength and firepower, killing Vietnamese and yet never seeming to clinch victory. Honest though the reporting was, and brave the reporters, the war in the living room was never anything like the real war in the jungles and rice paddies, which was a slow, patient wrestling match between the guerrillas and the government, in which all the fire and fury of American operations were in the end marginal.

From 1966 on, as the nightly bombardment of American homes with these puzzling images of war went on, new stories made their appearance more and more regularly on the nightly news: stories that were even less comprehensible to the viewer when they flashed on the screen for a min-ute and ten—two and a half minutes if you were lucky. After the urban riots and student demonstrations and mass protests against the war, there were stories about poverty and the Great Society and crime, which seemed, on top of all its old emotional undertones, to have become a political issue. And then came all the militant movements that, consciously or un-consciously, modeled themselves on militant black separatism: militant Chicanos, militant Indians, "ethnics," and—most disconcerting of all—the militant feminist movement. There were crusades for clean air and clean water and road safety and legalized abortion, and each came over from the television screen as more shrill and urgent than the last.

"Repent ye! Repent ye!" the endless talking heads seemed to be say-ing from the box. "The last day is at hand." There were few discussion programs or documentaries to explain these angry movements or to put them in context; only the evening news, if they could make their case shrilly enough, or devise a form of protest photogenic enough, to get on the air. The network news programs, by 1968–69, seemed to have become an immensely powerful bullhorn. Anyone who could get his mouth near the narrow end and shout loud enough could get through to the entire nation. "It is the development of the evening news as a social institution," wrote Byron Shafer and Richard Larson in the *Columbia Journalism Review*, "which has made social disorganization a realistic threat to the comfortably-off middle-class urbanites, to suburbanites, to rural residents—to all those, in short, who have seldom faced robbery, mugging, protest marches, chanting, blockbusting, black-power salutes, or perhaps even hostile questions about their values."

Television could not have avoided covering civil rights or the shooting war in Vietnam or the social tensions in American cities in the late sixties. And on the whole, television news presented the facts both fairly and faithfully, and certainly with great technical skill. "Was the journalism good enough?" Fred Friendly asked me, and answered, without boastfulness, that on the whole he thought it was. The journalism was often brilliant, and almost always conscientious. But the way television news worked, the configuration of the apparatus, made it not a lamp or a mirror but a burning glass.

For its own reasons, as we have seen, the television industry decided to go out for news after the quiz scandals. For its own reasons, essentially commercial reasons, its effort came to be concentrated above all on the nightly half-hour news programs. And for reasons partly commercial, partly journalistic, those programs beamed out atomistic images of vivid information with little explanation or discussion, so that the viewer was often left with little understanding of *why* these disturbing things were happening, or of what they meant.

From the beginning of the sixties, TV had become the primary news medium, and as the decade progressed its grip tightened. To a large degree it was television that defined the issues for the print media. It defined them, in any case, in terms of the mindset of the metropolitan elite of Washington and New York, and the process of concentration in the print media meant that there, too, the same attitudes were predominant. This new national elite, and its followers in the professional middle classes all over the United States, saw the news as the new national news media presented it, that is, in terms of a national psychodrama or myth. The eyes of the country were focused on the President, above all, as he wrestled with evil to perfect American society and to defeat the forces of darkness that threatened it from outside.

From 1959 to 1963, the effect of this nationalizing of the American consciousness was to reinforce the consensus. In those years, television and the national print media gave viewers and readers an exhilarating feeling of participation in the liberal crusade led and symbolized by John F. Kennedy. Even conservatives, in those years, criticized the President in terms of the liberal myth. They might argue that he was not mature enough to wrestle for America, or that he was not winning. The two wire services, the two news magazines, the two newspapers and the two networks all taught Americans to look to the White House as the place—so the closing phrase of Teddy White's book in 1960 called it—"on which an impatient world waited for miracles."

After the crisis began, in 1963, the unifying force of the news media still fastened attention on the moral drama of America, but now with a bewildered, frustrated sense that things were going wrong. People still waited for miracles. But each night, instead, television news battered them with doubts. Each morning, the newspaper reinforced them. The little glass screen began to act like a lens. Every evening for half an hour, it concentrated all the rays of heat from a world on fire, until they burned into the viewers' minds with an almost unbearable intensity. It was that, more than anything, that brought the United States to the brink of a nervous breakdown.

# 8

## The Crisis

In the fall of 1963 things were going well for America.

Or so it looked. More than ever before, the media had taught Americans to identify their country with their President and their own lives with the political drama of which he was at the center. And the President was riding high.

The Cuban missile crisis, a year earlier, swept two major doubts from the international horizon at one stroke: It disposed of the fear, which John Kennedy had skillfully exploited in his 1960 campaign, that the United States was vulnerable to Soviet pressure, and even to surprise attack, because of a missile gap. At the same time, it disposed of the fear that Richard Nixon had tried to make the most of, that the new President would prove too young and inexperienced to stand up to the Russians. Now, as Dean Rusk put it at the tensest moment of the confrontation, the United States had been eyeball to eyeball with the enemy, and it had been the other fellow who blinked.

The happy ending of the crisis ratified both the Administration's policy and its style. Here were all the ideas the defense intellectuals had been talking about: the need for a flexible, restrained response with conventional weapons; the concept of escalation ("if the naval blockade doesn't do the trick, we can always try an air strike"); the dialogue with the adversary, using both overt diplomacy and non-verbal signals; the sophisticated use of modern communications to keep the military forces as agents of the President's will. And it had worked. Rationality, restraint and logic had triumphed both over the Soviet challenge and over the atavistic military impulse to blow Cuba out of the water. The country felt safer and more confident. More important, the weathering of the crisis gave the President and his team confidence in themselves.

The first fruit of this new confidence was the nuclear test-ban treaty.

The Cuban missile crisis taught Kennedy "Mr. Khrushchev and I are in the same boat" when it came to nuclear confrontation. The contacts with Krushchev's emissary A. I. Mikoyan, who was sent to tidy up the residue of the Cuban episode, led directly into the first discussion of the test ban. Kennedy proposed the treaty in his American University speech on June 10. It was initialed in Moscow before the end of July, and it passed the Senate before the end of September.

Kennedy was no longer afraid of showing weakness to the Russians. And he was no longer afraid of being called weak by the American Right. His sensitive political judgment told him that now the American people trusted his confidence rather than the doubts of Senators Russell, Stennis and Goldwater. The test-ban treaty was only a limited step toward ending the danger of nuclear war. But as Kennedy said with one of those Massachusetts Chinese proverbs he loved to exhume or invent, "A journey of a thousand miles must begin with a single step."

Cautiously, but firmly, during those same months, President Kennedy was committing himself to two major domestic measures: a tax cut and a civil rights bill.

In so far as he had any very strong economic ideas before he took office, these had been conservative, influenced by his father's traditional wisdom about what made the stock market go up and down, rather than by the university economists and their Keynesian notions of using fiscal and monetary controls to manage the economy. (While he was in the Senate he confided to his aide Ted Sorensen that he had a hard time remembering which was which, fiscal and monetary.) In the White House, under the influence of such economists (in and out of government) as Walter Heller (chairman of his Council of Economic Advisers), Paul Samuelson, Robert Solow, and J. K. Galbraith, he became a convert to the New Economics. In June 1962, in a commencement address at Yale, he announced his conversion for the first time in public.

In August 1963, with the test-ban treaty before the Senate, and Washington waiting in mounting alarm for the arrival of the civil rights marchers, Kennedy announced that in the New Year he would propose to Congress a substantial tax cut. What he had in mind was the biggest stimulus the federal government had ever handed out to the private sector of the economy: the measure as eventually passed cut individual taxes by almost one fifth and corporate taxes by one tenth.

The Kennedy tax cut is a graphic illustration of my thesis that in the age of the liberal consensus there were in practice only two sides in politics: the center, and the Right. In this instance the liberals proposed a gigantic windfall for business and for the middle class. Conservatives opposed it on grounds of pure ideology. Whatever the merits of the tax cut, it did, after all, involve the government's handing out 12 billion dollars, most of it to the well-to-do. One might have expected some voices to be raised on the Left asking whether there were no social services whose improvement might be a higher priority even than economic growth. No such voices were heard.

The irrepressible Galbraith, to be fair, though he was in favor of the tax cut, did tell the President to his face that the speech in which he had announced the cut was "the most Republican speech since McKinley." But that was not a wholly unwelcome comment. For the tax cut put conservatives in general and the Republican leadership in Congress in particular on the spot, as it was intended to do. How could they be against cutting taxes? They had been complaining for a generation that taxes were too high. . . .

Their only way out was to call for cuts in the federal budget instead. This they did, raucously and quite unmindful of the fact that cuts of the magnitude they were demanding could come only out of the defense budget, something they would have denounced with horror.

But whatever criticism could be made at the time on grounds of social justice, or in retrospect on the grounds that an opportunity was missed to redistribute resources to the poor, the purpose of the tax cut was to stimulate the economy and reduce unemployment without causing inflation. And in all three of these objects, it was highly successful. The gross national product grew slowly in the Eisenhower years and in the early months of the Kennedy administration. By the spring of 1965, when the tax cut had been effective for a year, the GNP had jumped by more than one third in under five years. Inflation had been kept under 3 per cent a year while Kennedy was alive, thanks in part to the successful confrontation with the steel companies. Kennedy and his New Economists had started the American economy on the longest unbroken advance in its history.

A serious measure of civil rights legislation implied far deeper opposition in Congress, and therefore took courage of a different order, than a tax cut did. There, too, Kennedy moved to a commitment by gradual, cautious stages. His sympathetic phone call to Coretta King when her husband, Dr. Martin Luther King, was jailed at the climax of the 1960 campaign, aroused expectations that Kennedy would take a strong stand on civil rights. It was also an astute political move which offset a reputation for lukewarm attachment to the cause. Kennedy won 70 per cent of the black vote. The black turnout in Chicago alone, helped by a quarter of a million leaflets telling the story of his phone call, was enough to swing the election.

But, for the first two and a half years of his administration, those expectations were only meagerly fulfilled. The President's response to the civil rights crisis was strangely mixed. He appointed more blacks to high federal jobs than ever before, including the first black since Reconstruction to sit on the federal bench: Thurgood Marshall. He also appointed at least four southern segregationists to the bench. He decided against proposing any new civil rights legislation, and his aides coldly dissociated the White House from legislation proposed by others.

Instead Kennedy proposed to work quietly through the executive powers of the presidency and through the courts. He kept his brother the Attorney General out in front of him. The strategy was to rely on increased black voting in the South to break the power of the Congressional opposition in the long run, in the hope that with the vote southern blacks would acquire the political power to win the other changes they wanted. But progress was mortally slow, and he disappointed the civil rights movement by waiting almost two years before signing a mild executive order banning discrimination in federally impacted housing.

The President did go on television to appeal for order the night of the riot at the University of Mississippi in September 1962. But it was a conciliatory speech, and he appealed in the name of Senator Lucius Q. C. Lamar, a nineteenth-century defender of the Ku Klux Klan. The effect was a not altogether happy effect, though it was succeeded by relief when the 82nd Airborne arrived on campus ten hours later, after a night of wild rioting in which two were killed.

In the following February, Kennedy did propose a modest package of civil rights legislation to Congress. But it was not until the flagrant defiance of federal authority by public officials, from Governor George Wallace on down, in Alabama in the spring and summer of 1963 that the President seemed to grasp the scope and magnitude of the danger.

At last, on June 11, the night George Wallace's charade of defiance had brought federal bayonets onto the University of Alabama campus at Tuscaloosa (to the astute Wallace's lasting political advantage in that defiantly rebel state), Kennedy made his commitment in unambiguous language:

> I hope that every American . . . will stop and examine his conscience. . . .
>
> Today we are committed to a world-wide struggle to promote and protect the rights of all who wish to be free. And when Americans are sent to Vietnam or West Berlin we do not ask for Whites only. . . .
>
> Now the time has come for this nation to fulfill its promise. . . .
> The fires of frustration and discord are burning in every city, North and

South. . . . We face, therefore, a moral crisis. . . . It is time to act in Congress.

I watched that speech in the bar of the hotel in Tuscaloosa. As it ended, the man on the bar stool next to mine put down his glass. "White nigger," he sniffed contemptuously to the fading image of the President of the United States. Yet, at that moment, the President was still some way from total identification even with the more cautious wing of the civil rights movement.

It was not until the March on Washington, at the end of August, that Kennedy finally took the plunge and put himself at the head of the coalition for a historic civil rights statute to give the force of law to the rights he had listed in his speech. When the Administration first learned of the plans for the march, it did all it could to prevent it. As soon as it realized, however, that it could not be stopped, it set to work to transform it from a march *on* Washington to demand action from the federal government into a march *in* Washington to lobby for the Administration's legislation.

In one sense, that effort was triumphantly successful. A quarter of a million people gathered in peaceful brotherhood at the Lincoln Memorial to hear Martin Luther King's great peroration:

> I have a dream that one day this nation will rise up and live out the true meaning of its creed: We hold these truths to be self-evident, that all men are created equal.

That afternoon, President Kennedy at last pronounced his blessing. "The nation can properly be proud," he said, "of the demonstration that has occurred here today."

The nation did feel proud, and at a deeper level than mere relief that the marchers had behaved themselves. The march was one of the high-water marks of liberal optimism. All but an isolated handful of angry southern diehards, it was now hoped, would accept the march as a reaffirmation of the nation's fundamental ideals. The images of Bull Connor's firehoses and police dogs in Birmingham, the murder of Medgar Evers the night after the President's June speech, had shocked and shamed white America. To see working-class blacks in their best clothes linking hands with white clergymen and singing "Black and white together, / We shall overcome" was therapy for that trauma. It raised the hope that even this darkest stain on the American conscience could be erased without conflict. In political terms, the march was taken as evidence that a new national consensus was emerging to demand passage of the President's civil rights bill. But many people, and many newspapers, saw the march in more pentecostal terms. There was a hope that instantaneous conversion had taken place: that one hundred years after emancipation, racial inequality and injustice would soon follow slavery into oblivion.

It was a short-lived hope. Kennedy had moved so gradually and with such apparent reluctance to the conclusion that an all-out effort must be made to pass a civil rights bill not because he lacked sympathy with black aspirations (though it is true that his personal experience had made him slower to grasp the emotional urgency of the black revolt than that of, say, Lyndon Johnson) but because he knew all too well how much resistance there would be.

Already, in fact, by the late summer of 1963, an ominous dilemma was beginning to appear for liberal America and for its chosen instrument for social progress, the activist presidency. It had become urgent to take action effective enough and swift enough to meet the mounting surge of black impatience. "The fires of discord and frustration" were alight, and now not only in the remote South. There were riots and demonstrations in Harlem and Chicago that summer, as well as in Birmingham and Atlanta. A significant, though little noticed turning point was reached at the beginning of July. Just as the federal government stirred itself at last to enforce the abolition of *de jure* segregation in the South, the NAACP decided at its annual convention in Chicago to campaign against *de facto* segregation in northern school districts. Yet it was becoming clear that any action effective enough to satisfy black aspirations could not be taken without driving at least a substantial minority of whites, and not only in the Deep South, into bitter, unappeasable resentment.

A special issue of *Newsweek* on July 29, 1963, based on a nationwide poll of black leaders, documents with precision the point this emerging dilemma had reached a month before the March on Washington and four months before the assassination.

History would mark the summer of 1963 as a time of revolution, it bluntly reported. "Vast majorities" of blacks now demanded an immediate end to all forms of discrimination. "We have woke up," one Alabama woman said. Black leaders were all more or less militant to *Newsweek*'s eye, "partly by choice—and partly because they have no choice." Their followers wanted "complete equality, nothing less." They wanted it right away. And three out of four of them would not be deterred if that meant bloodshed. "Fights, shooting," said an unemployed black man in Miami, shrugging, "it takes that to make the world better."

If the mood of the black revolt was now insistent, though, its goals were still moderate. It was directed against segregation and inequality, not against white America. The great majority of blacks remained patriotic. They rejected separatism. They clung to the hope of winning equality without violence. So, at least, they told *Newsweek*'s interviewers that summer. By far their most popular leader was Martin Luther King, and President Kennedy was almost as popular: almost 90 per cent of those interviewed supported him. Only 15 per cent, most of them in the slums of northern cities, had a good word for Elijah Muhammad, the only separatist leader mentioned, and twice as many disapproved of him. The goal of the revolution was still integration. The overwhelming majority of black Americans, in spite of misgivings about how they would be treated, said they wanted not to get out of white society but to get deeper into it.

What was intolerably too slow for one angrily aroused tenth of the population, those figures meant, might be too fast for another six or seven tenths. What was fast emerging as the most urgent item on the agenda of practical politics, in other words, was none other than that "American dilemma," deeply rooted in history and habit, that Gunnar Myrdal had defined in his great book twenty years before:

> the ever-raging conflict between . . . the American Creed, where the American thinks, talks and acts under the influence of high national and Christian precepts, and, on the other hand, the valuations on specific planes of individual and group living, where personal and local interests: economic, social and sexual jealousies; considerations of community prestige and conformity; group prejudice . . . and all sorts of miscellaneous wants, impulses and habits dominate his outlook.

By demanding what in theory the national creed ought to allow them —equality—blacks had revealed the inconsistency between the egalitarian ideals of the American creed and the inequality of the actual condition of black people in American society. But not only that. The black revolt was changing as it spread and as the events of the summer of 1963 dramatized the issues. Now the demand was not just for legal equality, which was withheld only in the Deep South; it was for social and economic equality everywhere. The steps that would have to be taken if that demand was to be met would have to include economic measures, and they would touch every American, sooner or later, to some degree.

Something else had perhaps also become inevitable, which Myrdal had not foreseen and few yet understood. The black revolt, of itself, implied a crisis for the presidency as an institution. For it was now to the President, far more than to Congress or to any other agency, public or private, more even than to the courts, that Americans looked for the carrying out of their ideals. Where the fulfillment of those ideals demanded a course of action that would come into conflict with so many habits, assumptions, interests and emotions, then the resentment must backfire upon the presidency.

Even before the assassination, in fact, the culmination of the civil rights movement put the presidency in the center of the dilemma between the national ideal of equality and the national reluctance to do what would be necessary to achieve it. In the remaining weeks of John Kennedy's life the full implications of this dilemma were not plain. As long as the problem of achieving equality for blacks was still widely seen as something that could be solved by passing legislation, the risk for the presidency as an institution was not apparent. On the contrary, the presidency was enhanced. It appeared as the agent of the national conscience, embattled against a minority entrenched in Congress by seniority and the committee system. In the fall of 1963, the issue presented itself as a simple matter of practical politics. Could Kennedy pass a civil rights bill?

That question will never now be answered with certainty. But the probable answer is that he couldn't—not in his first term. The closer people were to the realities of Congressional power, the more skeptical they tended to be. Senator Hubert Humphrey, one of the bill's leading sponsors, said at the height of the euphoria after the March on Washington that he doubted whether it had turned a single vote. And one of the top lobbyists for the bill, the lawyer Joseph L. Rauh, told me in an interview, "The March was a beautiful expression of all that's best in America. But I would find it unreal to suggest that it had anything to do with passing the civil rights bill, because three months later, when Kennedy was killed, the bill was absolutely bogged down."

Until the test-ban treaty was voted by the Senate, and the tax cut by the House (its severest test), both in late September, the Kennedy administration had been singularly unsuccessful in getting major, innovative legislation passed. It was not always able to pass even routine appropriation bills. But that was the first Kennedy administration. It now looked increasingly certain that there would be a second.

The Democrats had held up well in the mid-term elections the previous fall. The President's poll ratings had dropped slightly from the peak they had reached after the Cuban crisis. (This almost certainly reflected the stand he had taken on civil rights.) But they were still high. Kennedy was now looking forward, with unconcealed pleasure, to the prospect of running against Barry Goldwater in 1964. (Richard Nixon, defeated for the governorship in California in 1962, was behaving in a way which suggested that he was not only finished but a little deranged as well.) Kennedy had a superstitious reluctance to tempt providence. But his aides and advisers looked forward to a second term, in which it would be easier to pass the domestic program Congress had balked at in the first.

The economy was perking up. The world situation looked less alarming than for many years. The love feast at the Lincoln Memorial drew the sting from the ominous evidence of racial strife. The mood of the country that fall was inclined toward optimism. And certainly that was the President's mood. On September 9 he felt able to say, on the Huntley-Brinkley show: "The country has done an outstanding job." In a speech written in late November he was to have said, "America is stronger than ever before." That sentence was in the speech he was to have delivered at the Trade Mart in Dallas on November 22.

At the death of a great prince, there have always been fear, superstition and panic. "Will anything ever be the same again?" people ask themselves at those moments. "Will the world go on as it did?" But the striking thing, in late November and early December 1963, was how many Americans were asking themselves, and asking each other, questions of a different sort. They boiled down to a single obsessive pair of alternatives. Was the assassination an act without meaning, a freak? Or was it the result and the ominous symptom of something rotten in the life of the country?

Among those who allowed themselves doubts of that kind, it would seem, were those acolytes of the liberal consensus, the editors of the New York *Times Magazine*. On December 8, 1963, the magazine published a long article that claimed to answer, in the specific context of the assassination, a notably comprehensive question. It was, one might think, a question of disproportionately comprehensive scope to be pegged on aberrations of Lee Harvey Oswald and Jack Ruby. But there it was in the headline: "What Sort of Nation Are We?"

The answers supplied in the article were neither startling nor original. They are worth some attention just the same. "We are, first and foremost"—the article ritually began—"a democracy. Indeed, of all the major countries in the world, we are probably most democratic in feeling and action." It was, the author conceded, a very special kind of democracy in which the United States led the world: "The will of the majority is not reflected in many of our political institutions. . . . Traditional ideas about innocence until guilt is proven . . . find little popular support. . . . There is the feeling that ideas can be corrupting and that accused enemies of society should be locked up with a minimum of formality." No, American democracy "must be interpreted as a social rather than a political phenomenon. It has meant that a greater and greater number of Americans have been able to ascend to a level of material security and a consciousness of personal worth that in other countries remains the privilege of exclusive minorities. . . . Critics of the American temper are, in reality, decrying the fact that social classes play so small a role in our national life."

Was this happy condition of classless social harmony even partially marred, then, by any other divisions: racial, for example, or ethnic rivalries of any kind? No, the author explained (in the year of Birmingham), "so long as one is a 'good American,' religious and ethnic considerations are viewed as secondary. The melting pot is doing its work . . . it must not be forgotten that graduation to the status of American is a marked advance for those who have succeeded in the climb."

One division the author did acknowledge: the contrast between a benighted "provincial America," well represented in Congress and in state and local government, and the wave of the future, "metropolitan America, typified by the new suburbs . . . by national corporations . . . [and] by the Executive branch of the Federal government."

What set the provincial and the metropolitan American apart, the article argued, were the two strongest American characteristics, "our commitments to a democratic society and to technological innovation." And since the suburbs, the big corporations and the executive branch were all in favor of technology and of "democracy" (defined as a more or less equal opportunity to enjoy material abundance), then . . . all was well. What of the "stunning events" which were, after all, the occasion for this remarkable essay in ideological chauvinism? The author dismissed them in two words: "unpredictable and unpreventable," and moved on serenely to his conclusion: "Our problems are those of success."

There they all were, the shibboleths of the liberal orthodoxy, all in one short article: a hubristic complacency modified only by a neurotic testiness about foreign critics, real or imagined; the confusion of democracy with economic abundance; the naïve repetition of the myth of classlessness; the inability to notice the black revolt that was moving the earth under the feet; the identification of the democratic tradition with the interests of the corporate elite and its unelected representatives in the executive branch. It was almost a caricature of the liberal ideology. And it was also almost a swan song.

The author of that article was none other than that same Professor Andrew Hacker whom we have already met, in Chapter 1, pronouncing a 1970 funeral oration over the death of America. In under seven years, he moved from the fatuous optimism of "our problems are those of success" to the fatuous pessimism of "America's history is at an end."

Never again, after the assassination, did the liberals pour forth their rapture in quite so artless a song. A far more representative reaction was to see the tragedy in Dallas as a symptom of, and perhaps even a punishment for, some tragic moral flaw in American life.

This was a Puritan reaction, and it was not surprising that Bishop Reuben Mueller, the newly elected president of the National Council of

Churches, should have argued that "fanatical and bigoted agitators . . . did not need to be linked directly with the assassination . . . their attacks on the integrity of our institutions and our leadership can trigger the irresponsible 'mad dog' acts of the Oswalds and the Rubys."

But it was not only churchmen who interpreted the assassination in these terms. Henry Steele Commager, for example, one of the most eminent of American historians, whose book *The American Mind* was a highly patriotic analysis of American thought, described the nation in an article for the Washington *Post* as "beset by division and the spectacle of hatred, and shaken by pervasive guilt." Rejecting easy interpretations—the nearness in time of the frontier, the inheritance of slavery, the wars of the twentieth century—Professor Commager diagnosed "deeply ingrained vanity and arrogance."

Senator Fulbright, who perhaps more than any man in Congress had constantly pointed to the great tradition in American public life, said in a speech: "It may be that the nation as a whole is healthy and strong and entirely without responsibility for the great misfortune that has befallen it. It would be comforting to think so. I for one do not think so. I believe that our society, though in most respects decent, civilized and humane, is not, and never has been, entirely so. Our national life, both past and present, has also been marked by a baleful and incongruous strand of intolerance and violence."

Earl Warren himself, Chief Justice of the United States, and a man as massively American as the redwoods of his native California, spoke strangely similar thoughts on an even more solemn occasion. In his formal eulogy of the dead President he said: "What moved some misguided wretch to do this horrible deed may never be known to us, but we do know that such acts are commonly stimulated by forces of hatred and malevolence, such as today are eating their way into the bloodstream of American life."

Now, there is a sense in which Andrew Hacker was right in saying that the assassination was a freak, and a sense in which Earl Warren's first, intuitive assumption, that it was not, was wrong.

Many months later, the Warren Commission reported that Lee Harvey Oswald had acted alone and not as the agent of any conspiracy. If one accepts that verdict (and I do, because, although the commission was often slipshod in detail and overeager to come up with a reassuring account, nevertheless I find it harder to square with the facts any alternative hypothesis I know of than to accept the commission's version), then Hacker was right in saying the assassination was "unpredictable and unpreventable."

And if, by "forces of hatred and malevolence," Warren meant, as I suspect he did, those forces of the radical Right that were busy plastering the highways of the Southwest with billboards calling for his own impeach- ment, it would seem that he was wrong. His own commission found no ev- idence that Oswald had been influenced by the Right.

In logic, in fact, the case for seeing the assassination as a symptom is weak. No human society has ever been so free from hatred and insanity that it could guarantee to produce no Oswalds. Queen Victoria was well beloved, and her subjects notorious for complacency and phlegm; but she was also lucky that the telescopic sight had not been invented in her life- time: there were half a dozen attempts on her life. There have been politi- cal assassinations in every major democracy in the twentieth century, from placid Britain and non-violent India to Weimar Germany and Third Re- publican France. There were too many political assassinations in America in the sixties: two Kennedys, Medgar Evers, Martin Luther King, Mal- colm X. It may be, again, that some quality of personal drama about American politics, as projected by the media, makes it more likely than elsewhere that some madman or halfwit will develop a psychotic compul- sion to destroy some leader whom he regards as symbolically to blame for his troubles, or simply to make himself famous. Most plausibly of all, it can be argued that there would have been fewer assassinations if the gun laws in the United States were effective enough to prevent potential assas- sins turning their rage into gunshot wounds.

But the wave of anguished national self-examination that followed the assassination was not, in any cause-and-effect sense, logical. It cer- tainly did not proceed from any judgment that the assassination had been literally caused by the prevalence of hatred in the country. It was more that the assassination was a metaphor for the fragility of national self- confidence. It expressed the deep divisions and bitter anger that even those who accepted the soothing myths of the liberal ideology knew at some level of their consciousness to be the darker side of the American in- heritance. In that profounder sense, the Warrens and the Fulbrights and the millions of other Americans who felt that the assassination was not wholly without meaning, were not mistaken. Dallas did present the Ameri- can people with a crisis of legitimacy, and the test of the authenticity of such a crisis is not logic, but feeling.

It was not only the death of a President that was traumatic. The iden- tity of his successor increased the feeling that the legitimacy of the presi- dency itself had been attainted. Under John Kennedy, both the power and the prestige of the institution had reached new heights. The presidency was something more than the central operational mechanism of the nation, something more, even, than the chief emblem of a powerful mood of nationalism. It had become the focus of the aspirations of two groups in particular. And now that Kennedy was gone, his successor was the national target of their fears and their resentment.

One group was the blacks. Kennedy had taken a long time to move on their behalf. But he had moved. The presidency was the one institution that seemed to have the power to coerce those who resisted their demands —in Congress, in state and local governments, in business, in the "power structure" generally. Under Kennedy, the presidency had become for blacks the one institution of white America that might still "come through."

The other group is less easily defined. It consisted of all those who accepted the liberal ideology, and especially its foreign policy. For them, the presidency had become the key institution of the American Government, and Kennedy had become the model of what a President ought to be. He exemplified the centrist ideal of the foreign policy Establishment: rational, restrained, stylish, yet fundamentally cautious, a man who accepted the Cold War verities without any public question, and who bet only on certainties. His handling of the Cuban missile crisis was taken as a final reassurance: he had shown himself both resolutely anti-Communist and unafraid to call the Russians' bluff, yet at the same time temperate in his use of the power that both exhilarated and awed liberal America. That was the way the leader of a great nation ought to behave: the United States was in an imperial mood, and Kennedy was an imperial President.

It wasn't only, or even mainly, the Establishment who liked him, though, or the intellectuals. He was the embodiment of the aspirations of the whole of the new, expanded upper-middle class: of the fellows, someone shrewdly said, who had been junior officers in World War II, of the younger corporate executives, the ones who had been the first in their families to go to graduate school. And that immensely powerful new class included the very people whose help Lyndon Johnson would need to establish himself with the nation: Washington reporters, New York television producers, book publishers, the more influential social scientists, the members of his own federal bureaucracy in Washington.

Perhaps someday a social psychologist will explain exactly why upper-middle-class Americans adored John Kennedy quite as intensely as they did. No doubt, elements of projection, of self-identification, of wish-fulfilling fantasy were all involved. Adore him, in any case, they did, in a way people rarely adore their political leaders. Their hostility to Johnson was therefore heartfelt. It was compounded of grief; of genuine—and, as it turned out, it must be said not wholly illusory—fears of his conservative side, of his simplistic anti-communism, and of his lack of experience in foreign policy; and of other feelings less justifiable and less rational.

Part of it can only be called snobbery. To a remarkable extent, Kennedy's appeal for the group I am discussing had been a class appeal. When such people talked about Kennedy's "manners," "polish," and "style," they meant prep-school manners, Ivy League polish and old-money style. Johnson, conversely, they dismissed as "cornball." (It is an intriguing commentary on the changes in American social attitudes that the connotations of the word "corny," mainly affectionate when "Oklahoma!" was produced, in the middle 1940s, had become mainly contemptuous twenty years later.)

More important than snobbery, however, was the resentment of what was felt as a usurpation.

All the things that had made John Kennedy an idol to his supporters, Lyndon Johnson was not. He was not young. He was not a Catholic. He had not been to Harvard. He was not the darling of the liberals; he could not talk the language of the intellectuals; the young didn't find him sexy. He seemed to look back to an older America. He wore not the cultivated grace of the national elite but the inelegant effectiveness of provincial America: not seersucker but serge.

He had succeeded in circumstances of tragic irony and horror. He took the oath "to perform the duties of the President of the United States" aboard an aircraft that was about to leave his native Texas carrying the body of the man who had been his rival before he became his leader. Symbolically, the fact that he was a Texan counted against him, identified him with the right-wing violence that people instinctively assumed was responsible for Kennedy's death. It was irrational, it was prejudiced. The Johnsons themselves had been spat on by right-wing fanatics in Dallas three years earlier, and John Connally, who represented Texan conservatism far more truly than Lyndon Johnson, had actually been a victim of the same assassin. Yet Johnson's own people felt it. His former aide Harry McPherson, a Texan too, then a Pentagon official, was awakened in the middle of the night in a Tokyo hotel. The President had been shot, the voice said on the phone, in Dallas. "Insane city; insane, wide-eyed, bigoted Dallas bastards," was McPherson's first thought. "A Texan becomes President after Kennedy is killed in Texas. There would be perilous suspicions."

The night of the assassination, Lady Bird Johnson drove home to her house in Spring Valley, on the western edge of the District of Columbia, with her friend Liz Carpenter, executive assistant to her husband.

"It's a terrible thing to say," Mrs. Carpenter said, "but the salvation of Texas is that the Governor was hit."

"Don't think I haven't thought of that," said Mrs. Johnson. "I only wish it could have been me."

A Secret Service agent said that even on the plane from Dallas to Washington "It was undeniably very, very sick, with a great deal of tension between the Kennedy people and the Johnson people."

The plane taxied to a stop at Andrews Air Force Base. A brutal glare of light flooded it. A stunned group of President Kennedy's friends lowered the coffin in a clumsy yellow caterer's lift, taking their orders from the dead man's brother, his face ravaged by controlled rage. Mrs. Kennedy was helped down the steps, still wearing a raspberry suit smeared vermilion with her husband's blood. Only after the gray naval ambulance had gone did the milling crowd of officials, the senators, congressmen, diplomats and reporters notice the tall man waiting quietly at the microphone.

He gave a sort of shiver. He looked gauntly down at his wife for encouragement. His first words were drowned by the roar of a helicopter, whose lights were flashing red, bloodying the scene. Somebody gave an order, and the new President could be heard. "I will do my best," he was saying; "that is all I can do. I ask for your help, and God's."

The great men pressed forward to shake his hand. Slightly apart, with an orange file folder or two under his arm, stood a wiry, fortyish man with thinning blond hair, a noticeably square jaw, and, behind light-rimmed glasses, quite unforgettably cold blue eyes. It was McGeorge Bundy, Kennedy's special assistant for national security affairs. With Robert McNamara, Johnson and Bundy climbed aboard the big army helicopter and flew to the White House lawn. Before they landed, Johnson let both men know that he meant to keep them on in their present jobs, and they sketched out for him the most urgent matters that needed his attention. At that moment, I thought as I watched them take off, power changed hands. At that moment, I now understand, the tragedy of Lyndon Johnson became inevitable.

It was a tragedy in the manner not of Aeschylus, whose heroes are destroyed, in spite of their titanic strength, by the blind, irresistible forces of fate and necessity, but of Shakespeare, whose victims are led on to their destiny by the forces of their own characters. Lyndon Johnson was a man of contradictions: a Southerner, yet one who intuitively understood the black revolution long before many northern politicians did; a Southerner, and at the very same time a Westerner; a man who understood poverty because he had known it, but who belonged also to a little rural oligarchy, a man with politics in his blood, and now also a man of self-made wealth. He was proud, domineering, insecure, persuasive, egotistical, subtle, coarse, sentimental, vindictive, intelligent (though not at all intellectual), insistent upon loyalty (yet capable of the most brutal ingratitude to those who had been loyal to him), needing love (yet not always able to repress upwelling bitterness and anger). Of the three very able and complex men who occupied the White House during the space of this story, he was perhaps the ablest, and surely the most complex. Yet the origins of his tragedy can be traced to two simple characteristics: he was passionately ambitious to be remembered as a great President. And, big and leathery as he looked, he was as sensitive to what others thought about him as a man with no skin.

From the moment when he first gathered his thoughts in the car on the way from Parkland Hospital to Love Field, in Dallas, he had grasped that his first aim must be legitimacy. Characteristically, a sure grasp of the main point was later wrapped in paranoid decorations. Later he persuaded himself that the main reason why his task would be so difficult was because of the invincible prejudice of the North and East against Southerners, and that the main reason for that prejudice, in turn, was the malevolence of the "metropolitan press of the eastern seaboard." Sometimes, too, he blamed "the Kennedys" for not giving him a fair chance, and wondered why they had been given so much credit for so little, and he so little for so much. But that was later. At the time, he saw the problem of legitimacy without illusions:

> Every President has to establish with the various sectors of the country what I call "the right to govern." . . .
> For me, that presented special problems . . . since I had come to the Presidency not through the collective will of the people but in the wake of tragedy. I had no mandate from the voters.

That was how he summed up the issue of legitimacy in his memoirs. In 1963 he seems to have seen it in significantly different terms. On the Monday after the assassination, he met the governors at the White House. It was one in the long series of meetings at which he tried to reassure people, to introduce himself, and to let everyone know where he stood. "This is the time," he told them, "when our whole public system could go awry, not just the Republican Party and the Democratic Party, but the American system of government."

What exactly did he mean? Did he mean that November and December 1963 were the time when things could go awry? Or was 1963 as a whole such a time? In other words, was the assassination itself the crisis? Or was the crisis there already before the assassination?

Johnson was talking to the governors about the civil rights bill. He tried to persuade them that "the nation could not live with racial tensions much longer." And then, as he recalls it, he started thinking aloud:

> "We have hate abroad in the world, hate internationally, hate domestically where a President is assassinated and then they take the law into

their own hands and kill the assassin. That is not our system. We have to do something about that. . . . The roots of hate are poverty and disease and illiteracy, and they are abroad in the land."

At the time, in other words, Lyndon Johnson's intuitive response to the assassination was very similar to that of Chief Justice Warren and Senator Fulbright: that it was not altogether a freak, not a wholly random act, but a sympton and a result of some larger social crisis. As to the nature of that crisis, they drew it very broadly indeed—too broadly: For Johnson it was hate, domestic and international. For Warren it was "new forces of hatred and malevolence" that were "eating into the bloodstream of American life." For Fulbright, with his historian's perspective, it was that "baleful and incongruous stand of intolerance and violence" that was, for him, no new element in American history.

They were right, I think, in their view that the crisis of legitimacy did not arise from the assassination, wrong in supposing that the assassination was a result of the crisis; for the crisis was not moral, but political. No doubt, there are hatred and violence and malevolence in American life, as there are in the life of every other society. But by ascribing the crisis to forces as broad and universal as hate, malevolence, or violence, people— and here the President, the Chief Justice and the Chairman of the Foreign Relations Committee were representative of millions of ordinary citizens— mistook the nature of the specific, historical crisis that had been on its way for some time. With the assassination and the accession of Lyndon Johnson, that crisis now broke in full force.

This was the great crossroads where the themes of this book intersect: the point at which the liberal ideology imposed a weight on the presidency that it could not carry; where the President, in turn, committed the country to two courses of action, which were to divide it until what was called into question was the legitimacy not of Lyndon Johnson but of the presidency, of the liberal ideology, and of almost every assumption and institution in the American system.

Two demands converged in the political system, and above all on the presidency, that they were not able to meet. Each sprang from the ideology of the liberal consensus. One was for limitless social progress: "poverty, disease and illiteracy" must be rooted out, and so must hatred. The other was the demand that the United States "root out hatred" internationally. In the liberals' terms, and in Lyndon Johnson's, that meant a world-wide commitment to resist communism, whether it appeared to threaten in the form of subversion in Latin America or as guerrilla warfare in Indochina. Both demands were to be presented to Lyndon Johnson, as it happened, within forty-eight hours of his accession.

There were times when, with that brooding intuition that those who saw only the tough, outer shell of his character never suspected, Lyndon Johnson understood that there was more to the crisis of legitimacy than the mere establishing of his own "right to govern"—difficult as that seemed in the first few days after the assassination. But he certainly saw no conflict between establishing his legitimacy as President and the demands of the larger task. There were, analytically, four phases to his strategy of self-legitimation: First, he had to calm the immediate panic after the assassination. Second, he meant to stress in every possible way the continuity between the Kennedy administration and his own. Third, he would win re-election in his own right by a margin so crushing that no one would remember or even care how he first came to office. And then he would venture out beyond the New Frontier, slaying the grizzlies that Kennedy had never even faced, and build a Great Society that would also be the perennial monument of a Great President. When one reviews the six furious weeks of his first brilliant political campaign as President, it is not always possible to break things down in that way—to say, "That was for the short term," or "That was politics for 1964." With daemonic energy, and surefooted tact, he called up a lifetime's knowledge of where the levers of power lay in Congress, and nudged them into the combination he wanted. When he disarmed Everett Dirksen by appealing to that sentimental old play-actor's patriotism, or softened the rancorous partisanship of Republican House leader Charlie Halleck by asking him to breakfast and serving *thick* bacon, "just the kind a fellow from Indiana would like," such touches served every purpose. They gave immediate reassurance that the country was in strong and skillful hands. They helped the passage of the Kennedy legislative program. They advanced the electoral fortunes of Lyndon Baines Johnson. And they were good for the country as he saw it.

Those who watched Lyndon Johnson in operation in his days as majority leader in the Senate used to joke about what was known as "the Johnson treatment." A legislator whose vote was needed would find himself literally surrounded by a one-man army of Lyndon Johnson. His birthday would be remembered, his vanity flattered, his shoulder squeezed. He would be reminded, subtly or brutally according to the estimate made of his temperament, of his political problems at home or of his hopes of advancement on Capitol Hill. Every scrap of information would be retrieved, every tactic used, until the wretched man did what was wanted of him; then he would be overwhelmed by signs of the majority leader's gratitude and admiration.

In the first six weeks after the assassination, the United States of America and a good part of the inhabited earth were given the Johnson treatment. A lifetime of knowledge was brought to bear, and a lifetime of debts called in. One of the first priorities was to set up the Warren Commission, its membership a masterpiece of the art of the balanced ticket: perhaps only Lyndon Johnson could have persuaded both Senator Russell and Chief Justice Warren, against their better judgment, to sit on it side by side. Almost equally urgent was the need to keep some at least of the Kennedy staff working for him: he told Arthur Schlesinger, only half in jest, that he would have him arrested if he didn't withdraw a letter of resignation. He saw Eisenhower, consulted Truman, talked with Meany and Reuther, kept his temper with De Gaulle, and wrote a dignified and conciliatory letter to Khrushchev, all within hours of the assassination.

He grasped the essentials of the politics of the tax cut, understood that it could not be passed unless it was combined with cuts in expenditure, and was convinced that it was worth going through the motions of cutting the budget if that was what was needed to produce a deficit that would stimulate the economy. "I understand," he told Walter Heller as the economist was spelling this argument out to him; "I always trade nickels for dimes."

He confounded those who thought that, because he was a Southerner, he would compromise away the guts of the civil rights bill. Such suspicions were ill-informed. Johnson had long shown great understanding of the civil rights movement. He had constantly pushed Kennedy to take it more seriously than he was doing. His speech at Gettysburg on May 30, 1963, went a good deal further than Kennedy had yet gone: "We do not answer those who lie beneath this soil—when we reply to the Negro by asking, 'Patience.'" They were understandable suspicions, given Johnson's Texas background and his often equivocal behavior under the pressures of Congressional expediency. Martin Luther King knew better, though. "As a Southerner," he said as he came out of his first meeting with the new President, "I am happy to know that a fellow Southerner is in the White House who is concerned about civil rights." And so did Senator Richard Russell, commanding general of the southern resistance. "The way that fellow operates," said the senator, "he means business. He'll get the whole bill." And he did.

The one driving purpose behind Johnson's tireless activity was the building of a consensus. That was the word he used. The idea of consensus, he complained in his memoirs, had been much misunderstood. It did not mean a mere "search for the lowest common denominator." To Johnson, it meant convincing the nation that "the time for positive action had come."

What kind of action? What kind of consensus? All the imperatives of Johnson's search for legitimacy dictated that he must take liberal actions;

it had to be a liberal consensus. He had to reassure the nation, and the world, that he was no Neanderthal Texas conservative. He needed to prove that he was free from the faintest trace of southern reluctance on civil rights. It was already clear that the Republicans would nominate Barry Goldwater; that left the liberal center open. To the Kennedy supporters and loyalists, Johnson must prove that he was no usurper, but as good a liberal as Kennedy—an ironic requirement, since in many respects he had perhaps always been a better one. Lastly, to the foreign policy community, including powerful members of his own administration, he must show that he was as good an "internationalist" as Kennedy, that he could be trusted to bear the burdens of "world responsibility."

That was why, when he turned away from the microphone that bleak evening at Andrews Air Force Base and climbed into the helicopter with McGeorge Bundy and Robert McNamara, the wheels of his presidential tragedy began to turn. For those two men symbolized—more than symbolized, would vocally represent—the tradition in which he must now establish his credentials. He must be more royalist than the King, more of a Kennedy than Kennedy himself.

It is unlikely that, in the blur of those first hours, all those meetings, speeches, telephone conversations, Lyndon Johnson fully appreciated it. But within forty-eight hours he had taken the two decisions that led to the dilemma that ultimately destroyed the consensus, and in so doing revealed the fatal weakness of the liberal ideology on which it was founded. Before Kennedy was buried, Johnson had committed himself to what became the War on Poverty. And he had turned down what may have been the last easy opportunity to end the war in Vietnam.

Before his death, Kennedy had been committed to asking Congress to pass a major piece of antipoverty legislation. In December 1962 he said to Walter Heller, the chairman of his Council of Economic Advisers, "Now, look; I want to go beyond the things that have already been accomplished. Give me the facts and figures on the things we still have to do. For example, what about the poverty problem in the United States?"

Heller set about getting the facts and figures. He put an economist called Robert Lampman, from the University of Wisconsin, to work on a memo which was finished in May 1963. Contrary to what most people assumed, Lampman showed, there were still a great many poor people in the United States, and the number of them was not declining but growing.

Kennedy read the memo. He had already read—that was perhaps what prompted his original interest—an article in *The New Yorker* by Dwight Macdonald that summed up the revelations in a newly published book by the socialist writer Michael Harrington, *The Other America.*

While America worried about the problems of affluence, said Harrington, between 40 and 50 million Americans were poor by any standards. Kennedy read Harrington, he read a paper by the economist Leon Keyserling —and he read an article in the New York *Herald Tribune* that hinted that the Republicans were planning to make poverty an issue in the 1964 presidential campaign. The President was definitely getting interested in poverty.

On October 29, Heller sent around the government a memo, prepared by his staff, on "the poverty cycle." There was no magic place at which the cycle could be broken, the paper argued. Instead, it recommended a three-pronged attack at 1) stopping people becoming poor in the first place, 2) rehabilitating those caught in the cycle, and 3) making life easier for those who could not be helped by rehabilitation to help themselves out of poverty. The next day, Heller was able to report that the President had asked to be sent, for his consideration, "a set of measures which might be woven into a basic attack on the problems of poverty and waste of human resources, as part of the 1964 legislative program."

On November 19, Heller asked Kennedy if antipoverty measures would be included in that package. "Yes," said Kennedy flatly, and asked for the proposals to be ready within two weeks.

All day on Saturday, November 23, a stream of visitors poured in and out of Lyndon Johnson's office. It wasn't until seven-forty that evening that Walter Heller got in to see him. Much of what he had to say seems to have been news to Johnson: that poverty was far more extensive than most people understood, that Kennedy had asked the different agencies of the federal government to come up with ideas for doing something about it, that three days before he was killed, President Kennedy had given Heller the go-ahead but without specifying any particular measures.

Johnson, he remembered later, looked out the window, and said, "I'm interested. I'm sympathetic. Go ahead. Give it the highest priority. Push ahead full tilt."

Walter Heller's recollection is almost identical. "That's my kind of program," he remembers Johnson saying. "Move full speed ahead."

Heller and Kermit Gordon, the director of the Bureau of the Budget, went down to the LBJ Ranch at Christmas, and there, on the kitchen table, began to work out the shape of a legislative program to attack poverty. In the meantime, one of Gordon's assistants, Bill Cannon, had contributed a fateful idea. It was not original with him; it was, in fact, fashionable among social scientists. But it was new to government thinking about poverty. The key to success, Cannon argued, would be to involve the poor themselves in decisions about efforts to help them, through what he called "community action."

Not all those the President talked to were enthusiastic. His conservative friends from Texas grumbled that what the poor wanted was a bit more hard work. But it was a relatively liberal Texan, the President's favorite free-lance speechwriter, sandy-haired Horace Busby, who gave the most prescient warning: Beware of the effects of a poverty program on "the American in the middle—the man who earns $3,000 to $9,000," he wrote.

> America's real majority is suffering a minority complex of neglect. They have become the real foes of Negro rights, foreign aid, etc., because, as much as anything, they feel forgotten, at the second table behind the tightly organized, smaller groups at either end of the U.S. spectrum.

Lyndon Johnson could see that danger, of course. In normal times, he would have been the first to protect that flank. But this was no normal time. This was his supreme test. He would show that Lyndon Johnson was not behind any rich man's son like Jack Kennedy when it came to caring about the poor. To do something about poverty appealed to his populist emotions. It suited his political purposes. It matched his ambitions for America. What prouder boast than to be able to say, as he did say when he signed the Economic Opportunity Act, on August 20, 1964: "Today, for the first time in all the history of the human race, a great nation is able to make, and is willing to make, a commitment to eradicate poverty."

It was one of Kennedy's men, just the same, who supplied the label for this tempting package. On January 8, in the State of the Union message, Johnson used a phrase contributed by Richard N. Goodwin. "This administration," he said, "today, here and now, declares unconditional war on poverty in America."

On the plane back from Dallas, Lyndon Johnson remembered afterward, he made "a solemn private vow" that for the remainder of John Kennedy's term of office he would try to do everything that Kennedy would have wanted to do. "That meant seeing things through in Vietnam," he added. The next morning, he had his first secret briefing on the state of the world. It was administered in McGeorge Bundy's office in the basement of the West Wing of the White House by John McCone, the director of the CIA. Two secretaries were openly in tears for John Kennedy as Johnson listened and asked a few questions. "Only South Vietnam," he later recalled, "gave me real cause for alarm." And the day after that, Sunday, November 24, he first came face to face as President with the reality of the situation in Vietnam at a meeting with the U.S. ambassador in Saigon, Henry Cabot Lodge.

Lodge had arrived in Saigon himself, just three months earlier, at the severest moment of crisis to date in the history of the effort to save South

Vietnam from communism. The regime of President Diem was locked in political conflict with the Buddhists, who represented not so much a religious community as a political movement of an equivocal kind, not Communist, certainly, but perhaps not adequately anti-Communist to worried American official eyes either. For months, American policy had rotated around a stale dilemma. Diem's government was corrupt, repressive and ineffective. But would the Buddhists be any better?

The week Lodge arrived in Saigon, Diem's brother and security boss changed all the terms of the game with one arrogant, overreaching mistake. He sent in his Special Forces, American-trained and paid for out of American aid, to sack Buddhist pagodas and rough up Buddhist bonzes all over South Vietnam. To add insult to injury, he pretended the Army had done it. This was the last straw for the generals. Already, as early as mid-July, the CIA's Saigon station had picked up rumors of a military coup. Now, in August, two separate officers contacted CIA agents and asked: if there was a coup, what would the U.S. attitude be?

Kennedy had chosen Henry Cabot Lodge because the U.S. missions in Saigon were riddled with faction and mistrust. They needed a man with independent standing and authority to give them a clear lead. Then again, by appointing a former Republican vice-presidential candidate, the dangerous issue of Vietnam might be kept out of presidential politics in 1964. "You have sent us a proconsul," said Madame Nhu when the appointment was announced. There was more truth in that than in most things the Dragon Lady said. Aristocratic, confident and aloof, Lodge immediately showed himself a masterful and crafty hand at the murderous game they were playing in Saigon that summer. He made up his mind that the war could not be won with Diem. Steadily he applied himself to stimulating a coup in Saigon, and patiently he reassured his masters in Washington—the President, Bundy, Dean Rusk—that it was in their interest to let a coup take place, perhaps to help it, just a little bit, around the edges.

August came and went, and then September, and still no coup. The situation became more and more tortuous. There were bluffs and double bluffs, provocations and rumors of betrayal. Lodge was due to fly back to Washington for routine consultations on October 30. (That was the day Walter Heller sent around his request for ideas to be woven into an anti-poverty program. Twin plots were gathering momentum, neck and neck.) At the last moment, warned that if he left Saigon, General Harkins, the head of the military aid command (MACV) and an advocate of giving Diem just one more chance, would be in charge of the mission, Lodge canceled his journey.

The coup took place on November 1. At 4:30 that afternoon, Diem telephoned Lodge from the presidential palace.

"Some units have made a rebellion," he said, "and I want to know what is the attitude of the U.S."

"I do not feel well enough informed to be able to tell you," said Lodge, the great New England gentleman. He had indirectly helped to plan the coup. He had supplied it with military intelligence. At that moment, he had a CIA agent, the legendary Colonel Lucien Conein, at the generals' headquarters, keeping him in touch minute by minute. He had discussed every nuance of the U.S. attitude, including what to say to Diem if he called up for help, in long cables, the last of them less than forty-eight hours before, to that other great New England gentleman McGeorge Bundy.

Lodge went on to compliment Diem on his courage, and to express, twice, his concern about his physical safety. The concern was not misplaced. Before dawn, Diem and Nhu had surrendered to the generals and been shot in the back of an armored vehicle on their orders.

On November 10, Lodge planned to reschedule his delayed meeting with President Kennedy, but it was remembered that most of the Cabinet was due in Tokyo for talks with the Japanese Government later that month. A conference was set up for November 20 in Honolulu. Rusk, McNamara, Bundy, General Maxwell Taylor (chairman of the Joint Chiefs of Staff), were there from Washington, and Lodge brought the whole of his "country team" from Saigon. Lodge was then to fly to Washington to see the President. He had got as far as San Francisco when he heard the news from Dallas.

Lyndon Johnson told him to come on anyway. They ought to talk. Johnson had disagreed with Lodge about the coup. He had met Diem, thought him the right kind of anti-Communist, had once even called him "the Winston Churchill of Asia." In any case, for Johnson, coups were a messy way of doing business. When they met, on Sunday afternoon, Johnson told Lodge as much. Still, he went on to say, all that was behind us. We must think of the future. And then he said something that showed he was also thinking of the past.

"I am not going to lose Vietnam," he said. "I am not going to be the President who saw Southeast Asia go the way China went."

The fateful decision had been taken. On the basis of the meeting with Lodge, and of the Honolulu conference, a national security action memorandum, NSAM 273, was drawn up to formalize policy. The purpose of the American involvement in Vietnam, it declared, was "to assist the people and Government of that country to win their contest against the externally directed and supported Communist conspiracy." It also requested plans for clandestine operations by South Vietnamese forces against North Vietnam. And finally it directed the State Department to produce a documented case "to demonstrate to the world the degree to which the Viet Cong is controlled, directed and supplied by Hanoi."

And so two chances were lost. The first had been that Kennedy, although he had made the commitment, although he shared the anti-Communist assumptions of Establishment policy, although he gave no sign of understanding the vast misapprehensions on which those assumptions were based, might have thought better of it. He was cautious, he was skeptical, he was pragmatic, and, after the Cuban missile crisis, his new confidence might have allowed him to cool it. That chance was lost on November 22.

The second chance was that the succession of Lyndon Johnson might have made it possible to reverse the direction of policy, and so to avoid the great mistake. After all, the government the United States had supported for eight years in Saigon had now fallen. Kennedy's policy was in ruins. And over the next few weeks, now that the terror of Nhu's secret police had been removed, new information was coming out about just how badly the war was going, how cruel and arbitrary a government the United States had been supporting in the name of democracy, how totally the strategic-hamlets program, on which U.S. hopes of winning the war depended, had collapsed.

A new President, confronting this new situation, could have decided, right at the start, before his personal prestige was committed, to cut his losses and get out. Given that the new President was Lyndon Johnson, with all the personal freight of ambition and insecurity that he brought to the office; given his imperative to show himself Kennedy's rightful heir; given the memory of China and Korea for his generation; given the empire that the illusion of omnipotence had over their minds—given all these realities, there was never more than the slimmest of chances, and it was gone by November 26, the day the decision to soldier on was set out in NSAM 273.

That particular formula was to be short-lived as a statement of policy. As the anonymous author of the relevant section of the Pentagon Papers was to write, "It was simply overtaken by events." No subsequent statement, however, was to dissent from the assumptions on which it was based. And so it marked one of the moments of decision both for Lyndon Johnson and for the United States.

Many years later, Daniel Ellsberg (who at the time of Johnson's fateful decision was still untroubled by doubts, a zealous laborer in the Pentagon vineyard) was to propound what he called Rule Number One of Vietnam policy. This was the principle, he argued, that in the last analysis three Presidents before Johnson—Truman, Eisenhower and Kennedy—had all obeyed. It was this: _"Do not_ lose South Vietnam to Communist control—or appear likely to do so—before the next election."

But the instinct of American Cold War policy had always been resolution tempered by moderation, and so there was also a second rule:

> _Do not,_ unless essential to satisfy Rule I . . .
> a. bomb South Vietnam or Laos;
> b. bomb North Vietnam;
> c. commit U.S. combat troops to Vietnam. . . .

Now Lyndon Johnson was the fourth President to yield to the force of Rule Number One. It would not be long before he discovered that he would have to choose between the first rule and the second. In the process, the nation would discover that, just as the black revolt had revealed the inconsistency between the ideals and the practice of American society, so events in Indochina, of all obscure, unlikely, peripheral places, would bring the foreign policy of the liberal consensus in conflict with the principles of the American creed.

# 9

## Black Uprising

What started as an identity crisis for Negroes turned out to be an identity crisis for the nation.

Howard Zinn, *The New Abolitionists*

We cannot be free until they are free.

James Baldwin, *The Fire Next Time*

In two hectic years, from the summer of 1963 to the summer of 1965, the momentum of events transformed the black uprising from a protest movement into a rebellion. Sweeping away the optimistic assumptions of the liberal consensus, it set processes in motion that reached into every corner of the country.

At the time of the March on Washington, in August 1963, the civil rights movement was still seen as the culminating affirmation of the liberal faith. It seemed to be not a bulldozer, flattening old structures so that something new could rise in their place, but just one of the garbage trucks of history, tidying away some ugly residual debris.

Its target then was the vestiges of legal segregation in the South. Its effect, people assumed, would be to bring a backward region in line with the American norm. Its philosophy and tactics, being non-violent, did not seem threatening. There was nothing in the movement's ideas, at that stage, that contradicted liberal orthodoxy, and its aims were championed by the whole breadth of the liberal consensus: White House, labor, churches, intellectuals, and the more modern-minded sectors of business. Its goal was to integrate black people more closely into white society. In the fall of 1963, it was still generally thought that this could be done without changing white society, as a consequence, in any major way.

By the time of the Watts riot, just under two years after the March on Washington, the rising was taking forms with which few liberals could sympathize. Four days after the riot, Martin Luther King was walking through the smoke-blackened streets of south-central Los Angeles with Bayard Rustin, the organizer of the march. They were accosted by a group of young blacks who boasted simply, "We won."

"How can you say you won," King asked them, "when thirty-four Negroes are dead, your community is destroyed, and whites are using the riot as an excuse for inaction?"

"We won," was the answer, "because we made them pay attention to us."

The battlefield had shifted, from the remote corners of the rural South to the centers of the greatest cities in the land. New black forces were making themselves felt. These were not whole communities welded together under the middle-class leadership of preachers like Dr. King. They were crowds. They came together in the flick of an eyelid after some random brush between the police and people from the angry streets. Their leaders were simply the boldest and the angriest people on hand. Instead of prayer, their characteristic language was the shrill, repetitive obscenity of the slums. And as the Molotov cocktails of Watts showed, neither their philosophy nor their tactics were non-violent.

In the South—it was a commonplace to say in 1965—the problems that blacks faced were legal and constitutional; in the North they were social and economic. The distinction was a rough-and-ready one, at best. It ignored the economic oppression of southern blacks and the precarious civil liberties of the northern ghettoes. While many saw that it might be harder to "solve the problems" of the northern cities, few blacks and scarcely any whites understood the full implications of the different situations.

In the South, for one thing, blacks were attempting to destroy a system that was already on the defensive. It not only offended the conscience of the nation, and the Constitution; it was also repugnant to influential groups inside the South. The situation in the North, on the other hand, was imperfectly understood. If any effort were to be made to improve the economic opportunities of ghetto blacks, some of the strongest interests in society—those of the real estate industry and of the craft unions, to name only two—would have to be infringed.

In the South, blacks were asking for things that whites, however reluc-tant, could give them. Where blacks were denied the right to vote, were legally obliged to go to segregated schools, or were excluded from public accommodations, then the law could provide redress. In the North, the operation of racism could be measured not by legal prohibitions but by very much lower statistical chances that blacks would enjoy in practice advantages to which in theory no one denied their equal right. To alter those chances, to achieve real equality of opportunity for blacks to get good jobs, good education, good housing, let alone to achieve anything approaching statistical equality of condition, might involve far more radical and complex forms of political and social action than were needed to abolish the formal traces of segregation in the South. And that had not been easy.

Things did change, and with remarkable speed. The federal government did move to positions that would have been unthinkably radical only a few years before. The poverty program is an example. The billions of federal money poured into compensatory education add up to another. The high-water mark of the liberal commitment to achieving social equality for black people came on June 4, 1965, at Howard University, in Washington. The standard President Johnson proposed there was not mere equality of opportunity but equality of condition: "not equality as a right and a theory, but equality as a fact and a result." The clear implication of that standard was that, to reach that result, the federal government and the other institutions of society must go beyond equality in their treatment of a historically disadvantaged minority. They must accept the principle of compensation.

That the quest for equality in the North would be even harder than the destruction of segregation in the South; that imaginative, radical strategies involving the spending of billions of dollars would be needed in a hurry; that government might have to discriminate in favor of black people—this was a great deal for people to have to learn in the brief years of the crisis, and even more for government to accept as the basis of policy. Yet, by 1965, the government had accepted it all. If the liberal policies failed, it was because they had failed to comprehend two even deeper and more paradoxical implications of the new crisis in the cities of the North.

There were clues to both of them in the brief exchange between Dr. King and the young rebels of Watts.

The first was that in the new phase of the black uprising, even more than in the civil rights phase, the motivation was at bottom neither political nor material; it was psychological. Of course, the inhabitants of Watts and of Harlem and North Philadelphia and the South Side of Chicago, wanted higher incomes and better housing and political power, but what they wanted even more, what they meant to have, was the attention and the respect of white people. It was no longer a matter of what whites could be persuaded to concede, if they were carefully not given an "excuse for inaction." That was what a group of boys on a shattered street corner understood better than the Nobel prizewinner. It was a question now of what degree of attention the angry young blacks of the northern ghettoes, and the educated blacks who now followed them, would demand.

It was a question of how much they could make white people respect them, and therefore also a question of self-respect. It was, in the word that was beginning to be used, a question of "consciousness."

In the process of achieving their own self-respect, the new wave of militant blacks made a discovery that had eluded men as wise as King and as lucid as Rustin. They found they could successfully demand the degree of attention that would be needed, in the estimation of white liberals in the federal government, in city hall, in the media, the universities and the foundations, to prevent them from expressing their anger. It was not the expression of their anger, they discovered, that frightened the liberals; it was the anger itself.

They had inadvertently exposed the secret fears of the white liberals: their fear of discovering that their own optimism might be unjustified; that their prescriptions for solving social problems might after all not work; and that racism might turn out to be not a relic of the past or a peculiarity of the South but a danger that could engulf metropolitan America itself. The result of this discovery was that the initiative passed temporarily from whites to blacks, and from those blacks who were most acceptable to whites to those who were most intransigent.

The shrill voices of the ghetto had somehow turned things inside out. In the civil rights movement, black people had been insisting that they were fit to be integrated into American society. Suddenly, they were asking whether American society was fit for them.

In 1964 and 1965, things moved so fast that the southern civil rights movement was almost forgotten. From the perspective of the later sixties, those nightly pictures in the living room were remembered almost like the stilted tableaux of a medieval morality play. Heroic virtue (clergymen, women, children) was put to the test of martyrdom by a series of Gothic villains ("Bull" Connor of Birmingham, "Hoss" Manoly of St. Augustine, Big Jim Clark of Selma). The civil rights movement came to be thought of as simple, united, tame, provincial and irrelevant.

It was none of those things. As in a Flemish primitive painting, what look like stilted groups dissolve on close inspection into spirited conflict: between blacks and whites, Northerners and Southerners, preachers and revolutionaries, black bourgeoisie and black proletariat, the children of privilege and the wretched of the earth. The pressure of near-revolutionary situations relentlessly exposed the divergence of interests that had seemed to be in harmony and the limits of commitments that had looked firm. In the end, they raised more and more searching questions about the underlying values of the liberal system.

The discrediting of any intellectual hypothesis usually begins with the discovery that it does not predict all the observable data. The first discovery the civil rights movement made was that the liberal account of American society simply did not predict what would happen in the Mississippi Delta or the Alabama Black Belt or southwestern Georgia. The more resounding generalities about democracy or abundance, for example, could not be recited in, say, Gee's Bend, Alabama, without provoking derisive laughter.

A second discovery went further. It wasn't only local institutions that didn't fit the theory; national institutions didn't either, when they had to confront the reality of the Deep South. Neither the decisions of the Supreme Court, for example, nor federal statutes were in practice effectively binding there. The FBI couldn't, or wouldn't, operate as a police force to protect civil rights workers, though it had no difficulty in arresting them on charges of illegal picketing. And the same turned out to be true of private institutions. National TV networks might take liberal positions, but their local affiliates continued to pump out segregationist propaganda. U. S. Steel might be willing to hire blacks for jobs in Pittsburgh or Gary that its subsidiary Tennessee Coal and Iron, in Birmingham, refused to hire them for. There were segregated locals in the South of the very unions that contributed money to civil rights organizations in New York.

And so, while northern liberals generally continued to believe that it was only a matter of time before the lamentable anomalies of southern life were brought into line with the national norm, the civil rights movement moved onto a third level of disillusionment. There gradually dawned on precisely those who were most committed to the cause of equality an appalling alternative explanation: that southern police, southern jails, southern institutions and southern racism might be not medieval extravagancies doomed to be reformed by the march of progress but mere variants of American police, American jails, American institutions and American racism.

To the young, white, upper-middle-class idealists in the movement, this discovery was especially traumatic. They had been assured by their parents, their teachers, the textbooks they studied, the newspapers they read, and the politicians they admired, that certain things didn't happen in America. Yet when they went South they saw these things with their own eyes, and sometimes felt them with their own bodies. Everyone in America, they had been told, had the right to register and vote. Murderers, they supposed, went to jail. Yet the man who killed Medgar Evers was to be seen treating his friends in the pleasanter bars of Greenwood, Mississippi: it was the people who tried to register and vote, and those who helped them, who were in jail.

There was naïveté in this reaction, no doubt, and even a touch of hy-

pocrisy. As Southerners never tired of pointing out, these young people
were more attuned to seeing evil in Mississippi than in Manhattan. But
that did not diminish the impact of the shock. It is no accident that the
origins of much of the political and cultural radicalism among young people in the later sixties can be traced to the eight hundred or so students
who went South to work for civil rights.

And so the civil rights movement had two faces: a public face of victory and a private face of disillusionment. The movement did play a decisive part in bringing about the passage of the Civil Rights Act of 1964 and
the Voting Rights Act of 1965. The successes of the Second Reconstruction were real. That was what the distant and the casual observer noticed. But those who were most directly involved had expected most, and
it was they who were the most disillusioned.

There had been a stirring in the airless world of the southern Negro
ever since the end of World War II. The new mood was compounded of
hope and discontent: hope, intensified after the Supreme Court's decision in *Brown*, because segregation seemed doomed; discontent, because it
was still the rule.

On December 1, 1955, Rosa Parks refused to move to the back of a
Montgomery bus. The young Martin Luther King had just come back
South from graduate school in Boston and had taken over his first church,
in Montgomery. In one of his characteristic phrases, he interpreted for
Mrs. Parks: she was "anchored to her seat by the accumulated indignities
of days gone by, and by the boundless aspirations of generations yet un-
born."

Mass nonviolent action for civil rights began in Montgomery. Still, it
was an isolated episode and might have had no significant results. In the
next three years, King grew in stature and wisdom. He visited India to
study *satyagraha* with the disciples of Gandhi, and he thought a good deal
about how this philosophy and technique of nonviolence could be applied
in America. He was becoming nationally known. But he had actually *done*
very little when, on February 1, 1960, Ezell Blair, Jr., Joseph McNeill,
David Richmond and Franklin McClain, four freshmen at North Carolina Agricultural and Technical College, sat down at the lunch counter of
Woolworth's in Greensboro, North Carolina, asked for a cup of coffee,
were refused it, and stayed right where they were.

"The waitress looked at me," Blair told me, "as if I were from outer
space."

Before they decided to act, Blair and McNeill had talked over carefully what they intended to do. They didn't know until later that the sit-in
technique had been used before, with indifferent success, both by the

Congress of Racial Equality (CORE) in the 1940s and more recently by youth branches of the National Association for the Advancement of Colored People (NAACP). They had read a comic book about the Montgomery boycott published by the Fellowship of Reconciliation, a northern pacifist group founded by the Christian socialist A. J. Muste. And they had also read a pamphlet by George House, one of the founders of CORE. So while their action was spontaneous, it was influenced by both northern ethical radicalism and the new, southern mass upheaval.

Within hours of the sit-in, local black leaders contacted CORE in New York, not the NAACP. Several representatives of CORE left immediately for Greensboro. Next, Martin Luther King arrived to speak. Only in third place, several days after CORE's response, did the NAACP respond. It sent its youth secretary, Herbert Wright; ironically, he was one of those who had pioneered the sit-in years earlier.

These responses were not an unfair illustration of the three organizations' contrasting styles.

CORE then was eagerly radical, interracial, and impatient to try out in the field the techniques of activist pacifism. It was northern-based, but it was beginning to attract radical-minded black professionals of the generation immediately older than the sit-ins: such men as Floyd McKissick, who arrived in Greensboro a few hours after the first sit-in.

The Southern Christian Leadership Conference (SCLC) was more slow-moving. Its strength lay in the unflinching support of the churchgoing middle-class and working-class blacks of the Deep South. Its principal weapon was the oratorical firepower of its preacher-leaders, such as Rev. Fred Shuttlesworth in Birmingham, Rev. Ralph Abernathy in Atlanta, and above all, Martin Luther King.

The NAACP's position and style are far harder to describe justly. It was the most venerable of black organizations, and the most powerful. With well over a thousand branches, it maintained some sort of presence wherever in the United States there were black people. With a membership of three hundred thousand, it was financially independent of white charity. That was to prove very useful.

Under Walter White, it had campaigned bravely and effectively against lynching in the 1930s. In the 1940s, under Charles Houston, James Nabrit and Thurgood Marshall, it had launched the legal siege of segregation that had culminated in the *Brown* victory. Its history, its resources, and the people working for it made the NAACP *the* national Negro organization.

Yet it was failing to rise to its great opportunity. The national board, especially, with autocratic power over the annual convention and the branches, was gradualist and cautious in a situation that called for flexibility of policy, speed of judgment, and daring in action.

The achievement of open enrollment in the New York high schools to black students in 1962 was an example.* Percy Sutton, then president of the Harlem branch of the NAACP (and later borough president of Manhattan), called in an independent attorney, Paul Zuber, to fight the case when the NAACP seemed not to be acting with enough speed or determination. For half a century, the NAACP had worked for a new day. Now it was dawning, and the NAACP was finding it hard to get out of bed.

In the first two weeks after Greensboro, there were sit-ins in fifteen other southern cities. By April, that number had risen to seventy-eight. By the end of the year, fifty thousand people had taken part in demonstrations. Three thousand, six hundred had gone to jail. At long last, spontaneously, the black people of the South had risen up. Their immediate target had been the pettiest of the restrictions that hemmed in their lives, the taboo against eating together with white people in public. They had been led in this revolt not by the NAACP or by Martin Luther King, and still less by the northern agitators of segregationist imagining; they had been led by their own teen-age children.

A number of unnoticed social changes had probably done more to prepare this moment than the more obvious powder train of political events. The combined effect of increased black enrollment in higher education and of the black migration to the North had brought into existence, for the first time, a large body of young blacks who could look forward to living outside the walls of southern segregation. Some were still in the South, concentrated in segregated colleges. There, racial politics were the main focus of intellectual interest, idealism and ambition. In the North, on the other hand, the very isolation of black students increased their feeling of solidarity. The great majority of black students were the first in their families to go to college. They were therefore the first generation to be aware of the full contradiction between the theory and the practice of liberal America.

The news from Greensboro hit this whole generation with a double impact. It offered a hope of what might be done. And it came as a reproach to those who were not doing it.

The Greensboro sit-in led to the foundation of the Student Non-

* See Louis E. Lomax, The Negro Revolt, pp. 170ff. Previously, students from Harlem, then a large majority of black students in New York, had a choice between two high schools, where, says Lomax, "the concentration of Negro high school students . . . constituted a kind of segregated schooling."

violent Coordinating Committee (SNCC) in the most direct way. Many of those who were to be its leaders, including Robert Moses and Julian Bond, said later that watching the Greensboro sit-in on television changed their lives. And yet, in another sense, it was an accident that a separate youth movement for civil rights ever grew up outside the three existing organizations: the accident that a single person was determined that it should be so. Both CORE and SCLC did their best to harness student commitment to their own organizations. The person who frustrated their ambitions was Ella Baker, a woman in her fifties who had worked for civil rights organizations all her life. Her position was anomalous. She was the executive director of SCLC. But she was determined that the young people should be free to act as they wanted.

She arranged for a conference of youth leaders at her own alma mater, Shaw College, in Raleigh, North Carolina, over Easter weekend, 1960, and she raised eight hundred dollars to pay for its expenses.

SNCC's first office was a corner of SCLC's office in Atlanta. To begin with, it was very much an offshoot of King's movement. There was a strong flavor of the Protestant ministry about both organizations. Many of the early SNCC volunteers were theology students. And at that first meeting at Shaw College they adopted a statement of purpose redolent of King's beliefs and King's rhetoric:

> We affirm the philosophical or religious ideal of nonviolence as the foundation of our purpose, the presupposition of our faith, and the manner of our action. Nonviolence as it grows from the Judaic-Christian tradition seeks a social order of justice permeated by love. . . . The redemptive community supersedes systems of gross social immorality.

SNCC was never a membership organization. It was always an elite group. About two hundred people came to that first conference in Raleigh, and at the height of its activity there were no more than a hundred fifty SNCC staff workers in the field in the whole of the South. If it was an elite, though, it was anything but elitist. It is true that many of the white volunteers came from upper-middle-class families and from famous northern colleges. But they were always a small minority. Four fifths of the staff were black. And most of those came from working-class families. (There was a small but totally tenacious and committed group of white Southerners, men and women.)

In the early days, SNCC tended to be dominated by recruits from two centers. There was the "Nashville group," from Fisk, Vanderbilt and the theological seminary there: Rev. James Lawson, Rev. C. T. Vivian, Rev. James Bevel, Diane Nash (who became Bevel's wife), Marion Barry, now president of the school board in Washington, D. C., and John Lewis.

And there was the "Atlanta group," mostly from the component colleges of Atlanta University, in which Julian Bond was outstanding. The Nashville group, in particular, was committed to nonviolence not merely as a tactic but as a Christian philosophy of ethics. Later, field secretaries were recruited from the various places where SNCC operated, and the influence of these two original groups was diluted. And later, too, the more radical, irreverent influence of the "Northerners" increased. They were black students from northern colleges; pre-eminent among them was the Nonviolent Action Group from Howard University, in Washington, led by Courtland Cox and Stokely Carmichael.

In the early sixties it was the fashion in the media to paint SNCC as an ineffective and even counterproductive group, spoiling the chances of "progress" by their "irresponsible" militancy. Rowland Evans and Robert Novak, in particular, used to write a recurrent column to this effect, seasoned with discreet innuendo about Communist influence. Because of their skill at public relations, the consensus held, the SNCC kids got more attention than they deserved.

It is clear, in retrospect, that the opposite was the case. The SNCC style, and the conclusions that its members reached in the crucible of their experience, were so unwelcome to the liberal mind that SNCC in fact got far less attention than it deserved.

For this handful of young civil rights guerrillas, black and white, young women as well as young men, were engaged in a task even more important than that of destroying racism in the Deep South. They were improvising a style and defining an ethic for a generation. In the process of dispersion, both the ethic and the style were to be distorted, diluted, corrupted, commercialized, vulgarized and plain misunderstood. Nevertheless, they changed America. Not in the way they set out to change it, but, in the end, perhaps in even more important ways.

It proved a little harder than the founders of SNCC had supposed to make the "redemptive community" supersede "systems of gross social immorality." But in their failure they discovered something that, ironically enough, their white southern enemies had been the only group in the United States to acknowledge: that success is not the only test, that since, in the end, failure is the fate of most human endeavors, what matters is with what enterprise and in what spirit one fails. For an ethic of success, they substituted an ethic of honesty and courage. Their style was not by results but by existential action. They found that it was sometimes more important not to call the jailer "sir" than to register voters; better, in certain circumstances, to stay in jail than to be bailed out to make a speech. They replaced their neat college clothes with denims and workshirts. They romanticized poverty in their revulsion from a "system" that knew how to produce great wealth but not, apparently, how to end great injustice. Gradually they came to reject most of the conventions and values of that system. Theirs was a highly moralistic antimorality, and they were among the makers of a counterculture.

They ended up rejecting the system. But they began as believers in the liberal creed. These young revolutionaries started out convinced of the relevance of the Christian gospel, of the promise of America, and of the righteousness of the federal government. Fear, pain, disappointment and betrayal changed them. They became more pessimistic, more skeptical, more scoffing—and more separatist. They lost faith in the political paradise. Instead, they came to believe in the necessity of individual salvation. And in those respects, they were pioneers on a trail that many of their fellow countrymen were to follow. The lessons that the rich, confident, successful America of the liberal consensus most needed to learn could best be taught by the poor, the unpopular, and the unsuccessful.

In 1961, however, the spearhead of radicalism was still not SNCC, but CORE. On January 31, 1961, the eve of the anniversary of Greensboro, the program director of the NAACP resigned and went to work as the national director of CORE. His name was James Farmer. Six weeks later, he announced that CORE would initiate nonviolent direct action to desegregate bus stations across the Deep South.

The Freedom Rides were consciously modeled on the Journey of Reconciliation of 1947, in which Farmer had taken part and for which Bayard Rustin had been sentenced to thirty days in a Georgia chain gang. Reconciliation, however, was not what the Freedom Rides achieved. They revealed more clearly than ever the hysterical ferocity with which at least a minority in the South would resist attempts to end segregation. At the same time, they revealed unsuspected schisms within the civil rights movement and between the movement and the federal government.

Two busloads of Freedom Riders, roughly half of them young blacks and half older white pacifists, left Washington on May 4. The violence gradually built up as they made their way south and west. On May 14 one of the buses burned to the ground outside Anniston, Alabama, and there were further savage attacks in Birmingham and Montgomery, where on May 20 a mob beat not only several of the riders but also President Kennedy's personal representative.

The original, CORE-initiated Freedom Rides disbanded in Montgomery on May 17, but new momentum was supplied by the Nashville group of SNCC, who arrived in Montgomery led by the tiny, indomitable Diane Nash and announced that, whatever anyone else proposed to do, they proposed to go on to Jackson, Mississippi. Escorted by the National

Guard, Riders from several organizations, including CORE and SCLC as well as SNCC, finally arrived in Jackson, where twenty-seven of them were promptly arrested and sentenced to sixty days on the state prison farm.

These events had consequences for all parties involved. The white South felt more than ever outraged by a deliberate breach of its law and customs with at least a degree of support from the federal government. At the same time, southern politicians, such as Governors Patterson of Alabama and Barnett of Mississippi were beginning to discover the political advantages of campaigning against the civil rights movement.

For the first time, the Rides involved white radicals, and notably white ministers and rabbis, in the movement, with momentous implications for the movement and even more so for the churches. The Rides turned the attention of SNCC toward the Deep-Deep South; specifically, they led to Robert Moses' decision to set up a black voter registration project in southwestern Mississippi. Finally, the Freedom Rides dramatized the dilemma of the Kennedy administration. The Kennedys personally and those who worked for them might all be in favor of desegregation (they were also very conscious of how much they had depended on black voters in 1960, and how much they would need them in 1964); in the meantime, between elections, they were desperately anxious not to alienate the Southerners in Congress. And so, at the end of May, having done something, though not enough, to protect the Riders' physical safety, Robert Kennedy called for a "cooling-off period."

Martin Luther King rejected Kennedy's appeal for a cooling-off period, but he did agree that there should be a "lull." This was the beginning of the rupture between King and SNCC. "They came back from the Freedom Rides," said Ella Baker, "with the terrible feeling that the angel had feet of clay."

All of these tensions contributed to the first of the many fierce strategy debates within SNCC. This came at the August 1961 staff meeting at the Highlander Folk School, near Nashville. The issue was a proposal by Tim Jenkins of the National Student Association that SNCC should drop direct action and concentrate on voter registration. The debate was confused. Radicals such as Jim Forman liked Jenkins' proposal because it meant getting into political action. On the other hand there was intense suspicion of Jenkins' motives. It was known that he had attended several meetings with representatives of the Taconic and Field foundations, and with officials of the Kennedy administration. Given what is now known about CIA penetration of institutions inside the United States, the intriguing possibility that Jenkins was working for the government cannot be dismissed out of hand.

It was obvious that the Administration's strategy was to concentrate on voter registration, which worked to its own political advantage looking to 1964, rather than on direct action, which offended its southern Democratic allies.

In the event, some of the most radical members of SNCC plunged into political action: Moses did in Mississippi, and so did Carmichael, later, in Alabama. But the episode increased suspicion of the Administration and of white liberals in general. It started SNCC on the path to a more radical version of political action, directed not toward helping but toward competing with the Democratic Party.

The Freedom Rides achieved one specific success. On September 22, the Interstate Commerce Commission ordered the desegregation of bus and train stations. The first day the order was supposed to be effective, two SNCC workers, Charles Sherrod and Cordell Reagan, traveled down from Atlanta to put it to the test in Albany, Georgia, a place still slumbering in a rigid, unchanged racial apartheid. In alliance with the local NAACP, they formed the Albany Movement. For the first time, the black citizens of a town in the Deep South, as a body, had decided to challenge the whole system of segregation.

The result was disappointing. There were two climaxes to the trial of strength between the Albany Movement and the white authorities. The first came just before Christmas 1961. A group of demonstrators (including Tom Hayden, who was then in process of drafting the Port Huron Statement, the first important manifesto of the New Left) was arrested. On December 16, more than seven hundred demonstrators, led by Martin Luther King, were arrested. Two days later, King was out on bail in return for an agreement that gave the black people of Albany nothing of substance. King had miscalculated. The result was what the New York *Herald Tribune* called a "stunning" defeat.

The second showdown came the following July. Again Dr. King was sent to jail, and again he was released within two days. The circumstances have never been explained: all that is known is that a mysterious, well-dressed black man showed up and paid the fine. Some suspected the Justice Department had reacted to King's arrest with a degree of concern that contrasted pointedly with its failure to respond to complaints about the continued flouting of federal desegregation rulings. A third time King marched. A third time he was arrested. This time the authorities were cunning enough to give him a suspended sentence. He left town, and the Albany Movement collapsed without achieving any significant concessions. Albany had been a defeat, one that resulted in large measure from the rivalries within the civil rights movement.

In 1973 I asked Stokely Carmichael what the conflict of tactics between SCLC and SNCC had been all about. He answered without hesitation, "Mobilizing versus organizing." What he meant was that, where King wanted to mobilize the black community for massive demonstrations that would impress public opinion, force the federal government to commit itself, and wring concessions from local power structures, SNCC wanted to organize black people to win power for themselves. There may be a touch of anachronism in Carmichael's applying this distinction to Albany. But it does explain the widening difference between King and the radicals. The trouble was that each needed the other and, knowing it, resented the fact. SNCC needed King's name and presence because he attracted the media, which both guaranteed a degree of protection from police brutality and, more important, spread the word. King needed the organizing energies of the SNCC volunteers.

But the dilemma between mobilizing and organizing went even deeper: To mobilize meant to rely, in the last analysis, on white help. To organize meant to stand or fall by what black people could do for themselves. The time of the organizers was coming. But first came the supreme example of what could be achieved by mobilizing. If Albany was King's most humiliating reversal, Birmingham was his greatest victory.

"Birmingham," he was to write in the open letter he wrote from its jail in 1963, "is probably the most thoroughly segregated city in the United States." Its white inhabitants were determined that it should be the last bastion of southern resistance. To blacks, it was the most menacing symbol of southern defiance.

King made his plans to breach its walls with a care that contrasted with the casual way he had walked backwards into trouble in Albany. Thanks to his lieutenant the Reverend Fred Shuttlesworth, an alliance was solidly bolted together with the city's black leadership. Money was raised in California and New York. The campaign was even delayed for almost a month to allow the city's white voters to reject their notorious commissioner of public safety, the Gothic, authentically frightening Bull Connor. It was still, however, Connor who commanded the Birmingham police, and it was with him that King would have to deal.

The first march, on April 6, Connor handled with circumspection. On April 12, Good Friday, King got himself arrested. In jail over the Easter weekend, he wrote his great *Letter,* with its scathing denunciation of those who asked black people to wait and its passionate argument for the morality of breaking unjust laws, an argument that would echo in surprising places before the sixties were out.

That same Easter weekend, his wife contacted the White House, and on Easter Monday the President called with his sympathy. The mobilization was beginning to work. There was a two-week lull, and then came the decisive days. On May 2, almost a thousand black children were arrested as they marched downtown from the Sixteenth Street Baptist Church. The next day, Bull Connor, who had so far been surprising everyone by imitating the relative restraint of Chief Pritchett in Albany, made his historic mistake: he let loose his dogs. That night, an appalled nation saw on television a snarling caricature of white racism savaging peaceful black children. The very next day, Assistant Attorney General Burke Marshall arrived in Birmingham to take personal charge of negotiations with a committee of white civic and business leaders. Bull Connor had succeeded in aligning a reluctant Administration with the civil rights movement.

The crisis came on May 7. Both the demonstrations and the police violence intensified. As King and Shuttlesworth prepared to launch waves of black children against Connor's men, now reinforced by hundreds of George Wallace's blue-helmeted state troopers, Robert Kennedy himself intervened, just in time to prevent what could have been a massacre. On May 10, in the courtyard of the Gaston Motel, a jubilant King announced the Birmingham power structure's acceptance of the movement's demands as a "great victory."

White violence, however, achieved more than black nonviolence in Birmingham. And not only the violence of the police. The Gaston Motel was bombed by white extremists, and so was the home of King's brother, a few blocks away. Bullets ripped through the rainsoaked leaves of the trees in the black neighborhoods of Birmingham that night, and not all of them were fired by policemen. Birmingham was a hard town. There were plenty of bitter, angry black men there who had watched with a curl to their lips as middle-class ministers shepherded schoolchildren in white shirts and clean, pressed dresses downtown to march. That night, the unwashed took a hand and spoke their language. It looked forward to Watts, and Newark, and Detroit, and to the defeat of King's hopes of nonviolent victory.

May 10, 1963, in fact, marked the beginning of the acute stage of the crisis of the sixties. After Birmingham, the presidency was committed to doing whatever could be done to meet the demands of the black rebellion while there was still time. And after Birmingham, it began to look as if there might not be all the time in the world. There were more than 750 riots in 186 cities and towns in the ten weeks after the bombing of the Gaston Motel. After Birmingham, in fact, the civil rights phase of the black uprising had almost done its work. But that fact was hidden from view by the triumph of the March on Washington.

The march was to be Martin Luther King's moment and his monument. But it was not originally his idea. A. Philip Randolph, of the Brotherhood of Sleeping Car Porters, had threatened to lead a black march to Washington back in 1941 unless something was done about the job discrimination and racial violence that black workers were meeting in war industry. But in the end, he agreed to set up the Fair Employment Practices Commission and the march was called off.

One afternoon in December 1962, Randolph, then seventy-three, was sitting in the brotherhood's office in Harlem talking over strategy with his friend and disciple Bayard Rustin.

Both men were socialists as well as pacifists. Both were connected with the labor movement. Both were essentially New York intellectuals of a certain sort of Left. More than twenty years younger than Randolph, Rustin had been jailed twenty times for demonstrating against war or racism in different parts of the United States. He had also worked with Gandhi in India, for nuclear disarmament in Britain, and for independence in West Africa. With Randolph he shared the belief that black people in America would achieve full equality only if they progressed hand in hand with underprivileged white people. And so it was natural that they should find themselves agreeing, that winter afternoon, that some dramatic new gesture was needed to extend the civil rights movement's field of action from the South to the North and to cement its solidarity with the labor movement.

When Rustin revived the idea of a march on Washington, Randolph was enthusiastic. But when Rustin showed him a draft plan, Randolph said it wouldn't do. The stress was too heavily on rights for black people: "I want you to go back and bring me a plan for jobs and freedom." Unemployment was still high in the winter of 1962–63. Intellectuals of the Left were concerned that much of it was a new kind of permanent unemployment, caused by automation. So Rustin planned a march for white demonstrators as well as black, for jobs as well as freedom.

There were two strategic problems to be faced. The first was the disunity of the civil rights movement. In theory, of course, the five main civil rights organizations—NAACP, the Urban League, SCLC, CORE and SNCC—all shared the same goals. In practice they were not only divided; they were competitors for members, publicity and money. Rustin's policy, spelled out in a shrewd memorandum, was to start with King. Once King was committed to the march, all the other civil rights leaders would have to go along. Then it would be possible to line up the white liberals, labor, and the churches.

The second problem was the hostility of the Kennedy administration. Harold Fleming, president of the Potomac Institute, was closely involved in the backstage negotiations. "It's no secret," he told me. "The Administration was eager to do anything it could to abort the whole enterprise. It was not a welcome event. But when they saw it was inevitable, they accommodated to it—or adopted it, depending on how you see it."

From the moment they took office, President Kennedy and his brother the Attorney General, while sympathetic, had been chary of the civil rights movement. Bayard Rustin was to tell a meeting of the American Socialist Party that summer that the dilemma of dissent in the United States was that most middle-class people believed in freedom and justice but they also believed in law and order. If it came to a choice between the two sets of values, law and order would win.

It was not a bad way of describing the Kennedy brothers' feelings when confronted with the prospect of mass demonstrations in Washington. Their strategy for meeting the demands of black protest centered on voter registration. The Justice Department had been energetically filing suits to register voters since the Administration took office. Only gradually and more reluctantly did it throw its support behind the desegregation of public accommodations. And just because it was committed, after Birmingham, to comprehensive civil rights legislation, the Administration was terrified of offending opinion in Congress.

Already at the time of the Freedom Rides, in May 1961, the Administration had worked secretly with private foundations to put money into voter registration and had tried to divert the civil rights movement in that direction and away from mass action. Robert Kennedy's civil rights lieutenant, Burke Marshall, contacted Harold Fleming and through him Stephen Currier, whose Taconic Foundation funded Fleming's Potomac Institute. (Currier's wife, a Mellon heiress, had inherited more than half a billion dollars.) At a meeting that June, Robert Kennedy personally told representatives of SCLC, CORE and SNCC that voter registration would be more constructive than Freedom Rides or other demonstrations. Later in 1961, the civil rights organizations were told of plans to channel money donated by Currier and other white-controlled foundations into voter registration under the aegis of a Voter Education Project, with headquarters in Atlanta. The episode made some civil rights leaders suspect that the Administration and wealthy white liberals were trying to buy the movement off.

In the winter of 1962–63, there was a series of meetings at the Taconic Foundation with the aim of hammering out an agreed set of priorities before approaching the federal government for money. Roy Wilkins of the NAACP, Martin Luther King, Whitney Young of the Urban League, James Farmer of CORE, and James Forman, John Lewis and Robert Moses of SNCC all attended at one time or another.

Then, on June 12, the day after George Wallace kept his promise to "stand in the schoolhouse door" and defy the federal government before he would see the University of Alabama desegregated, Medgar Evers, the most respected black leader in Mississippi, was shot. A week later, Stephen Currier called a breakfast meeting at the Hotel Carlyle in New York. It was attended by ninety-six top executives from banks, corporations and foundations. About $1.5 million was raised or pledged at that meeting. Slightly less than a month later, on July 17, a Council for United Civil Rights Leadership (CUCRL) was set up, with Currier and Whitney Young as cochairmen. The money was to be divided up between the organizations: SNCC got by far the smallest share.

On June 22, some thirty civil rights leaders gathered in the White House to discuss the march with the President. Kennedy argued that there was no need to upset Congress by marching on Washington, and that to do so might risk the passage of the legislation that had just gone up to Capitol Hill. Randolph countered by insisting that people were coming to Washington anyway (which was factually dubious but psychologically true) and that it was better they should come in an organized fashion. "Once Kennedy saw that we were determined to have it," Rustin remembers, "he said to every department of government, 'Co-operate fully with them, give them everything they want.'" A few days later, there were two meetings in the Hotel Roosevelt in New York. At noon there was a conference of the leaders of the march to confirm plans. An hour later, on the same floor of the same hotel, there was another meeting, with essentially the same people present, this time to hear Joseph L. Rauh, Jr., legal counsel to the UAW, and Andrew Biemiller, the legendary lobbyist of the AFL/CIO, explain the new civil rights legislation.

Gradually, almost imperceptibly, the march was being transformed from a March on Washington to a March *in* Washington. Where originally the idea had been to lobby the Administration, subtly it became a matter of helping the Administration by lobbying Congress.

Later there was to be much suspicion, not to say paranoia, among radical blacks about this transformation. "Now, what had instantly achieved black unity?" asked Malcolm X. "The white man's money." It was all, no doubt, less Machiavellian than he and the other radicals suspected. Stephen Currier is dead, but I have talked to several of his associates, and he seems from all accounts to have been motivated by an uncomplicated sense of the public responsibility laid upon him by his great wealth. He thought it would be a good thing if the civil rights organizations were relieved of the temptation to compete to raise funds. But essentially Malcolm was not wrong. The march was manipulated by the federal government and by white liberals for their own purposes, generous as these may have been. I asked Bayard Rustin, who is now regarded by the radicals as an archconservative, whether the march was taken over by the Administration, and found to my surprise that he did not disagree. "Of course," he said. "It would have been impossible to have any movement that big happen in the country without the Administration utilizing its strength to divert it into what it wanted."

Perhaps so. The fact remains that the Kennedy administration did manipulate the march to its own purposes. It is not surprising, therefore, that even that shining symbol of unity, upon closer inspection, hints at the instability of the liberal coalition.

What is best and most poignantly remembered about the March is Martin Luther King's peroration: "I have a dream that one day this nation will rise up and live out the true meaning of its creed: We hold these truths to be self-evident, that all men are created equal." Everybody had that dream. But King also said that day, "The whirlwinds of revolt will continue to shake the foundations of our nation until the bright day of justice emerges." One of the differences between the liberal majority and its new allies in the black movement was that the liberals were constantly tempted to suppose that the bright day of justice would arrive without the whirlwinds of revolt. Black people knew better than that.

The misunderstandings under the surface unity of the march surfaced unmistakably in the fuss over John Lewis' speech.

Each of the ten leaders was to speak for a fixed number of minutes. Lewis was to be the spokesman for SNCC. The night before the march, copies of his speech became available. It was, as even Jim Forman acknowledged, a "stinger."

From the Administration's point of view, the whole object of the march was to lobby Congress on behalf of the civil rights bill. And so it had been agreed that nothing must be said to annoy congressmen.

"In good conscience," Lewis' text began, "we cannot support the Administration's civil rights bill, for it is too little, and too late." He talked about "cheap political leaders who build their careers on immoral compromises," and he reminded everyone that the party of Kennedy was also the party of Eastland. "Which side is the federal government on?" he asked bluntly.

This was hardly likely to please senators or congressmen. And it seemed to the organizers that it violated the agreement that had been made. At about one-thirty in the morning of the day of the march, Rustin got a call from Walter Reuther. The archbishop had seen the text, and was threatening to boycott the march. This was Archbishop, now Cardinal, O'Boyle, who had consented to give the invocation and benediction at the Lincoln Memorial, a point of some importance to the White

House, where they were busy counting Catholic votes for the civil rights bill.

In the end, it was all right. Lewis agreed to change his speech, and the archbishop agreed to come. But it was a near thing. As the minutes ticked away, past the hour when the speeches were supposed to begin, a tense group was still huddled over a typewriter in a room inside the Lincoln Memorial. Jim Forman was rewriting the speech, while a committee peered over his shoulder: Randolph, Rustin, Reuther, and a tall, distinguished-looking white clergyman. This was Dr. Eugene Carson Blake, later head of the World Council of Churches, who had become involved in the civil rights movement only a couple of months earlier. Partly out of concern for his ecumenical contacts with the archbishop, he had emerged as the severest critic of Lewis' speech.

"There is one thing I remember," Dr. Blake told me; "he talked about the masses, and I said, 'Now, look, masses is Communist talk; we don't talk about the common people as the masses in this country.'"

"And John Lewis, I remember, said, 'I'm no Communist, I'm a Baptist preacher.'"

Telling me the story, Dr. Blake paused for a moment. Then he added: "He was right, you know, in what he said. I mean, that was always our way, in race relations. Pass a law, and then nullify it."

The difference between Dr. Blake's reaction to Lewis' speech at the time, and his reaction ten years later, is no bad measure of what the crisis did to the ideological confidence of American liberals. Dr. Blake himself has recognized just this in more general terms:

> I remember very vividly what we felt like at the end of World War II. We had a real hope in the best tradition of America—since we had come out so strong, ideologically, militarily, economically, at that time—that these next years, 25 years, were going to be an American age. . . .

The March on Washington was perhaps the last moment when that confidence was still possible. The magical moment when Mahalia Jackson's high note on the word "free" in the last line of the national anthem still hung in the air over the dusty crowd has been remembered by those who were there as the last glimpse of sunlit prospects glimpsed across stormy waters. The March on Washington did not represent the opening of a new period, but the end of the time of marching and praying.

Dr. Benjamin Mays gave the invocation on the great day, along with Archbishop O'Boyle. He was the president of Morehouse College when Martin Luther King arrived there as a fifteen-year-old freshman. When I talked to him, he was the chairman of the Atlanta School Board. "After the March on Washington," he told me thoughtfully, "and after Martin's speech, and the entire nation praising it as a great event, it was inevitable that black people should feel that this is the moment, and this is the time, and the things we've been struggling for, for centuries, are just about at hand now.

"Well," said Dr. Mays, "it's never so."

# Black Separatism

Hereditary bondsmen! Know ye not
Who would be free themselves must strike the blow?

> Byron, quoted by W. E. B. Du Bois
> in *The Souls of Black Folk*

On December 1, 1963, just over three months after what he insisted on calling "the farce on Washington," the man who had been known by many names but was now called Minister Malcolm X of Temple Number Seven of the Nation of Islam, was asked to comment on the assassination of President Kennedy. It was the result, he answered, of the general climate of hate and violence in the country. That was no more than the Chief Justice of the United States and the Chairman of the Senate Foreign Relations Committee had said. And then a sinister image fluttered out from the subconscious not of Minister Malcolm X nor of Detroit Red the Harlem hustler but from that of Malcolm Little, the six-year-old boy from Lansing, Michigan, who was to grow into both.

"Chickens come home to roost," he added. "Being an old farm boy myself, chickens coming home to roost never did make me feel sad; they've always made me feel glad."

Malcolm's father, Earl Little, was an organizer for the United Negro Improvement Association, founded by Marcus Garvey. The family lived in the country outside Lansing, because their home in town had been burned down by a Klan-style group called the Black Legion Society. The last time Malcolm saw his father, Earl Little lost patience with his wife because she was reluctant to kill a favorite chicken, and he wrung the bird's neck. As he reached the gate, he turned and waved to Malcolm and his mother. Or so it was important to Malcolm to remember. For, that same day, his father was lynched.

Whatever its subconscious source or private meaning, Malcolm's remark itself came home to roost. Elijah Muhammad thought it highly impolitic, at a time when all the white devils were in mourning for Kennedy. He suspended Malcolm and ordered him to keep silence for a year on public issues. The suspension pushed Malcolm into striking out on his own. And that decision, in turn, led directly to his death.

In less than a year, Malcolm had time to establish himself, alongside King, as one of the two great leaders of the black uprising.

It is easy to think of King and Malcolm as opposite poles: to compare the southern Baptist, preaching nonviolence, with the ghetto operator, skilled in the rhetoric of menace; contrast the polished scholar, quoting Tillich and Tolstoy, with the savvy hustler who learned his instinct for separation in poolrooms and prison. But, different as they were, both men had grabbed hold of the same truth. Both saw that before black Americans could win the victories they needed, they would first have to change themselves. At the heart of Malcolm's vision of black nationalism, and at the heart of King's existentialist nonviolence, there lay the same strategy: political self-assertion as social therapy. What is more, just as King, at the end of his life, came to understand the need for a degree of black separatism as a means; so Malcolm, before he was killed, accepted some form of integration as the ultimate end.

Fast as Malcolm himself changed in the eleven months between his break with the Black Muslims, in March 1964, and his death, in February 1965, the crisis was moving even faster.

In the brief space of time, four decisive developments came to a head:

First, white Americans woke up to the fact that blacks were demanding not just desegregation in the South but equality everywhere.

Second, George Wallace, by racking up between a third and a half of the vote in three northern Democratic primaries, served notice that there would be resistance to that demand everywhere.

Third, those months saw a chain of events that began with the murder of three civil rights workers in Mississippi and led up to the Democratic Party's refusal to unseat the all-white delegation from Mississippi at its Atlantic City convention. An influential fraction of the civil rights movement lost faith in the federal government, the Democratic Party and white liberals. And many blacks lost their faith in nonviolence.

Yet white liberals could be forgiven for feeling, as many of them did, that this reaction was unfair. For, fourthly, those very same months saw the climax of the liberal commitment to meet the blacks' demand for equality. Lyndon Johnson's speech at Howard University, the strongest statement of that commitment ever made by a President of the United States, came less than four months after Malcolm's death.

New currents of black thought—nonviolence, integration, separatism, black power—forced their way through the media to the attention of white Americans so fast in the sixties that it was easy to forget that this was, after all, a very old story. None of these alternative strategies was entirely new. Trapped by history half in, half out of American society, blacks had always twisted and turned painfully between the longing to be accepted, and the longing to reject.

In the generation of emancipation, Frederick Douglass stood for "ultimate assimilation through self-assertion, and on no other terms." In the next generation, Booker T. Washington took the opposite tack. The only hope of ultimate assimilation, he argued, lay in giving up all self-assertion. Blacks should become "hewers of wood and drawers of water," if that was the only way to earn the protection of the white business class. Then, in 1903, W. E. B. Du Bois started the pendulum on its slow swing back toward self-assertion. He ended a famous essay in *The Souls of Black Folk* with the words that may be said to have launched the civil rights movement: "By every civilized and peaceful method we must strive for the rights which the world accords to men."

Each of the three—Douglass, Washington, Du Bois—was thinking in terms of political realities. Since each had to start from the fact that black Americans were trapped as a permanent minority inside a predominantly white nation, assimilation was the ultimate goal for all three. Unlike politics, religion does not have to be bound by such realities. It deals in terms of deep, half-conscious longing. And so, from a very early date, and especially in times of trouble, some American blacks had always turned to religious movements that allowed them to express what the economic and political realities forbade as a practical program: the longing to reject the society that rejected them. Since that society was white by race, Christian by religion, and American by culture, it was natural that this rejection should take the form of a turning toward Africa. Early in the nineteenth century, free blacks in New York and Philadelphia founded the African Church. Early in the twentieth, millions followed Marcus Garvey and his "Back to Africa" movement. And in 1931, in the depths of the Depression, there came into existence the religious movement that called itself the Nation of Islam.

Wallace D. Fard and Elijah Poole, its founders, taught their followers a cosmology, a mythology, and a code of ethics all rooted in this instinct for rejecting the white man and all his works. They ordered them to cut themselves off as far as possible from the world of the white devils.

For more than twenty years, a few dozen poor families in Detroit and Chicago kept this faith. The Nation of Islam might seem little different from dozens of other churches that lightened the heavy load of their flock, and kept their shepherds in modest comfort, in the swelling black neighborhoods of the great migration. Like Daddy Grace and Father Divine, Elijah Muhammad, formerly Poole, was following a tradition of down-home syncretism that was as much part of the culture of the black poor as ham hocks or "the numbers." Then, suddenly, in 1959, the Nation of Islam was silhouetted by the glare of national publicity. Like that thrown by a mother's fingers on a child's wall, the silhouette was both more frightening and larger than life size. First came Louis Lomax's TV documentary for the Mike Wallace show, *The Hate Which Hate Produced.* Soon afterward, a full-length study, *The Black Muslims in America,* by Dr. C. Eric Lincoln, was published. White columnists raced each other to deplore what they called "hate messengers" and "black racists" and, inevitably, "possibly Communist-inspired." This wave of publicity alarmed white folks and middle-class blacks: poor black people flocked to join the Nation of Islam.

As usual when a movement suddenly swells like a leavened loaf, conditions were ripe, and a man was ready to use them.

Something like half of the ten million blacks brought by the great migration to the inner cities of the North and West were living there in a state of economic and social crisis. And no one else seemed to be talking straight about it.

In the spring of 1963, Herbert Hill, the labor secretary of the NAACP, pointed out: "What has been a mild and temporary recession for the white worker is a major crisis of unemployment for the Negro wage earner."

Behind this economic crisis there lurked a social crisis. Because unemployment was highest among teen-agers, many young black men and women never did win a foothold in the market for steady jobs. They went to swell the ranks of an underclass whose members could choose between a succession of ill-paid, short-lived, dirty but "honest" jobs as bus boy, maid, casual laborer; or take their chances as hustler, thief or pimp. Because blacks were discriminated against in the housing market, they were trapped in ghettoes. Because they were discriminated against in the credit market, those ghettoes became steadily more dilapidated. The interacting effect of many diseases—unemployment, poverty, crime, addiction and family instability—added up to a syndrome of social pathology.

There was indeed nothing new about this. In 1939 E. Franklin Frazier had written an essay about the Negro family in the northern ghetto and called it *In the City of Destruction*. James Baldwin remembered the pervasive sense of sin he grew up with in the Harlem of the 1940s:

> "in every wine-stained and urine-splashed hallway, in every clanging ambulance bell, in every scar on the faces of the pimps and their whores . . in every knife and pistol fight on the Avenue . . . the children parceled out here and there. . . .

It was not new. But it was getting worse, not better. As white Americans got richer and as liberal rhetoric raised the expectations of northern blacks, so the terrible reality came to look more and more obscene.

A handful of educated blacks joined the Nation of Islam. But its appeal was strongest for the inhabitants of the lower circles of these infernos. The Muslims were grudgingly admired even by policemen for their success at reclaiming heroin addicts. The explanation was simple: they were not shocked by addiction, because they could transfer the guilt from the addict to the devil white man. They were equally successful at recruiting in prison: those who had seen prisons at first hand found it easiest to see white society as a hierarchy of devils. The Muslims had been in jail. They had stood up to the Man. They had survived. They could therefore hope to cure the most deadly of all the afflictions of the ghetto: the loss of self-respect.

This was their opportunity, and Malcolm was the man to make the most of it. He, too, had been down low, and had had the strength to climb back up. He remained loyal to Elijah Muhammad long after it was obvious that it was he, Malcolm, rather than the old man in his mansion in Chicago, who was responsible for the Nation of Islam's swelling ranks. He was loyal because he credited Elijah with saving him from the slow slide into cornered ferocity that he saw as the inevitable fate of the aging hustler. The eventual breach was something more than the young stag banishing the old. The issue was political.

Black responses to the dilemma of being half in and half out of American society can be plotted along two axes. One runs from acceptance to rejection, or from integration to separatism. The other runs from self-assertion to passivity. Malcolm did not disagree with Elijah's prescription of rejection—not at first. But where Elijah taught passive rejection, Malcolm thought that the rejection must involve self-assertion.

In the end, the civil rights movement was overtaken by black separatism in the contest for black allegiance. But, at an earlier stage, Malcolm saw that the civil rights movement was a formidable competitor for the Nation of Islam. Young blacks in the northern ghettoes saw their southern contemporaries standing up for their rights, getting involved in the political process, and—contrary to what the Muslims taught—seeming to get something out of it. The Muslims preached black dignity, but what were they doing about it? In April 1962, the Los Angeles police shot seven unarmed Muslims, killing one of them, then arrested sixteen more on charges of "criminal assault against the police." Malcolm went out to handle the case, and wanted to organize a national protest campaign. Elijah Muhammad first agreed, then forbade it. In December 1963, when Malcolm first disagreed publicly with Elijah, it was on this issue.

> The Messenger has seen God. . . . He is willing to wait for Allah to deal with the devil. Well, sir, the rest of us Black Muslims have not seen God, we don't have this gift of divine patience with the devil. The younger Black Muslims want to see some action.

And so, in March 1964, he parted company with the Nation of Islam. He announced that he was ready to join in the civil rights struggle "in the South and elsewhere." That did not mean he had been converted to nonviolence. What had been called the black revolution, he said scornfully, was a deception: "There can be no revolution without bloodshed."

"Our political philosophy," he said a few days later, "will be black nationalism. . . . The political philosophy of black nationalism means we must control the politics and politicians of our community. They must no longer take orders from outside forces."

In the course of his last year, Malcolm made two trips to Africa. On a pilgrimage to Mecca he became aware of the parochialism of the Black Muslim version of the teachings of Islam; skin color, the obsessive concern of the Detroit version, was an irrelevance that had been foisted on black America by white racism. He also brought back from his African journeys a new understanding of the world situation of American blacks. He saw them now as belonging not only to a powerless minority in their own country but also to the world majority of the nonwhite. It is a measure of Malcolm's intelligence and also of his generosity that this discovery, which would have made some men more truculent, made Malcolm transcend narrow racism. In a speech at Columbia University, only four days before his death, he defined a position miles distant from that of black racists:

> It is incorrect to classify the revolt of the Negro as simply a racial conflict of black against white. Rather, we are seeing today a global rebellion of the oppressed against the oppressor.

In the last months of his life, Malcolm had become friendly with and interested in the ideas of the New York Trotskyists. No doubt their influence affected his thinking, though politically he had far more to give to, than to hope for from, that embattled fragment of the Left. Such speeches earned Malcolm X a place alongside Che Guevara and Frantz Fanon in the pantheon of the New Left. But it was to his own black audience that he was speaking. What he was trying to do, he said, was to build "an all-black organization whose ultimate objective was to help create a society in which there could exist honest black-white brotherhood."

Was he teaching hate? Louis Lomax had asked him.

> If there is a rattlesnake in the field who has been biting all your brothers and your sisters [Malcolm answered], then you go and tell them that that's a rattlesnake. . . . Well, then, that rattler will go back and tell the other snakes that this man is teaching hate. . . . But it's not hate . . . it's just that when you study people who have been harmed and discover the source of their injury . . . you must let them know what is wrong with them.

White people could not be expected to be pleased by the comparison. But, then, Malcolm was not primarily concerned with them. He was concerned with black people. The crucial matter, he saw, was their self-respect. If they could be brought to understand that they were not themselves "the source of their injury," then they would be able to respect themselves.

Malcolm had moved outward from psychology and religion to politics. He began, as a man self-educated in the hardest of schools, with certain discoveries about himself. He ended with a program for black Americans. Essentially, it was Frederick Douglass' program, "ultimate assimilation through self-assertion, and on no other terms." It was too much to expect white liberals to welcome a doctrine that seemed to be tearing down all they had so painfully achieved. But what Malcolm had to say, both to blacks and to whites, was perhaps as important as the Civil Rights Act of 1964, or even more important.

On March 20, 1964, just eight days after Malcolm broke with Elijah Muhammad, Joseph L. Rauh, Jr., was chairing a meeting on civil liberties when an unknown young black man stood up in the audience and asked a question. What chance did Mr. Rauh think there would be of seating a rival delegation from Mississippi in place of the regulars at the Democratic National Convention in Atlantic City?

Mr. Rauh, who is both a sanguine and a good-natured man, replied that he thought the chance would be good, and invited the questioner out to lunch. His name, Rauh discovered, was Robert Parris Moses.

Rauh was, and is, something more than one among many liberal Washington lawyers. He was counsel, political adviser and personal friend to Walter Reuther of the United Auto Workers. And Reuther was more than just the head of the most liberal big union in the country. He was financial angel to causes of all kinds, including some that were well to the left of anything that could be called Establishment liberalism. The first five thousand dollars for SDS's prototype community action program, for example, had just come out of the UAW's treasury. The most cherished of all the causes that Reuther supported, however, was Americans for Democratic Action. Through the lonely fifties, ADA, almost alone, had kept the flag of the Left flying in American politics. It was an anti-Communist Left, recognizably the heir of that native American radicalism that stretched far beyond the New Deal: a tradition of commitment to civil rights, civil liberties, and resistance to the monopoly of political power by "the interests." Rauh was a past president of ADA.

Born in a Manhattan housing project, Bob Moses went to Hamilton College on a scholarship, where he discovered Camus and commitment. He took a master's degree in philosophy at Harvard. He was working with Bayard Rustin when the Greensboro sit-in happened, and he went to work for SCLC in Atlanta. On a field trip across the Black Belt, he got the idea of helping black voters to register in Mississippi. The missionary journeys that resulted from this idea were as fateful for American society as anything that happened in those years of crisis.

In Mississippi, Bob Moses had learned how far the white planters and their agents in government and the police were prepared to go to resist change. He was beaten repeatedly. He was jailed. More than once, he narrowly escaped being killed. Two of those who helped him were not so lucky; they were murdered. In spite of all he had experienced, Bob Moses, at the beginning of 1964, still believed in integration as the goal and in nonviolence as a tactic and a philosophy. But now three new ideas had come to dominate his thinking:

Strategically, he had become convinced that voter registration was far more important than demonstrating against segregation, because it promised political power for poor people, white as well as black. Politically, he was impressed by the black sharecroppers, as opposed to the "Negro" middle class in the towns. He was intent on building institutions to express the rebellion of the black masses. Psychologically, he had reached a conclusion in rural Mississippi very like the one Malcolm had reached in Harlem: the key to the battle lay in the morale of the troops.

Moses' thinking was hardening into a Dostoievskian, almost mystical faith in the wisdom of the ignorant, the strength of the powerless. "The people on the bottom don't need leaders at all," he once said. "What they need is to have confidence in their own lives."

It was hard, though, to sustain realistic confidence about the prospects of winning political power in Mississippi. More than two out of every five people in the state were black. Only one out of every twenty black people of voting age was registered to vote. Not a single black person, therefore, had held elective office there since the collapse of Reconstruction, more than ninety years before. Every kind of intimidation was routinely practiced to keep things that way.

In 1962, Moses helped to set up the Council of Federated Organizations (COFO), an operating coalition among SNCC, CORE, SCLC and local NAACP branches to co-ordinate voter registration and other civil rights activities in Mississippi. The sheer rigidity of the resistance offered an opportunity if COFO could find a way to exploit it. Many white Mississippians were what was known as "yellow-dog" Democratic hereditary loyalists, that is, who would vote for a yellow dog on the Democratic ticket before they would vote for a Republican. But now white Mississippians were asking themselves whether even yellow dogs weren't one thing, and the national Democratic party, as represented by the Kennedys, quite another. So virulent had their disaffection become that the state Democratic delegation was actually pledged to support Barry Goldwater, the Republican candidate. This extravagance on the part of the Democratic regulars gave Moses his opportunity. It also commended his plan to those—such as Joe Rauh, Walter Reuther and Hubert Humphrey —who wanted the party to dissociate itself from extremist southern Democrats.

A fatal misunderstanding lay at the bottom of this apparent harmony, like a wasp in a basket of apples. But at first Moses' plan went well enough. In the fall of 1963, COFO organized a Freedom Ballot, to get blacks used to the idea of voting. Moses recruited students from Yale and Stanford to help with the registration drive. They were so successful that eighty thousand blacks voted. The decision was taken to bring students in by the hundreds the next summer, for a Mississippi Summer Project to register voters in support of a Mississippi Freedom Democratic Party.

There wasn't much that Moses or anyone else could do to prepare eight hundred students from Berkeley and Harvard, Swarthmore and Oberlin, for what they might expect in Mississippi. What little could be done was undertaken at two training courses, each a week long, on the beautiful campus of Western College for Women, in Oxford, Ohio.

As the boys and girls sat around in a circle on the grass, for all the world like good children at a church cookout, two black SNCC field secretaries demonstrated how to fall to the ground when the police were beating you: in the fetal position, with your hands behind the nape of your neck and your elbows covering your temples. Oh, and don't forget to cross your ankles, so they can't beat you between the legs. . . .

The black SNCC veterans treated the white college kids with the more or less affectionate contempt of the veteran for the raw recruit. Contempt was not justified. Fear hung over Oxford that hot week. The children of the most sheltered homes in the world were coming to terms with what it would be like not only to be hurt but to be hated. Every effort was made to persuade anyone who had second thoughts to go home. All but two of the eight hundred went to Mississippi.

The first morning of the second course, Bob Moses was talking quietly in the lecture theater. He was drawing an analogy from his favorite, Albert Camus. "The country is unwilling yet to admit it has the plague," he was saying, "but it pervades the whole society." There was an interruption. Moses listened like a man who has been told his mother was dead. Then, still quietly, he told the students. Three of the volunteers who had left that very hall two days before—two veterans, one recruit; two white, one black—had been arrested by police in Neshoba County, and were missing.

There was a search. President Johnson sent sailors from a local naval air station to help. He also assigned Allen Dulles, head of the CIA, and J. Edgar Hoover, of the FBI, to the case. The mutilated bodies of two other blacks were dragged from nearby rivers. After six weeks, on an informer's tip, the three bodies were found, bulldozed into the earth of a freshly made dam.

All three had been beaten, then shot. One of them, the black man, had been beaten with chains. The pathologist who examined his body said that he had previously seen similar wounds only as a result of high-velocity impacts in aircraft crashes.

The federal government's perfectly genuine eagerness to bring the murderers to trial was frustrated by the customs and feelings of Mississippi. On December 4, the sheriff and the deputy sheriff of the county, with nineteen others, were arrested on charges of violating the civil rights of the three men—by killing them. Six days later, the charges had to be dropped because the FBI brought in "incompetent," hearsay evidence.

The summer project went on. But it went on under the shadow of this evidence that the federal government either could not, or would not, protect civil rights workers. It went on, therefore, in an atmosphere not only of fear but of growing bitterness and anger as well. Fear alone might have glued black and white workers together. That was not what happened. The nightmare summer in Mississippi had two results: It divided the blacks in the movement from the whites. And it radicalized both.

A resentful feeling that, in a society in which they controlled so little else, blacks ought at least to control the fight for their own freedom, had been growing among black civil rights workers for some time. The issue surfaced openly, for example, at a SNCC staff meeting in November 1963.

Everything that happened in Mississippi was fitted into a pattern of increasing tension between whites and blacks. The black Mississippians assumed—wrongly, in most cases, as it turned out—that after the summer was over, the volunteers would be going back to pick up the threads of affluent careers in the North, leaving the blacks on their own to fight their unending battle.

The volunteers, on the other hand, were the children of the culture that had conquered Europe and built IBM. They were instinctively good at typing out checklists, paying phone bills, writing memos and drawing up organigrams. They admired their black contemporaries. They especially admired their black hostesses (who perhaps supplied the maternal support that their own mothers, for all their energetic adherence to the League of Women Voters in Beverly Hills or Connecticut, were rather weak in). But they couldn't help showing their impatience with their black hosts' lack of organizational skills. The black volunteers, wrote one upper-middle-class white girl volunteer, typically, resented "the smart, sharp, articulate" white volunteers (like herself), because they were so often "right."

There were other sources of tension. There was trouble, ironically enough in view of its later sanctification as the Eucharist of the counter-culture, over the blacks' use of marijuana. And there was trouble over sex. The black boys would say to the white girls, "Prove you're not prejudiced; come to bed with me." What could the girls do but prove it? The white boys would be jealous and say nothing. The black girls would be furious and show it. In some places, by the end of the summer, black-white tension had flared into open hostility.

In spite of everything—fear, heat, jail, quarreling and sand flies—most of those who went to Mississippi in 1964 remember it as the proudest campaign of their lives. But each group had been denied what it most wanted: the blacks, equality; the whites, gratitude. Both were radicalized, but in different ways.

The effect on the whites was to shake their faith in the benevolence of the system. Intellectually they became convinced that the injustice, defended with violence, that they saw in Mississippi was an inevitable consequence of the wider American system. Emotionally they were driven to prove to themselves and to each other, even if they couldn't prove it to skeptical blacks, that they were not "just white liberals." In the process they reassessed their deepest assumptions about liberal, bourgeois society in general. Teachers, lawyers, doctors, who had been in Mississippi, all felt forced to abandon the comfortable conventions on which their professional life could be based in the North. Students back from Mississippi looked on their universities with new, unsympathetic eyes.

Few blacks in the movement had ever totally shared the liberal confidence in the perfectibility of the system. Mississippi destroyed what was left of their confidence in the federal government, in white liberals, and in nonviolence. Had not the Supreme Court proclaimed, nearly seventy years before in *In Re Debs*, "The entire strength of the nation may be used to enforce in any part of the land . . . the security of all rights entrusted by the Constitution to its care"? Then, why was it that Burke Marshall and John Doar of the Justice Department so stoutly maintained that the federal government was powerless to protect the civil rights of citizens in Mississippi?

"How is it," John Doar was asked from the floor at the orientation session in Ohio, "that the government can protect the Vietnamese from the Viet Cong, and the same government will not accept the moral responsibility of protecting the people in Mississippi?"

Already, young blacks were beginning to make the connection between Mississippi and Vietnam. Already, young whites were getting ready to take that idea back to their campuses with them.

A specific irritant greatly heightened the suspicion of the "liberal Establishment" on the part of both black and white workers. This was the question of the National Lawyers Guild. It was by no means the piddling organizational jealousy it might sound.

If the summer project was to avoid disaster, it would need lawyers. The volunteers would be challenging the law of Mississippi, and the law would be used to parry their challenge. In the past, SNCC and CORE had relied on the legal arm of the NAACP, which is called the Legal Defense and Education Fund, Inc., or the "Inc. Fund." Some tension already existed between the fund and SNCC. Jack Greenberg, its head, resented the cavalier way the students seemed to expect that whenever they took it into their heads to break the law, they could count on the Inc. Fund to bail them out. The students, in return, thought the fund cautious and fussy.

The fund was in any case conspicuous by its absence in Mississippi. Robert Moses therefore accepted an offer of help from the National Lawyers Guild. The guild was anathema to orthodox liberals (including those on whom the fund depended for its support) because of its reputation as a "front" for the Communist Party in the 1940s. Admittedly, it had a number of former Communists among its members. Greenberg wrote angrily to Moses that if SNCC or COFO entered into any agreement with the guild, the fund would be unable to take part. In the end, it did take part, under the guise of a Lawyers Committee for Civil Rights, and so did the guild. But the subject caused friction all summer, and resentment long afterward. It was one of the reasons why later New Left institutions, to the horror of older liberals, always insisted on "non-exclusionist" policies, or "no enemies on the Left."

Most acutely of all, the Mississippi experience raised the issue of non-violence, which had been latent in the civil rights movement from the start. Not that anyone advocated the use of violence as a way of achieving the movement's objectives: the question was whether a member of the movement had the right to use a gun in self-defense. The division was between those who took nonviolence as an absolute principle, and those who adopted it merely as a tactic.

The issue surfaced as early as 1962. A SNCC field secretary called Charlie Cobb, who was organizing in Holmes County, Mississippi, found himself in a house that was shot into by white vigilantes. The people in the house had guns. Cobb picked one up to help stand guard. When they heard what had happened, the people at the SNCC headquarters in Atlanta were deeply shocked. An emergency meeting was called to decide the question of principle: were there any circumstances in which a SNCC member might touch a gun?

The younger, northern-educated blacks, such as Stokely Carmichael and his friends from the Howard University Nonviolent Action Group, accepted nonviolence as a tactic, not as an ideology. Those who were working at voter registration in the back country of the Deep South knew that they might find themselves in some situation on a lonely road where a gun would be their only protection. And so the meeting ended with an uneasy compromise. Publicly, SNCC maintained its allegiance to the principle of nonviolence. Tacitly, it was accepted that field secretaries might need to use a gun in self-defense.

By the summer of 1964, virtually every SNCC worker in the field was carrying a gun. Then, in Georgia, a SNCC worker named John Washington Cooley was arrested for possession of a firearm. Again, the leadership in Atlanta took the position that to bail Cooley out would contradict SNCC's fundamental principles.

Stokely Carmichael remembered what happened with wry amusement:

> When the story began to brim over to those who were in the field [he told me], it became obvious to everyone, like "I'm carrying a gun, you mean, if I get caught carrying it, they're going to let me rot in jail?" . . . The meeting was held in Holly Springs. We organized everybody who carried guns to come. . . . They argued back and forth, and tempers got hot. Finally, just to settle the argument, I looked around the room, and there were more people with guns than without. So I said, "What we should do is, all the people who are carrying guns should put them down

on the table." It wasn't a threat. It was just so those who didn't know what was going on should get a chance to see. And so all those guns came down on the table. . . .

Already, SNCC had come a long way from Shaw College in 1960 and the search for a redemptive community permeated by love.

All that Lyndon Johnson admitted to remembering, at the end of his life, about Atlantic City in August 1964 was that it was "a place of surging crowds and thundering cheers." He can hardly have forgotten Carol Channing, and the way her brass lungs drowned the biggest organ in the world when she sang, "Hello, Lyndon, why *hello*, Lyndon!" to the tune of the showstopper from *Hello, Dolly!* This was the coronation of the consensus, and "Hello, Lyndon" was the anthem of the day.

The convention was also, in retrospect, an occasion of haunting omens. It was meant to celebrate the unity of the great Democratic Party. Yet the portents of disintegration were all too visible. To spice the ceremonies with something for the journalists to write about, the President had carefully created doubt about his choice for Vice-President. One name he could not ignore: Robert Kennedy. And so he made sure that everyone knew that he had eliminated Kennedy beforehand. The two names on his short list were those of the two senators from Minnesota, Hubert Humphrey and Eugene McCarthy. Kennedy, Humphrey, McCarthy: only four years later, those names were to divide the Democratic Party as it went down to defeat.

Yet, in a longer perspective, the episode of the Mississippi Freedom Democratic Party was perhaps even more ominous. That was the moment when the more radical black leaders finally lost faith in the presidency, in the Democratic Party, and in the coalition between the liberal intellectuals and the labor unions. In the hour of its coronation, the liberal consensus began to fall apart.

Sixty-eight delegates from the Freedom Democratic Party arrived in Atlantic City. The President's original plan was to welcome them as "honored guests," while seating three members of the regular delegation. A secret understanding had been reached with Governor Paul Johnson of Mississippi, assuring the regulars of these three seats. The rest of the regulars could then allow themselves the luxury, desirable for their political reputations back home, of stalking out in protest during prime television time.

Fanny Lou Hamer spoiled that. On Saturday afternoon, the TV networks covered the hearings of the credentials committee. The nation found itself hypnotized by the testimony of this squat black woman, who spoke with the fervid rhythms of a country preacher and the haunting anguish of the blues, as she described what happened when she tried to register as a voter in Ruleville, Mississippi:

> They beat me and they beat me with a long, flat blackjack. I screamed to God in my mind. My dress worked itself up. I tried to pull it down. They beat my arms until I had no feeling in them.

This person called Fanny Lou Hamer was upstaging the coronation of Lyndon Johnson. This was the last thing in the world the President wanted to see on the networks as he strove to present the spectacle of a party united from the Bourbon South to the Jacobins of the West Side of Manhattan. He did his best to push it off the screen. He called a press conference, at the shortest of notice and on the flimsiest of pretexts. It was no good. Network news executives might have to cover the President of the United States live. But in television terms there was no way they could hold off Mrs. Hamer: she was compelling. They ran her again that night. The ragged army from Mississippi had won the first round: they had become the issue of the convention.

Two compromises were hastily put forward. One, aimed to assuage the horrified conscience of many delegates, came from two Congressional independents, Edith Green of Oregon and Robert Kastenmeier of Wisconsin. Their plan would have favored the MFDP: it would have seated all members of both the rival delegations willing to take an oath of loyalty to the Democratic Party. The White House refused to go that far. For the future, it was prepared to yield the main point of principle: no delegation would be seated from any state that practiced segregation in its delegate-selection procedure. But for 1964, the MFDP would have to be content with two seats, and not as delegates for the Magnolia State of Mississippi, but as delegates at large: take it, or leave it.

Why did Lyndon Johnson dig in his heels? He was, after all, committed enough to the cause of civil rights to have fought tooth and nail for the civil rights bill he had just signed. And he bore no love for the segregationist politicians of Mississippi. The obvious explanation was that he was afraid that the South as a whole would bolt. His friend John Connally, governor of Texas, said: "If you seat those black buggers, the whole South will walk out." It was an alarming enough prospect, with Barry Goldwater as the Republican nominee.

But a southern defection was not the worst Johnson had to fear if the Mississippi issue came to a floor fight, with delegations walking out and angry black faces framed by the TV cameras. George Wallace had proved it in Wisconsin, Indiana and Maryland that spring. It was not only in the South that black militancy might provoke a sharp reaction. There had been riots in Harlem and Rochester that summer. What the columnists were already calling the white backlash raised an appalling specter: the possibility that the Democratic Party as a whole would begin to unravel. Lyndon Johnson's victory that November was so complete that it is easy to forget how things looked that August. A column I wrote myself that weekend, after talking to White House staff and political lieutenants of the President, shows that the political opportunity which Richard Nixon was to exploit with such skill in 1972 was already discernible in 1964, if Barry Goldwater had been able to see it:

> The white backlash fits into a broader pattern of social and political change that may rewrite the most basic assumptions on which the dominance of the Democrats had been based since 1933.
> That dominance was built on the support of exactly the kind of people who voted for George Wallace in Indiana or Baltimore or Milwaukee. The people who are reacting most against the Negroes are working class. They are union members, many of them belong to the less-assimilated minorities—Poles, Greeks, Italians and other relative newcomers. To a great extent they are strongly Roman Catholic. . . .
> . . . Those who have most to thank the Democrats for, can most afford to vote Republican. Economically, these working-class groups have prospered. Emotionally and socially they are insecure.
> Far more than the mythology of the melting-pot would suggest, they have already chosen segregation for themselves. Poles cling to Polish neighborhoods, Italians tend to marry Italians. And now along comes the Negro, moving into beloved neighborhoods, threatening jobs, and stirring up unsuspected prejudice.

The polls that he studied so avidly that summer told the President that he had no need to worry, unless . . . These ominous tendencies would not eat away his long lead over Goldwater so long as public suspicion of black militancy were not aroused by some highly visible incident. But if the Democratic convention dissolved into nationally televised chaos on the issue of race, then all bets might be off. At the very moment that he had so carefully scheduled as the coronation of consensus, in other words, Lyndon Johnson could see in the Mississippi challenge a potential threat to each of the three main divisions of his army. If he leaned too far toward the challengers, he would lose the South. If he gave them nothing, then he would outrage the middle-class "conscience liberals." And if there was a bitter floor fight in which black militants seemed to be asking too much, there might be a backlash from labor. At all costs, the challenge must be contained.

The importance of the affair in Johnson's eyes can be judged from the resources he threw into the battle. He kept himself in the background and put Hubert Humphrey in charge of the operation, giving him a strong impression that his chances of the vice-presidential nomination would depend upon how he handled the assignment. Every then-powerful figure in the Democratic Party was given a role in the script: Governor David Lawrence of Pennsylvania, John Bailey of Connecticut, Johnson's confidential adviser Clark Clifford, among them.

At midnight on the Monday, Walter Reuther flew in from Detroit, breaking off critical contract negotiations with General Motors in order to use his influence on civil rights leaders to get them to persuade the MFDP to accept the White House's compromise. "Look, Martin," Reuther was heard to say to Dr. King, "we've given you all this money. . . ."

Every conceivable pressure was used on those members of the Credentials Committee who supported MFDP. For three full days, everything else in Atlantic City stopped while the President of the United States brought the entire weight of the Democratic Party to bear in the effort to persuade sixty-four black and four white people from Mississippi to accept two seats at the convention.

By Tuesday, the MFDP's support on the Credentials Committee had been gnawed away, and the committee voted for the White House position. Still the MFDP refused to give in. That night, the MFDP staged a sit-in. On hasty orders from White House aides over the walkie-talkies, the stewards handled it with kid gloves. But Lyndon Johnson's political nightmare was perilously close to coming true, right there on everybody's TV screen.

The climax came the next morning at the church where the MFDP delegates were staying. Now the civil rights establishment took over where the politicians had failed. Martin Luther King spoke for acceptance, and so did Rustin. But the delegates wouldn't have it. They had come to Atlantic City to unseat the other delegation. They were particularly incensed that the President should have presumed to nominate which of them should be seated, and all the more so because he had made the tactical blunder of insisting that one of the two chosen should be a white man. They remained irreconcilable.

The Mississippi challenge left lasting bitterness on both sides. Many liberals simply could not understand why MFDP had refused to accept the compromise. They could only suppose that the delegates had been misled by extremists.

The MFDP, on the other hand, and the young black leaders of SNCC, and black radicals in the country generally, read the pressure they had been subjected to by the President and the Democrats as conclusive confirmation of their emerging thesis that "the system" was ineradicably permeated by racism. They had seen the Democratic Party in action, and it had been solidly aligned against them, or so they could be forgiven for thinking. And they regarded the behavior of their friends—Reuther and Rauh, King and Rustin—as no better than treason.

The bitterness only revealed the chasm of genuine misunderstanding that separated what had now become two adversary positions: that of the liberals, and that of the radicals. To orthodox liberals, the behavior of the radicals in Atlantic City was both inexplicable and unforgivable. (MFDP, wrote Theodore H. White, "had stained the honor that so much courage and suffering had won it.")

A statement issued by the MFDP afterward shows how very differently radicals saw things. "The compromise was not designed to deal with the issues raised by the FDP," it argued. ". . . The FDP delegation came to Atlantic City to raise the issue of racism, not simply to demand recognition. It could not accept a token decision which had as its goal the avoidance of the question of racism." The MFDP and some of its supporters, in other words, saw the Democratic Party and liberals generally, white or black, no longer as the hope of a solution, but as part of the problem.

About a week after the convention, ten leading members of SNCC, together with Fanny Lou Hamer, left for Africa. They had been invited as guests of Sekou Touré, the Marxist President of Guinea. The journey itself had no special significance. It had been planned before the convention and was meant as a vacation. Nevertheless, it was a parting of the ways. Some of those who went to Guinea came home and went on working within the system, such as John Lewis and Julian Bond. Some, such as James Forman, moved toward a commitment to revolution. Robert Moses abdicated his leadership in Mississippi, which had been won by sheer courage and force of personality. Afraid that black Mississippians would think he had come to lead them to the Promised Land, he took his mother's name and called himself Robert Parris. A year or so later, he turned up late at night at a white radical friend's house in Washington. The friend asked him in. No, said Moses, he just wanted to say that he had come to the conclusion that "this black-white thing doesn't work." He was off to Africa.

After he left Mississippi, Moses had one more major effect on the history of the decade. He spent the summer of 1965 traveling around the country on behalf of an organization called the Committee of Unrepresented People. He was trying to get the students who had been to Mississippi, and others like them, to work for other causes, and especially against the Vietnam War. So Moses, who had come to civil rights from the peace movement, played a crucial part in shifting the focus of the nascent student rebellion from civil rights to the war. Shortly after that, he went to live permanently in Tanzania. He is still there.

By that time, it was indeed sadly clear that "this black-white thing" was going to be more difficult than it had seemed in the heady days of the March on Washington. In the spring of 1965, the civil rights movement stood on the eve of its culminating triumph. It was also on the point of falling to pieces.

The final act of the drama that had begun at Greensboro on February 1, 1960, ended five years later in another previously obscure southern town: Selma, in the heart of the Alabama Black Belt, fifty miles west of Montgomery. "The paths of Negro-white unity that had been converging," Martin Luther King wrote afterward, "crossed at Selma and like a giant X began to diverge."

On December 10, 1964, King received the Nobel Peace Prize in Oslo. On his return to New York he was the guest of honor at a reception in Harlem attended by Vice-President Humphrey, Governor Rockefeller and New York's Mayor Robert Wagner. On January 2, he arrived in Selma to announce that he was going to lead a voter-registration drive there.

Stokely Carmichael was one of the young fire-eaters in SNCC who had been against the attempt to work with the Democratic Party from the start. After the convention in Atlantic City, he moved his duffel bag from Mississippi, where he had been organizing the Second Congressional District for the MFDP, to the Freedom House in Selma, and started to organize voter registration in Lowndes County, which had a fearsome reputation for intimidation and violence. Late in December, he heard that King was going to Selma. He was furious.

SNCC had some reason to be annoyed with King's choice. They had been operating a voter registration project in Selma since early 1963. Once again, it seemed, King would move in, reap the harvest SNCC had planted, and walk off with the glory, and the fund-raising potential, that SNCC workers felt they had earned. Some of them wanted to snub King openly. Carmichael and the other leaders knew that couldn't be done: King was too much loved in Alabama. But feelings were bitter to start with, and they were not improved by the course of events.

Demonstrations began in mid-January, and on February 1 Dr. King and 770 other demonstrators were arrested. Five days later, he was released. He went straight to Washington, and was promised by Vice-President Humphrey and the new Attorney General, Nicholas de B. Katzenbach, that the Administration would bring in a voting rights bill to enforce black registration of qualified voters in such places as Alabama, where fewer than a quarter of qualified blacks were on the voting rolls.

The showdown came with three marches. The first was on March 7.

King was in Selma the night before, urging the people to march. "I can't promise you that it won't get you beaten," he said. But he did not march himself.

Why? He said he could not leave his own congregation in Atlanta for yet another Sunday. That consideration had hardly impeded his travels in the past. It is possible that he was anxious not to court arrest on a state charge, and probable that he had been asked not to take part by Attorney General Katzenbach, a New York patrician with but the dimmest comprehension of southern realities or black politics.

Whatever the reason, King's absence was a serious mistake. As the marchers streamed across the Pettus bridge onto Highway 80, appropriately the Jefferson Davis Highway, they were halted by a line of state troopers. Without warning, the sheriff's deputies and city police fell on them from behind with tear gas, clubs, whips and electric cattle prods. The marchers ran for their lives; more than fifty were seriously hurt.

The scene at the Pettus bridge, like many scenes in the history of the civil rights movement, had different meanings for different audiences. For the national television audience, it seemed a nightmarish dramatization of brutal southern resistance to dignified, nonviolent black protest. It helped to fill the sails of the Administration's voting-rights bill. But to activists, and to some extent to blacks generally, it suggested quite a different moral: the futility of Dr. King's conciliatory approach, and of his reliance on the federal government. It also raised questions about King's judgment and even his courage.

Two days later, King did lead a march. That did him no good either. In the meantime, a federal judge had issued an injunction forbidding it. This put King in a dilemma that was a sort of parable of his whole precarious political position. If he defied the injunction, he risked losing the support of the White House and of white liberals. If he obeyed it, he would infuriate SNCC and perhaps many other blacks. The march duly reached the eastern end of the Pettus bridge. There George Wallace's troopers sprung an additional trap for King. They stood aside, leaving him free to march on, if he was willing to ignore the injunction. He was not. Singing, "Ain't Goin' to Let Nobody Turn Me 'Round," the marchers turned around.

SNCC's disillusion with King had become absolute. But, once again, King was lucky. That night, a white Unitarian minister was murdered by whites outside a Selma cafe, shouting "Nigger lover" as they beat him with iron bars. Two days later, when the man died, Lyndon Johnson was more angry than he had ever been. At a meeting with George Wallace at the White House on March 13, the President made it very plain that if the National Guard was not called out, federal troops would go in to pro-

tect the marchers. And two days later, again, on March 15, LBJ went up
to the Capitol and there pronounced, to a Joint Session of Congress, the
strongest commitment an American President had ever made to the struggle for black equality:

> . . . It is not just Negroes, but really it is all of us who must over-
> come the crippling legacy of bigotry and injustice. And . . . we . . . shall
> . . . overcome.

When James Baldwin wrote, two years before, "We cannot be free
until they are free," he can hardly have imagined that his thought would
have been echoed so soon, in that place, by that man, in that office.

The third march, which set out from Selma on March 21, was a tri-
umphal celebration, its free passage guaranteed by the Alabama National
Guard, called by the President into federal service.

When Martin Luther King, at his most paternal, urged his supporters
as they left to "walk together, children, don't you get weary," few of his
children could hear him for the noise of the army helicopters overhead.
They walked. And on the fifth day they came proudly into Montgomery,
thirty thousand strong. There were white ministers, and rabbis, and the
wives of senators and famous men, and representatives of the coalition of
labor and liberals who had pushed through the Civil Rights Act. At a concert on the last night of the march there were so many stars of show business that you might have thought you were at the Academy Awards dinner. In the grounds of the Capitol in Montgomery, Martin Luther King
was at his most eloquent. "How long?" he asked again and again, and each
time he answered, "Not long." It was the rhetorical equivalent of whistling in the dark. They had reached Montgomery. But the Promised Land
was as far away as ever. And they were no longer walking together.

Over the fifteen months from Selma to the middle of 1966, both
SNCC and CORE fell apart. There were three main theoretical questions
at issue. Could the movement remain nonviolent? Could blacks continue
to work with whites and, if so, on what terms? Was the movement
reformist, or was it revolutionary? But, on those issues, bitter divisions of
race or class or politics, and personality, fought it out in hundreds of angry
meetings.

In SNCC, the transformation from an interracial, nonviolent group
working for civil rights into a black separatist one that rejected nonviolence and, at least in theory, worked for revolution, can be traced through
a series of increasingly angry staff meetings.

The first was held in October 1964, just after the leaders had come
back from Africa. One problem was what to do about some two hundred

white volunteers who had disproved cynical predictions by staying on after the Mississippi Summer Project. Eighty-five of them were made members of the staff. This caused resentment among the working-class black veterans, who were afraid they would be swamped by middle-class, mainly white college students. One scathing paper circulated about the time of the October meeting illustrates these fears very plainly. It was an attack on "bourgeois sentimentality." "Some of the good sisters and brothers," it said scornfully,

> . . . think that our business is the spreading of "the redemptive warmth of personal confrontation," "emotional enrichment," "compassionate and sympathetic personal relationships," and other varieties of mouth to mouth resuscitation derived from the vocabulary of group therapy and progressive liberal witch doctors. But we ain't got enough redemptive compassion and cultural enrichment to go around.

As a result of this sort of feeling, a negative decision of the greatest importance was taken. There had been a plan for repeating the Mississippi voter registration project on a huge scale, covering the whole of the southern Black Belt in 1965. It never happened.

At the second meeting, at Waveland, Mississippi, in November 1964, Robert Moses was already abdicating his leadership. Stokely Carmichael was beginning to emerge, alongside James Forman, as challenger for the vacant place. By February 1965, when a third major meeting was held, in Atlanta, the opposition between the black working-class element and the middle-class liberals was overt. "If this organization is going to be revolutionary," said Ella Baker, "we are going to have to do certain things." A white staff member jumped up. "This is a liberal democratic organization," he said, "and it's not going to be pushed into violence."

Then came Selma.

The march from Selma to Montgomery passed through Lowndes County, where fewer than a hundred white families owned more than 90 per cent of the land and not a single black person was registered to vote. Stokely Carmichael and his friends had already decided to start a voter registration campaign there, Mississippi style, before the events in Selma.

When he had to choose a symbol to put on the ballot, Carmichael chose the black panther. It was a brilliant stroke of public relations. The panther was just the bogey to scare the white folks: lean, black, hungry and dangerous. Not long after, when Carmichael was out in California, he told me, no fewer than five groups wanted to adopt the black panther as their badge. The group he said yes to was led by Huey Newton and Bobby Seale. That, according to Carmichael, was how the Black Panther Party got its name. But the black panther first became the badge of black militancy not in Oakland but in rural Alabama in that decisive spring of 1965.

The night after King's triumphant speech in Montgomery, the wife of a Detroit labor union official, Mrs. Violet Liuzzo, who was ferrying marchers back to Selma in her car, was murdered by the Klan. For the radicals, her death was just one more in a long series. Had she been black, they reflected bitterly, there would have been no fuss about it. For them, the lesson of Selma was that it was simply hopeless to rely on the White House or the Justice Department to protect black people who challenged the code of the Deep South. And there was another consideration in their minds, too, that was less easy to acknowledge: the passage of the Civil Rights Act of 1964 and, soon, of the Voting Rights Act of 1965 made much of the organizing they had been doing so far obsolete. They had to move on.

At the SNCC staff meeting in November 1965, Carmichael's friend Courtland Cox chalked on the blackboard: "Get power for black people. The people want power, power to control the courthouse, power to control their own lives." (He was specifically not talking about power over white people.) "Something clicked in me," wrote Jim Forman. "I felt we had emerged from the internal disorder. . . . I went up to the blackboard and wrote down, 'Power, Education, Organization.'" The black militants had found the slogan they would be shouting to the world in six months.

At the same meeting, SNCC discussed the Vietnam War. Two strands in its tradition met here: one from the top down, the other from the bottom up. Many of SNCC's leaders had long been pacifists. Nonviolence itself grew out of an international pacifist tradition. Its roots went back to Gandhi and Tolstoy. At the same time, the casualties of the war were being disproportionately borne by black communities. The very black youths SNCC was trying to reach were those most likely to be drafted and killed in Vietnam. As early as the spring of 1965, Bob Moses had been speaking against the war. In January 1966, SNCC went further and expressed sympathy for draft resistance.

By the spring of 1966, the process of radicalization was complete. At the staff meeting in May that year at Kingston Springs, Tennessee, Stokely Carmichael was elected chairman in place of the nonviolent John Lewis, who had said, "I'm no Communist, I'm a Baptist minister." The executive council was renamed the "central committee." A resolution was passed that fell short of expelling white members, but ordered them to work thenceforth only in white communities. Nonviolence, both as a philosophy and as a tactic, had long been dropped.

The evolution of CORE paralleled that of SNCC. As early as February 1965, before Selma, a Long Island chapter leader said, "Nonviolence is coming to an end." The split was to some extent personalized in the competition between James Farmer, who was committed to integration and nonviolence, married to a white wife, and moved easily in the urbane world of the national civil rights leadership; and Floyd McKissick, a tough-talking black lawyer from North Carolina. After Farmer's departure, in late 1965, essentially the same conflict was personalized again in the contest between McKissick and George Wiley for national director; McKissick won. At about the same time, the even more outspoken black separatist Roy Innes, of New York CORE, became national chairman. Ultimately, in 1968, Innes squeezed McKissick out, too.

It would be a mistake to focus too much on the politics of the national CORE organization, however; as a membership organization with chapters all over both North and South, CORE was battered by all the swirling winds of change in both black and white communities. The new division first became obvious at the national convention that was held in Durham, North Carolina, in the summer of 1965. The proceedings were dominated, as CORE's historians August Meier and Elliott Rudwick put it, by four questions: "the growing gap between the southern field staff and the national organization, the question of the legitimacy of violence, the black-white issue and the Vietnam war." Just the same four issues, we saw, were dividing SNCC at just the same time.

The trend toward radical black nationalism seemed irresistible. Community organization seemed in practice to stimulate black separatism. Just as SNCC workers in Mississippi had long taken to carrying guns, so CORE field staff in Louisiana, where CORE's main southern effort was deployed, struck up an alliance with the Deacons for Defense in Bogalusa, a black vigilante group who went openly armed. Already in the spring of 1965 there was opposition to white staff appointments. By the fall of that year there was opposition even to white membership in many chapters. At the 1966 convention, CORE formally repudiated nonviolence, denounced the Vietnam War, and endorsed the slogan "Black power."

On June 5, 1966, James Meredith, the black air-force veteran who had integrated the University of Mississippi in 1962, set out to march the length of the state from North to South as a one-man demonstration that blacks in Mississippi were still not free. The next day, a certain Aubrey James Norvell, a white man, rose from the brush at the side of the road and emptied a shotgun into him.

Meredith was taken to a hospital in Memphis, and there, the same day, Martin Luther King, Floyd McKissick and Stokely Carmichael met around his bedside. Then and there began one of the most bizarre ideological debates of the twentieth century.

Before leaving the hospital, the three leaders agreed to carry on with

Meredith's march, and they called on people to join them in the name not only of their own three organizations, but of others, such as the NAACP, which had joined in the great demonstrations of the past. But those days were over. The mood had changed. The old unity had gone.

Within an hour, they were marching. On the road, and in a motel that night, the debate went on. When they stopped marching, someone started singing "We Shall Overcome." But when they reached the line "Black and white together," the younger marchers stopped singing, and when they got to the chorus, they sang, "We shall overrun."

There were two points on which King could not get the radicals to give in. They refused to commit themselves to nonviolence. And they did not want white people along.

The climax came in Greenwood on the eleventh day of the march. That was where Carmichael's friend Willie Ricks first shouted, "Black power!" The crowd deliriously chanted it back to him, drowning the authorized slogan, which was "Freedom now!"

The next day, King, Carmichael and McKissick met to thrash things out in the parish house of a Catholic church in Yazoo City. King had nothing against black power, he said. But the connotations of the phrase would give the impression that they were talking about black domination rather than black equality. Carmichael was impatient with connotations. "Power," he said, "is the only thing respected in this world, and we must get it at any cost."

The meeting ended with a compromise: neither slogan should be used. But that didn't hold. The media had picked up black power. And they were right to see it as marking the end of an epoch.

The civil rights movement was over. Something else had begun. Whether it would bring blacks real power, of course, was another matter.

# Vietnam: the Beginning

At the end of January 1965, Lyndon Johnson had succeeded in the first stages of his task beyond anyone's expectation. He had taken the power of the presidency into his hands masterfully, and on the whole—even the Kennedy people had to admit—he had used it wisely as well as effectively. Now he had been re-elected with a majority that even he found satisfactory. This was the moment, before the prestige of victory could be dissipated, to stake his claim to the respect of the historians.

Johnson was so conscious of the eye of history that a joke went around Washington about the style of his speeches:

Q: Why does LBJ talk so slow?
A: Because he thinks he's dictating to a stonemason.

Yet his ambition to build a Great Society was not the vulgar megalomania it has been drawn as. Here was a political leader in a position of apparently impregnable strength. He had to decide how to spend national resources that were growing at the rate of 5 per cent a year. His economic advisers were telling him that they had discovered the secret of perpetual growth. "Both our increasing understanding of the effectiveness of fiscal policy," they wrote in that month's economic report to Congress, "and the continued improvement of . . . our economic information, strengthen the conviction that recessions can be increasingly avoided and ultimately wiped out." Here was one of the rare moments when a government seemed to have real freedom to compose a national agenda with some assurance that it would be able to do most of the things it chose to do. Lyndon Johnson's agenda was neither unwise nor unworthy.

The package of legislative proposals that he put forward in his State of the Union message that January was drafted with a virtuoso politician's hand. There was something in it for every group that had gone to make up the motley army of his majority. There was an education bill for the young, and a medical-care bill for the old; an arts foundation for the sophisticates, and a change in the immigration laws for the folks from the Old Country. Business was to be placated with large cuts in excise taxes, and labor with repeal of the hated "right-to-work" clause of Taft-Hartley. The desert West was to get water, and the crowded Northeast was promised trains running at two miles a minute.

But the program was more than just a political balancing act or another dip in the old bran tub. It was a venture into what might be called the metapolitics of postaffluence: the politics, that is, of a country where the number of chickens comfortably exceeded the number of pots. The President invited Americans to start work on the building of a society that would ask "not how much, but how good; not only how to create wealth, but how to use it; not only how fast we are going, but where we are headed." His speech echoed the language in which Alexis de Tocqueville, a century and a quarter earlier, had described what seemed to him the essence of the American character: "Forever seeking, forever falling to rise again," Tocqueville had written, "often disappointed but not discouraged, he tends unceasingly towards that unmeasured greatness so indistinctly visible at the end of the long track." In that same spirit Johnson (and his speechwriters) saw the Great Society they wanted to build not as a stable condition of pluperfect affluence but as "the excitement of becoming—always becoming, trying, falling, resting and trying again—but always trying and always gaining."

If it was something more than just politics, Johnson's program was also something more than just rhetoric. In a real sense he was proposing to carry out the agenda of the liberal consensus.

It was not only Johnson's program, after all. The proposals were based on the recommendations of the fourteen task forces he had set up, back in August, to follow up the speech at the University of Michigan, in May, with which he had launched the good ship Great Society. The membership of those task forces was like an honor roll of the liberal intellectual community. Far more than under the Kennedy administration—more than ever before or since, indeed—this was a moment when the intellectuals, especially the social scientists, had the run of the domestic departments of the federal government as recruits, consultants, idea men, kibbitzers and mandarins. With the ambrosial scent of presidential approval in the air, they fell over each other to fund studies and to back the most promising of those studies with massive federal action programs. It can be said without injustice to the clever and ambitious men who descended on Washington by every plane, many of them sharpened by years of committee work devoted to fighting for far smaller scraps of funding from foundations, that it had not escaped their notice that the premium would be on those studies that confirmed that problems could indeed be solved by spending federal money and in ways that did not ruffle too many presidential or Congressional feathers.

Even in foreign affairs this was a time of growing hope—for those not privy to the tightly held secret of just how bad things were in Southeast Asia. Since the Cuban missile crisis, there had been a steady downgrading of earlier estimates of the threat from the Soviet Union, military, economic or ideological. "Well-informed Americans," I reported in a column in mid-January 1965, after a round of interviews in the White House, the State Department and the Pentagon, "now no longer fear the Communist power, nor do they expect the Cold War to last forever." The State of the Union message avoided the subject of Vietnam except for a perfunctory pledge, or so it seemed: "To ignore aggression would only increase the danger of a larger war."

Khrushchev had fallen the previous October, at the height of the presidential campaign, and on the same day the Chinese had exploded their first nuclear weapon. The first reports of open confrontation between the U.S.S.R. and China in the Far East had begun to reach Washington; it looked as though the split between the two Communist great powers might be both serious and permanent. The Administration was determined to improve its relations with Khrushchev's successors; and both the Sino-Soviet split and the Chinese bomb seemed on the whole favorable omens for this enterprise.

"This, then," Lyndon Johnson felt able to report that January, "is the State of the Union: free, growing, restless, and full of hope." In this mood of euphoria, on January 27, just one week after the beginning of his first full term in office, he received a memo that appeared like a ghost at the feast and set off the train of events that soon extinguished the high hopes of his inaugural honeymoon.

The memo was signed by McGeorge Bundy but it arose out of a conversation between him and Robert McNamara. It therefore represented the concurrent opinion of the two forceful men whose help and good opinion Johnson had needed so badly that night when the three of them climbed aboard the symbolic helicopter at Andrews Air Force Base.

So far, they now told the President, they had gone along with his reluctance to change his fundamental policy in Vietnam. Dean Rusk, the third-most-powerful of his advisers, they acknowledged, still thought that the consequences of all alternatives to the existing policy were so bad that it simply had to be made to work. They disagreed. Things were going so badly in Vietnam that the present course could lead only to "disastrous defeat." And so, the memo said, "the time has come for harder choices." With the election behind him and with the danger of a decisive Viet Cong offensive at any moment, the President must choose between "escalation and withdrawal," between abandoning the American commitment to prevent a Viet Cong victory and making that commitment good with American air power. As a last step before the final decision they proposed that Bundy be sent to Saigon to see things for himself.

He left on February 2 with a team of Vietnam experts from the Pentagon, the White House and the State Department. It was one of the fateful moments when the threads of this story spun together as if they were being twisted from on high by a President of the Immortals with a malicious sense of humor and a taste for bad theater.

On February 1, Martin Luther King, back from receiving his Nobel Peace Prize, was carted off to jail in Selma.

On February 2, Alexei Kosygin, the new Soviet Prime Minister, left Moscow for Hanoi. One widespread fear was that the Russians now thought a final Viet Cong victory was so imminent that they were trying to claim a share in the credit for it. President Johnson, in any case, took this opportunity to announce that he hoped to meet Kosygin at the summit in a year's time or so.

On February 3, two U.S. destroyers were scheduled to sail on what was called a DESOTO patrol in the Tonkin Gulf, for the first time since the previous September. Like the ships that had set off the Tonkin Gulf incident in August 1964, their mission included electronic intelligence. But this time there was more than a hint of provocation about its rationale. U.S. aircraft were standing by with orders to bomb carefully chosen targets in North Vietnam if the destroyers were attacked. The plans had been drawn weeks before, under the heading "Punitive and Crippling Reprisal Actions on Targets in North Vietnam," and the code name for the operation was Flaming Dart. At the last moment, however, the DESOTO patrol was first postponed for four days and then countermanded. Washington was reluctant to bomb North Vietnam while Kosygin was in Hanoi.

Flaming Dart was not to be wasted, though. Hanoi did not have any matching inhibitions about attacking Americans in South Vietnam while the President's personal representative was in Saigon. On the night of February 6 (February 7 local time) a Viet Cong unit mortared an American advisers' barracks at Pleiku, in the central highlands, killing nine and wounding one hundred Americans.

The American response, both in Saigon and in Washington, was unhesitating. "We have kept our gun over the mantel and our shells in the cupboard for a long time now," said the President. "And what was the result? They are killing our men while they sleep in the night." Flaming Dart was ordered immediately.

This was not the first time that U.S. aircraft had bombed North Vietnamese territory; that had happened after the Tonkin Gulf incident. This was the moment, just the same, when—as Chester Cooper, a veteran CIA official, then working in the White House, who had gone to Saigon with Bundy, put it—"the die was cast."

Bundy visited the victims of the Pleiku attack in a hospital that afternoon. He seemed greatly perturbed by what he saw—a little illogically, perhaps, since he had succeeded in maintaining his famous detachment through some hundreds of thousands of Vietnamese casualties.

That same day, in any event, Bundy and his experts boarded *Air Force One* and set off back to Washington. When they landed, Bundy went straight to the White House and handed the President a report he had drafted in mid-air, with an annex drafted by another former Harvard professor, McNamara's right-hand man, John McNaughton. With his first glance, the President could see that the debate in which his advisers had agonized for a year was over.

> The situation in Vietnam is deteriorating [Bundy's own report began], and without new U.S. action defeat appears inevitable . . . within the next year or so. There is still time to turn around, but not much. . . .
>
> The stakes in Vietnam are extremely high. . . . The international prestige of the United States, and a substantial part of our influence are directly at risk in Vietnam. There is no way of unloading the burden on the Vietnamese themselves, and there is no way of negotiating ourselves out of Vietnam which offers any serious promise at present.

A negotiated withdrawal, Bundy said, would in his judgment constitute "surrender on the installment plan." Instead he recommended as "the most promising course available" what he called a policy of "graduated and continuing reprisal."

The phrase did credit to the Harvard training in verbal skills, for what Bundy and McNaughton were saying was that the time had come to move beyond reprisals in the natural meaning of the words, namely retaliation for specific acts, such as the attack on U.S. ships in the Tonkin Gulf or on the barracks at Pleiku. Now they were urging the President to take the momentous decision, long contemplated and long deferred, to make systematic use of American air power so as to strengthen Saigon and weaken Hanoi. It was perhaps McNaughton, the lawyer, who devised the

semantic *léger de main* by which a decision to retaliate could be made to
slide unnoticed into a decision to go beyond retaliation:

> Once a program of reprisals is clearly underway [the annex began],
> it should not be necessary to connect each specific act against North Viet-
> nam to a particular outrage in the South. . . .
> This reprisal policy should begin at a low level. . . . At the same
> time it should be recognized that in order to maintain the power of re-
> prisal without the risk of excessive loss, an "air war" may in fact be neces-
> sary. We should therefore be ready to develop a separate justification for
> the destruction of Communist air power. The essence of such an explana-
> tion should be that these actions . . . in no sense represent any intent to
> wage offensive war. . . .

In no sense?

After Pleiku, it was as if some membrane of inhibition in Lyndon
Johnson's mind had been pierced. One by one, in a few weeks, he ordered
actions that he had resisted for as many months of Talmudic analysis and
agonized debate inside the bureaucracy.

There was a second Flaming Dart reprisal after a Viet Cong action at
Qui Nhon on February 11. This time, it was justified publicly in accord-
ance with the Bundy-McNaughton formula as a generalized response to
"continued acts of aggression." Only two days later, on February 13, the
President abandoned the fig leaf of retaliation completely and ordered Operation Rolling Thunder, continuous air war on North Vietnam, though
what with an Anglo-Soviet peace initiative, poor bombing weather, and
political instability in Saigon, the bombing didn't actually begin until
early March.

A propaganda campaign to represent the war as almost wholly caused
by acts of aggression built up step by step with the "punishment." The
campaign was orchestrated around a State Department white paper issued
on February 27. This grossly exaggerated the importance of arms supplied
to the Viet Cong from outside South Vietnam as opposed to the weapons
they captured from government forces, and flatly stated, "The war in Vietnam is *not* a spontaneous and local rebellion against the established government."

This last statement, indeed the white paper as a whole, illustrated just
how far the government was now prepared to go in the direction of deceiv-
ing the American people not only about its own intentions, which might
be justified by the need for operational secrecy, but about the nature of
the situation to which it claimed it was obliged to respond. For in a secret
paper written to guide the thinking of the President and his top advisers
only three months earlier, the interagency Vietnam working group had

conceded, "Despite a large and growing North Vietnamese contribution to the Viet Cong and insurrection, the primary sources of Communist strength in the South remain indigenous."

The decision to launch an air war had been taken on political and psychological grounds—though the President's advisers did not agree among themselves what those grounds were. Walt Rostow, who was still head of the policy planning staff in the State Department but was later to move over to the White House to replace McGeorge Bundy, argued that to bomb Hanoi would be a signal of American resolve to Hanoi. General Taylor, on the other hand, wanted bombing because he thought it would stiffen morale in Saigon. The Bundy-McNaughton report added a third psychological target to these two: "the minds of the Viet Cong cadres."

The military had been arguing for bombing all along for reasons of a wholly different kind. They wanted to destroy, physically, the enemy's ability to wage war, both by bombing military installations in the North and by "interdicting" the lines of communications by which men and munitions were infiltrated into the South.

It did not take long after Rolling Thunder began, in March, for the military's view to triumph. There was a gradual shift from politically and psychologically chosen targets to the lines of communication that the military thought most critical to infiltration.

McGeorge Bundy had not so much as mentioned the sending of U.S. combat units to Vietnam in his post-Pleiku memorandum. (This was no new idea, however. Robert McNamara had written in a memorandum for President Kennedy as early as November 1961 that he agreed with the Joint Chiefs of Staff that "the chances are against, probably sharply against, preventing [the fall of South Vietnam to the Communists] by any measures short of introduction of U.S. forces on a substantial scale.")

On February 22, only two weeks after Pleiku, the new U.S. commander in Vietnam, General William Westmoreland, asked for troops to defend the perimeter of the bases from which Flaming Dart sorties were being flown. Thus did the ladder of escalation lead upward, simply and logically: bombers to protect the destroyers, troops to protect the bombers, and all with "no intent to wage an offensive war." On March 8 two marine battalions splashed ashore at DaNang. The first American combat units had arrived in Vietnam. It would be wrong to suppose that the Administration regarded those two battalions as a decisive commitment of U.S. ground forces. It is not clear whether the civilian officials in Washington saw through the thin pretense that the marines were there just to protect DaNang. The military certainly did. They knew that it would have needed at least five times as many troops to hold a perimeter wide enough to keep the Viet Cong out of mortar range of the airfield. Westmoreland understood that the two battalions must be the entering wedge of American military commitment, whether that was what the government in Washington wanted or not.

At this critical juncture there was one dissent, and it came from a surprising quarter. General Maxwell Taylor had been the first American official to recommend sending in American troops. Back in 1961 he had proposed to President Kennedy that combat troops be smuggled into the Mekong Delta under the guise of army engineers working on flood relief. Later, again, he was to be a dogged defender of the American presence in Vietnam. But now his reaction to Westmoreland's request was instant and skeptical.

He cabled to Washington the same day that, once U.S. troops were there, the temptation to use them would grow insatiably. He warned that what he called "white-faced soldiers" wouldn't be able to tell the difference between friendly and unfriendly Vietnamese; that the marines were neither trained nor equipped for jungle warfare; and that, like the French before them, they would fail at it.

He was right on every count. But he didn't press his dissent. And no one in Washington, with the single exception of Under-Secretary of State George Ball, took it up.

Now the dam broke. The President, the military and the civilian officials seemed almost to be vying with each other to see who could think up the best reason for pouring in more troops. Westmoreland asked for more marines to secure other bases, and at the beginning of April the President said yes. Even before that, Johnson had asked the Joint Chiefs at a meeting to come up with ways "to kill more VC." He was getting his blood up.

On April 20, McNamara and the other top civilian officials concerned met the chairman of the Joint Chiefs of Staff, the Pacific commander (Admiral Sharp), and Westmoreland in Honolulu. After six weeks of Rolling Thunder, they agreed that air war on the North was not going to prevent Viet Cong victory in the South and decided to try another way of "breaking the enemy's will." They would send in enough U.S. troops to hold four coastal enclaves. This would prove to the enemy that he couldn't win. It was reckoned that a total of ninety thousand American, Korean and Australian troops would achieve this effect.

In May the President's zeal for liberty was diverted by the "crisis" in the Dominican Republic. In the meantime things went from bad to worse in Vietnam. Another government fell in Saigon. The Viet Cong seemed on the point of cutting the country in half. And at the battle of Dong

Xoai, in June, the South Vietnamese Army was closer than ever to abject rout. Westmoreland asked for more troops: either thirty-three or thirty-five battalions, depending on how you calculated. The Joint Chiefs offered him forty-four battalions, and the President agreed to this higher figure by mid-July. By the end of July the Pentagon was planning in terms of a total American strength of 193,000, or more than twice the number that had been thought necessary at Honolulu three months before. That higher force level was actually reached before the end of the year.

Two similarities with the decision to bomb North Vietnam are striking. The first is that, just as Washington decided to bomb before it made up its mind why bombing would help, so troops were poured into Vietnam before it had been decided how they would be used. First they were to be sent to protect bases. Then they were to man enclaves. By mid-June Westmoreland had received permission to commit U.S. forces outside the enclaves, and the first major "search and destroy" operation was mounted in War Zone D north of Saigon.

Secondly, once again the Administration did not tell the American people the truth about what it was doing. On July 28 at a press conference the President said that "the lessons of history" showed that "surrender" in Vietnam would not bring peace. In one breath he wrapped together the Munich myth and the domino theory:

> We learned from Hitler at Munich that success only feeds the appetite of aggression. The battle would be renewed in one country and then another country. . . .
> We intend to convince the Communists that we cannot be defeated by force of arms or by superior power. . . .
> I have today ordered to Vietnam . . . forces that will raise our fighting strength from 75,000 to 125,000 almost immediately. Additional forces will be needed later, and they will be sent as requested.

That was a disingenuous way of describing plans that were already made for sending close to two hundred thousand troops. A reporter asked:

> Q: Mr. President, does the fact that you are sending additional forces to Vietnam imply any change in the existing policy of relying mainly on the South Vietnamese to carry out offensive operations and using American forces to guard installations . . . ?
> A: It does not imply any change in policy whatever.

One last point is worth noting. This decision to send an American expeditionary force to South Vietnam to preserve its government had been taken with a minimum of consultation with that government and certainly in no meaningful sense at its request. The succession of governments in

Saigon during the first half of 1965 represented little except fractions of the officer corps and the civilian bureaucracy. They did not ask for this American help, and they were in no position to refuse it. Just how eagerly Washington rushed to their support is perhaps best suggested by a desperate cable, from the always realistic General Taylor, sent to McGeorge Bundy in April:

> This mission is charged with securing implementation by the two month old Quat government of a 21 point military program, a 41 point non-military program, a 16 point Rowan USIS program and a 12 point CIA program. Now this new cable opens up new vistas of further points as if we can win here somehow on a point score. . . .
>
> Mac, can't we be better protected from our friends?

In that spirit, ever activist, ever statistical, the eager bureaucrats of the New Frontier rushed headlong into disaster. In a little under six months, they had committed the United States to an undeclared air war on North Vietnam and an undeclared land war in the South.

Were the decisions taken in the spring and early summer of 1965 real decisions? Hadn't the decision to bomb North Vietnam, at any rate, been taken in reality months earlier? Didn't the President merely defer executing it until the 1964 election was safely behind him?

In one sense, the debate that led up to those decisions can be traced back over more than a decade and through four U.S. administrations: as far, for example, as the moment in 1950 when Dean Acheson, already under attack for having "lost" China, asked the French Colonial Government in Indochina what help it would need to defeat the Viet Minh. Early in 1952, a statement of policy by the National Security Council laid it down as the formal goal of U.S. policy in that part of the world "to prevent the countries of South-East Asia from passing into the Communist orbit." In 1954 the Joint Chiefs of Staff formally recommended the bombing of Communist forces in Indochina. They specifically approved the use of atomic bombs "in the event that such course appears militarily advantageous."

For a year before the order was given for Operation Rolling Thunder, the Administration had been seriously contemplating the bombing of North Vietnam. As early as the end of May 1964—two and a half months before the Tonkin Gulf incident—the new assistant secretary of state for far eastern affairs, William P. Bundy (who happened to be Dean Acheson's son-in-law as well as McGeorge Bundy's brother) produced a laboriously worked-out "scenario." It was rejected by the President's senior advisers. But it came uncannily close to predicting the course events actually took:

1. Stall off any conference on Vietnam until D-Day.
2. Intermediary (Canadian?) tell North Vietnam in general terms that US does not want to destroy the North Vietnam regime (and indeed is willing "to provide a carrot") but is determined to protect South Vietnam from North Vietnam. . . .
3. (D—20) Obtain Joint Resolution /from Congress/ approving past actions and authorizing whatever is necessary with respect to Vietnam. . . .
8. (D—13) Release . . . full documentation of North Vietnamese supply and direction of the Viet Cong.
15. (D-day) Launch first strikes (See attachment C for targets). . . .

In August the Tonkin Gulf incident not only gave the President a joint resolution textually almost identical to the one Bundy drafted in connection with this scenario; U.S. aircraft did actually bomb North Vietnam, thus removing important psychological and political inhibitions against sustained bombing later on. In early September there was open discussion among the President's advisers of the advantages of deliberately provoking Hanoi into some act that could be used as a pretext for bombing. The fact that the South Vietnamese, with both help and encouragement from the United States, had been carrying out clandestine raids on North Vietnam for months meant that provocation would be neither ethically unthinkable nor difficult to arrange.

By November, with the election past, the debate within the Administration had refined down to the discussion of three alternative "options," A, B, and C—each of which involved bombing North Vietnam!

Even when the Viet Cong blew up a U.S. officers' billet in Saigon on Christmas Eve, he ignored the opportunity to order bombing as a reprisal. In his memoirs, he treats the memo from McGeorge Bundy on January 27, reflecting as it did the latter's talk with McNamara, as the event that led to the decision to retaliate for Pleiku. Once that threshold had been crossed, the decisions—to order continuous bombing of North Vietnam and to send in first a few and then more and more American troops—seemed almost automatic.

Ultimately, then, the fateful decisions were taken by the President. But they were taken in the context of the "institutionalized presidency" which had grown up in response to the supposed demands of the Cold War and which was virtually isolated by recruitment, style, intellectual tradition, and above all by secrecy from electoral politics. The American people were not consulted. Lyndon Johnson had gone to great lengths to conceal from the electorate the nature of the decisions that were being debated. On September 28, for example, in a speech in Manchester, New Hampshire, right in the middle of the policy debate inside the national security apparatus on the very question of bombing, and after it had become plain that at the very least a decision might be taken to bomb North Vietnam, he said this:

> Some of our people—Mr. Nixon, Mr. Rockefeller, Mr. Scranton, and Mr. Goldwater—have all, at some time or other, suggested the possible wisdom of going north in Vietnam. As far as I am concerned, I want to be very cautious and careful, and use it only as a last resort, when I start dropping bombs that are likely to involve American boys in a war in Asia with 700 million Chinese.
>
> So just for the moment I have not thought we were ready for American boys to do the fighting for Asian boys. What I have been trying to do, with the situation that I found, was to get the boys in Vietnam to do their own fighting with our advice and with our equipment. That is the course we are following. So we are not going north and drop bombs at this stage of the game, and we are not going south and run out and leave it for the Communists to take over. . . .

Now, that is a fairly remarkable piece of demagoguery by any standards. Connoisseurs will appreciate touches such as "some of our people" for the Republicans, and "with the situation that I found." The last sentence actually succeeds in confusing invasion and withdrawal! Confusing as they were, however, the net effect of such speeches was to leave the average American voter with a very clear idea. He was being asked to choose between a President who was against both bombing North Vietnam and sending American boys to fight in South Vietnam, and a Republican challenger who was not only in favor of both those things but apparently did not even rule out using nuclear weapons.

The President had gone to similar lengths to deceive the press. Only the very best-informed reporters and columnists in Washington had any inkling of the issues that were being debated inside the national security apparatus. Even those that did were inhibited by a professionally improper but very real dilemma: should they reveal that Johnson *might* be a bomber, and so risk helping Goldwater, who certainly was?

Finally, Congress was largely kept in ignorance. The President made a considerable show of consulting "Congressional leaders," especially those members of the armed services committees who could be relied on to go along with anything that the military wanted. But the information that congressmen and senators as a whole were given was simply not adequate to support serious critical discussion.

The President had armed himself with authority to do virtually what-

ever he thought necessary in the form of the joint resolution rushed
through after the Tonkin Gulf incident. It is doubtful whether, even at
the time, the resolution would have passed with only two dissentient votes
in the two houses (those of Senators Morse and Gruening) if the Administration had told Congress the truth. By suppressing the fact that South
Vietnamese patrol boats, supplied by the United States and with the Administration's approval, had attacked North Vietnamese shore targets only
a few hours before the North Vietnamese attacks on the American destroyer, the President totally transformed the character of what the North
Vietnamese had done. The Administration's version of events turned a
tough but natural response to an invasion of sovereignty into an unprovoked "act of aggression." That would justify U.S. retaliation and could be
relied on to close ranks in Congress and in the country. And the Tonkin
Gulf episode was only the most flagrant instance of the way in which
Congress was manipulated.

The Pentagon Papers historian of the decision to bomb North Vietnam reports, "The question of constitutional authority for open acts of
war against a sovereign nation was never seriously raised." The President
and all his advisers, civilian and military, simply assumed that in practice
the absolute power to make war belonged to the presidency.

The secrecy and isolation of the national-security bureaucracy were to
have many results. One of the first of them was a certain stale quality
about the bureaucracy's own work. It is depressing to open the Pentagon
Papers and see how the written arguments of men with a reputation for
clarity and intelligence—McNamara, John McNaughton, the Bundy
brothers—were dominated by *cliché*, fixed ideas, unexamined assumptions
and a persistent tendency to argue backward from predetermined conclusions.

The best known of the assumptions is the so-called "domino theory."
As early as the hearings on the Mutual Security Act, in 1951, Dean Rusk
was arguing that since the Viet Minh rebels in Indochina had help from
China, then their war against the French was tantamount to Chinese ag-
gression and would in turn encourage further aggression elsewhere. In
June 1964 the President asked his advisers whether this was still true:
would the rest of Southeast Asia fall if South Vietnam came under North
Vietnamese control? Back came the considered response of the CIA's
Board of National Estimates:

> With the possible exception of Cambodia, it is likely that no nation
> in the area would quickly succumb to communism as a result of the fall
> of Laos and South Vietnam. Furthermore a continuation of the spread
> of communism in the area would not be inexorable, and any spread which

did take place would take time—time in which the total situation might change in any number of ways unfavorable to the communist cause.

That expert judgment destroyed the whole rationale for U.S. policy. It was not, so far as the Pentagon Papers reveal, discussed or challenged. But here is all that remained of it in the final draft of the Working Group's report, a single qualifying clause as the archaeological vestige of an argument buried under mounds of assertion:

> The so-called "domino" theory is oversimplified. . . . Nonetheless Communist control of South Vietnam would almost immediately make Laos extremely hard to hold, have Cambodia bending sharply to the Communist side, place great pressure on Thailand . . . and embolden Indonesia to increase its pressure on Malaysia . . . could easily, over time, tend to unravel the whole Pacific and South Asian defense structures . . . the loss of South Vietnam [would not necessarily be as serious as the loss of Berlin] . . . there would almost certainly be a major conflict and perhaps the risk of nuclear war.

Closely related to the domino theory was the Munich analogy: the fixed idea that anything less than total victory in Vietnam must be abject surrender, that the United States must fight wherever its will was challenged to the slightest degree. Both the President and the Secretary of State were much given to drawing the Munich analogy (naturally with Ho Chi Minh in the role of Hitler). This befitted men of an age to have lived through the dangers of isolationism and appeasement; but the analogy was also part of the standard kit of concepts for many of their younger advisers.

The perception of Vietnam itself in Washington was bizarrely unreal. Here and there, among CIA veterans or in the lower ranks of the State Department, it was possible to find men who remembered that the two Vietnams had been parts of the same territory only a decade before, and that complex and substantial transfers of population had taken place that were scarcely irrelevant, for example, to the quarrel between Diem and the Buddhists. In the higher ranks of the bureaucracy, however, such a pedantic insistence on local peculiarities was suspect. It smacked of the type of foreign-service officer who has gotten too much involved with his post, gone native, even, and blurred the grand simplicities of struggle and duty. There is no trace in the Pentagon Papers of any awareness that the Catholics who had gone South after 1954 and who made up a disproportionate part of the support for the Diem regime might seem to most Vietnamese in the South every bit as foreign as Communist "infiltrators" returning to their native province after training in the North. The Administration, in its inner debates just as much as in its statements for outside consumption, stuck to the rigid notion that a country called South Vietnam was being invaded by its "neighbor," North Vietnam, exactly as if Mexico were being invaded by the United States. This notion contradicted the facts of Vietnamese language, ethnology, politics and history, but it had the simple merit of providing a legal rationale for American intervention.

A similarly unshakable assumption was that the Viet Cong were controlled by Russia, or China or both. Long after the Administration's policy toward the Soviet Union and Eastern Europe had come to be based on a realistic appreciation of the implications of Sino-Soviet tension, the myth of monolithic communism seemed to survive in the darker corners of even the most luminous of bureaucratic minds. In March 1965, for example, John McNaughton jotted down, in a rough draft for his own guidance, an extraordinarily revealing little formula for "U.S. aims" as he saw them:

70%—To avoid a humiliating U.S. defeat (to our reputation as guarantor).
20%—To keep SVN (and then adjacent) territory from Chinese hands.
10%—To permit the people of SVN to enjoy a better, freer way of life.
ALSO—To emerge from crisis without unacceptable taint from methods used.
NOT—To "help a friend," though it would be hard to stay in if asked out.

It is disturbing to learn that the most trusted of Robert McNamara's advisers, in the very moment of weighing the crucial decision whether to advocate committing U.S. troops to South Vietnam (which he did advocate, successfully, a few days later), privately supposed that they would be going there to prevent it being occupied by the *Chinese!* From that one scribbled note, in fact, a good deal of the intellectual climate inside the bureaucracy at that critical period can be reconstructed. There was the pseudorational quality lent to arguments by expressing them in numbers. This was a particular habit of McNaughton's. In perhaps the most important of all the papers he drafted, the annex to McGeorge Bundy's memo written on the plane home after Pleiku, he estimated the chances of success for bombing as "somewhere between 25% and 75%." It is amusing to speculate what grade Professor McNaughton would have given to a student who expressed such a hopelessly noncommittal opinion, even on the most trivial of subjects, and then tried to dress it up with false precision by expressing it as a percentage. But, then, McNamara loved statistics. The Pentagon ran on them. In Saigon the war was all but fought by numbers. As General Taylor had scathingly put it, it was as if the war could be won on a points score: so many KIA, so many defectors, so many hamlets cleared, so many tons of ordnance dropped. The process by which in the end these statistics came to blot out reality started inside the heads of clever people in the Pentagon.

Then there was the primacy given to the matter of prestige. It was seven times more important, for McNaughton, to avoid humiliation than to help the people of South Vietnam. That was frank enough. In another of his papers he put the same point even more pithily:

Our stakes in South Vietnam are:
a) Buffer real estate near Thailand and Malaysia and
b) Our reputation.

It was not only with America's reputation for toughness among the Communists that the President's advisers were so preoccupied; it was also her reputation for toughness among her allies. "We must maintain," said the final draft of the Working Group's report in November 1964, perhaps the most thorough position paper of this whole period, *"particularly to our key Nato allies,* the picture of a nation that is stronger and at the same time wise in the exercise of its power." In the background there was a specific concern with asserting American world leadership now that it seemed to be challenged by General de Gaulle. In the top-level discussion of that same paper, Dean Rusk argued that Vietnam must be held because other nations would lose confidence in the United States if it was not. "If we did nothing to affect the course of events in Vietnam," he went on, "it would have the effect of *giving more to de Gaulle."*

Lastly, to squeeze one more inference from the text of poor McNaughton's scribble, whatever might be maintained in public, there was no pretense inside the bureaucracy that the United States was in Vietnam because anyone in that country wanted an American presence. "It would be hard to stay in if asked out," McNaughton wrote—not that it would be hard to get out if asked to stay in. It was Washington's constant preoccupation, from the time of the Buddhist crisis in the summer of 1963 on, to ensure that the government in Saigon not ask the United States out. In every discussion of any hypothetical negotiated settlement, the irreducible minimum American position was that the government of South Vietnam that resulted from such a settlement would accept American aid. This was not the policy of the reluctant benefactor. It was the superpower intent on preserving world leadership.

There has been much discussion of the nuances of opinion within the national-security bureaucracy, and correspondingly little realization of where the essential division lay. This was above all a debate between the civilians and the military. And it was one in which—notwithstanding the widespread belief that Kennedy and McNamara established civilian control in the Pentagon—the military habitually won their point.

There were several reasons for this. The military fared very well as bureaucrats, for one thing. The Joint Chiefs of Staff were consistently adept at presenting the military alternatives in such a way that their preferred solution was likely to be chosen in the long run.

One cannot read the documents without a sense of the superior drive and vitality of the military case. The Joint Chiefs made up their minds by the end of 1963 that "the root of the problem is in North Vietnam and must be dealt with there." They were probably wrong. The root of the problem was an insurgency in South Vietnam, and it was not until after the American escalatory measures of 1965 that North Vietnamese support became crucial to it. Nevertheless, over twelve months of tortuous and sometimes fluctuating debate, the civilians were drawn to the military position.

It was almost as if the imperative to escalate had a life of its own. It steadily wore down arguments *against,* and seemed to call forth arguments *for.* Both in the case of bombing and in the case of sending in troops, the decision seems to have been reached before the bureaucracy could make up its mind exactly why it had been reached. In both cases, after the decision had been taken, military strategy quickly asserted itself and pushed aside the tenuous rationales of the civilians. Once General Westmoreland had gotten his troops, he stopped keeping them to protect air force bases, nor did he leave them in enclaves to communicate messages of American determination. He went hunting the Viet Cong with them. And once they had gotten orders to bomb, the Joint Chiefs used those orders to bomb the enemy's lines of communications, not to exert psychological pressure on the politbureau in Hanoi.

The military had one great advantage: they knew what they wanted. Once—it was in a discussion of the possibility that a certain course of action might lead to the danger of a nuclear exchange—General Maxwell Taylor silenced the Secretary of State's hesitations by declaring brusquely that there was "a danger of reasoning ourselves into inaction." Reasoning, to the military men, was something that ought to end in action, not a way of deciding whether action was desirable or not. The fundamental question, whether the United States was right to be committed in Vietnam, was not much discussed in the meetings recorded in the Pentagon Papers. But on one of the few occasions when it was, the discussion was summarily ended by the Joint Chiefs' representative present, Admiral Mustin. He didn't like the implication that there was any alternative to defending South Vietnam, he said: "There isn't."

One reason why the military won their point so often and so easily was that the civilians tended to be deferential toward the men in uniform. In part this may have been an automatic response subconsciously caused by the fact that so many of them had been junior officers themselves—"captains and majors, telling the whole world what to do." "Twelve years ago," wrote Harry McPherson of his feelings in the Pentagon mess when he was a civilian officer there in the middle 1960s, "you were a corporal in the Air Force. . . . Now you were sitting across from a major general who survived the Bataan death march. He embodies the military virtues of stamina, courage, allegiance to country." Not all of McNamara's civilian staff, notoriously, felt that way about generals. But on the whole, the civilians were trying harder to show the military that they understood the military point of view than the military were trying to show the civilians that they understood theirs.

There was another reason why the military case should prevail. It was in the logic of the debate. On one side were those who favored swifter movement to higher levels of military force, on the other those who argued for the slower application of more restrained levels of force. The fundamental alternatives—that the United States had no vital interests at stake in Indochina that were worth fighting for, that it could not effectively advance its interests by using force, and that it should lessen its commitment and withdraw—these arguments were never heard. In an argument between men who agree that they must use force to prevent something happening and disagree only on when to use it, it is not hard to predict that force will be used in the end. In the absence of a Left, the men of the center will always be drawn to the Right. Only thorough debate, in Congress, in the press, and in politics, could have prevented any other result. And public debate was the last thing the presidential elite wanted.

John McNaughton's special assistant at this time was a young man named Daniel Ellsberg. He helped to draft many of the papers in which the question whether to bomb North Vietnam was discussed. He did not read those papers, he said in a lecture in a Boston church many years later, with the same eyes that his wife and children brought to them when they eventually read them:

> Here is some of the language they read in the Pentagon papers about our bombing policy:
> "We all accept the will of the DRV as the real target";
> "Judging by experience during the last war, the resumption of bombing after a pause would be even more painful . . ."
> "water-drip technique . . ."

"It is important not to 'kill the hostage' "

"fast/full squeeze" option versus "progressive squeeze-and-talk . . ."

"the hot-cold treatment . . ."

"our salami-slicing bombing program . . . ratchet . . . one more turn of the screw."

It was, Patricia Ellsberg said, "the language of torturers."

There is a difference between the way a torturer uses force and the way a soldier uses it. A torturer may not need to use much force; just enough to inflict pain, for he is in no danger himself. The soldier uses as much as he needs to destroy his enemy and make himself safe. The case the Joint Chiefs were arguing was the soldier's case. If the United States was at war with the Vietnamese Communists, as the civilians said, then let its military power be used as it has always been used in war, to defeat the enemy as swiftly as possible.

The civilians' model was not war but the imposition of the will of the United States on people who might frustrate and humiliate the United States in the sense that a victim can humiliate a torturer by refusing to obey his will but could in no circumstances hurt the United States. The position of the civilian officials, therefore, when they argued for just enough bombing to "break the will" of Hanoi, may have been more "restrained" than the policy of the Joint Chiefs, who wanted the immediate destruction of North Vietnam's capacity to make war; at the same time, it was more "godlike," more arrogant. And, worse than a crime, it was an error.

For in spite of the voluminous analysis and the pseudorational discourse, the President's civilian advisers were quite simply wildly wrong. They consistently overestimated their own strength. They underestimated the strength of the enemy. They overestimated their ability to prevent infiltration. They underestimated Hanoi's ability to match the build-up of American manpower: the ratio between Saigon's forces and the guerrillas was less favorable to Saigon after half a million Americans had been injected into the war than it had been at the beginning. And above all they underestimated their own weakness.

There is no mention, in all the voluminous debate about escalation, of the possibility that frustrating the Viet Cong might involve any serious cost for the United States other than the ordnance expended and a few casualties. The cost of allowing the Viet Cong to win was always present in that debate. The cost of trying to prevent that victory was not even seriously discussed. And yet it was to shake American society to its foundations.

# Economic Consequences

The President's mood at his cabinet meeting on July 27, 1965, as he remembered it later, was a contradictory one: self-congratulatory about the past but overshadowed by the presentiment that things would not go so well in the future.

The previous week, he told the men around the coffin-shaped table, had been "the most productive and the most historic week in Washington during this century." He was exaggerating, but less than he often did. He was thinking of the Medicare and voting-rights bills, both near final passage in Congress, and more generally of the major pieces of legislation he had either already succeeded in persuading Congress to pass or else knew from his long experience would pass soon: the tax cut, the Civil Rights Act of 1964, the Economic Opportunity Act, the pioneer Elementary and Secondary Education Act, and the rest. It was, Tom Wicker commented a few weeks later in the New York *Times*, a more substantial record of reform legislation than most Presidents put behind them in two full terms, and it had been done in a bare eighteen months.

There were two reasons for the President's suspicion that the summer was now nearly over. One was what he himself called the unmistakable sound of dragging feet on Capitol Hill. No one had more sensitive antennae for the mood of Congress, and now, with the first signs of hostile reaction to the new black militancy and the community action program beginning to show, Johnson's instinct told him that, if he himself was becoming irritated by the ingratitude of those he was trying to help, then a lot of his old friends would soon grow mighty weary of doing good.

The second cause for gloom, as the President saw it, was "the lowering cloud of Vietnam." That was his private nemesis. As he reeled off the good news to the Cabinet on July 27, he had a paper in front of him that listed the alternatives he had to choose between at a meeting of the National Security Council that same afternoon. The next day, he announced his choice. He told a press conference that the 101st Airborne Division would be leaving for Vietnam. He was not, as we have seen, altogether frank about how many other troops would be needed. But the open-ended nature of the commitment was plain enough. That was the day the Rubicon was crossed.

It was an economic as well as a military turning point. That same day, he sent to Congress a request for additional appropriations to pay for the war, together with a warning that more money would be needed in the new year. In the whole of the fiscal year that had just ended, the fighting in Southeast Asia had cost $100 million. In May, the Administration had asked for $700 million more. The August and January requests between them came to more than $14 billion. "So," as Johnson himself put it later, "on that July 27, 1965, two streams in our national life converged—the dream of a Great Society at home and the inescapable demands of our obligations halfway around the world."

He did not at the time see any contradiction between domestic reform and foreign war. Certainly he saw none at the philosophical level. And it would have been strange if he had. For he was the heir and champion of the liberal consensus, and he was surrounded by advisers who were its true believers. His ideology and theirs had always taken it as a fundamental assumption that the economic strength of the American system could produce the resources both to improve society at home and to resist communism and spread the American gospel abroad: both were inseparable parts of America's duty and privilege.

Nor did Lyndon Johnson and his advisers at first see any necessary conflict between the war and the Great Society in terms of economics. Some of his advisers had their doubts, but they suppressed them dutifully. On January 12, 1966, the President went before Congress to sketch his legislative program and at the same time to ask for the supplementary appropriations for the war. "I believe," he said, and the congressmen applauded, "that we can continue the Great Society while we fight in Vietnam." More than a year later, Robert McNamara was asked during a Senate hearing how much longer the country could afford the war. "I think forever," he answered, "and I say it for this reason: that there are many things, many prices we pay for the war in Vietnam, some heavy prices indeed, but in my opinion one of them is not strain on our economy."

They were wrong.

But there was no need for them to have been wrong. It was quite true that the American *economy* could have afforded to pay both for the war and for a sweeping program of domestic reforms at the same time. Over the four years from 1965 to 1968, which covered the main period of escalation of the American war effort, the total of federal spending on domestic social services did rise almost as fast as the military budget. And in the early years of the Nixon administration, while the war was still going on, though at a lower level of intensity in terms of costs of the U.S. defense budget, domestic social expenditure did catch military spending up and pass it. The *economy* could afford both guns and butter. The snag was that the federal *budget* could not, unless it transferred resources from the private sector (which was some six times larger), without running a deficit. And at a time when the economy was approaching full employment, a deficit could only mean inflation. In other words, the federal government could not afford to fight a war without raising taxes. And this, until it was too late, it did not have the courage even to attempt.

The real dilemma the Johnson administration faced, in short, was not between the war and the Great Society; it was how to carry on with both without asking people to pay more taxes. They tried to hide the cost of the war from the people, and so in economic terms they made its cost far higher than it need have been. They knew it was an unpopular war, and so they hesitated too long before asking Congress to raise taxes. Then Congress hesitated too long before increasing them; and this was understandable, since the same President and the same economists who now called for higher taxes had only just finished beseeching Congress for lower ones. The result was inflation, and a balance-of-payments crisis, and in the end the Great Society had to be put off until another day. In the end, indeed, it was to a great extent the poor who paid for the war. But not before it had done a great deal of economic harm to almost every other group in American society, and indeed to the economic equilibrium of the whole world.

In the summer of 1965 the professors of the New Economics—the Walter Hellers and Paul Samuelsons, the James Tobins and Gardner Ackleys and their friends—had every reason to feel like men who after long search have found the famous stone that turns all things to gold. When they were in the wilderness, if that is not too bleak a term for their chairs in the economics departments at Harvard, Yale, Columbia and other great universities, they had boldly asserted a remarkable claim: if they could get their hands on the levers of federal fiscal and monetary policy, they said, then they could manage the American economy, according to principles outlined by the late Lord Keynes and interpreted by their collective selves, in such a way that everyone could have his cake and eat it too. Specifically, they claimed that if tax policy was used to stimulate aggregate demand and induce full employment even at the risk of budgetary deficits, then there was no reason why you shouldn't enjoy steady economic growth and falling unemployment and minimal inflation all at the same time. First Kennedy, and then Johnson, gave them a chance to put their theories into practice.

Their "Keynesian" doctrine sounded novel and shocking to conservatives in Congress, in the press and in business, who had been brought up to believe that balanced budgets were the ark of the covenant for sound public economics. It was therefore embraced by liberals as the height of economic daring. What very few people realized was that the version of Keynes that was being put on offer by most of his American disciples, and in particular the version that was to triumph as the new orthodoxy in the Kennedy and Johnson administrations, was a highly cautious selection from the great man's teaching.

Once again, in fact, in the domestication of the Keynesian economics, we are confronted by the persistent tendency of American politics in this period to array themselves into a conflict between the Right and the center: the Right in this instance being those conservatives who opposed the tax cut on the old-fashioned ground that budget deficits were always wrong, and the center being represented by the liberals who proposed it. Once again, in the very act of bringing into the political marketplace what looked like a daring, radical new idea, the liberal intellectuals subtly transformed it, and the political process transformed it still further, so that it ended up as that peculiar phenomenon, a radical reform whose chief practical effect was to redistribute wealth *toward* the well-off!

Keynes had pointed out that in order to reduce unemployment a government could use fiscal policy to stimulate demand and thus expand the economy even at the cost of running a budget deficit. But a government can follow this prescription in only one of two ways: by spending, or by cutting taxes. The government can either spend the money where it decides it is most needed, and thus take care of particular needs while at the same time stimulating the over-all level of activity; or it can leave the money in the hands of private citizens, to spend it as they want. A debate raged on precisely this issue among the Keynesian economists consulted by the Kennedy administration. In effect it was a special case of a more fundamental argument: Could one rely on economic growth alone to meet social needs? Or, while aiming for as much economic growth as compatible with this second objective, should one first attempt to meet priority needs?

One group, led by J. K. Galbraith, wanted higher public expenditures to meet the vast unmet need for public services which had been one of the themes of his book *The Affluent Society*. But the key man in the Kennedy administration, Walter Heller, chairman of the Council of Economic Advisers, was a tax cutter, if only because he thought that a tax cut was politically possible and in his judgment public spending programs of an adequate magnitude were not. Since he believed, with reason, that it was vital to expand the economy, then a tax cut it must be.

In the end, Heller and his allies won. The economic stimulus proposed by the Kennedy administration took the form not of an attack on "public squalor" but of two successive tax giveaways. That was what they became. Each reduction in tax was supposed to be accompanied by tax "reform," that is, by the closing of tax loopholes. The reductions happened. The reforms didn't. Walter Heller, it must be said, accepted this philosophically. "The dream of a thorough tax reform," he once observed, realistically, no doubt, but with perhaps a shade too much resignation, "is just that: a dream."

First there was the investment credit of 1962, then the tax cut, which was proposed by President Kennedy in his lifetime and passed by Congress early in 1964.

The investment credit was billed as an incentive to business to expand. But that was not very convincing. The cash flow of all American corporations that year was greater than the sum they invested in plant and equipment: the investment credit simply added to profits. And this, too, Heller accepted. He later told businessmen proudly that they had been able to hide billions of dollars in profits under depreciation allowances. And he was quite right. Corporate profits did double between 1961 and 1966 If the upsurge in the economy was the major reason for this, the tax breaks helped, too.

At first glance, the cut in income tax looked more equitable than the investment credit. But that, too, unaccompanied by any serious tightening at the loopholes that enabled the well-to-do to reduce their theoretically high level of income tax, had the over-all effect of favoring the upper-income groups. Writing in the *National Tax Journal*, no radical sheet, in December 1965, a tax authority, S. O. Hermansen, delivered what may be read as an epitaph on what was touted as an era of liberal reform: "Changes in federal tax laws since January 1, 1963," he estimated, "by 1968 will overwhelmingly have benefited the higher income groups in relation to the lower income groups."

It wasn't, of course, that the New Economists, or anyone else in the Kennedy administration, consciously meant to sell out tax reform or equality. On the contrary, they thought of themselves to a man as idealists, even as do-gooders. This in itself may have made them too anxious to placate business. They had lived through the 1950s. Just as the professors in the Pentagon were a little too anxious to show the generals what red-blooded, patriotic Americans they were, so the professors in the Executive Office Building were at pains to prove to business that they were no soft-boiled eggheads.

And, then, they really did believe, with a fervent and simple faith, in the religion of growth: seek ye first the kingdom of GNP, and all else will be added unto you. There was nothing misguided about the policy of growth in itself, of course. The full-employment policies of the Kennedy administration and the economic surge that followed from them really did raise the living standards of the great majority of Americans, and not only by paying higher wages. In the private sector they made possible better housing, better pensions, and, for example, less inadequate health insurance. In the public sector they gave the government a bigger revenue, because though rates of tax were low, they were levied on a greater volume of taxable income. This "fiscal dividend" made possible the Great Society programs of the early years of the Johnson administration.

But the price of economic stimulus through tax cutting, which was the easy way of doing it, was a drop in the rate of tax on an already seriously eroded tax base. And that drop was going to be hard to reverse. By 1966 the proportion of the U.S. GNP taken by all federal, state and local taxation had fallen to just over 28 per cent. By way of comparison, the average rate in the four main Western European countries, Britain, France, West Germany and Italy, was 33.5 per cent: more than five percentage points higher. If the United States had taxed itself at the same rate as the four nearly comparable non-socialist developed economies in Western Europe, it would have had by 1969 $50 billion more in tax revenue. Even if the United States had simply continued to tax itself at the same rate as during the Eisenhower years, from 1953–61, it would still have had $25 billion more to spend. That would nearly have covered the incremental cost of the war in Southeast Asia that year. And half of that sum, simply handed out in cash, would have raised every family then living below the official, statistical poverty line (thirty-five hundred dollars a year for four people) above it. It can be seriously argued, therefore, that the Kennedy administration's decision to stimulate the economy through cutting taxes rather than through higher public expenditure was responsible for the fiscal dilemma of the Johnson administration. Even more plausibly, it can be argued that that dilemma was caused by the unwillingness of those who exercised political power both in Congress and in the executive branch to pay the level of taxes required by the policies they chose to follow.

So much for the achievements of the New Economics in the field of redistribution. Still, Americans didn't want redistribution. (Perhaps they might have if anyone had explained to them that it was possible, but nobody had.) They wanted prosperity. The heart of the claim the New Economists had made was that they could unlock the wasted potential in the economy, and in the summer of 1965 it looked as if that was exactly what they had done. They had said that they knew how to expand the economy, reduce unemployment, and still keep prices stable, and the statistics showed that they had done all three things.

Unemployment had been close to 7 per cent when the Kennedy administration took office, and the New Economists got their chance to show what they could do. Now it was down to 4½ per cent and the topic of the hour was whether it could be brought down to 4 per cent without inflation. The GNP had soared by more than a third from the last quarter of 1960 to the second quarter of 1965. It had been $500 billion in 1961; it would be $685 billion in 1965. In May the statisticians in the Executive Office Building chalked up another record: fifty months of unbroken expansion. And $25 billion of that increase, they reckoned, was due to the tax cut. Finally, there was still no sign of inflation. The consumer price index had risen by less than 2 per cent in each of the previous three years.

It was in the second half of 1965 that the dream of the New Economists, the optimistic vision of expansionist roses without any of the thorns of inflation, was destroyed. Was Vietnam the cause? One should be careful here. It is in the New Economists' interest now to blame the war. Walter Heller has been quite explicit about this:

> The prickly dilemmas posed by inflation could bring setbacks to the public acceptance of the economist and his wares. This could happen if those who have a vested intellectual or political interest in doing so manage to establish the 1964–65 tax cuts rather than Vietnam as the inflationary culprit—or scapegoat—in today's economy.

The New Economists, in other words, must insist that inflation was caused by the war, lest anyone should think it was caused by their policies.

Again, and also for their own respective purposes, both the conservative Dr. Arthur Burns (appointed by President Nixon in 1970 as head of the Federal Reserve Board) and Marxist critics of the New Economics orthodoxy have argued that inflation would have broken through anyway as the economy approached full employment, that the signs of it had even started to appear. Thirdly, it can be argued that, even with a war, swift and effective deflationary action by the federal government, planned as part of the war effort from the beginning, might have prevented inflation from taking hold.

What is clear, without attempting to resolve technical or theoretical arguments, is that the sharp rise in military spending in late 1965, not balanced by any deflationary countermeasures, did set the inflationary snowball moving.

By December 1965, the Johnson administration's economists may not have known how bad the situation was, but they knew inflation was loose, they knew why, and they were saying so—but only inside government.

In public, however, they remained blandly reassuring. The very next month, the Council of Economic Advisers' annual report to Congress said: ". . . our vigorous economy is in a strong position to carry the new burdens imposed by expanded national defense requirements." The President did ask for, and quickly got from Congress, a minor increase in excise taxes. Not until a whole year later, in December 1966, did he admit that his projections of the cost of the war had been too low: he said that there had been "a $10-billion error" in forecasting. In January 1967, therefore, he asked Congress for a 6 per cent tax surcharge, but when the economy showed temporary signs of slowing down, he dropped that. It was not until August 1967 that he finally asked Congress for a 10 per cent tax surcharge.

By that time, the horse had long gone out the stable door. Inflation had taken firm hold.

But not only that. By the winter of 1967, the mood in Congress had so hardened against the social programs of the Great Society that Congressman Wilbur Mills, chairman of the strategic Ways and Means Committee, felt constrained to insist that the tax increase should be matched with cuts in domestic programs. It was Mills's judgment that he could not pass a tax surcharge unless it was linked to deep cuts in social programs to appease conservatives. He was therefore able to bargain his support for the tax increase against a commitment from the President to cut progressively more and more from the domestic side of the budget: first two, then four, five and ultimately six billion dollars.

After a bitter struggle, Lyndon Johnson faced a painful dilemma. He must either cut the cherished Great Society programs, including urban spending which he believed urgently necessary to prevent further rioting, or he must do without a tax increase. And he needed that just as badly not only now because of the effects of inflation at home but also because of the implications for the international position of the dollar. If there was no tax increase, both his Secretary of State and the chairman of his Council of Economic Advisers were now telling him, then he might have to put up the price of gold, which would amount to devaluing the dollar. In the end, the President decided that he had no option but to pay Wilbur Mills his six billion dollars' worth of flesh from the domestic budget. At that heavy price, he finally signed the 10 per cent tax surcharge into law, on June 28, 1968, almost three years after the decision that made it inevitable.

Why did the Administration wait so long before asking Congress for a tax increase?

Lyndon Johnson maintained all along that it was because, as a simple matter of political realism, he knew he couldn't get one. Business was against it. Labor was against it. His Congressional experts told him that, out of the twenty-five votes in the Ways and Means Committee, he would get four for an increase in taxes if he was lucky, and those four would not include the all-important vote of Wilbur Mills.

There is no question that a tax increase was not popular. Tax increases rarely are. In this instance, what was more, it was unusually hard for the Administration to go back up to the Hill and ask for taxes to be put up so soon after it had triumphantly succeeded in persuading Congress to cut them. Logically, of course, the fiscal policy of the New Economics implied raising taxes just as often as cutting them. Somehow, though, in the long campaign to educate Congress and the public, the New Economists and their two President-converts had understandably laid a good deal more stress on the times when the New Economics meant that taxes should go down than on the cases where they would have to go up. Even so, the President's explanation is not altogether satisfying. Given that it would have been unpopular to ask for a tax increase in 1966, would it have been more unpopular than it was in 1968? Given the President's formidable standing and prestige in 1965–66, would he have had to pay as high a price to persuade Congress to go along with a tax increase then as he had to pay in 1968? No one can be sure. But I think not.

There were probably two deeper explanations for the disastrous delay. One was that the Administration did consistently, and quite genuinely, underestimate the cost of the war. For one thing, it always underestimated both the time and the number of troops it would take to win it. When George Ball, back in 1961, told President Kennedy that if he wasn't careful he'd have three hundred thousand troops fighting up to their waists in mud in Indochina, Kennedy's reply was: "George, you're crazier than hell!" The number, Ball commented later, was "a ludicrous underestimate." When Lyndon Johnson and Robert McNamara took the decision to meet Westmoreland's request in July 1965, they knew they were committed to sending some two hundred thousand before they were through. But if anyone had suggested that less than three years later there would be more than half a million American troops in the Big Muddy, and no end in sight, they would assuredly have answered him as Kennedy answered Ball. Not having any idea that it would take so many troops so long to win, the President and his advisers naturally had no idea it would take so much money.

Even so, the Administration's spokesmen repeatedly played down both the cost of the war and its impact on the federal budget, both in public statements and also in testimony to Congressional committees. This consistent undercounting cannot all plausibly be attributed to the honest error that Professor Okun is perhaps a little too quick to plead guilty to. It is far more likely that Edwin L. Dale, Jr., for example, was right when he reported in the New York *Times* in December 1966 that people in Washington believed that "the original understatement of expenditure [on the war] was political, to make the war seem cheaper than it was." Interviews with high officials then in the Treasury confirm this judgment.

If Lyndon Johnson, then, never dreaming that the war could last as long or cost as much as it did, hoped against hope that he could get it over with before people woke up to how much it had cost; if, just because he had so wholeheartedly taken over Kennedy's economists and Kennedy's tax cut, he was trapped when it came to reversing direction; if, above all, he hoped to avoid choosing between the war he regarded as his duty and the domestic programs he hoped would be his memorial: there is a tragic irony to the story. For in the end, he came close to getting the worst of all worlds. The war went on. The Great Society programs did have to be cut back. And the tax increase came too late to check inflation.

What, then, were the economic consequences of Mr. Johnson and of his decision to go to war without raising taxes?

First, inflation. Prices rose, and so did costs. Whichever indicator you look at, 1965 marks a sharp break. The true cost of labor to American industry, for example, had remained remarkably stable, in spite of rising real wages, through the early 1960s, because of the improvement in productivity due to better training, better education, higher capital investment per worker, and automation. Labor cost per unit of output, the indicator that takes account of these improvements in productivity, was still in 1965 no more than five percentage points higher than it had been back in 1958. Less than one percentage point up each year for seven years is a remarkable record of stability. Then, suddenly, in the four war years from 1965 to 1969, labor cost per unit of output shot up some seventeen points, partly because of wages continuing to rise but more because of a decline in productivity.

Prices rose in an exponential curve. The consumer price index went up less than 2 per cent in 1963, 1964, and 1965. It rose almost 3 per cent in 1966, over 3 per cent in 1967, more than 4 per cent in 1968, and over 6 per cent in 1969.

Wages rose, too. But here the graphs reveal a fact whose significance for the politics of the later 1960s literally cannot be exaggerated. It helps to explain everything. For while wages continued to rise, their value was eroded, chiefly by the rise in prices but also by the fact that as inflated-money wages took people into higher tax brackets, income tax began to bite even on middle-income workers.

If you look at the graph of raw wages—average hourly wages in private, nonagricultural industry measured in current dollars—you will see that they climbed steadily, and almost in a straight line, from a fraction over two dollars an hour to just under three dollars an hour in 1969. But suppose, instead, that you take into account inflation: suppose you plot real, spendable wages for industrial workers; if you take, for example, the weekly earnings, after tax, of the average production worker with a family of four, measured in the uninflated dollars of 1957–59, then you will notice a strange and highly significant peculiarity. And 1965 was the year when it happened. From 1958 until 1964 the graph rises, again more or less in a straight line, except for a hiccup caused by the recession in 1959, from sixty-eight dollars to seventy-eight dollars a week. Then, abruptly, in 1965, it turns right and runs dead level with only minor fluctuations, for four years.

From 1965 to 1969, then, the value of the pay packet of Mr. Middle American, of the blue-collar working stiff who, in the mythology of the new, liberal American capitalism, was doing better and better every year . . . did what? It stood still.

While the war boom was helping businessmen to higher profits; while professional men and women, lawyers, doctors, accountants were all seeing their incomes rise; while the stock market was rearing up like a wave in a Japanese woodcut; at a time, also, when the media were full of what government was doing for the poor, and above all for the black poor, in terms of higher wages, higher welfare, programs for this, funding for that—Mr. Middle American was marking time.

Can it be wholly a coincidence that precisely in these years Mr. Middle American began to show a puzzled resentment, inexplicable to those who studied him but strangely enough directed at just those two groups who were, indeed, now moving ahead economically while he stood still? Somehow, in those unhappy years, the average blue-collar worker got the idea that he was being screwed and that somehow the war was at the bottom of it even if you did have to support the President and stand up to the Communists. The statistics suggest that he was exactly right.

The second economic price the United States had to pay for the decision to crush the Viet Cong insurgency was in terms of the balance of payments. The problem of balance-of-payments deficits was much older than the Vietnam War. But the decision to escalate the war in 1965, which had both directly and indirectly a negative effect on the balance-of-payments position, came at the moment when a long-standing imbalance—itself largely the price of the imperial role the United States had played in the world since 1945—would otherwise have been cured by the successful economic policies of the Kennedy administration.

In the late 1940s the United States as an international trader was in the happy position of a poker player who, without having had to reach deep into his own roll and indeed without having seemed to concentrate more than a fraction of his mind on the game, has gotten most of the other players' chips in a stack on the table in front of him.

In 1949 the official gold reserves of the United States stood at the imposing total of $24.6 billion. No other country had as much as $3 billion in reserves, and the stack in Fort Knox and at the Federal Reserve Bank in New York represented well over half the entire world's monetary gold.

Nor was there any reason then to think that this would be a temporary pre-eminence. The Bretton Woods and Dumbarton Oaks agreements had formalized the dollar's predominance by making it the foundation of the new monetary system. The world's money was backed by the dollar.

The U.S. quota in the new International Monetary Fund was set at 41 per cent, a figure that, if anything, substantially underestimated the dollar's strength. And that strength was based on economic realities. In 1948, the United States exported one quarter of the rest of the world's imports. And the superiority of American industry in price, design, and quality was such that the world would have bought more American goods if it could have afforded them.

From 1950 on, the United States began to show a deficit on her overall balance of payments. These modest deficits can be regarded as the direct price of the imperial policy of "world leadership" and the decision to contain communism in those years. Over the whole of the period 1945–64, the United States advanced $27 billion in loans and grants to Western Europe for reconstruction and development (practically all of it before 1957). It spent $21 billion on foreign military assistance, including NATO. And on the maintenance and supply of U.S. forces in Europe, it spent $21.3 billion in addition. All together, over the whole of the twenty years after World War II, the United States spent $67 billion on military assistance and direct military expenditure overseas, plus $77 billion on total economic aid: a mind-bending total of $144 billion. In the same period, accumulated deficits came to $35 billion. One quarter of what the U. S. Government spent abroad was not covered by exports or the supply of services.

Those deficits of the 1950s—they averaged $1.5 billion a year from 1950 to 1956—were reasonably regarded, both in the U.S. and elsewhere, as further evidence of American strength and American benevolence. The United States was the world's banker. An outflow of dollars from the American reserves increased the liquid capital available for a world desperately hungry for reconstruction and development. "Up to the mid-50s," a staff study for the Senate Banking and Currency Committee put it in 1965, "the great problem for the whole world was the dollar gap, and we were doing our best to close it."

It was all too successfully closed. In just twenty years, from 1949 to 1969, the gold reserves melted from just under $25 billion to less than a third of that figure. By 1971, the German Government alone held more dollars than there was gold in Fort Knox. Liabilities in the hands of foreigners far exceeded the U.S. reserves. But the worst had not then even begun to happen. There was an over-all deficit of $8 billion in 1970 in spite of the fact that the trade balance was modestly in surplus. Then, in 1970, even the trade balance, the hard-core positive item that had sustained years of deficits on other items, went into the red by almost $3 billion. The result was catastrophic. The combined deficit on current and long-term capital account was $9.3 billion. The "net liquidity deficit"— which had been the classic way of looking at the accounts in the early 1960s—reached $22 billion. And on the "official reserve transactions" basis, a new way of looking at things which had been adopted precisely so as to prevent things looking worse than they really were, the deficit reached $29.8 billion!

On August 18, 1971, the Nixon administration moved in and, in effect, suspended the convertibility of the dollar, which had been the central feature of the American-led postwar monetary system. Just before Christmas, at the Smithsonian meeting, as quietly as possible, the dollar was devalued. It was the first time since the depths of the Depression, forty years earlier. But it was not to be the last time.

Why, though, if the U.S. balance of payments had been almost constantly in deficit and the U.S. gold reserves steadily melting away for fifteen years before 1965, is it fair or reasonable to seize on the decision to escalate the Vietnam War in that year as the decisive event that made the ultimate devaluation of the dollar inevitable? The answer is that, unperceived except by a handful of experts, the cause of the U.S. deficit had changed over the course of time so that, though the men who took the decision to escalate the war thought that the dollar could stand the strain, they were wrong.

The Kennedy administration faced a balance-of-payments problem when it took office. The gold reserves declined by $8.75 billion over the last three Eisenhower years, and in the month before the 1960 election there was an international gold crisis. One of the first things the Kennedy administration did, therefore, after its inauguration, was to announce a package of measures designed to correct the balance of payments. The prescription was that government spending abroad should be curtailed and

U.S. commercial exports encouraged. Reinforced by further measures in 1963, these actions "worked." By 1964, the trade accounts had improved by more than $5 billion.

But the over-all deficit had not disappeared. The balance on current transactions moved steadily up to a surplus of over $7 billion in 1964. But the over-all deficit remained at over $3 billion. What had happened was that those components of the accounts that had not been thought of as problems in 1959–61 had now turned sour. The balance of investment had worsened by more than three billion a year. Two new and ominous long-term trends had made their appearance: One was the tendency of U.S.-based multinational corporations to export capital in order to set up manufacturing operations in foreign countries with lower labor costs, thus replacing direct exports of goods from the United States. In time, such operations could be counted on to yield repatriated profits from overseas. But in the short term the whole weight of the capital required flowed out through the exchanges. The second development was the remarkable growth of the so-called "Eurodollar" market. By 1970 the Bank for International Settlements estimated that the enormous sum of $57 billion, most of it held in dollars, was available as a pool to be borrowed from banks in Europe, many of them newly formed affiliates of U.S. banks. Higher interest rates than those obtainable in the United States made it attractive to U.S. corporations, especially the growing multinationals, to leave their balances in this Eurodollar pool; and high rates of growth in Europe meant that there was no shortage of opportunity for the money. These two trends combined to swell the capital-outflows item in the U.S. balance of payments.

Beginning with voluntary constraints in early 1965, but moving toward tougher and tighter controls, the federal government set itself to cut back this loss of capital. Once again, the measures "worked." They did deal with what seemed to be the problem. But again the over-all deficit refused to respond to the treatment. Two different components of the over-all balance of payments had begun to go wrong. And in each case the deterioration resulted from the illusion that the United States could afford to fight the Vietnam War without sacrificing any other desiderata of policy.

The less important of the two was the direct cost of the war in foreign exchange. "Beginning in mid-1965," a Pentagon official testified in 1971 to the Joint Economic Committee of Congress, "our expenditures have increased, due primarily to the conflict in Southeast Asia," to a total of foreign-exchange expenditure directly caused by the war of around $1.5 billion. In the same hearings, Congressman Reuss made the point that the gross foreign-exchange costs of the American military establishment abroad were enough to account all by themselves for the basic deficit in the balance of payments.

Far more important, however, was the indirect effect of the war. By 1971, the deficit on "merchandise trade" had reached $2.9 billion. One reason was the steady increase in imports. In sober language the *Federal Reserve Bulletin* of April 1971 recorded the "greater acceptance of foreign imports by American consumers and business in the last ten years":

> The continuous availability of an increasingly wide variety of foreign products of good quality, attractively designed and sold at competitive prices, and the expansion in facilities to market and service those products, have made imports an increasingly more important part of domestic markets.

You had only to walk down Fifth Avenue, or window-shop in the new "upmarket" shopping centers that had sprung up in upper-income suburbs, or turn over the pages of any glossy magazine to be taught the same lesson: foreign manufacturers were succeeding, and sometimes defeating their American competitors, in the very field in which the original miracle of postwar American capitalism had been achieved: in the mass distribution of well-made, attractively designed and relatively cheap consumer goods. U.S. imports of capital goods—machine tools and other industrial equipment—also more than doubled over the decade of the 1960s.

Moreover, the resilience of American industry's response to this challenge seemed to have been reduced. Whereas in 1960–61 the introduction of Detroit-built compact cars sharply reduced imports, in 1970 the second wave of American "sub-compacts" failed to do the same. Imports of automobiles took, on the average, 5.6 per cent of the U.S. market in the first half of the 1960s. In 1970 and 1971, they took over 16 per cent.

One of the reasons why American imports rose so much faster than exports was the fading of what had once been the special glory of American industry, the magical American secret that, in Marshall Plan days, teams of missionaries had gone forth to teach the Europeans: productivity. Between 1965 and 1970, output per man-hour in manufacturing, the measure of productivity, rose on the average 14 per cent each year in Japan, more than 6 per cent in France, and even in Britain, plagued with industrial troubles, 3.6 per cent. In the United States it rose 2.1 per cent.

All these troubles—buoyant imports, lagging exports, sluggish investment leading to mediocre productivity—could be traced to one grand cause: inflation. And inflation was caused by the Vietnam War. In that sense, economists and bankers came to acknowledge that the U.S. balance-of-payments crisis of the early 1970s was caused by the Vietnam War. As Robert Roosa put it, "The effects of the so-called Vietnam inflation upon the balance of payments had proved to be far more damaging than even the direct impact of the Vietnam military operations across the exchanges."

There is another sense, however, in which both the Vietnam inflation and the dollar crisis it brought to a head were themselves only the surface symptoms of an underlying historical shift. The pendulum of relative economic power, which had tilted so sharply toward the United States after both world wars, had swung back toward the rest of the world.

The American economy remained vast, growing, productive, in some respects the most innovative and incomparably the largest of any single country in the world. But, taken in comparison with the world as a whole, it was no longer alone and unchallenged as it had been after World War II. The U.S. share of world trade had declined inexorably, from 25 per cent in 1948, to under 15 per cent in 1964, to little better than 10 per cent at the end of the decade. The United States was no longer the largest trading entity: the European Economic Community could make that boast. It was no longer the fastest-growing major economy: Japan had wrested that crown.

In a world where the pressure of rising population and rising living standards was eliminating food surplus producers one by one, the scale and productivity of American agriculture guaranteed an important source of revenue from food exports, and one that would continue to expand. And the sheer scale of government-subsidized defense and space orders meant that the rest of the world was hard put to it to compete with U.S. industry at the top end of the technology scale: in aviation, in computers, and in the most sophisticated electronic system. But, over the whole range of manufactured products intermediate between raw materials which America had exported even before the industrial revolution began and the high-technology, space-age jumbo jets and advanced computers, it was American industry that seemed progressively less able to compete.

And the United States was no longer as self-sufficient as it had been. Imports of oil were expanding several times faster than the economy, an omen of future dependence where the United States had historically been most advantaged, namely in the abundance of cheap power. Economists could also foresee in the not too far distant future an increasing dependence on imported nonferrous metals, beginning with bauxite for reduction to aluminum.

There were those, such as the banker and economist Robert Roosa, who even likened the evolving patterns of the American economy in relation to the rest of the world to that of Britain in the late-nineteenth century and foresaw that the United States would come to rely less and less on directly competitive exporting and more and more on the income earned from investments made in more competitive days.

In the late sixties, as the war ground on, inflation mounted, and the dollar steadily weakened, such long-term prognostications were still speculative. If the hopes of the early sixties had been dupes, some of the fears of the second half of the decade proved to be liars. The spread of inflation elsewhere in the world, the revaluation of the dollar, shifts in the ratio of prices between raw materials and food and manufactured goods, and more or less successful economic management on the part of the U. S. Government all improved the relative situation of the United States, and war in the Middle East and the subsequent rise in the price of oil catastrophically affected the situation of other industrial powers, even more dependent on oil imports than the United States.

But whatever was to come, one thing was unalterably plain. The men who made the decision to escalate the war had committed a historic error. Those men—Robert McNamara, Walt Rostow, the Bundy brothers, Lyndon Johnson himself—had come to political maturity and formed their view of the world during the brief, exceptional period when the economic position of the United States was such that its policies could be framed in virtual disregard of economic consequences. They had failed to observe that that time had now gone. They had all subscribed to, and the consensus of the nation had endorsed, the rhetorical pledge in President Kennedy's inaugural to pay any price to assure the survival of liberty. (He did not go so far as to say Americans would pay any *tax* in that cause!) They and the nation had subconsciously assumed that, for a nation as powerful as the United States, there would not be any significant economic price to pay. And in this, events were to prove them grievously wrong.

# PART III

# Fragmented Consensus

In March 1965, the month of Selma and Rolling Thunder, one hundred copies of a document were printed and bound in Washington. Its publication has been called "the great event of the sixties."

It was originally intended only for circulation among the policy-making circles of the Johnson administration. It was called *The Negro Family: the Case for National Action,* and its author was Daniel Patrick Moynihan, a young social scientist then serving as assistant secretary of labor. He had been one of the Administration's chief strategists in planning the "War on Poverty." Now he was proposing a new strategy for the struggle for black equality.

It was a time of general awareness that that struggle was moving into a new phase. Only the previous month, Bayard Rustin had written in *Commentary:* "The civil rights movement is evolving from a protest movement into a full-fledged *social movement.* . . . It is now concerned not merely with removing the barriers to full opportunity but with achieving the fact of equality."

This awareness was given urgency by the first urban riots in the summer of 1964. But Moynihan had begun to formulate his analysis even earlier. In an impromptu contribution to the discussion at a conference in April 1964, he brought up what were to be the two main themes of his report. One was the idea that government would have to give blacks preferential treatment if they were to overcome their inherited disadvantages: the conference should reflect, he said, whether "if you were ever going to have anything like an equal Negro community you are . . . going to have to give them unequal treatment." The second was the relationship between unemployment, the other problems of the ghetto, and the Negro family.

In a sense, there was nothing new in what Moynihan was saying. His conceptual framework drew heavily on the work of two well-known black social scientists: Thirty years before, E. Franklin Frazier had described the prevalence of deserted mothers and broken families in "the city of destruction." In 1964, in his report on youth in Harlem, Kenneth B. Clark had shown the interconnected effects of what Moynihan called the "tangle of pathology" in the ghetto. Much of Moynihan's report was made up of statistical data. But what figures they were! One third of nonwhite children, they showed, lived in broken homes. In Harlem, the illegitimacy rate for blacks, only one of the causes of such homes, was well over 40 per cent. And "unemployment among Negroes outside the South has persisted at catastrophic levels since the first statistics were gathered in 1930."

At the head of the deterioration of black society, Moynihan argued, there lay the deterioration of the black family. Not all black families. There was no one black community. The evidence suggested that while a disorganized lower-class group was falling further and further behind, a growing middle class was succeeding. "Nonetheless," he maintained, "at the center of the tangle of pathology is the weakness of the Negro family."

On the one hand, Moynihan suggested that this weakness had its roots in the experience of slavery. "It was by destroying the Negro family under slavery," he wrote, "that white America broke the will of the Negro people." On the other hand, he also insisted on the causal relationship between unemployment and the breakup of families. Cyclical swings in unemployment, he pointed out, were followed, one year later, by increases and decreases in matrimonial separations.

The report was primarily concerned to define a problem and to bring it to the attention of the government. But it did end with a policy recommendation: that the federal government's policies aimed at bringing blacks into equality should be designed to strengthen the stability of black families.

The two main points of Moynihan's analysis seemed to have been accepted as the Administration's policy when they found their way straight into the speech the President decided to give at Howard University on June 4, 1965. Indeed, Moynihan actually wrote the first draft of it; it was then reworked by Richard N. Goodwin. The President accepted the principle of compensatory policies intended to achieve equality not just as "a right and a theory" but "as a fact and a result." And he accepted the proposition that black inequality was the result of a "devastating heritage of long years of slavery," and in particular of "the breakdown of the Negro family structure."

But what did the Administration propose to *do*? A public speech, and a highly rhetorical one at that, was not the same as an internal policy document. It would not be enough for the President to diagnose. He must prescribe. Goodwin found the upbeat ending that all good speeches should have by proposing a White House conference on the theme: "to fulfill these rights." The President was committed. As another White House aide put it, he had said, "Y'all come."

The President still occasionally called up black leaders and asked them what they wanted him to do. But, already, the White House was turning to white liberals far more frequently, to ask them what ought to be done *for* blacks. And so, in July, when a preliminary series of meetings was held to plan the White House conference, those who were invited were the cream of the social-science elite: Erik Erikson, Robert Coles, Kenneth Clark, Urie Bronfenbrenner, and the venerable Talcott Parsons himself. Of those who attended, five were professors from Harvard: only Clark was black. Already, at this stage, the opinion was being expressed that it would be politically unwise to devote the conference as a whole to the touchy matter of the black family.

These meetings were going on at the exact moment when the President was confronted with the failure of his spring decision to escalate the war in Indochina. On July 20, Robert McNamara came back from a tour of inspection to report, "The situation in South Vietnam is worse than a year ago (when it was worse than a year before that)." On July 27, after a weekend of reflection and debate at Camp David, there took place the historic National Security Council meeting at which Lyndon Johnson made up his mind neither "to bring the enemy to his knees by using our Strategic Air Command" nor to "pack up and go home" but to "give our commanders in the field the men and supplies they say they need." That was the fatal decision.

Once again, the war and the fate of the cities were bound together by a coincidence of timing.

On August 6 the President signed the voting-rights bill. The civil rights leadership was invited to be present at the signing ceremony, Martin Luther King among them. At this point, King's biographer says, "A malfunction in the transmission of political signals occurred . . . one that was never to be repaired." King thought it essential to press the President into turning his attention to the plight of the northern ghettoes; and he considered it his duty to raise the issue of the war. Johnson thought the time had come for a pause in the pressure on the black issue; he was angered by what he regarded as King's presumption in speaking about the war. Above all, the President was increasingly preoccupied with Vietnam: from the middle of 1965 on, the war monopolized his time, his patience and his mental energy.

Then the second shoe dropped. On August 9, the first leaks from the Moynihan report surfaced in *Newsweek*. Two nights later, a traffic officer arrested a young black man in Los Angeles. A crowd gathered and began to attack white motorists. Thirty hours later, and two miles away, in Watts, heavy firebombing began. Watts being a black ghetto, it was apparently aimed at property owned by whites rather than at white people. Given the traditions and attitudes of the Los Angeles Police Department, that hardly made much difference. Police, and later, national guardsmen, moved in. Thirty-four people were killed. All were black.

The newspapers said it was the worst riot in the United States since the Detroit race riot of 1943. Clearly it marked the beginning of a new and darker time. Perhaps the worst thing of all about it, though, was that it marked the beginning of a period when the same events took on utterly different meanings for white people and for blacks.

To whites, or most of them, what happened in Watts was that the blacks rose, and rioted, and sniped, and killed white people.

Lou Smith, a former CORE worker from Los Angeles, described how it felt to black people. He called it a "tremendous community tantrum."

> What happened was that people had sat here and watched all the concern about black people "over there." And there wasn't a damn soul paying one bit of attention to what was going on in Watts. So the black people in Watts just spontaneously rose up one day and said:
> Fuck it! We're hungry. Our schools stink. We're getting the shit beaten out of us. We've tried the integration route. It's obvious the integration route ain't going to work. Now we've got to go another way.

After Watts, it was rare for black-white exchanges not to be dialogues of the deaf.

The riots confirmed the worst fears of those who had never really accepted the aims of the civil rights movement.

They also appalled many who had accepted every one of those aims, who thought of themselves as liberals, who really believed that injustice was still being done to black Americans and that the government ought to do something to right that injustice. One such person was the President of the United States.

Before the end of his life Lyndon Johnson came to understand something of the gap between white and black attitudes. "Black power," he even wrote in his memoirs, "had a different meaning to the black man, who until recently had had to seek the white world's approval and for whom success had come largely on white people's terms."

But, in 1965, he was not fully capable of understanding what had happened in Watts. "Neither old wrongs nor new fears can justify arson and murder," he said at the time. He either didn't understand, or couldn't acknowledge, that if blacks had committed a good deal of arson in Watts, the killing had been done by white men, and by white men in uniform at that.

He was not alone in this misconception. The vivid, unexplained images of rage and hatred that appeared on TV news from each successive scene of rioting gave the majority of the white population the same distorted understanding of the nature of what was happening. To take one notorious example, it was generally imagined that black snipers were widespread and indeed, it was assumed, organized. In fact, there is very little solid evidence of any sniping by blacks in any of the riots of the middle 1960s. Most of what was at first reported to be sniping turned out on investigation to be the result of wild firing by police or national guardsmen. The result was that from the time of Watts on, the President and all other elected officials had to concern themselves with a wave of panic about "black crime." To some extent, this fear was justified by a real increase in crimes of violence. To a far greater extent, it was caused by a misunderstanding of the ghetto rioting which, from 1965 to 1968, dominated newspaper headlines and TV screens each summer.

By mischance it was in this deteriorating climate of fear, anger and misunderstanding that the Moynihan report became public, and not by official publication but at first through partial and muddled leaks.

A column by Rowland Evans and Robert Novak, just one week after the Watts riot broke out, was an influential and disastrous example: influential because of the inside knowledge they were credited with, disastrous because of the use they made of it. The columnists erroneously implied that the Moynihan report was a response to the 1964 riots. They failed to mention its crucial argument that the breakdown in black family life was a result of unemployment. And the ending of their column managed at once to be opinionated, incendiary . . . and sadly prescient:

> The implied message of the Moynihan report is that ending discrimination is not nearly enough for the Negro. But what is enough?
> The phrase "preferential treatment" implies a solution far afield from the American dream. The white majority would never accept it.

As the fall of 1965 wore on, the controversy over the report continued. It was bitterly criticized both by white liberals (especially in the churches) and by black leaders, largely, it must be said, for things it did not say, often for not saying things it did plainly say.

The White House conference "To Fulfill These Rights" had originally been planned for November. In this climate it was not thought wise to go ahead with it. Instead, an elaborate planning conference was held in Washington. The government went to great lengths to play down the Moynihan report. It produced an agenda paper, written by the distin-

guished black sociologist Hylan Lewis, which argued against Moynihan's
central thesis that the black family was "crumbling." The family, it was
decided, would be only one of eight topics to be discussed at the full conference in the spring. And one government spokesman, only half in jest,
maintained, "No such person as Daniel Patrick Moynihan exists."

Increasingly the President's attention—and therefore, given the nature
of presidential government, that of the White House as a whole—was
being absorbed by the escalation of the war. By the end of the year, the
war had added nearly $5 billion to the federal budget and was expected to
add $10 billion the following year. By January the White House was ex-
pecting to have to commit over four hundred thousand men. "You know,"
one high official is reported to have said about this time, "there are less
than twenty men in the government who can get something new done,
and they really have to work and fight to do it: with Vietnam building
up, they just had to drop this other thing." The remark is a graphic illustration both of how centralized presidential government had become and
of how directly the government's commitment to achieve equality for
blacks was seen by insiders to have fallen victim to the Vietnam War.

Preoccupied by Vietnam, the President was also out of sympathy
with the new, separatist militancy and profoundly irritated by black
leaders' opposition to the war, which he saw as none of their business. His
breach with Dr. King became more or less absolute after King denounced
the war in a volume published on New Year's Day 1966.

Five months later, on June 1, the White House conference met at
last, almost a year after the President had promised in his Howard speech
to make the achieving of equality for black people, "as a fact and a result,"
the "chief goal" of his administration. No doubt the President still
devoutly desired that consummation. But it hardly had the same priority
now. At times, he and his staff seemed more concerned with minimizing
political embarrassment from black militants and antiwar demonstrators
than with fulfilling rights.

In the planning of the conference, both black leaders and white intellectuals had been shunted aside in favor of "concerned" big businessmen.
The chairman was one of these, Ben Heineman, of the Chicago and
North Western Railway. As one of the President's aides put it, these were
men whose success in making money reassured the public that they were
not revolutionaries. Quite so. On the other hand, to be fair, they were not
reactionaries. With more than two thousand participants, all the conference delegates could do was comment briefly on recommendations
prepackaged by Heineman and his committees, and these proved relatively
liberal. On the other hand, the black Justice Department aide Roger
Wilkins commented at the time, "There is widespread belief among

Negroes interested in civil rights that there will be no significant follow-up to or implementation of the recommendations of the conference by this administration." They were right.

Not surprisingly in the circumstances, fewer than half the delegates bothered to attend the formal sessions of the conference. The President, to his delight and to the relief of his staff, was able to pay a surprise visit without untoward incident. Everything passed off without mishap. But that was all. That this was the most that any of the organizers dared hope is in itself the best commentary on how things had changed in the twelve months since the Howard speech.

Less than a week later, James Meredith was shot.

Soon Willie Ricks was shouting, "Black power!"

Later that same summer, Martin Luther King went to Chicago and was routed.

At about the same time, Lyndon Johnson discharged a social obligation. He invited the committee and staff of the civil rights conference to the White House to thank them for their efforts. After a few sentences, he dropped the subject of the conference. For an hour, he rambled on obsessively about the Vietnam War: how he was misunderstood, how often he thought about Abraham Lincoln, how Lincoln, too, had been misunderstood.

The symbolism was perfect.

The controversy over the Moynihan report was more a symptom than a cause of what had happened.

When it was written, the assumption was that the President was at the head of a great liberal coalition in which the Democratic Party, and the intellectuals, and the unions, and the more enlightened leaders of business, would march shoulder to shoulder with the black organizations "to move beyond opportunity to achievement." The goals, the methods, the political strategy, the optimism, were those of the liberal consensus.

Now, by the middle of 1966, the coalition had been fragmented. That movement was stalled. That consensus was no more.

The Vietnam War was one reason for what had happened.

The rise of black militancy, the beginning of the riots, and the consequent backlash among even previously well-disposed white people—those were all other reasons. But even more fundamental was the fact that events had revealed the inherent contradictions of the liberal ideology itself.

Wasn't it inevitable that the civil rights coalition should fragment and fade away? Civil rights, surely, was no longer the issue. If the Johnson administration failed to follow up the promise of the Howard University speech, wasn't that because it was already doing so much, in concrete and more relevant ways, to diminish black inequality?

It is perfectly true that blacks were, disproportionately, beneficiaries of the "Great Society" social legislation: of the Economic Opportunity Act, of the Elementary and Secondary Education Act, of Medicare, and of a dozen other programs. It is also true that, from 1965 to 1969, not only the absolute amount of money but also the proportion of the federal budget devoted to these domestic social programs rose sharply, while the proportion of the national budget spent on defense went down.

Yet the same pattern of disillusionment can be traced in the Administration's attitudes to programs intended to help poor people, many of whom, of course, were black, as can be seen in its attitude to the civil rights movement. And there is no question that in this respect the Administration was responding to a shift in public opinion.

The War on Poverty, in fact, was the archetypal liberal program. It was inspired by a characteristic blend of benevolence, optimism, innocence and chauvinism. ("Today," said Lyndon Johnson when he signed the Economic Opportunity Act, "for the first time in all the history of the human race, a great nation is able and is willing to make a commitment to eradicate poverty among its people.") It was to be carried out essentially by the authority of the President (though of course Congress would have to appropriate the funds). In other respects, its strategy had been devised by intellectuals virtually without reference to the process of electoral politics. It was greatly influenced by the theories of social scientists, but it was also intimately related to the belief of the New Economists that they had discovered the secret of constant, non-inflationary growth and that they had therefore created new resources with which poverty could be abolished without anyone's pocket suffering. He set out, in other words, to achieve the millennium without changing the system. This miracle was to be worked through consensus. Business would do its part, and so would labor. ("The concept of consensus took over," according to the best-informed account of the task force's work on drafting the Economic Opportunity legislation. "Shriver busied himself touching every conceivable power base, especially in the business community.") It was, in short, both ideologically and in practice a very much more conservative program than it was supposed to sound. In every one of these particulars it was typical of the liberalism of the consensus years.

Both this consensus approach and ordinary political considerations brought it about that many and various programs that one department or another had long been wanting Congress to pass found their way into the six titles of the Economic Opportunity Act. The main decision of principle had been settled before that. The Labor Department, and its representative on the task force (none other than Moynihan), maintained that what the poor needed most was money and that they could best be given it by giving them jobs. At a cabinet meeting in March, however, the President decided against imposing a cigarette tax to raise more than $1 billion for creating new jobs.

The White House preferred "community action" to a jobs program. The idea had been picked up by the Bureau of the Budget from the enthusiasm of the President's Commission on Juvenile Delinquency, which in turn had adopted the theory that the causes of youth crime lay in the community, not in the individual, from the thinking of the social scientists at the Ford Foundation and the Columbia School of Social Work.

The Council of Economic Advisers liked community action. The White House originally wanted it to be the whole of the poverty program. And it was Sargent Shriver who insisted that it be tried not just in a few experimental centers but all over the country. Both intellectually and politically, community action was the heart of the poverty program.

The Office of Economic Opportunity set up shop late in 1964 in a mood of intellectual excitement reminiscent of the mood in which the larger body of intellectuals had come down to Washington to work for Kennedy at the end of 1960.

The President remained enthusiastic until the middle of 1965. At a cabinet meeting that summer, with Vietnam expenditure already looking like a threat to other programs, he went around the room and asked each cabinet officer in turn to see what savings he could make. Then he pointed dramatically to Shriver and said: "You-all give the money to him!"

In September 1965, according to the historian of OEO, Robert A. Levine, this all changed "sharply, abruptly and traumatically." In the first year, OEO's budget had been $750 million. In the second year, Congress appropriated $1.5 million. The agency's own five-year plan envisaged a massive, nationwide community-action strategy with programs in both urban slums and rural depressed areas and a total budget of $3.5 billion. In the new climate, the Administration asked for just half of that figure, or $1.75 billion, and Congress finally appropriated even less: $1.625 billion. There was a drastic change in the mood of Congress starting early in 1966. And OEO seemed to have lost the President's confidence as well. Many of the idealists and ideologues departed. They were replaced by hard-faced administrators put in to tidy up the ship.

What had happened? Why had the climate changed? Levine's answer is clear:

> It changed because of the rapidly increasing fiscal demands of the Vietnam war, but it also changed because the political fruits had fallen off the trees of administrative chaos and program excess.

The mayors of the United States had descended upon Vice-president Hubert Humphrey, Mr. Johnson's envoy to the cities, and given him the word as to what had been happening in their cities and what they thought about it. Their thoughts were pretty pungent. The poor were being organized against the establishments and, not surprisingly, the establishments didn't like it a bit.

No doubt the merits of the case varied greatly from one program to another. It is easy to sympathize with the Mississippi Child Development Group, which succeeded in giving preschool education to a large number of desperately disadvantaged children, even if the Mississippi senators and congressmen were right in their allegation that some of its funds had been used to campaign against them. The Mississippi Congressional delegation had never been backward in using public money to improve its own political position. In general, the Head Start preschool program was a notable success, and with few scandals. On the other hand, it is hard to disagree with criticisms of the decision to give public money to a Chicago street gang, the Blackstone Rangers—"kooks and sociologists!" the President is said to have exclaimed when he heard this had happened—or even to the subsidizing of LeRoy Jones's talented, but openly anti-white, theater in Harlem.

Whatever the merits of the particular case, elected politicians could hardly be expected to tolerate the use of federal money to subsidize the opposition to them. Full of their ideology of community action and participatory democracy, the OEO intellectuals arrogantly ignored the existing elected officeholders. In other words, they were so infatuated with the black, the poor and the powerless, that they ignored the sensibilities, and the collective political power, of the white American majority. That hubris was to bring its nemesis soon enough.

It is possible to disagree about the relative importance of the causes of the withdrawal of support from the poverty program. For Daniel Patrick Moynihan, for example, "The underfunding was at least as much associated with the war in Vietnam as with any political difficulties the War on Poverty might have caused." There can be little argument, though, about the two causes themselves. It is too clear what happened. The poverty program ran into exactly the same crossfire as civil rights.

After the middle of 1965 the Vietnam War meant that resources—tax revenue and the attention of the President and his men—were scarcer for programs aimed at helping the poor and blacks. At the same time, such programs became less popular—with the President, with elected politicians, and with the public.

The two wings of the liberal ideology were being simultaneously exposed. The liberals were revealed as being more interested in containing communism in Indochina than in abolishing poverty or achieving equality at home. At the same time, the elitist character of the liberal strategy at home was also becoming apparent. Under fire from the twin crises in Southeast Asia and in American ghettoes, consensus was breaking up. It gave way to bitter polarization.

## 14

## *The Great Schism*

Societies have a need to find ways of checking their own tendencies.

Richard Hofstadter

On May 11, 1965, Dean Rusk called the Soviet ambassador to the United States, Anatoly Dobrynin, down to the State Department. He told him that the United States was willing to stop bombing North Vietnam, which it had then been doing for just over two months, if Hanoi would order the Viet Cong to halt its activity in the South. It was the beginning of what was to be a weary, seven-year dialogue of the deaf, doomed to frustration. Each side saw the other as a blackmailer, cynically asking to be paid to stop doing what it should not have started in the first place. But there was another, ironic resonance to the conversation. Rusk strove to convince the Russian that the United States was in deadly earnest. "Hanoi appears to have the impression they may succeed," he said, "but the U.S. will not get tired." One illusion in particular Rusk did all he could to dispel. The Russians would be making a bad mistake if they supposed that the U. S. Government would be affected in the slightest by what Rusk dismissed as the "very small domestic pressure" against the war.

It was a startling misreading of the situation. The truth was that Lyndon Johnson and his advisers underestimated the political cost of the war even more disastrously than they underestimated its economic cost. Precisely in the two months before Rusk's conversation with Dobrynin, domestic opposition to American involvement in Vietnam made a quantum jump. It broke out of the tiny shell of the traditional peace movement and began to reach its first wider constituency, on college campuses. For the first time since the beginning of the Cold War, the foreign policy of the liberal consensus met serious opposition from the Left. Within less than three years, the opinion polls were to show more than half the population opposed to the war. Vietnam would make it impossible for Lyndon Johnson to fulfill his plans for building a Great Society, impossible for him to be re-elected, impossible, even, for him to travel freely around the country.

The war became the organizing principle around which all the doubts and disillusionments of the years of crisis since 1963, and all the deeper discontents hidden under the glossy surface of the confident years, coalesced into one great rebellion. Those "very small domestic pressures" grew and grew until the United States did get tired of the war. And then they grew and grew again until they had polarized the country into two opposed camps, two mutually hostile cultures, even: those who accepted and those who rejected the assumptions of 1960. That evening, as Rusk tried to impress upon Dobrynin the unity of American purpose, the age of consensus was on the very eve of giving way to the Great Schism.

On Lincoln's Birthday in 1947, between four and five hundred American men publicly destroyed their draft cards in protest against the imminent passage of the new Selective Service Act. Sixty-three of them did so at a meeting in New York City where the speakers included A. J. Muste, Dwight Macdonald, David Dellinger and Bayard Rustin. Muste, veteran preacher and pacifist, had founded the American Workers Party in the 1930s and had helped to found CORE in the 1940s. Macdonald had by 1947 successively renounced the Communists, the Trotskyites and Marxism itself but was still to perform his greatest service to the American Left when his *New Yorker* article drew President Kennedy's attention to the problem of poverty and put it on the agenda of American politics. Dellinger had been to jail as a conscientious objector in World War II, and in 1947 Rustin still had a thirty-day sentence on a Georgia chain gang hanging over him for his part in the Journey of Reconciliation, precursor of the Freedom Rides, earlier the same year.

That 1947 meeting is a reminder that the New Left of the 1960s had its roots in an older tradition. Even its most spectacular techniques were not always new. The peace movement in the United States was older than the Vietnam War, older than the draft, older than the Cold War. Indeed there had been a radical peace movement in America for a hundred years. At times there have been conservative peace movements as well: Copperhead in the Civil War, German- or Irish-American in the First World War, isolationist between the wars.

The roots of the radical peace movement have always been entangled with those of the civil rights movement. The ideals, and many of the idealists, have been common to both. They have been ideals of personal conscience and liberation, perhaps, more than aspirations to acquire political power in order to change society. But they have had a political base of sorts in two, uneasily allied, minority traditions: the Marxist Left, and the tradition of radical religious conscience—especially, though not exclusively, Jewish, Quaker and Unitarian.

This is the native American Left. It can claim, and for me persuasively, to represent much of what is truest and best in the American political tradition. But in so far as it has represented itself as a peace movement and nothing more, it has been disingenuous. It has always been a critique of the moral justification of the American *status quo*, and of the morality of those who wielded power in America.

The influence of this radical peace movement has ebbed and flowed according to the degree to which the times favored its ability to recruit support from other, less conscience-directed groups. In 1947, with fear of Stalinism building up to a climax, the peace movement was near its lowest ebb. Its influence hardly stretched beyond the tiny circulation of A. J. Muste's paper *Liberation*.

By the late 1960s, it seemed to have reached a zenith. More than half the population opposed the war. But that was deceptive. It did not mean that half the population had joined the peace movement. The draft, the war, and the crisis had indeed led millions to re-examine the moral basis of American power. But millions of those who opposed the war had no sympathy for any such re-examination. They simply wanted the war to end.

In the late 1950s, as the fear of McCarthyism and of the Soviet Union began to recede, the peace movement slowly began to expand beyond these twin bases on the Left and in the church groups. A more affluent strain had been added by the World Federalists. One of the founders, Cord Meyer, went on to become a senior official at the CIA. Another was Norman Cousins, editor of *Saturday Review*. With Norman Thomas of the Socialist Party and Clarence Pickett of the American Society of Friends—the Left and the churches again—Cousins was behind the founding of the National Committee for a Sane Nuclear Policy (SANE), which put its first advertisement in the New York *Times* on November 15, 1957.

"Sociologically," SANE's director, Sanford Gottlieb, told me, "SANE recruited from the business and professional middle class. These were issue-oriented, educated, middle-class people. They were concerned about nuclear weapons, nuclear testing, fall-out and related issues."

The best-known of these converts, and yet quite typical of them, was Dr. Benjamin Spock, pediatrician to a generation. "I was a hawk in 1960," Dr. Spock said in an interview. "I thought there was a missile gap. There was nothing pacifist about me then. I thought we had to be strong to stand up to the Soviet Union."

In 1962 he joined SANE—at the *third* invitation. It was a small thing that changed his mind. President Kennedy had announced that he would meet with his experts to decide whether the United States needed to go on testing nuclear weapons or not. The experts met, and the President announced that they all agreed that the United States was ahead in nuclear weapons technology . . . but that he was going to go on testing anyway, so as not to fall behind.

"I thought that was odd," said Dr. Spock. "You were damned if you didn't, and damned if you did. It was quite clear that if all the experts said we were behind, we would go on testing. But we were also going to go on testing when the experts said we were ahead. So when would we stop? I thought of all the children who would die of leukemia and cancer, and of the ultimate possibility of nuclear war, and I joined SANE."

He was asked to collaborate with Bill Bernbach, of the Doyle Dane Bernbach agency, in writing the copy for an advertisement in the New York *Times*. "I was thrown into intellectual and emotional turmoil," he told me. "It was having to write that ad which made me examine all aspects of American foreign policy."

"Dr. Spock is worried," the text began. And he was. The next year, he became one of the two cochairmen of SANE. The other was the Harvard history professor H. Stuart Hughes, who ran for the Senate against Edward Kennedy on the peace issue in November 1962. The Hughes campaign was the first attempt to inject the peace issue into mainstream electoral politics.

In the advertisement, Dr. Spock wore a suit with a waistcoat, and he was looking down at a little girl with a frown of concern. The furrowed brow was the style of SANE and the other middle-class peace groups in the early sixties. But even before the Kennedy assassination, another wing of the peace movement was growing up, whose style was the clenched fist of anger. The Student Peace Union was founded in Chicago in 1959. By 1962 it had seventy chapters and more than thirty-five hundred members. Affiliated to it were radical groups at the two most influential universities in the country, TOCSIN at Harvard and SLATE at Berkeley.

A breath was stirring the elms on campus. The young people who joined the SPU were concerned with more than just the issue of "peace" as such. They joined peace groups partly because there were no other radical groups for them to join. (The Communists' Labor Youth League, for example, was dissolved in 1957; the Trotskyite Young People's Socialist League, the once famous YPSLs, had almost ceased to exist.) The concern of the SPU was with building a new society, not just with protecting the existing one from fall-out and nuclear war.

Yet the Student Peace Union was short-lived. It disbanded in 1964. Many of its members moved on to the group—organization is not, perhaps, the right word—that eventually took up the running as the spearhead of the radical peace movement: Students for a Democratic Society.

SDS was born in wedlock as the child of those poor but honest parents the Old Left and the American labor movement. But it wasn't long before, like many another child of the sixties, it ran away from home. It didn't like the compromises it felt the old folks had to make to earn their living. And it needed to find its own identity.

To grasp how the New Left and the peace movement developed, you need to understand their parentage. The New York socialist Left at the beginning of the 1960s was a tiny world. It was riven by family quarrels and love-hate relationships that no outsider can quite hope to fathom. And yet, through its influence over parts of the labor movement and over certain intellectuals, it exercised infinitely more power than its numbers warranted, or than most Americans imagined.

One of the obsolescent institutions of the Old Left was the League for Industrial Democracy. It had known more glorious days, as a platform for Jack London, for Upton Sinclair, and later for Norman Thomas. But now it existed on the charity of the New York needle-trades unions. A group of socialists, including Michael Harrington, now proposed to revitalize it as a center for discussions among labor people, blacks and intellectuals. They were what was called in the family the Schachtmanites: followers of the veteran Marxist theoretician Max Schachtman.

In 1960, as part of their plans for revamping the LID, they equipped it with a student wing. In 1961 this was taken over by a group of students led by Al Haber, a radical from the University of Michigan.

Over the winter, a good deal of energy went into discussing drafts of a paper written by the editor of the student newspaper at Michigan, Tom Hayden. In June 1962 fifty-nine members from a dozen campuses met with Harrington (who had then just finished writing *The Other America*) as a sort of camp counselor, at a UAW conference center at Port Huron, north of Detroit. There they issued a sixty-four-page statement, largely written by Hayden, which has often been called the manifesto of the New Left.

The most often-quoted passage (partly perhaps because it is the first!)

stresses the perplexity of a new generation before the twin issues of race and peace:

> We are people of this generation, bred in at least modest comfort, housed now in universities, looking uncomfortably to the world we inherit.
> When we were kids the United States was the wealthiest and strongest country in the world . . . many of us began maturing in complacency.
> As we grew, however, our comfort was penetrated by events too troubling to dismiss. First, the permeating and victimizing fact of human degradation, symbolized by the Southern struggle against racial bigotry, compelled most of us from silence to activism. Second, the enclosing fact of the Cold War, symbolized by the presence of the Bomb, brought awareness that we ourselves, and our friends, and millions of abstract "others" we knew more directly because of our common peril, might die at any time.

There was little in what the statement had to say about these two grand issues that could have troubled their mentors in the labor movement. It was when it touched on the immediate experience of students, that is, on the university, that the statement's analysis departed most sharply from orthodoxy.

In the past few years, it noted, thousands of students had begun to demonstrate against racial injustice and the threat of war. The real significance of these demonstrations lay in the fact that students were at last "breaking the crust of apathy and overcoming the inner alienation that remain the defining characteristics of American college life." It is an interesting formulation: it comes close to implying that the causes of student concern over peace or civil rights lay in the unhappiness of their own lives. And what were the causes of apathy and alienation? Again, the statement answers that they are to be found, at least partly, in the university: in "cumbersome academic bureaucracy" and in "social and physical scientists" who work "for the corporate economy" or "accelerate the arms race." Five years before the accusation became commonplace that universities were guilty of complicity in Vietnam, and more than two years before the first student revolt at Berkeley, SDS was already depicting the university and its (predominantly liberal) professors as substantially to blame for student alienation. From the start, the New Left had a tendency to be more outraged by what it conceived as the hypocrisies of the liberals than by the grosser sins of the Right.

In the next section of the Port Huron statement, the key passage in the entire document, the liberal intellectuals are even more explicitly treated as mere apologists for a structure of oppression:

> Some regard this national doldrum [sic: i.e. apathy] as a sign of healthy approval of the established order—but is it approval by consent

or manipulated acquiescence? Others declare that the people are withdrawn because compelling issues are fast disappearing,—perhaps there are fewer breadlines in America, but is Jim Crow gone, is there enough work, is world war a diminishing threat, and what of revolutionary new peoples? Still others think the national quietude is a necessary consequence of the need for elites to resolve the complex and specialized issues of modern industrial society—but why then should *business* elites decide foreign policy, and who controls the elites anyway, and are they solving mankind's problems?

The apathy here is, first, *subjective*—the felt powerlessness of ordinary people. . . . But subjective apathy is encouraged by the *objective* American situation, the actual structural separation of people from power.

Long before the escalation of the Vietnam War, then; before the disillusionment of the civil rights movement in 1964; even before the assassination; *some* young people, when they looked at the institution they knew best, which was the university, were ready to question the liberal ideology and its ever-prompt apologetics for the *status quo*. Something in the air that generation had breathed—television quiz shows, perhaps, or the revolution of rising expectations, or sheer boredom with the pious repetitions of consensus—had predisposed it to skepticism.

Yet it was so far only a predisposition. Tom Hayden's long and candid account of the evolution of his own political states of mind, in an interview in *Rolling Stone* in 1972, has something of the pathos of an archaeological dig. Right at the bottom of the trench, under all the strata of his later radical career, beneath the Chicago trial, and the peace movement, and community organizing, there nestled the unmistakable fragments of the lost innocence of a Kennedy liberal. Lower still lie the carbonized traces of a rebel who was once without a cause.

> I was a college editor, very influenced by the Beat Generation. My thing was to hitchhike all over the country. . . .
>
> And so that summer [it was 1960] I went to North Beach [where the Beats had lived on love and poetry and cheap red wine, in San Francisco] and my justification for it as an editor was that I was going to cover the Democratic convention [in Los Angeles]. I was always very divided between being what now you would call a radical and what then didn't have a name . . . it was mainly like trying to mimic the life of James Dean or something like that. . . . And then the other half of me was in the Establishment—ambitious young reporter who wanted to be a famous correspondent.
>
> I got to Berkeley and immediately went to the first person who was giving out leaflets, because I'd never seen anything like this before . . . and being political, they took me home and gave me a room to stay in for a few weeks and tried to educate me politically. . . .

Brought up in a working-class family in the suburbs of once-militant Detroit, and after three years at one of the best universities in the country, Hayden had never come in contact with the Left. To question the ethics of nuclear war, to organize unorganized workers, these were new thoughts.

> You know what they were doing? They were organizing farm workers. . . .
>
> He drove me out to Livermore one day and showed me the nuclear reactor, where all the hydrogen bombs were made. And then another day [he] drove me out into the fields and the valleys, and he told me about the Chicanos. . . .
>
> On the other hand, I was in part tied to the Kennedy image also, the appeal of the New Frontier and the Peace Corps was pretty great.

There would be causes and to spare for rebels in the sixties. No doubt, if he had gone into the Peace Corps, it would have made him a rebel just the same. That was what it did for Paul Cowan, a representative figure of upper-middle-class dissent if ever there was one. Son of the producer who thought up quiz shows, alumnus of Choate and Harvard, he wrote an angry, strangely self-pitying book about the Peace Corps called *The Making of an Un-American*. But whether you grew up at Choate or in working-class Detroit, it was hard not to be "in part tied to the Kennedy image." They all started out as believers. Or at least they all once wanted to believe.

It is usual to speak of a generation radicalized by external events: by Dallas, and Mississippi, and Vietnam. And the relentless succession of external traumas did have its effect. Hayden mentions all those three among the stations of his personal journey. But even more, perhaps, they were driven into radical rebellion by their personal experience of those whom they expected to be their allies: by what they saw as the liberals' equivocations and manipulations. Hayden was no exception.

In the summer of 1961 he and his Michigan friend Paul Potter, a future president of SDS, visited McComb, Mississippi, with Bob Moses. While they were watching a nonviolent demonstration, they were pulled from their car by whites whom they believed had been set on them by the sheriff. Then they were told to leave town, or go to jail, by a high state official. They flew to Washington, expecting to be met with indignation and help from the Justice Department. Politely they were told by John Doar that there was nothing the federal government could do and that they should stay away from Mississippi. "From that time on," Hayden comments, "it was clear."

An even more embittering lesson was to come. That same autumn, Hayden and several others of those who later became the national leadership of SDS ran for national office in the National Student Association. They had no means of knowing that it was controlled by the CIA. But they did come up against what they described, with more truth than they realized at the time, as "the foreign policy elite" of the NSA: mysteriously well-heeled and well-briefed "students" in their thirties who always seemed to have plenty of money for flying around Europe.

> It all became a little more chilling [Hayden added] when one day we were in the office of the president of the NSA just before the congress and found on his desk a chart written in his hand. His name was Richard Rettig. He was a CIA agent from the University of Wisconsin, and he had a chart of the congress. Me, Haber, and other people, SDS people, were listed as being the Left on this chart, and there was a Right and a Center, in terms of power blocs. And at the top there was a group called the control group.

Eleven years later, Hayden laughed as he remembered the shock and disillusionment of that discovery.

"Control group," he repeated. "Capital C, capital G!"

This, as the young radicals saw it, more than any other factor meant that there had to be a New Left. For a long time they hoped that they would be able to work with labor and the Left liberals, that they shared common ideals about peace and civil rights. But what was unmistakable was that in practice those whom they expected to be their allies were afraid of them. The Old Left "retained a liberal or radical rhetoric, but their real job was to be the Left gatekeeper of American radicalism."

And so the next SDS manifesto, *America and the New Era*, published in 1963, was more radical than the Port Huron statement. And the main difference was precisely on the issue of the liberal establishment:

> . . . the capture of liberal rhetoric and the liberal power base by the corporate liberalism of the New Frontiersmen means that the reformers and the democratically oriented liberals are trapped by the limitations of the Democratic Party, but afraid of irrelevancy outside it.

The young radicals refused to limit themselves to writing pamphlets. They believed in action. "The whole soul of the New Left idea of politics," Carl Oglesby, another of the pioneers, wrote later, was the "concentration on process rather than on institutional end-points." And so they decided to try to contact the working class directly, in the most literal sense: by knocking on doors.

This was the logic behind the next phase of SDS's activity: "community organizing." It might be true, as Todd Gitlin, president of SDS from 1963 to 1964, wrote, that "the under-class has its most abrasive contacts with the ruling elites less at the point of production than outside it." The unions, in any case, controlled contacts at "the point of production," and they were not about to let young student radicals interfere with their power there. And so the community organizer knocked on doors, and talked about "bad housing, meager and degrading welfare, irrelevant schools, inadequate community facilities." As it happened, SDS was helped to do this with a grant from the UAW. But the constituency the young radicals were trying to reach was not the same as that of the big unions. The "communities" where they worked—defined, in fact, by their sad lack of community—were not inhabited by members of the UAW, the Teamsters or the building-trades unions, but by the unorganized and, all too often, by the unemployed. Rennie Davis and Todd Gitlin worked with poor white Appalachian migrants in the Uptown neighborhood of Chicago, Tom Hayden and Carl Wittman mainly with blacks in Newark. They discovered a world that had simply not been described by the liberal social scientists: a world where alienation meant not apolitical complacency but anger, deprivation, and poverty every bit as desperate as they had witnessed in the South.

The idea that a mass movement for social change through participatory democracy could be built by organizing the unorganized around local issues has proved to be a delusion. But it was a heady and a transforming experience for those who threw themselves into it. It was a time of apostolic hope and purity of motive. And for a while it distracted the attention of young radicals from what was happening in Vietnam.

In the late summer of 1964, shocked by the bombing of North Vietnam after the Tonkin Gulf incident, SDS did call a protest demonstration, to be held in Washington the following spring. When it took place, on April 17, 1965, the war had been escalated, and at least fifteen thousand young people joined the SDS march. It was one of the first signs that opposition to the war was spreading beyond the ranks of committed radicals. Yet, even then, SDS remained reluctant to give the war priority over the attempt to build a grass-roots radical movement in the United States. At the SDS national convention at Kewadin, Michigan, as late as June 1965, the foreign policy workshop, chaired by Todd Gitlin, recommended *against* concentrating on Vietnam. So, far from whipping up the movement against the Vietnam War, SDS took a leading part in it only with reluctance and after it was clear that there would be a mass movement against the war among young people anyway.

The dream of a multi-issue coalition lay behind the reasons why older radicals, too, were slow to take up the issue of Vietnam. But where the New Left had plunged into community organizing because they were pessimistic about the chances that labor would ever give a radical lead, the older Left was deterred from speaking out against the war for the opposite reason.

"In 1964 and 1965," Michael Harrington has written, "it seemed to us socialists that political realignment in America was about to come true. . . . The landslide of 1964 had elected the most liberal Congress within a generation. With an activist president of New Deal inclinations, that provided the setting for the most hopeful period of reform since Franklin Roosevelt." The anguished debate within the New York Left paralleled the dilemma with which liberals in general wrestled as the war gathered momentum and seemed to threaten the prospects of the Great Society.

Harrington has described one particular meeting at which Max Schachtman "launched into a Marxist attack on pacifism and the moralistic approach to politics. In Max's view, a condemnation of the Vietnam war primarily on the grounds that it was immoral was an exercise in phrase-mongering." Schachtman and his friends argued, on spurious Marxist grounds, that because the peace movement was largely middle class, which it was, *ergo* it must be acting in a manner contrary to the interests of the working class. There was a profoundly pessimistic assumption that the mass of the working class would inevitably support the war: an assumption that was, in spite of some dramatic and highly publicized symbolic events, only partially borne out, and which might have been even less justified if the Left, in 1965 or even earlier, had thrown its considerable influence with organized labor into the scales against the war.

That did not happen. The Left was to be divided on this issue as bitterly as the country as a whole. Certainly, even within his own immediate circle, Max Schachtman's arguments did not go unchallenged. Michael Harrington, in the end, broke with Schachtman on this issue and finally resigned his cochairmanship of the Socialist Party rather than "pretend any solidarity with people who, in the name of Marxism, were helping Richard Nixon." Bayard Rustin, on the other hand, found himself in the tragic posture, for a lifelong pacifist, of justifying the war in the name of a radical coalition that never materialized. Puzzling and even perverse as these almost theological arguments may seem to outsiders, they do explain why the Old Left did not take the lead, as it might have been expected to do, in the movement against the war.

If people on the Left were reluctant to attack the war because of their high hopes for Lyndon Johnson's domestic programs, the same was even more true of the liberals. The negative form of the proposition carried most weight: if we don't back Johnson, we might get Goldwater.

Even the hard-core peace movement felt the force of this. "We were outspoken enough about Johnson and the war in 1964," David McReynolds of the War Resisters' League acknowledged in an interview, "but we did discourage demonstrations. We thought it important to elect Johnson."

"We were so eager to have Johnson over Goldwater," Dr. Spock told me, "that there was what the psychologists call a halo effect. If you think someone is on your side, you ignore his defects. I campaigned actively on radio and TV for President Johnson."

SANE had organized two demonstrations on Vietnam in front of the White House when President Kennedy was still in it, but in those days the issue was Diem's autocratic behavior as much as it was American involvement. In Washington, under the influence of the Franco-American writer Bernard Fall, *The New Republic* had taken up the issue even earlier, with a special issue, in April 1962, headlined "No Win in Vietnam." In 1964 there had been a SANE petition, organized by Hans Morgenthau among others, calling for the neutralization of both Vietnams. Nevertheless few liberals were deeply concerned before the escalation decisions of early 1965.

"There wasn't very much evidence that we had cause to be worried until February of 1965," Sanford Gottlieb of SANE told me. "On the morning of February 7, Bernard Fall called me at 7 o'clock in the morning and said, 'They did it.'"

"Sandy Gottlieb called up early that Sunday morning," Dr. Spock remembers, "and said the U.S. was bombing North Vietnam. He read over the text of a denunciatory telegram he wanted Hughes and me to send to Johnson. . . . In the end I agreed, and he sent it in our name. A commentator said the White House says the move is approved by all Americans except Dr. Spock and Professor Hughes."

That was a considerable error on the White House's part. But the reaction to the decision to escalate the war did not explode all at once. "The successive nations in this country reacted to the war one after another," Sanford Gottlieb put it, "and the big sophisticated universities were first."

As it happened, the first of them was the University of Michigan. It was at Michigan that the technique was invented that linked the peace movement to the mass of students who were uneasy about the morality of the war and threatened by the draft. The technique was the teach-in, and it happened by accident.

Dr. William Gamson, a sociologist, was one of the four leaders of the teach-in movement at Ann Arbor. "The idea came from something that happened in the civil rights movement," he said. "I was a Democrat but not actively involved in politics, but I had been vice-chairman of CORE in Boston. There was a school boycott in the Boston area. As well as asking children to stay away from school, a Freedom School was set up to teach black history and civil rights: this was more positive than just asking kids to stay away from school."

"After the bombing in February 1965," Gamson went on, "a group of about fifteen faculty members met at one of our homes on March 11 to discuss what action we should take." The group included the philosopher Arnold Kaufman, who had actually been the chairman of the local Citizens for Johnson/Humphrey group three months before.

"Some wanted to put a protest ad in the paper. Some called for a hunger strike. Most of us wanted something more drastic than an ad. We hit on the idea of a one-day cancellation of classes and the holding of an all-day Vietnam symposium on the model of the Freedom School I just mentioned."

On March 17 the *Michigan Daily* reported that thirty-five faculty members were willing to walk out on March 24 to protest the Administration's policy in Vietnam. Selma was also mentioned. Two days later, the headline was "Faculty Group Cuts Off Walkout, Plans Teach-in." It was a new word. What had happened in the intervening two days was that there had been an angry reaction from the state legislature. The university administration, scenting trouble, persuaded Kaufman, Gamson and their friends to modify their plans.

On March 24 the following ad appeared in the *Michigan Daily*, signed by 216 members of the faculty.

### AN APPEAL TO OUR STUDENTS

We the faculty are deeply worried about the war in Vietnam.

We think its moral, political and military consequences are very grave, and that we must examine them and find new alternatives before irreparable actions occur.

We are devoting this night, March 24–25, to seminars, lectures, informal discussions and a protest rally to focus attention on the war, its consequences, and ways to stop it.

It was an appeal from the faculty to the students, moderate in tone and signed by many who could not by any stretch of the imagination be called radicals. There was even a note at the bottom of the ad that today has a period flavor: "Women may obtain overnight permission from their house directors" to attend the teach-in. It went off peacefully. Two speakers from the State Department were given a hearing. It was, in fact, a pretty mild affair.

And yet the idea spread as if a spark had been thrown onto dry straw. "It spread because the mood at Michigan prevailed in other places," says Gamson simply. Michigan faculty called friends at fifty other universities.

The very next day, there was a letter in the *Daily* from ten Stanford professors saying they planned to hold a teach-in there. Within a couple of weeks teach-ins had taken place at dozens of colleges. The movement culminated in a national, televised teach-in from Washington in June.

A few days after the first teach-in at Michigan, there was one at the University of Wisconsin. A graduate student, James Gilbert, later described what he had found so impressive about it. Not all the lectures were about Vietnam, he said; in fact, the most important was probably a speech on the meaning of commitment by the French existentialist and *résistante* Germaine Brée. He added:

> This, I think, hints at the central meaning of the teach-ins; that the Vietnam war has implications for every aspect of life; that it actually means something for the university itself. . . . Vietnam was for some, then, a symbol for the deeper ills of American society.

# Telegraph Avenue, Son of Madison Avenue

Asking why it happened in Berkeley first is like asking why Negroes, and not Americans generally, are involved in securing access for all to the good which America could provide for all her people.

Mario Savio

The events at Berkeley proved exceptionally difficult to interpret with balance and candor.

Report of President Nixon's
Commission on Campus Unrest.

Americans believe the world spins from east to west, that America's destiny is to supersede what they alone still call the "Old World." California is America raised to the $n$th power, the superlatively American part of America. It is only natural that Californians should commonly assume that they stand to the East Coast as America stands to Europe. They take it for granted that the way they live is a preview of the new society that must come to birth.

In general, this Californian assumption can be disputed. But in one particular case there is no arguing with it. Not only did the student revolt of the 1960s begin in California; each successive phase of it began there too. The whole story of the rise and fall of student rebellion in the country as a whole can be traced in miniature in the sequence of events at one campus: Berkeley.

Those fortunate people who live in the Berkeley Hills, on the eastern rim of San Francisco Bay, rarely bother to toss a casual glance at the view. But a visitor feels he is in the gallery, looking down onto a superhuman stage. The great oval of water is crisscrossed with bridges and sprinkled with islands. The smoky outline of Mount Tamalpais and the low silhouette of the peninsula are the backdrop. Center stage, he sees the hills and towers of San Francisco.

Around the beginning of the 1960s, an imaginative visitor looking out from the crest of Grizzly Peak could have peopled that landscape with the symbolic characters of a vast allegorical drama. In it, all the great forces and conflicts of contemporary America would have been represented: Technology and Abundance, Opportunity and Exploitation, Consensus and Alienation, and Ideology incarnate in perhaps its most characteristic institution.

Somewhere in the eucalyptus trees at his feet was the Lawrence Radiation Laboratory of the University of California, where nine synthetic elements and one third of all known atomic particles were discovered between 1945 and 1961. Just over the hill (but hardly out of range for the eye of the imagination) was the laboratory's stepchild at Livermore, where Edward Teller and his colleagues had developed the hydrogen bomb. And beyond that stretched the endless expanse of the Central Valley. If our visitor had the sardonic, caricaturist's turn of mind of a Chaplin or a René Clair, he could hardly have invented a more ironic metaphor for the economics of the liberal society than the agribusiness of the valley. Capitalism and technology, applied to resources on an imperial scale, were producing unprecedented abundance; and yet, two hundred miles and five years away, Cesar Chavez would demonstrate that the social cost was a petty autocracy of the growers.

Straight ahead across the water, the naked eye could see the city in which the contradictions of America were exaggerated with almost operatic bravura. There stood the Bank of America, ultimate confirmation of the most cherished of all American myths: the greatest agglomeration of private capital in the world, heaped together by the son of Italian immigrants, A. P. Giannini. And not half a mile away, in North Beach, you could hear the angriest of the voices that were trying to puncture the myth: the blues, lovingly preserved at the Jazz Workshop; Lenny Bruce at the hungry i across the street (he was to be arrested there for saying "cocksucker" in 1961); and the rambling poets foregathering in Rabelaisian conclave at the City Lights Book Shop.

To the left of a watcher on the Berkeley Hills, Oakland was already beginning to show what the leapfrog race to the suburbs would do to a city abandoned by its middle class. As poor black people silently filled up the devastated streets of West Oakland, Senator William Knowland's Oakland *Tribune*, which had once braced the nation for battle against the distant menace of communism across the water, now rallied conservatives against this new menace on their doorstep.

But the most potent and the most promising of all the symbolic pres-
ences on his imaginary stage, a visitor might well have supposed at the beginning of the 1960s, was the University of California at Berkeley, hum-
ming purposefully around its campanile like the armature of a dynamo
around its spindle. The best sociological thinking endorsed this view.
"The university," Daniel Bell, the sexton of ideology, was to write in his
*Notes on the Post Industrial State*, "becomes the primary institution of
the new society. Perhaps it is not too much to say that if the business firm
was the key institution of the past one hundred years . . . the university
will become the central institution of the next hundred years because of
its role as the new source of innovation and knowledge." San Francisco,
after all, was a city of the first rank only for bankers, poets and connoisseurs of seafood; Berkeley was a world-class university. A survey by the
Chicago *Tribune* in 1957 had placed it third in the United States, after
Harvard and Yale. Others' estimates put it in second place. It was already
pre-eminent in what, in 1960, were regarded as the respective queens of
the physical and social sciences, nuclear physics and sociology. Surely
Berkeley was destined to be the university of the future, the most powerful
and most prestigious among the key institutions of the new society.

Its new president, Clark Kerr, was the paragon of the liberal statesman in the academic world. His own scholarly work had been done in the
field of labor relations; and was not the taming of the unions the key
event in the creation of the liberal consensus? Kerr and his university had
both been among the pioneers of this healing science.

Kerr had indisputable credentials as a liberal in the civil-libertarian
sense. As early as 1952 he had incurred the hostility of conservative Republicans in the state legislature at Sacramento. In 1958, ironically enough
in view of what was to come, he was accused by the Un-American Activities Committee there of being pro-Communist—because of his policy of
allowing free speech on the campus! The employers' organizations were
suspicious of him because of his ties with labor. And right-wing hate
groups were circulating slide shows to the luncheon groups comparing him
to Marx and Lenin. Kerr had run real risks on behalf of free speech.

Kerr was an administrator, a planner, a practical man, with no mean
grasp of the political skills. The conception of the "uses of the university"
that he put forward in his famous Godkin lectures in 1963 was that it
should be the servant of the larger society. That implied that it should be
a provider of trained manpower, of usable research, and of practical expertise for government and for corporate business in the first instance.

If Kerr was the archetypal liberal, Berkeley had good claims to be considered the archetypal liberal institution. Like the institutions of liberalism
in general, it was far more heavily embroiled than its admirers realized in

trying to serve two masters: its own ideals, and the interests of the established powers in society. Thus, for example, it was impeccably democratic in the sense that it stood at the apex of the California system of higher education, genuinely the first attempt in the world to make higher education of the highest possible quality available to every young man and woman in the state. It was less democratic in the sense that the students were treated by a sometimes autocratic and often unimaginative bureaucracy like a work force—while the federal and state governments, the military, large foundations and corporations in a position to pay for research were treated like valued customers. The university was deeply involved in the Cold War: it had built the H-bomb. "The humanities," says a semiofficial history, with unconscious wit, "were represented by such units as the Russian and East European Studies Centers. . . ." The federal government provided 58 per cent of its research budget. In the land-grant tradition, the university thought of itself as the servant of the state government, and properly collaborated with the state government at every level in innumerable projects. Equally traditionally, though less properly, it was obsequiously responsive to the big economic interests in the state, especially the oil, real estate, utility and agribusiness interests, as made known through powerful business representation on the Board of Regents. The agricultural-research departments of the university had consistently toed the line of agribusiness interests: in 1964, when there was serious discussion of banning the importation of bracero labor from Mexico, the university's economists and labor-relations experts rushed out reports to show what a terrible thing this would be for the economy of the state.

James Ridgway, in a bitterly critical book, called the University of California "the largest dummy corporation in the world." The comparison might seem too harsh—until one remembers that Clark Kerr himself had called the university a "knowledge factory" and defined the faculty—the heart of any university—as "a series of . . . *entrepreneurs* held together by a common grievance over parking." That was a joke, of course. But it mockingly echoed Professor Bell's insight. Could it be that the way in which the university was destined to succeed the business firm as the central institution in society was by becoming indistinguishable from it?

Universities were drifting in that direction in the late 1950s and the early 1960s. Some universities, indeed, were setting a deliberate course in that direction under purposeful skippers. It was a course, in any case, that was to be reversed. There was a mutiny below decks.

Berkeley was the logical place for a reaction against the corporate domination, the utilitarian values and the bureaucratic order of the age of the liberal consensus, because Berkeley was the perfect microcosm of liberal America. Along with the glittering façade of earned success, the wealth, the growth, the confident assumption of future pre-eminence, the University of California shared one other characteristic with the society it epitomized. At Berkeley, as in the larger society, the experts all agreed, the inhabitants ought by rights to be contented beyond the common lot of man. And yet at Berkeley, as elsewhere, a disconcertingly large proportion of these fortunate beings perversely refused to feel as contented as the experts said they were.

Just as Berkeley was the archetype of liberal America, so the rebellion in Berkeley, not just in 1964 but throughout the decade, was the prototype of the younger generation's rebellion. Imitation, helped by television, played a part. But, for whatever reason, a sort of natural history of upheaval could have been written. New issues, new tactics, new moods and new fashions repeatedly showed themselves first at Berkeley. They then spread very quickly to the other centers where thousands of young people were clustered in youth ghettoes around the great graduate schools: in New York City, in the Boston area, in Madison and Ann Arbor and so on. Then they spread by stages to every junior college and high school campus in the land. There was no inflexible rule about this process, but it was consistent enough for it to be possible to sketch the whole shape of the youth rebellion in the three acts of the Berkeley tragedy.

The first act is the best-remembered.

In June 1964, the Bay Area sent more people to Mississippi than any other section of the country, more than Cambridge, more even than New York. On September 4, an ad hoc committee began to picket the Oakland *Tribune* for racially discriminatory practices. An executive of the newspaper telephoned the university administration to ask whether it was aware that the picketing had been organized on university property, namely the strip of sidewalk immediately outside the main gate on Bancroft Way, the traditional university "Hyde Park," where political and other organizations solicited money, recruited, and advertised themselves. Ten days later, the university closed the strip, alleging that it was enforcing its "historic policy." On September 17 this ruling was protested by a united front of campus organizations broad enough to include Youth for Goldwater. And on September 21, the first day of classes, the university announced a new "historic policy." Groups could man tables on the holy ground; but there was to be no fund-raising, no recruitment, no advocacy —none of the activity, in short, that would make it worth anyone's while to man them. Within a week this regulation was being openly flouted, and when, on September 30, five students were summoned to the dean's office as a result, a graduate student in philosophy named Mario Savio turned up at the head of five hundred students who protested that since they had all broken the rules, they ought all to be punished. Ignoring this ominous evidence of rumbling solidarity, the administration suspended eight students.

The next day was the Boston Tea Party of the student revolution. Or, rather, it was more like the day when Charles I made the fatal mistake of going down to the House of Commons with a file of soldiers to arrest the Five Members. "The birds have flown," he said, but these birds stayed put. A young man called Jack Weinberg was manning the CORE table. (A graduate student in mathematics, he had temporarily dropped out of school and had been active in several civil rights demonstrations.) The deans told him that if he was a student he was breaking the rules, and if he was not he was trespassing. He said nothing, and the deans called the campus police.

"Will you come peacefully?" he was asked, "or if not we'll take you."

By this time, a crowd had gathered. "Take all of us!" was the answer.

The cop went off to get help, and while he was going Weinberg explained his position. (If only a tape recording had been made of the Boston Tea Party!) He made two highly significant points.

"This is a knowledge factory," he said. "If you read Clark Kerr's book, those are his words. . . . This is mass production; no deviations from the norm are tolerated."

And then, a little later, in answer to a heckler, he said this: "We feel that we, as human beings first and students second, must take our stand on every vital issue of discrimination, of segregation, of poverty, of unemployment."

A moment later, the police came back with a car and started trying to drag Weinberg into it. He went limp. And spontaneously, but also of course because many of them had had nonviolent technique drilled into them in the civil rights movement, the crowd sat down round the car. In seconds it was immobilized, and there it stayed for thirty-two hours, the first rostrum of the student movement.

Speaker after speaker climbed onto the roof of that car that evening to debate what should be done. But one thing that was said from there had a prophetic significance.

Professor Seymour Martin Lipset, head of the Institute of International Studies and expert on student movements around the world, was one of the most respected of social scientists, the most eminent of liberals. Only four years earlier, he had written near the end of his *magnum opus, Political Man,* "The very triumph of the West ends domestic politics for those intellectuals who must have ideologies or utopias to motivate them to political action."

Now here he stood, physically surrounded by intellectuals who seemed unaware that social revolution had in all respects triumphed, in

Mississippi, for example, or in Oakland, and still less agreed that domestic politics were at an end. Prophetically he followed the logic of his own argument and ignored the palpable reality around him in the Berkeley dusk. The students, he told them, were "acting like the Ku Klux Klan." In one respect at least, as those who had been in Mississippi could have told him, he was exaggerating: for he was allowed to climb down unharmed.

The next day, Clark Kerr proclaimed in a speech: "The rules will not be changed in the face of mob action." Almost one thousand police from Oakland, from the county, and from the State Highway Patrol arrived on campus; but after a day of tension a compromise was reached. The next two months were consumed by political wrestling. On one side, at this stage perhaps one tenth of the twenty-five thousand students at Berkeley supported the radical leadership, now organized (or at least labeled) as the Free Speech Movement (FSM). On the other, the campus authorities, the president, and the regents disputed and misunderstood one another about the meaning of the rebellion, the regulations that ought to be enforced, and the disciplinary measures appropriate for enforcing them. Members of the faculty tried, more or less tactfully, to mediate. And the Democratic governor of California, Edmund G. Brown, looked on unhappily at an imbroglio whose mischievous potential for his opponents was all too apparent.

Inevitably, perhaps, given the passion on one side and the misapprehension on the other (one campus official thought he was dealing with "a civil rights panty raid"), it was a messy period. Even so, the tension might have died away had not Kerr, on November 23, threatened Savio and another student leader, both of whom had been promised amnesty, with expulsion. It was this mistake that recruited mass support for the FSM.

On December 2, six thousand turned out in support of a sit-in at Sproul Hall, the administrative center; fifteen hundred actually entered the building, and eight hundred were arrested. The university was brought to a halt. Students went on strike. Classes stopped. And the faculty, shocked by the invasion of its academic groves, rediscovered a sense of common interest with the students and—with a few exceptions, prominent among them the liberal social scientists Lipset, Nathan Glazer, and Lewis Feuer—rallied to their support. On the afternoon of December 8, the faculty voted decisively, 824–115, to concede the Free Speech Movement's essential demands. No restrictions were to be imposed on political activity on the campus beyond those applied in the community at large. That went further than Kerr or the administration had been willing to go, and it ended the first phase of the conflict.

The previous morning, a memorable scene had taken place, an

allegory of what was at stake. Clark Kerr had announced that he would speak in the Greek Theater, donated by those prime beneficiaries of free speech the William Randolph Hearst family, and in that evocative setting among the evergreens on the hill eighteen thousand members of the university community gathered to hear him. His speech was, for some at least, a little overseasoned with the industrial metaphor. "Today," he said, "we decide whether we shall move ahead productively and in peace." Growth, he said, must never stop. Then, the meeting ended, Savio stepped to the rostrum to announce a mass rally to discuss the situation, and to which, he had announced beforehand, he planned to invite Kerr. As he opened his mouth to speak, he was grabbed by two policemen. One of them pinioned his arms. The other yoked him around the throat. Thousands of students started angrily forward. A wave of sympathy ran through the faculty. Kerr was persuaded to let Savio speak, and a riot was avoided.

One minute Clark Kerr, the champion of liberalism, had been talking about "the powers of persuasion against the use of force." The next minute two armed men, his agents, were literally choking his opponent, the symbolic representative of free speech. It would have been hard for a script-writer to have invented a scene that would have more powerfully illustrated the mutual misunderstanding between an institution that thought of itself as the embodiment of liberalism, and a generation whose leaders were beginning to think of that kind of institution, and of that kind of liberalism, as repressive.

On February 3, the lead story in the campus newspaper, the *Daily Cal*, announced that the Free Speech Movement was "for all practical purposes dissolved except for legal and political defenses." And indeed, with the vote of the academic senate on the afternoon of the Greek Theater drama, the demands that had ostensibly brought the Free Speech Movement into existence had essentially been met. But a confused ferment of debate and protest continued on other issues for the next three months. It was as if, in the very weeks when the disillusionment of the civil rights movement was reaching its climax at Selma, and the Johnson administration was taking its fateful decision to escalate the war, a rebellion was already in being and searching for a cause.

On February 15 an editorial reported, "The campus and the entire nation has recently been immersed in conversation about the confusing situation in North and South Vietnam." That was one week after the Flaming Dart reprisal raids, and three days before the President decided, in secret, to order sustained bombing of the North. "Student groups have conducted marches, pickets, rallies and debates on the subject," said the *Daily Cal*, and added with a sniff, "We now have one or more moronic individuals running around campus with spray cans of red paint scrawling

'Get the troops out of Vietnam' and other phrases to this effect." On February 18, more than two weeks before the President announced that the marines were going in, one hundred Berkeley students led by Art Goldberg, one of Savio's chief lieutenants in the Free Speech Movement, marched in protest to the Oakland army terminal. On March 1, eighty members of the Berkeley faculty were among one hundred fifty residents of the Bay Area to sign a full-page ad in the New York *Times* against U.S. involvement in Vietnam. There was another march to Oakland on March 9, and a third, with fifteen arrests, on March 23. That same day, the draft authorities dismissed as "childishness" the action of the son of a Berkeley professor who had torn up his draft card in Sproul Plaza. And the next day, March 24, more than one thousand turned out at a meeting held in support of the Michigan teach-in.

In the meantime, Art Goldberg and others had found a bizarre new issue. The Free Speech Movement had won for Berkeley students the same rights of free speech on campus as the law allowed off it. The Dirty Speech Movement went further. On March 3, a young man from New York, John Thompson, unconnected with the university, stood on the steps of the student Union with a poster on which he had inscribed the word FUCK. The next day, Goldberg and others were arrested for shouting the same verb over a loudspeaker.

For the rest of the spring, the banner with the strange device provided a good deal of innocent amusement. Some ingeniously maintained it was a loyal acronym for "Freedom Under Clark Kerr." Ed Sanders, later song writer and guitarist with The Fugs, the group (mealymouthed only in name) that tried to levitate the Pentagon in 1967, and historian of the Manson family, made his name by starting a literary review with the most evocative of all Anglo-Saxon words in its name. Most students were bored or embarrassed by the issue. But the "FUCK" furore was not without consequences. It destroyed Savio's leadership, handed the tactical initiative back to Kerr, and provided a heaven-sent opportunity for conservatives, notably the archtraditionalist Max Rafferty, state superintendent of education and a regent of the university, to dismiss the Free Speech Movement and everything else that was happening at Berkeley as no more than guttersnipery. The "FUCK" issue was an early warning sign of the inner division inside what people were already beginning to call the Movement: between political dissent and cultural revolution. It was a hairline crack that spring. By the fall, it had become wide enough for all to see when Ken Kesey and his busload of Merry Pranksters did their best to turn the big Vietnam Day rally into psychedelic vaudeville.

In the spring and summer of 1965, that fork in the road was still well ahead. With Jerry Rubin working like an old-style organizer at the Viet-

nam Day Committee, and Marvin Garson researching the business affiliations of the regents while Barbara wrote *MacBird*, "Make Love Not War"
was a slogan that neatly united both wings of the revolution. On May 21,
ten days after Dean Rusk told the Russian ambassador he could ignore domestic opposition, feeling against the war culminated in a rally of fifteen
thousand in Berkeley. The campus was being politicized.

Already what was happening at Berkeley was beginning to spread
to other campuses. There were student demonstrations at Yale, Brooklyn,
Florida State, New Mexico State, Illinois, Michigan, Wake Forest,
Fairleigh Dickinson and the University of Vermont that spring, *none
of them about Vietnam*. The issues mentioned were largely matters of student discipline such as drinking and parietal rules, and student participation in university administration. It seems clear that the upsurge of indignation about the war was superimposed on a climate of frustration and
discontent, and here, too, Berkeley showed the way.

The first phase of the Berkeley experience, then, from the fall of 1964
to the summer of 1965, lights up in sharp focus several points that were
true of the origins of the student rebellion generally.

1. The Free Speech Movement was the bridge between the civil
rights movement and the antiwar movement. In the specific case of Berkeley, the issue behind the original picketing was specifically racial. In a
broader sense, the mood, tactics, and personnel of the FSM came out of
the civil rights movement.

As it happened, the Johnson administration decided to escalate the
war, after the Pleiku incident at the beginning of February 1965, precisely
when the Berkeley students had learned the techniques and acquired the
habit of rebellion. The Bastille of "free speech" had fallen before them.
They made an army in being for the antiwar movement. There would in
any case have been protest against the escalation of the war, as the swift
spread of the teach-in technique from Michigan showed. Inevitably, too,
many of those who threw themselves into it would have been the same
people who had joined the civil rights movement. As we have seen, the
civil rights movement and the radical antiwar groups had been interconnected for a generation and more. What the particular course of events
at Berkeley did was to stamp on the antiwar movement, for better and
for worse, a sort of anti-ideology of radicalism that challenged the liberal
ideology not simply on the issue of the war's ethical justification but at
every point.

2. The Berkeley episode of 1964–65 played a crucial part in the
radicalization of students generally. It did this partly by the force of example and the glamour of success. But a more specific dialectic was also at
work. In the South, a handful of middle-class white students had seen the

liberal orthodoxy contradicted. They learned that Mississippi was not so completely the exception in American life as they had been taught. "At first," Tom Hayden said later, "you thought, well, the southern system is some kind of historical vestige. . . . Instead, we found out that the structure of power was very tied into the structure of power in the whole U.S. You'd find that Harvard was investing in Mississippi Power and Light, which was a company that economically dominated Mississippi. You'd find that the southern wing of the Democratic Party held all the seniority positions in Congress."

But there were, after all, no more than a thousand who went South in 1964. The struggle in Berkeley contributed to the radicalization of millions because it suggested that perhaps the proposition must be inverted. No doubt the comparison was overdrawn, self-indulgent, even a little paranoid. But when they saw—and thanks to TV, they did *see*—cops in riot gear looking remarkably similar to the cops of Mississippi dragging student sit-ins out of Sproul Hall, it suddenly became possible for students on every campus in America to ask themselves whether there wasn't a little bit of Mississippi in all America.

They began to compare their own situation with that of the poor blacks in Mississippi. More, they began to liken whatever authority there was over their own lives—and there was perhaps less than over any comparable group of young people in the history of the world—with the repressive forces that maintained white supremacy in the Deep South. The more sensitive they were, the more they had agonized over their own privilege and compared their situation with that of the sit-ins they had watched being manhandled on TV.

The Mississippi metaphor, therefore, had appeal in the autumn of 1964. The fact that white people were noticeably less welcome in the black movement by 1965 did not lessen that appeal. If you could no longer go to work for black people without being made to feel uncomfortable, at least now if you were a student you could sit in, and march, and even get arrested on your own behalf, while fighting the same enemy. But what decisively confirmed the force of the metaphor was the escalation of the war. The government of the United States not only underpinned the discipline of the campus. In a harsher and more literal way, it threatened young men in the shape of the draft. As the war dragged on and the draft calls increased and the stories of what was really happening in the rice paddies and villages of South Vietnam trickled back, the image of the United States and especially the image of the President of the United States as a Mississippi sheriff, unctuous and sadistic, meting out death and terror in the name of law and order, gained a hideous plausibility.

In Barbara Garson's play the stage directions specify: "The 1st WITCH is dressed as a student demonstrator, beatnik stereotype. The 2nd WITCH is a Negro with the impeccable grooming and attire of a *Muhammad Speaks* salesman. The 3rd WITCH is an old leftist, wearing a worker's cap and overalls."

|  |  |
|---|---|
|  | They dance around the caldron, and chant: |
| 1st Witch: | Stench of Strong and tongue of Kerr, |
|  | Picket, sit-in, strike, and stir, |
|  | Regents raging, Reagan hot, |
|  | All boil up our protest pot. |
| All: | Bubble and bubble, toil and trouble, |
|  | Burn baby burn and caldron bubble. |
| 2nd Witch: | . . . |
|  | Club and gas and whip and gun, |
|  | Niggers strung up just for fun. |
|  | Black men beat and burnt and shot, |
|  | Bake within our melting pot. |
|  | . . . |
| 3rd Witch: | Taylor's tongue and Goldberg's slime, |
|  | McNamara's bloody crime, |
|  | Sizzling skin of napalmed child, |
|  | Roasted eyeballs, sweet and mild, |
|  | Now we add a fiery chunk |
|  | From a burning Buddhist monk, |
|  | Flaming field and blazing hut, |
|  | Infant fingers cooked and cut, |
|  | Young man's heart and old man's gut, |
|  | Groin and gall and gore of gook, |
|  | In our caldron churn and cook. |

Berkeley, said *MacBird*, equals Mississippi equals Vietnam. That double equation was the shibboleth of the schism that split America after 1965. If you assented to it, you were on one side; if it stuck in your throat, then you were on the other.

3. Something else is clear, however, from the sequence of events at Berkeley. The students' discontent was not wholly a response to national or international events. Nor was it wholly caused by conditions on the campus. They brought their discontent with them from their prosperous suburban high schools.

The civil rights movement supplied leaders, techniques, a new mood. But the FSM would hardly have aroused students as it did unless it had spoken to feelings shared by far more than the small proportion who had been actively involved in civil rights. As for Vietnam and the draft, the

FSM was over before the antiwar movement got going. And on other campuses, too, disturbances over local issues preceded demonstrations against the war.

The early student leaders talked both about the civil rights movement and about conditions on the campus. Clark Kerr, understandably, argued to me that conditions on the campus actually had little to do with what happened in the 1960s. I suggested that students did feel that universities were too big, too remote. He conceded that there was dissatisfaction with teachers. Then he made a telling point. "But bigness?" he asked. "Then, why do the students always want to go to the big campuses? Do they really dislike bigness? It's the little campuses that die.

"There are two polar theories about what went wrong," he went on. "One is that the campuses went wrong. Nixon and Reagan believe that, and to some extent the people of California believe that. Or, two, the whole of American society went wrong. I think 85 per cent of the students felt that. It wasn't a revolt against the campus; it was a revolt on campus against things that were happening in American society—including the war."

Vietnam, said James Gilbert, the Wisconsin graduate student I quoted earlier on the teach-in, was for some "a symbol of the deeper ills of American society." John Searle, now a professor of philosophy at Berkeley, was involved in student protest at the very beginning, in the HUAC demonstration of 1960. He was a sympathetic counselor to the Free Speech Movement. Later he observed the confrontation from the other side, as a member of the university administration. "What happened in the FSM," Searle has written, "was a kind of shock of recognition as people became aware that they no longer believed in the official beliefs they had thought they believed in; and most surprisingly they found that thousands of others shared their new beliefs. People suddenly discovered that they no longer had to go on repeating the same old social lie; they found a new social lie."

A revolt against the things that were happening in American society, a new awareness of the deeper ills of American society, the discovery that people no longer believed in the old beliefs—these are three different ways of saying that the age of consensus was coming to an end.

The second phase of the Berkeley story began in the autumn of 1966, just two years after the first. Superficially, 1966 looked like a replay of 1964, but the conflict moved through its stages faster and to a grimmer rhythm. The mood was angrier, the parties more irreconcilable. It was as if both sides knew their lines now and moved according to a scenario toward confrontation. The university was becoming polarized, and in this, too, it was a prototype for society as a whole.

Again it began with a recruiting table, set up this time in the student Union by the U. S. Navy. From one point of view, nothing could have been more normal: from another, nothing could have been more provocative. From the teach-in of May 1965 through the massive Vietnam Day demonstrations of October 1965 and into the campaign to send Robert Scheer to Congress on a peace ticket, which had failed only by a surprisingly small margin earlier that same month, the Berkeley community had been caught up in a crescendo of moral fervor and political activity against the war. And so, two days later, the radicals took up the challenge. A girl, put up to it by the SDS, asked for permission to set up a table to advertise "Alternatives to Military Service." The request was refused, but she went ahead just the same, SDS pickets arrived, and so, a few minutes later, did the police. The inevitable scuffle led to another marathon confrontation. Six people were arrested; they included Mario Savio and Jerry Rubin. None of them were students. At one o'clock in the morning, the great majority of the many hundreds of students present voted for a strike, and on December 2 the decision was ratified by a meeting of some eight thousand students. On December 5, the Academic Senate met. It was far less sympathetic to the students than it had been in 1964 but still criticized the university administration by condemning the use of police on campus and calling for amnesty. The administration was under pressure from the regents. The regents, in turn, were under pressure from the new governor-elect, Ronald Reagan, who had made the turmoil and radicalism at Berkeley one of the main issues, and perhaps the decisive issue, in his victorious campaign. The regents voted to support "all necessary action to preserve order on all campuses of the university." Reagan was blunter. The students, he said, ought to "obey the prescribed rules or get out." The strike ended that same night with the teaching assistants singing "Solidarity Forever" and an impromptu coalition of radicals and hippies singing "We All Live in a Yellow Submarine." Cultural impasse had been reached.

Two members of the political science department, Sheldon Wolin and John Schaar, pointed out the contrasts between 1964 and 1966 in an article in *The New York Review of Books,* for the eyes of the country were on Berkeley by now. In 1964, they wrote, the politics of the Free Speech Movement had a kind of "radical purity," an idealism like that of the civil rights movement in its "heroic phase." By 1966, student attitudes had been hardened by the war and the spread of New Left doctrine. Where in 1964 they had claimed constitutional rights, in 1966 they demanded "student power." "Another and more exotic element entered

the movement," said Wolin and "the cool and hippie culture of Telegraph Avenue" (the main drag running south from the gates of the campus). By 1966 in Berkeley "a new culture had come into being." Most
striking of all to every observer was the change in mood. Idealism, hope,
good nature and good humor had been replaced by exhaustion, bad
temper, disillusionment, and fear.

In the third week in April 1969, the following announcement appeared in a small box in the Berkeley *Barb*:

### HEAR YE, HEAR YE

A park will be built this Sunday between Dwight and Haste. The
land is owned by the University which tore down a lot of beautiful houses
in order to build a swamp.

The land is now used as free parking space. In a year the University
will build a cement type expensive parking lot which will fiercely compete
with other lots for the allegiance of Berkeley's Buicks.

On Sunday we will stop this shit. Bring shovels, chains, grass, paints,
flowers, trees, bull dozer, soil, colorful smiles, laughter and lots of sweat.
. . . This summer we will not be fucked over by the pigs' move-on fascism,
we will police our own park and not allow its occupation by the imperial
power.

"We began building a park last Sunday," next week's *Barb* reported:

"Several hundred Berkeley Freemen showed up for work. . . .

First the land was bulldozed and then we shoveled the rocks and
assorted shit into barrels. . . . A truck arrived with grass—that is, sod. . . .

Flower and vegetable gardens were planted around the trees and it
was like a small universe of beauty being created at the roots of a giant
one. . . .

At some point in the afternoon a pig appeared and wasn't sure if our
park was disturbing the peace. It looked like those guys liked what was
going on but a lifetime of conditioning made it impossible for them to act
it out. . . .

The Black Panthers showed up and loved it. Bobby Seale kept laugh-
ing in total and happy amazement. "Are you going to call it People's
Park? Listen, we got to have some Panthers down here working, this is really socialistic."

As the afternoon turned late, the chill returned but with it rock
music and a warming fire, people danced and celebrated, the weed was
passed and an appropriate height of achievement was part of what we vi-
brated to. . . .

For the first time in my life I enjoyed working.

In such a mood of euphoria began what was perhaps, of all the symbolic confrontations between rebellion and authority, between the old values and the new, the strangest and the most pathetic.

The first response of the university authorities was to announce that People's Park would be dismantled on July 1. Then, in a series of chaotic meetings with the self-appointed representatives of "the people," it appeared to waver. A series of compromises were entertained: the land might be left in part under the "creative control" of the park people, it must be used for softball or soccer, it could be used as an environmental "field experiment station," so long as the university's title was respected. On May 13 the vice-chancellor responsible pledged that "the university will not move in the middle of the night." In the middle of the next night, the university moved.

Shortly after three in the morning, two hundred campus and city police moved in, arresting three street people they found in the park. Construction crews began to put up a fence. At noon, a women's rally turned into a mass meeting, which turned into a march down Telegraph Avenue toward the park. "We must show Heyns and the other bums who run this campus that the park belongs to the people," shouted the president-elect of the student government, "and I say, 'Take the park!'"

Rocks and bottles were thrown at the police. They replied first with tear gas, then with revolvers and shotguns. More than thirty demonstrators were wounded: one young man, not a student, died later in hospital. Six policemen were injured, one of them stabbed.

For the next week, police and the National Guard, called out by the governor, occupied the campus. They were taunted and occasionally stoned by students and street people. Helicopters flew low over the campus, on occasion emitting CS gas, the extratoxic substance used in Vietnam to flush out guerrillas from their bunkers. First and last, almost eight hundred students, street people and bystanders were arrested. Many of them, especially those wearing what police chose to identify as "hippie" clothes, were savagely beaten in Santa Rita prison.

The situation became almost totally polarized. On the one hand, the governor and the police authorities at various echelons treated the students and the street people, without differentiation, as if they were armed revolutionaries. The commanding general of the National Guard defended his actions, including the indiscriminate laying down of CS gas, as "an inescapable by-product of combating terrorists, anarchists and hard-core militants." The governor maintained that People's Park had been built expressly as "an excuse for a riot," at the initiative of what he termed "a professional revolutionary group."

Impotent to match the state's capacity for physical violence, the radicals vented their feelings in recklessly extravagant rhetoric. In an equally undifferentiated way, they lumped the university, the police and the state of California together as so many bloody oppressors. "You've pushed us to the end of your civilization, here against the sea in Berkeley," wrote one Ishmael, who had presumably gotten to Telegraph Avenue of his own free will, either by hitchhiking or with the help of his father's credit card. "Then you pushed us into a square-block area called People's Park. It was the last thing we had to defend, this square block of sanity amid all your madness. . . . We are now homeless in your civilized world. We have become the great American gypsies, with only our mythology for a culture."

One result of the heavy-handed police action was to make this mythology acceptable to people who would never have swallowed it before. The original diggers of the park had numbered a couple of hundred, few of them currently registered as students at Berkeley. After a week of watching the National Guard standing around the campus with fixed bayonets, 85 per cent of some fifteen thousand students voting in a referendum said they wanted the park left alone.

Between these two opposed poles, the self-righteous imposition of law and order, and the ranting rhetoric of liberation, there wavered and quavered the authorities and the faculty of the once proud and confident University of California. The president of the university, Charles Hitch, himself a former high official at the Pentagon, criticized the police and sought to dissociate the university from their actions, though the university had called them in. The Berkeley chancellor, while shocked at the excesses of the police and the Guard, blamed these on the "unjustified aggression" of those who had laid sod and planted flowers in a car park not their own. The faculty voted to condemn the police and military as "irresponsible,"—and in the same breath voted to uphold the chancellor who had called them in.

Both administrators and faculty were, on the whole, moderate and rational men. They needed each other, though there was a nuance of difference between them. The administrators did not dare to flout the governor, the regents and the legislature. The faculty was reluctant to offend the students. (Some of the best-known members were an exception, devoting much ingenuity to drawing elaborate parallels between their students and the Nazis. But these were men whose true constituency was in the New York foundations, not in the Berkeley classrooms.) Both administrators and faculty were appalled by the behavior of the students, and terrified of what the governor might do. Their instinct, therefore, was to search for compromise, to rely on logical analysis, to stand on legal justification. These tendencies, however admirable, weakened their position still further. They confirmed the radicals' suspicion that the university was run by hypocritical agents of bourgeois oppression, without allaying the stereotype in Sacramento that it was run by a bunch of weaseling pinkos. Archetype of liberalism, the university was caught in the classic predicament of the moderate once a situation has been polarized between two extremes.

No dialogue was now possible except that of the jabbed club and the thrown stone. Each side now openly questioned the other's sanity. And each side had an unfortunate knack of acting in such a way as to bear out the other's most paranoid suspicions.

The governor and the police had acted, step by step, as if they were following the script of some crude radical satire on the "pig nation." First the cops with their shiny plastic helmets and their shotguns; then the helicopters and the CS gas: the whole scene might have been staged on purpose to verify the radicals' contention that Berkeley equals Mississippi equals Vietnam.

And perhaps it was. For if there was paranoia and overkill in the university's and especially in the state government's reaction to People's Park, those same characteristics were conspicuous in the propaganda for it. ("You pushed us into a square block . . . your land title is covered with blood.") Behind the innocent love of nature and humanity there was aggression, and even class arrogance. ("A pig appeared . . . a lifetime of conditioning"; poor pig, no Berkeley education for him.) And perhaps there was just a trace of blood on the squatters' title, too. For while in all innocence people turned up to build the park, somebody thought of turning that lot into People's Park. And whoever thought of it knew very well that the university could not give up its title. And when they marched to "take the park," after nearly five years of Berkeley rituals, they knew how the police would respond. If the system was as repressive, as bloody, as the radicals insisted, then it was all the more certain that people would be hurt.

And so there was, somewhere behind the Whitmanesque vision of a People's Park, a manipulative disingenuousness worthy of the slickest corporation lawyer: Telegraph Avenue, son of Madison Avenue.

In 1964 the liberal orthodoxy had been challenged at one of its strongest and most sensitive spots by the Free Speech Movement. By 1966 the process of polarization had begun in Berkeley, where the future, like spring, arrives earlier than elsewhere. By 1969 the schism was complete in that microcosm. Two societies, two cultures, two myths glared at each other in total hostility, utter incomprehension. And yet they were as alike as father and son. It is time to examine the origins of the Great American Cultural Revolution.

# An Invasion of Centaurs

> An image comes at once to mind: the invasion of centaurs that is recorded on the pediment of the Temple of Zeus at Olympia. Drunken and incensed, the centaurs burst in upon the civilized festivities that are in progress. . . . The image is a potent one, for it recalls what must always be a fearful experience in the life of any civilization: the experience of radical critical disjuncture, the clash of irreconcilable conceptions of life.
>
> Theodore Roszak, *The Making of a Counter-Culture.*

One of the strange side effects of the black rebellion on American minds was a persistent tendency to draw analogies between the black minority and other groups, such as women, and the young. The young are not an ethnic minority, though it was fashionable for a while to write about them as if they were. Nor are they a social or economic class. They come from all backgrounds, all regions, all traditions. In the end, of course, the young inherit the earth. But by then they will no longer be young.

Not all of the young are students, not even in America. Rapidly though higher education expanded, still, even by the end of the sixties, fewer than half of any age group started college at all. The student rebellion started at Berkeley among the most privileged of the privileged, in a minority within a minority. Yet the student rebellion was not an isolated phenomenon. It was a concentrated form of a wider revolt against all the assumptions and orthodoxies of American life.

Throughout the sixties and beyond, there has been a constant tendency for the ideas and fashions that started in the great elite graduate schools of the East and West coasts gradually to spread both geographically and also down the scale of age, class and educational advantage. There was an epidemiology of dissent. Berkeley or Harvard or Columbia would toss the stone into the pond. The ripples would spread, first to other universities and colleges, then to junior colleges, small denominational colleges, community colleges, and finally to high schools, growing feebler as they spread.

Eventually the cultural revolution that began among a tiny minority at a few great graduate schools in the middle sixties will have affected an entire generation of Americans. Most will have been affected only distantly and slightly. Only a handful of lives were drastically changed. Only a tiny minority ever joined communes or experimented with psychedelic drugs. But few lives were wholly unaffected by the ideas that motivated those who did make those experiments.

By the end of the sixties two mountainous literatures on the rebellion of the young had accumulated. On the one hand there was the rebellion's own literature: tracts, pamphlets, guides, exposés, prophecies, and even cookbooks. The literature was fantastically varied, but it was also notably "unitarian": All change, it generally assumed, would be part of the One Big Change. An attack on any outwork of the system, the rhetoric implied, was a blow to the system as a whole. The dream was that the converging rebellions of students, pacifists, draft resisters, black militants, Mexican farm workers, welfare mothers, frustrated suburban housewives, reservation Indians, penitentiary inmates, hippies from the California beaches and the western wilderness, and bored workers on the General Motors assembly lines would all roll together into one millenarian Mississippi of revolution.

The literature *about* the rebellion of the young was hardly less voluminous. By 1970 the bibliography of the Scranton Commission, which made no claim to be exhaustive, listed 176 works relevant to campus unrest and then appended a bibliography of bibliographies that ran to another six pages. Some of these academic studies were naïvely sympathetic to student protest. Others were shrilly hostile. One generalization can be made about them, however. The great majority followed the instinct of social science; to chop the subject up into small pieces before putting it under the microscope. And something else: so far from drawing parallels with other movements in American life, the tendency was to subdivide, to draw distinctions, to insist that each kind of student rebellion must be separately studied.

A good example of this is the work of Kenneth Keniston, perhaps the most perceptive of all these academic writers about the rebellion of the young and certainly one of the more sympathetic. First, in 1965, he pub-

lished a study of disturbed students at Yale, whom he diagnosed as
"alienated," and called it *The Uncommitted*. Then, two years later, he
turned his attention to a group of students active in the Vietnam Summer
campaign of 1967 and published a book about them, *Radical Youth*,
which he subtitled *Notes on the Committed*.

Now, it is certainly true that in the late 1960s there was a conflict between cultural and political rebellion. Moreover, in the early 1970s this
conflict was one of the reasons for the failure of political protest. The fact
that the McGovern candidature was so intimately associated with the
movements for abortion-law reform and for guaranteed representation for
women, young voters and blacks, fatally weakened the movement for more
radical change in the strictly political arena.

But this very example reminds us that the cultural rebels and the political radicals were to a very large extent the same people. And there was a
good reason for this. At the heart of the political rebellion there was a
deep feeling that something was wrong not just with political leaders or
with their policies but with American society itself.

To emphasize, as Keniston has done, "the distinction between activist
and alienated students as psychological types" ignores the strong conviction of both groups that they were fighting the same battle. Underground
newspapers gave sympathetic treatment both to political radicalism and to
drugs, rock music and mysticism. It also fails to explain why, while only a
tiny proportion of students could be described as either political or cultural radicals, nevertheless whenever the moderate majority felt that it was
being forced to choose between either group and authority, the majority
invariably sided with the radicals. That's what happened at Berkeley over
People's Park, at Columbia in 1968 and at Harvard in 1969. This tendency
earned the radicals an undeserved reputation for diabolical manipulative
skill. It more truly represented latent sympathy with the radical position
among the lukewarm majority.

In practice, the same people passed from cultural rebellion to political
activism and back again. Jerry Rubin, for example, the clowning leader of
the Yippies in 1968, started out as the earnest tactician of the Vietnam
Day Committee in Berkeley in 1965. Tom Hayden was a cultural rebel,
influenced by Jack Kerouac, before ever he came under the influence of
political radicalism.

"When I appear in the Chicago courtroom," Abbie Hoffman wrote
of his impending trial for conspiracy in the summer of 1969, "I want to be
tried not because I support the National Liberation Front—which I do—
but because I have long hair. Nor because I support the Black Liberation
Movement, but because I smoke dope." He was not saying that long hair

and marijuana were more important than radical politics. He was saying that they were, to him, inseparable.

One of the frankest descriptions of the interaction between cultural rebellion and political commitment came from David Harris, who married Joan Baez and was one of the leaders of the draft-resistance movement. He was talking about his life as a Stanford undergraduate in 1966:

> There began to develop a synthesis of the style developed [i.e. in the civil rights movement] in the South and . . . a vision of self. . . . I went through a big Nietzsche thing: Nietzsche's talk about the *Uber-mensch*, the idea that a man could build himself into anything he could see, talking about the base of power being the self, consciousness. I re-member going through a very heavy existential thing, reading lots of Kierkegaard, lots of Sartre. . . . We were all into a motorcycle thing. It's the most existential position possible. . . . We were riding life like a mo-torcycle, on top of it, opening it up as far as it would go. . . . The curi-ous thing about my attachment to nonviolence is that it came in the same period when I was reading Nietzsche, riding motorcycles, and visiting women late at night by the back door.

Commitment to the civil rights movement or to draft resistance, Harris was saying—whether he fully realized what he was saying or not—was among other things a way of competing, a way of showing off, a way of being in the fashion and of setting it; it was the rebellion of the ag-gressive young male animal against the old leaders of the herd. "Nonvio-lence," Harris actually went on to say, "came as a function of a vision of adventurous, hell-bent, wild-west manhood."

Young men like David Harris were overtly rebelling against the fact that American society was too dangerous—for the Vietnamese and for inner-city blacks. They were also subconsciously rebelling against the fact that it had become too safe for them. Not that the commitment was not genuinely risky: Harris himself served a long jail term for his draft resist-ance. It was just that political commitment, for him and for very many others of his generation, sprang from the same sources as the urge to let a big motorbike rip without a crash helmet.

What gave unity to all these different forms of rebellion, joining rebels and radicals in a common cause, was their shared conviction, vague but unshakable, of the unity of what they were rebelling against. Behind each specific movement of the sixties there was one underlying Movement, because behind each specific injustice there was perceived, shadowy but all-powerful, one System. All voices that shattered the decorum of con-sensus were welcome, because the ultimate enemy was consensus itself. There was, no doubt, a paranoid flavor to this view of society. But, then, the rebellious young were scarcely the only group in America to be afflicted with a touch of paranoia in the late 1960s. And it was this sense of being locked in battle with a single giant enemy—*Amerika,* the radicals called it—which gave the rebellion not only its unity, but its special quality of rage.

When the political hopes of the radicals had petered away, in any case, there often remained an apolitical alienation even in those who had once seemed most committed to the political millennium. Of all the radicals of the sixties, for example, it would have been hard to find one who seemed more completely the dedicated political organizer than Rennie Davis. Yet, in January 1973, Davis traveled to India and there became a disciple of the Guru Maharaj Ji, the sleek adolescent whose puppet-masters call him the Perfect Master of Divine Light.

One of the most thoughtful of Davis' former colleagues in SDS, Carl Oglesby, was appalled by the news. Many would feel that the wretched of the earth had been betrayed once more by spoiled middle-class radicals. Yet Oglesby couldn't bring himself to condemn Davis. "What was the struggle of the past decade," he asked, "if not the struggle of the values of the spirit against the values of Leviathan?" Perhaps the new spiritualism would

> continue the march that the new politics took up in the '60s, when politics itself (so I would argue) . . . continued the march formerly begun in art, in the consciousness which the black and white jazz and the white and black poetry of the '50s began to instill and focus.

Transcendental meditation and oriental religion are never likely to be more than minority fads. But about the past, Oglesby was surely right. The great political rebellion of the sixties was rooted in cultural alienation. And its specific character can be traced back to the ideas of a tiny *avant-garde.*

It was not until near the end of the decade that the historian Theodore Roszak suggested the most satisfactory name for the whole complex of new patterns of behavior and belief. "It would hardly seem an exaggeration," Roszak wrote, "to call what we see arising among the young a 'counter culture': meaning, a culture so radically disaffiliated from the mainstream assumptions of our society that it scarcely looks to many as a culture at all, but takes on the alarming appearance of a barbarian intrusion."

As early as the spring of 1965, in a talk on the campus at Rutgers in New Jersey, the critic Leslie Fiedler sought to explain the race of barbarians who "sit before us in class, or across from us at the dinner table, or who stare at us with hostility from street corners." Some called this new race of young people beatniks, Fiedler said. Some called them hipsters, or layabouts, or dropouts. (The word "hippie" was to be minted by a reporter for the San Francisco *Chronicle* some two months later.) Fiedler called them the "new mutants." And he argued that they were dropouts not simply from college but from the whole Western intellectual tradition. In rebelling against the university, he said, they were also rebelling against "the whole notion of man which universities sought to impose: that bourgeois-Protestant version of humanism, with its view of man as justified by rationality, work, duty, vocation, maturity and success." In so doing they were attempting to disavow "the very idea of the past."

Nor were they interested in the future. They lived for the moment. They were prepared "to prolong adolescence to the grave," and like the mystics, they thought the enlightenment of the moment more precious than the slow accumulation of wisdom or virtue for the future.

But these were non-Christian mystics. Christianity was rejected, because it was seen as the tribal religion of the white Western bourgeoisie and as the ideological justification for capitalism, for imperialism, even for racism. The mutant young therefore sought expression for their religious yearnings among the symbols and mysteries of the non-white world: in Japanese Zen Buddhism, in the legends of the Plains Indians, and in the lamaseries of Tibet.

To this list Fiedler might have added the Tantric tradition of Bengal, with its sacramental view of sexual experience, and the picturesque superstitions of the *I Ching*. Even the religious traditions of the European past were to become acceptable to the counter culture, so long as they were sufficiently cleansed by antiquity and irrationality from any taint of association with Christianity or scientific rationalism. Young Americans who could not conceivably be persuaded to read Milton or Pascal pored with scholarly patience over theses on the Druidic cults at Stonehenge. Their eyes watered with excitement over wild hypotheses about the legend of Atlantis. (If these are barbarians, they are barbarians with access to excellent libraries!) The successive fads for a whole mishmash of superstition and occultism, from the oriental allegories of Hermann Hesse to the pathetic Victorian satanism of Aleister Crowley—all fit Fiedler's tests. No beliefs were too outlandish for the mutant culture, so long as they were neither rational, nor irrational in any tradition too closely connected with the mainstream of Western culture.

Of all non-white people, of course, the most accessible were American blacks, and Fiedler observed "an attempt to become Negro" as one of the marks of the new culture. Here he was picking up an idea suggested several years earlier by Norman Mailer in an essay called *The White Negro*. The hipster, Mailer said, was the American existentialist. He—for the hipster, in Mailer's usage, was a suspiciously masculine concept—reacted to the new dangers facing man in bourgeois society, to "the pyschic havoc of the concentration camps and the atom bomb," and to the alternative of "a slow death by conformity," by deciding to live dangerously. But this, said Mailer, was what black men in America had always learned to do. "Any Negro who wishes to live must live with danger from his first day. . . ." And so,

> In such places as Greenwich village, a *ménage à trois* was completed —the bohemian and the juvenile delinquent came face to face with the Negro, and the hipster was a fact of American life. If marijuana was the wedding ring, the child was the language of hip. . . . And in this wedding of the white and the black it was the Negro who brought the cultural dowry.

Back to Professor Fiedler, on the Rutgers campus in the spring of the teach-ins, trying to psychoanalyze the centaur in the classroom. The mutation went beyond race to sex, he maintained, "to become new men, these children of the future seem to feel, they must become not only more black than white, but more female than male." In a sense, he blamed abundance: in a postindustrial society the obsolescence of the distinctively male functions—making things, making money, making war—had induced "a radical metamorphosis of the Western male." Freed from the need to be Puritans, "all around us, young males are beginning to retrieve for themselves the cavalier role once . . . surrendered to women: that of being beautiful and being loved."

Fiedler linked this "revolt against masculinity" with the cult of drugs. "What could be more womanly . . . than permitting the penetration of the body by a foreign object which not only stirs delight but even (possibly) creates new life?" It is amusing, in view of the fact that Fiedler himself was later to be the hero of a famous marijuana bust, that in 1965 he could write of drugs: "Here is where the young lose us . . . what we really cannot abide, hard as we try." With drugs, in any case, he wrote then, "we come to the crux of the futurist revolt, the hinge of everything else:"

> The widespread use of such hallucinogens as peyote, marijuana, the "Mexican mushroom," LSD, etc. . . . is not merely a matter of a changing taste in stimulants but of the programmatic espousal of an antipuritanical mode of existence—hedonistic and detached—one more strategy in the war on time and work.

If that were true, then the barbarians really were at the gates of American civilization.

American Protestants, Catholics, Jews and agnostics have all been Puritans. Work, progress, economic growth, saving, investment, self-denial, self-improvement, sodbusting, the designing of better mousetraps and even rationality itself were all held to be good because they would all help to build a more abundant world in the future. On that fundamental preference for present sacrifice in the hope of future reward was founded the whole structure of American belief. The respect for law, the instinct for order, the sanctity of the family, even the self-regard of the white race, were all related to this religion of accomplishment. The Puritan looked for a city. And as his faith in the hereafter weakened, he came to look for an earthly city of future abundance, as George F. Babbit dreamed of the day when Zenith would have a million inhabitants.

The counter culture denied the values of Americanism at this fundamental point. Instead of the striving, planning, saving, "uptight" man, it preferred the "cool," passive, self-indulgent personality. In practice, as David Harris with his throttle out reminded us, there was often a good dose of the old competitive Adam in the messiahs of the new gospel. But that only goes to reinforce the point that the counter culture was not confined to any particular type. Its fundamental tenet was the rejection of the Puritan emphasis on the future. On that, the passive and the aggressive, the hip Hindu and the Hell's Angel, could all find common ground. The meaning of life is here and now, in *this* experience, in *my* head *now*.

That is why drugs were so central to the counter culture. It was not irrelevant that they were illegal and therefore dangerous. "Half the fun of grass and acid," one user told the author of a Harvard thesis on drug use, "is that they're illegal. If they suddenly became legal, the bottom would drop right out of the whole scene." It was important, too, that they were—more or less accurately—associated with those who lived outside the code of respectability: with blacks, Mexicans, American Indians, with prostitutes, pimps, jazz musicians. And it was attractive that they were so shocking to middle-class morality, to mothers and teachers and policemen. But the crucial thing about drugs was that they were culturally associated with, and to some extent actually did induce, a state of mind in which the present was everything. Nothing could have more radically rejected the whole future-oriented system of Puritan values.

The counter culture, of course, also reacted against the sexual code of Puritanism. It tolerated homosexuality, most unmentionable of abominations in traditional, middle-class society, and homosexuals and bisexuals were disproportionately represented among its heroes and spokesmen. This reinforces the theory of some psychiatrists, such as Keniston, who have suggested that one of the sources of alienation, and therefore of the counter culture, was the combination of emotional, dominating mothers with fathers who were seen as weak and uninterested. The counter culture, if this theory has any validity, may have drawn many of its recruits from the same psychological backgrounds that have classically produced homosexuals. And this combination, the close mother and the distant father, may well have been commoner in the middle-class suburbs of the fifties and early sixties than in earlier times and places. Still, homosexuals made up only a small fraction of those who were attracted to the counter culture. The change was not in general in the direction of homosexuality so much as it was away from the classic masculinity of the paterfamilias, aggressive in search of a mate and authoritarian and competitive in enforcing her monogamy. The search was, rather, for a sexuality of companionship and sensation, divorced from family structure and responsibility—sex now, in short, with no future.

At the same time, there was a revolt against femininity. Just as men, under the influence of the counter culture, became less different from women, physically and symbolically, with their long hair and brightly colored clothes, and later with bags, high heels and even cosmetics, so women became more "male." Their clothes became less distinctive. Elaborate coiffure and, for a time, makeup went out of fashion. First pants came in, then denims, then boots, and heavy leather belts. By the early seventies, the fitted coats, ladylike silks and bouffant hair styles of the ladies of Camelot had been replaced by something more akin to combat gear. One should beware of extrapolating sociological trends from fashion. Such is the commercial cunning of the rag trade that what looks like a spontaneous migration to the butch style may all have started inside one male-chauvinist head. With a big enough advertising budget, one sometimes suspects, half the women in the country could be put back into crinolines in six months. But if unisex fashion was not part of the counter culture, it was certainly an imitation of it. No other influence on fashion was so powerful. In the later sixties, both the masculine woman and the feminine male were gaining prestige.

The Great American Cultural Revolution was born, like the rest of us, of the coming together of a seed and an egg.

The passive, receptive element was the subjective dissatisfaction the new generation felt when they looked at the world they had inherited. The seed was the particular bundle of ideas they took over from the handful of rebellious spirits in their parents' generation who gave them a pattern for dissent.

The causes of the new generation's dissatisfaction lay back in the 1940s. We have named some of them: the fear of the Bomb, the flight to the suburbs, the migration into the ghettoes, the rise in the birth rate.

This was, for one thing, a much bigger generation. Betty Friedan's upper-middle-class housewives, taking advantage of their new economic security, obeyed the feminine mystique by having big families. Those who were more modestly off still had on the average more children than people felt it was safe to bring into the world in the thirties.

Then, as we have seen, a higher proportion than ever before went to college. The outbreak of student protest in the autumn of 1964 came exactly eighteen years after the peak of the postwar bulge.

When they got to college, the institution itself had been changing. It had been growing larger, necessarily, in order to accommodate them. It had also been growing more bureaucratic and impersonal. (I AM A HUMAN BEING, said the most popular button in the Free Speech Movement, DO NOT FOLD, SPINDLE OR MUTILATE.) The emphasis of the faculty's interest had shifted from teaching to research, and all too often to a kind of entrepreneurial speculation in research. Faced with this professionalized "scholarship," the students retreated into their own world.

Most undergraduates' routine problems were now handled not by the faculty but by graduate teaching assistants, in order to leave the faculty more time to press on with the mining of knowledge. Now came a crucial shift in the alignment of the graduate students. Once, they had been a hand-picked few with excellent prospects and naturally tended to follow the attitudes of the professional elite they hoped to join. Now, in the early sixties, especially in the overcrowded social sciences and liberal arts (just the disciplines where relativistic and critical attitudes to the social *status quo* were in any case most likely), the graduate students began to take on the psychology of the disinherited. They became the leaders of the undergraduate masses in the rebellion against adult authority.

It was in any case getting harder for the university to impose its traditional pseudoparental discipline on the students. More and more, they were being concentrated into youth ghettoes almost as segregated as those of the blacks—or indeed as the suburbs where their middle-class parents had brought them up. Around most universities, whether they were in such leafy college towns as Ann Arbor and Madison, or in such run-down urban neighborhoods as West Philadelphia and Morningside Heights, and in purest form where, as in Cambridge or in the Bay Area, there were several large universities with a combined population of dozens of thousands of students, there grew up self-sufficient communities dominated by the tastes and needs of young people. Nothing could have been more natural than that these "dinky towns," with their shops full of cheap, original clothes, their coffee shops and their headshops, their folk-music cellars and their rock dances, should act as a magnet for young people whether they were students or not. It was in this kind of neighborhood that the first un-

derground newspapers were born: first *The Village Voice,* then the Berkeley *Barb,* the *East Village Other,* and the rest. In this new and specialized
environment, then, grew up a new culture for the young with its emphasis
on the exploration of sexual and personal relationships, on adventures in
fashion of every kind, and on radical dissent from the values of the adult
world.

Very often, the youth ghetto was physically next door to the black
ghetto. This was not wholly accidental. The effect of the university's
"edifice complex" on real estate values made it inevitable that its gleaming
new towers should rise out of a morass of urban decay. Proximity encouraged the growth of a sense of solidarity between students and blacks.
It also fostered a misleading analogy between their respective social situations.

For the student in his run-down apartment house was after all in a
very different situation from his black neighbor. Youth City was not a permanent ghetto. It was a decompression chamber between the sheltered
world of the suburban home, where a dollar was what your mother gave
you to buy fifteen cents' worth of soda, and the more or less harsh reality
of the adult world.

John Searle, in his book *The Campus War,* has chosen a telling illustration of the cultural chasm between those two worlds. Young, middle-
class Americans, he pointed out, had been brought up in a "warm, permissive, forgiving, child-centered style of home life," very different from the
life for which the child was being prepared. "The characteristic organization of our society is not the cosy suburban household, it is the large bureaucracy." Such organizations are not cosy. "Take a close look, for example," Searle wrote, "at Form 1040 of the Internal Revenue Service: it is not
a warm, loving, permissive or forgiving document."

This dichotomy between home and work, childhood and adult life,
the city and the suburb, is not new. It goes back to the time when the Industrial Revolution first drove men to rescue their wives and children from
the cruel, polluted streets of the city, where they made their money, and
to use *it* to buy an artificial Arcadia for them in the suburbs. Charles
Dickens described an early stage of the process in *Great Expectations,*
which was published in 1861:

Mr. Wemmick earns his living as a lawyer's clerk near Newgate Prison
in the City of London. Pip, the young man with great expectations, is
aghast when he first comes up from the country and sees the neighborhood, with its gallows and its whipping post, its beggars and drunks,
and the slaughterhouse "asmear with filth and blood and fat and foam."
He is even more terrified of Mr. Wemmick, with his light way of talking
about hanged clients and perjured evidence, his "mechanical appearance

of smiling," and his "air of knowing something to everybody else's disadvantage." But when Pip asks him for friendly advice, and Wemmick asks him home, Pip is amazed to find him a different man. Wemmick has built himself a little cottage with a garden, symbolically decorated as a castle, only a mile or so south of the Thames, but in those days on the edge of open country. There, in his own castle, Wemmick is open, jovial, loving to his father and girl friend, and a wise and kind friend to Pip.

Dickens had discerned that there is a dichotomy not just between the physical surface of life in the city and life in the suburb but between their moralities as well. When the Anglo-Saxon bourgeois began to move to the suburb, he split his morality in two. By keeping away from his home everything that was not idyllic, pure and healthy, it was as if he could keep his aggression unrestrained and his heart hard for his day at the office. "No," says Mr. Wemmick, "the office is one thing, and private life is another. When I go into the office, I leave the Castle behind me, and when I come into the Castle, I leave the office behind me."

After World War II, when the American middle class migrated en masse to the suburbs, it took this split-level morality, as it took so many other things, to its logical extreme. Never had businessmen been prouder than the American executives of the fifties of their competitive drive, their tigerish aggression. Never had men tried harder to be sweet, affectionate and tolerant at home.

By the late 1960s, after a decade of prosperity in the suburbs and of decay and despair in the inner city, the physical contrast between the two environments had swollen to the dimensions of an allegorical fantasy, and the moral schizophrenia kept pace. A statue to Mr. Wemmick might appropriately have been erected at the entry to each of the freeways, parkways, and expressways that were being built, with 90 per cent federal funding, to take the fathers of America every day from the Castle to the office and from the office to the Castle.

The wives raised the children in the artificial Arcadia of the suburbs, and the children went to high school there, stifling with boredom and resentment against the cloying security of life there, and seizing any opportunity that came along to raise hell. And then, often enough, a truly extraordinary thing happened. Did the upper-middle class, which had gone to such lengths to protect its children from the dangers of the city, cocoon them away in even more idyllic retreats for the perilous passage from childhood to adult life, from the Castle to the City? In the case of the brightest and the most gifted, and therefore of the most influential, of the younger generation, it often did exactly the opposite. It packed them off to find their identity in that very inner city from which their parents had fled, and left them to the tender mercies of an environment almost as harsh, and as dangerous, and as shocking in its social contracts and hypocrisies as Victorian London itself.

The two points at which the Newtonian world system of the liberals had first showed itself vulnerable were foreign policy and the future of black people in America. Specifically, as the unhappy decade went on, it became increasingly doubtful whether the liberal majority could achieve what it wanted in Southeast Asia without flagrant departure from its own moral code. It became questionable whether black Americans would be willing to accept as little as the white majority was willing to concede. And so there was growing reason for doubting the sincerity of the commitment to abolish racism and for doubting the motives of the commitment to contain communism. By the end of the year 1967 these doubts had grown in the minds of tens of millions of Americans into two ominous, lowering issues: "the War," and "the cities." But the essence of the cultural crisis that was about to burst was the apprehension that these two issues were at bottom the same issue: that what was happening in Southeast Asia and what was happening in American cities were subterraneously connected by certain moral flaws in American society. That idea in turn carried with it the implication of a terrifying possibility: What if Vietnam and Mississippi, "the war and the cities," should turn out to be not aberrations from the central tradition of American history but logical consequences of certain strands of that tradition?

The challenge to the authority of institutions, Daniel Patrick Moynihan has written, "reached endemic proportions towards the close of the decade. . . . But it tended to be most conspicuous among upper-middle-class youth, and the urban poor, with some apparent interaction between the behavior of the two." Why did those two groups take the lead in this assault on authority? The answer, I think, has to do with the fact that these were, for different reasons, the first large groups in society to make a connection between the war and the domestic crisis and to attribute both to underlying moral causes.

Some blacks, of course, did continue to support the war. But survey data show that blacks were quicker to give up their support for it than whites. By the spring of 1971, a Gallup survey showed that 83 per cent of blacks, as against 67 per cent of whites, thought that the United States had made a mistake in sending troops to Vietnam in the first place. Black leaders were far quicker than white politicians to link the war and domestic issues. The leaders of SNCC, who had all individually opposed the war all along, went beyond that position and issued a joint statement condemning the draft as early as January 1966, primarily because of the impact of the war on the black community. Even before that, in his column in the

Chicago *Defender* for New Year's Day 1966, Martin Luther King had come out against the war both on purely pacifist grounds—"I believe that war is wrong"—and also with the argument that blacks had special reasons for being wary of the argument that "might makes right." "Morality," he answered when I asked him about this in an interview for British television that same spring, "is indivisible." Then, in his famous sermon at Riverside Church in New York on April 4, 1967, King committed himself openly to the peace movement. He explicitly gave as one of his reasons his fear that "the Great Society has been shot down on the battlefields of Vietnam."

From 1965 on, all black leaders and organizations came under increasing pressure from below to oppose the war. One reason for this was the working of the draft. Relatively very few young blacks could qualify for the 2-S deferment in order to finish college. As a result, black casualties in Vietnam were roughly twice as high as those of whites in relation to population. Secondly, there was the feeling that the war was absorbing resources that were desperately needed at home. (As we have seen, this suspicion, while economically oversimple, was politically justified.) Most important, there was a vaguer, less tangible alienation from the aims of the war, rooted in the whole experience of slavery, segregation and racism. The thought was crudely expressed by a poster often seen at peace demonstrations: NO VIETNAMESE EVER CALLED ME NIGGER. A University of Michigan survey that found that, while 85 per cent of white respondents referred to the U. S. Government as "we," two out of every five blacks spoke of it as "they." American blacks remained a strongly patriotic group. They believed in the ideals of American democracy all the more strongly because they needed to believe in them more than most people did. But they knew that those ideals were not always lived up to. They were therefore quicker than white people to see the war as one more piece of evidence of a strain of ruthlessness of which they had all too much experience at home.

But why should the children of the upper-middle class, the most privileged group in American history, have been equally quick to see the war and the urban crisis as symptoms of deeper moral failure?

One answer is: "Because they were so privileged."

If one tries to understand the lost children of the suburbs, it is hard to better Jules Feiffer's cartoon of 1966:

Paterfamilias speaks:
> WHEN I WAS A KID WE LIVED IN A SLUM, MY FAMILY WAS ON RELIEF, I HAD TO QUIT SCHOOL AT TWELVE. AND I USED TO SAY TO THE WORLD: LISTEN WORLD! YOU'RE NOT GOING TO LICK ME WORLD! I'M OUT TO BUY ME A DREAM! A GOLDEN DREAM, WORLD! A STEADY JOB! YEAH! WHERE A MAN CAN

USE HIS HANDS! YEAH! AND BUY CLOTHES FOR HIS WIFE! YEAH! AND FOOD FOR
HIS CHILD! A LOVERS DREAM WORLD! A SMALL HOUSE IN THE COUNTRY!
YEAH! A WHITE PICKET FENCE! YEAH! A DOG FOR OUR KID! A FAMILY CAR!
YOU LISTENING, WORLD? I'M GONNA SEND ROCKETS TO THE MOON! TEAR
STARS OUT OF THE SKY! PUT MY NAME UP IN LIGHTS! YEAH, WORLD, YEAH!
AN AMERICAN DREAM.

SO NOW I MAKE 50,000 A YEAR, OWN A TOWN HOUSE AND A COUNTRY
ESTATE, KEEP AN EXPENSIVE SECOND WIFE AND RAISE A HANDSOME TALL SON
—WHO HAS GONE TO EUROPE FOUR TIMES, TO THREE DIFFERENT PRIVATE
SCHOOLS, ONE IVY LEAGUE COLLEGE AND HAS OWNED FIVE DIFFERENT CARS
SINCE HE WAS SIXTEEN.

AND HE SAYS TO THE WORLD—
"I'M DROWNING!"
SON OF THE DREAM.

It was one thing for those who had lived through the Depression and
fought through the war to hug prosperity to them with pride as something
they had earned. It was something else for the sons of the dream.

To them, the abundance of their own and their parents' lives often
seemed not the fulfillment of the ethical values they had been taught but
their negation. The children of the upper-middle class saw their parents'
behavior and their declared values as being in conflict. If they continued
to respect their parents as individuals, they saw the behavior of society as a
whole as a betrayal of its principles.

This was where the widespread assumption that equality meant equality of opportunity was crucial. So long as you accepted that definition, it
was possible to make fifty thousand dollars a year without seeing any contradiction of the national belief in the value of equality. But if you knew
that your own opportunity had not been equal, that it had in fact been far
better than other people's opportunities, because your father had been
making fifty thousand dollars a year and had sent you to an Ivy League
college so that it would be comparatively easy for you to make fifty thousand dollars a year if you set your mind to it, then the conflict between the
reality of privilege and the theory of equality became intolerable. The biggest and most prosperous middle class in history quite naturally developed
the biggest case on record of middle-class guilt.

This prevalent social guilt was accentuated by the draft. Just because
it was so easy for upper-middle-class children to get college deferments, it
became a psychological necessity for some, and not for the least admirable,
to find something dangerous to do instead. For them, draft resistance,
drugs, and radical political activity became in a sense "the moral equivalent of war."

There were others whose reaction to the draft was a mixture of fear

and reluctance to fight in a war that seemed pointless, compounded sometimes with sheer outrage that anyone should have the presumption to ask
them, the most talented children of the greatest nation on earth, to do anything they didn't want to do. Something of this emotion comes over in an
autobiography, *The Making of an Un-American,* by Paul Cowan. He just
couldn't believe, he says he told a friend in the summer of 1965, that the
government would be so crazy as to draft married men and graduate students "and make enemies out of a generation whose loyalties they need."

The children of the dream, then, were drowning in it. They were
shocked by what seemed to them the conflict between the values they had
been taught and the privileged complacency both of their parents' own
lives and of their parents' expectations for them. They were frightened of
the draft, and ashamed of being frightened of it, and then again quite
honestly appalled at the work they would have to take a part in if they
were drafted. And they had been exiled from the gentle myths of suburban Arcadia into the angry squalor of the inner city.

It was not so surprising that they should have rebelled. But why did
their rebellion take the particular form it did? Why should so many of the
best-educated Americans have rejected the whole tradition of their own
culture so totally as they seemed to be doing? Whence the infatuation
with black style? Why the revolt against masculinity, against Puritanism,
against work? Why the affinity for the occult and for the East? It was one
thing to understand that the soil of a generation might be rich with disillusion. But what seeds had been thrown into it to bring up this particular
crop, this peculiar combination of frivolity and despair that was the badge
of the counter culture?

For a hundred years, in every industrialized bourgeois democracy, the
intelligentsia had been at odds with the accepted doctrines of the dominant middle class, and American intellectuals were no exception. Chopped
up smidgens of the dreams and arguments of every *avant-garde* movement
of the century went into the stew that was cooking. There was a generous
dollop of the ideas of German *émigré* intellectuals, especially those of the
socalled Frankfurt school, who had tried to achieve a synthesis of Marx
and Freud. From France there was a seasoning of existentialism, a craze
for Camus, a pinch of Dada. Timothy Leary himself has pronounced,
"The American psychedelic movement was almost completely a British
import": he was thinking of the novelist Aldous Huxley, of the psychi-
atrist Ronald Laing, and of the Anglican orientalist Alan Watts, who
popularized, if that is the right word for such hard matters, the teachings
of Zen Buddhism. And then of course there were the Four Evangelists, as

Leary called them: John Lennon, Paul McCartney, George Harrison and Ringo Starr.

Nevertheless the seed that fertilized the discontents of the 1960s was of native breeding. The moment of its germination can be dated to 1955, the year before the Rockefeller brothers commissioned their wise men to write a new testament for liberal America. It was in that year that certain bohemians of San Francisco received through the mail a postcard inviting them to a poetry reading at the Six Gallery in North Beach. The invitation had been sent out by Allen Ginsberg, and it promised "a happy apocalypse." Jack Kerouac, Gary Snyder, Lawrence Ferlinghetti, and Michael McClure were among those who listened to him read, swigging burgundy from a jug. But the poem Ginsberg had written, two weeks earlier, on a mixture of dexedrine, amphetamine, and peyote, was not happy. It was apocalyptic. He called it *Howl*.

I saw the best minds of my generation destroyed by madness, starving hysterical naked,

dragging themselves through the negro streets at dawn looking for an angry fix,

angelheaded hipsters burning for the ancient heavenly connection to the starry dynamo in the machinery of night,

who in poverty and tatters and hollow-eyed and high sat up smoking in the supernatural darkness of cold-water flats floating across the tops of cities contemplating jazz,

who bared their brains to Heaven under the El and saw Mohammedan angels staggering on tenement roofs illuminated,

who passed through universities with radiant cool eyes hallucinating Arkansas and Blake-light tragedy among the scholars of war

* * *

Moloch whose mind is pure machinery! Moloch whose blood is running money! Moloch whose fingers are ten armies!

* * *

Moloch whose love is endless oil and stone! Moloch whose soul is electricity and banks! Moloch whose poverty is the specter of genius! Moloch whose fate is a cloud of sexless hydrogen! Moloch whose name is the Mind!

* * *

Moloch! Moloch! Robot apartments! invincible suburbs! skeleton treasuries! blind capitals! demonic industries! spectral nations! invincible madhouses! granite cocks! monstrous bombs!

* * *

Real holy laughter in the river! They saw it all! the wild eyes! the holy yells! They bade farewell! They jumped off the roof! to solitude! waving! carrying flowers! Down to the river! into the street!

Better poems have been written, some of them, indeed, by Allen Ginsberg. What makes *Howl* remarkable is how accurately it expressed what few felt then, and so many would feel so soon. No poem written by a thirty-year-old, surely, has ever so totally rejected so many of the beliefs of the society it was written in. No poem, certainly, has lived to see so many of its heresies so widely accepted before its author turned forty.

When *Howl* was written, it would have been hard to imagine a grosser blasphemy against the whole gospel of Americanism. Not only machinery and money, this incensed and drunken young centaur was saying, are Moloch: so is Mind. He dares to liken not just the American gods of technology and abundance but rationality itself to an ancient idol, Milton's

> . . . horrid king, besmeared with blood
> Of human sacrifice and parents' tears.

What America calls sanity is madness, Ginsberg was saying, and the invincible panoply of American might and right no better than so many madhouses. It was the scholars of war who were truly hallucinating (prophetic insight). The mad, with their wild eyes and their flowers, were truly holy.

Even the first audience of *Howl* seems to have realized that it was hearing the beginning of something. The journalists called it the Beat Movement. The Beats are taught in college now. In America people are in such a hurry that they speed up their own history so that the past will seem safely further away. Jack Kerouac is dead, of drink. But Allen Ginsberg only turned fifty in the bicentennial year. The idiosyncratic brew of ideas and interests and obsessions that were inside his head in 1955 became the ideas, interests and obsessions of a generation.

The Beats never were really a movement, so much as a group of friends held together by their various relationships with Allen Ginsberg, poet of talent and publicist of genius. Ginsberg was a freshman at Columbia at the end of the war, when he met Kerouac, who was older, French-Canadian and trying to make it as a writer after a tough-guy life as a merchant seaman. Then he met William Burroughs, Harvard graduate, heir to the adding-machine fortune, and addict of every drug he could hustle or scrounge. Picaresque is the word for the adventures of Ginsberg, Kerouac and Burroughs over the next ten years. Burroughs killed his wife by mistake, trying to shoot a glass of water off her head, and went down to Peru in search of drugs of fabled potency and secret enlightenment. Kerouac set off with his friend Neal Cassady, the poetical brakeman of San Jose, on the travels he described in *On the Road*. After various wanderings Ginsberg fell in love with Cassady and went to California to find him, only to discover that Cassady had, of all things, married. That was when Ginsberg drifted up to San Francisco, to Berkeley, where he worked as a bus boy, and to *Howl*.

In the rest of the fifties he traveled all over Europe and the Americas, reading vastly, experimenting with various drugs, and writing poems. In the new decade he moved on to Israel, and then to India. Nothing freed him from the despair he described in another poem:

> erk, I'm stuck with this familiar rotting ginsberg.

It was in Japan, on the Tokyo-Kyoto express, that he experienced the religious conversion he described in one of his finest poems, *The Change*. Whatever went into that change, it brought Allen Ginsberg to accept himself. He came back to America with an implacable commitment to do battle in his own way against the ten armies of Moloch. In August 1963—three months before the shock that for most Americans brought on the Crisis—he described the search that had led him through three continents and God knows what "poverty and tatters and hollow-eyed and high . . . smoking in the supernatural darkness of cold-water flats."

> In the midst of the broken consciousness of mid twentieth century anguish of separation from my own body and its natural infirmity of feeling its own self one with all self, I instinctively seeking to reconstitute that blissful union which I experienced so rarely I took it to be supernatural and gave it holy Name thus made hymn lament of longing and litanies of triumphancy of Self over the mind-illusion mechano-universe of un-feeling Time in which I saw my self my own mother and my very nation trapped.

That was not only a credo. It was a manifesto. It has been said that all revolutionary movements must have their utopia. It was Allen Ginsberg and his friends, more than anyone else, who were responsible for the fact that many millions of young Americans joined a movement whose utopia was between the ears. He was in truth the prophet of a new consciousness.

He himself is well aware of the connection between the Beats and the counter culture. "Sure," he once told an interviewer, "there are many elements of continuity from the Beats to the present." He mentioned drugs, music, the interest in the East, the preoccupation with the tradition of Whitman and Thoreau, the rediscovery of the land and of the body. What was at the heart of the movement, then? "Well," he answered, "there was the return to nature and the revolt against the machine."

Exactly those impulses lay at the heart of the counter culture. By the second half of the sixties, a growing number of Americans had come to picture American society itself as a cruel, impersonal machine into which their own lives would be fed unless they could struggle free. They had, whether they knew it or not, adopted Ginsberg's metaphor. Robot apartments and invincible suburbs had become Moloch. There were many direct lines of influence between the tiny Beat group in the fifties and the mass diffusion of their ideas in the sixties. For example:

Item: In August 1960 Timothy Leary and Richard Alpert, two Harvard instructors, with four of their friends, first tasted the sacred mushroom at Cuernavaca, in Mexico. The experience decided them to devote the rest of their lives to investigating and propagandizing for psychedelic drugs. In 1963 Leary and Alpert left Harvard, and shortly after, their International Foundation for Inner Freedom, radiating its influence from a four-thousand-acre estate in upstate New York, became the most energetic source of propaganda for the coming revolution through acid. "During the next few hundred years," as Leary put it with characteristic bombast, "the major activity of man will be the scientific exploration of, and education in, the many universes of awareness that have been opened up by psychedelic drugs." Leary always acknowledged himself a disciple of Burroughs and Ginsberg. "Burroughs was Mr. Acid before LSD was invented," he said (though with typical inaccuracy, since lysergic acid diethylamide was first synthesized in 1938, long before Burroughs was interested in psychedelic drugs). In December 1960, Ginsberg was one of the first people invited by Leary to join his experiments. "Ginsberg came to Harvard," Leary has said, "and shook us free from our academic fears."

Item: After Leary, the second-most-effective of the salesmen of pharmacological enlightenment was Ken Kesey. His first novel, *One Flew over the Cuckoo's Nest*, published in 1962, was very much in the Beat tradition. The famous bus trip around the United States by Kesey and his Merry Pranksters in 1964 was modeled on Kerouac's odyssey. And who drove the psychedelic Paisley-pattern Day-Glo bus? Old Neal Cassady, Kerouac's original companion and Ginsberg's inamorato.

Item: At all the well-publicized ceremonial gatherings of the hippies, and of the political radicals, especially but not only in the Bay Area, between 1964 and 1968, the Beat veterans were on hand. Ginsberg, Snyder, McClure, Corso, Ferlinghetti, were consulted by the impresarios of chaos and the gurus in the ashrams of the Haight-Ashbury. From the Vietnam Day happenings in Berkeley in 1965 to the great assembly on the day California made LSD illegal a year later, and again at the Gathering of the Tribes in Golden Gate Park in January 1967, and even at the march on the Pentagon that same October, almost alone among the over-thirties, the Beats were accepted by the young as teachers and guides. And wherever the clowning was most furious, the bald head of Allen Ginsberg tossed in the thickest of the fray.

# Triumph and Failure of a Cultural Revolution

We tell ourselves we are a counterculture. And yet are we really so different from the culture against which we rebel?

Jon Landau, *Rolling Stone*, 1971.

1

The heyday of the counter culture coincided with the buildup of the Vietnam War from the President's decision to escalate in the spring of 1965 to the Tet offensive of 1968. It also coincided with the climax of racial confrontation, from Selma to the death of Martin Luther King. But if the twin crises in foreign policy and the cities were the occasion of the youth rebellion, the actual process of recruitment to the counter culture probably owed more to three factors that had little enough to do with politics except as symbols—to drugs, to rock music, and to the underground media: the sacrament, the liturgy and the gospel of a religion that failed.

The youth culture liked to remind older Americans that they, too, were insatiable consumers of various stimulants and depressants. That was why young people were so fond of the Rolling Stones' song *Mother's Little Helper:*

> And though she's not really ill,
> There's a little yellow pill.
> She goes running for the shelter
> Of her "mother's little helper."

There was no getting away from the fact that, lashed on by advertising agencies, distillers, brewers, cigarette manufacturers and pharmaceutical companies, the ordinary American had long thought it perfectly normal to be more or less addicted to alcohol, nicotine, barbiturates and tranquilizers. American physicians were prescribing more and more drugs, and sometimes, indeed, behaving almost as if they were drug salesmen. Neither the U. S. Army nor the CIA, those two pillars of the "straight" society, saw anything wrong with using LSD long before it had become a fashion in the counter culture. The drug culture of the 1960s certainly did not grow out of a society that was totally new to the idea of chemical aids to the pursuit of happiness.

In a more literal sense, the drug users were the children of whiskey drinkers and cigarette smokers. There is some statistical evidence that marijuana smokers, for example, are more likely than non-users to be the children of parents who smoke tobacco or drink alcohol. In the circumstances, it is worth asking why the "drugs" of the youth culture aroused such vehement indignation and fear.

Historically American attitudes to the taking of drugs, in the wider sense, for "pleasure," have always reflected a deep dichotomy in the culture between the inhibitions of Puritanism and the imperative to pursue happiness. More recently, two other factors have been at work to modify these attitudes: the pressure of business interests, and ethnic prejudice. Business pressures were largely responsible for removing the ban that twenty-one state legislatures imposed on cigarettes between 1895 and 1921. And only the absence of effective restraint on business interests can explain the overproduction and overprescription of barbiturates.

Ethnic prejudice was certainly involved in the temperance movement during the campaign for Prohibition. The drys were nativists and Protestants as much as they were teetotalers. The same is true of the history of legislation against narcotics. In 1900, according to the Nixon administration's Shafer Commission, approximately 1 per cent of the population was addicted to opium, morphine, heroin or cocaine. But these were predominantly middle-class people. It was only the increase in the "pleasure" use of these narcotics by ethnic minorities, especially the Chinese immigrants in California, that led to the Harrison Narcotics Act of 1914.

Marijuana was introduced in the next decade by Mexican laborers and West Indian sailors, and spread up the Mississippi Valley in step with the first wave of the black migration. By the 1940s its use had become fashionable among white bohemians in New York and Los Angeles, partly because of its association with jazz musicians. Hostility toward it was perhaps based on fear of the unknown as much as on racial prejudice. But there is in any case a sad contrast between the escalating penalties for marijuana use and the reluctance of Congress to take action against the manufacture and advertisement of cigarettes, though the evidence for the dangers of cigarette smoking was accumulating throughout that period, while "a careful search of the literature . . . has not revealed a single human fatality resulting solely from the ingestion of marijuana."

This is not, however, either a treatise on pharmacology or a moral tract. From a historical point of view, four drugs or groups of drugs are relevant to the spread of the counter culture: marijuana, the hallucinogens, the amphetamines, and heroin. The use of all these increased dramatically during the second half of the 1960s.

The amphetamines ("speed") can be dismissed with merciful brevity. "Speed kills," the lore of the drug subculture warned, and it did not exaggerate.

Each of the other three drugs, or groups of drugs, had a special symbolic importance: the hallucinogens, especially "acid" (LSD), for the "hippies," that is, for those who were fully committed to the counter culture; marijuana for the great army of lukewarm converts and partial sympathizers; heroin for its enemies.

From the early days of the Beat Movement, the idea that hallucinogenic drugs could create a new consciousness had been "at the crux of the futurist revolt." In America, it was never in the cards that such an idea could long survive as the prerogative of an initiate elite. If Ginsberg had been the prophet of using chemistry to change consciousness, and Leary the salesman of the idea, its Henry Ford was "Owsley"—a University of California student, grandson of a United States senator from Kentucky, with the sonorous name of Augustus Owsley Stanley III. It was on February 21, 1965, ten days before Operation Rolling Thunder began, and the month before the first teach-in, that Owsley's primitive acid factory in Berkeley was raided. In March he moved to Los Angeles and went into mass production of lysergic acid monohydrate. The business was profitable by any standards: he is said to have paid twenty thousand dollars for the first shipment, of five hundred grams, which was converted into one and a half million tabs at one to two dollars apiece *wholesale!*

With massive supplies of acid guaranteed by this pioneering venture in hip capitalism, the next three years—those same three years of schism from 1965 to 1968, when the war and the urban crisis seemed to be tearing the country in two—saw the illusion that chemistry could free the human mind spin through the full cycle from frenzied hope and bombastic prophecy to panic, paranoia and catastrophe.

In the spring of 1965 the word went out that they had discovered peace and love in San Francisco. To a depressing extent, this was an illusion resulting from the chemical effects of lysergic acid. People tried it, one researcher has concluded, as "a relief from boredom, an enhancement of sentience, a source of fusion, an escape from the sheltered life, an initiation, a way to express anger or withdrawal, an answer to loneliness, a substitute for sex, a moving psychological, philosophical or religious experience, and, most importantly [for] fun." It was all of those things, no doubt. It was also a supreme example of the power of fashion in American life.

The speed with which the craze took hold is a tribute to the needs of a generation that "had everything." It was also a remarkable illustration of the fine-tuned efficiency of the American social machine for distributing *any* new idea, fashion or product.

LSD was launched by a handful of Berkeley and San Francisco bohemians. Madison Avenue itself could not have handled the launch more successfully.

"It all came straight out of the Acid Tests," according to Tom Wolfe, the social historian of anti-fashion, "in a straight line leading to the Trips Festival of January 1966. That brought the whole thing out in the open." In other words, the craze was publicized by the spectacular mass turn-ons organized by Kesey and his friends. In 1965 and 1966, LSD was still the esoteric rite of initiation into a relatively small company of the enlightened in the Haight-Ashbury district in San Francisco and the East Village in New York. That was still true even as late as January 1967, when Allen Ginsberg, Timothy Leary and the Zen poet Gary Snyder were among the organizers of the Great Human Be-In at Golden Gate Park. Thousands of devotees, in a state of beatific hallucination, turned to face the sunset over the Pacific while Ginsberg blew on a ram's horn and recited a propitious mantra.

The omens were not favorable. The Summer of Love in 1967 turned into a nightmare. The runaways poured into the Haight-Ashbury and the East Village from every campus and suburb in the United States: the bored, the delinquent, the psychotic, and the mere followers of fashion. They were followed by tourists, journalists, sociologists and undercover agents. And they met bad acid, bad vibrations, uptight cops, Mafia peddlers, chiselers, stranglers, hepatitis and VD.

There was a phrase the acid freaks used about a bad trip: they called it a "horror show." By 1968 the psychedelic paradise itself was turning into a horror show. The older and more serious seekers were horrified at what publicity was doing to their private cult. They began to move out physically from the hippie ghettoes, and to experiment with less instant paths to truth, with communal living, macrobiotic diets, group therapy and transcendental meditation.

One way station on the road out of the Haight-Ashbury that summer was Esalen, in the Big Sur country, which emerged as a kind of ashram where a bizarre assembly of sadhus and disciples searched for peace and wisdom with the help of LSD, folk and rock music, naked bathing, Tai

Chi exercises and the *Gestalt* therapy of Dr. Fritz Perls as interpreted by Paul Goodman. But even on the sunny cliffs of Big Sur, the quest for truth and beauty was haunted by bad vibrations. One disciple recalls a sinister evening at Esalen that summer when one of the flower children around the campfire was heard to be muttering "Blood! Blood! Blood! Hate! Hate!" And no less a symbol of the dark potentialities of Dionysian rebellion than Charles Manson was lurking around Esalen that same summer.

"If I had to summarize in one word what has happened to the street scene in the last two years," said one literate hippie in 1969, "it would be 'decay.' It's not so much love any more, it's survival." That was the year of the Woodstock festival. Three hundred thousand turned up, and the media discovered the "Woodstock Nation." But in fact, by 1969, the use of hallucinogens had already started to level off among college students in the trend-setting regions, California and the Northeast. Not long afterward college students elsewhere and high school students followed suit. As a pilgrimage in search of new freedom, the great acid trip was over before the end of the sixties.

It was during precisely these same three years, from 1965 to 1968, that marijuana first caught on as a mass habit, first among students and then among young people generally. The first studies of drug use among college students date from 1965. In that year a survey of graduating seniors from Brooklyn College found that only 4.2 per cent had ever used marijuana, and in a sample of graduate students at "a large urban university in Southern California," where the habit was most deeply established, the proportion who had ever tried marijuana was still only 10.7 per cent.

By 1969 the lowest reported incidence of marijuana use in *high schools*, in conservative Utah, was higher than the rate for graduate students in Los Angeles only four years before. By the last week of 1969, a survey of full-time college students on fifty-seven campuses in the United States conducted by The Gallup Organization and reported in *Newsweek* found that 31.9 per cent said that they had used marijuana.

Surveys of students at individual universities reported even higher rates of response: 44 per cent, for example, at Michigan in the autumn of 1969, and 48 per cent at four Massachusetts colleges, one of them Harvard, the following spring. The higher the social class from which young people came and the higher the standing of the college they attended the more likely they were to have tried marijuana. The Massachusetts study found that only 26 per cent of young people between sixteen and twenty-three in jobs had smoked marijuana, as against 48 per cent of those who were in college. And a 1970 survey of students at a wide variety of educational institutions in the Denver-Boulder area of Colorado found that the percentage who had used the drug declined roughly in proportion to the academic and social standing of the college: from 35 per cent at the University of Colorado at Boulder, to 16 per cent at Loretto Heights College, a small local girls' college. While the craze for LSD was beginning to die down, the marijuana habit was steadily spreading to new groups of the youth population.

This remarkable change in taste, involving as it did, at last, the symbolic rejection of many of society's strongest values, was essentially spontaneous. The great majority of those who used marijuana were first given it, for free, by a friend. No large commercial organization for handling the trade and distribution ever seems to have developed. Some 80 per cent of the weed was brought in over the Mexican border. The rest was grown locally, either wild, or in cultivation in Oregon and California communes, city window boxes or, once, with heroic bravado, in the median strip on Park Avenue in New York.

Some small-scale "hip capitalists" did organize shipments of grass from Mexico and of hashish from the Near East and India. But the stereotype of the evil pusher luring adolescents into the grip of addiction for his own profit was always, as far as marijuana was concerned, a myth.

Even an official publication put out by the Nixon administration in 1971, at the height of its crusade to stamp out drugs, conceded, "In general adolescents are introduced to marijuana by others in their groups. There is little evidence to confirm the belief that 'pushers' are needed to 'turn on' a novice. His friends do it for him."

Once a boy or girl had tried marijuana, he or she was automatically a potential recruit for the culture of opposition, not because of the pharmacological effects of the drug but because of its cultural associations and above all because it remained illegal. And since, unlike LSD or the amphetamines, marijuana is mild, pleasant, no more harmful than coffee or wine, and relatively cheap, the human chain effect by which millions of young people were introduced to it by their friends became a powerful recruiting network for the counter culture.

Heroin had never been central to the ideas of the counter culture, as the hallucinogenic drugs were. Nor was it ever anything like as popular as marijuana. The major prophets disapproved of it (though they disapproved more vocally of punishing people for using it), and few hippies used it. A study of the drug subculture in the East Village in 1967, at the height of the acid craze, for example, found that where 100 per cent of those sampled had used marijuana and 90 per cent had used acid, only 13 per cent had ever experimented with heroin. No mass survey of college students ever found that as many as 0.5 per cent admitted to having ever tried heroin.

As an opiate, heroin is a "depressant," a "downer," like alcohol. At best, it induces not excitement or visions but a sense of relaxed satiation. Nobody would ever take it in search of enlightenment; nobody could seriously argue that it expanded the field of human consciousness.

Except at the lowest levels of the capillary system by which it reached the addict on the street, the supply of heroin, unlike the supply of marijuana, was always firmly controlled by professional criminals operating on a fairly large scale. For this reason, and because there was no competition from domestic production, heroin remained extremely expensive. It therefore notoriously became connected with crime in a second sense: the addict was driven to steal in order to support his habit.

Leaving aside the special and apparently temporary problem of heroin use in the military services, which was related to special factors such as fear, boredom and the availability of cheap supplies in Vietnam, heroin addiction was essentially a problem of the ghetto. In 1969 just under half the known heroin addicts in the country were black. Well over one third of the rest were either Puerto Rican or Mexican.

Indeed heroin was above all a problem of the New York ghettoes. Almost half the sixty-two thousand narcotics addicts known to the authorities in 1967 were in New York, and while the spread of heroin apparently accelerated subsequently in other cities, notably in Detroit, it was still true in 1971 that thirty-three thousand out of eighty-two thousand known addicts in the whole country were in the single city of New York. Unknown addicts presumably bore approximately the same relation in numbers to those known in New York as they did elsewhere. A whole series of studies reported that heroin users overwhelmingly came from the most underprivileged, crowded and dilapidated sections of the city, and spelled out the connection between heroin and the whole syndrome of crisis in the inner city.

After about 1969 some middle-class white graduates from other drugs did experiment with heroin. "Everyone just got so that they weren't turned on to tripping [i.e. to LSD] any more," a New Jersey teen-ager explained, with all the moronic logic of the man who explains that he drinks in order to forget that he is an alcoholic; "they just decided that downs were the best kind of experience to have." But these young white boys and girls who drifted into heroin because they had tried everything else remained a small minority among heroin users. More typically, heroin was just one among the many ways in which those at the very bottom of urban society, and especially urban black society, exploited each other's desire to escape, to the ultimate profit of others outside the trap. If the

LSD craze was an episode in the mythology of bohemia, heroin was part of the psychic and social pathology of the ghetto.

Unfortunately, however, those whom the counter culture dismissed as "the straight world" made no such distinction. For middle-aged conservatives, drugs were drugs. Among slightly less rigid sectors of public opinion, any awareness of differences between various drugs was canceled out by the power of the myth that all drugs were one great slippery slope; that once you took the first drag at a joint of marijuana, you would be lucky not to slide all the way down to end up as a heroin addict.

The specter conjured up by the word "drugs" in the minds of middle-class parents was above all the specter of heroin: the Big H. The myth of the insidious pusher and the innocent victim crystallized into a morality play of enticement, addiction, withdrawal, relapse, overdose and death. There was just enough truth in this melodramatic stereotype to give it the power to trouble the sleep of half the parents of teen-age children in the country. It *did* happen that kids from "nice homes," having first tried marijuana, ended up dead in a pool of vomit after an overdose of heroin. But it happened infinitely less often than middle-class families, in their terror, imagined. Perhaps the myth, on balance, did more harm than the drug.

By the early 1970s, heroin had clearly become a surrogate target for the fears and anger of a society that was passing through a terrifying period of shocks and disillusionment. The Nixon administration—in this, at least, reflecting the feelings of a large majority of middle-class opinion—had become almost obsessional on the subject. Few issues occupied more time in the White House. In the State Department, a high official there told me late in 1971, roughly one third of the cable traffic in and out of the department was about drugs. Nelson Rockefeller, supposed champion of Republican liberalism, proposed to introduce a mandatory death penalty for selling drugs. Not that the situation did not justify serious concern: it did. But the form the hysteria about heroin took was largely unrelated to the real problems of increasing addiction in the ghetto.

Heroin had become the convenient outward symbol for deep, irrational fears: for the white man's fear of the black man, for the fear (never far below the surface in a society of immigrants) of losing beloved children to an alien culture, for the Puritan's Manichaean fear of the lurking powers of darkness. In a way, heroin had taken the place of communism.

Not the least of the ways in which America was divided in this period was by the emotional harmonics of the word "drugs." To millions of younger people, drugs meant first and foremost marijuana, which in turn meant nothing much more than fun. To some few of the intellectuals of the counter culture, drugs meant the hallucinogens, which seemed to offer the hope of achieving a "new consciousness." But to by far the largest number of Americans, drugs meant heroin. And heroin symbolized all they most hated and feared.

2

On the last Saturday night in August 1965, Bob Dylan was booed at a concert in Forest Hills, New York. It wasn't quite the first time; the same thing had happened at the Newport Festival a month earlier. Both times, Dylan knew what his offense had been. He had played a new kind of music. He had mixed in with his well-loved repertoire of folk songs, written by himself in the Old Left-Greenwich Village tradition of allegorical political protest, accompanied by himself on acoustic guitar, and sometimes echoed by his plaintive harmonica, a new group of songs. (The best-known of them was "Like a Rolling Stone.") The words were less political and more personal. The music had a driving beat supplied by a group with amplified electric guitars. The critics called it "folk rock." The devotees of folk music called it sacrilege. Even so, Dylan seemed incredulous at the ferocity of the audience's anger.

"You scumbag!" one woman screamed.

"Ah, come on," he said, "was it really that bad?"

The audiences weren't booing because they didn't like new songs played in a new way, or even because they didn't like amplified electric guitar. They were booing because they suspected that a hero had betrayed them, and because they sensed that a certain hope was fading.

The first phase of Dylan's career had coincided exactly with the years of pell-mell crisis from 1963 to 1965. It was in the spring of 1963, the spring of Bull Connor's police dogs, that all America was first whistling one of Dylan's tunes. The song was *Blowin' in the Wind*. It was a perfect song for the year that began with Birmingham and ended with Dallas. It captured the disillusioned impatience, hardening into anger, of those who had been liberals and were turning into radicals. And especially it caught the mood of those in Dylan's own generation—he was not twenty-one when he wrote it—who had retained their parents' determination that the world must be cleansed of its sundry imperfections but were losing their parents' confidence that this could be done by fiat of the President and Congress of the United States.

How many seas must a white dove sail
Before she sleeps in the sand? . . .

> How many years can some people exist
> Before they're allowed to be free?
>
> The answer, my friend, is blowin' in the wind,
> The answer is blowin' in the wind.

Dylan was always a complex and subtle man, an artist, whatever you think of his work, and not a propagandist. There had always been since the seven times he ran away from home as an adolescent in Hibbing, Minnesota, to wander the roads like a Kerouac hero, as much of the cultural rebel in him as there was of the political radical. As early as 1964, he had turned far enough from political protest to write the poetic, introspective *Mr. Tambourine Man*, which anticipated most of the major themes of the counter culture: its preoccupation with states of consciousness, with the present as opposed to the future or the past, with hallucination as a road of escape:

> Take me on a trip upon your magic swirlin' ship . . .
>
> Then take me disappearin' through the smoke rings of my mind
> Down the foggy ruins of time, far past the frozen leaves
> The haunted, frightened trees out to the windy beach
> Far from the twisted reach of crazy sorrow.
>
> Yes, to dance beneath the diamond sky with one hand wavin' free
> Silhouetted by the sea, circled by the circus sands
> With all memory and fate driven deep beneath the waves
> Let me forget about today until tomorrow.

But that side of Dylan's personality was not obvious during his period as a folk singer in the tradition of Woody Guthrie and Pete Seeger. A high proportion of his songs then, such as *Masters of War*, were overtly political. He was committed to the civil rights movement. He even went to sing in Mississippi in the summer of 1963, a whole year before that was a fashionable thing to do. That same year, he wrote what was to become the anthem of the generation gap:

> Come mothers and fathers
> Throughout the land
> And don't criticize
> What you can't understand
> Your sons and your daughters
> Are beyond your command.
> There's a battle
> Outside and it's ragin'

It'll soon shake your windows
And rattle your walls . . .
For the times they are a-changin'.

By 1965, when Dylan adopted the idiom of rock, the times had changed again. An illusion had died. It was soon to be replaced by another illusion.

Throughout the sixties, the changing phases of popular music did coincide uncannily with changing political moods. First came the unworldly moralizing and naïve political idealism of the folk-music movement: Judy Collins, Joan Baez, Pete Seeger, and Dylan the folk singer were at the height of their popularity between 1963 and 1965, the years of high hopes for the New Frontier and the Great Society.

Then, in 1965, came rock. The words of the folk songs had been full of radical implications. The singers themselves were men and women of the Left. They sang about peace and war, poverty and injustice, and sometimes, as in *The Times They Are A-Changin'*, they looked forward to the coming of revolution.

The rock singers sometimes sang about revolution, too. But the word meant something different for them from the literal, political revolution of such New York Marxist folk singers as Pete Seeger and Phil Ochs. The music itself was to be the revolution. In the first dizzy years of rock, in 1965 and 1966, and above all in 1967, the promise that intoxicated initiates was that of a wider revolution of consciousness and culture, of which political revolution would come as a by-product.

Rock music is American on both sides of the family if you trace its pedigree far enough. Its technical elements have come down through the commercial rock-and-roll and rhythm-and-blues of the 1950s from the two deepest fountains of American popular music, black blues and white country music. But, in 1965, two traditions fused to create the rock music of the late sixties: one come back to America from Britain, and one out of San Francisco.

Beginning, like so much else, in 1963, first the Beatles, and then a succession of other British pop groups, of whom the Rolling Stones eventually became almost as important as the Beatles themselves, re-exported American popular music to America and proved that their kind of it could be a commercial success on a far bigger scale than the originals it came from. Folk music, rock-and-roll, and urban blues all sold to fractional markets: to campus and coffee house and to the black "race" market. The Beatles' formula, compounded of driving rhythm, sophisticated musical craftsmanship, fresh and often exquisite melody, and literate, irreverent lyrics about real life, unlocked the American youth market as a whole. After the

Beatles had made the breach, a host of imitators, British and American, poured through it.

Technical and economic factors contributed to the staggering commercial success of rock music. The improvement in electronic amplifying; the development of eight- and sixteen-track tape recorders; the spread of FM radio; the marketing shift from 45-rpm singles to 33-rpm albums (itself predicated on the new prosperity which meant that even teen-agers were used to spending four dollars on an album once a week or more and could afford elaborate stereo equipment); the rise of such aggressive new recording companies as the Ertegun brothers' Atlantic Records to compete with the stodgy giants of the industry—these made the rock boom possible.

But in the end the phenomenal success of the Beatles was due to psychological compatibility. They came from an Irish working-class background in Liverpool, where irreverence toward all established authority, and especially toward national and military authority, is endemic. They grew up knowing some of the things that young Americans were discovering with pained surprise in the 1960s: that industrial society uses people as well as makes them more affluent, that there is a good deal of hypocrisy about politicians' patriotism, that a lot of middle-class virtue is a sham. When a generation of young Americans emerged from Birmingham and Dallas, Mississippi and Vietnam, into disillusionment and cynicism, the Beatles were waiting there with a grin on their faces. They were as disillusioned and cynical as anyone, but they were cheerful about it; they had never expected that life would be any different.

It would be hard to exaggerate the influence the Beatles had on the generation of Americans who grew up in the sixties. But the Beatles were influenced by America, too, and in particular by the other stream that went into creating the vitality of rock music. That was the San Francisco influence.

In San Francisco in 1965, 1966 and 1967, Jon Landau of *Rolling Stone* has written, "rock was not only viewed as a form of entertainment." It was "an essential component of a 'new culture,' along with drugs and radical politics." That hardly does justice to the fervid claims that were made on behalf of the new music. The leading San Francisco band, The Grateful Dead, was at the very center of the general ferment in the Bay Area in those years. It had played at Ken Kesey's legendary "acid tests." Augustus Owsley Stanley III had personally bought the band its equipment out of his LSD profits. And the Dead had actually lived in a commune in the Haight-Ashbury until driven out by the sheer squalor into which that neighborhood declined after 1967. The other San Francisco bands, such as the Jefferson Airplane, shared this "underground" style. In

1967, for their own various reasons, the three unarguable superstars of the new music—Bob Dylan, the Beatles, and the Rolling Stones—all stopped touring America. In their absence, after the Monterey festival of that summer, it was the "underground," San Francisco style that emerged triumphant. Soon even the Beatles were imitating the San Francisco underground style: a peculiar blend of radical political rhetoric, of allusions to the drug culture, and of the excited sense of imminent, apocalyptic liberation. After 1967 the equation between rock music and "revolution" became firmly anchored in the minds of all those who listened to the one or hankered after the other.

It was perhaps always an absurd idea that a new kind of music could change society as Hamelin was changed by the Pied Piper. It was in any case a short-lived idea. The episode which, more than any other, revealed the sheer nastiness that was the antithesis to the claim that rock music was liberating came at the Rolling Stones' concert at Altamont, California, in the last month of the sixties.

It was part of the Stones' carefully polished image to be "their satanic majesties," the naughtiest boys in the world. That winter, they toured the United States. Audiences and critics agreed that their music was as exciting as ever. To end the tour, they planned to give a free concert in San Francisco. It was to be a royal gesture, and at the same time their acknowledgment of the city's role in the culture that had crowned them.

The coronation was as satanic as any press agent could have wished. "Hustlers of every stripe," wrote the relatively sympathetic Michael Lydon in *Ramparts*, "swarmed to the new scene like piranhas to the scent of blood." And so did three hundred thousand for them to prey off. Lydon saw "the dancing beaded girls, the Christlike young men and smiling babies familiar from countless stories on the Love Generation." But another side of the culture was unmistakable, too: "speed freaks with hollow eyes and missing teeth, dead-faced acid-heads burned out by countless flashes, old beatniks clutching gallons of red wine, Hare Krishna chanters with shaved heads and acned cheeks."

Four people died. One, a young man with long hair and a metal cross around his neck, was so stoned that he walked unregarding into an irrigation ditch and drowned. Another was clubbed, stabbed and kicked to death by the Hell's Angels. What were those dangerous pets of the San Francisco *avant-garde* supposed to be doing at the concert? It turned out that they had been hired as "security guards" by the Rolling Stones, on the advice of none other than The Grateful Dead, the original troubadours of love, peace and flowers. "Regrettable," commented the Rolling Stones' manager, "but if you're asking me for a condemnation of the Angels . . ." It sounded eerily like President Nixon discussing Lieutenant Calley's conviction for the massacre at My Lai.

"Altamont showed everyone," wrote one of the most levelheaded of the rock critics, Jon Landau, in *Rolling Stone*, "that everything that had been swept under the rug was now coming into the open: the greed, the hustle, the hype. . . ." Only four months earlier, the national media, always quick to seize on some dramatic but complex event and shape its ambiguities into the oversimplified symbol of a new trend, had celebrated the Woodstock Festival as the birth of a new "nation." Then, after Altamont, the boom jibed brutally over onto a new tack. Where the news magazines, the networks and the commentators had managed to ignore the hype, the hustle and even the mud, and had portrayed Woodstock as a midsummer night's dream of idyllic innocence, Altamont was painted as Walpurgisnacht, a witches' sabbath.

Those who were most sympathetic to the counter culture had been aware of its deep and dangerous ambiguities even long before Woodstock. It was as if, wrote Andrew Kopkind, a wholehearted convert to the alternative life style, "some monstrous and marvelous metaphor had come alive, revealing itself only in terms of its contradictions: paradise and concentration camp"—it was quite typical of the fashion of the time in radical journalism to compare a wet weekend with the Final Solution—"sharing and profiteering, sky and mud, love and death. The urges of the ten years' generation roamed the woods and pastures, and who could tell whether it was rough beast or speckled bird slouching through its Day-Glo manger to be born?" For Landau, more realistically, Woodstock was not a new birth but an ending. It was "the ultimate commercialization" of the underground culture at the very moment when it seemed to be in process of being transformed into a mass culture, and perhaps indeed into *the* mass culture. Since it demonstrated "just how strong in numbers the rock audience had become, and just how limited its culture was," he thought Woodstock "a fitting end to the sixties" and the satanic events at Altamont only a parody and an anticlimax.

One reason why it was absurd to equate rock music with revolution, political or cultural, was because it was so very much a commercial product and one that was marketed with single-minded cynicism by individual entrepreneurs and corporate business alike. Behaving in this instance, for once, just as pragmatically as Marxist lore would have predicted, the entertainment industry put up with whatever the musicians and their admirers chose to inflict on it. It tolerated outrageous arrogance, boorishness and unreliability. It raised no demur at long hair on stage and clouds of marijuana in recording studios. It even shelled out royalties far higher than the deferential blacks and crooners who ground out the hits of the past had ever been paid. It would have put up with far more—just so long as the records kept selling. And sell they did.

In the very month of Woodstock *The Wall Street Journal*, no friend of revolution, psychic or political, looked upon rock music and found it good. Over the past several years, it reported, record sales had been rising at the rate of between 15 per cent and 20 per cent annually. The previous year, they had passed the $1-billion mark. The fundamental cause of this sales boom, no doubt, was prosperity: that very "Great Society" prosperity that the counter culture so bitterly affected to despise. But it was rock that was making those burgeoning sales. "Five years ago," the *Journal* found, meaning 1964, "Columbia Records . . . did about 15% of its business in rock. Today rock (using the term loosely) accounts for 60% or more of the vastly increased total."

In 1967 *Rolling Stone* magazine was founded, by Jann Wenner, age twenty-one, with seventy-five hundred dollars borrowed from family and friends. He could not have been a more characteristic product of the counter culture. He had dropped out of Berkeley, where he had been caught up in the Free Speech Movement. He knew Ken Kesey. He had been one of the early hippies. He had been involved with drugs. By the end of its first year *Rolling Stone* had a circulation of sixty thousand. By the end of the decade, with a circulation of over a quarter of a million, it was attracting lush advertising from the big record companies. Less than three years after it was floated, *Rolling Stone* was spending a sum of money roughly equivalent to its original capitalization in order to advertise on the back page of the New York *Times*. "If you are a corporate executive," the ad said, "trying to understand what is happening to youth today, you cannot afford to be without *Rolling Stone*."

"Several large Establishment-oriented corporations," the New York *Times* reported as if to confirm the effectiveness of this pitch, "are interested in cashing in on the youth market that Woodstock proved exists. These firms are hiring highly paid youth consultants to advise them on forthcoming trends that percolate from the deepest underground to . . . the silk-shirt hippie types from Forest Hills who do so much of the buying." "The Establishment," one underground journalist complained in 1970, "is slowly but steadily finding ways to exploit the radical movement."

To call this development revolution was to pervert language. Some of the adherents of the counter culture were uncomfortably aware of the incongruity of what was happening. They saw it, however, almost without exception, as evidence that "the Establishment" was taking their thing over. The more optimistic saw in the trend a portent of ultimate victory. The counter culture, wrote Andrew Kopkind, had grown out of the "vinyl and aerosol institutions that carry all, the inane and destructive values of privatism, competition, commercialism, profitability and elitism." He conceded, however, that since the new culture had yet to produce its own, alternative institutions on a mass scale, it must be content with feeding the old system "with rock and dope and love and openness," so as to receive these precious gifts back "from Columbia Records or Hollywood or Bloomingdale's"—or, in other words, from the very "vinyl and aerosol institutions" that the new culture was supposed to be superseding.

Others were unable to foresee any such spectacular conversion of the plastic Babylon. "So effective has the rock industry been in encouraging the spirit of optimistic youth takeover," wrote Michael Lydon in a bitter little essay called *Rock for Sale*, "that rock's truly hard political edge, its constant exploration of the varieties of youthful frustration, has been ignored and softened. Rock musicians, like their followers, have always been torn between the obvious pleasures that America held out and the price paid for them. Rock and roll is not revolutionary music, because it has never gotten beyond articulation of this paradox."

It was true enough that rock musicians made a beeline for the obvious pleasures of fame and fortune, and true, too, that many of them paid full price for them in the coinage of neurosis, crackup, and overdose. It is less clear that more than a handful of them ever had much of a hard political edge. Each of the three superstars of the sixties, as it happens, put himself on record on this point with brutal clarity.

"I was much more political before I started music," said Mick Jagger. "At the London School of What's-'is-Name, I was big on it, big arguments and thumping on tables—like everybody in *college*, man."

"Even though you've more or less retired from political and social protest," Nat Hentoff asked Bob Dylan in an interview for *Playboy* in 1966, "can you conceive of any circumstances that might persuade you to reinvolve yourself?"

"No," was Dylan's answer, "not unless all the people in the world disappeared."

"You say you want a revolution," sang John Lennon, "well, you can count me out."

Janis Joplin was of almost the same mind. "My music isn't supposed to make you riot," she once said. "It's supposed to make you fuck."

Rock music was never, except in the minds of a handful of its adherents, an attack on the values of "privatism, competition, commercialism, profitability and elitism." By the end of the decade it was hard even for them to deny that it had become a glorification of each and every one of those.

3

Like the counter culture itself, the underground press of the sixties
could trace its pedigree back to the handful of bohemian intellectuals and
political radicals who held out against the consensus of the late 1950s.
Like rock music, it developed as it did because of technological innova-
tions. But it caught on because in the high years of the Great Schism,
from 1964 to 1969, millions of people no longer believed what the television networks and the established papers and magazines were telling them.

The grandfather of the underground papers was *The Village Voice*,
which first appeared in January 1956. Norman Mailer was one of its
founders and wrote a column for the first eighteen issues, after which he
fell out with the other editors. "They wanted it to be successful," he complained later; "I wanted it to be outrageous." It did in fact become immensely successful only after it had ceased to be outrageous: which only
goes to show that the consensus of the time was real enough. But it did
make one crucial connection. The socialist weeklies of the Old Left had
been remorselessly heavy in style and timidly puritan about such matters
as drugs, art and sexual freedom. The *avant-garde* magazines, on the
other hand, were utterly apolitical. What was new about the *Voice* was
that it always understood that the hip style and the nascent civil rights
and peace movements had their sources in the same emotions. Its stance,
however, was analogous to that of the folk songs of protest that were being
sung around the corner from the *Voice*'s office; like them, it had a minority audience mainly concentrated in what had become the very prosperous
heirs of New York radicalism. By the middle sixties, the heartland of the
*Voice*'s readership had moved uptown from Greenwich Village to the
West Side of Manhattan. In the same years two publications that combined superb journalistic quality with a consistently radical stance
acquired great influence with the same educated, upper-middle-class
readership: *The New York Review of Books*, closely associated with major
New York publishing houses, and *I. F. Stone's Weekly*, which became
more and more widely admired by journalists within the established media
the more often its dogged skepticism about the Johnson administration
proved justified.

But both the review and the newsletter were created by men (and
women) trained in the old media. The possibility of an entirely new kind
of journalism, made by a new kind of journalist for a new readership, was
opened up by the development, also originally in 1956, of photo-offset
typesetting. Photo offset did away with the need for expensive printing

plant and for highly skilled linotype operators on high union wages. Any
intelligent eighteen-year-old could learn in a couple of days to make up a
page with bold headlines and elaborate artwork, and after about two thousand copies, an attractive, professional-looking paper produced by photo
offset was cheaper than mimeograph. Even so, the two papers that pioneered the true underground press of the late sixties by using this new
technology both had their roots in the older traditions of dissent, one in
the New York Marxist Left and the other in the Beat bohemia of the Bay
Area.

Art Kunkin, the founder of the Los Angeles *Free Press*, was educated
at the New School for Social Research in New York; he was on the national committee of the Socialist Party; he was active in civil rights demonstrations in the early days of CORE. Then he went out to California
and worked as a machinist. In the late fifties he started a small left-wing
print shop, and later he did some journalistic work for a Mexican-
American paper in East Los Angeles. It sounds like a jumbled career, but
it couldn't have been better chosen if he had been consciously preparing
himself for running an underground paper. His years on the Left had disillusioned him with the old radical papers, such as *The Militant*, which sub-
ordinated every other subject to the class struggle. His shift work as a machinist had left him free to spend hours in the Los Angeles coffee houses,
getting to know the people who would read, write, sell and advertise in the
*Free Press*. And from his print shop he had learned that you could produce five thousand copies of an eight-page paper for $125. Above all, when
Kunkin launched the *Free Press* in May 1964—before Mississippi, before
the escalation of the Vietnam War, six months before the Free Speech
Movement, and before the word psychedelic had been coined—he had already sensed that a new community of dissent was coming into existence
in California. When I asked him why he started the *Free Press*, he answered: "I wanted to find some way of connecting the various aspects of
this community together."

Max Scherr is a melancholy-looking man, with a straggling beard
down to the middle of his chest like an eminent Victorian author. He was
already forty years old when he founded the Berkeley *Barb*, in 1965. He
had practiced law for a few years in Baltimore before he went into the
Navy in World War II. After demobilization he studied sociology at
Berkeley, and in the early sixties he was running a bar in Berkeley called
the Steppenwolf. Scherr is proud that he discovered Hermann Hesse, as he
was to discover so many other trends, ahead of the herd. The *Barb* started
out as, in a loose sort of way, the Vietnam Day Committee's paper, in the
days when Jerry Rubin, still a political militant and not yet a Yippie, was
planning to stop the troop trains. Scherr's reason for starting a paper was

simple: he got tired of having to walk down to the campus every day to find out what was going on. His formula was simple, too: he suspected there were a lot of people in Berkeley who were interested in the same things as he was. He proved to be right.

In 1965 and 1966 the new papers sprang up like mushrooms in the lush manure of bad news. Their epidemiology followed the familiar pattern. The capitals of the counter culture in California and New York came first, with the *Oracle* in the Haight-Ashbury and the *East Village Other*. Then the big university centers: the Boston *Phoenix*, *The Paper* in East Lansing, home of Michigan State. Then the metropolitan cities away from the East and West coasts: the *Seed* in Chicago, the *Fifth Estate* in Detroit, the *Great Speckled Bird* in Atlanta. By 1968 there was hardly a city or a campus of any size in the country that did not boast at least one underground paper. Their mortality rate was fairly high, but by the early 1970s it was calculated that there were three–four hundred underground or alternative papers, with a total of some 9 million readers.

In 1962 a group of liberal Catholic laymen began to publish a review called *Ramparts*. Originally it was mainly literary, printing poetry by John Berryman and Conrad Aiken as well as by Allen Ginsberg and Lawrence Ferlinghetti, and its political aims stopped short at chiding the hierarchy for its reticence on such issues as racism, poverty and nuclear weapons. In October 1964, however—the month after the birth of the Free Speech Movement—it changed its format, and began to tackle major political stories. *Ramparts* was in the forefront of the revival of investigative journalism, which had virtually atrophied in conventional U.S. newspapers except for periodic razzias against trivial corruption in local politics. The recurrent themes of *Ramparts'* concern were the civil rights struggle and the Vietnam War, but a survey of the major articles it published over the next four and a half years is a sound guide to the evolving political interests of the counter culture. In 1964 and 1965 *Ramparts* printed long, committed reports from Selma, from Mississippi and from Harlem. In July 1965 it published Robert Scheer's classic analysis of the "Vietnam lobby"; in April 1966 it revealed the involvement of Michigan State University in training President Diem's secret police in South Vietnam; and in January 1967, in an illustrated twenty-five-page report called "the Children of Vietnam," it did much to set off national discussion of how U.S. tactics in the war were causing unnecessary civilian casualties.

Gradually *Ramparts'* political interests broadened from the specific issues of racism and war to a more generalized suspicion of "the system." In March 1967 it published perhaps the most influential scoop of the decade: an exposé of how the National Student Association had been secretly financed for fifteen years by the CIA. In 1968 it followed that with its last two major coups: the revelation that the CIA had engineered the death of Che Guevara, and the publication of his diary. Over this same period *Ramparts* also showed a remarkable flair for social trends and fashions. To take examples almost at random, it published the first major articles on Marshall McLuhan, on LSD, on the hippies, the Black Panthers (whose Eldridge Cleaver was a *Ramparts* editor for a time), and on the women's liberation movement.

Unlike *Ramparts*, which always aspired to a national readership, the proliferating underground papers were essentially neighborhood papers. Their small ads provided the basic network of information for those who lived in the East Village, in Berkeley, in the Haight-Ashbury or in Chicago's Old Town: they were sold by hand at street corners. They also served a community that was defined by its decision to live the new life; and so they provided such useful information as where to live, and whom you could live with, as well as what was on at the neighborhood movies and how to get a ride to a rock concert. The *Barb*'s Dr. Hip Pocrates, and a hundred imitators, offered advice on the little inconveniences of liberation: what to do if you got pregnant, or if the dog swallowed some marijuana, and how to cure nonspecific vaginitis. They catered to their readers' inexhaustible fascination with drugs: the Los Angeles *Free Press* never fully recovered from the effects of a $25-million lawsuit brought against it by the state of California for identifying some hundreds of its undercover narcotics agents by name. At their best, they also reported superbly the news of the community: the *Free Press*'s coverage of the Watts riot and the *Barb*'s coverage of the People's Park episode were models, because virtually every bystander was not only a reader but a potential reporter. This was not only community journalism, it was participatory journalism. At its best, it produced perceptive and moving reporting. At its worst, it was a prescription for exhibitionism, parochialism, lying and chaos.

In the years from 1965 to 1968 those who lived in all the little communities of dissent still felt that they also lived in a larger community. Those who went to rock concerts and bought waterbeds also wanted to know what was "really" happening in Vietnam and in South America and in Washington. There was exhilaration in the work of the best of the underground journalists. It was as if they were digging up a mint-new world that had been hidden by the world they told you about in sociology classes and on the nightly news. It was logical that there should come into existence an alternative wire service to help the alternative press report this alternative world.

It was in the summer of 1966 that the idea was first floated in the offices of the *East Village Other*, and at a conference the next Easter at

Stinson Beach, north of San Francisco, eight papers, including the *Barb* and the *Free Press*, agreed to form the Underground Press Syndicate, in order to communicate "news that the middle-class press won't print or can't find." There were ambitious plans for national clearing houses to distribute underground features and underground advertising, and there was to be a free exchange of all materials among member papers. "Copyright," wrote John Sinclair in the syndicate's directory, "is just another bullshit Western ego trip and a capitalistic greed-scheme. Nobody can own the fucking words."

Sinclair was one of the Universal Men of the counter culture. He was the manager of the MC5 rock group, and introduced them, so one of its members once explained, "to the whole concept of energy which is essentially, man, if you take everything in the universe and break it down, you can only go as far as energy." A photograph of the MC5, utilizing its energy in collective intercourse with a groupie, and published in the *Barb*, nearly brought the end for that enterprising journal. Sinclair went on to found the White Panther Party, dedicated to bringing the revolution "by all means necessary, including rock music, smoking dope and fucking in the streets."

In 1967 the underground media took the next logical organizing step. Two student editors, Ray Mungo and Marshall Bloom, founded Liberation News Service. Its coverage of the march on the Pentagon that October was used by more than one hundred papers. But, within a few months, a bitter factional dispute had broken out among LNS's staff, a dispute that was both a classic example of the dilemma the underground media faced after 1968 and a forewarning of the ultimate disintegration of the counter culture itself.

When it was started, in 1967, LNS reflected the hip, rather than the radical, attitude. The liberation that interested it most was inside people's heads. One faction on the staff demanded that the news service should commit itself more heavily to radical politics, and specifically to the SDS position. The arguments grew so bitter that, in the summer of 1968, Marshall Bloom, who took the antipolitical side, walked off with the printing equipment and physically moved LNS to a farmhouse in western Massachusetts. Depressed over a pending prison sentence for draft resistence, Bloom later committed suicide. A rump of LNS stayed in New York, little more than an appendage to what by then had become only one among several quarreling factions of SDS.

"And so it went," Ray Mungo wrote sadly much later. "The college editors were interested mostly in campus revolution, the pacifists in the war, the freaks in cultural revolution and cultural purity. . . . Our glorious scheme of joining together the campus editors, the Communists, the

Trots, the hippies, the astrology freaks, the pacifists, the SDS kids, the black militants, the Mexican-American liberation fighters, and all their respective journals, was reduced to ashes."

What was happening from 1968 onward was that the progressive fragmentation of the underground culture was reflected in the underground press. The whole style of the counter culture, informal, participatory, and yet intensely concerned with the ethics of action, encouraged the constant quarrels, mutinies and defections that plagued every underground paper. Almost always, issues of principle were invoked; almost always, personalities were also involved. The more closely a paper approached the ideal of apostolic simplicity, eliminating bureaucracy and functioning as a commune of brothers and sisters, the more certain it was that editorial disagreements would turn into personal rancor, and vice versa. On the other hand, where the old capitalist Adam survived, that could mean trouble, too. In the summer of 1969, for example, the staff of the *Barb* mutinied against Max Scherr. The ostensible issue was a demand for participatory democracy in editorial decisions. Scherr refused, saying, "A committee of friends is still a committee," an almost sacrilegious proposition to those of the SDS faith. Friends they might be, but behind the mutiny there was resentment that the staff was working for no more than the legal minimum wage, while they suspected, not without some reason, that Scherr was becoming a rich man.

As the radical movements proliferated and new causes competed with each other for the attention, the support and the money of the radical community, each movement and cause brought new papers into existence. Originally, for example, SDS published the intellectually distinguished *New Left Notes*, showing underground influence in format and style but a serious political review in content. Then local SDS chapters started their own papers, such as *Notes from Maggie's Farm*, in Ohio, its name taken from a Dylan song. By 1969 the Weathermen (their name taken from another Dylan song) were tussling openly with the Progressive Labor faction in SDS for the body of *New Left Notes*. The Black Panthers had their paper, *Black Panther*, and then, when the Eldridge Cleaver faction broke with Huey Newton, they started their own paper and called it *Right On!* There were high school underground papers, and underground papers on army bases, and American Indian papers, and *Chicano* papers in Spanish, and truly underground papers in prisons. There were homosexual papers, one with the happy name of *Fag Rag*. Then a whole crop of women's papers came along; one of them was called *Off Our Backs!*

As the underground papers got angrier, and more numerous, and less united, and smaller, they began to run into economic pressures. By the summer of 1972, the plight of LNS summed up the plight of many of its subscribers. A desperate notice appeared in the *Radical Media Bulletin Board:*

HELP US IN OUR HOUR OF NEED!

LNS is flat broke. We have to pay an $800 phone bill tomorrow. (All those collect calls for antiwar actions piled up.) We'll make that, but there won't be any money for lunch or dinner tomorrow or salaries, and last week everybody got $20 instead of $35. All in all we've got about $2,000 of back bills and worst of all we're out of film.

The underground papers that survived in the end were those that found some way of making themselves useful to the rich, capitalist society they had failed to overthrow. *Rolling Stone* continued to thrive on advertising from CBS and the other record companies, and it was painfully noticeable that its tone was more kindly, even deferential about even the most mediocre new issues than on any other subject. Stewart Brand's *Whole Earth Catalogue,* bible of the flight from commercialism, was sold to Random House and duly became a national best-seller. The *New Times* in Phoenix raised one hundred thousand dollars by a stock issue, helped by local financiers, few of whom, no doubt, could be called totally committed to a radical position. And the *Straight Creek Journal,* in Denver, hit upon an even more ingenious scheme: it sold part of its stock to businessmen who needed tax losses.

Saddest of all the ways the underground press found to make its middle age comfortable in the Age of Nixon was by printing sex ads. Art Kunkin's dream when he founded the *Free Press* had been that it would help to connect people together, so that those who were trying to liberate their lives could communicate about new music, new films, new ideas in psychology and religion. Instead, the *Free Press* ended up connecting people together in the most coarsely literal way:

*Institution of Sexual Intercourse.*
*(No tests required.) Come and learn to make love. The hottest lovemakers in town.*

*The Academy of Nude Wrestling invites you to wrestle with a beautiful nude girl.*

*Eager young sexy girls make your sex life* HOT *and* NASTY. *Private rooms.*

A large proportion of the hundreds of ads in the classified section of the same issue were no less blatantly commercial. "Get laid! $5 tells you where," was the bluntest. "Perverts, Fetishists, Freaks and their admirers," said another, "somebody had to do it, so we're compiling the most disgust-

ing book in the world." Sometimes the approach was marginally more subtle. But subtle or blunt, straightforward or perverted, heterosexual or homosexual, it was plain that a very substantial proportion of the *Free
Press*'s revenue was derived not just from sex, which would perhaps have
been compatible with its original ideals of liberation, but from the marketing expenditures of the commercial sex industry. The *Barb*, the Boston
*Phoenix*, and many other surviving underground papers, in becoming dependent on this type of advertising, in effect made themselves cogs in the
pornography industry. From 1969 on, control of the *Free Press* slipped
gradually into the hands of one of the two biggest pornography tycoons in
Los Angeles. It now belongs to two San Diego businessmen who are interested in it purely as an investment. It seems something more than an
ironic footnote to the story of what began as an attempt to liberate people's lives from the chains of sexual taboos and money.

4

The years from 1965 to 1968 were years of polarization for America
partly because they were years of unity for the counter culture. In the beginning, those who played rock music or took LSD, even those who
smoked marijuana, bought a rock album or read an underground newspaper, felt themselves part of the same great army as those who went to
jail for resisting the draft or dropped out to work for radical political
change. Indeed the cultural revolutionaries and the political radicals often
were the same people, in the beginning. They had a single enemy, as they
saw it in the first, innocent days, whether they called it capitalism, or the
System, or Pig Nation, or Amerika. There was a conviction that all rebellions, however trivial or bizarre, were parts of one grand war of liberation
against the infanticidal thing that Carl Oglesby, the politician, called
Leviathan, and Allen Ginsberg, the poet, called Moloch.

It was in 1967 that the underground papers first began to talk about
"the Revolution." The confusion between the political and the cultural
was compounded by the popularity of this metaphor. At its silliest, it led
to the sad delusion that you could change society by smoking marijuana
and listening to amplified electric guitars (provided they were loud
enough). Neither Ginsberg's mantras nor the Fugs' chords budged the
walls of the Pentagon. It was a revolution that existed only in rhetoric, a
linguistic escalation born of the radicals' shame at their impotence to do
anything in practice either to help the blacks or to end the war, let alone
to change any society but their own.

In political terms, the counter culture's claim to be revolutionary was always tenuous. Even in its political aspect, it was a subjective culture, more interested in the ethics and feelings of its members than in changing the outside world; more concerned for the morality of American policies toward Vietnam, for example, than by the future fate of the actual Vietnamese. Even the political radicals, we saw, had often been formed by a sense of alienation from a society that seemed to have gone tragically wrong in moral terms, rather than by adherence to even the broadest of programs for action.

The schism between political radicals and cultural rebels opened very gradually. As early as 1965 the underground papers were already showing signs of boredom with political issues. In the same year, Dylan, admittedly always a pathfinder, turned from his political ballads to the smoke rings of his mind. Increasingly, those who were serious about political change became exasperated by the dreamy narcissism of those who sought a personal salvation, while those whose hearts were set on a new consciousness and a new style of living were repelled by the obsessional commitments, the squalid compromises, of those whose goal was revolution.

That was one axis: between the search for salvation and the hope of revolution. But there was another sense in which both the heavily committed political radicals and those who took seriously the search for a private salvation were tiny minorities surrounded by the half-serious multitudes of their occasional followers. While an inner minority plunged deeper and deeper into alienation from society either through commitment to political extremism or through withdrawal to the north woods of Oregon or to some Oregon of the mind, for the majority the counter culture soon degenerated into a complex of fashions and attitudes. The fashions and the attitudes were not without powerful symbolic content. It was not for nothing that the mystic signs for peace and love became the most banal decorative motifs. You could even say that if the counter culture failed to change American society in any more definite way, it did make both militarism and racism unfashionable. Still, by the end of the decade, for a majority the counter culture had degenerated into a mere youth cult. Its values were often no longer determined by the aspiration to build a freer society so much as by an Oedipal hostility to the older generation.

In a song written by Jim Morrison of The Doors in 1967, and much praised at the time, "the killer" comes to a door (or to a Door?) and looks inside:

> "Father?"
> "Yes, son?"
> "I want to kill you.
> "Mother, I want to. . . ."*

* Lyrics from "The End," words by Jim Morrison. Copyright © 1967 Doors Music Co. Used by permission of the author and publisher.

"I think kids should kill their parents," said Abbie Hoffman.

The one idea that seemed never to occur to either side in these Freudian wars of the suburbs was how much the parents and the children were alike. The children said they loathed the uniformity of the suburbs, where your personality was defined by the size and style of your house and by the make and year of your car. But they allowed the record industry and the fashion trade to define their collective personality every bit as rigidly as Detroit had ever done for their parents. Their long hair, their blue denim, were every bit as much a uniform as the crew cuts and chinos of the fifties. Even their alienation from their parents may have owed more than they realized to their similarity. If children felt that their parents didn't understand them, it may have been less because of any deep clash of values than because the parents were often too busy having a good time or getting on in the world to spare much time for their children.

Tom Wolfe described how it felt to be a middle-class teen-ager in the fifties, cruising in Dad's car on the new highway on the edge of town, looking for some action:

> The first wave of the most extraordinary kids in the history of the world . . . with all this Straight 6 and V-8 power underneath and all this neon glamour overhead, which somehow tied in with the technological superheroics of the jet, TV, atomic subs, ultrasonics—Postwar American suburbs, glorious world! . . . To be Superkids! The world's first generation of the little devils—feeling immune, beyond calamity. One's parents remembered the sloughing common order, War & Depression—but Superkids remembered only the emotional surge of the great payoff, when nothing was common any longer—the Life! A glorious place, a glorious age, I tell you!

The children who were born in those same postwar suburbs and were of college age in 1965 to 1968 did not, perhaps, feel themselves beyond calamity, even though they enjoyed a greater immunity from the sloughing common order than their parents had. They certainly had the conviction that they were "the most extraordinary kids in the history of the world." They were Superkids, Mark II.

By the end of the sixties it was plain enough that whatever the people who flocked to rock concerts or read underground newspapers wanted, it would be doing violence to the language to call it revolution. Their problem was the no-problem society—not of the United States but of the relatively privileged part of American society from which they came. They were bored because there was no problem about money, no problem about sex, no problem about college, and no great problem if you dropped out; only the inescapable bleakness of being young and insignificant, a pebble on the infinite beach of America, but a pebble bombarded with information about the gratifications of others. They turned to the life style of the counter culture for all the things they had missed in the sheltered, affluent suburbs where they grew up: excitement, purpose, a feeling of community, and some measure of individual worth. When Mick Jagger swayed in the spotlight and promised them, "We're gonna get some satisfaction," dams burst. A frightening intensity of emotion flooded normally sulky faces. It was hardly the fault of the musicians if all they had to give was excitement without purpose, an illusion of community, when the individual's yearnings were lost in the contrived explosions of mass hysteria. It wasn't revolution; it was only show business. But, then, bored, lonely, angry though they might intermittently be with a world they never made, the Superkids of the second generation wanted to change it as little as their parents had. Telegraph Avenue was indeed the child of Madison Avenue.

# The End of Consensus

In the early spring of 1968 there was a heady scent on the air: the smell of impending change. Everywhere, assumptions that had gone unchallenged since 1945 were being called into question. Institutions that had long looked invincible cracked and crumbled. Spontaneous shoots of freedom in Prague had pushed up through the ugly gray concrete of the Soviet system, and in those spring months it looked as if they had cracked it for good. In France a coalition of students and labor unions, with apparent ease, toppled the colossus who had dwarfed Europe for just ten years. As sober and cautious men around the world lifted their heads from their own, immediate problems, the realization dawned on them that the unthinkable might be on the point of becoming reality: The United States might lose a war. The dollar might be devalued. The United States, the bastion and exemplar of stability since 1945, might be torn apart. People asked themselves in all earnestness whether they were living through another 1848, a second Year of Revolutions.

It was true enough that in the United States all the clouds that had been gathering since the spring of 1965—the growing strength of the peace movement, the growing student militancy, the growing alienation of the black ghettoes—all burst together in what seemed a single electric storm of terrifying force. As in 1963 and 1965, the threads of war, of racial conflict and of presidential politics seemed to have been woven together into a single, intricately constructed national drama on an epic scale. The triple crisis that had opened with the confrontation in Birmingham, the fall of Diem, and the assassination in Dallas now reached its third and most ominous climax.

On January 30, forty-eight hours before the Tet festival, the Vietnamese New Year, Hanoi abruptly dropped its patient strategy of protracted war and threw all its resources into a gambler's throw for sudden victory.

Mobilizing more than eighty thousand front-line troops, the North Vietnamese and the Viet Cong attacked virtually every city and town of any importance in the country simultaneously. The Administration claimed later that it had been expecting an offensive. Later still, it also alleged that the CIA had deliberately underestimated the enemy's strength. In any case, the timing, the scale, and the ferocity of the attacks took the American high command completely by surprise.

For some weeks, feinting a repeat of his famous victory over the French at Dienbienphu, the North Vietnamese commander, General Vo Nguyen Giap, had been investing the American outpost at Khe Sanh. Now, while every military pundit in the United States was still dusting off the clippings from 1954, Giap reversed his tactics, sidestepped the prepared position, and walked almost unopposed into the northern provinces of South Vietnam, capturing Hué, the historic capital of Annam, and flying the flag of the Viet Cong from its citadel. While U.S. troops up and down the country improvised the defense of their own camps, Viet Cong suicide squads broke into the presidential palace, the national radio station, and even the American Embassy compound in Saigon.

When Lyndon Johnson and General Westmoreland later claimed that the Tet offensive had been a military disaster for the Communists, they were greeted with general derision. Yet there was some truth in what they said. Once the U.S. forces had regained their balance, they proceeded to inflict appalling casualties on the Viet Cong, and in the process on any civilian Vietnamese, whatever their loyalties, who happened to get in the way. The guerrillas had not fully recovered from these losses, not so much in raw numbers as in quality, by the time of their second major surprise offensive, in 1972. What was even more discouraging from Hanoi's point of view was that the general uprising that their theoretical analysis led them to predict, and which they had briefed their men to expect, never happened.

But if the Tet offensive was a tactical setback for Hanoi, strategically it was the most brilliant of victories. It sowed the seeds of demoralization in the U.S. forces. Increasingly, this expressed itself in corruption, drug use, insubordination, racial brawls, "fragging"—attacks on officers by their own men with fragmentation grenades and other weapons—and in the end in actual mutinous disregard of orders, to the point where in May 1971, even as cautious an observer as McGeorge Bundy concluded, "Extrication from Vietnam is now the necessary precondition of the renewal of the U. S. Army as an institution." It is hard to go much closer than that to an admission of defeat.

At the same time, the shock of Tet intensified the ferocity of the military's behavior toward the Vietnamese. Long before Tet, sheer frustration at the difficulty of fighting a guerrilla enemy who lived among the people —in Mao's phrase, like a fish in water—had suggested to some American officers a drastic solution: drain off the water.

This frustration was reinforced in the worst officers by a callous contempt for the lives of "gooks" and "slopes," and in the best by a proud determination that no problem was too tough for Americans. It was played upon by the obsession with numerical criteria for success which reached all the way up through the military bureaucracy to its civilian masters, Robert McNamara and Walt Rostow.

Already in 1966 and 1967, these factors had produced ruthless "free-fire" and "free-strike" tactics, torture of prisoners, napalm and defoliation, and a moral climate in which such ambitious officers as George S. Patton III encouraged their units to "kill, kill, kill," and helicopter pilots hunted down scurrying civilians like Texas ranch hands shooting jackrabbits from a Jeep.

After Tet, anger and fear, added to frustration and indifference, made up a prescription for atrocity. It was on March 16, 1968, some ten weeks after the outbreak of the Tet offensive, that a company of the notoriously shaky American Division dropped like messengers of death on the hamlet of My Lai 4 in Quang Ngai province. Eighteen months later, in a far less publicized but even more sinister case, a court-martial at Long Binh altered the conviction of one Lieutenant Duffy for murder to a conviction for manslaughter. Duffy admitted that he had kept a prisoner tied to a stake all night and then ordered or allowed his sergeant to shoot him in the morning. But he pleaded that it was his understanding that it was army policy to maximize the "body count" by taking no prisoners. Four other officers so testified in his defense. The court's decision can only be taken as a tacit acknowledgment of a systematic policy of ignoring the laws of war and the Geneva Conventions. This, too, may be counted among the consequences of Tet.

The immediate, decisive effect of the Viet Cong's gamble, however, was not in South Vietnam but in the United States. "I was surprised and disappointed that the enemy's efforts produced such a dismal effect on various people inside government, . . ." wrote Lyndon Johnson. "Hanoi must have been delighted; it was exactly the reaction they sought." Oddly enough, he was wrong. Many months later, a North Vietnamese official confessed to an American delegate in Paris that the Tet offensive had been planned with little thought of American political repercussions. The objective had been to bring down the government in Saigon. The result was to bring down the government in Washington.

In times of crisis it sometimes happens that a single image, a tiny radioactive particle of the truth, has the power to start a chain reaction in millions of brains. These sudden illuminations of the truth or, rather, of one part of the truth, have been one of the *Leitmotive* of this book. The power of television, in particular, to change a significant fraction of public opinion overnight by emitting one of these political charged particles does a lot to explain why people feel they live in an age of accelerated change. But television does not have a monopoly of this power of political radiation. Sometimes a still picture or even a phrase can flash through the nation with the same effect. Within a few hours of the outbreak of the Tet offensive not one but three of these splinters of the truth of what was happening had embedded themselves in the minds of millions of Americans. The process was not logical, rational or consistent. But it was decisive.

The first was not a visual image at all. It was a remark made by an American artillery officer after half the town of Ben Tre, in the Mekong Delta, had been destroyed by American shelling, and it was recorded in an Associated Press wire-service message. "We had to destroy it," the officer said, "in order to save it."

The second was a picture, though it was not, so far as I have been able to discover, shown on television. It was published in *Life* magazine, and it showed the mission co-ordinator of the U. S. Embassy in Saigon, George Jacobson, looking out of his bedroom window with an automatic pistol in his hand. In the very sanctuary of American power in Vietnam, he was going to have to fend for himself.

The third, and most powerful, image was conveyed both by live film, shown on NBC, and by still pictures taken at the same moment by Eddie Adams of the AP. As the NBC bureau chief in Saigon described the film in a telex to his office in New York:

> A VC OFFICER WAS CAPTURED. THE TROOPS BEAT HIM. THEY BRING HIM TO [Brigadier General Nguyen Ngoc] LOAN WHO IS HEAD OF SOUTH VIETNAMESE NATIONAL POLICE. LOAN PULLS OUT HIS PISTOL, FIRES AT THE HEAD OF THE VC, THE VC FALLS, ZOOM ON HIS HEAD, BLOOD SPRAYING OUT. IF HE HAS IT ALL ITS STARTLING STUFF.

The impact was so startling, in fact, that when battle-hardened producers and reporters watched it screened in NBC's New York headquarters they were speechless, and for reasons of "taste" trimmed seventeen seconds of the bleeding corpse from the film. With this omission it was seen by an estimated 20 million viewers. Adams' simultaneous still picture was carried on the front page of virtually every newspaper in the country. Its impact was arguably the turning point of the war, for it coincided with a dramatic shift in American public opinion, and may well have helped to cause it.

From time to time, the Gallup poll had been asking its sample whether they were "hawks" or "doves." The graph line of both groups makes one of the most startling jumps ever recorded on a national public opinion poll. Between February and March 1968 the doves jumped from around 25 per cent to over 40 per cent. At the same time, the hawks dwindled from 60 per cent to 40 per cent. After three years of war, roughly one American out of every five changed his or her mind about it in a single month. That is one crude measure of the effect of Tet. Behind that apparently simple, massive shift of opinion, there were swirling currents and crosscurrents. But that was less obvious at the time than the fact that where, before Tet, a majority of the American people had supported the war, now, suddenly, a majority opposed it.

It did not take long for that shift in opinion to be translated into a new political reality, both in electoral terms and in the closed politics of presidential Washington. On March 6 the regular Democrats in New Hampshire put an advertisement in the local press saying, "The Communists in Vietnam are watching the New Hampshire primary." If so, Hanoi must have been overjoyed. For on March 12, in the first and most publicized primary of the new presidential contest, if Republican crossover voters were counted, the President of the United States led Senator Eugene McCarthy, clearly identified as the peace candidate and the leader of a movement to "dump Johnson," by less than one full percentage point. Four days later, Robert Kennedy, the Hamlet of Hickory Hill, ended months of hesitation by announcing that he, too, was a candidate for the Democratic nomination. By March 29, the President's confidential advisers had taken soundings in Wisconsin, the state with the next primary, and had told him that he must expect to be beaten there by McCarthy by as much as two votes to one.

It was not only the bewildered French-Canadian mill workers of New Hampshire, the German farmers and Polish factory workers of Wisconsin, who were shaken by Tet. The leaders of the foreign-policy Establishment prided themselves on their personal intelligence sources, their overview of the world. They had been the staunchest champions of the President's policy. Indeed he could have complained (though he never did) that he had adopted it partly to guarantee with them his credentials as a statesman. Now they, too, were having second thoughts.

In the summer of 1965, faced with the first serious dissent within the upper ranks of his own administration on the war, from George Ball, the President had formalized the support of the Establishment by inviting a group of senior men, such as Dean Acheson, Clark Clifford, and John J.

McCloy, all of whom had played leading roles in laying down and carrying out the policy of containment in the early years of the Cold War, to consult with him. Unanimously they supported his policy against Ball's cogently argued skepticism; earnestly they urged him to stand firm. "They were for bombing the be-Jesus out of them," one eyewitness recalled.

Once more, in November 1967, the President called in a larger, more formal group of these senior advisers, the Wise Old Men. The Administration was in a buoyantly optimistic mood. Only a few days before, Ambassador Ellsworth Bunker and General Westmoreland had been back in Washington talking publicly about "light at the end of the tunnel" and about the possibility of bringing some troops home soon. Once more, that winter, the Wise Old Men endorsed the President's policy and his optimism.

Then came Tet.

As early as February 7, General Westmoreland, while stoutly maintaining that the Viet Cong had met with a disaster, was calling for studies of how many more troops would be needed to beat them now than would have been needed before the disaster. No question, now, of sending men home. By February 25, General Wheeler (chairman of the Joint Chiefs of Staff) was on his way back to Washington from a hasty visit to Vietnam with a request for some 206,000 men.

On March 1, Clark Clifford was sworn in as Secretary of Defense. The President had chosen him not only as one of his own oldest personal advisers but also as a hard-headed hawk who would not suffer from the tortuous doubts and scruples that had latterly plagued Robert McNamara and led the President to fire him in November.

Clifford had been a hawk all along. In many private meetings with the President he had consistently supported the war and argued against ending the bombing. A tour of Southeast Asia in the summer of 1967 had sowed the first seeds of concern in his mind, and after Tet he actually hinted at some of this concern during his Senate confirmation hearings. But these were only hints.

The day after he was sworn in, Clifford ordered a comprehensive review of policy in the Pentagon. He soon learned two things: that many of the civilian officials there now had strong doubts about the wisdom of sending more troops, and also about the bombing; and that the Joint Chiefs of Staff, who did not admit to sharing these doubts, nevertheless seemed unable to give straight answers to his questions. The report that this review produced still did not bring Clifford's change of mind into the open. Sent to the White House on March 4, it accepted the need to send some twenty thousand more troops to Vietnam immediately and deferred a decision as to the rest. But, in fact, by that time Clifford had changed his mind. He set himself to change the President's.

It was Clifford, whether he fully foresaw the result or not, who suggested to the President at one of his Tuesday working lunches in mid-March that he should reconvene the Wise Men. On the evening of March 25, they foregathered at the State Department for briefings and dinner. The next day, they were to go over to the White House and meet the President.

Dean Acheson was there, with Arthur Dean, George Ball, McGeorge Bundy, Douglas Dillon, Robert Murphy and Cyrus Vance—all down from their law offices, foundations or banks in New York. The President's friend Abe Fortas, then a Supreme Court justice, was there, and so were two legendary generals from World War II, Omar N. Bradley and Matthew B. Ridgway. Others, who were not less important in their standing in the Establishment, were there by virtue of the office they held in Washington: Dean Rusk, Clark Clifford, Richard Helms of the CIA, Walt Rostow, Nicholas Katzenbach, Henry Cabot Lodge, Averell Harriman, and William Bundy. It was—for those who are moved by the romance of power—a sort of Round Table of the sedentary chivalry of the Cold War, or, if you prefer, a board meeting of the most powerful enterprise on earth. It was also the last occasion on which so many leading members of the Establishment ever found themselves in agreement, and so perhaps in effect the last plenary session of that mythical but once potent body.

They read all the briefing papers. They listened to all the briefings. The next day, with McGeorge Bundy—the man who had first briefed Lyndon Johnson, on board the helicopter from Andrews Air Force Base, on the decisions that had to be taken in Vietnam, and whose advice had been decisive at the moment of escalation—acting as their *rapporteur*, they proceeded to strip the President of their confidence, and perhaps to strip him of his confidence in himself.

They were deeply discouraged by the way military victory seemed to recede into the future like a mirage. They were horrified by the war's failure to meet their own test, as rational men of business: cost effectiveness. They were shaken by the passionate opposition to the war they had encountered in their law partners, their banking correspondents, and in their other, somewhat limited contacts around the country. Some of them were besieged by the moral fervor of their wives and especially their children. All of them, as "internationalists," were appalled at what might happen to the threatened dollar on the world's exchanges. And so they remained faithful to their instinct for the center. The Establishment made a characteristic decision: not to send good money after bad.

The result of the New Hampshire primary, and the prognosis for Wisconsin; the prospect of running against Robert Kennedy; the disillusionment of Clifford, and the defection of the Wise Men; a dozen forgotten problems crowding in on him, such as the tension in the Middle East, in Berlin, and with Korea over the *Pueblo* incident; his own bitter sense of frustration and political isolation, which prevented him from dealing decisively with any of them; his moral tiredness and his wife's protective awareness of it—all these several factors converged to play their part in Lyndon Johnson's decision to announce that he would not seek re-election.

There was another factor, however, which should not be too cynically discounted and which was perhaps decisive in his own mind: his desire to preserve the integrity of the presidency as an office. He had first entered political life more than thirty years earlier by campaigning in favor of Roosevelt's plan to pack the Supreme Court, the boldest assertion up to that date of the primacy of the executive over another branch of government. All his political life, even when he was the embodiment of the power of the Congress, he had watched, and had accepted, the steady growth in presidential power until, for the whole of his generation, it was unchallenged as the supreme symbol of the nation.

Now, in the storms of 1968, the consensus presidency that had emerged in the 1940s and 1950s seemed to be threatened. Naturally he did not blame his own policies. But Lyndon Johnson could not fail to see that he had failed to keep intact the bipartisan foreign policy that had been one of the pillars of the modern presidency. With Robert Kennedy moving to the assault, he had failed in his effort to establish his own legitimacy with the "Kennedy people." The "Roosevelt coalition" in the Democratic Party, which had done so much to put the presidency at the head of the liberal consensus as its chosen instrument, now seemed in danger of disintegration. The Great Society seemed to have fallen a casualty to black frustration and to the war. And so did the prestige of the presidency. The effort to justify the war was responsible in the first place for the "credibility gap." Now public skepticism had spread to other issues. The President no longer had the right to expect that he would be believed. He no longer had the freedom to travel around the country without risking demonstrations, perhaps not without risking actual physical danger. It was as a last bid to save the integrity of the presidency that Johnson decided to abdicate. That was what he meant when he said in his television speech to the nation, "I shall not permit the presidency to be involved in the partisan divisions that are developing." The presidency had always been involved in limited partisanship within the broad consensus; now Lyndon

Johnson thought he saw more dangerous and more irreconcilable divisions ahead.

He spoke on March 31. That same day, the Gallup poll revealed that his popularity had fallen to its lowest level: 35 per cent. Three days later, Lyndon Johnson met Robert Kennedy: as it turned out, for the last time. They faced each other across the cabinet table in the White House in response to the President's offer to brief all major Democratic candidates on the situation. It was a painfully strained occasion. Both men were doing their best to suppress the bitter rivalry each had often felt for the other. Neither was altogether successful. After the formal briefing was over, Senator Kennedy asked about the political situation. Would the President marshal forces against him?

"I expressed it in my speech," Johnson said. "I want to keep the presidency out of this campaign. I'm not that pure. I am that scared. The situation of the country is critical."

The worst had not yet happened.

On March 31, the day of the President's speech, Martin Luther King had preached at the National Cathedral, in Washington. His mood was somber. The technique of nonviolent confrontation which had brought him triumph in Birmingham had not worked in the North. He had just come from Memphis, where he had experienced the worst setback of his career to his faith in the effectiveness of nonviolent tactics. A march he led had turned into an ugly little riot, with young blacks shouting black-power slogans and tossing Molotov cocktails, and police shooting into the crowd. "If nothing else is done to raise ghetto hope," King said in his sermon, "I feel this summer will not only be as bad but worse than last time." He seemed to accept the pessimism of his militant rivals, who warned that, next time, it would be the fire.

On April 4, the next time came. Dr. King was shot, by a white ex-convict named James Earl Ray, in Memphis. Within a quarter of an hour crowds of black people who had heard the news on their transistor radios had gathered at the busiest intersections in every black neighborhood in the United States. They were beside themselves with grief and anger.

"This is it, baby," said one man on upper Fourteenth Street in Washington, a mile or so north of the White House. "The shit is going to hit the fan. We ought to burn this place right down."

By the end of the week, there had been riots in more than a hundred cities. Thirty-seven people had been killed, twelve of them in Washington, where looting crowds of black rioters swarmed through wide swaths of the city, setting fires not only in the ghettoes but in the downtown shopping streets as well. By dawn on April 6, a pall of black smoke from those fires hung over the national monuments. The capital of the United States was under military occupation. For those who had dreamed the dreams of the New Frontier, and shared the hopes of a Great Society, this was perhaps the darkest moment of the entire decade.

In those feverish spring days, the peace movement seemed to have flexed its muscles and driven a President from office. On Robert Kennedy's campaign trips to California, all the groups and forces that normally controlled American life seemed to have been stunned into immobility. A great new coalition of the young, the black, the alienated and the radical seemed to have the strength to sweep Kennedy into the White House. It was an illusion, a tragically short-lived illusion. But, for a moment, it was persuasive. Black militancy, too, seemed to be building up to a climax, perhaps even to an ultimate test of armed strength. Finally, before the end of April, the third and oldest of the three movements that appeared to be uniting to overthrow the *ancien régime* reached its own climax. It was, characteristically, only a climax of rhetorical violence. But that was not immediately obvious to those who had to deal with the "rebellion" at Columbia.

There came an intriguing moment, in the confused guerrilla theater of events on the Columbia campus, when the mayor of New York was deliberating whether to send in police to make arrests. John Lindsay had saved the situation at the beginning of the month by his coolness. After King's murder he had walked with patrician nonchalance and real courage through Harlem streets seething with anger, and it had worked. Now, as if half persuaded by the students' exalted rhetoric, he hesitated to give the arrest order until his representatives had checked with their contacts in the black community that Harlem would not rise in sympathy with Columbia! The mayor of New York was not the only American, in that mad month when anything seemed possible, to ask himself whether the revolution had arrived.

Even for steadier souls, it was hard to get away from the feeling that consensus had now been replaced by polarization: that the nation was splitting, indeed had to an alarming extent already split, into two antagonistic camps with irreconcilable views on almost every issue.

Once, in a private conversation with Robert Kennedy, across his big desk in the Justice Department, back in 1963, I happened to suggest that the future of American politics might lie in polarization between liberals and conservatives. He looked at me sharply and, reaching in the deep bottom drawer of his desk, he fished out a box full of file cards in his own handwriting to show me how much he had read and thought about the question. He proceeded to take issue with me. The gist of his argument was that a nation that was already so deeply divided vertically by race, ethnic origin, religion and geography simply could not afford to be divided horizontally by class and ideology as well.

That was the orthodoxy of consensus. Now, in 1968, just that dangerous division seemed to be appearing. Ironically, Robert Kennedy's own "New Politics" was predicated on something very like the horizontal realignment whose dangers he had warned me against. But he could hardly be blamed for the movement of the political earth beneath his feet. Nor did the realignment take the form of shuffling all the traditional liberals into one party and all the traditional conservatives into the other.

What had happened was that, first, the two issues, Vietnam and civil rights, which—as we have seen—were regarded by most well-informed and right-thinking Americans, as late as the spring of 1963, as peripheral—swelled until they shoved all other matters out of mind. Domestic policy, the whole future of the Great Society, came to be dwarfed by the linked problems of black pauperization and black militancy. All other issues of foreign policy had come to revolve like dead satellites around the blazing question of the Vietnam War.

Second, these two issues themselves were perceived in 1968 and 1969 as evidence that there was a larger question to be answered: Has something gone wrong with America? Had there, indeed, always been something morally flawed about American power and success?

On these questions, the intellectual elite divided in a bitter schism. It raged in university faculties, in newspaper offices, on the boards of foundations. Three hundred and twenty professional economists signed a petition in support of the President's surtax bill; three hundred twenty other economists signed an antisurtax petition, denouncing the President's policy as "an economic Gulf of Tonkin resolution." Almost every other corner of American intellectual life was transformed into a similar bitter debate.

The schism went deeper than mere political disagreement. It was as if, from 1967 on, for several years, two different tribes of Americans experienced the same outward events but experienced them as two quite different realities. A writer in *The Atlantic* put the point well after the October 1967 demonstrations at the Pentagon. Accounts of that happening in the conventional press and in the underground press, he pointed out, simply didn't intersect at any point. It was as if they had been reporting two different events. "The older reporters, who were behind the soldiers' lines, or on the Pentagon roof, or inside the temporary war room, wrote about hippies and Maoists; the kids, on the other side of the line, wrote about the awful brutality of the U.S. marshals. Each wrote with enough half truth to feel justified in excluding the other."

The two parties could soon be distinguished by outward badges, almost by uniforms: by the style of their clothes and the length of their hair. Professor Charles Reich, of the Yale Law School, analyzed the whole country, with the exception of an anachronistic rump of hayseeds and stick-in-the-muds, into two warring cultures, the liberal and the radical, which he called Consciousness II and Consciousness III. His book was a runaway best seller—less, perhaps, because of its intrinsic merits than because people could see the schism all too well and were willing to listen to any theory that offered to explain it.

It was not only those who felt, as Reich apparently did, that the country's problems could be solved if only enough Americans would learn to wear bellbottom pants and to say "Oh, wow!" with the correct intonation who acknowledged that America was fundamentally divided over the question, has something gone morally wrong with America? Conservatives worried over this question as much as radicals. A writer in the October issue of *Fortune*, for example, addressed himself to the "crisis of national perception" and concluded, "The more passionate discussers of the four commanding topics of 1968—Vietnam, poverty, race, and law and order—regard each as a symptom of some deeper and more general moral sickness in contemporary U.S. society."

By that test, the ultimate boss of *Fortune* itself would have to be reckoned among the "passionate discussers." For, early the next year, in a public speech, Hedley Donovan, editor in chief of Time Inc., and as such the heir of Henry Luce, who had proclaimed the American Century less than a quarter of a century before, pronounced this recessional:

> We look out on this world of 1969 as a deeply confused country. It is easy to say that it is the cruel question of Vietnam that has got us so mixed up. . . . But I believe the causes of our confusion go much deeper than Vietnam. Indeed the Vietnam experience . . . has in a sense masked a more fundamental change in the underpinnings of American foreign policy. That change, very simply, is the loss of a working consensus, for the first time in our lives, as to what we think America means.

At about the same time, a professor of journalism at the University of Montana, Nathan Blumberg, summed up in cogent sentences how consensus had yielded to schism:

> It emphatically is not simplistic to suggest that the central political fact of our times is that there are only two sides: Those who do not want to see any fundamental change are pitted against those who find the status quo intolerable. Of course there are degrees and nuances on both sides, but it is useless to deny that when large numbers of our citizens are frustrated and angry with the established system, those who are not on their side are against them. Thus "you are either part of the problem or part of the solution."

# The Discovery of Middle America

"Most censorship on television is self-censorship."
NBC producer Fred Freed.

Can the outcome, for the near future, be in doubt? The people, the majority of the people in the affluent society, are on the side of that which is—not that which can and ought to be.
Herbert Marcuse, "Political Preface"<br>to Eros and Civilization (1966).

In 1968 it did look as if America was being polarized, as if all the issues had to come together as One Big Issue. A struggle of some kind seemed inevitable, as a result of which one of two rival, irreconcilable conceptions of the nation must triumph at the expense of the other.

But that was not what happened. Schism and polarization gave way to fragmentation. By 1973 it was clear that the pattern of the future would be neither revolution nor reaction.

Not that the upheavals that had divided the nation between 1965 and 1968 came to an end in the latter year. On the contrary, the intensity of dissent actually increased. The antiwar demonstrations of November 1969 dwarfed anything of the kind that had happened earlier. At the time of the invasion of Cambodia and the killing of students by the National Guard at Kent State and by police at Jackson State in Mississippi, in May 1970, the country was even more bitterly divided than it had been in the spring of 1968. Among students, a degree of alienation that, before 1969, had been virtually confined to a handful of elite universities—Berkeley, Columbia, Harvard and a few more—had become commonplace in the early seventies. A special Harris survey in 1970 found that 76 per cent of a national sample of students believed that "basic changes in the system"—

whatever that might mean—would be needed to improve the quality of
American life; that 80 per cent of the colleges attended by those interviewed had experienced demonstrations in May 1970; and that 75 per cent
of the students were in favor of the goals of those demonstrations. Indeed
nearly three out of every five students said that they themselves had taken
part in protest actions.

Although there were no ghetto riots on a scale comparable to those in
the spring of 1968, in many cities militant young blacks were engaged in
what amounted to guerrilla warfare against the police. A series of incidents
—the trial of Bobby Seale, the death of George Jackson, the Angela Davis
case and the Attica mutiny—polarized opinion in the most literal sense.
According to preconceptions, each could be taken as confirmation of the
dangers of anarchy or of the dangers of repression. Black separatism,
though by no means universal, became more pronounced. Black opinion,
at least in the inner cities (and in spite of a trickle of middle-class blacks
escaping to the suburbs, that was where most blacks still were), continued
to grow more and more alienated—from the federal government, from
City Hall (except in the handful of cities with black mayors), and from
the institutions of white society generally. In rhetoric, at least, the mood
of the National Black Political Convention held in Gary, Indiana, in February 1972 was far more intransigent than that of any but the most extreme fringe of black leadership in Martin Luther King's lifetime.

In the press, overground as well as underground, and in the stream of
best sellers analyzing the state of the nation which poured from the New
York publishing houses, the pessimism was more desperate and the rejection of traditional American values even more total in 1969–71 than anything from the middle sixties.

In politics, too, the insurrection reached its zenith not in 1968 but in
1972. With George McGovern as the Democratic nominee; with the
"McGovern rules" enforced on the party, so that the Democratic convention was dominated by women, by blacks, and by the peace people; with
Richard Daley symbolically rejected and replaced by the Reverend Jesse
Jackson as the leader of the Illinois delegation—the Movement succeeded
in 1972 where it had failed in 1968. The schism between the two cultures
had at last become the central issue of a presidential election.

With what result . . . is well known. The old culture inflicted a
crushing defeat on the new.

Even before 1968, the partisans of change had not in reality been the
mighty, united army that both they and their opponents tended to take
them for. They had started out divided, and as time went on the divisions
in their ranks grew wider and wider.

It was in any case simplistic to imagine that there were two sides, and only two sides, in the United States. It did not follow that, because large numbers of citizens were frustrated and angry, as indeed they were, in 1968 and in 1970 and even in 1972, that they must therefore see themselves as obliged to choose between aligning themselves with those who found everything about the *status quo* intolerable and aligning themselves with its defenders.

There was another reason. Just as the rhetoric of the liberal consensus exaggerated the perfectibility of American society, so the radical rhetoric of the late sixties exaggerated the irreconcilability of its divisions. Radicals spoke of revolution, and conservatives took them at their word. But it never was true that American society was polarized, if that word is taken to mean "split into two mutually hostile and utterly irreconcilable camps," in the sense in which Russia was split in 1917 or Spain in 1936 or Chile in 1973. In those truly tragic situations in which actual revolution or civil war is a practical possibility, all the problems of a society—moral, political, economic and institutional—become so entangled that the society is on the point of choking to death. At that point, at least one great party in the state—in the case of Russia it was the Left, in Chile it was the Right, and in Spain it was both sides—sees no way out unless the Gordian knot is cut with the sword.

No more than a handful of Americans seriously thought that the United States had even approached that point between 1965 and 1972. People certainly lost confidence in accepted ideas and institutions. It was plain that liberalism had failed to carry out its program, either in defeating communism abroad or in creating the Great Society at home. Liberals, radicals and conservatives who agreed on nothing else, agreed that the country faced real and terrible dilemmas of policy. But there was only one level at which all these separate problems—the war, race, crime and poverty—could be perceived as the same problem. That was if they were all interpreted as so many symptoms of "some deeper and more general moral sickness." The question was not that with which Lenin had launched his revolution: What is to be done? It was more introspective, less urgent, more of a luxury than that. It was: Is America morally sick?

To misquote T. S. Eliot, human kind cannot bear very much morality. Even in a country as deeply marked by Puritanism as the United States, it is hard to interest the majority for very long in the proposition that they are miserable sinners. The American majority was certainly troubled by the moral implications of war, riots, crime and pollution, and was troubled most of all by the moral implications of racial inequality; it refused to see these things, as a vocal minority insisted they must be seen, as proof of a deeper, more general flaw. It was not that the majority defended war, or "racism," or even the *status quo*. It just didn't disapprove of them strongly enough to feel that the ultimate remedies that were being recommended—unilaterial withdrawal from Southeast Asia, busing, redistributive taxation—were justified, let alone demanded by the state of affairs. In the end, a concrete political choice drew the line between the pragmatic majority and the moralist minority with painful clarity. It wasn't that the majority liked Nixon; its members just didn't feel that things were bad enough that you had to put up with McGovern.

The war and the racial crisis of the sixties had both put moral issues in the forefront of the political agenda. But the third strand of the crisis, the crisis of the presidency, suggested that this tendency to see political issues in moral terms on the part of the American elite was perhaps intrinsic. We saw how, after the assassination and before even the sketchiest background on Lee Harvey Oswald and his killer was available, many of the wisest and most prominent of Americans had jumped to the conclusion that the assassination was evidence of a general moral flaw.

From—roughly—1963 to 1968, at any rate, the attention of the United States had been all but monopolized by two groups. One consisted of those—the poor, blacks, other underprivileged minorities—whose interests were served by posing the moral issue; the other—the young, intellectuals, and the professional upper-middle class—was made up of people whose interests were in any case so securely protected by the *status quo* that they could afford the luxury of interpreting politics in moral terms. These two groups joined forces to put the issue of national morality at the center of American politics. Together, for the five years from 1963 to 1968, they almost succeeded in blotting out the humdrum issues that interested the pragmatic majority.

The mechanism by which this question of the moral nature of American society came to obsess the nation's political attention from the time of the Kennedy administration on, was the media. Just as the media, by their coverage of civil rights and then of the war, had been primarily—if largely unintentionally—responsible for raising grand questions of morality in the first place, so, too, it was the media that led the retreat. There was nothing mysterious about what happened. Mass media are ultimately dependent on communicating with masses of people. In 1968 the mass media were abruptly reminded of the existence of the mass of ordinary working Americans and their families, of that majority that had been, for a decade, not so much silent as ignored.

1

Sometime in 1970, after Spiro T. Agnew had unleashed the wrath of Middle America on the heads of the news media, a certain vice-president of CBS was talking to a colleague at CBS News. He was unsympathetic about the flak the news people had run into. Network news divisions, he reminded his colleague, owed their budgets and their ten years of power, and glory to the fact that the networks had once had a public-relations problem. Now, he said, it was the news divisions themselves that were the problem.

"There was a time," he is remembered to have gone on, "after the quiz-show scandals, when this industry had egg all over its face. Now, mark you, you didn't do much for profits even then. You still don't do much for the profits, and now it's you who get us into trouble."

From 1967 on, all three networks ran into more difficult years in profit terms. News operations, always expensive, cost more than ever in 1968, both because of the tremendous expenditure on covering the presidential primaries and the two conventions, and because of the long sequence of unscheduled events that had to be reported in the course of that tumultuous summer. It wasn't long before *Fortune* was reporting that the networks were having second thoughts about the cost of their news operations.

Money, however, was not the true cause of this re-evaluation. For one thing, ever since the quiz-show scandals of the late fifties, the networks had thought of their growing news budgets as a necessary investment in public relations. They had paid them, and increased them, as a sort of guarantee that their licenses would be renewed; without their licenses they would be out of business. And then again, while it was true that all three networks lost some millions of dollars on their news operations, for CBS and NBC, the two stronger brethren, the loss was hardly catastrophic. The flagship nightly news programs, in particular, were respectable earners: NBC's *Huntley-Brinkley Report*, for example, on a budget of $7.2 million in 1968, generated revenue of $34 million; and while all such figures were fairly meaningless because of the arbitrary nature of internal accounting, it wasn't because they "didn't do much for the profits" that the network managements began to look askance at their news operations. It was because they had begun to "get us into trouble."

Between the summer of 1968 and the spring of 1969 there was a crucial shift in the policy both of network television news and, to a lesser extent, of the more influential of the print media. "Policy" is perhaps the wrong word; it may suggest that the change was more conscious than it was. It was more a new atmosphere in which decisions were taken, a new awareness of pressures that those taking the decisions had not previously felt concerned about.

The shift was subtler than the new emphasis on news after the quiz-show scandals at the beginning of the decade. But it was just as real, and it helped to end the crisis just as surely as the earlier changes in media policy had helped to begin it.

What happened was that the media became aware that, in their coverage of the war, of racial conflict, and of dissent generally, they had gotten a long way out in front of the mass of their viewers and readers; and that the audience, being frightened, was getting ready to blame the bearers of bad tidings. Subtly, but also decisively, the mood changed.

Three points are worth making briefly about the nature of this change before we look at it more closely. The first is that, once again, there was no simple relationship of cause and effect among media policy, public opinion, and political events. There was, rather, a complex process of feedback. Thus, for example, the election of Richard Nixon in November 1968 was both in part an effect and in part a cause of this new atmosphere.

The second point, however, is that the new mood was definitely not simply the result of the attacks on the media's objectivity by Vice-President Agnew and other members of the Nixon administration, or of the new constraints imposed on the media by the courts, the Congress and the executive branch in the early seventies. Before anyone ever tried to censor the media, some of those with authority in the media had decided that it would be prudent to censor themselves.

And yet, thirdly, it was not wholly or even mainly a matter of self-censorship. It was, just as much, a matter of editors and producers, and columnists and commentators, becoming aware that the picture of the world they had been transmitting was not the whole truth. In the process of trying to correct their omissions, and so trying to do their job better, as they saw it, they moderated their emphasis on certain aspects of the news and stressed certain new aspects of it. The effect was that the picture that the nation had of itself and its situation was swiftly modified.

2

The first, and perhaps the crucial, episode in this transformation of the mood of the media was the Democratic National Convention in Chicago, in the last week of August 1968.

Until around the beginning of 1968 it could not be seriously maintained that the great national institutions of the news industry had shown any noticeable signs of bias in favor of dissent. On the contrary, the rise of the underground press was largely due to the fact that young people, troubled by the war and the racial crisis, could find in the great majority of newspapers very little coverage at all, and certainly no sympathetic cov-

erage, of movements that seemed to many of them to be the most important things that were happening in the country. This was especially true of
the peace movement. Newspapers and wire services consistently described
any and all participants in peace demonstrations as "beatniks," "hippies,"
"peaceniks," and so on. When SANE, for example, held its overwhelmingly middle-class, middle-aged, middle-of-the-road march in Washington
in November 1965, what appeared on TV news and in news photos were
Viet Cong flags, interruptions by the tiny American Nazi Party, and the
handful of marchers, out of several thousand, who were wearing beards
and sandals. A few days later, the New York *Times*, greatly daring, found
it news to point out that the typical marcher was "a middle-class adult!"

After the Tet offensive, and with the antiwar presidential campaigns
of Eugene McCarthy and Robert Kennedy making rapid headway, however, these orthodoxies began to change rapidly. Some newsmen were
themselves sympathetic to the peace movement and to other forms of dissent. Others began to show at least an open mind to the ideas of the peace
movement and political radicalism.

Then came the Chicago convention.

Mayor Daley's police behaved as they had often done before in the
spreading black neighborhoods of the South Side and the West Side, and
as other policemen had behaved often enough in the streets and jails of
other cities and small towns from Florida to California. But this time the
police were doing it in front of the Hilton Hotel with the flower of American journalism there as witnesses and sometimes as victims.

It was hard not to be radicalized by the arrogant brutality of the
Chicago police. Later it became fashionable to point out that these were
poor men beating the children of the rich. They were also large, armed
men beating old men, women, and children, few of them rich.

"The truth was," wrote Tom Wicker in the New York *Times*, "these
were our children in the streets, and the Chicago police beat them up."

But the Chicago police not only cracked the heads of peaceniks, and
hippies, and Yippies, and middle-aged demonstrators, and clergymen, and
delegates to the Democratic National Convention, and any bystanders
unlucky enough to happen upon the scene; they also beat newspaper reporters and photographers and television news camera crews. The cries of
outrage from the media were deafening.

"Miraculously," wrote *Newsweek*, "no one was killed by Chicago
Mayor Richard Daley's beefy cops, who went on a sustained rampage"—
and here you can almost feel the malice as New York (where the cops are
well known to be wilting wallflowers) reaches for the comparison that will
be most wounding to the Second City—"unprecedented outside the unreconstructed boondocks of Dixie."

"In Chicago," as the normally urbane and serenely patriotic Stewart Alsop wrote in his column, "for the first time in my life it began to seem to me possible that some form of American fascism may really happen here."

In the Washington *Post* a column by Leroy Aarons compared Daley's real-life Chicago to the mythical gangland Chicago of Bertolt Brecht's play *The Resistible Rise of Arturo Ui* and quoted the play's last line. The actor who plays the gangster-dictator takes off his Hitler mustache and warns the audience that, though Hitler is dead, "the bitch who bore him is in heat again."

It would be unjust to suggest that the ferocity of these denunciations was inspired only by the fact that the police were beating newsmen. But surely only the fact that, as Chet Huntley said on the air on the Wednesday night, "the news profession in this city is now under assault by the Chicago police," could have produced one of the most remarkable joint *démarches* ever made by the acknowledged peerage of the American news media.

Arthur Ochs Sulzberger of the New York *Times*, Katharine Graham of the Washington *Post* and *Newsweek*, Otis Chandler of the Los Angeles *Times*, and Bailey Howard of the Chicago *Sun-Times* and the Chicago *Daily News* joined the top executives of the three networks and Hedley Donovan, editor in chief of Time Inc., in sending a telegram to Mayor Daley that alleged that newsmen "were repeatedly singled out by policemen and deliberately beaten . . . the obvious purpose was to discourage or prevent reporting of an important confrontation between police and demonstrators which the American public as a whole has a right to know about."

That telegram may pass as the historical high-water mark of the radicalization of the Establishment of the American news media; even before the end of the convention, the waters of righteous wrath had begun to ebb.

That night, Mayor Daley was interviewed on CBS News by Walter Cronkite. The fatherly Cronkite had been genuinely shocked by what he had seen, and particularly angry that a CBS cameraman had been among the injured. He had allowed his feelings to show.

Now, suddenly, he was transformed. Perhaps he had been called to heel by the management. Perhaps he felt that he had erred and strayed from the hard path of strict professionalism. Whatever the reason, his manner with Daley was almost obsequious. He repeatedly addressed him as "sir." He introduced him with the ingratiating remark, "Maybe this is a kiss-and-make-up session, but it's not intended that way. . . . I think we've always been friends." And he proceeded to allow Daley to smear the organizers of the demonstrations as Communists and to pass off, unchallenged, the absurd tale that the police's behavior was justified because he, the mayor, had secret intelligence of an assassination plot. As one top CBS executive said with an unbelieving shake of his head: "Daley took Cronkite like Grant took Richmond."

The Chicago convention, in fact, was traumatic for the media. Not only the reporters, for once, but a good proportion of the publishers and executives and editors, too, had seen what happened. The instant reaction, angry condemnation of the police, was from the heart. But then came the disorienting experience of discovering that, in this reaction, they were in a minority. They felt proud of the courageous way they had done their job: and to their amazement, thousands of abusive letters poured in from their readers and viewers, denouncing the way they had done that job and commending their enemies. "We got thousands of calls," Bill Small, Washington bureau chief of CBS remembers, "from people saying they didn't believe their eyes, accusing us of hiring cops to beat up kids. That produced a profound impression."

Almost to a man, the journalists had been shocked by what the police did. To their astonishment, the polls showed that a large majority in the country were shocked by the demonstrators, and sympathetic to the police. Nine out of ten of the seventy-four thousand letters sent to Mayor Daley in the first two weeks after the convention, commended the police. And bumper stickers blossomed across the country: WE SUPPORT MAYOR DALEY AND HIS CHICAGO POLICE.

No discovery could have been more disconcerting for the masters of the media. Here they were, supposedly experts on the state of public opinion. They had been united, as rarely before, by their anger at Mayor Daley. Now they learned that the great majority of Americans sided with Daley, and against them. It was not only the humiliation of discovering that they had been wrong; there was also alarm at the discovery of their new unpopularity. Bosses and cops, everyone knew, were hated: it seemed that newspapers and television were hated even more.

Their reaction revealed how abruptly their confidence had detumesced. In theory, after all, they might have reacted to the letters, and the criticisms, and the polls, by redoubling their efforts to convince the public that their reporting had been right all along. They might have rerun film of unprovoked police charges, for example, or investigated and exposed the flimsy fairy tales put out by the police and the Daley machine to excuse their behavior. They might, in short, have stuck to their guns.

They did none of these things. Abruptly the mood in the media changed from righteous indignation to self-doubt, apology and even penitence. Less than three weeks after the convention, the Washington *Post* was half-apologizing for police brutality with the remarkable argument that "of course" policemen must be expected to be annoyed by the sight of men in beards! The editor of the Chicago *Daily News* was even more abject. His own publisher had joined in the protest telegram to the mayor. Now he publicly criticized one of his own reporters who had shouted, "For God's sake, stop that!" to policemen who were beating three young girls, and had been two days in the hospital as a result of the beating they gave him. "He acted as a human being," the editor regretted, "but less than professionally. He was there as a reporter and not to involve himself."

### 3

There may have been a touch of guilt about these reactions; editors and executives may have felt that they had failed to control the bias of their own reporters. There was certainly the reflection of an internal conflict between reporters and their bosses both on newspapers and on TV. Edward Jay Epstein, interviewing network TV news correspondents and news executives in 1968–69, found a clear nuance of difference between the political attitudes of the two groups, with the reporters predictably more left-wing in their attitudes than the executives. Most of the reporters, for example, expressed sympathy with black-power leaders and called themselves doves on Vietnam. Few of them liked either Humphrey or Nixon. Failing a Kennedy, their favorite politician was Edmund S. Muskie. The executives were distinctly less far to the Left. More than two thirds of them preferred Humphrey. Nevertheless, the great majority of producers thought of themselves as liberals and certainly felt more sympathy for the peace movement than the majority of their viewers seemed to do. Had they committed the ultimate sin of unprofessionalism, they asked themselves, and allowed their preferences to color their objectivity?

Then there was the old, deep-rooted fear of the yahoos in the hinterland. Of the thirty-six producers and news editors Epstein interviewed, twenty-four came from New York City or Chicago and most of the rest from other big cities. "A majority," Epstein found, "came from middle- or upper-class families, in which the father usually was a businessman. Twenty-one were of Jewish descent; none were black or came from lower-class backgrounds. . . . Nearly two-thirds attended such competitive city colleges as CCNY, NYU, Chicago, Northwestern and Columbia"— colleges, moreover, where left-wing ideas were far more strongly established in the period when these men would have been in college than they were in most American universities. These were, in fact, precisely the people who had learned in the McCarthy period to fear the dormant right-wing anger of that sleeping beast, the great American majority.

Within a week of the convention, this new doubt was exemplified in a famous column by Joseph Kraft which is worth quoting at some length because it was both a sensitive account of what many people in the media felt after Chicago and an important turning point in its own right.

The violence in Chicago, Kraft began, showed that the police were no neutral custodians of the public order. But what of the media?

> Are we merely neutral observers, seekers after truth in the public interest? Or do we, as the supporters of Mayor Richard Daley and his Chicago police have charged, have a prejudice of our own?
>
> The answer, I think, is that Mayor Daley and his supporters have a point. Most of us in what is called the communications field are not rooted in the great mass of ordinary Americans—in Middle America. And the result shows up not merely in occasional episodes such as the Chicago violence but more importantly in the systematic bias towards young people, minority groups, and the kind of presidential candidates who appeal to them.
>
> To get a feel of this bias it is first necessary to understand the antagonism that divides the white middle class of this country. On the one hand there are highly educated upper-income whites sure of themselves and brimming with ideas for doing things differently. On the other hand, there is Middle America, the large majority of low-income whites, traditional in their values and on the defensive against innovators.
>
> The most important organs of press and television are, beyond much doubt, dominated by the outlook of the upper-income whites. . . .
>
> In the circumstances, it seems to me that those of us in the media need to make a special effort to understand Middle America. Equally it seems wise to exercise a certain caution, a prudent restraint, in pressing a claim for a plenary indulgence to be in all places at all times the agent of the sovereign public.

That was it. After Chicago, the media were in a chastened mood. Prudent restraint was the new watchword.

The different directions in which feelings ran on either side of that watershed can be seen, for example, in changed attitudes at NBC News. After the riots in the spring of 1968, but before Chicago, Reuven Frank, the president of NBC News and originator of the Huntley-Brinkley partnership, was one of the executives from all three networks who attended a conference sponsored by the federal government at Poughkeepsie, New York, the purpose of which was to enlist the networks' help in cooling down tensions in the ghettoes by what was euphemistically called "better news treatment." Frank objected, and wrote to Roger Wilkins, the Justice Department official who had arranged the conference, that in his opinion "the discussion was asking a medium of journalism to act as an instrument of social control. We must never accept such a request." Yet in fact, after Chicago, all three networks did accept the guidelines for reporting racial disturbances that were suggested at Poughkeepsie. (Some of them had already adopted similar, voluntary guidelines of their own.)

"We finished up Chicago in 1968," Wallace Westfeldt, who was then shortly to become the executive producer of NBC's evening news, told me subsequently, "feeling we had done a very good job. The first indication I had that NBC News was getting some kind of pressurizing was the first discussions over 'First Tuesday.'" (This was a once-a-month current-affairs program that went on the air in January 1969; the discussions Westfeldt referred to would therefore have been in the fall of 1968.) "I was asked what were the three most important stories in the country, and I said, 'The war, the blacks, and the economy.' And somebody said: 'I don't want to see a single black face on "First Tuesday."' So I said, 'Hell, that's ridiculous, they're 14 per cent of the population. How about every seventh talking head?'"

To be fair to NBC, when Westfeldt became executive producer of the evening news, which was that same January, he "bore down" on those three stories and no one ever told him not to do a particular item. "Looking back on it," he added, "there must have been times when my bosses must have gone up the wall."

The effect of Chicago on policy can be measured by this: In the spring of 1968, Reuven Frank was loftily rebuking the government for suggesting that NBC co-operate in playing down civil disturbances; within the year, NBC News and the rest of the media were doing exactly that.

4

The new policy was plain for all to see or, rather, because of what all could not see, at President Nixon's inaugural in January 1969. In Chicago the previous summer, CBS had shown only thirty-two minutes of demonstration footage in more than thirty-eight hours of convention coverage; NBC had shown even less, fourteen minutes in more than nineteen hours. It was not much, but it had been enough.

At the inaugural, NBC showed no footage whatsoever of the demonstrations against the war and against the President, which included some minor violent incidents. (CBS did show some of these incidents briefly, but, curiously accepting the public's view of the bringer of bad tidings, apologized to viewers for doing so!) NBC's action was apparently the result of deliberate network policy. According to Epstein, who was studying NBC News from within at the time, "NBC gave strict orders that there was to be no live or film coverage of the 'counterinauguration' which was being held by antiwar dissidents; and NBC relayed orders to its field producers, editors, correspondents and camera crews not to cover or film any of these protests."

A few days earlier, on a Public Broadcasting Laboratory program, Reuven Frank had made an interesting admission: "There are already controls of a very insidious nature," he said; "an atmosphere is building up that concerns me a great deal, that news people, acting according to their best lights, keep feeling that their almost conditioned actions and decisions may be subject to review. And I am afraid of a process of self-censorship developing."

Self-censorship was nothing new, of course, even before Chicago. But Frank's fears proved justified. Less than a year later, the networks made a surrender that dwarfed the decision to ignore the unpleasantness at the inauguration.

In October 1969, the peace movement announced plans for a "moratorium" and mobilization of massive demonstrations in November. On November 3 President Nixon went on the air in an address to the nation in which he rallied the "silent majority" in support of the war. On November 13, with the White House's full knowledge and help, Vice-President Agnew, in a speech in Des Moines, launched his campaign against the media in general and the networks in particular. The point got a little lost in the excitement that the onslaught generated in the executive offices of the media, but the timing of Agnew's speech was in no way accidental. It was intended to affect network coverage of the antiwar demonstrations, and in that intention it was brilliantly successful. For the demonstrations were the largest in American history. They were the high-water mark of the movement that had been snowballing since the teach-ins in the spring of 1965. In Washington alone, more than half a million people took part in the largest and most impressive demonstration of all. And there was no live coverage at all by any of the three networks. . . .

In this way, the networks almost convinced the American people that the peace movement was dead, at the moment of its greatest popularity. Yet even this was hardly more important than their feat of persuading the American people that the war was over when it had in truth almost four years to run and was still to claim over a million more lives.

Typically this was the result not of conscious policy so much as of decisions flowing naturally from the professional values and journalistic instincts of the news bureaucracy itself.

"Let me tell you a negative thing," said Robert J. Northshield, who was executive producer of the Huntley-Brinkley program from 1965 to the end of 1968. "The executive producer sits down every morning to plan his show. He aims at having five segments. He talks to Brinkley in Washington, to other guys. And very often his feeling is, 'Oh, God, not Vietnam again!' By early 1969 that feeling was very marked. The trend was away from Vietnam."

"About the time, in early 1969, when we got tired of combat footage, we said, 'Let's get some pacification footage,' and that was soft stuff, so it went out at the tail end of the show. So straightaway people got the impression that the war was less important. The American voter is willing to vote for Nixon now"—this conversation was in 1972—"because the voter, who is also the viewer, thinks that Nixon has ended the war." Northshield is anything but a naïve man, and he was passionately against the war. But he added, as if it was obvious, an undeniable concomitant of the power of television: "And he *has* ended the war, because you don't see the war on the tube any more. So the war has ended, though we are bombing the hell out of these poor people, more than ever."

After President Johnson announced the complete halt to the bombing in November 1968, in fact, Northshield told his news staff that the "story" was now the peace negotiations, not the fighting, and although combat footage continued to come in from Saigon almost every day, it was used on the evening news only three times in two months, as against three or four times a week the previous year, with a similar quantity available.

Northshield was not the only producer to make the same judgment. On becoming executive producer of the ABC evening news in March 1969, Av Westin wrote to his correspondents, "I have asked our Vietnam staff to alter the focus of their coverage from combat pieces to interpretative ones, pegged to the eventual pullout of American forces. This point must be stressed for all hands." And in a telex to his Saigon bureau he spelled out the kind of footage this new policy was expected to produce:

> I think the time has come to shift some of our focus from the battlefield . . . to themes and stories under the general heading: We Are on Our Way Out of Vietnam.

Now, it was quite true that American ground forces were to be progressively reduced and that, less than four years after these decisions were taken in New York, a cease-fire agreement of a sort was reached. It is also true that, when the television networks decided that the time had come to shift attention from the battlefield, some of the heaviest fighting and *the* heaviest U.S. bombing of the war were still in the future. Nevertheless by the spring of 1969 the war was over, because you didn't see it on the tube any more. And the reason why you didn't see it on the tube was because certain television executives had decided, conscientiously following their own professional logic, that it wasn't the story any more.

## 5

President Nixon and Vice-President Agnew were to complain bitterly about the power of "a small group of men" in the media to impose its liberal bias on the news. And the response to Agnew's intemperate speeches to this effect in 1969 and 1970 suggested that tens of millions of Americans shared his suspicions. In one respect, Agnew had a point. The growth of TV, the pre-eminence of the nightly network news over any other source of information, and the concentration of control over the media in so few hands did indeed give great power to a small group of men, and one woman.

But from 1968 to 1972 Nixon and Agnew had little serious reason to complain of the way that power was used.

It is true that the men who ran the great media empires of New York and Washington did not share the personal style and attitudes of the Nixon administration. They might be conservative enough, in all conscience; but it is true that few of them were "conservative," either in the sense in which the President's wealthy backers used the word to rationalize their self-interest or in the various ways in which it was embraced as a label by Protestant fundamentalists, Roman Catholic working men, many U. S. Navy officers, or the nationalist-anti-Communist school of political philosophy graced by Professor Robert Strausz-Hupé and William F. Buckley. Most of them, in fact, were "liberals," in the broad sense in which the word has been used in this book.

But in practice the Nixon administration suffered less at the hands of these hated liberals than it might have suffered if the networks, the news magazines and the great national newspapers had all been in the hands of avowed conservatives.

It was at all times professionally safer for a journalist working for these supposed liberal cabals to be known as a committed conservative than to come under the suspicion of leaning toward the New Left. Even such papers as the New York *Times* and the Washington *Post*, to obviate the suspicion of liberal bias, hastened to employ conservative columnists. The New York *Times* hired the former presidential speechwriter William Safire, whose background was in advertising, to write a regular column. In New York and Washington from 1969 to 1972, a literate conservative was more precious than fine gold.

Relations between the Nixon administration and the working press were not always friendly, partly because of the highhanded contempt with which White House officials treated all but the most servile reporters. Yet the Administration, all things considered, got a remarkably easy ride from the press.

Although William Beecher of the New York *Times* published as early as 1969, for example, the fact that the Administration was secretly bombing targets in Cambodia, for three years the press never bothered to follow the story up. Few officials in the history of the U. S. Government, again, have ever been as consistently sympathetically treated as Dr. Henry Kissinger, partly, perhaps, because both in talent and in charm he stood out so sharply from the flatness of the surrounding country. In the 1972 election campaign the press overwhelmingly favored Nixon both in the tenor of its reporting and in formal endorsements. By that year, Patrick Buchanan, who had co-ordinated the Administration's campaign against the media from inside the White House and actually wrote the famous Agnew speeches, was openly claiming in an interview in the New York *Times* that victory had been won. One of his severest critics, Ben H. Bagdikian of the *Columbia Journalism Review*, was disposed to agree with him:

> A sample study of leading papers and network specials during the presidential campaign makes it clear that the Nixon Administration's three year war against the media has succeeded. There has been a retrogression in printing newsworthy information that is critical of the Administration and a notable decline in investigation of apparent wrongdoing when it is likely to anger or embarrass the White House. This, coupled with the shrewd manipulation of the media by Nixon officials, has moved the American news system closer to becoming a propaganda arm of the administration in power.

Perhaps the most striking evidence of the truth of this proposition is to be seen by looking closely at the two cases which, at first glance, look like the two supreme instances of the watchfulness, the audacity, and the liberal animus of the American press: the Pentagon Papers and Watergate.

With the exception of the Washington *Post* and two or three other papers, the American press virtually ignored the New York *Times*'s scoop of the secret history of the Vietnam War. The first installment of the story appeared, with a deliberately dull headline, reading "Vietnam Archive: Pentagon Study Traces 3 Decades of Growing U. S. Involvement," on Sunday morning, June 13, 1971. The Associated Press carried not one line on this, perhaps the most important scoop of the decade, until Monday afternoon, and not a single one of its forty-five hundred subscribers registered any protest or interest. UPI did carry a brief item on the Sunday afternoon but didn't think it important enough to mention in its daily news budget! Few of the clients of the New York *Times* News Service, who had been given exclusive early warning of the story, bothered to take advantage of it, and the Chicago *Tribune*, which claims to be the "World's Greatest Newspaper," never did carry a word of the story. Both *Time* and *Newsweek* learned of the story in time to include something on it if they had wanted to, but only at the cost of an expensive last-minute change. Neither magazine's editors thought the change justified.

Of the three networks, NBC did lead with the story that Sunday on the nightly news. But the other two ignored it, in the case of CBS after deliberate veto in New York of a suggestion from the Washington bureau. Senator Hubert Humphrey was not asked a single question about the Pentagon Papers on ABC's "Issues and Answers" that afternoon. Nor was the Secretary of Defense, Melvin Laird, on CBS's "Face the Nation."

Eventually, of course, the Pentagon Papers snowballed into a major story and a *cause célèbre*. But the initial media reaction can hardly be squared with the Agnew picture of the liberal media, on the qui vive for any opportunity to embarrass the Nixon administration and ever ready to seize any opportunity to attack the Vietnam War.

Still less can the media's handling of Watergate be reconciled to the widely held preconception of an aggressive, liberal-tilted media establishment.

All over the world, "the American press" was praised for breaking the Watergate story. That credit is misplaced. It belongs essentially to one newspaper, the Washington *Post*, and in a very much lesser degree to a handful of other news organizations. Although, once the *Post* had broken the story of the Watergate burglars' links to the White House and to the Nixon re-election campaign, anyone with the wit to hold down the lowliest job on the obscurest weekly could see that there was a case to investigate, and one that might lead into the White House, few papers dared to look into it. The New York *Times* followed up the *Post*'s disclosures but mounted no investigation of its own until much later. All together, according to a study by Ben Bagdikian in the *Columbia Journalism Review* in May 1973 (almost a year after the arrest of the Cubans), out of twenty-two hundred reporters in Washington, only fourteen had done any substantial work on the Watergate story!

6

Why had the media allowed their teeth to be drawn to the point where their reactions were as cautious as they were in these two famous instances and in many others?

Part of the trouble perhaps was the defect of a virtue. The press and television prided themselves *above all* on their fairness and objectivity. Agnew's and Buchanan's charges of bias piqued them on the touchiest spot of all. Punctilio and self-respect made them lean over backward to disprove those charges.

Then . . . the world had become so complicated. Again and again, with variations, this point was made to me in interviews. Editors and columnists and television producers and commentators looked wistfully back to the simplicities of the sixties. The bold drama of right and wrong that had impressed the civil rights struggle on the mind and conscience of the nation seemed to have dissolved into an angry confusion of arguments and statistics that were hard to understand and harder still to put across with clarity in a newspaper column or a minute and a half on the evening news.

One veteran television producer put it like this: "Civil rights," he said, "was a *safe* one for us. People, the great majority of white Americans, really agreed that blacks should have the right to vote.

"When it became a question of northern ghettoes and *de facto* segregation, that was tougher.

"Then Vietnam came along, and that was a little tough. We were accused of hanging an antiwar picture on the wall in every living room in America. As a matter of fact, I don't think we were antiwar enough.

"Let me summarize it: Police dogs, that was easy. Vietnam, that was not so simple. And then we got into stuff like inflation, and busing, and the balance of payments, and economic stories; that was really tough."

There was also something else. That was fear. Not fear of the federal government, though it was alarming that reporters were being investigated and taken to court and asked to reveal their sources, and that papers were being threatened with prior restraint in spite of the First Amendment guarantee of freedom of speech, and that pressures of all kinds were brought against management by the government.

No: the real fear was that which haunts all elites, and the national news media are an elite in America. It was the fear of being out of touch with the majority, the fear of being unpopular. It was in Chicago in 1968 that the face of this unpopularity first appeared, and it had done its work before ever it occurred to Patrick Buchanan and a few others to reinforce it with the grimaces of the federal government.

Six weeks before Agnew's first salvo in Des Moines, *TV Guide* reported a change in the emphasis of television news and news specials. They were shifting away from emphasis on the militant Left, it said, and veering toward the center and the Right. All three networks, the article predicted, quite accurately, would be "exploring middle and lower-middle class Americans."

That was on September 27, 1969. On the very same day—there could hardly be a better example of the intellectual lockstep that Agnew complained of in the media, but in this instance it worked for him—*Editor & Publisher*, quite independently, summarized the coming trends in newspapers. "The shift," it found, "is a reflection of the views of what is called 'the silent majority' who feel that television has devoted too much time to the role of the militant and the agitator and has given too little coverage to the quiet hard-working Americans of all races."

The media and the intellectuals had rediscovered the working class, whose abolition they had prematurely announced in the fifties. That rediscovery was the hinge on which the door of the period of polarization swung shut. During that period the attention of the United States had been monopolized by the claims of certain minorities. Now the time of the majority had come.

# War, Peace and Two Americas

> Amongst democratic nations, in time of peace, the military
> profession is held in little honor and practiced with little spirit.
>
> Alexis de Tocqueville,
> *Democracy in America*

After the Tet offensive, the peace movement could have been forgiven
for imagining that its prayers had been answered and that the day of
Jubilo had dawned at long last. There was a sudden, massive and unprecedented swing of public opinion against the war.

In January 1968, immediately before Tet had printed on the national
retina its pictures of frustration and defeat, the Gallup poll had reported
that a clear majority (in fact 56 per cent) of the American people, as
measured by its usually reliable sample, still classified themselves as hawks
and that they still outnumbered the doves (28 per cent) by just two to
one.

Just three months later, the balance of opinion had jibed over to the
other tack. The doves had overtaken the hawks. They now led by only the
narrowest of margins, it was true (42–41 per cent). But the trend was unmistakable, and at first glance it seemed to show that the peace movement
had succeeded in converting the nation. By early 1969, for the first time,
more than 50 per cent of Gallup's respondents had concluded that American involvement in Vietnam had been a mistake from the start. In 1965
fewer than a quarter of the sample had taken that view. After Tet the proportion who maintained that the war had always been a mistake grew continuously. It passed 60 per cent in the spring of 1971, and by the end of
President Nixon's first term had approached two thirds of the American
people. Within two years of Tet, to put it neatly, the ratio of doves to
hawks had swapped over: from 56–28 per cent in favor of the hawks in

January 1968 to 55–31 per cent in favor of the doves in November 1969.

Even to think of that month, however, is to remember that the state of American opinion was anything but neat. For November 1969 was the month in which the strength of the peace movement seemed to reach its peak; and it was also the month in which Richard Nixon, in a television speech to the nation, successfully counterclaimed that, against the great mass meetings demonstrating for peace, he could appeal to a silent majority.

There are in any case inherent difficulties in the attempt to measure how public opinion has moved on a given issue over a period of time. It is rare, for one thing, to find a long series of polls in which the same question has been asked in the same words. If the question has not been asked in the same words, the results are not comparable. Even if it has, they may not be very enlightening, because events may have changed so much that the same words no longer refer to the same reality. "Isolationism" in 1940 meant something very different from what it meant when Dean Rusk and others tried to revive it as a bad word for the opponents of American military intervention abroad.

In the particular case of Vietnam, the effort to divine the mind of America was even more fraught with booby traps than usual. In the early days of the war there were a good many reports in the press, and not least in such "liberal," "Establishment" papers as the New York *Times*, the Washington *Post* and *Newsweek*, to the effect that if President Johnson was under any pressure to modify his policy on Vietnam, that pressure came from the Right. In part, this confirms the general observation we have made that politics in the age of consensus was often in effect a conflict not between Left and Right but between moderate-right- and extreme-right-wing policies. It reflected that determination to have "no enemies on the Right" which the pundits of the foreign policy Establishment, the media, and so many politicians seem to have acquired as the legacy of fear in the McCarthy period.

Whatever this idea may tell us about the political psychology of Washington, however, it had no basis in fact. Elaborate analysis of poll data and of a specially devised 1966 National Opinion Research Center survey by Sidney Verba and other social scientists found that those who supported the President anyway were likely also to support further escalation of the war, while those who opposed him were statistically likely to favor de-escalation. In scanning the horizon to the Right of him with such care, posting no pickets to the Left, Lyndon Johnson had made the political mistake of his life. It was from the Left that the Indians had been creeping stealthily upon him.

The implications of the data were chaotic. Few Americans, it showed, could truthfully be called either hawks or doves. Their views were simply not that consistent. Nor did it seem possible to discover any strong correlation between attitudes to the war and any of the sociological and demographic characteristics that traditionally predict political loyalties in the United States. It wasn't possible to say that the rich were for the war, or that the poor were; or that the young took any one view of it, or that the old did. Neither religion nor the strength of religious belief seemed to have anything to do with it. And while the southwestern states, as one might expect, were more in favor of a tough war policy, the South, as one might not have guessed, was most in favor of de-escalation.

There were two very interesting exceptions to this negative rule. Men were more likely to be hawks than women. And blacks, whatever their level of education, were significantly more opposed to escalating the war than whites with the same amount of education.

But what were tidy-minded social scientists, let alone politicians, obliged by the coarse needs of their trade to deal in broad, marketable generalizations, to make of the confusing, and sometimes apparently contradictory pattern of public opinion on the war? The NORC survey showed, for example, that no fewer than 88 per cent of the American people would be willing to negotiate with the Viet Cong, and that a majority, 52 per cent, would go so far as to hand South Vietnam over to a coalition that included the Viet Cong. And yet equally imposing majorities rejected any policies that smacked of scuttle. Eighty-one per cent said they would disapprove if the President were to announce tomorrow that the United States is going to withdraw from Vietnam and let the Communists take over. The same data could be read to sustain the view that America was either a nation of hawks or a nation of doves.

It might be thought that this confusion was the result of ignorance and indifference. If so, as the war went on—as more Americans were killed and as the peace movement's campaign of education took effect and as people read more about the war and saw more of it on television—one might have expected opinion to become less confused and shake out into some clear pattern. That didn't happen. To some extent opinion did at least seem to become more polarized. Morris Janowitz, a sociologist at the University of Chicago, wrote that the nightly spectacle of the war on television "hardened and polarized public sentiment" so that by the end of 1967 "those people who are skeptical of the war now have a vehemence in their skepticism. Those who are for the war see Americans being killed and they don't want those sacrifices to be in vain." That was true. But the pattern never did become a simple one.

Two stereotypes, in particular, came to be so universally accepted that they became crucial shibboleths in determining political attitudes in the early seventies. These were two related ideas: that young people were more likely to oppose the war than their elders, and that the more highly educated people were the more likely they were to oppose it. The peace movement, disproportionately recruited from the young and highly educated, took both propositions for granted, not without a touch of arrogance. But so, too, did its enemies. Richard Nixon and Spiro Agnew, by campaigning against kids and snobs, showed that they accepted both propositions as true. They were not.

In May 1971, for example, Gallup found that two thirds of those with a college education thought that the war had been a mistake; three quarters of those with only a grade-school education thought the same. "If we divide a sample of the American public roughly into thirds on the basis of how attentive or informed they are about Vietnam," wrote three social scientists in a report commissioned by SANE and the Commission for a Livable World, and so hardly prejudiced against middle-class liberalism, "we find that the top third tends to show the most hawkish attitudes, the bottom third the most dovish, with the middle third falling somewhere in between."

Nor did the data support the assumption that the young were disproportionately doves. As of 1968, data from the University of Michigan's Survey Research Center showed that college-educated white people in their twenties were more likely than older people with only grade-school education both to justify the war and to favor intensification of it, in both cases by the very substantial margin of twenty percentage points or more. In the *American Journal of Sociology*, late in 1972, Michigan's Howard Schuman summed up the evidence like this: "A careful review of public opinion data over the last seven years [i.e. 1965–72] shows that on most war-related issues, the greatest opposition to continued American involvement has come from the least educated parts of the population. A related finding is that when it comes to Vietnam, the 'generation gap,' at least in a simple form, has been largely a myth."

How can these findings be squared with the evidence of campuses on fire with rebellion against the war? Were the polls simply inaccurate? No. Was the upheaval of student feeling against the war, then, an illusion? Of course not. But things were nevertheless not quite as they seemed.

The Tet offensive, so decisive a turning point in so many other ways, produced the first clue to the meaning of this riddle. For it was after Tet, as we have seen, that the decisive swing in public opinion against the war took place. And Tet was a defeat for American policy. The sharpest increase in mass public opposition to the war, then, followed the clearest indication to date that the United States was not winning it.

The peace movement had not been born of the response to Viet

Cong offensives. It had sprung up in protest at American aggression. Its first great surge came after the escalation of American offensive action in the spring of 1965, and it flared up with its most incandescent intensity after the invasion of Cambodia in the spring of 1970.

The key to the riddle, in fact, lies in grasping the fact that the peace movement and mass public opposition to the war were two different phenomena. They sprang from different emotional roots, they affected different kinds of Americans, and they responded to different events. Indeed, they were to some extent mutually opposed movements.

Once this is understood, the poll data can indeed be made to fit with the fact that the great universities and certain other groups who shared their culture—intellectuals, journalists, publishers, clergymen, and some politicians and business leaders—went on fire against the war. Then many of the other apparent paradoxes in the politics of the seventies can be resolved. The answer to the riddle of the Vietnam polls, in fact, becomes in turn the clue to the larger riddle of the Nixon majority.

Many of the characteristic habits of thought of the liberal consensus, and of the national media which had been so largely converted to that ideology, played their part in creating this confusion about the nature of American attitudes to the war. There was the media's tendency to generalize from examples. A student demonstration against the war at Berkeley, a second at Michigan and a third at Columbia became projected as an image of "youth in revolt against the war." Then there was the rhetorical exaggeration of liberal optimism. "Everyone," people under this influence liked to say, "goes to college in America now," when the fact was that less than half of the Americans born in any given year even started to attend any kind of college. And lastly there was the liberal myth of the abolition of class, the false egalitarianism that pretended that there was no difference between the young people who went to Berkeley, Michigan or Harvard, and those whose experience of college meant state colleges, or community colleges, or small denominational colleges, or other institutions which were largely untouched by the fervor against the war.

It is quite true that after the invasion of Cambodia in the spring of 1970, sentiment against the war spread rapidly to many colleges where there had been previously very little sign of dissent. It is also true that, even then, fewer than 30 per cent of the institutions of higher education in the United States were affected. There is a mass of evidence of the deep cultural divide, on the issue of the war and in fact on other issues too, between the leading universities, and particularly those with large graduate schools, on the one hand, and attitudes at smaller colleges and among young people who did not go to college at all.

In an article in *Scientific American* in June 1970, for example, Philip

Converse and Howard Schuman reported the results of one study of the difference between opinion at what they called "leading universities" and at other colleges. They grouped the respondents in the Survey Research Center's sample according to a rating of the quality of the university they attended, based on factors such as faculty salaries and information about the academic quality of students. This was their conclusion: "Throughout the entire period from 1964 to 1968, alumni of the smaller colleges"—by smaller, interestingly, Swarthmore and Oberlin notwithstanding, they meant "non-quality"—"although they came [eventually] to see the war as a mistake, clung to a harder line than even the non-college population. It is this constituency from smaller colleges more than any other that has served as the backbone of popular support." And of course, since there were far more students at "smaller colleges" than at "leading universities," this explains why, in spite of what was happening at Berkeley or Harvard, college students and recent graduates did not appear nearly so dovish in national surveys as one would expect. Before the silent majority, there were the forgotten students.

There were two classes of college, then, with different attitudes to the war. There were also two different classes of students in this respect.

A survey done by Daniel Yankelovitch for *Fortune* in January 1969 revealed this very clearly. Yankelovitch divided young people between eighteen and twenty-four into three groups in an ingenious way. One group consisted of those who didn't go to college at all. Those who did go to college were shown the two following statements and asked which came closer to their view:

1) "For me, college is mainly a practical matter. With a college education I can earn more money, have a more interesting career, and enjoy a better position in society."

2) "I'm not really concerned with the practical benefits of college. I suppose I take them for granted. College for me means something more intangible, perhaps the opportunity to change things rather than make out well within the existing system."

Those who preferred the first statement, Yankelovitch called the "practical-minded" students. The second group—there is a revealing value judgment concealed here—he called "the forerunners." The practical-minded students were more likely to come from blue-collar families—a third of them did—and more than half of them were enrolled in business, engineering or science programs, with clear vocational implications. Four out of five of the "forerunners" were in the arts or humanities, and only a quarter of them came from blue-collar families.

Not only, Yankelovitch found, were the "forerunner" students far more likely to be doves, and correspondingly far less likely to be hawks, than either the "practical-minded" students or those who didn't go to college at all (actually, 47 per cent of the latter, 37 per cent of the "practical-minded" and only 20 per cent of the "forerunners" called themselves hawks); even more revealing were the different attitudes, indeed you could almost say the different cultures, that lay behind that bottom-line decision to be for or against the war.

The "forerunner" group was far more committed to bringing about change and far less committed to living "the good Christian life" than the other two groups. It was far more critical of parents and the older generation, far less inclined to identify with the middle class (a poignant point, since the "forerunners" were by definition members of the middle class, while the others, who were in danger of exclusion from it, clung to it). Only 17 per cent of those out of college, and 36 per cent of the "practical-minded" thought that draft resistance was justified under any circumstances; 67 per cent of the "forerunners" did. And the "forerunners" were far less likely to admit to feelings of patriotism and far more disposed to state, "There are worse things to fear politically than the threat of Communism," than those who did not go to college. In each case, the "practical-minded," hoping for "a better position in society," show up halfway between the two poles. They appear like so many poor souls in limbo trying to scramble out of the harsh realities and stern beliefs of the American working class into the loose, cool freedom of that upper-middle-class culture in which, not needing to "make out," a fellow could afford to think, with an idealism perhaps tinged with condescension, about "the opportunity to change things."

The contrast between the attitude toward the war of the more privileged students and that of other young people showed up also when such students were compared with a broad sample of the population. Again, the work was done at the University of Michigan, naturally enough, since it is both one of the two or three chief homes of public-opinion research and the cradle of the campus peace movement. In the summer of 1971 the university's Detroit Area Study asked a sample of the general population of the city and its surrounding suburbs not only whether they thought the war had been a mistake but also why. Their answers were then coded in terms of the main themes that respondents mentioned as reasons against U.S. intervention. These responses were then compared with those of students in three sociology classes at the university. The results were very striking. There were sharp differences between the students' views and those of the general Detroit population. And those differences followed a coherent and extremely suggestive pattern

The students were far more likely than the Detroiters, for one thing, to be concerned by Vietnamese as well as by American casualties. In the general sample, 73 per cent of those who mentioned war casualties as one of their reasons for thinking that the war had been a mistake, meant by that *American* casualties only. No less than 85 per cent of the students referred either to Vietnamese casualties in this context or to those on both sides.

Again, of those who argued that the United States should not have become involved because the conflict in Vietnam was a civil war, 84 per cent of the Detroiters turned out on further analysis to mean, "We should get out because *they* are causing *us* trouble," whereas 57 percent of the students thought the United States should get out because the war was a civil war and *"We* are causing *them* trouble."

Most revealing of all, only 11 per cent of the Detroit sample opposed the war on the grounds that U.S. policy in Vietnam was morally questionable. And of those, more than half (6 per cent) did so only in the sense that they asked in effect, "Who are we to say what is right there?" a type of response that might reflect isolationism or even racism, rather than moral doubt. More than a third of the students, on the other hand (35 per cent), said that their opposition to the war was based on what were classified as moral or politicomoral grounds, saying, for example, that the war was "imperialist" or simply "immoral." Again, more than three times as many of the students as of the Detroiters (10 per cent as against 3 per cent) cited negative feelings toward the government of South Vietnam among their reasons for opposing the war.

In all the whole period from 1964 to 1972, the most massive shift in public opinion against the war came after Tet. Two years later, there came news from South Vietnam which, if moral revulsion were the basis of such surges of antiwar feeling, ought to have set off an even more massive defection. Seymour Hersh broke the news of the My Lai massacre in February 1970. Its implications were just those which might most have been expected to disillusion those whose support for the war had survived Tet. My Lai meant that the distinction, on which the whole case for the war rested, between Viet Cong and villagers was even more tenuous than it had seemed. And it also meant that the ambiguities and frustrations of the war had damaged the morale and the discipline of the American military to the point where it was seriously doubtful whether they could still claim to be upholding the values of international law or democracy. Did the news of My Lai send a second seismic wave of opposition to the war through American public opinion? It did nothing of the kind. On the contrary, President Nixon, a few months later, saw and seized an opportunity to bid

for popularity by intervening on behalf of Lieutenant Calley, who had
been found guilty of the massacre.

There were, in short, two oppositions to the war, one moral, the other
pragmatic. The widespread popular disillusionment with the war from
1968 on, which showed up not only in public-opinion polls but also in
support for "peace" candidates such as Robert Kennedy and Eugene
McCarthy in the 1968 presidential primaries and George McGovern in
1972, came from people who were not even speaking the same language as
those who organized those campaigns. The opposition to the war on the
campuses of the great universities, among intellectuals, in the media, and
even at the comparatively "grass roots" level of state and local leadership
in political campaigns, reflected moral considerations. Whether because
they sympathized with Vietnamese nationalism or because they believed
America had no right to intervene or—which was most often the case—
because they were horrified by what would have to be done, both to Vietnamese and to American society, if the war was to be won, those who
shared the humanist, humanitarian culture of the American intelligentsia
thought that the war was a crime.

To the great majority of Americans the war was worse than a crime,
as a cynical Frenchman once said: it was a mistake. The swing of public
opinion against the war did not mean that the peace movement had succeeded in achieving its dream of mass conversion. It reflected the cannily
realistic judgment that winning the war didn't seem worth the price.
Some measured that price in American lives, in boys they knew who
had gone over there and not come back. Others measured it in squandered
resources that would have been better spent at home: on economic problems and inflation. Others, again, thought in terms of the realization that
the war was dangerously dividing the country and diverting its attention
from more urgent priorities. No doubt the judgment also reflected the fact
that the broad mass of public opinion had never embraced the stern joys
of America's world role quite as wholeheartedly as the politicians, the intellectuals, and the cheerleaders of the liberal ideology in the media. It
was at the point, in any case, where they could see that it was affecting
their own lives that the majority of Americans made up their minds, pragmatically and, as usual, very sensibly, and certainly not out of any sense of
moral guilt, that the war was a mistake.

By 1971 some two thirds of the American people had come to this
conclusion. An unknown but very large proportion of them used another
word for it. The war, as they saw it, was a "mess." The word was a refrain.
It recurred again and again, in public opinion surveys, in *vox pop.* interviews on television, in ordinary conversations the length and breadth of
America, in country clubs and corner taverns. Welfare was a mess, and the

cities were a mess, and nobody knew what to do about them. The war was a mess, and there at least the answer did not seem hard to find. It was past time to get out of it.

Few people realized it at the time, as the polls recorded higher and higher percentages against the war, but this mood was deeply ambivalent. Opposition to the war was spreading out from Berkeley and Cambridge, New York and Washington, into every corner of the country. But the farther you went, geographically and culturally, from those places, the smaller the proportion of moral compunction in that opposition and the larger the dose of sheer gruff impatience and irritation.

There was a good deal of academic consternation in 1968 when political scientists discovered that a high proportion of those who, in Indiana for example, had voted for Robert Kennedy in the primary, went on to vote for George Wallace in November. For the war was the great issue. How could you vote in May for a man who asked, "Are we like the God of the Old Testament that we can decide what hamlets in Vietnam are going to be destroyed?" and then vote in November for a man who said, "Pour it on . . . there's no sense in talking peace to that crowd until you've got 'em whipped"? From the logical perspective of political scientists or national political editors, that might be baffling and even perverse behavior, but from the standpoint of someone who didn't honestly much care what happened in Vietnam as long as it stopped affecting his life, it made a great deal of sense. And there were a great many such people.

In 1968 the Survey Research Center showed just how many. By a margin of roughly five to three, it found, people said they thought it had been a mistake to intervene in Vietnam in the first place. But by almost the same margin, they called for a "stronger stand," even if that meant invading North Vietnam! Almost as many of those who thought it had been a mistake to get involved wanted to get out by escalating the war as wanted to get out by simply withdrawing.

The same study documented another point of the greatest importance. Not only did ordinary people not turn against the war for the reasons that had made students and intellectuals rally to the peace movement; most of those who disliked the war, disliked the peace movement even more. The SRC asked people to evaluate a number of political groups and leaders on a scale that measured their feelings about them, from highly positive to highly negative. Reactions to "Vietnam war protesters" were by a wide margin the most negative shown toward any group. Three quarters of the sample reported negative feelings toward them, and the remarkably high proportion of one third went so far as to put the peave movement at the extreme negative point of the scale, a penalty box rating that was rarely used for any other group. Most extraordinary of all: more than half even of those who themselves favored immediate and total withdrawal from Vietnam recorded negative feelings about those who publicly advocated this same position!

"The campus peace movement has . . . tended to assume," one study of public opinion and the war concluded, "that the 30 per cent or 40 per cent of the public [who wanted to get out of Vietnam as quickly as possible] are their devoted followers. Sad to say, the truth is very near the contrary."

Father Andrew Greeley, of the National Opinion Research Center, has elaborated on this feeling with all the understanding of a priest who knows the white "ethnic" neighborhoods of Chicago and perhaps shares some of the feelings he describes:

> In the eyes of the white ethnic, "peace" has been identified as a "radical" cause. The ethnics want no part of contemporary radicalism, especially when it is advocated by long-haired college students. . . . However moral or virtuous the present radical movement may be, it has turned off between 60 per cent and 90 per cent of the American population. If the white ethnic is told in effect that to support peace he must also support the Black Panthers, women's liberation, widespread use of drugs, free love, campus radicals, Dr. Spock, long hair, and picketing clergymen, he may find it very difficult to put himself on the side of peace.

One may well ask, of course, who was purveying this misinformation to the people who believed it. It is an open question whether the Abbie Hoffmans or the Spiro Agnews were more assiduous in insisting that peace and drugs were inseparable. But that only goes to confirm Greeley's point. In any case, the most interesting part of Greeley's description is his insistence on a point that also emerges clearly from the survey data: the class basis of this hostility to the peace movement. True, Greeley is sufficiently steeped in the tradition that denies the importance of class in American society that he talks about "the white ethnic" rather than about the working class, and about "the Establishment" when another might write the bourgeoisie. But with these translations the class analysis could not be plainer if the passage had been written for Pravda:

> From the point of view of the Polish television watcher on Milwaukee Avenue on the northwest side of Chicago, the long-haired militants and their faculty patrons are every bit as much part of the Establishment as are the presidents of corporations. . . . Richard Nixon, to some extent, and Spiro Agnew, to a very considerable extent, are anti-Establishment figures and someone like David Dellinger with his Yale degree is very much an Establishment personage. The protesters and the militants are the sons and daughters of the well-to-do.

. . . The peace movement is seen as very much of an Establishment movement, working against the values, the stability and the patriotism of the American masses, which masses incidentally are seen as footing the bill for Establishment games and amusements.

There were, then, after 1968, two movements in American opinion relative to the Vietnam War. Both worked in the same direction for some abrupt change in policy that would end the war. With an ill grace, they traveled the same road.

One movement—the one we usually call "the peace movement"—was numerically small though immensely influential. Its motivation was essentially moral; its basic attitude was that the war was not only unjustified, futile, dangerous, corrupting and wasteful, but that it was *wrong*. Its basic policy therefore was to end the war as soon as possible and at whatever cost. Ironically, since many of the founders and leaders of this movement were radicals and socialists who believed as a matter of faith in the potential radicalism and pacifism of the working class, in practice its appeal was almost exclusively to those who, whatever their family background or financial status, belonged in cultural terms to the upper-middle class.

The other movement was sprawling, inchoate, and so unorganized that it is taking a liberty with language to call it a movement at all. Its dominant tone was not idealistic but realistic. Its members were all those Americans, many tens of millions of them, who said—some stressing one reason, some another—"whatever we might like to think, let's stop kidding ourselves. This war is a mess, and it's got to stop." They were to be found in every socioeconomic class. But the largest number of them were to be found in the ranks of the working class. George Wallace, bidding for their support, talked about "this average man, this man in the textile mill, this man in the steel mill, this barber, the beautician, the policeman on the beat . . . and the little businessman," and that was a good list of some of the people who belonged to this movement, though Wallace could have added the farmer, the office worker, the engineering student at night school and the retired couple in Tampa or San Diego. Only a fraction of this movement was to respond to Wallace. Its chief heir and destined beneficiary was Richard Milhous Nixon.

In March 1968 a young conservative intellectual named Richard Whalen (best known up to then for a biography of President Kennedy's father) was taken onto Nixon's campaign staff to help formulate the candidate's policy and write his speeches on Vietnam. Already in early 1968 Nixon was being advised, by Melvin Laird in particular, that military victory might be impossible. After Tet he could see as well as anyone, and better than most, that the war was becoming increasingly unpopular. On

March 29, which was a Friday, Whalen was working with Nixon on putting the final touches to what was to be his first policy statement on Vietnam, which was to be taped the next day, Saturday. As Nixon thought aloud about Whalen's draft, Whalen made notes. Suddenly he found that his pen had stopped. The full implications of what Nixon had just said sank in:

> I've come to the conclusion that there's no way to win the war. But we can't say that, of course. In fact, we have to seem to say the opposite, just to keep some degree of bargaining leverage.

According to Whalen, the speech was to have called for a summit meeting with the Soviet Union as the first step toward negotiating an end to the war in the context of general détente. It was never given, however. Within hours before he was to have gone to the studio to tape it, Nixon learned that President Johnson had taken network time for a speech of his own on Sunday night, March 31. That was the fateful night when Johnson announced his decision not to run for re-election. Nixon promptly cancelled his own speech, and from then on until the campaign was over and he had entered the White House, he adroitly kept silence on the specifics of his Vietnam policy.

A few days after the inauguration, he was talking to National Security Council staff in the White House when he suddenly turned to Henry Kissinger and said, "You and I are going to end this war." At that moment in time, the lengthy process of hammering out in detail how it would be done had only just begun. There had been position papers, written by Kissinger and other experts while Nixon and his advisers were still at the Hotel Pierre in New York, between election and inauguration. They spelled out every option, from immediate withdrawal to massive escalation. There had been the NSSM-1 study, based on a questionnaire sent around the departments, brainchild of Daniel Ellsberg. And on January 25 there was a formal meeting of the National Security Council, at which the decision was taken to withdraw U.S. troops from Vietnam, not immediately but gradually, and to withdraw them unilaterally, in advance of negotiations with Hanoi.

That was only the first signpost to a rough and winding road. It would be almost four years before Richard Nixon and Henry Kissinger had discovered exactly how the war could in fact be ended, and on what terms. It would take secret diplomacy of Byzantine ingenuity, and some disingenuousness. It would take public showmanship, and the discovery of a real, if limited, harmony of interest, at summit meetings in Moscow and Peking. It would take the discreet help of the Communist superpowers themselves. The conflicting but convergent interests of the Soviet Union and China, the fears of Saigon and the stubborn will of Hanoi, the suspicions of the Pentagon and the impatience of the American electorate—all had to be fitted into that improvised formula. And still it would take years of ambiguous action and dogged killing in Indochina; open troop withdrawal and secret escalation of the air war; the rundown of the draft to disarm the peace movement and the extension of the war to Laotian and Cambodian sanctuaries; the frequent deception of Congress, and the American people, and the South Vietnamese ally; years of "Vietnamization," and then a climactic application of American strategic air power: it would take all that before the war could be ended or, rather, before American withdrawal could be portrayed as the end of the war.

The purpose had been there in Nixon's and Kissinger's minds all along. It was rooted in three conclusions, which their very different minds both found inescapable. First, the American people wanted the war ended. Second, the war could not be "won." Third, the war dare not be "lost." Those simple rules defined the limits within which Nixon could maneuver to keep American political support in line for whatever solution Kissinger could negotiate, and within which Kissinger could find a solution that would be politically acceptable to American public opinion. Those rules had been laid down by the emergence of three clear majorities in American public opinion after Tet: a majority that held that it had been a mistake to get involved in Vietnam in the first place, a majority who wanted that involvement ended, and an even larger majority that rejected the peace movement's policy of immediate and unconditional withdrawal.

In 1968, in the mysterious way in which two hundred million people contrive to communicate their dominant mood, the American people had spoken. It was public opinion that laid down the terms on which Richard Nixon had to find an end to the war. In so doing, public opinion, the new voice of the American majority, had brought a whole era of foreign policy to an end.

Nixon's own personal predilections, of course, were those of a hardline anti-Communist. In 1966 he had said, "This is a war which has to be fought to prevent World War III," and until 1968 there was little evidence to suggest that he thought in terms of anything short of military victory. But if he stood at the right-hand end of the foreign-policy consensus, he did not stand outside it. There were differences of nuance and style, but not differences of substance, between his position on the war and those of President Kennedy, President Johnson and the other liberal Democrats who had helped to deepen the American involvement.

When it spoke out for an end to the war not at any price but as a more urgent national goal than victory, the new voice of the American majority rejected the old consensus on foreign policy, which had for some years largely ignored the opinion of the majority or, rather, taken its continued support for granted. Even more decisively, as we have seen, the majority had also rejected the radical alternative as proposed by the peace movement.

It would be natural to attribute this evolution of majority opinion on the war to the specific history of Vietnam, in isolation from what was happening in the U.S.A. But to do so would be to fail to explain the fact that, at exactly the same time, the same shift was taking place in opinion on domestic issues. There, too, a new majority simultaneously rejected the liberal program for perfecting society, and resisted the radical attack on that program. It is time, therefore, to take a closer look at the mood and composition of that new majority.

# PART IV

# More Movements than Movement

Let the reformers descend from the
stands where they are forever bawling.

> Walt Whitman,
> *Transpositions.*

A California song. . . .
Voice of a mighty dying tree in the redwood forest dense.

> Walt Whitman,
> *Song of the Redwood Tree.*

Of the interminable sisters,
Of the ceaseless cotillions of sisters,
Of the centripetal and centrifugal sisters. . . .

> Walt Whitman,
> *A Song of the Rolling Earth.*

1

Within roughly four weeks in the late summer of 1969, *Time, Newsweek, Life* and *Look* magazines all carried major stories on the proposed new jet airport in Florida Everglades National Park. The project was being opposed on two grounds. It threatened to destroy a unique ecological complex, and to deprive southern Florida of water, in order to benefit the Walt Disney interests, which were getting ready to open their Disney World entertainment complex nearby and naturally wanted to shovel in the paying customers as fast as possible.

Within a few weeks, ABC had put out a documentary on the same subject, and so had CBS. NBC, not to be left out, covered the story on its top-rating "Today" show. A new issue had forced its way to national attention: the environment, or—as it was often called by people who seemed to have only the shadowiest notion of what the word meant—"ecology." Politicians, adjusting hastily, found that they had to beware of the strength of yet another new constituency: "environmentally conscious people."

There was nothing new about natural resources being an issue in U.S. politics, of course. What was new was that American attitudes toward the issue entered a new stage abruptly in the late 1960s. It was the third stage of a long evolution. Environmental Consciousness One, the log-cabin, frontier tradition, was one of unrepentant exploitation. To the pioneer, the riches of the continent had been put there by God for his (the pioneer's) use. The forests were there to be logged, the plains to be plowed, and the bison to be hunted.

Environmental Consciousness Two was the traditional conservation movement. Born in the years after the Civil War, when the Sierra Club was founded and the first national parks set aside, it was an important element in the thinking of the Progressives in the early 1900s. It passed from such men as Teddy Roosevelt and Gifford Pinchot into the philosophy of the New Deal.

This classic conservationism still thought in terms of conserving the land for *use*. One of its key slogans, in fact, was "multiple use." Philosophically the distinctive idea of the third stage of environmental consciousness was the feeling that some resources should not be used: that as well as protecting the resources for the people, you should protect some resources *from* them.

Several strands converged to bring about the state of affairs, by the fall of 1969, when suddenly it seemed that every journalist in New York had turned with relief from worrying about "the war and the cities" to worrying about "the environment" instead.

For many years there had been growing awareness within the scientific community that technological progress implied new dangers for the human environment. There was serious concern about radioactive waste from the 1950s on. A gifted group of publicists began to draw wider attention to this and related problems. After the publication of Rachel Carson's *Silent Spring*, in 1962, which led forty states to pass legislation restricting pesticides within two years, no educated American could be unaware that the wonders of technology might have to be paid for in sinister ways. Two object lessons of the middle sixties reinforced the warning. Public awareness of air pollution was sharply heightened by the debate over nuclear fallout before the signature of the test-ban treaty in 1963. And the Surgeon General's report, confirming reports on the dangers of smoking, which came out at Christmas 1963, not only frightened people but reminded them that vast economic interests might be involved in pollution. After three days of smog alerts in southern California in October 1965, smog became a major political issue there.

The late sixties saw the rapid growth of citizen pressure groups concerned about a variety of different threats to the environment. Such long-established national organizations as the Wilderness Society, the Sierra Club and even the National Audubon Society, traditionally a conservative body dear to New England gentlefolk and retired admirals, suddenly found they were attracting a very different kind of member: young, aggressive, energetic, and politicized. Literally hundreds of local, highly participatory and sometimes militant action groups sprang up to raise local issues and combat specific threats, from the Florida keys to the redwood groves of northern California. These new environmentalists overlapped sociologically and ideologically with the middle-class peace movement. They began to look for a philosophical basis for their opposition to the sacrificing of natural beauty to industrial or residential development.

They found it in a new skepticism about economic growth. A high-water mark of some kind was reached early in 1972, when the Commission on Population Growth and the American Future, appointed by President Nixon, reached the conclusion, "No substantial benefit would result from continued growth of the nation's population." Obviously, several distinct and highly complicated issues are involved here. But the upshot was that by the end of the sixties a large slice of educated opinion had been brought by environmental considerations to reject that unquestioning faith in economic growth that had been one of the load-bearing pillars of the liberal ideology ten years before.

From 1968 on, influenced more or less consciously by the tactics of the civil rights and peace movements (which many of them had passed through), the militant environmentalists courted, and skillfully publicized, a series of confrontations. There were the saving of the (remaining) California redwoods and the saving of the Grand Canyon. In January 1969, within ten days of the Nixon administration's taking office, an oil rig off the coast near Santa Barbara, California, spilled, causing a physical mess on an epic scale, and a public outcry to match. Later that same year came the affair of the Everglades jetport. And then followed the most dramatic clashes of all between the new environmental lobby and traditional technological and economic values: the case of the Alaska pipeline and the case of the supersonic air transport.

By the spring of 1970, the environmental movement seemed to have become a true mass movement. On Earth Day, in April, Congress adjourned and ten million schoolchildren took part. Fifth Avenue in New York was closed to traffic for two hours.

The political system responded to this demonstration of concern. By the end of 1969, Congress had passed the National Environmental Policy Act (NEPA), and in his State of the Union message, President Nixon was at pains to put himself at the head of the new movement. He even went so far as to give utterance to the heretical proposition, "Wealth and happiness are not the same thing."

In the spring of 1970, suit was filed under NEPA to block the building of the pipeline the oil companies wanted to build across the Alaskan and Canadian wilderness. In September the President set up an Environmental Protection Agency (EPA). And in December the Senate voted against continued funding of the supersonic air transport on environmental grounds. It was finally killed by Congress the following May.

That was the high point. By 1971, the tide of political responsiveness to the environmental movement had begun to ebb. In a series of confrontations with industrial interests involving issues as varied as strip mining in the West and Great Lakes pollution, the Administration either backed off or openly took the anti-conservationist side. In late 1969 President Nixon had intervened to support his Interior Secretary, Walter Hickel, when he killed the Cross-Florida Barge Canal, a venerable boondoggle, on environmental grounds. In 1970 Hickel was fired. And now, in late 1971, Nixon flew to Mobile, Alabama, to shake George Wallace's hand at the ceremonial dedication of a remarkably similar project, the Tombigbee-Tennessee Waterway. Soon White House policy was openly anti-environmentalist. By 1972 the President had gone over to openly attacking the environmental lobby. "We are not going to allow the environmental issue to be used," he declared, "sometimes falsely and sometimes in a demagogic way, basically to destroy the system."

Successful though it was for a brief while, the environmental lobby was hardly threatening to destroy the system. Yet Nixon's reaction was less irrational than it might seem. Certainly it was less dissonant with his basic sympathy for business than his flirtation with the environment had been. In a way, he was right. The environmental movement was a challenge to the interests and even to the legitimacy of business. It was perhaps the most serious challenge to the reputation, and therefore ultimately to the power, of business since the labor struggles of the thirties, with one possible exception: the consumer movement.

2

The moment when, on March 22, 1966, the president of General Motors apologized publicly to Ralph Nader was one of the great David and Goliath scenes of the twentieth century. Here was a man whose position, power and salary made him, in the eyes of many Americans, more enviable than the President himself, making humble submission; here was the greatest corporation in the land admitting that it had been reduced to the most ignominious snooping on an obscure young lawyer. As a scene, it was a little spoiled by the fact that Nader, like many another Washingtonian before and since, couldn't find a taxicab and so arrived too late at the hearing to hear the apology. But that didn't stop him becoming a national hero overnight.

Nader himself has suggested that one reason for his extraordinary popularity was that his contemporaries were "starving for acts of the individual in a conflict situation outside the sports arena." That was part of it, no doubt. But Nader was also a twentieth-century Horatio Alger hero, the immigrants' son who had triumphed over the big boys by clean living and hard work.

There is, in fact, a distinct ambivalence about Nader's relationship to the "system." That is one of the reasons why he appeals both to radicals and to those who detest radicals. Partly this is a matter of externals. Nader may be, in serious ways, more radical than Abbie Hoffman. But he doesn't look it. He doesn't wear his hair long, he wears suits, and he has no use for marijuana. Such things matter to people. But there is also ambiguity in what he is saying.

Sometimes Nader sounds as if he were attacking corporate capitalism as a system. "Air pollution," he has written, for example, "is a new way of looking at an old American problem: concentrated and irresponsible corporate power." That sounds, if not like a socialist, at least like an old New Dealer of the trust-busting school talking. But at other times he comes on more as if he wants to do no more than point out to the defenders of the *status quo*, for their own good, where they are falling down. "I am trying to tell people," he has also said, "that if they can just organize to make the establishment obey its own rules, they will have created a peaceful revolution of tremendous proportions." In this vein Nader does not talk about who should have power but only about smoothing out the marginal inefficiencies of the system. The explanation, I suspect, is that Nader thinks analysis is less important than action. He knows that his effectiveness has been enhanced because he calls for change ostensibly in the name of the system's own values.

Nader's first handful of Raiders, financed out of the $425,000 GM paid him in settlement of his lawsuit, arrived in Washington in the summer of 1968. The next year, he had over a hundred volunteers at work. The reports they produced were aggressively conceived, meticulously researched, outspoken in presentation. In 1970 he had more than three thousand applications for two hundred places in teams investigating dozens of subjects. His activities had proliferated into half a dozen separate institutions grouped around his Center for the Study of Responsive Law, and imitators were springing up around the country. The consumer movement had arrived.

Nader's first target was strategically chosen. He began by investigating the federal regulatory agencies, starting with the Federal Trade Commission and the Food and Drug Administration in 1968, then moving on to others. These agencies were the incarnation of that "harmony of interest" between government and business that was so dear to the prophets of the liberal ideology. They had become sad illustrations of what that harmony had come to mean in practice. Originally intended to bring the power of business under public control, in practice they had handed out the power of government to business. Some were well-intentioned but ineffectual; others had almost totally capitulated to the interests they were supposed to police.

Gradually the consumer movement spread its net wider. Some of its concerns, as we have seen, overlapped with those of the environmentalists. Others were more clearly political in their thrust: a study of landowning and political power in California, for example, and another of the domination of the state of Delaware by the DuPonts.

Nader did not forget his first antagonist, however. With his backing, a group called Campaign GM bought stock in General Motors in order to appear at the 1970 annual stockholders' meeting and press for the corporation to become more responsive to the new range of concerns. For six hours they pelted the chairman with hostile questions about pollution and safety; they also wanted GM to get involved in checking population growth and in ending the Vietnam War. A black woman law student asked: "Why are there no blacks on the GM board of directors? Why no women?" At the end of the day they had won what one newspaper, usually friendly to GM, called "an enormous psychological and publicity victory." They had also won just 3 per cent of the votes.

The confrontation between the world's largest manufacturing company and its tormentors at Cobo Hall in Detroit that day epitomized the consumer movement of the early seventies in its strengths, and also in its weaknesses. Even James M. Roche, the chairman of the board of GM who had been humiliated by Nader, conceded that Campaign GM was impressively well briefed. There was a mixture of commando bravado and earnest idealism about its members that was immensely appealing to the media. It was less well thought out in terms of grand strategy.

Campaign GM underestimated the obstinacy of its opponents and also their commitment to a set of values, articulated in terms of "free enterprise," that were at least as strongly held as those of the consumer movement. The men who ran the world's largest corporation might talk like fools to ears trained in university liberal arts programs, but that did not mean that they were going to be easily pushed into handing over any significant part of their power. Campaign GM overestimated its opponents' vulnerability to the amorphous pressure of "public opinion." Whatever their failings, automobile executives were at least as popular with the American public as public-interest lawyers. The consumerists made no serious attempt to form an alliance with GM's own workers, either at the shop-floor level, in spite of a good deal of evidence of seething hostility to the management there, or through the UAW, which is, after all, the second-biggest union in the United States.

Perhaps in the end the most Campaign GM could claim to have achieved was to have shaken up the corporation's public relations program. Some such result was inevitable in what was, after all, a contest between amateurs, however talented, and professionals, however inept. Campaign GM, like Nader's Raiders generally, was largely recruited from the same upper-middle-class background that had provided the activists for the white civil rights movement, the peace movement, the environmental movement, and such political campaigns as those of Eugene McCarthy and Robert Kennedy. Such people moved on from one cause to another. Their commitment to challenging the power of General Motors was not as firm as their opponents' commitment to defending it.

The consumer crusaders, like the environmentalists, frequently impressed even their opponents with their intelligence, hard work and dedication. It was incredible, people said, how much more they could learn about a business in a short time than people who had been in it all their lives. What was equally remarkable was how little they seemed to know about America. Sophisticated about their research, their legal tactics, and their public relations, they were capable of being astonishingly naïve about politics, class and power.

After 1970 the consumer movement continued to expand. It kept up its pressure on business to behave more responsibly in various ways: to hire more women and members of minorities, to avoid the more blatant marketing abuses. It continued to be a force of which congressmen, for example, were very aware. But it became clear that Nader's original hope that it would be the core of a mass political reform movement would never be fulfilled. In 1968 he had told college audiences that the United States would see "consumer demonstrations someday that will make civil rights demonstrations look small by comparison." It hadn't happened by 1972, and it hasn't happened yet. And if the civil rights movement proved anything, it was that it takes more than even the most massive demonstrations to change deeply rooted patterns of power.

3

Between 1968 and 1972 a series of movements arose that among them challenged virtually every accepted assumption of the American ideology. Almost all of them were either consciously modeled on, or at least powerfully influenced by, either the peace movement or the black rebellion.

Some of them, such as the environmental crusade, aimed at drawing attention to what were seen as grave problems for the nation as a whole. These followed the model of the peace movement. At first, that is, the need to dramatize the issue in order to catch the attention of the media and awaken public interest favored the more extreme proponents of the case. And so, just as the more moderate opponents of the war were upstaged by the militant draft-resistance movement, so those who stated other problems in the most alarming form and those who were prepared to use direct-action tactics to win attention tended to outbid moderates. But usually this extreme statement of the case—the prediction of Earth Death and Eco-doom, for example, in the case of the environmental movement—failed to win many converts. Instead the role of the extremists was often to persuade almost everyone that there was some case to answer and that the issue should be added to the national agenda, though not to the degree or with the urgency that the original enthusiasts insisted it deserved.

Survey data on attitudes to pollution illustrate the sort of pattern that opinion followed on many other issues. In 1959 and again in 1964 The Gallup Organization carried out surveys on behalf of the Institute for International Social Research to find out which issues Americans were most concerned about. In both years, the surveys recorded zero concern about pollution. Then, between 1968 and 1970, the environmentalists succeeded in putting pollution on the national agenda. Books and articles predicting disaster if American society didn't mend its spendthrift ways had been coming out for many years. But in the late sixties demonstrations and environmental activism suddenly made pollution an unavoidable issue. By 1971, when Albert H. Cantril and Charles W. Roll, Jr., used a similar survey as the basis of their book *The Hopes and Fears of the American People*, they found that 9 per cent of the Gallup sample spontaneously mentioned pollution among their fears for America, making it the sixth-most-frequently cited danger. Virtually overnight, pollution had come to frighten as many Americans as racial conflict. These 9 per cent, moreover, were heavily concentrated among the wealthier and the better educated; 16 per cent of professional and business people, for example, mentioned pollution as a problem, as against 7 per cent of manual workers.

Only a year later, a follow-up study, *State of the Nation*, by William Watts and Lloyd Free, found that concern about pollution, "whether based on fact or fad," was now "well-nigh universal" and rather evenly distributed throughout the population. But it was a moderate concern. When people were asked whether they would be in favor of deliberately holding back the growth of the U.S. economy in order to reduce pollution, only 27 per cent said yes, and a resounding 60 per cent said no. The environmentalists had succeeded in spreading a practical concern with reducing pollution: they had not succeeded in converting the majority to their philosophy.

The parallel with the success and failure of the peace movement is striking. There, too, a minority stated an issue out of passionate moral conviction: a majority agreed that, pragmatically, there might be something in what they said.

The resemblance between another category of movements that sprang up in the late sixties and the black rebellion, though, was even closer. These were movements that aimed not at drawing attention to some specific problem that concerned the nation generally (the war, pollution, inadequate health care) but at claiming a new status in American society for particular groups, whether these were defined biologically (women), socially (homosexuals), or ethnically (Mexican-Americans, American Indians).

These movements imitated the black movement so closely because, like the blacks, their constituencies were in a posture in relation to the majority* that was fundamentally ambiguous.

Black Americans have always been ambivalent about white America, unsure whether what they wanted was to be more in it or more out of it. Some, at least, therefore, of those blacks who chose separatism in the middle sixties did so as a tactic. They hoped that separatism would ultimately make them less separate from the mainstream of American life. In an analogous way, the new movements for the rights of women, Chicanos, Indians and homosexuals were ultimately concerned with the status of these groups. Their goal could only be conferred by the majority. But before the

---

* I apologize for writing as if women were a minority. Statistically, of course, they are a majority. But the error is not mine. The leaders of the women's movement in the United States have consistently behaved as if women were a minority, either because they have been hypnotized by the black example or because when they speak of women, privately they mean "women", that is, women who accept the goals of their movement, and these are, to date, still a minority.

attention of the majority could be caught, it was first necessary to improve the morale of the minority. Women, for example, had to be made to think of themselves as women rather than as whites or as Americans or as members of a particular ethnic group or class. This was the process called "consciousness raising." The phrase, too, was borrowed from the black movement.

The prestige of the black movement and this concept of consciousness raising explain a great deal that is otherwise puzzling about these movements. A favorite argument among some of the leaders of the women's movement even made the comparison explicit. Gloria Steinem, for example, liked to say that women were niggers. It is a metaphor that ignores almost every important ethnic, economic and sociological truth about race in America, but it becomes less idiotic when it is understood that its purpose was not to persuade men but to arouse women.

The same factors explain what might seem at first glance an irrational preoccupation with words and names in all these movements. Red power succeeded black power. Gay lib mimicks women's lib. Perhaps the Chicano movement illustrated the importance of words best. Blacks, in order to free themselves of the connotations of inferiority and patronage that hung around the word "Negro," had to embrace the more insulting associations of the word "black" before they would feel free to say "black is beautiful" with the pride that would both raise their own morale and win white respect. In the same way, the genteel terms "Mexican-American," "Spanish-speaking," and "Spanish-surname" had to be dropped and replaced by the street slang "Chicano" before discontent could be welded into a movement.

As early as 1966, the discontent had been hot enough to boil over. That was the year of Cesar Chavez's grape pickers' strike in California, and also of Reies Lopez Tijerina's guerrilla raid on a courthouse in northern New Mexico. But it was not until the spring of 1969, when Rodolfo "Corky" Gonzales, at a conference in Denver, gave them a name (Chicanos), a language (*pochismo*, the street slang of the *barrios*), and a myth (the legend of the lost homeland of Aztlan), that an effective movement was born and Spanish speakers from the Rio Grande to the Sacramento began to think of themselves as a *raza unida*, a united race.

Names, languages and myths played a crucial part in the creation of all these movements.

But, in each of them, a deadly paradox was at work. They had to keep the cause in the forefront of the nation's attention. They had to compete for money and support. They therefore had to provoke and keep the curiosity and if possible the sympathy of the media. All these requirements strengthened the hands of militants as against moderates. If the goal was pride and status, then in any case the skills of the negotiator and the politician were in less demand than panache, charisma, and rhetoric. It was as bad to be a Tio Paco as to be an Uncle Tom. And in the women's movement, such moderate leaders as Betty Friedan, who advocated working for specific gains for women through legislation, political action and pressure, and who were willing to form alliances with men for this purpose, found themselves upstaged by their more intransigent sisters.

The paradox was this: a bias toward radical rhetoric was built into these movements by their need to attract attention: yet the more the radical rhetoric predominated the less they were able to enlist the full support of their own constituency, let alone have that effect on the opinion of the majority which was their ultimate purpose.

The issues raised by the environmental and consumer movements concerned the health and well-being of all Americans, whatever their socioeconomic class and wherever in the country they lived. Smog gets in everyone's eyes. The women's movement, too, saw itself as raising issues that affected all women. It set out to raise the consciousness of working wives in the industrial cities of the Middle West as much as that of career women in New York. Objectively, the movement had more to offer to girls with high school diplomas in small southern towns than to women at the great graduate schools on the East and West coasts.

The bald fact is, however, that these movements did not sweep the country. Essentially they remained upper- middle-class movements. The press loved them. Students responded to them. Some professional and business people found their consciences touched by them. They raised new issues, and in some cases they significantly altered American norms and values. But they never acquired the mass following which, routinely, the media forecast for them. Like the peace movement and the black rebellion, whose examples they followed so closely in other respects, they turned more people off than they turned on.

In foreign policy, the peace movement was dwarfed by the pragmatic, non-moralistic revolt against the war. At home, all the movements inspired by moral revulsion from the assumptions and the institutions of liberal America, put together, did not equal the vaster revolt of the pragmatic majority.

# The Capture of the New Majority

"Sam's right. There won't be any revolution. You're just a lot
of damn fools."

Senator Marcus A. Hanna, 1894.

1

One crude measure of the shift of the majority against liberalism was
the vote in successive presidential elections.

In 1964 Lyndon Johnson had established himself as the leader of the
liberal consensus on racial and social issues. He had not yet escalated the
war. He won 61 per cent of the vote. The combined vote for Nixon and
Wallace in 1968 was 57 per cent, and that swing certainly underestimated
the movement that had taken place, since although Hubert Humphrey
had long been identified with liberalism, by election time he had been
sharply contrasted with the new champions of the left wing of the Democratic Party, Robert Kennedy and Eugene McCarthy. Many of those who
voted for Humphrey in 1968, especially labor union members and their
families, did so out of past loyalty. In other respects, they shared the mood
of rebellion. If the Democratic candidate had been anyone other than
Humphrey, they might have voted for Nixon or Wallace. To say that in
1964 three fifths of the electorate voted for liberalism, and that four years
later three fifths of it voted against liberalism, is to oversimplify; but it
gives some indication of the scale of the rebellion.

For a time, this shift was hidden from sight by the more fashionable
idea that the wave of the future in politics was a coalition of "kids, blacks
and women," or, as Jack Newfield of The Village Voice put it, of "campus, ghetto and suburb." There was loose thinking in that formula,

though. Not all suburbs, or even all campuses, displayed any marked sympathy for the inhabitants of the ghetto. The "New Politics" alliance was between the upper-middle class and lower-class blacks. Arithmetically, it was not a very promising combination. But it was given an artificial boost by the Democratic primaries in 1968 and then revived by the success inside the Democratic Party of George McGovern in 1972. The illusion is easily explained: A coalition between upper-middle-class radicals and minorities might be able to make an impressive showing in a primary, in which a candidate who won no more than a plurality in one party—which is to say often far less than half of one half of the electorate—could be, and often was, projected by the media as a power and a portent. Nixon's victories in 1968 and 1972 brought such illusions tumbling down. They emphasized the cold arithmetical truth: a coalition that reached no farther than lower-class blacks and the upper-middle class was doomed to failure. An unassailable majority of Americans were neither rich nor poor, and neither black nor radical.

2

As early as 1967 the new reality had been described in a remarkably prescient speech by Robert C. Wood, a social scientist from M.I.T. who was then under-secretary at the new Department of Housing and Urban Development in Washington. Over recent years, Wood said, a union had developed "between the central city poor, more and more Negro, and the educated, economically secure, mostly white, Protestant suburbanite." This union, to Wood's mind, had much to commend it, especially its concern with social justice. But it had one defect. It was a union of minorities. It was not a majority.

The majority, he pointed out, was not made up of "the agitator, not the dissident, not the intellectual, not the educated housewife, nor the conscience-stricken executive—but the working American." And he offered a definition that is worth quoting at length:

> Statistically, he is a white employed male . . . earning between $5,000 and $10,000. He works regularly, steadily, dependably, wearing blue collar or white collar.
>
> This definition of the "working American" involves almost 20 million American families.
>
> The working American lives at the "grey area" fringes of a central city or in a close-in or very far out cheaper suburban subdivision of a large metropolitan area. He is likely to own a home and a car, especially as his income begins to rise. Of those earning between $6,000 and $7,500,

70% own their own homes and 94% drive their own cars. 94% have no education beyond high school and 43% have only completed the eighth grade.
The picture of these families is not exactly one of deprivation:
—87% have refrigerators
—77% have washing machines
—97% have television sets—18% of them color.
But he does not necessarily live well. In terms of debts the working man's family owes around $5,000—$700 of which is in installment debts.
A recent study by the Department of Labor concludes that it cost, in 1966, $9,200 for a family of four to live at a moderate standard (neither subsistence nor luxury) in urban areas of the United States. . . .

There was a fundamental difference of attitudes, Wood pointed out, between the "union of minorities" on the one hand and the "working Americans" on the other. What brought the most privileged and the least privileged together, he suggested, the Negro and the Puerto Rican with the Jew and the WASP, was a "yearning for community." The average working American, in contrast, was preoccupied not with the nation or the community or even the neighborhood, but with the protection of his job, his family and his home.

A couple of months before Wood made that speech, a young aide to a congressman sent to the publisher the draft manuscript of a book that started from the identical observation that Wood had made but drew from it very different conclusions. The young man's name was Kevin Phillips, and the book was to be called *The Emerging Republican Majority*. Wood was pleading with his liberal "union of minorities" to stretch out the hand of understanding and help to the majority before it was too late. Phillips was coldly telling the Republican party that if it could woo the majority it would be able to afford to kiss the liberals off.

Phillips' book appeared in January 1969. It landed with the explosive effect of a book that has an answer to the question everyone is asking. The question was: Is Nixon's victory a freak? Phillips' answer was that it was not. This was equally startling to conservatives, who had been secretly afraid since the Goldwater debacle that no candidate with their views could ever get to the White House, and to liberals, who had taken it for granted since Franklin D. Roosevelt's time that the White House was theirs by divine right.

Not so, said young Kevin Phillips. Two mighty movements were at work, he argued. Between them they would convert the historic Democratic majority, which had lasted from the Great Depression to the crisis of the sixties, into a natural Republican majority. Given ordinary luck and prudence, that, too, could last for a generation. One of these two movements was geographical—out of the Northeast and the Middle West into what Phillips called the Sun Belt, which stretched from Florida across Texas and the growing Southwest to southern California. The second was sociological—the movement of newly arrived members of the middle class, most of them of immigrant stock, out of the cities into the suburbs, but not into the liberal suburbs of Jack Newfield's and Robert Wood's imagining. "The silk stocking liberal suburbs of Boston, New York, Philadelphia, San Francisco and (to a lesser extent) Chicago and Washington," Phillips wrote scornfully but with undeniable truth, "cast only a minute fraction of the ballots wielded by the preponderance of unfashionable lower-middle-class and middle-income suburbs." And then over the grave of one kind of New Politics he pronounced the credo of another.

"The corporate welfarists, planners and academicians of the Liberal Establishment," he said, were no better than a privileged elite. Their interests in high government spending on social programs and on education were as much vested interests "as those of Coolidge-Hoover-era financiers and industrialists. The great political upheaval of the nineteen-sixties is not that of Senator Eugene McCarthy's relatively small group of upper-middle-class and intellectual supporters, but a populist revolt of the American masses who have been elevated by prosperity to middle-class status and conservatism. Their revolt is against the caste, policies and taxation of the mandarins of Establishment liberalism."

Suddenly, in 1968 and 1969, this was an idea whose time had come. Journalists, social scientists, pollsters and politicians all discovered the new majority. Each traced its profile a little differently. And each stressed those of its characteristics which suited his argument. Catholic writers, such as Father Andrew Greeley, Msgr. Geno Baroni and Michael Novak, often wrote as though the majority were largely made up of predominantly Catholic "white ethnics," though at least a half of the working American majority was made up of Protestants, most of them of southern white descent. Kevin Phillips put his emphasis on the prediction that the emerging majority would be Republican. Richard Scammon and Ben J. Wattenberg, being regular Democrats, drew from the (dubious, if not meaningless) proposition that the average voter was a forty-seven-year-old white truck driver the conclusion that the Democrats ought to stop running after blacks and "Movement" people and stick to the good old pocketbook liberalism of the New Deal. Radical populists, on the other hand, such as Senator Fred Harris, argued that the people, like a sleeping giant, were ready to be roused to a new crusade against war and big business if only the right politician could wake them with a kiss.

On one point, all these accounts agreed. It was common ground that the new majority was in revolt against "the mandarins of Establishment liberalism." All versions stressed how an alliance between the militancy of the ghetto and the idealism of an elite that could afford to have a social conscience had been forged at the expense of the majority in the middle.

There was a good deal of truth in this. The "radical chic" of the late sixties was an outward and visible sign of the alliance. The community-action programs of the War on Poverty were a perfect example of it. Upper-middle-class intellectuals devised them. Ghetto leaders, usually self-appointed, were their main beneficiaries. They were often directed against the elected leaders of the white working class in city hall. And the working majority, on whose behalf no such efforts were being made, bitterly resented them.

### 3

The classic instance of the new alignment was the Ocean Hill-Brownsville affair, which brought New York teachers out on strike three times in 1968. Ocean Hill was an angry knot in which many threads of educational, civic, and ideological history were twisted together, but this is not the place to try to disentangle them. It was the moment when the balance of power among the five main ethnic groups in the city—blacks, Irish, Italians, Jews and Puerto Ricans—pivoted. Alarmed by what they took as evidence of black anti-Semitism (which was, however, exaggerated and misunderstood, not to mention exploited), a substantial fraction of the Jewish middle class swung away from their traditional emotional and voting alliance with the blacks and the poor, into a new alliance with working-class and Irish and Italian homeowner sentiment. That tipped the balance from liberal to conservative predominance.

Besides all else, Ocean Hill was the perfect example of the new way in which the racial politics of urban America were being polarized into something remarkably similar to the traditional tacit alliance of plantation owners with blacks against the poor and middling whites of the South. On one side of the line, in the Ocean Hill affair, there now stood, in surprising alliance, the small, immensely powerful WASP upper class, as represented by the mayor, former "silk-stocking" Republican congressman John Lindsay, and McGeorge Bundy, new president of the Ford Foundation; some liberal intellectuals; and a majority of a vast, mainly black and Puerto Rican, underclass. By 1971 the number of welfare recipients in New York City alone was over 1.2 million; at least as many of the working poor lived in similar circumstances. On the other side, despised and to a remarkable degree ignored by the upper class and the media which it largely controlled, and feeling alternately resentful of the limited successes and alarmed by the general desperation of the under-class, were the embittered and embattled working classes in between. By the end of the sixties, a chasm icier than the East River in February flowed between the mind of Manhattan and the mind of Queens.

The immediate issue at Ocean Hill was the decentralization and "community control" of the New York public schools. These had been administered by a highly professionalized bureaucracy under a board of education ever since the schools were prized from the grasp of Tammany Hall by middle-class reformers early in the century. Something similar had happened in most of the older large U.S. cities. In the fall of 1966, black parents in Harlem boycotted Intermediate School 201. They were infuriated that a new system of intermediate schools, brought in to reduce *de facto* desegregation, had turned out to be as segregated as ever.

From that moment on, three strands of thought began to run rapidly side by side. Black parents (and some black educators), influenced by the black-power movement and feeling that the schools were so bad that they had little to lose, began to demand community control. So did many liberal intellectuals influenced by the ideology of "community action" (which had surfaced both in SDS and OEO). Thirdly, those powerful people whose concern was with the over-all tranquillity and economic prospects of New York City and whose children would not be attending the public schools in any case, took up the idea of community control, too. More moved to penitence at the situation of the blacks than to sympathy with the less dramatic plight of middle-class and working-class parents and teachers, and more or less openly fearing racial Armageddon, such people as Lindsay and Bundy found that community control suited both their emotions and their policies.

It is a startling illustration of the power of private money in the United States that the Ford Foundation could insert itself into the most delicate issue in the politics of the city, as if it had every bit as much right to be consulted as the parents, the teachers, the voters or the taxpayers. Its personnel sat down with the school superintendent, union representatives and "community leaders" (some, at least, of whom owed their status to the Foundation's patronage) to discuss a plan for decentralizing the schools. In the spring of 1967 this plan was adopted by the Board of Education. Local boards were set up to run the schools in three pilot districts. One of them was Ocean Hill-Brownsville, a forlorn wasteland of tenements in Brooklyn and, with Harlem and the South Bronx, one of the three worst slums in the city.

Mayor Lindsay appointed a panel of prominent citizens, headed by Bundy, to prepare an over-all decentralization plan. The pilot boards were given money by the Ford Foundation to get started, and "community workers," paid by the Ford Foundation, rounded up voters to elect members to the boards. A few weeks after the Ocean Hill board went into operation, the Bundy panel announced its recommendations: all schools in New York were to be handed over to between thirty and sixty small local school boards.

The reaction was immediate, and largely hostile. The teachers' union, already rebellious both about money and on the issue of teachers' power to expel "disruptive" students from the classroom, insisted that it did not oppose some measure of decentralization but attacked the Bundy plan as "Balkanization." The stage was set for confrontation.

There is no need to follow in detail all the moves and countermoves, the angry claims and counterclaims. The city Board of Education and the Ocean Hill board never agreed on how powers should be shared between them. The Ocean Hill board ordered "involuntary transfers" for nineteen teachers and administrators. The union promptly claimed that they had been fired, and struck.

By the fall, the lines had been drawn. The union struck a second time for the teachers to be reinstated, and then again, claiming that an agreement had been violated. In October there was a fourth strike (the fifth in fifteen months), because teachers were intimidated by what could be called either "black-power militants" or "community leaders," according to predilection.

The precise fortunes of the struggle are less important, in the context of the newly emerging political alignment, than its symbolism. The teachers and their allies took their stand, in effect, on the traditional principles of the Old Left. They saw themselves as defending the hard-won job security of union members. They refused to acknowledge that to their opponents this might look very much like defending a privileged middle-class position against the interests of the black and Puerto Rican poor.

The supporters of community control, in answer, pointed to the failure of the existing schools and to the success of the "street academies" run by black militants and young white radicals. These experiments suggested, perhaps deceptively, that with the right motivation on the part of both teachers and students, ghetto youngsters could get to college. Teachers sometimes seemed to imply that they were ineducable. Their parents naturally preferred to conclude that the teachers were incompetent, or racist, or both; and they were not always wholly wrong.

In an article in *Commentary*, Maurice J. Goldbloom made an equally serious countercharge: that the advocates of community control, knowingly or not, were playing the game of interests more privileged and more powerful than those of the teachers' union. More generally, he said:

> There is a widespread movement now afoot to ally the bottom and the top layers of American society against those in the middle. . . . Com-

munity control of schools . . . can offer quite tangible benefits to certain sections of the economic elite; for example, it affords an excuse for not increasing expenditure and taxes. . . . But to the people of the community, the actual community, it offers only the simulacrum of power—for they have no command over the economic resources that real power requires. . . .

### 4

That was not the only reason why community control, in practice, proved disappointing. Blacks were learning about its limitations on a larger scale as, from 1968 on, they began to acquire political power at the city level.

The Hatcher administration, in Gary, Indiana, is a case in point. Richard Hatcher was elected mayor in 1968, by a few hours the first black mayor of any major city in the country. Gary was a test case both for black power and for the doctrine of community development: both militant blacks and the liberal Establishment had the most powerful incentive to do all they could to make the Hatcher administration a success. And so, for the first three years after Hatcher took over, a stream of federal officials, consultants, urbanologists, and journalists flowed through the shattered streets of the city. Studies were generated, projects proposed, programs funded, and concerned articles written. "Whatever program we thought up," one member of the new administration remembered with a gleam in her eye, "they sent us the money for it, and if we couldn't think up a program, why, they sent us the money anyway." By 1972, the federal infusion had reached a total of $150 million, or close to one thousand dollars for every living soul in the city. And this federal blitz was matched by a second golden shower of money and concern from the big private foundations.

This largesse was not wasted. Things did happen. A good deal of excellent low-income housing was built. Innovative education, health and job-training programs were started. But after some four years, Richard Hatcher and his administration were ruefully aware of the limits of their power.

Unemployment was still too high. Crime was a menace. Downtown neighborhoods looked as if a war had been fought there. The schools were threatened with closing down for lack of money. And white people were leaving town.

Some of the power to tackle these interrelated problems lay with the federal government. Some lay with the state of Indiana. Neither was automatically sympathetic to the difficulties of Gary. The mayor of Gary, it turned out, didn't even control his own revenue. The city depends for the whole of its income—aside from what it is given by the federal government—on its share of a property tax. Other public jurisdictions—the school district, the township, the county—take a share of this property tax. And valuation is assessed not by the city but by an official elected in the *county* (and therefore by a predominantly white electorate, in this case) according to formulas determined by state law. The city of Gary does not have that most elementary of the powers of government, the power to raise its own revenue.

That is not the end of the ways in which the people of Gary lack power over their own life. Roughly half of all the property tax paid in Gary, for example, is paid by a single taxpayer: U. S. Steel, with headquarters in Pittsburgh, Pennsylvania. The company's plant is assessed at a fraction of its replacement-cost value. The other half of the tax base is constantly being eroded by white flight and the consequent decay of the city's commercial center. Moreover, the mayor does not even control his own police; that function lies with a police commission. The vital decisions that affect the level of employment in the city, of course, are taken elsewhere, mainly in Pittsburgh.

There is a sense in which a place like Gary is not really a true city: it is only one part of an organic urban region whose economic reason for being there is the string of steel plants along the shore of Lake Michigan. This urban region has sprawled back from the shore to the point where what lies within the city limits is only an arbitrary and declining fraction of the whole. It is also the fraction with a disproportionately big share of the social problems of the whole and a disproportionately small share of its resources. The liberals believed that economic growth would generate the resources for solving social problems, but that won't happen if the growth is in one place and the problems are left behind in another.

Hair-raising though Gary's problems are, they are in no way exceptional. Gary is almost an exact model, on a smaller scale, of the other great lakeside cities of the Middle West: on a 1/5 scale, of Cleveland; on a 1/10 scale, of Detroit; on a 1/20 scale, of Chicago. But the problem is not confined to the half-moon-shaped cities along the Great Lakes. Everywhere, middle-class white people, new investments, and therefore tax revenues were moving out to the suburbs, leaving economically declining core cities to cope with exploding problems of poverty, welfare, inadequate schools and slum housing. At the precise historical moment when the inner city began to run into trouble, the city limits of most older U.S. cities stopped expanding. The inner cities became imprisoned in an iron collar of white suburbs. And this was no accident. It was, on the one hand, the direct consequence of the black migration from the South, and on the other, the result of the conscious, if veiled, efforts of middle-class whites, especially the real estate and credit interests who controlled suburban governments.

Hatcher and the black majority in Gary, in fact, like black leaders and black people in cities all over America, were discovering that black power at the lowest tier of a federal system, and black power at the lowest level in an economy dominated by national institutions and national corporations, is limited, if not illusory, power. It may have valuable effects on black people's morale. It may be able to achieve elementary decencies that were refused before it was won. It is not to be despised. But it cannot tackle fundamental problems unless the white majorities at the upper tiers of the system are willing to share their power.

The learning of that lesson leaves black people and their strategists with a hard choice. Should they go all out for power at the level of the cities, only to risk finding that when they have won it, most of it has slipped through their fingers? Or should they bargain for whatever share of power they can get at the higher levels, knowing that all they can hope for there is the limited voice a minority can acquire through the political bargaining process unless it can form alliances on the basis of common interests with sections of the majority. And at first glance, in the hardening racial climate of the late sixties and early seventies, such common interests looked hard to find.

## 5

There was some truth, then, in the perception that an alliance between black people and the liberal elite would leave blacks without real power. There was even some truth in the idea that liberalism itself was a doctrine that tended to preserve the *status quo*. But what was far more significant than the alliance between black militancy and the liberal elite was the alliance between the rebellious Middle Americans—whether they came from a fundamentalist Protestant tradition in the South and Southwest or were mainly Catholic "ethnics" in the urban Northeast and Middle West—and a conservative economic elite whose most noticeable characteristic was emphatically not its social conscience.

The revolt of the Middle Americans, that is to say, was captured by the conservatives. It was not intrinsically conservative. The best single label to describe it is perhaps "populist." It was a revolt against the indifference and the condescension of the liberal elite. That made it easy to mistake it for conservatism. And it made it easy for the conservatives to capture. That is what Richard Nixon did, with consummate tactical skill.

Nixon and his confidants had an aversion to serious discourse with the press that amounted almost to phobia. That is why an article by James Reichley published in *Fortune* magazine in December 1969 is such precious evidence. It was based on discussions with the Nixon administration's strategists that were far less disingenuous than usual. And there can be no doubt of its accuracy, for the simple reason that the strategy it outlined was the strategy that was actually followed for the next three years.

Nixon and his chief strategist, John Mitchell, Reichley reported, were hoping to build "a national majority which will long survive their own tenure": by invoking "the traditional values of middle class America—hard work, individual enterprise, orderly behavior, love of country, moral piety, material progress." For these beliefs and attitudes, Reichley proposed a new symbol: not Wall Street, citadel of big business, not Main Street, stronghold of the local elites and small-town conservatism, but Elm Street, the quiet residential street where "the best people," doctors, lawyers and leading businessmen with Anglo-Saxon names, had their homes. That, said Reichley, was where most Americans wanted to live. "The essential image of Elm Street," he wrote almost lyrically, "has been lovingly reproduced in bedroom communities from New England to California. Steamfitters and firemen and taxi drivers, as well as accountants and engineers, have swarmed into the new suburbs. . . . And wherever [they] have gone they have sought to re-create the remembered ideal of Elm Street."

Even Kevin Phillips had pointed out that the groups from among whom a new Republican majority might be recruited were not so much conservative at heart as populist. Now, after Nixon's victory, that was forgotten. The voters who had deserted Humphrey for Nixon and Wallace, and the millions more whom Nixon and Mitchell hoped to win in 1972, were said to be moving away from their populist past:

> They have at least temporarily become conservatives, in the sense of believing that they are more likely to lose than to gain from social change. The economic issues that now concern them most, inflation and high taxes, reinforce their social conservatism. More deeply, they are disturbed by challenges to the system of values that has guided their lives.
>
> Hippies and black power militants, drug addicts, Mafiosi, "welfare mothers"—and to some extent expense account executives—are perceived as transgressors against the moral verities that have always been accepted by most Americans, poor as well as rich and middle class, black as well as white.

Nixon and his strategists, in other words, were banking on exploiting the new polarization and pitting the new Middle American majority against *both* radicalism or black militancy *and* "Wall Street" or "big business" or "expense account executives." "Large elements within the middle class," Reichley quoted them as believing, "suspect that the business elite is now prepared to sacrifice the interests of middle-class whites in order to quiet the protests of discontented blacks."

After Watergate, that strategy is rich in unintended irony. It is amusing that the Nixon people were counting on "an impression of widespread ethical misconduct in high places in government and business" to help their fortunes. John Mitchell was quoted, hilariously in retrospect, as saying: "Watch what we do instead of listening to what we say." But the fact is that the strategy worked. Nixon did capture the lion's share of the Middle American majority.

The talk about his being against "big business," "expense account executives" and the "business elite," of course, was so much cynical propaganda. With the exception of a handful of wealthy individuals mostly in New York City and in California, just about everything and everybody that could be described as "big business" were for Nixon in 1972, some reluctantly but more with enthusiasm.

It was not even true, as was often said, that Nixon championed a new class of self-made men against old, established wealth. Nixon might feel personally more at home with such men as Bebe Rebozo, Robert Abplanalp the aerosol patentholder, and J. Willard Marriott of Hot Shoppes. But if W. Clement Stone, the self-made Chicago insurance man, was the biggest contributor to his 1972 campaign (so far as we know), the second-largest was Richard Mellon Scaife. The prized embassies in London and Paris went, respectively, to Walter Annenberg, heir of an eastern media fortune, and to Arthur Watson, heir of the family that controlled the sixth-biggest corporation in the United States, IBM. All the great agglomerations of capital in the United States—the oil people, the insurance people, the banking people, the automobile people, the real estate people —were for Nixon. And now that we know something of how the President's fund-raisers went about making the milk producers and the people who wanted federal banking licenses, and the air lines, cough up for the President's re-election; now that we know what we know about Spiro T. Agnew's financial ethics and about the President's relations with Howard Hughes, not to mention his income tax returns—Richard Nixon's claim to represent the little fellow against the money power of the economic elite has become a shabby fraud.

That only makes the rest of the Nixon-Mitchell strategy for winning the hearts and minds of Middle America all the more audacious. For

Nixon and Mitchell believed that, as James Reichley put it, few average Americans would base their political choice "on desire to improve their economic lot." Instead, they were betting that, for the majority of the voters, the highest priority was to save the nation from hippies and black-power militants, from drug addicts and welfare mothers.

It was, on a moment's reflection, an amazing proposition. Yet it proved absolutely correct.

The Nixon administration made campaigning against those four categories of people its highest policy priority.

No doubt there was a side to Richard Nixon that had immortal longings and dreamed of peace and national unity and of President Nixon's place in the history books. But a more skeptical reading of his administration suggests that this amounted to little more than the banal Puritan dualism between the Sunday-suited Nixon of the White House prayer meetings and the workaday Nixon who had learned that in a wicked world, unworthy of his dreaming, it was often wiser to kick the ungodly in the groin first and pray for them afterward.

He did want peace, and he was prepared to take diplomatic and political risks to get it: to cut U.S. forces in Vietnam, to talk to Hanoi, to go to Moscow and Peking. But when he couldn't have it as he wanted, he was prepared to invade Laos and Cambodia and to bomb more ruthlessly than ever Lyndon Johnson had, and then to lie to the American people about it.

Nixon was flattered by Daniel Patrick Moynihan's invitation to become a second Disraeli and steal the liberals' clothes with "Tory men and radical measures." But the radical measures somehow never got the President's wholehearted support. The Tory men could always count on it.

Moynihan's own Family Assistance Plan staked the Administration's main claim to a reputation for radical measures, and although Moynihan did his best to blame the liberals for its failure to be enacted by Congress, he had to admit that in the hours of crisis for welfare reform, the President's attention was "usually elsewhere." When it came to pressing for bills to fight crime or stamp out drug addiction, the President's mind was never so absent.

Somehow, it was always the liberals who got squeezed out, a long, sad line of them: Robert Finch, John Knowles, Leon Panetta, Walter Hickel, in the end Moynihan himself. It was the hard men with mouths like scars who drew steadily closer to the throne: John Mitchell and big John Connally, Spiro Agnew with his contempt for liberals, Patrick Buchanan with his contempt for all but servile newsmen, H. R. Haldeman and John Ehrlichman with their contempt for everyone. As time went on, the President became more and more confident of the soundness of his strategy of campaigning against blacks and radicals. The plan was revealed in all its coarseness at the Senate Watergate hearings in August 1973. Haldeman, who had finally edged out even Mitchell as the archadvocate of the hard line, was interrogated by Senator Lowell Weicker (R.-Conn.) about some annotations Haldeman had made on a report about plans for a presidential visit to Charlotte, North Carolina, in October 1971. Weicker read it aloud:

> Q.: "1. The most recent intelligence that has been received from the advance man Bill Henkel and the United States Secret Service is that we will have demonstrations in Charlotte tomorrow. . . . They will be violent—with a penciled underlining of 'violent'—They will have extremely obscene signs"—underlining "obscene." And next to the word "obscene," penciled in writing which . . . seems to be the same as the writing below your initial, appears to be yours, saying "Good."
> Is that your writing where it says "Good"?
>
> A.: I believe it is.
>
> Q.: "As has been indicated by their handbills, it will not only be directed toward the President, but also toward Billy Graham." Underlining "also toward Billy Graham" where you penciled in "Great."

Now, why did Haldeman think it would be good if the President was to be attacked by demonstrators, and better still if they were violent and waved obscene signs, and best of all if they waved them at Billy Graham as well as at Richard Nixon? Because the more demonstrators, and anyone who opposed Nixon, could be portrayed to Middle America as militants, radicals and hippies, the better for the President's hopes of winning those Middle American votes. The heart of Nixon's strategy was to distract attention from the causes of dissent and to campaign against the dissenters themselves. It cannot be said that it was unsuccessful.

## 6

George McGovern campaigned on many issues. He campaigned for withdrawal from Vietnam, and he campaigned for a new attack on privilege and inequality in American society. He got almost no response from the electorate. A survey carried out by Albert H. Cantril and Charles W. Roll for the public employees' union AFSCME, showed that "over half (52%) expressed confidence in Nixon on the matter of 'keeping the big interests from having too much influence over the government,' as against only 35% expressing confidence in McGovern [on that issue]"! Even more astonishing: on McGovern's chosen issue, the war, which he had been speaking out about since 1967, "less than a third (29%) trusted McGovern when it came to getting out of Vietnam 'honorably' as compared with 70% for Nixon."

McGovern proposed an (admittedly ill-considered and poorly prepared) plan for a one thousand dollar per person per year "Demogrant" in place of welfare. He suggested that all inheritances of over five hundred thousand dollars should be taxed, at first at 100 per cent and later at only 77 per cent. Middle America showed only negative interest in the "Demogrants," although many Middle Americans would have benefited from them. And McGovern himself was bemused by the opposition of blue-collar workers to the inheritance tax. "They must think they're going to win a lottery," he said. And of course in a sense they did. The idea that in America anyone may make a fortune by striking oil or inventing a better mouse trap dies hard.

The issues that did count with Middle America, counted against McGovern. There were three of them in particular: amnesty, abortion and pot. McGovern was on record as supporting amnesty for those who had gone to Canada to avoid the draft but not as favoring either abortion or legalized marijuana. Near the end of April, however, the Evans-Novak column quoted "one liberal Senator" (unspecified) as saying, "The people don't know McGovern is for amnesty, abortion and legalization of pot." Three days later, James Reston picked this up in the New York *Times,* writing, "McGovern carries a heavy load of promises: to slash the defense budget steeply, legalize pot and abortion, and grant amnesty to Vietnam expatriates." Reston subsequently apologized for the mistake. Evans and Novak never did. The agonized denials of McGovern's staff never did quite catch up with the suspicion that McGovern was a kook and a friend to—Reichley's list of the bugaboos the Nixon people had picked out to campaign against, three years earlier, had proved deadly accurate—a friend to hippies, and drug addicts, and welfare mothers.

The TV coverage of the Democratic convention reinforced the image. There was Mayor Daley, the working man's friend from Back of the Yards, bounced from the Illinois delegation by eloquent, militant, black Jesse Jackson. There were all the Women, and the Kids, and the Blacks and the Browns, but where were the middle-aged, middle-class, Middle Americans? Labor delegates from Pennsylvania were especially bitter about I. W. Abel, president of the United Steelworkers. In 1968 he had probably done as much as any other man to mount the labor drive that came within a hair of stopping Nixon. In 1972 he wasn't even a delegate. In every state there were I. W. Abels.

"Campaigning," said a little manual used by the Nixon political staff in 1968, "is symbolic, i.e. it is not what the candidate actually does as much as what it appears he does." In 1972 the whole campaign to re-elect the President was a gloss on a slightly different axiom: It is not what the opposition candidate actually stands for, it is what it appears he stands for.

It would be wrong to attribute Nixon's success with Middle American voters in 1972 entirely to this strategy of tagging the McGovern Democrats with extremism. There had been signs for twenty years that some working-class voters, especially Irish-Americans, were drifting away from the Democratic Party and voting Republican, especially in presidential elections. Many other factors were going Nixon's way. The success of the Nixon-Kissinger foreign policy, with its bold rejection of conservative taboos about détente; the approaching "end" of the war; the Democrats' disunity; and the contrasting impression of a strong and capable President —these all contributed to Nixon's victory. Yet, the centerpiece of his strategy, which made all the rest possible, was the appeal to Middle American fears of extremism. And it worked.

Nixon won 61 per cent of the vote. Contrary to many prior predictions and subsequent analyses, he did *not* do so merely by adding Wallace votes to his own. In the first place, his share of the vote was higher by some four percentage points than the combined Nixon-Wallace vote in 1968. Secondly, the best estimate is that Nixon won no more than 60 per cent of the Wallace vote.

No: what made the Nixon landslide possible was the deep cut he made into the Democratic Party's own territory. Many Democrats split their tickets, voting for Nixon and Agnew but for no other Republican candidate. Richard Nixon, as the politicians say, had short coattails.

A computerized Election Day survey by CBS, based on the exceptionally large sample of seventeen thousand voters, calculated that Nixon captured no less than 36 per cent of the "habitual" Democratic voters. These votes came exactly where Kevin Phillips said they would. Nixon's biggest gain was in the South. Helped by the absence of George Wallace —shot and paralyzed on June 11—his vote in the South rose 38 percentage points from 1968 to 70 per cent in 1972.

Even more decisive was his showing in the traditional Democratic heartland, among urban and suburban Middle Americans. His share of the blue-collar vote rose from 35 per cent in 1968 to 54 per cent in 1972.

The vote was, to a decisive extent, as Cantril and Roll demonstrated in a mid-October survey, a vote *against* George McGovern rather than a vote *for* Richard Nixon. They found 62 per cent of the electorate supporting Nixon, which was close enough to the final tally. Only 37 per cent of these, not much more than half, supported Nixon because they positively liked him. The remaining 25 per cent who supported him did so because they would "hate"—that was the word the survey used—to see McGovern win. "For the most part," Cantril and Roll commented, fairly, "Richard Nixon's 'new American majority' was the creation of George McGovern."

True. But here we should apply the Nixon people's own axiom: what matters is not only what the opposition candidate stands for but what he appears to stand for. The "George McGovern" whom so many of the voters would have hated to see President was to a considerable extent the creation of Richard Nixon, and of four years' steady, crafty and unremitting work by Nixon's propaganda machine to identify the liberal wing of the Democratic party with radicalism.

One should not exaggerate. Many voters disliked McGovern because they found his personality cool and elusive. Blue-collar, "ethnic" voters may have been especially prone to this feeling. They were certainly suspicious of McGovern's upper-middle-class radical supporters, and who is to say that they were wrong? Others doubted McGovern's competence. After the Eagleton affair, in particular, many voters reacted strongly against McGovern's earlier image as a man above politics, and put him down as "just another politician." In two weeks after the revelation of Senator Eagleton's history of mental stress, wrote McGovern's own press secretary, Richard Dougherty, the candidate was transformed by his own errors of judgment "from a possibly too radical, possibly too righteous, but interesting new political leader, who would be worth watching, into an undoubted bumbler and probable liar."

Yet when one has given all due credit for the achievements of the Nixon administration and made all due allowance for the shortcomings of his opponent, a residual impression is left. The revolt of the Middle American majority against liberalism was captured by Richard Nixon and yoked to the service of a cause that was not their own.

## No Crystal Stair

"Generally, to date, the 1970s have been characterized by a mixed pattern of development as compared with the 1960s, the decade when major social and economic advances were made by blacks."

U. S. Bureau of the Census, 1973.

"Well, son, I'll tell you:
Life for me ain't been no crystal stair."

Langston Hughes, *Mother to Son.*

1

By the spring of 1972, four years had passed without major urban riots.

In December 1971 the U. S. Bureau of the Census marked in the unexcited prose of one of its current population reports the passing of a statistical milestone with dramatic implications: "There was no apparent difference in 1970," it reported, "between the incomes of white and Negro husband-wife families outside the South where the head was under 35 years old."

And in the next month, January 1972, Elliot Richardson, then Secretary of Health, Education and Welfare, released a set of figures that suggested that, at long, long last, almost eighteen years after the Supreme Court, in *Brown*, had condemned it, the dual school system in the South was being dismantled and that legal segregation must soon be a thing of the past. As recently as 1968, more than two thirds of the black children in the South, or some two million children, went to all-black schools. By

1972, that number had fallen below three hundred thousand, or less than one in ten of the South's black children. The proportion of black children there who went to schools where a majority of the children were white had risen from less than one fifth in 1968 to more than two fifths in 1972. One other fact that Secretary Richardson recorded that day had more ambivalent implications: For the first time, the South, with roughly half of the nation's black population, had both a smaller absolute number and a smaller proportion of black children in segregated schools than the rest of the country. Still, credit where credit was due: the South was at last coming into compliance not with Richard Nixon's southern strategy but with the decision of the Supreme Court in *Brown* v. *Board of Education of Topeka.*

What did the passing of those milestones mean? They meant what they said, of course. It was true that rioting had subsided, that some blacks had made rapid economic progress, and that school desegregation in its southern form was on its way out. It was tempting to go further and take these signs of improvement as portents of a larger victory, and to claim that American blacks were on their way to economic and social equality. Yet to each of these hopeful propositions, at the beginning of the seventies, it was necessary to oppose its gloomy antithesis.

The riots were over. But the conditions that were supposed to have produced them were little changed. If anything, in certain respects they were a little worse.

Some blacks had made rapid economic progress. But, over all, blacks were not catching up to whites in income in the early seventies; they were falling further behind.

Segregation, in the traditional southern form of the dual school system, was on its way out. But *de facto* segregation was almost unchanged. The proportion of black children attending schools that were 80 per cent or more black in the North and West declined from 69.7 per cent in 1968 . . . to 68.3 per cent in 1971. Busing—the main device by which such segregation could be quickly remedied—was meeting with growing opposition. And the hope that the schools would be the means of abolishing social inequality between whites and blacks had been abandoned.

2

Early on Sunday morning, July 23, 1967, police raided a "blind pig" after-hours club on Twelfth Street in Detroit's West Side black ghetto. To their surprise, they found it full of more than eighty people at a party for two veterans just home from Vietnam. It took unusually long to get the prisoners into police vehicles, and before the job was finished, someone broke the window of a police cruiser with a bottle. Within minutes, the riot had begun. By the following Thursday, when General Throckmorton and elements of two airborne divisions had restored order, the whole center of the city looked as if it had been bombed, and forty-three people were dead.

Nationally the explosion of grief and anger that followed the death of Martin Luther King in the spring of 1968 was more spectacular. But the crescendo of spontaneous rioting that began in Watts in 1965 reached its true climax in Detroit in 1967. The question is "Why hasn't there been rioting on the same scale since?"

In 1967 everybody had an explanation of the riot, and all the explanations were a little different. Detroit, for a while, was the most analyzed city in the United States. There were polls, surveys, reports, commissions, television documentaries and countless articles. They fell roughly into three categories of explanation, which can be called the radical theory, the conservative theory, and the liberal theory.

The radical theory, in its pure form, was that what happened in Detroit that week was a spontaneous revolutionary insurrection. "The civil rights movement," wrote Jimmy Breslin after a night in the Detroit streets, "is becoming a rebellion." "It was the colonized reacting to colonization," a young black-studies teacher at Wayne State University told me.

The trouble with the radical theory is that if what happened in Detroit was an insurrection, it was one of the most aimless and incompetent insurrections imaginable. Most of the damage was done to black neighborhoods. Most of the victims were black. Most of those who were shot, were shot by white people.

The conservative theory surfaced almost before the shooting died away: it was that there was a revolutionary insurrection, but not a spontaneous one. On July 28, with troops still patrolling the streets, the Detroit *News* splashed across eight columns a story by-lined by Tom Joyce: "Police and military officials," it led off, "trying to unravel the vicious pattern of deadly sniping that prolonged Detroit's racial maelstrom say there already is strong evidence to suggest a national conspiracy."

Most of the speakers at a convention of police associations in Toronto that week agreed. The president of the Los Angeles association asserted that the riots had been "stirred by traveling agitators, perhaps hundreds of them." And the Republican Coordinating Committee in Washington lent its authority to this theory by passing a resolution condemning "hatemongers . . . traveling from community to community inciting insurrection."

There were two substantial difficulties about this explanation, however. No one ever found any evidence of agitators at work. And if there were any snipers, no one ever found them.

In September 1967, a careful analysis of the forty-three known fatalities in the rioting by three reporters in the Detroit *Free Press* concluded, "Only three of the victims may possibly have been killed by snipers, two of them doubtful."

In March 1968 the report of the National Advisory Commission on Civil Disorders (the Kerner Commission), appointed by President Johnson while the troops were still on the streets of Detroit, concluded after taking testimony from dozens of witnesses, "Rioters were responsible for two and perhaps three of the deaths." None of them were caused by snipers. By contrast, the police killed at least twenty and perhaps twenty-one people. The National Guard killed seven and perhaps nine. The U. S. Army, which distinguished itself for discipline, killed one.

Of the seventy-two hundred people arrested during the riot, twenty-seven were initially charged with sniping. Cases against twenty-four of these were dismissed, and no one has been convicted of sniping.

The following vignette, reported on July 25 by the Detroit *News*, disposes of any possible suggestion that the reason for this might be any softness toward the accused on the part of the courts. Recorder's Court Judge Robert J. Colombo told one man accused of looting:

> "You can't get personal bond in this court. You're nothing but lousy thieving looters."
> When the accused replied, "You'll have to prove that," Judge Colombo reddened and shot back, "We will."

Peter Clarke, publisher of the Detroit *News*, which on July 26, 1967, splashed a story beginning "Negro snipers turned a 169-square block area north of West Grand Boulevard into a bloody battleground last night," told me in an interview in 1973 that he was now inclined to the view that "there may not have been [any] snipers."

So much for the conservative theory of sniping organized by radical agitators.

That leaves the third of the theories that were current to explain the riot, the one I have called the liberal theory, as the orthodox explanation today. The Kerner Commission's analysis is fairly typical. The root causes of the riots, the commission thought, were "imbedded in a massive tangle of issues and circumstances . . . which arise out of the historical pattern of Negro-white relations in America." It listed many of these causes: discrimination and segregation; black migration and white exodus; the pathology of the ghetto. It spoke of:

> men and women without jobs, families without men, and schools where children are processed instead of educated, until they return to the street—

to crime, to narcotics, to dependency on welfare, and to bitterness and resentment against society.

To sum up all these historical and societal causes, the Kerner report used a famous phrase which has given deep offense and drawn forth shocked denunciation: "White racism," it said, "is essentially responsible for the explosive mixture." And when it came to recommending policies to prevent a recurrence of riots like the one in Detroit, the commission laid its emphasis on long-term social measures: more jobs, more welfare, better housing, better education.

This classically liberal theory is obviously both subtler and more serious than the crudities of radical rebellion and conservative conspiracy. But it, too, presents one major difficulty. The rioters, or looters, rather, for that is what most of them were, cannot be called "men and women without jobs" or children of "families without men."

Detroit Police Department records show that only 10 per cent of those arrested were juveniles, and of the adults arrested, 83 per cent were employed. Half of those in jobs were UAW members working for one of the Big Three auto companies—members of the very union that the liberals of the 1950s constantly cited as evidence of the absorption of American labor into the middle class.

Although the riots began in a neighborhood that has "gone downhill" and where there is a good deal of prostitution, narcotics and other crime, in general the areas to which the rioting spread were not the city's worst black slums. They were black working-class residential neighborhoods with a fairly high proportion of owner-occupied property and a median income, at over six thousand dollars a year, not far below the median of white income. More than three quarters of the households in the neighborhood had male heads, which is above the national average for blacks.

The classic liberal theory, that rioting is caused by social deprivation, does not apply in Detroit. The rioters there, or at least those arrested for looting, were not the most deprived. They were mostly typical members of the black working class who, by the standards of the poorest or of unemployed teen-agers, were "making it."

The Detroit riot was not caused by "white racism" except in a sense so remote as to be almost meaningless. In a more real sense, it was caused by the police.

The background to it was one of bitter hostility between the police and the black community, dating back at least as far as the 1943 riot, in which police shot seventeen black rioters and no whites. It was revived in 1963 by the Cynthia Scott case, in which a black prostitute was shot by a white policeman. In November 1965 Judge George Edwards of the U. S.

Court of Appeals for the 6th Circuit, a former commissioner of the Detroit Police Department, wrote in the *Michigan Law Review:*

> Though local police forces generally regard themselves as public ser-
> vants with the responsibility for maintaining law and order, they tend to
> minimize this attitude when they are patrolling areas that are heavily pop-
> ulated with Negro citizens. There, they tend to view each person on the
> street as a potential criminal or enemy, and all too often that attitude is
> reciprocated.

About a month before the 1967 riot, another black prostitute was
murdered. Police said she had been killed by a pimp, but there were persistent rumors in the black community that she, too, had been killed by a
vice-squad officer in plain clothes. (John Hersey's account of the *Algiers
Motel Incident*, in which three black men who were supposed to have
been with two white girls were murdered by police officers at the height of
the riot, explores a poisonous mixture of sexual jealousy, sadism and racial
antagonism in the relations between black prostitutes and white policemen.)

At about the same time, a black veteran was killed, in front of his
pregnant wife, by a gang of white youths shouting, "Niggers, keep out of
Rouge Park." The widow lived very near the blind pig over the Economy
Printing Co., on Twelfth Street, where the riot began.

The immediate cause of the riot was the neighbors' resentment of the
police's mass arrest of black people at a party which, while technically illegal, would in all probability not have been raided if it had taken place at a
country club in a prosperous suburb.

The next stage, spreading rapidly from the site of the original incident, was looting, a "property riot." (The first casualty was a white looter,
shot by a Syrian-American store owner.) Even at this stage, the emotional
tension between the black community and the police seems to have been
crucial to the way the riot developed. White observers stress the "carnival
atmosphere" at this stage. Blacks do not remember the atmosphere as
being so cheerful. No doubt many looters, mostly black but many white,
were glad enough to get beer or TV sets or whatever they could lay their
hands on for free. But it was also an opportunity to defy a system of law
and order which seemed to many blacks fundamentally biased against
them.

Because of past relations between the police and the black community, there was nothing the police could do. For the first crucial hours, Police Commissioner Ray Girardin ordered his men not to move in and arrest
looters. "If we had started shooting," Girardin told the Kerner Commission, " . . . not one of our policemen would have come out alive."

But they did start shooting. Regulations in Detroit, as in most other U.S. jurisdictions, permit officers to shoot a felony suspect who disobeys an order to stop. Covered by this absurd regulation, which means that the death penalty survives for suspected thieves though not for convicted murderers, and makes all policemen potentially prosecutor, jury and executioner, they started shooting looters. Because they were afraid of snipers, they started shooting out street lights. The great majority of the reports of sniper fire, it is now generally agreed, were caused by this wild, panicky firing by police and the National Guard. Heavy-caliber machine guns were played on apartment houses. A four-year-old child was shot because a guardsman mistook her father's lighted cigarette in the window for a spurt of fire from a sniper's gun. It seems unlikely that this would have happened in a predominantly white neighborhood.

The first phase of the great Detroit riot, then, was a street scuffle provoked by heavy-handed behavior on the part of the police in a tough black neighborhood. The second was looting that the police did not control in time, again because of their bad relations with black neighborhoods in general. And the third was a full-dress police riot. Of course black anger and black violence were to be seen on the streets once the riot was under way. But it is plain that a disciplined police force, on reasonable terms with the black half of the city's population, could have prevented rioting on anything like the scale on which it occurred.

So, why hasn't there been a riot in Detroit since 1967?

If you accept the orthodox liberal explanation of what happened then, you would expect the answer to stress the progress the city, and particularly its black citizens, have made: less white exodus, less unemployment, better education, and a decline in crime, narcotics and welfare dependency.

Let us take those points, by way of example, one by one.

White flight has continued. In 1950 the Detroit metropolitan area as a whole, three counties with the city as their center, had just three million people, 60 per cent of them in the city. In 1960 the area as a whole had grown faster than any other metropolitan area in the country except Los Angeles. But the city of Detroit had shrunk by 10 per cent to 1.67 million, the suburbs growing in population from 1.2 million to 2 million. By 1970 the metropolitan area had 4.2 million people, but the city had shrunk again, to 1.5 million—less than in 1940. Blacks, 16 per cent of the population in 1950, after the great in-migration of the forties, had reached 44 per cent of the population by 1970.

Between 1960 and 1970, in fact, more than 350,000 white people, or one in three, left the city. The black population, meanwhile, grew by two hundred thousand, or more than 40 per cent.

"The whites léft rather than live with blacks," said Harold Varner, the director of the Detroit Housing Commission, who is black. "Don't fool yourself; they didn't leave because of the good life in the suburbs, but rather because a black family had moved into their neighborhood or was expected to arrive shortly."

Businesses and manufacturing plants are also steadily leaving town for the suburbs. Because Detroit has no rapid-transit system and poor public transportation generally, this has had a negative effect on black employment opportunities.

Unemployment has continued to be a problem for black people. In February 1972, according to a survey commissioned by the Detroit *News*, "Black recruitment and hiring at major Detroit area industries has dropped off." The previous month, unemployment in the city of Detroit was almost exactly 10 per cent for whites, 15 per cent for blacks. A year later, the unemployment rate for blacks in the inner city was estimated at 20 per cent. And the unemployment rate for black teen-agers hovered around 30 per cent.

A "Detroit Plan" for increasing the number of black construction workers has been only partially successful. Many blacks find jobs on the assembly line at the big auto plants, which is hard and monotonous work, but relatively well paid. Few blacks have won promotion to management in the auto industry.

A Market Opinion Research poll published by the Detroit *News* in early 1972 showed that few blacks attributed the difficulty in finding work to discrimination: nearly half thought the trouble was that there were not enough jobs in the Detroit area, and over a quarter thought the trouble was that blacks didn't have enough education and training. And this is also the view of the experts at the Michigan Employment Security Commission and in industry.

Then, how is the educational situation for blacks in Detroit?

Not good, according to former School Superintendent Norman Drachler, who pointed out to me that schools in the inner city have higher costs, lower staffing ratios, more truancy (much of it due to social problems), and lower incomes, than suburban schools.

Not good, agreed Dr. C. L. Golightly, who has been president of the Board of Education since 1961. At the time I went to interview him, the city's schools were in imminent danger of closing for lack of money. Thirteen times in ten years, the school board had gone to the voters to ask for a "millage" increase in the property tax which is its main source of income; eleven times, the voters had turned it down. In the end, a compromise was worked out with the state, and the schools did not close. But the fact that they came so close suggests how desperate their chronic financial position is.

Then, has there been a decline in welfare dependency, in narcotics, in crime?

There has not as of this writing.

In 1968 there were 50,000 families in Michigan receiving Aid to Dependent Children. According to an authoritative estimate, at least 70 per cent of these were in Detroit. In 1969 there were 82,000 ADC families. In 1970 there were 101,000. And in 1971 there were 129,000, an increase of well over 150 per cent in four years.

On February 20, 1973, Judge George W. Crockett, of the city's Recorder's Court, who is black, filed a complaint in his own court calling for a one-man grand jury to investigate the operation of the narcotics trade in the city. He cited a number of reports in the city's press and television over the previous twelve months as reason to believe that policemen and former policemen were involved in the heroin trade, had been extorting payoffs running into thousands of dollars, and had on more than one occasion committed murder to enforce their rackets.

Crime in general is probably the biggest single worry for black citizens, as for white citizens, of Detroit. Market Opinion Research, in the previously quoted 1972 survey, asked a sample of Detroiters: "What do you think are the most important problems facing the city of Detroit at the present time?" Easily the commonest type of answer was that grouped under the heading "Crime/Robbing/Mugging/Stealing." More than 35 per cent of those polled gave answers in that category. Next came "Dope/Drugs," which 26 per cent cited.

The fact that Detroit has not seen a major riot since 1967, then, is not necessarily reassuring for those who accept the liberal theory that the riot happened then because of general conditions for blacks in the city, since most of the specific conditions mentioned in the Kerner Commission report are either worse now or not significantly improved.

What of relations between black people and the police? There is no great comfort there either.

In the spring of 1971, after theft had increased by 67 per cent in two years and faced with an outcry from all sections of the community to do something about street crime, Police Commissioner John F. Nichols started a new program, with the acronym STRESS: Stop The Robberies; Enjoy Safe Streets. Tough policemen in plain clothes were sent out as decoys, with orders to shoot thieves if they couldn't arrest them. In the first six months, STRESS officers had killed ten people and wounded another nine. Ten out of the first eleven killed by STRESS men were black. Not all black people opposed the program, nevertheless; the fact that 54 per cent of blacks in a 1972 poll said they approved of STRESS is a measure of just how badly black Detroit was plagued by crime. STRESS officers continued to be involved in a series of bizarre and violent incidents, one of them a shoot-out with what turned out to be deputies from a neighboring jurisdiction. Then, at the end of 1972, came the incident that showed just how touchy the black community still was about the police, and just how understandable it was that it should be touchy.

It began with a shoot-out between police and three young blacks in which four officers were wounded. Police claimed that the young men, two of them college students, were escorting a big shipment of drugs. The word in the black community was that, on the contrary, the three were vigilantes, surprised by police with a kidnaped drug dealer in their car. In any case, police launched the biggest manhunt in the city's history, which was redoubled after another officer was killed in a second gun battle. Two months later, a judge granted an injunction restraining the police from unconstitutional searches on the grounds that officers had broken into fifty-six homes of friends and relatives of the wanted men without warrants. They there abused people, beat people, and in at least one case forced a young woman to strip. The result was a hornet's nest of anger in the black community. Perhaps only the fact that the manhunt took place in December and January prevented the outbreak of another major riot.

It is hard not to feel some sympathy with the police. Everyone was screaming for something to be done about crime. They responded in what was after all more or less the traditional way. They were exposed to violence from criminals: fifty-six STRESS officers were injured in the first six months of the program, and one killed. Yet, as of 1973, with Commissioner Nichols openly making a political issue of STRESS and police behaving in exactly the way most calculated to alarm and anger black people, it would have been a rash prophet who would have predicted that never again would police make the mistakes they made in July 1967.

The original question is still unanswered: Why has there been no riot since 1967?

There was a surprising concurrence in many of the answers I was given. "One reason," said the young black militant Lorenzo Freeman, "is because a lot of black people experienced a lot of grief."

The effect of the riot, said the white newspaper publisher Peter Clarke, was "moral and psychic exhaustion" in both blacks and whites. "It took the edge off people's desire to start more riots," he said, "and off their desire to shoot more blacks."

Forty years ago, in his classic study of southern racial violence, Walter White showed that lynchings very rarely happened twice in the same town in a generation. It was as if, he suggested, anger and hatred built up over the years to a climax, and then, once released, took many years to reach the danger level again. Lynching, as such, has disappeared from the South. But something of the same kind, I believe, rather than any major improvement in the relative circumstances of black people, or in the way they are treated, for example by the police, explains why the riots of the mid-sixties have not been repeated—so far.

Given the immense resources, in money and people and goodwill, available, there is no question that Detroit's problems can be overcome. That will mean eliminating the relative social disadvantage of black people, as liberals assume, of course. But it seems doubtful if it will be done without transferring some of their burden to the shoulders of white people. It does not seem likely that the education in Detroit schools, for example, will improve dramatically, with consequent effects on the cycle of unemployment and limited job opportunities, so long as Detroit taxpayers vote down millages, and suburbanites fight busing, and Washington hesitates to launch massive compensatory expenditure programs. In each field —employment, transportation, public finance—it seems clear that the city cannot hope to make it without help from the suburbs which have sapped so much of its wealth.

Detroit, in fact, like many old U.S. cities, is dying from the center outward. It can be saved. But to save it will take structural and institutional change on a scale that will require sacrifices from the very people who have fled the city to leave its new, black inhabitants to their own devices. Over the seven years since the riot, however much has been done within the city, there has been little sign of any such fundamental change in the terms of the problem, still less of any such willingness to make sacrifices in order to solve it.

3

It is true, then, that there have been no major urban riots since 1968. But a close look at the circumstances of the black community in the last place where a major riot did take place (except the outbreaks that followed the death of Martin Luther King) suggests how dangerous it is to extrapolate from such a simple statement of fact. Behind it there lies such a tangle of interpretation, and behind that again such a stubbornly noncomparable complexity of people's lives and feelings, expectations and disappointment, that as a measure of the general condition of black people after the upheaval of the sixties, it breaks in your hands. The statement means what it says; it does not mean what it is often taken to imply.

The same is true of a statistical "fact" like the Census Bureau's announcement, at the end of 1971, that the income of young black married couples, outside the South, had virtually caught up with that of comparable white couples. In itself it was true, of course. The temptation was to take it as a sign that the persistent gap between the average incomes of blacks and whites would soon disappear.

Attempts were made to argue just that. In April 1973, for example, the theme of rising black income was developed by a former director of the Census Bureau, Richard Scammon, and Ben J. Wattenberg in an article in *Commentary*. "A remarkable development has taken place in America over the last dozen years," they began impressively.

> For the first time in the history of the Republic, truly large and growing numbers of American blacks have been moving up into the middle class, so that by now these numbers can reasonably be said to add up to a majority of black Americans.

On the face of it, this was a startling claim. It becomes less impressive when one understands their definition of "middle class." "What does middle class mean in this context?" they asked, and answered that it referred to the condition of the "vast majority of working class Americans," who were defined as those not actually starving, naked, or deprived of sanitary shelter. "Middle class," for Scammon and Wattenberg, meant "working class."

This trifling difficulty removed with the simplicity of genius, they went on to cite figures to show black progress in income, jobs, unions and education.

> Income for white families in America went up by 69% in the 1960s, while income for black families went up by 99.6%.
>
> The *ratio* of black family income to white family income also changed dramatically in the period, climbing from 53% in 1961 to 63% in 1971.

Black unemployment rates, they conceded, had been twice as high as unemployment rates for whites for two decades. But this, they argued, was not as bad as it sounded:

> A cross-tabulation of married men over age 20 reveals a far sharper drop in unemployment among blacks than for the population as a whole.

If you exclude black women, black bachelors and black teen-agers, that is (which might seem to be fairly arbitrary exclusions), then where in 1962 there were 2.5 times as many black people (proportionately) out of work, in 1972 the ratio was only 1.7 to 1.

"Here, too, then," Scammon and Wattenberg commented, "we see a steady and powerful movement into the middle class."

It is an extraordinary interpretation, for two reasons. First, it identifies any job whatever—however dirty, however ill-paid, however temporary—with membership in the "middle class," a definition which, if generally accepted, would finally deprive that much ill-used concept of its last shreds of meaning. Secondly, it ignores precisely the two problems that give most concern. Behind the demure jargon "cross-tabulation of married men over age 20," there lurk, left out of account, the three black families out of ten that are headed by women and the appalling rates of unemployment for black teen-agers. Only if one were recklessly concerned with drawing attention to those areas in which progress had been made and unconcerned with those areas in which it had not, would one choose to present the evidence in that way.

Herbert Hill is the national labor director of the NAACP and an acknowledged authority on black labor in the United States. To hear him talking about what was happening to black incomes after reading the Scammon and Wattenberg article was to wonder whether he and they were talking about the same country.

"I have examined the data carefully," he told me. "The general pattern is quite clear. At the beginning of the decade of the seventies, black family income for the nation was 61 per cent of white family income. That is an increase from 57 per cent in 1945. This means that between 1945 and 1970 the increase in black family income as a proportion of white family income was 4 per cent. Black family income gained four percentage points in twenty-five years."

At that rate, black families would be able to look forward to catching up to whites in 250 years. Even that is no cause for congratulation, because since 1970, the gap has been moving the other way.

By 1973, according to the Bureau of the Census, the ratio of median black family income to that of whites had moved downward again, to 58 per cent. Helped by the general recessionary conditions of the economy, the Nixon administration had succeeded in getting things back almost to where they were in 1945. At the rate it maintained over nearly thirty years of furious reformist activity since World War II, the average income of black American families was due to catch up with that of whites in forty-two centuries.

"Look," Hill said, "the only thing that matters is not how far we've come since the day of emancipation 108 years ago, but what is the status of the black wage earner in relation to the white wage earner. And here the data is very significant: not only have we not narrowed the gap, but in dollar terms it is getting greater and greater and greater."

This is confirmed by the Bureau of the Census' report on the *Social and Economic Status of the Black Population in the United States*, issued in July 1974. The report noted:

> The upgrading of the income levels of black families which was associated with the narrowing income gap which occurred in the 1960s was not as evident in the last four years.
>
> From 1969 to 1973, the median income of black families (in constant 1973 dollars) did not grow, after an appreciable increase during the preceding four year period. On the other hand, white families showed gains in the median levels for both periods.

Why was it, I asked Herbert Hill, that in spite of equal employment opportunity commissions and legislation and prosperity and all the changes in public attitudes, black incomes caught up with white incomes so slowly?

At the bottom of the trouble, Hill explained, was the fact that all too often black workers and white workers were climbing different ladders.

"You must begin with the assumption," he said, "that there is in this country a dual labor system. There are jobs for whites and jobs for blacks. We have not destroyed the basic pattern of the system, although we have improved benefits."

Although unions indignantly deny discriminating, the double job ladder is codified in collective bargaining arrangements. This is just as true of industrial jobs as of the craft unions, only the system works a little differently in the two cases. In the craft unions, especially in the building trades, the union itself does the hiring and can simply exclude blacks from certain jobs. In industrial unions, where the industry hires its own work force, blacks find it easier to get hired in the first place, but they often find that it is far harder for them to get promotion than it is for whites.

There have been changes, Hill says, but the two main ones have been, on the one hand, "tokenism"—that is, "a minimum strategic accommodation by labor organizations to the entire body of federal and state antidiscrimination laws"—and on the other hand, practices that were once "openly racist and acknowledged to be such . . . have now become covert and subtle."

This is a startlingly gloomy picture. But Hill has evidence to back it up. He has carefully compared the hearings held by the Equal Employment Opportunity Commission since 1966 with those held by the Fair Employment Practices Committee set up in 1941. In many cases, he found, the Equal Employment Opportunity Commission investigated and found . . . the exact same discriminatory practices . . . cited by the FEPC more than a quarter of a century ago.

Most incredible of all is the Dobbins case, in Cincinnati. The plaintiff tried to join Local 212 of the International Brotherhood of Electrical Workers in 1956 but was refused in spite of the facts both that he was a certified journeyman electrician and that he had a bachelor of science degree. In 1968 a federal judge ordered the local to admit him, but the local went back into court for relief. "After twenty-six years," Hill comments, "exactly two black men have been admitted to membership in Local 212 of the Electrical Workers in Cincinnati, and we are back in court on the very same issue which was first presented by a government agency in 1945."

There are, as Hill sees it, two separate, though related, problems working to prevent blacks from progressing through the jobs they can get. On the one hand, working-class black men with jobs cannot get better jobs. On the other, young lower-class blacks are finding it increasingly difficult to get jobs at all.

"You can go for miles and miles of brownstone row houses in Brooklyn," he said to me. "The black people who live in those houses brush their teeth every morning, they have breakfast with Smith's Premium Ham, they go off to their jobs. They go to church. And they pay their taxes. They are the stable black working class. They will continue. They will even expand. But there is also another class developing, a permanent black under-class."

Within that black under-class there is one particular group which Hill, looking to the future, finds worrying, both on its own account and on society's. He expects a massive increase in the number of young, unemployed members of this under-class, with high expectations and correspondingly low real prospects. He has estimated from census data that the number of black men coming into the adult labor market will grow about twelve times faster over the seventies than the number of white men coming into it will. Or, rather, "They should be entering the labor force in the decade of the seventies, but, because of changes in the economy, the technology, and restrictive practices of organized labor and big business, too many of them will not enter the labor force."

This army of young men will be lucky if they even get a job, let alone make it into the middle class. And yet they are different from the young men born into the under-class in every previous society in one respect. From television, and from the sight of those who have made it, either by getting into college or by hustling themselves a long white Cadillac Eldorado in the ways of the ghetto, the members of this new and peculiar under-class will know what they are missing. In them, Hill soberly warned me, "we have the classic preconditions for large-scale social turmoil."

At first sight, we seem to have here two utterly different pictures of what is happening to black Americans in terms of jobs and income. But there is, on close inspection, one important respect in which the two pictures agree. Scammon and Wattenberg, after all, claimed only that "a slender majority" of blacks are now "middle class." Making allowance for their peculiar use of the term "middle class," we can translate their claim into an indisputable statement: half or more of all American blacks are now in stable working-class jobs or better. Shorn of Scammon and Wattenberg's Panglossian rhetoric, that statement is perfectly reconcilable with Herbert Hill's picture of a black population dividing into two classes. One large group makes slow progress in hard, stable work in spite of the obstacles put in its way by continuing discrimination. Another group, which may grow with frightening speed, sinks into the condition of a permanent under-class, tormented like Tantalus by the sight of the good things few of its members will ever reach.

Such a model of a black population no longer excluded as a whole from the mainstream of American life by the taboos of caste but divided into two classes, one rising, the other sinking, has a familiar look about it. It is the model forecast in Daniel Patrick Moynihan's famous paper on *The Negro Family*, as long ago as March 1965. "While many young Negroes are moving ahead to unprecedented levels of achievement," Moynihan wrote then, "many more are falling further and further behind."

Moynihan was naturally quick to sense that new data would confirm his presentiment of what was happening. As early as the spring of 1970, he asked the Census Bureau to "break out" the very data on black family income that were quoted at the beginning of this section. In the spring of 1972 he published in *The Public Interest* an analysis of the black income crux with the apt title "The Schism in Black America." In the early 1960s, he reminded his readers with pardonable self-justification, he had begun to get the feeling from the data that while some blacks were moving upward, a "marginal lower working class group was being left behind and was being transformed into a genuine lower class." This, he suggested, was exactly what now seemed to be happening. And to the question "Are things getting better or worse?" he returned this answer:

> First, things are going in two directions at once. Second, considerable energy is devoted to denying either trend.

The title of this 1972 essay of Moynihan's was borrowed from a speech by the black economist Andrew Brimmer, now a governor of the Federal Reserve Board. Brimmer made a speech at Tuskegee Institute in 1970 which he called "The Deepening Schism." In it he said:

> During the 1960s, Negroes as a group *did* make significant economic progress . . . in terms of higher employment and occupational upgrading as well as in lower unemployment and a narrowing of the income gap between Negroes and whites.
>
> However, beneath these over-all improvements another—and disturbing—trend is also evident: Within the Negro community, there appears to be a deepening schism between the able and the less able, between the well-prepared and those with few skills.
>
> This deepening schism can be traced in a number of ways . . . above all in the dramatic deterioration in the position of Negro families headed by females.
>
> In my judgment, this deepening schism within the black community should interest us as much as the real progress that has been made by Negroes as a group.

Moynihan's original thesis, back in 1965, associated the schism in black society with the growing proportion of black families headed by women. The thesis was bitterly denounced, but events would appear to have confirmed it. The Census Bureau's report on *The Social and Economic Status of the Black Population in the United States 1973*, issued in 1974, showed that black family income had moved down in relation to white family income, but it also showed that this movement was largely caused by the increase in the number of black families headed by women:

> The overall income position of black families relative to white families . . . has declined. Although the overall ratio declined between 1969 and 1973, the income ratio remained unchanged for male headed families. . . . Thus the changes in the overall ratio reflect, in part, the changes in the mix of the population, such as changes in . . . the proportion of families headed by women.

The percentage of white American families headed by women, for whatever reason—whether because they were widows, or never married, or their husbands were away in the service or in prison, or because they were divorced or permanently separated—went up from 9 per cent in 1965 to 9.9 per cent in 1974. The proportion of black families headed by women went up from 23.7 per cent in 1965 to 34 per cent in 1974, or from under a quarter to over a third.

Whatever the reasons for this trend—and the explanations that have been put forward for it range from the legacy of slavery, through the availability of welfare, to the liberation of women—its consequences are clearly catastrophic both for the women themselves and their children, and for the chances of the black population as a whole catching up to whites in income.

4

There is no more graphic illustration of the way the liberal consensus split apart than the debate over education and equality after the publication of the Coleman report, in 1966.

Education, in the American tradition, was the high road to equality. If liberals believed that social problems could be solved by spending the incremental resources produced by growth, education was one of the main kinds of spending they had in mind. For education was opportunity; and equality of opportunity appealed to the liberal mind because it meant giving a chance to the have-nots without taking anything from the haves that they would notice losing.

As a tool of reform, it had the advantage that it also appealed to the ideology of conservatives: to the traditions of Protestantism and to the ethic of self-improvement that stretches back down the American tradition through Horatio Alger and McGuffey's *Readers* to Benjamin Franklin himself.

In the age of the Great Migration, the public schools of New York and other cities really did provide a measure of equality of opportunity to the immigrant poor, if only by opening to them the language and the basic skills by which they could qualify for jobs. By the time the New Deal coalition was formed (and educators of one sort and another were to be a significant part of that coalition), these assumptions about education were so deeply rooted as to be unquestioned. They were certified with the authority of social science and transferred to the special arena of racial equality by the Supreme Court's 1954 desegregation decision in *Brown*.

When, in the late 1930s and 1940s, the NAACP and its lawyers began to lay siege to segregation, they wisely chose education as the sector to attack, precisely because they knew that it was so firmly associated in the public mind with equality that it would be an easier point of attack than, say, housing. In *Brown*, Thurgood Marshall and his colleagues deployed social science evidence in support of their contention that segregated education was inherently unequal. In particular they cited work done by the psychologists Kenneth and Mamie Clark with black children and black and white dolls. The Clarks' conclusion was that segregation inflicts psychological harm. The great majority of liberals came to suppose not just that "social science proved that segregated education was inherently unequal," the proposition the Court endorsed, but that if you wanted to achieve equality, education could do the job for you.

In the mid-sixties another development tied the fate of liberal doctrine even more tightly to the efficacy of education. President Johnson's Great Society was to be built without alienating Congress. From the start, education was an important part of his administration's strategy for reducing poverty and racial inequality. But as other approaches, especially "community action," ran into political opposition, the Great Society's reliance on education programs grew accordingly. In the end the Johnson administration, committed up to the eyebrows to reducing inequality, was almost equally committed to education as the chief way of doing it.

Professor James Coleman himself has confessed he does not know exactly why Congress, in section 402 of the Civil Rights Act of 1964, ordered the Commissioner of Education to conduct a survey "concerning the lack of availability of equal educational opportunities for individuals by reason of race, color, religion or national origin." A handful of social scientists had hinted, before Coleman, that the effect of schools on equality of opportunity might have been exaggerated. But such work had simply made no dent on the almost universal assumption to the contrary. Coleman himself took it for granted that his study would show that "the difference in the quality of schools that the average Negro child and the average white child are exposed to" would be "striking."

He was exactly wrong. What was striking was how little difference there was.

When the results were in, from about six hundred thousand students and sixty thousand teachers in roughly four thousand schools, they turned out to contradict all previous assumptions.

They were a quarry in which the material for many conflicting theses could be mined. But there were four major points that, taken together, pointed almost with the logical drive of a syllogism toward certain conclusions:

First, most black and white Americans attended different schools.

Second, the "inputs" into those schools—the physical facilities, the formal curricula, and the measurable characteristics of the teachers—were far more similar as between the schools blacks went to and the schools whites went to than anyone had imagined.

However, third, there was very little correlation between the difference in these "inputs" and the "output" of the schools, as measured by how students performed on standardized reading tests.

Lastly, the one characteristic of the schools that showed a consistent relationship to the students' performance in tests was the one poor black children were denied access to: classmates from affluent homes. As Coleman himself put it, the sources of inequality lay, first, in the home, and, second, in the schools' ineffectiveness in forcing achievement from the impact of the home.

Here is how Coleman himself summed up the 737 pages of his report (not to mention the 548 pages of statistical explanation):

> Children were tested at the beginning of grades 1, 3, 6, 9, and 12. Achievement of the average American Indian, Mexican American, Puerto Rican and Negro . . . was much lower than the average white or Oriental American, at all grade levels . . . the differences are large to begin with, and they are even larger at higher grades. Two points, then, are clear: (1) these minority children have a serious educational deficiency at the start of school, and (2) they have an even more serious deficiency at the end of school, which is obviously in part a result of school.

Coleman added that the survey showed that most of the range of variation in students' achievement was to be found within the same school, and that there was very little range of variation by comparison between schools. Family background—whatever that might mean—must, he concluded, account for far more of the variation in achievement than differences between schools.

If quality were measured, as it had tended to be measured by administrators and educational reformers alike, in material terms, then the quality of the school, on Coleman's data, counted for virtually nothing.

When other things were equal, the report showed, factors such as the amount of money spent per pupil, or the number of books in the library, or physical facilities such as gymnasiums or cafeterias or laboratories, seemed to make no appreciable difference to the children's level of achievement.

Moreover, as between the schools that black children and white children went to, these facilities *were* far more nearly equal than anyone had supposed. For example, it was true that black children had less access to chemistry labs than white children did. But the difference was that only 94 per cent of them, as opposed to 98 per cent of the whites, went to schools with chemistry labs. That was hardly enough to explain the gap between average black and white performance at school, let alone the gap between the average status and income of whites and blacks after they leave school.

The day Daniel Patrick Moynihan arrived at Harvard, in the spring of 1966, he ran into some of his new colleagues at the Faculty Club. One of them was Professor Seymour Martin Lipset, whom we last met haranguing

the infant Free Speech Movement from the roof of a police car in Berkeley "Hello, Pat," Lipset said, "guess what Coleman's found?" And he proceeded to give his swift summary of the Coleman findings: "schools make
no difference, families make a difference." No, said Professor Thomas Pettigrew of the Harvard School of Education when I quoted this summary
to him, "the belief that Coleman hit was the belief that you could make a
difference with money." It is hard to say which interpretation contained a
greater challenge to liberal orthodoxy, which had tended to see education
as a mechanism for transforming inputs of money into outcomes of
equality.

In the fall of 1966, installed at Harvard, Moynihan began to apply his
talents to making sure that the Coleman report should not be ignored. He
and Pettigrew organized a seminar on equality of educational opportunity.
It became the focus of an extraordinary welling up of intellectual excitement. Harvard had seen nothing like it since the arms-control seminars of
the late 1950s, at which the future strategic policies of the Kennedy administration were forged and the nucleus of the elite that was to operate
them in government was brought together. But in the intervening decade
domestic social questions had reasserted their urgency. Education had
emerged as the field where all the agonizing problems of race, poverty and
the cities seemed to intersect.

If schools, as Lipset paraphrased Coleman, made no difference, then
what could explain the inequalities of achievement between blacks and
whites? A school of thought was waiting in the wings with an answer: the
geneticists. A controversy of great heat and passion blew up after Professor
Arthur Jensen's article in the *Harvard Educational Review*, in 1969,
suggesting that genetic factors might "play a part" in explaining the lower
average performance of blacks on various tests. Before long, a geneticist
like Jensen could find himself in danger of being chased around campus by
a mob that considered what he was saying racist; while Jensen's opponent,
the Princeton experimental psychologist Leon Kamin, could jump in a
matter of paragraphs from painstaking analysis of the IQ scores of identical
twins in Denmark to ringing appeals to build a better society. The once
sedulously "objective" academic life of the fifties had been politicized; the
once purposive march of social science had broken up in doubt and division.

The Coleman report did not discuss these vexed issues, and it gave
only three of its 737 pages to an even more political question: the effect of
desegregation. Harvard's Professor Thomas Pettigrew persuaded the Civil
Rights Commission to reanalyze the Coleman data to see what light they
cast on the effects of desegregation, and, with David Cohen, was the main

author of the resulting survey, which came out in 1967 as *Racial Isolation in the Public Schools* and gave the impression that the Coleman data supported desegregation. This was true as far as it went. Coleman had concluded that desegregation did indeed have an effect on black educational achievement. But his report also showed that social class had a greater effect.

Professor Pettigrew is not much troubled by this point, because of the close connection between race and social class in America. "Two thirds of the whites are middle class" is his way of putting it, "and two thirds of the blacks are working class." He also draws a sharp distinction between desegregation and true integration. By integration he means an atmosphere of genuine acceptance and friendly respect across racial lines, and he believes that mere desegregation won't help blacks to do better in school until this kind of atmosphere is achieved. He argues that no one can say that integration hasn't worked, for the simple reason that it hasn't yet been tried.

Given the prevalence of residential segregation in American cities, desegregated arrangements implied, first and foremost, busing.

Desegregation proceeded so slowly, Pettigrew put it to me, that the courts "got mad and started ruling for busing in 1969 and 1970." Two different factors, roughly simultaneously, drove the courts to consider busing as a remedy. Judges did become impatient at the sophisticated devices with which southern school districts, fifteen years or so after *Brown*, were still succeeding in evading the obligation to destroy dual school systems. At the same time, both in such newly grown southern cities as Memphis, Richmond and Charlotte, and in such northern and western metropolises as San Francisco, Denver and Detroit, the courts were beginning to meet the new form of educational segregation implied by increasing concentration of blacks in a predominantly black inner city surrounded by overwhelmingly white suburbs. The same shift of emphasis that hit the civil rights movement in early 1965, from concern with legal segregation in the South to concern with patterns of discrimination and *de facto* segregation outside it, reached the courts after 1968.

The result was a whole series of court decisions. The circumstances were different in each case, and often complex, and so were the precise points of law they raised and decided. But the direction of judicial opinion was plain enough. Faced with the continued survival of dual school systems in the South, the judges were ready to demand immediate compliance with *Brown*. Faced with *de facto* segregation brought about by housing patterns and by the isolation of the inner city jurisdiction in a ring of white suburbs, they were ready to order busing, both within the city and between it and the suburbs.

When the Supreme Court decided the *Green* case (*Green* v. *County*

*School Board of New Kent County, Virginia*), in May 1968, very little progress had been made toward desegregating dual school systems in many parts of the rural South. The immediate issue in *Green* was so-called "freedom of choice" plans, a species of tokenism widely adopted in the South to stave off genuine desegregation. Their usual effect was that a few hand-picked black students attended previously all-white schools, and all-black schools stayed that way. In its *Green* judgment the Court did not stop at ruling out freedom of choice. It moved the burden of proof onto school boards to come forward with a workable desegregation plan. The Court used the word *now*, with emphasis, and it set deadlines for final and effective desegregation: September 1969 for schools with a majority of white students, and one year later for the black schools. In practice, for many of the larger districts, *Green* meant busing.

In order to be elected, however, and indeed in order to be sure of being nominated by the Republicans, the incoming President Nixon had given the South the impression that he would preserve it from the horrors of school desegregation. As soon as he was inaugurated, deputations of southern Republicans arrived in Washington to hold him to the bargain. Above all, they demanded the rescinding of the hated "guidelines" under which, they believed or affected to believe, southern school districts that failed to comply with the law by desegregating would have their federal education funds cut off.

For the first nine months of the Nixon administration, a sort of battle for its soul went on within the bureaucracy. On one side were the civil rights and education officials in HEW, led by a vacillating Secretary Finch and supported by liberal Republicans in the Senate and scattered liberals in the executive branch. They pointed out that the fund cutoffs were required not by some nebulous bureaucratic guidelines but by federal status. The slightest retreat, they argued, would invite further demands from the Southerners. On the other side stood the formidable Strom Thurmond and his ally Harry Dent in the White House, backed by the Southern Progressives who had delivered to Nixon the nomination and the election; the White House's political and Congressional experts; the Justice Department under John Mitchell; and—it eventually became all too clear—the President himself. Their position was summed up by Robert Mardian, later rewarded for his part in the struggle by promotion to assistant attorney general. "You can't just tell the South to stuff it," said Mardian. The President himself preserved the suspense about his own position until late September 1969, when he called at a press conference for a "middle course" between the "two extremes" of "instant integration" and "segregation forever," which was like appealing for a middle course between breaking the law and obeying it.

Just under a month later, the government's lawyers for the first time shared the defense table in the Supreme Court with John C. Satterfield, the gentlemanly strategist of white supremacy from Mississippi, in the case of *Alexander* v. *Holmes County*. The government was asking for yet more delay. But the court would have none of it. With the concurrence of Chief Justice Burger, newly appointed by the President, it held unanimously, "The obligation of every school district is to terminate dual school systems at once and to operate now and hereafter only unitary schools."

The Nixon administration and its supporters were to make considerable capital out of the fact that it was in its time, and not under the Democrats, that the back of school segregation in the South was broken. A great leap forward in compliance did take place between 1970 and 1972. But to the extent that school desegregation did occur (for it is worth remembering that as late as 1971–72 almost one third of black children in the South were still in 80–100 per cent black schools), the fact is that it occurred in spite of, and not because of, the efforts of the Nixon administration. It happened because the Nixon administration lost a battle to prevent its happening, and so failed to keep a pledge to prevent its happening. The turning point was the Supreme Court's decision in *Alexander*. Only then did the southern diehards realize that they had reached the last ditch. Or, rather, almost the last ditch: for had not their most sagacious champion, Senator John Stennis, told them that they could win if only they could get the issue into the North?

And it was getting into the North. If the fate of dual school systems, a southern issue, was settled at last, after *Alexander*, busing, the form the issue took in the North, was only just beginning to come before the courts.

"The clause reprobating the enslaving the inhabitants of Africa," wrote Jefferson of the debates over the drafting of the Declaration of Independence itself, "was struck out in complaisance to South Carolina and Georgia. . . . Our northern brethren, also, I believe felt a little tender under these censures: for though their people had very few slaves themselves, yet they had been pretty considerable carriers of them to others." On busing, the northern brethren felt a little tender under southern censures, for segregated schools, they were just beginning to realize, were not exclusively a southern phenomenon.

In October 1970 the Supreme Court heard arguments in *Swann* v. *Charlotte-Mecklenburg Board of Education et al.*, and on April 20, 1971, it gave its decision. The Court rejected the goal of racial quotas, saying in its unanimous opinion, "The constitutional command to desegregate schools does not mean that every school in every community must always reflect the racial composition of the school system as a whole." But that was the court's only deviation from the strictest enforcement of *Brown* that any civil rights lawyer could have asked. The Supreme Court fully upheld the District Court's contention that the dual school system in Charlotte could not be dismantled without "the remedial technique of requiring bus transportation as a tool of school desegregation." Only if the busing needed involved so much time or such distances that the children's health would suffer could it be objectionable, the court found, and in Charlotte, it pointed out, the busing required for desegregation would compare favorably in those two respects with the busing already practiced under segregation. For the first time, the Court had endorsed busing specifically, and in the South.

A year earlier, the Detroit Board of Education had adopted a plan for distributing black and white children more evenly among its schools by changing attendance zones. Within three months the plan had been blocked by the state of Michigan and the members of the school board who had supported the plan voted out of office after a recall petition. Shortly afterward, the NAACP brought suit, in *Bradley* v. *Milliken,* alleging that the Detroit public school system was segregated on the basis of race. It called for busing as a remedy. On September 27, 1971, in U. S. District Court, Judge Stephen Roth ruled that the Detroit school system was indeed segregated and as a result of unconstitutional proceedings on the part of the city's school board and of the state of Michigan. In March 1972 Judge Roth ruled that no plan limited to the city of Detroit alone could eliminate segregation and that a plan would have to be drawn up for assigning and busing pupils in the whole of the three counties of the metropolitan area around Detroit. In June 1972 he ordered a panel to draw up plans for integrating the city's school system with those of fifty-three suburban districts. And in December of the same year, the Court of Appeals accepted Judge Roth's main point, saying, "Big city school systems for blacks surrounded by suburban school systems for whites cannot represent equal protection of the law." Only on the narrow grounds that all the school districts affected had not been heard as parties to the action did the court overrule Judge Roth, and so the action stood as it waited to go to the Supreme Court, where it was to be decided in the summer of 1974.

The Detroit case was only the largest in its implications of a whole flotilla of cases slowly winding their way toward the Supreme Court by the end of 1972. In October 1972 the court heard arguments in a Denver case, the first segregation case it had ever heard from a city outside the South. The same month, the Appeals Court ordered the city of Atlanta to devise a broad new desegregation plan which would almost certainly involve busing on a massive scale. And in Richmond, the Supreme Court was waiting to review a case in which the Appeals Court had ruled that Judge Merhige, in the District Court, had exceeded his authority by ordering that, to eliminate *de facto* segregation, the school system of Richmond, Virginia, of all places, must be merged with those of the two adjacent counties.

By election day 1972, in fact, the courts seemed headed for a major constitutional showdown on this issue with the President or the Congress or both. For while the judges were maintaining and developing the doctrine that if what was required to achieve desegregation was busing, then busing there would have to be, a mounting swell of opposition was making itself felt in the country and in Congress. The President, subtly but unmistakably, was putting himself at its head.

In the fall of 1971 school buses in Pontiac, Michigan, were burned by rabid opponents of busing. Just a decade after the Freedom Rides, it was understandably seized on by the media as an ominous symbol of the way attitudes that had once seemed exclusively southern had now become national. Busing dominated the Florida primary, in the spring of 1972, and was generally thought to have accounted for George Wallace's coming easily at the top of the poll there. By the fall of 1972 both houses of Congress had passed anti-busing legislation in one form or another. There was growing talk of a constitutional amendment to prohibit busing, though it seemed doubtful if it could ever secure the two-thirds vote necessary for passage in the Senate. In June 1972, accordingly, senators and congressmen voted gratefully for a compromise that satisfied neither the supporters nor the opponents of busing: no court-ordered busing should go into effect until 1974 except where all appeals had been exhausted.

Already in March President Nixon had moved to make the issue his own with a long message to Congress. It was carefully drafted to straddle the two principles of support for desegregation and opposition to busing. The President said his aims were both to "give practical meaning to the concept of equal educational opportunity" and at the same time to "downgrade busing as a tool for achieving equal educational opportunity." To this effect he proposed two separate pieces of legislation, an Equal Educational Opportunities Act and a Student Transportation Moratorium Act, the one to set new criteria for equality in education and the other to halt busing until its fate could be permanently decided either by legislation or by a constitutional amendment.

By then, politicians at every level and in all parts of the country were under intense pressure to stop busing. In the Detroit area, for example, no candidate who favored busing survived the August primary elections. Passions in the South were as high in some places as when token integration first arrived, in the early 1960s. On the other hand it is impossible to avoid a suspicion that the popular feeling against busing was a little less strong than the politicians, responding to an outspoken minority, sometimes inferred. Wherever busing began, North or South, a similar, contradictory pattern of response was reported. It was plain, for a start, that the great majority of whites, and at least a substantial proportion of blacks, both in northern and southern cities, didn't like busing. A vocal minority of whites demonstrated against it. The number of white children in city public school systems dropped by around 10 per cent initially as the more prosperous parents either put their children in private schools or moved to the suburbs. There were sporadic reports of fist fights and more general reports of tension inside the newly desegregated schools, with here or there a bomb threat or some other hint of more serious violence.

But these incidents soon dropped off. The great majority of the students, of both races, got along together at least tolerably, and a substantial proportion of them soon began to pay more or less grudging tribute to the merits of the other group. At the beginning of the second year school almost invariably opened with far less trouble than the first. Only a vocal minority, it would seem, opposed busing unappeasably. The majority were apprehensive before it happened, unhappy with it, but determined to make the best of it if it had to happen. Public opinion, in fact, was nervous and confused, as a Potomac Associates survey in 1972 showed. While support for increasing public spending to help blacks was generally low, the survey found that when people were asked to choose between busing and higher spending on education, a large majority plumped for higher spending.

Perhaps too much should not be made of such survey data. It seems clear, however, that by 1972 the great majority, without any rabid racist opposition to busing, nevertheless didn't like it and were prepared to consider most other alternatives. No doubt this same majority had accepted the *Brown* decision and the goal of educational equality. They would therefore seem liable to the charge of being ready to will the end but not to will the means—except that at this very moment the experts were casting doubt on the efficacy both of busing and of higher expenditure as means of achieving greater equality through education.

It was, in retrospect, ironical that Professor Pettigrew should have suggested to one of his junior colleagues at the Harvard School of Education that he might do a study on busing. The colleague's name was David Armor, and Pettigrew's idea was that he take a look at Project Metco, a scheme for busing children out of Roxbury, the main Boston ghetto, into nearby white surburban schools.

That was in 1969. Three years later, as the public controversy over busing was boiling to its climax, a paper by David Armor called "The Evidence on Busing" was published in *The Public Interest*. Armor said he had concentrated on the question whether "induced integration"—that is, busing—"enhances black achievement, self-esteem, race relations and opportunities for higher education." Armor said that it did not. Armor found, "The available evidence . . . indicates that busing is *not* an effective policy instrument for raising the achievement of blacks or for increasing interracial harmony."

He did not limit himself to reporting the results of his own or other studies. His article was a sweeping, slashing attack on the whole tradition of liberal social science, a frontal assault on "forty years of studies," as one of his opponents put it. At one point Armor came close to accusing his opponents of deliberate dishonesty: "There is the danger that important research may be stopped when the desired results are not forthcoming. The current controversy over the busing of schoolchildren affords a prime example."

The response was severe. Pettigrew and three colleagues called Armor's paper "a distorted and incomplete review." They argued that the studies Armor had cited as "*the* evidence on busing" were highly selective: he had not discussed seven other studies, which reported positive results for busing blacks, though they met his own methodological criteria.

Tempers, in short, were comprehensively lost over the Armor affair. But it would be wrong to dismiss the episode as a mere squabble among professors. It shows just how traumatically a world where, half a dozen years before, consensus reigned had been affected by the pressures of political division and intellectual doubt. And the issue, after all, was the relationship among education, race and equality in the United States, which is not exactly an obscure academic quibble.

The Coleman report came out in 1966. It was not until 1972 that two major books were published, each an attempt to reassess the whole subject in the light of the Coleman data and their disconcerting implications.

The first was a collection of papers arising out of the Harvard seminar, with Frederick Mosteller (professor of mathematical statistics at Harvard) and Daniel Patrick Moynihan as its coeditors. Most of the leading participants in the debate contributed papers: Pettigrew and Armor, Coleman, and Christopher Jencks among them.

Later in the year, Jencks and seven colleagues published an only slightly less massive book: *Inequality: a Reassessment of the Effect of Family and Schooling in America.*

The enormous body of analysis and reinterpretation in these two books represents the first stage of the reaction to the Coleman shock. The nub of the new thinking, derived from the Coleman report, which has set off the whole prolonged, disturbing, confused and sometimes bitter debate, can be expressed as a simple syllogism:

(1) The "quality" of the schools attended by black and white children in America was more nearly equal than anyone supposed.

(2) The gap between the achievement of black and white children, as measured by standard tests, got wider, not narrower, over twelve years at school.

(3) Therefore there was no reason to suppose that increasing the flow of resources into the schools would affect the outcome in terms of achievement, let alone eliminate inequality.

Among the social scientists, the central ground of debate about the meaning of those findings lay between Jencks and Moynihan. It was a strange debate, for the two protagonists have much in common, even if one does have New Left loyalties and the other served Richard Nixon in the White House. The rift between a Christopher Jencks and a Pat Moynihan, indeed, is a kind of paradigm of the fission of liberalism. Both use the same data. Both agree on many of the implications and even on many of the conclusions to be drawn from them. Yet those who lump the two professors together, as many practical educators and civil rights lawyers do, as "Moynihan and Jencks and those people up at Harvard," could hardly be more wrong. The two men are divided by temperament and ideology, in the preconceptions they bring to the data, and ultimately also in the policy prescriptions they draw from them. In them as individuals, two divergent fragments of the liberal tradition can be seen embodied.

Perhaps the very heart of their disagreement, after all, comes down to a matter of temperament. Is a glass half empty, or is it half full? A pessimist will say it is half empty, while an optimist will say it is half full.

One of the specific recommendations of the Mosteller-Moynihan essay is optimism. If the differences in quality between the schools attended by different groups of children in the United States were so much smaller than anyone had expected to find them, then surely the United States had come much closer to realizing the goal of equality of educational opportunity than most people realized. And so the electorate should maintain the pressure on government, the essay urged, "with an attitude that optimistically expects gains, but, knowing their rarity, appreciates them when they occur."

On examination, this is a strange use of the word optimism. Optimism usually connotes an attitude toward the future. The emotion that is being evoked here has more to do with the past. It is not so much optimism as pride. "The nation entered the middle third of the twentieth century bound to the mores of caste and class. The white race was dominant. . . . Education beyond a fairly rudimentary point was largely determined by social status. In a bare third of a century these circumstances have been extensively changed. *Changed!* Not merely a sequence of events drifting in one direction or another. To the contrary, events have been bent to the national will." We should accentuate the positive, say Moynihan and Mosteller: "It truly is not sinful to take modest satisfaction in our progress."

It would be easy to make the mistake of concluding from this that Moynihan thinks that the policies that have achieved this progress should be pressed to the utmost. But he does not. When I asked him why not, he replied promptly, if cryptically: "Production functions." In an article in the fall 1972 issue of *The Public Interest* he spelled out what he meant. The argument was characteristically simple, forceful and provocative.

Proposition 1: "The most striking aspect of educational expenditure is how large it has become." It has now reached one thousand dollars per pupil per annum, and it has been rising at 9.7 per cent annually for the past ten years, while the GNP has been rising at 6.8 per cent.

Proposition 2 (the Coleman point): "After a point, school expenditure does not seem to have any notable influence on school achievement."

There are, Moynihan conceded, considerable regional, class, racial and ethnic variations in achievement, and he would like to see them disappear: "But it is simply not clear that school expenditure is the heart of the matter."

This is where the production functions, or what is more familiar to laymen as the law of diminishing returns, come in. The liberal faith held that expenditure of resources on education would produce not merely a greater equality in scholastic achievement but greater equality in society as well.

On the contrary, says Moynihan, additional expenditure on education (and also on other social policies) is likely to produce greater *inequality*, at least of income.

"Any increase in school expenditure," he wrote in *The Public Interest*, "will in the first instance accrue to teachers, who receive about 68% of the operating expenditure of elementary and secondary schools. That these are estimable and deserving persons none should doubt"— Brutus is an honorable man—"but neither should there be any illusion that they are deprived." With teachers earning some ten thousand dollars a year on the average, he argued, and with many of them married women with well-paid husbands, "increasing educational expenditures will have the short-run effect of increasing income inequality."

That may be literally true. It is a peculiar argument, nonetheless. Leaving aside the matter of their spouses' incomes, teachers are not, relatively, a highly paid group. Marginal increases in their salaries, especially if accompanied, as they actually were during the Nixon years, by corresponding increases in the income of some other lower-middle-class groups such as policemen, have an imperceptible effect on the inequality of national income distribution.

Whatever its merits, Moynihan's position is plain. It is also an interesting example of a new awareness of the class interest of those reform-oriented groups—in this case teachers, but the argument is also applied to social workers—who have traditionally been supposed in liberal doctrine to be motivated only by idealism but who are no longer accorded that courtesy. It is worth noting, however, that this position fits oddly with an exhortation to optimism. There is indeed nothing sinful about taking satisfaction in past progress. But when this attitude is combined with skepticism about the benefits to be expected from future public expenditure, it is usually called not optimistic but conservative.

Like Moynihan, Christopher Jencks is concerned with equality not only in the schools but also in the world after school. The originality of his thinking lies in his emphasis on two crucial, though not in themselves original, distinctions.

The first is a distinction we have encountered again and again. It is one of the great intellectual cruxes that have challenged the complacency of American liberalism: the distinction between equality of opportunity and equality of condition. Most Americans, said Jencks, say they are in favor of equality, and so no doubt they are. But what most of them mean by this is equality of opportunity. What we have learned from the Coleman report, said Jencks, and indeed from the fate of the reforms of the 1960s generally, is that, contrary to the conventional wisdom, you cannot have equality of opportunity without a good deal of equality of condition —now, and not in the hereafter.

This is where the second of Jencks's distinctions comes in. Where the Coleman survey and most of the work published in the Mosteller-Moynihan volume looked at the degree of equality among *groups* (and especially between *racial* groups) Jencks was more interested in inequality among individuals. It is cause for shock, he said in the preface to his book, "that white workers earn 50% more than black workers," but it was a good deal more shocking "that the best-paid fifth of all white workers earn 600% more than the worst-paid fifth. From this point of view, racial inequality looks almost insignificant"—by comparison with economic inequality.

Is the glass half empty, or half full? If Moynihan's instinct seems to be to emphasize the real progress that has been made to reducing certain forms of inequality in America, Jencks's is to stress how much inequality remains not only in educational opportunity, in learning skills and in educational credentials, but also in job status, in job satisfaction, and in income.

The trouble is, he pointed out, that whatever measure you take, income or socioeconomic status or education, there is plenty of inequality among Americans, but the same people by no means always come out at the same point on each measure. That, too, can be taken as a point of pride, if one wants to take it so. But it does follow that school reform is not likely to effect much greater equality outside the school.

He concluded that the egalitarian trend in American education over thirty years had not in fact made the distribution of either income or status outside the schools much more equal. The school must be abandoned as an instrument of social equalization, but only in favor of what Jencks hoped would be stronger and more effective instruments.

"As long as egalitarians assume that public policy cannot contribute to economic equality directly, but must proceed by ingenious manipulation of marginal institutions like the schools, progress will remain glacial."

"Marginal institutions like the schools!" The phrase sets Jencks every bit as far outside the liberal orthodoxy as Moynihan's suggestion that spending money on schools may actually increase inequality. And fourteen words from the end of his book, Jencks unfurls a word that must have startled most of his readers, the word that a generation of liberal intellectuals had been trying to avoid. "If we want to move beyond this tradition, we will have to establish political control over the economic institutions that shape our society. That is what other countries usually call socialism. Anything less will end in the same disappointment as the reforms of the 1960s."

By the time of President Nixon's second inauguration the challenge to the case for spending money on education was beginning to echo down the halls of Congress, ominously for the supporters of federal aid to education, who include both Representative John Brademas, Democrat of Indiana, the chairman of the House Select Subcommittee on Education, and one of his Republican colleagues, Representative Albert Quie of Minnesota. In a speech Quie made it plain that he remained to be convinced that compensatory education made no difference. And Brademas told me that he was afraid that the findings of the social scientists, misunderstood or deliberately misrepresented, would be used to justify cuts in federal aid to elementary and secondary education and to make opposition to such programs respectable. He is deeply skeptical of the case against the efficacy of educational spending, pointing out that federal aid still amounts to only 7 per cent of the cost of elementary and secondary schooling and that in addition funds intended under Title I to pay for compensatory education for underprivileged children had been indiscriminately spent for political reasons on middle-class children, so that few valid conclusions, in his opinion, could be drawn from the experience of compensatory spending to help the disadvantaged under Title I.

"The Jencks report" was freely cited by the Nixon administration's Office of Management and Budget on Capitol Hill in justification of cutting the budget for fiscal year 1974. There was a widespread feeling that "Coleman and Jencks" provided a respectable rationale for giving a low priority to spending on education.

Money is one issue. Integration is another. Yet, although, as Christopher Jencks put it to me, "the impact both of the Coleman report and of the Moynihan-Mosteller book is to put the support of social science behind integration," and even though a majority of the social scientists who have spoken up on the issue remain integrationist, there was no mistaking the chill that the Armor paper, supported as it was to some extent by influential figures in the intellectual community, sent down the spines of the integrationists. In November 1972, for example, Harold Howe, U. S. Commissioner for Education in the Johnson administration, and subsequently an official of the Ford Foundation, conceded that what he called, with a perceptible nuance of dislike, "the lively researches of statistically oriented social scientists have cast some shadows on conventional assumptions about the benefits of integration, particularly in the schools."

Would those shadows fall in due course across the courts, jammed as they were with cases arising from the desegregation orders made by federal judges all over the country after the *Green* and *Alexander* decisions in 1968 and 1969?

It is too soon to say. Yet what seems to be in doubt is not the principle established in *Brown*, but the practical possibility of enforcing it, and indeed the possibility of enforcing even the "separate but equal" principle acknowledged in *Plessy* v. *Ferguson* eighty years ago, in the new circumstances of the largely black inner city hemmed in by a ring of white suburbs.

Already the Supreme Court has decided against two strategies which, however drastic, seemed the most promising. In the *Rodriguez* case, from Texas, over a vigorous dissent from Mr. Justice Thurgood Marshall, the hero of *Brown*, the court turned down the requirement that educational expenditures be equalized as between the different school districts in a state. And finally, in the summer of 1974, the court overturned Judge Roth's plan for merging the increasingly segregated school system of Detroit with its predominantly white suburban neighbors.

In each case, it can well be argued that the court was doing no more than take prudent account of the political realities and the tolerance of the majority. Yet, after those two decisions, it is hard to see how the black

children of the inner city—those very children who are in danger of sinking into a permanent under-class—can be given an education that is anything other than separate and unequal.

## 5

Some years ago the great historian of the South C. Vann Woodward
compared the civil rights movement of the 1960s to the Reconstruction
after the Civil War. He feared then that the second Reconstruction was
ending. He was right. The momentum of the black advance has slowed,
though it has not stopped. Since 1965, blacks have made enormous social
and political gains. They continue to consolidate their political power, and
all the time individual blacks, in increasing numbers, have been making
it in economic terms. Like the mother in Langston Hughes's poem, they
have been reaching landings, and turning corners, and they are still climbing. But for blacks as a group, life is still no crystal stair. New gains for
some have been offset by new predicaments for others; and at the end of
the day, a split-level utopia, in which one half of the black population
moves on into relative security and affluence while the other half drifts
into deeper and deeper spirals of misery, is not good enough for anyone.
It is not safe, even for those who are making it. For those blacks who have
advanced, by their own tenacious efforts, to some prosperity or even modest security know in their marrow that as long as there are ten million, or
twelve million, of their brothers and sisters who are still trapped without a
ladder out of the flooded basement of American society, all blacks are
trapped with them.

In spite of all that was achieved in the 1960s, the scale of the black
migration and the scope of its effect on the human and political geography
of the country leave no alternative. There will have to be a third Reconstruction. It cannot be limited to the South next time. It will have to be
national. Its goal must be to succeed where its predecessors in the 1860s
and the 1960s both ultimately failed: to bring black Americans into full
equality, psychological as well as economic and political, and so to remove
the impediment that has so long obstructed the fulfillment of the promise
of America for white people as well as black. If the experience of the sixties proved that the confident assumptions of the old liberalism were too
facile, it only proved all the more the need for a new philosophy and a
new coalition for change. The third Reconstruction will have to fulfill the
hopes of the black minority and the white majority together. Nothing less
will be enough.

## Ideology and Consensus

"They want you to be a frontier for them."

Walter Prescott Webb

Once, in the early sixties, I sat in an office in the White House listening to one of President Kennedy's science aides, the late Dr. Nick Golovin, checking off on his fingers with irrefutable clarity the several reasons why manned flight to the moon was unnecessary, wasteful and technologically inelegant compared to instrumentation. At the same time, he was insisting that there could be no doubt about it: by the end of the decade, the United States would put a man on the moon. But why, I eventually asked, if it is so pointless? "Mr. Hodgson," was my reproof, "in this country we like to win our ball games."

Who doesn't? What was peculiar about the generation of Americans who grew up in the forties and into whose hands the destiny of the country had fallen by 1960 was not that they liked to win; it was that, being accustomed to victory, they expected it. It was not that they were impervious to the thought that there were problems to be solved; they were impervious to the idea that they would not be able to solve them.

There was hubris in this mood. But the roots of it were in the experience of real success.

"There we were," said Carl Kaysen of the memory that the intellectuals of the Kennedy administration had of World War II, "there we were, captains and majors, telling the whole world what to do."

"All was free," wrote Theodore H. White of his arrival in China in 1945, "room, food, liquor, girls—because we were Americans. The whole world belonged to America."

"Postwar American suburbs," wrote Tom Wolfe, "glorious world. One's parents remembered the sloughing common order, War & Depression—but Superkids knew only the emotional surge of the great payoff."

By 1960 American athletes expected victory, and so did American military men. The economists expected uninterrupted growth, and the businessmen—once they had overcome their suspicion of the economists—expected uninterrupted profits.

The doctors expected to conquer disease. There was so much publicity about the cure for cancer, the cure for heart disease, one expert recalled to me, reminiscing about the Kennedy years, that people began to feel "it was only a matter of time before the brilliant, dedicated doctors discovered a cure for death."

By the time the 1970 United Nations *Demographic Yearbook* was published, the United States was seventeenth in the international league table in infant mortality. Twelve sovereign countries, plus two of the constituent republics of the Soviet Union, claimed a higher life expectancy for females, and another six came within one year of the U.S. figure of seventy-four years. In life expectancy for males, in spite of all the money spent on research into cancer, heart disease and stroke, the United States ranked thirtieth, behind Spain, Greece, and five Communist countries in Eastern Europe.

In respect of the most vital statistics of all, the descendants of those who had migrated to America to find a better life had done worse than the descendants of those who had stayed behind. The reason, of course, was not that American medicine was less skillful; but that it was less available.

How inconceivable that unfavorable comparison would have seemed in the fifties! Then, American intellectuals galloped ahead of the irresistible march of technology like skirmishing Cossacks, waving their shining hyperbole around their heads. The European, wrote Leslie Fiedler in 1952, almost contemptuously, after a visit to Italy, finds it impossible to reject the reality of death, and difficult to believe in anything else; where, in America, "only death is denied and everything else is considered possible."

It was indeed a miraculous vision that Fiedler's contemporaries in the American elites of the age of consensus had seen. The social scientists were confident that they could explain the mechanisms of society without implying any serious criticism of its institutions. The politicians and the bureaucrats believed that they could use this new knowledge and the wealth it would help to create to abolish poverty and inequality—without upsetting the less-poor or the more-equal-than-others by redistributing wealth or increasing taxes.

A state of sociological hygiene, they believed, could be attained as directly, as *technologically*, as the U. S. Army public-health people, in wartime Naples, had abolished typhus and malaria. The poor could be sprayed with money, and the enemy sprayed with lead, it was assumed, just as efficiently as the Italians had been sprayed with DDT. The result would be just as gratifying. Poverty and communism would become extinct, like typhus.

It took the twelve years from 1960 to 1972 to learn that life is not quite as simple as that. Society and politics, like the biological world, are neither as easily understood nor as easily changed as it seemed to the American elite of the confident years. Immune strains of mosquitoes soon appeared. Worse, the possibility had to be faced that DDT might cause diseases as deadly as those it had helped to suppress. In the same way, in American cities and in Southeast Asia, each campaign to eradicate social problems or political dangers seemed to leave some of the old infections immunized against treatment, and to create new infections into the bargain.

There was something even worse than that. The American governmental and intellectual elite made a discovery in those years that can be compared to Heisenberg's uncertainty principle. They had assumed that they could study the world with objectivity. They had also assumed that they could change it by exerting money, or force, or both, with surgical dispassion, without themselves being changed. They found that can't be done.

They supposed that they could intervene in Indochina as if from Mount Olympus and that their intervention would have no effect on the United States. They were wrong.

They supposed that it would be possible to eliminate segregation in the South without changing the social relations or political institutions of the country as a whole. That was wrong, too. And when they discovered that mistake, they went on to imagine that they could get rid of the poverty and discrimination that they had rather belatedly discovered in the North without that effort, either, having any great effect on themselves. And that was the worst miscalculation of all. They discredited their own doctrines. They lost the confidence of the majority. And so they put into the presidency, the office on which they counted as their instrument, at the head of a rebellion of the very people whom they thought of as their followers, Richard Nixon, who became their archenemy.

Such a dénouement, I began this book by suggesting, raises the possibility that it wasn't so much that something went wrong with their plans as that there was something wrong with the liberals' perception of reality all along. And in fact if we look once again at the major assumptions of the liberal consensus, one by one, it is plain that each of them has been at least apparently or partially discredited in one way or another by the events of the sixties. As a system, the liberal ideology is in ruins. Let us look briefly at some of its key assumptions, and see how they fared.

1. *American capitalism works: more than that, it is the truly revolutionary force in the world.*

By 1973 several other economies had been relatively more successful than that of the United States. American capitalism was still working. But it was no longer the wonder of the world. Its future did not look as unclouded as it had looked in 1945 or even in 1960. Inflation, the loss of its competitive position in many industries, the probability of shortages both of energy and key raw materials, and inadequate investment all threatened that future. And certainly in theoretical terms few intellectuals were hailing American capitalism as a revolutionary force for social change in 1973.

The GNP had more than doubled since 1960. Median family income, even taking inflation into account, had almost doubled. But most of that growth had come in the first part of the period. Latterly, industrial workers' real incomes had stood still. Not only Kuwaitis, but the Swiss, Swedes and West Germans now earned on average more than Americans. Where, in 1965, industrial wages in the nine other leading industrial countries had been less than half the level of U.S. wages, by 1975 workers in five of the nine got more than 80 per cent of the U.S. average wage. A historic gap was closing. Many European economies had been growing steadily faster than that of the United States since the early sixties. Japan's had been growing much faster. By the tests that American economists and ideologues themselves had proposed to the world, GNP growth and average earnings, the United States was no longer setting the pace.

It was possible to argue that those other economies had succeeded only because they had successfully imitated the American pattern. Increasingly the world economy was dominated by multinational corporations that were mostly either U.S.-controlled or at least steeped in the U.S. business culture. That might be a consolation for nationalists. It was a poor basis for arguing, as so many intellectuals had argued in the early 1950s, that U.S. capitalism was about to change the face of the world. The fact that executives of state-owned oil companies, or European private banks, or Japanese *zaibatsu* dressed and lived and talked and, on certain subjects, thought like Middle Western businessmen, suggested the opposite. Everywhere, local elites were finding how well they could get on with American corporate business, and American businessmen were deciding they didn't really want anything to change. The businessman as revolutionary, never a very convincing figure, was fading from view.

The growth of multinationals had menacing implications for U.S. labor. Complaining that perhaps as many as one million jobs in U.S. manufacturing industry had been shifted abroad by U.S.-controlled multinationals, labor shifted from its traditional support for free trade to the tough protectionism of the Burke-Hartke bill. Just as jobs had fled South from New England and the Middle West to escape unions and taxes and safety regulations, so now jobs were escaping from the United States, first to Western Europe, then increasingly to low-wage, low-tax, low-regulation areas in Latin America and the fringe of Asia.

Some, such as the banker Robert Roosa and the sociologist David Riesman, wondered whether the U.S. economy was not slowly beginning to follow the example of nineteenth-century Britain, exporting capital and jobs rather than goods, and living increasingly on the repatriated profits of the exported capital. If so, the outlook was not good. U.S. industry would become progressively less and less competitive. Eventually there was the risk that foreign countries, tired of watching U.S.-controlled corporations shipping out massive profits, would begin to expropriate U.S. interests. In 1971 the Allende government in Chile, computing that two U.S. copper companies had taken out of Chile, since the early-twentieth century, a sum equivalent to the rest of the Chilean national product over that period, proceeded to nationalize the mines without compensation. The oil companies' ownership of the producing fields was disappearing. Increasingly, the United States would have to relate its foreign policy to defending foreign investments. In that case, U.S. blue-collar and white-collar workers would find themselves paying more and more for the relative affluence of the stockholders, the executives and the military men who owned, operated and protected the multinational corporate economy.

That was perhaps an exaggerated view. While manufacturing industry as a whole did seem to be getting steadily less competitive in world markets, the agriculture and high-technology sectors looked as strong as ever.

Still, if the U.S. economy had performed solidly for a decade, the outlook was far less promising than in the early sixties. Inflation had taken hold. Recession threatened. The balance-of-payments deficit was horrendous. The United States was becoming ominously dependent on foreign oil and raw materials and on foreign markets. And these objective problems bred new attitudes. For the first time since the thirties, people were no longer sure that corporate business was beneficent. For a generation, it had provided jobs. Now unemployment was beginning to rise. Rates of actual unemployment remained fairly low until the energy crisis bit hard in 1973–74. But the unemployment rate, which measures the number of people out of work on a given day, seriously underestimates the number of workers with reason to fear for their jobs. In 1969, for example, 18 per cent of all operatives were out of work at one time or another; in 1970 the rate rose to 23 per cent, and their unemployment lasted on the average for three months. In other sectors, such as construction, as many as three workers out of ten were out of work at one time in the year.

To the old fear of unemployment, there were added new reasons for doubting the benevolence of corporate business. Since 1945 business had gone to great lengths to persuade people that it was public-spirited, and on the whole it had succeeded. Now the environmental movement was accusing it of ruthless indifference to people's health and the beauties of nature. The consumer movement was challenging its honesty. The fall in the stock market cast a new light on the dream of a People's Capitalism. "No policy is likely to benefit business itself," Peter Drucker had written, "unless it also benefits the society." Now, for the first time in a generation, Americans in large numbers had begun to question the social benefits of corporate capitalism.

2. *American capitalism has discovered the secret of economic growth. And growth, the supreme touchstone of a healthy society, will lead us to a New Frontier.*

First the Soviet Union, in the late 1950s, then the European Common Market, then Japan, then Spain, then Brazil, and finally the oil-producing countries showed that it was an illusion to imagine that American capitalism, or American technology, or American management had any monopoly on the secret of economic growth. The environmental movement pointed out the limits to growth. Inflation and the Arabs limited it in practice. But growth was more than a desideratum for the liberals. It provided them with their most characteristic metaphor, and with the goal of their mission.

Back in 1890, as Frederick Jackson Turner reminded the American Historical Association three years later in his famous lecture, the Superintendent of the Census announced the closing of the frontier of settlement.

By the end of the 1960s, Americans had come to terms with the painful fact that the metaphorical frontiers to which they had looked were also closing.

The idea of the New Frontier was not just the election slogan of the Kennedy administration. It was both a far older and a more widespread idea than that. Turner's famous thesis interpreted American history, and accounted for what he regarded as the distinctive American characteristics of mobility, strength, acuteness, individualism and democracy, in terms of a geographical frontier. He defined it as "the existence of an area of free land, its continuous recession, and the advance of American settlement westwards."

In the hungry, radical thirties, Turner's thesis was much derided. But in the forties it reappeared in a new form. And this time it was not advanced just as an explanation of past superiority. It was a prescription for future hegemony.

The frontier, said the historian Dixon Ryan Fox, was not just free land. It was in far more general sense "the edge of the unused": all the boundless resources of the universe that remained to be exploited by science and technology. It was an idea perfectly fitted for the new wave of American nationalism. Most influential of all was Joseph Schumpeter, conservative intellectual godfather to the liberals. He was in the right discipline, economics, and at the right university, Harvard, to sell this second, metaphysical version of the frontier thesis to the American elite. "We must not confuse geographical frontiers with economic ones," Schumpeter wrote in *Capitalism, Socialism and Democracy*, which was published in 1942. "Technological possibilities are an uncharted sea."

Long before John Kennedy borrowed them for his acceptance speech in Los Angeles in 1960, in fact, both the phrase "a New Frontier" and its promise of an American future of boundless resources and limitless expansion made possible by science and technology, had become familiar. They reappeared like a *Leitmotiv* in the literature of the consensus. The New Frontier is there in Daniel Bell's *The End of Ideology*, and again as a chapter heading in the Rockefeller panels' *Prospect for America*.

As early as 1951, indeed, the idea was prevalent enough to draw forth a stinging and memorable rebuke from Walter Prescott Webb, whose thesis was that four hundred years of frontier were coming to an end for Western civilization in general. "Less thoughtful people," he warned his readers in the *Atlantic Monthly*, "speak of new frontiers":

> The businessman sees a business frontier in the customers he has not yet reached. . . .
> The social worker sees a human frontier among the suffering people whose woes he has not yet alleviated. . . .
> If you watch these peddlers of substitute frontiers, you will find that nearly every one wants you to buy something, give something, or believe in something. They want you to be a frontier for them.
> They are all fallacies, these new frontiers, and they are pernicious in proportion to their plausibility and respectability.

Poor Walter Prescott Webb was a prophet before his time, a pessimistic conservative in a time of surging liberal boosterism, a voice crying in the Texas wilderness. Walter Prescott *who?* By the early sixties, the new elites, in business and academia as well as in government and the media, those graduate sodbusters, were lighting out for the territory.

The New Economics would fine-tune the motor, and the American economy, firing on all eight cylinders, as Otto Eckstein put it, would be "the mightiest engine of human progress the world has ever seen." The small change of incremental resources from its uninterrupted growth would be enough to abolish poverty—without putting up taxes. The frontiers of scientific research and technological development would recede continuously into an infinitely distant future: electronics, automation, cybernation, aerospace, and then the ocean. And then think what the sciences of the mind and of society could do, once they, too, were harnessed by corporate organization and the profit motive! Public opinion surveys, motivational research, advertising, scientific marketing, all would bring new acreage of demand under the corporate plow. They would create service industries, each of which would make the open range of the old West look like a paddock. There would be a leisure industry and a knowledge industry, each rich enough to make old Spindletop look like a dry hole. And even those rich new gushers would be nothing compared to the new frontiers that would open up as government and academia worked hand in hand with business.

There was the great Cold War frontier, which poor President Eisenhower was *passé* enough to fear and call the military-industrial complex. That would go on. But behind it there stretched, virgin and unsurveyed, the consultancy frontier, the health-care frontier, the nursing-home frontier, the poverty frontier, the crime-and-police frontier, and finally—conceptual California—the study of future possibilities, the frontier frontier itself.

None of these infinitely receding frontiers need be bounded by the confines of the United States. Just as in the nineteenth century American settlement had spread inexorably westward across the free land, so in the second half of the twentieth the frontiers of American influence and American corporate business would spread around the world, promising a boundless bonanza of limitless growth.

That dream has faded now.

The certainties of the New Economics were shaken first. Each of its two central tenets, the paramount desirability of economic growth and the possibility of achieving it by economic management without either excessive inflation or excessive unemployment, has been severely challenged by theoretical critics. And each has also come under fire from the artillery of events.

Two schools challenge the old faith in growth. One of them asks whether for the individual the advantages of economic growth in the society outweigh its disadvantages. This case was made formally in E. J. Mishan's 1967 book *The Costs of Economic Growth*. It is the subject matter of a now fashionable branch of economic science, welfare economics. And in terms of ordinary people's lives, the same question underlies the world-wide rebellion against more superhighways, more high-rise buildings, more new plastic products, and so many of the other blessings that liberal America had promised to bring forth so abundantly.

The other school, exemplified by Donella and Dennis Meadows and the team at M.I.T. who wrote *The Limits to Growth*, asked not whether growth was desirable but how long it would continue to be possible. They projected five factors into the future up to the year 2100: existing trends of population, industrial output, food supplies, mineral resources, and pollution. While population and demand would increase exponentially, food and other supplies would not. That must lead to world-wide economic collapse. Critics pounced on the Meadows thesis. Their model did indeed seem oversimple. Yet their central point was becoming generally accepted. Theoretically, the possibilities of future growth must be *finite*. The whole economic and intellectual system of the New Frontier had been predicated on the assumption that growth could be virtually infinite.

Everywhere, by the early seventies, the expansive vision of boundless frontiers was giving way to the metaphor of Spaceship Earth. The world was seen not as virgin prairie awaiting the plow but as a fragile nest whose brood must fight for scarce resources.

At the same time, there was a new awareness of the predatory side of the frontier tradition. The new sympathy for the American Indian, illustrated, for example, by the fantastic sales of *Bury My Heart at Wounded Knee* in 1971, helped to make people realize how the West was won: by fraud and genocide as well as by courage and determination. A whole anti-chauvinist literature, inspired by the Vietnam War and beginning with Norman Mailer's *Why Are We in Vietnam?* elaborated more or less masochistic variations on this theme. The result was a new popular understanding of what was implied by the New Frontier dream. Unlimited growth of American consumption in a world of poor people and scarce resources: that had always been a glutton's dream. Now it seemed a fantasy into the bargain.

The New Economists, meanwhile, were coming under fire in their own theoretical backyard. A "monetarist" school, led by the University of Chicago's Professor Milton Friedman, attacked from the Right, challenging their faith in the effectiveness of fiscal policy for managing the economy. A new generation of neo-Marxists poured in stiff volleys from the Left. In a new edition of his *History of Economic Thought*, published in 1973, Eric Roll found that he had to add another chapter, called "The

Age of Doubt": the section that described what was happening to the certainties of the sixties, he called "From Authority to Disaffection." In the preface to the ninth edition of his famous textbook, also published in 1973, Professor Paul Samuelson laid all his emphasis on change, doubt, and the new critiques of the orthodoxy of which he had once been the acknowledged champion. "In this edition," he explained, "I have particularly emphasized unsolved problems in modern economics: cost-push inflation; the quality of life versus mere GNP growth"—mere GNP growth! That was as if St. Paul, in an updated edition of his Epistles, suddenly started writing about the "mere" kingdom of heaven—"Net Economic Welfare (NEW) *versus* Gross National Product (GNP); Zero Population Growth (ZPU); Zero Economic Growth (ZEB) and ecological doomsday . . . and the principal criticisms of mainstream economics." Doubt had gnawed its way into the very citadels of certainty.

The most anguished debate of all among the professional economists was over the question whether, as they put it in the jargon, "the Phillips curve had shifted to the right." Had the level of prices and wages, in plain English, become less responsive than previously to changes in the level of employment? It seemed that they had. That meant that governments were faced with a more agonizing choice than ever before between unemployment and inflation. It also meant that economists knew less than they thought they knew, in the first flush of the Keynesian triumph, about how to control a modern economy.

It was not these moral arguments or technical debates, however, that did most to discredit the New Frontier's faith in boundless growth. It was inflation.

As we saw, inflation first began to get out of control in late 1965, as a result of the escalation of the war, and more specifically as a result of President Johnson's unwillingness or inability to raise taxes to pay for it. For a time it was mild, though even in the late sixties there was enough inflation to cast doubt on the fundamental liberal assumption that decisive social change could be paid for out of the new resources created by growth. As long as government was not prepared to take those resources from the private sector through taxation, it found itself creating growth artificially by printing money, and so also creating inflation.

By August 1971, inflation was rampant enough to force President Nixon to reverse his economic policy overnight. Three years to the month later, in the month of Nixon's final fall, Dr. Arthur Burns, now the chairman of the Federal Reserve Board, wrote the epitaph of the New Economics. At the end of twelve months in which the consumer price index had risen by 11 per cent and the take-home pay of the typical worker in real terms had fallen by nearly 5 per cent, Burns had to record that inflation "comes to dominate every aspect of economic life."

No doubt the energy crisis after the Yom Kippur War, in the fall of 1973, steepened the inflationary gradient. No doubt it could be argued that the Arab decision to increase oil prices was not predictable. (Certainly it was the one factor ignored in a pretentious survey of the future by that archetypal conservative liberal Dr. Herman Kahn and his Hudson Institute.) By the spring of 1974, the United States, which had been self-sufficient in fuel a decade earlier, was importing almost one third of its oil and natural gas at an annual cost approaching $30 billion. The deficit in the U.S. balance of payments would have been correspondingly hair-raising, had it not been for another inflationary factor, which, in balance-of-payments terms, happened to be favorable: the sharp rise in the world price of food.

But if shortage of food and shortage of fuel help to explain the unforeseen onset of inflation, they only further showed up the fatuity of those who had seen the world, only ten years before, in terms of New Frontiers of boundless economic growth.

3. *Out of the incremental resources created by economic growth, we will solve social problems. Nor will we have to make hard choices. For, given adequate inputs of resources, the solution of problems is the outcome. And our resources, now that we know how to manage the economy, will be boundless.*

No American was more involved in the detailed, practical work of planning and steering through Congress and then administering the social reforms of the sixties than Wilbur Cohen. He was assistant secretary at HEW under a succession of Secretaries, and then briefly Secretary himself. When I went to talk to him at the University of Michigan in 1973, his mood was sober and chastened. He was aware of the crisis in liberalism. But he refused to accept that the reforms of the sixties had failed in terms of any realistic expectations. People wanted the instant millennium, he grumbled, whereas in reality "most problems involving human beings take twenty years." "We're going through a period of antithesis," he said, "but I'm optimistic enough to believe that we will see a new synthesis before long. In the year 2000 historians will look back and say that the 1960s were the great watershed."

He singled out four "long-range conceptual achievements" as the basis for this belief, each symbolized by a major piece of legislation but transcending it in its implications for American society.

First he put the implementation of the concept of civil rights for blacks: not just the belated acceptance of the principle, but the greater practical implementation that had been achieved, with its implications for politics (voting) and for the texture of racial relationships (the desegregation of schools and public accommodations).

Second, the long-term effect of the war on poverty. Not only had many millions of Americans been helped to move up out of poverty; there was a greater consciousness of the existence of poverty and of the need to do something about it.

Third, the question of public responsibility for health care. The passage of Medicare, besides being a major reform in itself, had transformed public attitudes so that the concept of national health insurance was no longer controversial: "Everyone is for national health insurance now."

Fourth, the nation had come to accept the principle of "doing something for the disadvantaged in education."

The Civil Rights Acts of 1964 and 1965, the Economic Opportunity Act of 1964, Medicare, and the Elementary and Secondary Education Act of 1965—those four great measures, conceived by the liberal consensus of the late 1950s, prepared by the Kennedy administration, and carried out under the leadership of Lyndon Johnson, together form the main struts of an imposing structure of social reform that has humanized American society and will inevitably clarify the course of social policy in the future.

And yet . . . You have only to think of those four areas of triumphant liberal reform, one by one, to be reminded how deeply the liberal program has been challenged on the plane of theory, and how the liberal coalition has been divided in terms of practical politics.

The key idea behind the civil rights movement of the early 1960s was integration. This is now very widely rejected by both whites and blacks. While the great majority of Americans accept the goal of equality for blacks in theory, equally massive majorities oppose most of the specific policies that have been advocated for making that equality a reality. By two to one, Americans reject the idea of increased public expenditure to help blacks improve their situation.

The number of poor people was dramatically reduced in the 1960s, more, no doubt, as a result of general prosperity than as a direct consequence of the War on Poverty. But, in the seventies, that reduction has stopped. The master idea behind the liberal strategy against poverty, that of community action, is intellectually discredited and politically a pariah. The Office of Economic Opportunity was dismantled, unlamented. New strategies for eliminating poverty, whether it was the Nixon-Moynihan Family Assistance Plan or George McGovern's vaguer talk of redistributing wealth and guaranteeing a minimum income, have all so far failed to command substantial political support.

The way in which Medicare was introduced, and specifically the fact that a huge new flow of public money was entrusted to the existing private-health-care industry, unleashed an inflation of health costs that convinced even President Nixon that "we face a massive crisis in this area." This was the situation that made everyone suddenly come out for national health insurance. As Dr. William McKissick reported in the *New England Journal of Medicine*:

> The year 1969 witnessed advocacy of universal health insurance from political quarters that ranged from Representative John Dingell [on the medical Left] . . . to the American Medical Association . . . Governor Rockefeller, the Aetna Life Insurance Company . . . Senator Kennedy . . . Walter Reuther.

And, he might have added, the AFL/CIO. By 1970, when President Nixon added his endorsement of the principle, it truly seemed that national health insurance was an idea whose time had come.

It soon transpired, however, that what both the Nixon administration and Chairman Wilbur Mills of the House Ways and Means Committee understood by national health insurance was an obligatory extension of private insurance policies to the whole population, with the federal government stepping in only to fill those gaps that the industry did not find profitable. That would not only have the effect, as Secretary Richardson calculated, of swelling insurance companies' premium incomes by at least 30 per cent, or $7 billion, in the first year; it left the structure of the health-care industry, as a privately owned, profit-oriented enterprise, essentially unchanged. No more fundamental reform, as both Senator Kennedy and the labor unions soon found out, had any hope of surviving the Congressional process as of the early seventies. So while the principle of some kind of national health insurance was accepted by "everyone," the opportunity for a more fundamental reform of the health-care delivery system was missed.

As for doing something for the disadvantaged by means of education, so far from being one of the long-range conceptual achievements of the 1960s, it is the classic instance of the disintegration of the liberal consensus. The liberal philosophy was a centrist one. It looked for a maximum of reform with a minimum of institutional change. And it depended on the belief that social problems could be solved by the scientific application of the resources created by economic growth. Whatever else the Coleman report and the ensuing debate proved or didn't prove, it cast doubt on that belief.

Did liberalism fail?

Did it work, in which case it seemed to have failed only because its successes had raised people's expectations or because a sort of law of diminishing returns had set in?

Or was it simply never tried?

Each of these positions was clearly staked out in the debate about education and equality. More generally, by the early seventies, the liberal consensus had split into three. And those three questions marked out its three major fragments.

There are still plenty of bitter-end liberals. To the question "Did liberalism work?" they answer: "We don't know yet; it was never tried." They continue to believe that busing would make true educational integration possible, if it were tried. More generally, they maintain that poverty could be abolished, wealth redistributed, equality achieved, within the framework of the existing system. They may be right. But they have largely lost their audience. They are caught between the exhaustion of the political majority and the skepticism of the intellectuals, most of whom now prefer one of the two more fashionable positions.

There are the radicals. Liberalism failed, they say. It was bound to fail. So now let us try stronger medicine!

But what medicine? Radicals, for example, accept that money spent on education may not bring equality any nearer. But they disagree about the remedy. Is it to change the pattern of political and economic power, and achieve equality that way, rather than by "tampering with marginal institutions like the schools?" Or is it to create an entirely different kind of school, and so "deschool society"? As heirs of the counter culture of the sixties, radicals suspect authority, institutions, programs, plans, rules, committees, and experts. Sometimes they even seem to suspect rationality itself. But they have also inherited the fatal dilemma of the counter culture, between personal and political liberation as a goal, or between salvation and revolution. They are therefore torn between rejecting existing society so totally that they can have no influence over it (going to live on a commune in Oregon, for example), and accepting it so far that you are inevitably drawn into compromise (going to lobby in Washington for radical causes). While radical ideas leaven America more than ever before, and radical individuals have learned how to use the judo principle and move public opinion by its own weight, as a group the radicals are too few, too divided, and too much against the American grain to be the heirs of liberalism.

"Liberalism did work. But people's expectations have risen. Because of the law of diminishing returns, further efforts may not yield worthwhile results. And there are limits to how much society can be reformed." Something like that is the characteristic response of the third fragment of the consensus, which might perhaps be called Positivist.

After the French Revolution, with the Bourbons, who had learned nothing and forgotten nothing, restored to their throne, there grew up in France the philosophical movement called Positivism. The name was a kind of pun—or at least it referred to two distinct kinds of positiveness. On the one hand, Positivism was a methodological posture of skepticism, especially toward schemes for radical political and social reform. You must believe only, said the Positivist, what science can positively affirm. At the same time, he was called a Positivist because he believed in being positive as opposed to negative. This combination of skepticism about drastic reform, and a kind of optimism, made Positivism an attractive creed for those who were tired of Jacobin excesses, and still dreaded the backlash of reaction.

American intellectuals in the early seventies had not seen their loved ones carted off in tumbrels to the guillotine. Hopes had been the casualties, and the wounds had been to self-esteem. Still, they did have the feeling that they had lived through a revolutionary period, and many of them reacted in a way that was strikingly similar to that double response of the nineteenth-century Positivists. Like them, they scrutinized proposals for reform with a new skepticism. And like them, they tended to accentuate the positive, eliminate the negative.

The skepticism was intellectual, and applied to future proposals for reform. The yearning for faith in the past was emotional. "It is frequently said that ours is a sick society," wrote Irving Kristol, one of the chiefs of the Positivist school, "and this may be so. But it is awfully hard to arrive at a convincing conclusion, because one of the ills we are certainly suffering from happens to be hypochondria."

This was something different from the old liberal optimism. The old liberal's brow was permanently furrowed by the thought of all the menacing problems that must be solved without delay. There were not enough science teachers, and too many juvenile delinquents, in the schools. There was a missile gap. Civilization was threatened by advertising, alienation, anomie, automation, communism, coexistence, cybernation, hunger, materialism, obesity, poverty, materialism, and nuclear fallout. Yet the old liberals never doubted that these problems could all be solved. Given the inputs of federal legislation, brains, programs, money, the outcomes must follow. The liberals of the heyday of consensus were intellectual Sea Bees: the impossible took a little longer.

The new Positivist attitude was subtly different. Liberal programs had worked. One should be positive about that. Yet it was not clear that they would go on working. Moynihan's position on education is a classic example. "It is simply extraordinary," he wrote, "that so much has been done. . . . No small achievement! In truth, a splendid one. . . . It truly is not sinful to take modest satisfaction in our progress." Yet, what was that progress? In a third of a century, education, once determined by social status and class, had become generally available. Should the same policies be pressed further, then? No: for further expenditure on education would produce greater *inequality*.

And so the abounding optimism of the liberal consensus about the perfectibility of society went out of fashion. It was replaced by philosophical pessimism, sometimes modified by an attitude to the *status quo* so Positivist as to be in practice hard to distinguish from conservatism.

"In our competitive efforts to win his attention, we too often build up his expectations to unrealistic levels and must share the blame when he is disappointed. There is no doubt that promotional excesses have come back to haunt us and we are paying the price for these indiscretions." The speaker was the president of American Motors, and he was speaking about the disappearing customer. But his words might have been composed as an epitaph for liberalism. Summing up the debate over the failure of the Great Society in *The Public Interest* in early 1974, Lance Liebman found that four overlapping reasons had been most often put forward:

1. Things improved, but not enough to meet the rise in expectations.
2. There are things we don't know how to do. Teaching poor children to read may be an example.
3. Urban public services are inefficient.
4. Adequate resources were not provided, because of the Vietnam War, and also because the middle class resisted taxation.

Or, to use the terminology I have been using, because there was a political revolt against liberalism on the part of the majority of working Americans. It was this which demonstrated the most glaring of all the flaws in the liberal picture of American society: the myth of the abolition of the working class.

4. *Class, as the basis of political conflict, has been abolished in America. The American working class is becoming "middle class."*

"Steamfitters and firemen and taxi drivers as well as accountants and engineers," wrote James Reichley in his summary of Nixon's electoral strategy for *Fortune*, "have swarmed to the new suburbs [and] sought to re-create the remembered ideal of Elm Street."

"Something has happened in the United States in recent years," wrote Ben J. Wattenberg in *The Real America*, "that has never happened before anywhere: The massive majority of the population of a nation is now in the middle class. . . . The head of the household may not be a doctor, lawyer, accountant or professor, but rather a plasterer, lathe operator, steelworker, routeman or salesman. But—in our judgment—these Americans are very much part of the middle class."

Those two quotations suggest how very much alive the myth of the abolition of the working class still was in the early seventies. It suited everyone. Republicans used it as the basis for strategies designed to broaden their electoral catchment area. Democrats turned to it to show that their policies had not failed, after all. Positivist intellectuals embraced it because it enabled them to argue, in the same breath, how well past reforms had succeeded and how little need there would be for reform in the future. Even radicals were well content to be told that the working class was wallowing in unseemly prosperity, for then they could pursue their own dreams of salvation or revolution with a good conscience. Yet the disappearance of the American working class was simply a myth: a popular story not supported by reality.

The myth can be broken down into several related parts, each of which, at best, was only partially true. Together, they composed a picture of American society so distorted that, once it is realized that virtually all political strategists and social commentators were looking at the myth rather than at the reality, that fact alone explains much that is baffling about the rise and fall of American liberalism.

First, it was endlessly asserted that blue-collar workers have become a minority in the American work force. That is true only if the definition used is that of the Census Bureau, rather than the common-sense meaning of plain language. Furthermore, even if it is ever true at some time in the future that blue-collar workers are a minority, the difference between the status of blue-collar workers and a large proportion of white-collar workers is not such that it makes any sense to talk of those who have moved from one group to another "moving into the middle class."

Second, it is widely believed that the wage differentials between blue-collar and white-collar workers have disappeared. That, too, follows from the misleading categories used by the Census Bureau. It is not true. Still less is the inference that is often drawn from that assertion true, namely, that American workers in general enjoy a "middle-class" standard of living. To imply, as Ben Wattenberg, for example, does, that plasterers or lathe operators enjoy the same life style or economic situation as lawyers and doctors is pure fantasy.

Third, it is incessantly repeated that blue-collar workers, having "moved to the suburbs," have become culturally indistinguishable from the middle class: that "steamfitters and firemen" have not only sought to re-create, but have actually succeeded in re-creating, "Elm Street." The majority of working Americans, that is, are alleged to enjoy the economically easy and culturally spacious life of the upper-middle class. But they don't.

Steamfitters don't live on the same block as surgeons. The truth is less dramatic, though nothing to be ashamed of. It is that, if all goes well for them as individuals—no accidents at work, no long illness, no divorce, no sudden layoff—a substantial fraction of the working population can aspire to a level of material comfort that is impressive compared to that of workers in most other countries, and compared to that of American workers forty or even twenty years ago. But that level no more resembles the life of the established American upper-middle class, either in economic or in psychological comfort, then a stamped tin eagle over the door transforms a cheap tract house into an ante-bellum mansion, or owning a secondhand Cadillac makes a man a millionaire.

It is obvious enough why these illusions became so widespread. But how have they been so little challenged?

The first—the myth of the middle-class majority—is easily enough explained. The U. S. Bureau of the Census divides all occupations into ten broad categories. The first four of these are 1. "Professional, technical and kindred"; 2. "Managers, officials and proprietors"; 3. "Clerical"; and 4. "Sales." All the jobs in these four categories are further classified as "white collar" occupations. The next three categories are called "blue collar," and only the next three. They are 5. "Craftsmen and foremen"; 6. "Operatives"; and 7. "Laborers (non-farm)." And finally there are three categories of occupation that are classified as neither "white collar" nor "blue collar": 8. "Service" jobs; 9. "Farmers"; and 10. "Farm workers."

First of all, to take 1970 figures (those of the last census), 9.7 million "service" workers are excluded from the "blue collar" categories. These include janitors, guards, watchmen, policemen, firemen, waiters, waitresses, cooks, bus boys, dishwashers, maids, porters and gas-station attendants—a list of the least-middle-class jobs in America, most of which have been universally considered classic working-class jobs since the Paris Commune of 1870 and before.

Second, the "white collar" category includes 3.5 million male clerical workers and 2.8 million male sales workers. Most of these jobs are subordinate, entirely repetitive and less well paid than the majority of those listed as "blue collar" jobs. Checkout clerks in a supermarket, for example, cannot be said to be in "middle-class" jobs without doing violence to the language.

Third, the "white collar" ranks are swollen by the wholesale conscription of women. They include no fewer than 10.2 million women clerical workers and over 2 million women sales workers. Think of the ones you know or meet. The vast majority of them, working as secretaries, typists, filing clerks, salespersons in stores, come from the same backgrounds as men in blue-collar or service jobs. A high proportion of them (roughly 70 per cent) are married women who work part time because their family needs extra income to make ends meet. They are poorly paid. Perhaps the best way to show how absurd it is to claim them as members of the middle, as opposed to the working, class is to guess that more than a third of them are presently married to men in blue collar jobs; many of the others either have been married to such men or will be one day.

It is not easy to discover a "middle-class majority," in fact, without either playing games with census categories or changing the common meaning of the term "middle class." Excited rhetoric about the disappearance of the working class or the emergence of the middle-class majority should be measured against two stubborn facts. Six out of every ten American men earn their living with their hands. And only two Americans out of every seven work in what the census calls "professional and technical" jobs or as "managers, officials and proprietors." In terms of income, status and life style, the proportion of Americans who belong to the middle class as that term is used in common speech cannot be above, and may be well below, one out of every three.

An equally exaggerated view of working-class income has become current. Much has been written about the unionized workers who earn ten or twelve dollars an hour. Some men in the construction trades, especially, mainly in the Northeast, do earn hourly rates as high as that and even higher. But there are not many of them. Hourly rates exaggerate annual incomes, especially in trades in which layoffs are frequent and long, as they are in construction. Few union workers earn as much as craftsmen in the building trades. And in any case, fewer than a quarter of all U.S. workers are union members at all. In industry, the proportion has fallen since 1950 and has scarcely risen since 1940.

The same conceptual peculiarities that give rise to misleading statements about class also make statements about average income derived from the U. S. Census hazardous as well. If you identify the working class with the census's "blue collar" categories, and exclude low-paid clerical, sales, service and farm workers, then you are systematically exaggerating working-class income, and this is often done. One scholar has gone even further. In an article called "A Profile of the Blue Collar American," drawing on census data, Herman P. Miller stated, "By 1969 the median annual income of white families headed by blue collar workers was $10,700." It is an impressive figure. It turns out, however, that to arrive at it Miller not only left out blacks, and service workers, but also laborers, and counted only "foremen, craftsmen and operatives"!

By the beginning of the seventies, as the economy staggered under the double impact of inflation and rising unemployment, there was a growing awareness that twenty-five years of high wages had not brought on the earthly paradise for the American worker. But, even in labor circles, there was a tendency to explain working-class discontents in racial terms and to ignore the fact that large numbers of workers had a hard time making ends meet. "Integration of schools, jobs, neighborhoods, poses problems," said Nathaniel Goldfinger of the AFL/CIO, "that the elitist managerial crowd knows nothing about." That was true, no doubt. But what far fewer people talked about, either in management or in labor, was the fact that in raw economic terms blue-collar workers were actually worse off after the reforms of the Great Society than they had been before.

The data are unambiguous. According to the Bureau of Labor Statistics, the average worker with three dependents earned $95.80 a week in 1965. By 1969 this had risen to $115.44. But in 1957–59 dollars, after taking account of federal tax and social-security deductions, the average worker took home $78.49 in 1969, as compared with $78.88 in 1965. And that was an average. Some were worse off. General Electric workers at Schenectady, for example, with a high average of skill and employed by one of the half dozen biggest corporations in the country, took home $93.96 a week in constant dollars in 1969 as against $101.21 in 1965.

In the memorandum in which domestic counselor Moynihan proposed a guaranteed annual income to President Nixon in 1969, he pointed out, "The amount of money a low skilled male family head can earn in a city such as New York is not enough to maintain a family at what are now expected standards." Nor were "expected standards" as plush as the advertising industry likes to suggest. Every year, the Bureau of Labor Statistics calculates three "standard budgets," which roughly correspond to the cost of living respectively of the poor, of the working class, and of the comfortable middle class. In 1970, the lower budget for a family of four came to just $7,000 a year. The intermediate budget came to $10,670. And the higher budget came to just under $16,000. A study by the United Auto Workers gives the feel of what it would be like to live on the intermediate budget:

> It assumes, for example, that the family will own:
> . . . A toaster that will last for 33 years.
> . . . A vacuum cleaner that will last 14 years.
> The budget assumes that a family will buy a two-year-old car and keep it for four years.
> . . . That the husband will buy one year-round suit every four years . . .
> . . . Take his wife to the movies once every three months . . .
> Finally, the budget allows nothing whatever for savings.

Such, for millions of families, was the intermediate standard. Not desperate, but hardly affluent. And in 1970, 60 per cent of all working-class families lived *below* that standard.

Firemen and plasterers, then, like accountants and doctors, may have moved to the suburbs, but not to the same suburbs. Anybody who has traveled in America with his eyes open knows this to be true. Chester, Pennsylvania, is not Villanova, Pennsylvania. Homestead is not Sewickley. Fairfield, Alabama, is not Mountain Brook. And so it is from Miami to Seattle, from Boston to Los Angeles. The geography of every metropolitan area is class geography. Indeed, in many a middle-sized or old city, the gap between the working class and the middle class is still symbolized, as it was in the novels of Theodore Dreiser and Sinclair Lewis, by the railroad tracks. The affluent live in pleasant, older neighborhoods near the city center; or miles out on the nice side of town. In northwestern Atlanta, they live in an area where magnificent trees have survived. In Minneapolis, they live around the lakes on the southern fringe of the city. In Los Angeles and Birmingham, they live in the hills. Steamfitters and lathe operators, everywhere, are more likely to live in the sonic path from the new airport, or downwind from a chemical plant. If they live in older neighborhoods, it won't be in those with a politically powerful neighborhood association but in those that are being sliced through by interstate highways or eroded by urban blight. If they live in suburbs, the trees will be fewer, the houses smaller, the infrastructure of public services less adequate, the whole atmosphere instantly recognizable, at first glance, as . . . not middle class.

In other ways, in the late 1960s, the working class was being squeezed. Advertising, and especially TV advertising, the most powerful single influence on all Americans from infancy up, made them want, and even feel they should be ashamed not to have, goods and services of every kind that they couldn't afford to pay cash for, and that they had far more trouble than middle-class people in buying on credit. (The criteria for creditworthiness drip with class bias, not to mention sex bias.) Too much should not be set down to rising expectations, however. For in many ways, even if incomes were higher than they had been a decade earlier, life was objectively harder.

The cost of health care rose steeply. Many of the very trends on which liberal commentators congratulated themselves had the effect of making life more difficult for working-class people. Commentators exaggerated the move to the suburbs, for example. But to the extent it was taking place, it was destroying all those informal institutions that made a neighborhood livable, and separating people from friends, cousins, grandparents, landsmen, and the people they had grown up with.

Working-class people had to bear the brunt of the pressures, in ordinary life, caused by the great in-migration of blacks: competition for jobs, the disruptions caused by block-busting and changing neighborhoods, and all the fear that the great change caused. They had to live through these strains at a time when the strongest traditional working-class institutions—the family, the parochial school, the labor union, and the political machine—were all either declining or undergoing transformations that made them less able to cope. To cap it all, not only had no real redistribution of income toward the working class as a whole taken place; working-class income, in real terms, began to decline in the second half of the sixties.

Nothing about the political history of the 1950s was more eerie than the silence of the American working class while the liberal intellectuals proclaimed its contentment to the world.

"The workers," wrote Daniel Bell, "whose grievances were once the driving energy for social change, are more satisfied with the society than the intellectuals." It would have been hard indeed to be more satisfied with it than some intellectuals were. "The workers have not achieved Utopia, but their expectations were less than those of the intellectuals, and the gains correspondingly larger." They had never, in a word, been expected to eat cake.

Still, wrote Richard Hofstadter, "the jobless, distracted and bewildered men of 1933 . . . have become homeowners, suburbanites, and solid citizens. . . . Among them the dominant tone is one of satisfaction, even of a kind of conservatism."

"When the cost of fulfilling a people's aspirations can be met out of a growing horn of plenty—without robbing Peter to pay Paul," wrote the economist Walter Heller, distilling into a single sentence the liberal hope and the liberal illusion, "ideological roadblocks melt away and consensus replaces conflict."

The horn of plenty has continued to grow. But conflict replaced consensus. The great political event of the sixties was not the elimination of inequalities. It was the revolt of the very people who seemed—to the eye of the liberal intellectuals—so satisfied, so contented. The great riddle is why that revolt took the form that it did take.

Politics polarized, but not, as might have been expected, between the economic elite on the one hand and the angry majority on the other. What happened was that the majority, or a decisive fraction of it, showed a startling tendency to join forces with the economic elite against, on the one hand, unpopular minorities, and on the other, the liberals. Richard Nixon was the supreme example of the politician who harvests the votes of working people at election time by blaming all their troubles on people even less powerful than themselves, and then serves the interests of the business community once in office. But he was not the only one. George Wallace's performance as governor of Alabama was a classic example of the same process. Richard Daley's long career as mayor of Chicago is another. Sam Yorty in Los Angeles, John Connally in Texas, Frank Rizzo in Philadelphia—there is hardly a major state or city in the country that has not experienced the technique at some time in the past ten years. The pattern is so familiar that, behind the political riddle, there must lie a deeper constant in American society and psychology.

Short of rewriting the whole history of American politics, one can only put forward theories to account for this puzzling tendency.

The first might be called the Southern Theory. "You are kept apart," said the populist leader Tom Watson in 1892 to the poor whites and the poor blacks of the South, "that you may be separately fleeced of your earnings. You are made to hate each other because upon that hatred is rested the keystone of the arch of financial despotism which enslaves you both." There is no older theme in the history of southern politics than the perception that the true interests of poor whites and poor blacks coincide, unless it is the perception that the loyalties of race feeling are more easily exploited than those of class; so that, as Lyndon Johnson used to say, the politician who proposes change in the common interest can always be beaten by the politician who just "hollers nigger, nigger, nigger." At the heart of the mind of the South, wrote Wilbur Cash in 1941, "the ancient fixation on the negro" was still perhaps primary. The pride and will of the southern white man, Cash wrote, and especially the pride and will of the common white man of the South, were concentrated on maintaining superiority to the black man as the paramount thing in life. "What fixes his gaze to the eclipse of everything else," said Cash, "was the spectacle of himself being reduced to working side by side . . . with the black man . . . his one incontestable superiority, threatening to plunge finally and irretrievably to extinction." And in 1949, at the conclusion of his great study of southern politics, V. O. Key argued that the key to southern conservatism was the way in which this fear was turned to advantage by the holders of economic power:

> Sustained effort to improve the Negro's economic and political status costs money, and upper-class southerners, like upper-class non-southerners, dislike to part with cash. . . .
> The almost overwhelming temptation . . . is to take advantage of the short-run opportunity to maintain the *status quo* by using, or tolerating the use of, the race issue to blot up the discontents of the lesser whites. . . .
> It would be naive, of course, to interpret southern politics as a deliberate conspiracy among the better class whites to divide the mass of people by Negro-baiting. Nevertheless with a high degree of regularity those of the top economic groups—particularly the new industrialists—are

to be found in communion with the strident advocates of white supremacy. In the political chaos and demoralization that ensue alert men with a
sharp eye for immediate advantage take and count their gains.

That analysis of the reason for the conservatism of southern politics
twenty-five years ago is uncomfortably close to the truth about national
politics in the age of Nixon.

That is not to say that personal racism, raw and obsessional, of the
kind Wilbur Cash diagnosed in the hearts of fellow Southerners of his
generation, has spread around the country. Such evidence as there is suggests just the contrary. Racism in personal attitudes has declined, and the
improvement has been as great in the South as anywhere. In 1972, for example, a Potomac Associates survey found that white people were actually
more likely to welcome black families of their own income and educational level as neighbors than to welcome lower-class white neighbors.
Again, the proportion of those surveyed who told the Gallup poll that
they would vote for a well-qualified black candidate for President increased
from 38 per cent in 1958 to 59 per cent in 1965 to 70 per cent in 1971.
The great majority of other statistical indexes of racial prejudice—as opposed to indexes of feeling about specific policies, such as busing, with
more or less clear-cut racial undertones—have moved consistently and
rather rapidly in the same direction.

What is more, working-class Americans are right to resent the suggestion that they are more prone to racism than other groups. ("It has not
gone without notice," Michael Novak has written, "that the same elites
that once called white ethnics Polacks, Hunkies, Micks and Guineas now
call them racists, fascists, and pigs.") Polls have consistently found Catholic voters more liberal than the population as a whole on racial issues, and
the same has been broadly true of union members. Working-class Americans are no more likely, and may be less likely, to have racist views than
the professional and executive classes.

No, if there is a sense in which racism has spread across the country
in the wake of the great black migration out of the South, it is not personal, but institutional, racism. It can take many forms. In political terms,
one of the forms it has taken is that issues and decisions which, thirty
years ago, had no racial content—decisions about zoning or school-board
policies or public housing or police corruption—are now seen as at least
partly racial. The concerns and fears of ordinary people, for their job, for
their home, for their neighborhood, now often take a racial shape. Inevitably an undercurrent of racial feeling is felt under the surface of politics.

As black people came to be found in cities everywhere, so the urban
politics of the nation as a whole began in the sixties to imitate, in discreet

ways, the classic politics of racial division that were once peculiar to the South. And nationally the career of Richard Nixon teaches that in the ensuing chaos and demoralization, "alert men with a sharp eye for immediate advantage" may count even the White House among their gains.

The second theory is the Immigration Theory. There is an element of conscious choice and personal commitment about American patriotism that is exceptional. And this is natural. For Americans are a self-chosen people. Every white American is either someone who voted with his feet to become an American, or he is the descendant of someone who made that conscious and often arduous choice. Not only is that a historic fact. The symbolism and rhetoric of American patriotism have always kept it in the forefront of the national consciousness.

There are other countries now with an equal or even higher proportion of immigrants, and other countries that are peopled entirely by the descendants of immigrants. What gives a special intensity to American patriotism that is lacking in the national feeling of, say, Brazilians or Australians (two peoples, incidentally, with very considerable patriotic traditions) is the exceptional success and power of the United States, and, more importantly, the special American sense of historical mission and destiny. The purpose of America, in a sense so essential that it seems almost part of the definition of America, has been from the start to create a new pattern of life by means of a new political and social system.

So there is a peculiar quality to American patriotism which is at once unusually intense and exceptionally insecure. It attaches not just to the land, but to the system, and to the system as a whole. While to a Frenchman, for example, France under the Revolution or the monarchy or Napoleon, and even tragically under Nazi occupation, is still France, to many, if not most, Americans there seems to be a sense in which the Constitution, and the presidency, and even some form of private-enterprise capitalism, are inseparable from the idea of America.

It is a short step, for some at least, from the idea that free enterprise is an essential part of the American idea, to the conclusion that anyone who doesn't express a suitable degree of enthusiasm for the free-enterprise system is un-American.

This interpretation of patriotism, broadening it to extend not just to the nation but to specific features of its organization, would in any case be a powerful pressure in the direction of conservatism. Plenty of demagogues in American history have manipulated the symbols of patriotism for the advantage of the established economic interests.

This tendency, caused by the exceptional features of national self-consciousness in America which date back to Colonial and Revolutionary times, was accentuated by the Great Migration of the nineteenth century. Roughly half of all Americans are the descendants of immigrants who came to the United States between 1865 and 1924. A very large proportion of the rest are the descendants of Southerners who fought against the Union in 1865. Both groups feel a strong impulse to show themselves "good Americans" in a way in which Italians, for example, do not need to prove themselves good Italians. (Southerners, it seems to me, feel about the *South* the same instinctive, my-country-right-or-wrong-and-God-knows-it's-often-wrong sort of patriotism that Englishmen feel about England and Frenchmen about France. About the United States of America, I suspect, they feel the need to believe, and it is this which often makes them superpatriots.)

The "ethnic" immigrant, especially, had to go through an Americanization process in which everything was unfamiliar. It was also on the whole greatly preferable to anything in his own previous experience. It was natural for him to see the vote and free enterprise as inseparable parts of one "American way," and to attach his gratitude and his patriotism to all things American alike. Nothing could be more natural than for Americans brought up in this tradition, the tradition of "only in America," to take any radical criticism of any aspect of the system as disloyalty to the whole, and so as an affront to their patriotism. Some such instinctive reaction lies behind the distaste that so many working-class Americans feel for dissent. It does them credit. But it has had a distorting effect on the shape of American politics. It helps to explain why ordinary people so often vote for demagogues like Richard Nixon or George Wallace, who do not represent their real interests but who at least seem to understand their moral and patriotic feelings, rather than for the proponents of change, who uphold their interests, but outrage their feelings.

"They must think they're going to win a lottery!" said George McGovern when he realized how bitterly hostile most working-class people were to his proposal for an inheritance tax.

It just showed how little he understood. For that is exactly what they do think.

Working-class Americans are quite well aware that their situation in life could be a lot better. They know, better than any middle-class sociologist, how dreary work is in a factory or an office. They haven't looked up the figures in a book, but they know, too, that real wages have not risen as much as all that, and that no major redistribution of income either has happened or is likely to happen. But they are not particularly interested in a redistribution of income. And they don't look to the unions, or community action programs, or the federal government, or to any other political change to uplift their collective situation. They plan to make it on their own.

It is hard to make the point better than it is made by anecdotes from a book by the former New York *Times* writer Tad Szulc, *Innocents at Home*. The first is about an elderly widow in a blue-collar neighborhood who has gone out to work scrubbing floors for years to send her boy through college. I won't leave him any money, she says, but I hope he'll be able to leave some to his children. "Now this fellow McGovern wants to pass laws against inheriting money," she says. "He's against the American Dream!"

Again, Szulc, who was born in Poland, recalls how he and his wife, who comes from Akron, Ohio, were watching on television the yachts and the private jets bringing the millionaires to the Republican National Convention in Miami in 1972. That was going to antagonize all the people who could barely make ends meet, said Szulc. "No," says his wife, "you're wrong. It's much more complicated. In a way, people do resent this sort of thing, but, on the other hand, they admire it and identify with it, and hope for the same things for themselves, even if it is a dream they know will never come true. That may be a contradiction, but it's the way people are."

It is the social ethic of Horatio Alger. Working-class Americans don't hate the rich; they envy them. They don't want to take their money away from them; they just want to have as much themselves. Nothing is harder for a European to understand than the fact that the name Rockefeller is an asset, not a liability, with the voters. And it's not just because, as they say, "With all that money they can afford to be honest." For exactly the same reason, the ultimate hero of blue-collar America is perhaps . . . Sinatra. Looking at a Rockefeller or a Sinatra, the ordinary American is looking at a big winner in the lottery in which he also believes that he owns a ticket. He believes, in fact, in equality of opportunity, not in equality of condition.

In the past, the opportunities to move up, to make it, to strike it rich, even, have been real enough to keep the myth alive. And so the ordinary American is easily persuaded that any attempt to increase equality of condition threatens his and his children's opportunity. The truth nowadays is probably the exact opposite: the only way to increase equality of opportunity may be to increase the equality of condition, as Christopher Jencks concluded in his study of *Inequality*.

Yet the Middle American is not a true conservative. His objective situation, and the odds against his winning in the lottery, do not allow him to be that. As long as he cuddles the dream that he and his family will be the ones who make it, he may not be ready to vote for collective efforts to change the rules: for more equitable taxation, or for redistributive policies generally. Yet his dream clashes daily with the reality of his discontents. His children may make it to Palm Springs. In the meantime, he is still living in Bluesville.

Anger and confusion result from the conflict. In the late sixties and early seventies, much of that anger was displaced onto blacks, students, and radicals. But its real cause is the failure of the political system to represent the needs and grievances of the majority. And for that failure, the myth that class interests have been abolished in the United States and that the aspirations of all will be automatically fulfilled out of the growing horn of plenty, must bear a large part of the blame. People talked about "the revolution of rising expectations" as though everything that had gone wrong could be explained away by the lag between expectation and fulfillment. But there was nothing wrong with rising expectations, and nothing new about them either. America was built on rising expectations. It was false expectations that did the harm, and false measures of how far those expectations had been fulfilled.

## Puzzled and Prospering

The point of departure of this book was the idea that, for a few years on either side of 1960, American politics and society had been ruled by a consensus, and that this consensus in turn rested on an ideology. What happened in the twelve years separating the beginning of Kennedy's and the end of Nixon's first terms in the White House, I have argued, can best be understood in terms of impact of events on that interlocking body of ideas and beliefs.

With misgivings, and for want of any word that would not cause worse confusion, I have called that ideology "liberal." The adjective is misleading in several ways. The ideology was not the exclusive property of liberals. There could have been no consensus if that had been the case. Consensus stretched right across the broad center of the political spectrum. Only the extremes to Left and Right remained aloof from it. The "liberal ideology," in fact, was the ideology of the center. It was born of a fusion of certain elements from both liberal and conservative tradition. Specifically it came into existence in the middle 1950s, when most conservatives came to accept some of the economic and domestic policies of Rooseveltian liberalism, while many liberals adopted a foreign policy whose major premise was the kind of anti-communism that had once been the mark of conservatives. "Liberal" has another misleading connotation, too, when applied to the dominant ideology of 1960. It suggests the beliefs of "the liberals," in the sense of "the intellectuals." The "liberal ideology" was not confined to intellectuals. It was also taken for granted by bankers, industrialists, clergymen, politicians and even by many military men, some of whom, in all those categories, would have been properly indignant at being described as intellectuals. Systematic attempts to arrive at a set of first principles by the editors of *Fortune*, by the Rockefeller panelists, and by the Eisenhower administration's Commission on National Goals arrived at conclusions that were both remarkably similar to each other and completely in conformity with the main themes of the ideology I have called liberal. It was, in fact, the ideology of the elite.

The ideology was liberal. But it was not just the ideology of liberals. The same themes could be picked out on almost every stave of the score played by the orchestra of American life at the beginning of the sixties. The same phrases were repeated in the antiphonal trumpet solos of politicians, in the fugal intricacies of academic argument, and—such was the grip of the elite on the organs that formed opinion—in the ground bass of popular belief. The liberal ideology was more than the dogma of a faction or a school. It was the operational creed of a great nation at the height of its confidence and power.

The great events of the years covered by this book tore consensus to shreds. Both the triumph and the ultimate frustration of the black rebellion tended to disprove the comfortable assumptions the consensus had made about the ability of governmental action to "solve" social problems without unleashing a chain reaction of unwanted social change; at the same time, the Vietnam War discredited the foreign policy of the consensus. In practical terms, it demonstrated the limits of American ability to affect events in spite of theoretically invincible strength. In moral terms, it raised doubts about American disinterestedness. In political terms, it revealed the bankruptcy of the American model for most of the developing world. Moreover, the decision to escalate the war without raising war taxation allowed inflation to get out of control and eventually frustrated the New Economists' dream of perpetual growth. And growth had been both the intellectual first premise of the liberal ideology and the practical prerequisite of the liberal program.

All these disappointments combined to lay an impossible burden on the institution on which the consensus had counted to carry out that program, and to which everyone turned to put things right when it became apparent that they were going wrong: the presidency. In response to the demands of war, of economic crisis, and then of a generation of Cold War, the office had stretched its powers and its scope far beyond what was traditionally envisaged in the constitutional scheme. Yet it had still not become a rational, self-perpetuating modern bureaucracy. It remained a personal office. Its power to intervene was limited by the ideas or the interest of the incumbent. Under Kennedy and Johnson, as much as under Nixon, the White House was a court, and its staff essentially not bureaucrats but courtiers. Ultimately, as a result, the crisis of the sixties posed questions about the legitimacy of the modern presidency, and therefore—since the presidency had become so much the most visible piece of the political system—about the legitimacy of that system itself.

Under such blows, the consensus disintegrated, and the liberal ideology fell into discredit. That alone would have been important, even traumatic, enough. Yet the crisis would not have been so profound had it not also called into question, not just the prevailing assumptions of a particular generation, but older and more fundamental American beliefs.

America has always been both an enterprise and a pilgrimage. American culture, that is, unlike the cultures of Europe, is essentially political. There is admittedly apparent paradox here. A society that has laid so heavy an emphasis on the freedom of the individual is nevertheless ultimately concerned, not with the happy or virtuous individual, but with the good society. The American system of values has rotated around two aspirations, almost two imperatives. The individual must both be free, and have equality of opportunity, to seek abundance. So society must be perfected by political action.

The central myth of the American culture is the myth of the frontier. It is often overlooked that there are two sides to that myth. The pioneer ventured forth to cut a homestead for himself and his family from the wilderness. But he was not left there long in isolation. The preacher, the teacher, the salesman, and the politician soon followed—figures just as archetypal as the frontiersman, and who have long survived him. The individualist may be free to take what he can get. But then he must give his new freedom back to the community.

Both aspects of this tradition, the enterprise and the pilgrimage, demanded, and bred, optimism. Experience justified confidence. It also made confidence necessary. Because the enterprise really did achieve in each generation material abundance undreamed of by the generation before, Americans came naturally by the belief that oceans could be crossed, wars won, and wildernesses tamed. The struggle was mortally hard, though, for many individuals. And the pilgrimage never reached the city the Puritan sought. So it became a psychological necessity to suppress doubt and adopt the religion of healthy-mindedness. The Puritan, the pioneer and the immigrant, out of their different experiences, and for their different reasons, shared the conviction that for "the American, this new man," everything must be possible.

The idea of the New Frontier, I have suggested, was a dubious metaphor from the start. It cheapened the real achievement of the American past, while promising an illusory vision of the American future. In the New Frontiersman, the sober, self-reliant confidence with which a man tells himself that he can complete a task, too often degenerated into the cocky, chauvinist optimism with which a man tells others that he can solve a problem. It was characteristic of the liberal ideology that it believed problems could be solved. The debunking of that facile ideology was bound to call into question the ancient American confidence that society could be made more perfect.

The burned child dreads the fire. Americans had gone into the age of Kennedy and Nixon convinced that their government's action—*their* action, that is, multiplied by the immense collective power of the federal government—could make over the world, at home and abroad. Now they had been burned. It was not just that they had learned how much harder it is to change the world than the elite they had listened to had told them. The lesson was more painful than that. They had learned that there was moral ambiguity where they had once thought that the issues of right and wrong were clearest; that their own motives were not above suspicion; and that there seemed little that political action could achieve, however idealistic its intentions, without evoking unforeseen and unwanted reaction.

Three recurrent themes have run through this history. There was the war. There was the question of the position of blacks in American society. There was the central role of the presidency in the drama of American life. It so happens that three vignettes from the month of Richard Nixon's triumph illustrate, in terms of these three themes, in the lives of individual Americans, this new prevailing mood of impotence and loss.

On January 8, 1973, just twelve days before Nixon's inauguration, Henry Kissinger met Hanoi's representative Le Duc Tho in Paris. There, at last, terms were negotiated for American withdrawal from the Vietnam War. The announcement that the talks were to take place coincided with the end of the bombing of Hanoi, the heaviest and most ruthless bombing of the war.

Nixon and Kissinger maintained that the bombing brought the end of the war and the promise of a generation of peace. In little more than two years, the hollowness of this pretense was exposed. Peace with honor meant defeat with dishonor. For the majority of Americans, perhaps, the bombs of Christmas 1972 signified no more than relief that the whole wasteful business was over at last. But there were others, millions of them, for whom the way the war ended brought something else: the end of a certain hope and the death of a certain vision they had once had of what their country could be.

With eloquent brevity, *The New Yorker* expressed what such an end to such a war meant to such people:

> Our leaders have often told us they can see the light at the end of the tunnel. They have been wrong about the light, of course, but they have been right about the tunnel.

It has been ten years. The historians call ten years an era; the ten years just past will be the Vietnam era, no doubt. For ten years, death has had us in its grip, and now it is we, the killers, who are beginning to die.

On January 8, again, the day the final peace talks began in Paris, police stormed a sniper's nest on the roof of the Downtown Howard Johnson's Motor Lodge, across the street from the civic center in New Orleans. It was, said William J. Guste, the attorney general of Louisiana, as the police waited to go in, part of "a nationwide conspiracy against the police."

It was nothing of the kind. The night before, police in a marine helicopter scoured the roof with rounds from a heavy-caliber machine gun. One sniper stood up and fired back at them. Before he fell, they heard him shout: "Power to the people!"

All night, police continued to pour fire into the sniper's position. When the light came, and they went in to the assault, they found they had been shooting at a dead man and at each other all night. There was no conspiracy; just one 23-year-old black man called Mark Essex. He had been dead for hours when Guste spoke. Six other people were dead. Some had been shot by Essex. But not all. The others had been hit by police crossfire or by ricochets. The dead included a hotel employee, two guests, two policemen, and the deputy police commissioner, Louis Sirgo.

Mark Essex grew up the son of a churchgoing widow in Emporia, Kansas. He went into the Navy, where he came up against what he found intolerable racial discrimination. He went to New Orleans. He rented a cheap apartment. He bought a rifle, and he scrawled his philosophical conclusions on the wall:

"Revolutionary justice is black justice!" he wrote. "Shoot to kill! My destiny lies in the bloody death of racist pigs!"

Would it have made any difference to Mark Essex if he had known how hard one of the men it was his destiny to kill had tried to understand him?

"The greatest sin in American society," Louis Sirgo had said in a speech a couple of months earlier, "is the status of the American Negro." And he went on: "We have got to get our heads out of the sands, for after all it is an unsafe position. An ostrich buries his head in the sand, and that part of his anatomy makes a very good target for a sniper."

The week Mark Essex and Louis Sirgo died, of a mutual misunderstanding, you might say, Washington was busy with last-minute preparations for the inauguration. A reporter from the Washington *Post* paid a call on the home of the young man who had been put in charge of the arrangements for it.

It was a lovely home, of course, in one of Washington's nicest suburbs. The young man wasn't home when the reporter arrived, but his pretty young wife was playing with the babies. She made her guest welcome, her legs crossed at the ankle, until husband got home from the office.

It was a charming scene, the reporter felt, and when he did arrive, he seemed such a nice young man. Yes, he said, he had considered some good offers to go into private business and make some money, but government service was more of a challenge. Just before the end of the interview, he turned serious for a minute. "I think the country's on the upturn," he said. "I think we are seeing our way ahead through a lot of the problems that have existed. As the war winds down, the country's spirits are up."

The nice young man's name was Jeb Stuart Magruder. Ten months later, he was sitting in an apartment in Manhattan with the Reverend William Sloane Coffin. To those who knew of them both only through the newspapers, the two men might have seemed oddly assorted. Coffin had been an activist in the peace movement, and one of Dr. Spock's codefendants. Magruder was one of the President's brisk young conservatives. In fact, they knew each other of old. Coffin had been Magruder's ethics teacher at Williams College; had flunked him, as it happens, for ethics. Now Magruder had pleaded guilty to a felony charge of obstructing justice. He was in good company; more than a dozen of the leading men in the law-and-order administration were under indictment. The Vice-President of the United States, stern champion of the ancient virtues, had pleaded guilty to corruption. Only forced resignation was to save the President himself from impeachment.

At the time of his meeting with Coffin, Magruder faced imprisonment, as Coffin had done for very different reasons in his time. The two men talked about what had happened to the country to bring it about that the two of them, on opposite sides of a cultural and political abyss, should both have found themselves in a situation that would have been unimaginable when they were at Williams.

"We don't have a democracy of the people any more," Magruder concluded after they had been talking for several hours.

The cost of those years was high. For many, it could be reckoned only in terms of loss. There were many who wondered, like Jeb Magruder, whether the meaning of what had happened to the American political system was simply that democracy had been lost. For Mark Essex, and for others, the quest for justice ended in death on a bullet-swept rooftop. Louis Sirgo was not the only man to die in a crossfire from men who thought they were fighting to protect society. Millions more, like *The*

*New Yorker's* editorial writer, asked in their moral anguish, whether all that was best in America had not deserved to die a murderer's death.

For many, the political drama had been a morality play, in which right ought to be ultimately triumphant. For them, despair was inevitable.

Yet there is another view. It is that a price must always be paid to be free from illusions, and that if the illusions are dangerous enough, the price is well paid.

The disasters of the sixties, foreign and domestic, can be traced to a body of beliefs, to an ideology, and to the body of people who held them. While it was more or less widely accepted by ordinary people, that ideology was the creation of an elite which, for the first time in American history, controlled enough of the expanding, powerful institutions of society to be without effective check or balance. It was not a mere clique. Still less was it a conspiracy. Its ideals were of the highest. It was a liberal elite. Part of its strength, indeed, came from a certain magic inhering in that word, a pervasive implication that one had better not criticize whatever the liberals did, for any alternative would be worse.

This new national elite and its ideology caused the United States to come under the sway of two dangerous illusions. The first was that the inequalities and injustices of American society were residual, and could be abolished by the expenditure of resources on a scale that need not involve any hard choice between priorities—"without robbing Peter to pay Paul," in Walter Heller's revealing phrase. The other was that the United States could use its military power to change the world in conformity with its wishes and not itself be changed in the process.

Now, it is not impossible, though it is not easy either, to bring about real changes in social conditions by governmental action. And military power is indeed all too effective. What you cannot do, ever, is to get what you want without paying for it in some coin or other. You cannot abolish poverty if you won't pay higher taxes. Only if a real transfer of resources has taken place has relative inequality been diminished; it is the relative, not the absolute, situation of the poor that must be changed if poverty is to be abolished. Again, you cannot make selective efforts to favor certain groups in society, however deserving, unless you are willing to antagonize other groups. You cannot win a war without seeing people killed on both sides. And you cannot use torture if you don't want to hear the screams. Such axioms are the political equivalent of the law of gravity. Those who ignore them think they know how to walk on water.

The cost was high. But the lesson has been learned. The illusion of omnipotence has been destroyed. In the same month in which the war "ended" and Richard Nixon called on his countrymen "above all" to be proud of themselves, two of the men who had worked for him drew wiser lessons from the experience of the decade.

Daniel Patrick Moynihan had already left government to return to Harvard when he gave a lecture at his son's school, Andover Academy. "We are getting back to earth," he said. "Ours was a society fifteen years ago which was almost impervious to the thought that it had many problems of its own; it was much too eager to see problems in other countries."

Elliot Richardson left the Department of Health, Education and Welfare that same month to become Secretary of Defense. At the ceremony that is held to mark such resignations, he said this: "We must recognize, as we have with both foreign affairs and natural resources, that resources we once thought were boundless—human, financial and intellectual resources—are indeed severely limited."

Down to earth. Limited resources. Those phrases distilled the lessons that the American majority learned from the twelve years from 1961 to 1973—lessons that have since been driven even more painfully home by events outside the scope of this book. They might have been deliberately chosen to mark the formal ending of the New Frontier, as the Bureau of the Census in 1890 announced the exhaustion of the frontier of unsettled land. The very kernel of the New Frontier was the idea that limitless intellectual resources could make the United States indefinitely an open-ended society, and could free American man from the need ever to set his sights lower than the stars.

That is why what was changed by the experiences of the sixties was more important in the perspective of American history than the humbling of a certain hubris or the discrediting of particular assumptions. It implied a permanent change in the way Americans see the future of their society.

In America, wrote Leslie Fiedler, only death is denied; everything else is possible. No doubt he wrote that with irony. It still expresses the historic American conviction that American society is not bounded by the common human limitations of equivocal success, inevitable compromise, insoluble dilemma, and ultimate mortality.

In individual lives, there comes a stage when a person has to recognize that death is indeed an undeniable fact, and that not everything is possible. To believe otherwise is the mark of the adolescent. To persist in that belief in adulthood is a sign of psychopathology. Sooner or later, individuals adjust to the reality of their limitations. They learn to choose. Nations, like individuals, that do not learn to accept their limitations, or to choose, are dangerous, to themselves and, especially if they are as powerful as the United States, to others.

To adjust to a future of limited, though magnificent, resources will demand a historic shift in American values. Yet the prize will be worth it.

There will have to be less emphasis on equality of opportunity, and more on equality of condition. The traditional goals of absolute freedom and maximum economic abundance will have to be modified in the more intricate equilibrium of a society that accepts the limits of human possibility and strives for the greatest possible measure of justice and equality. It will not be easy. Yet, sooner or later, the American people will have no alternative but to attempt it. They will succeed if the political system can find ways to harness those most precious of all resources, which the liberal elite consistently underestimated: the energy, good sense and generosity of the majority of ordinary people. Then a new consensus will be built on the ruins of illusion, and the United States will go on, in Thomas Jefferson's affectionate phrase, "puzzled and prospering beyond example in the history of man."

# NOTES ON SOURCES

## CHAPTER 1

Although I spent some time in Washington when I was a graduate student in 1955–56, I first worked there as a correspondent, for the London *Observer*, in March 1962. From then until the present time, I have worked in Washington, on and off, for rather more than half of the time. In particular, I was living and working there as a reporter and commentator both at the time of the assassination of President Kennedy and at the time of Richard Nixon's 1972 triumph and of the breaking of the Watergate crisis.

The picture I have drawn, therefore, of the change in political mood and attitudes over the twelve years from 1961 to 1973 is essentially drawn from my own, firsthand impressions, recollections and conversations, checked against the files of the New York *Times* and the Washington *Post* and against my own notes and clippings accumulated for the purposes of my work over that period. I did not, however, have firsthand knowledge of the period of the 1960 election or of the first fourteen months of the New Frontier. My impression of the time when Camelot was still a musical was therefore supplemented by an intensive reading of the newspapers and magazines of the time, and especially of the New York *Times*, the Washington *Post*, *Time*, *Newsweek*, *Fortune* and *The New Yorker* from October 1960 to February 1961. The orthodox, not to say hagiographical, version of that period is to be found in many books, notably Theodore H. White, *The Making of the President 1960*; Arthur M. Schlesinger, Jr., *A Thousand Days*; and Theodore M. Sorensen, *Kennedy*. I found Henry Fairlie, *The Kennedy Promise*, a refreshing corrective to these courtly works.

The intriguing fact that far more people believed that they had voted for Kennedy after he was dead than actually voted for him when he was alive is taken from William Manchester, *The Death of a President*, and confirmed by National Opinion Research Center data. The extracts from the files of the Nixon administration's American Revolution Bicentennial Commission were quoted by Erwin Knoll in *The Progressive*, of which he is now the editor, in summer 1972. The quotation from William L. Langer comes from his essay in *Goals for Americans*, the report of President Eisenhower's Commission on National Goals. The quotation from an earlier presidential commission, reporting to President Hoover in September 1929, was drawn to my attention, as a corrective against supposing that cosmic alarm was a recent phenomenon among leaders of American thought, by Michael Lacey, on the staff of the Woodrow Wilson International Center for Scholars, in Washington. The Congressional

documents relating to the New Orleans massacre of 1866 are quoted in A *Documentary History of the Negro People in the United States*, edited by Herbert
Aptheker.

### CHAPTER 2

The more I thought about the political preconceptions with which Americans entered the 1960s, the more clearly it seemed to me that these had been
shaped by the great events of the 1940s and the early 1950s: by World War II
and by the Cold War, by the end of the Depression and the coming of
affluence, by the emergence of the United States as a global power, by the
Stalinist threat and the McCarthyite response to it in the United States, and
finally by the great migrations from country to town, from city to suburb, from
East to West, and from South to North.

I got a certain scaffolding of chronology and "fact" from well-known general histories such as Samuel Eliot Morison and Henry Steele Commager, *The
Growth of the American Republic*; S. E. Morison, *Oxford History of the
American People*; and Stephen E. Ambrose, *Rise to Globalism*. I got more conceptual help from two popular works, one by a journalist and the other by a
professional historian: F. L. Allen, *The Big Change*; and Eric F. Goldman,
*The Crucial Decade*.

There are two books I read long before I first set foot in the United States
in 1955 and that I have absorbed at so deep a level that it is hard for me to say
how much of my understanding of American politics is owed to them: D. W.
Brogan, *An Introduction to American Politics*; and Samuel Lubell, *The Future
of American Politics*. I must also acknowledge a debt to André Fontaine, *History of the Cold War*, for its qualities of fairness and lucidity; and to William
Appleman Williams, *The Contours of American History*, for opening my eyes
to new interpretations. This was especially useful since so much of the postwar
history of the United States has been written in terms of the very preconceptions I wanted to re-examine.

I read a great many of the memoirs of the period. Those of Presidents
Truman and Eisenhower are both outstanding sources. Among others I found
particularly useful were Dean Acheson, *Present at the Creation*; Henry L.
Stimson and McGeorge Bundy, *On Active Service in Peace and War*; and
George F. Kennan, *Memoirs*.

The memoirs gave what was for a long time the orthodox account of the ori-
gins of the Cold War. So, too, did, for example, Herbert Feis, *Between War
and Peace*. I found the "revisionist" view of the same events in W. A.
Williams, *The Tragedy of American Diplomacy*; D. F. Fleming, *The Cold
War and its Origins*; and Gar Alperovitz, *Atomic Diplomacy: Hiroshima and
Potsdam*. Critiques of these "revisionist" historians, in turn, are to be found in
Robert W. Tucker, *The Radical Left and American Foreign Policy*; Robert
James Maddox, *The New Left and the Origins of the Cold War*; and J. L.

Gaddis, *The United States and the Origins of the Cold War, 1941–1947*. See also the 1954 paper by the British nuclear physicist P. M. S. Blackett *America's Atomic Dilemma.*

On the development of nuclear weapons and the American nuclear monopoly, I found accounts comprehensible to the lay reader in Robert Jungk, *Brighter than a Thousand Suns*; Ronald W. Clark, *The Birth of the Bomb*; and Len Giovanetti and Fred Freed, *The Decision to Drop the Bomb*. Henry L. Stimson's own account of the decision to drop the first atomic bombs was given in *Harper's Magazine* in 1947.

The best book on McCarthy is still Richard H. Rovere, *Senator Joe McCarthy*. On the Hiss case, Alistair Cooke, *Generation on Trial*, is trustworthy, and Richard M. Nixon, *Six Crises*, revealing. On the McCarthyism episode as a whole, I. F. Stone, *The Truman Era*, is a compendium of contemporary articles in the author's best vein, perspicacious and combative. Eric F. Goldman's *The Crucial Decade* contains a useful brief history of the episode. Three books were especially helpful in interpreting McCarthyism: Richard Hofstadter, *The Paranoid Style in American Politics*; Theodore W. Adorno and others, *The Authoritarian Personality*; and Leo Lowenthal and Norbert Guterman, *Prophets of Deceit.*

Besides books already mentioned, on the origins of the American commitment to global containment and interventionism I must mention Ronald Steel, *Pax Americana*, and Joseph Jones, *The Fifteen Weeks*. An article by former Senator J. William Fulbright, "In Thrall to Fear," in *The New Yorker* for January 8, 1972, is interesting as the repentance of a former interventionist on the origins of the commitment. Acheson's memoirs are, of course, essential reading.

### CHAPTER 3

The fundamental source for this chapter is the United States Bureau of the Census and its cornucopia of information dispensed annually in the successive volumes of the Statistical Abstract of the United States. I could not hope to enumerate all the authors who have drawn my attention to one intriguing or significant atom or another in that statistical ocean. I am especially grateful to the editors of *Fortune*, and of *U.S.A., the Permanent Revolution*; to F. L. Allen, *The Big Change*; and to David M. Potter, *People of Plenty.*

Out of all the innumerable descriptions of the Great Depression, in history, fiction, statistical compilation and personal recollection, the two that have given me the most graphic understanding of what it was like to live through are James Agee, *Let Us Now Praise Famous Men*, with its haunting pictures by Walker Evans; and—a generation later—Studs Terkel, *Hard Times.*

For the politics of the New Deal and the effort to revive the economy, I used Arthur M. Schlesinger, Jr., *The Age of Roosevelt*; James McGregor Burns, *Roosevelt: The Lion and the Fox*; and Raymond Moley, *The First New Deal*. The three quotations about the danger to democracy as long as unemployment remained at such high levels, from Berle, Hopkins and Hoffman, all come from W. A. Williams, *The Contours of American History*.

On labor unions and their history, I interviewed many people in Washington, New York and elsewhere, notably Bayard Rustin of the A. Philip Randolph Foundation, Jerry Wurf of AFSCME, Frank Wallich of the UAW, Haynes Johnson and Nick Kotz of the Washington *Post*, and John Herling, veteran labor columnist. I found two biographies especially useful: Joseph Goulden on George Meany, and Frank Cormier and William Eaton on Walter Reuther. Of other works on American labor, I found J. T. Dunlop and Derek Bok, *Labor and the American Community*, excellent as a statement of the consensus view, and Jeremy Brecher, *Strike!* a lively presentation of the radical tradition.

On the expansion of higher education, I interviewed many academics and university administrators, the most illuminating, perhaps, being President Kingman Brewster of Yale and former President Clark Kerr of the University of California. But the principal source of my account of the expansion of the universities is Christopher Jencks and David Riesman, *The Academic Revolution*.

There is, interestingly enough, far more literature on the black migration out of the South than on the white. The two classics on the black migration are *They Seek a City*, by Arna Bontemps and Jack Conroy; and E. Franklin Frazier, *The Negro Family in the United States*, especially part four, which is subtitled "In the City of Destruction." On the white migration, I found the most helpful book to be Robert Coles, *The South Goes North*, the third volume of his great trilogy *The Children of Crisis*.

There are three contemporary stores of information about the South from which both blacks and whites were migrating: the National Emergency Council's report on the economic condition of the South, published in 1938; Howard W. Odum's *Southern Regions* (1936); and Gunnar Myrdal, *An American Dilemma* (1944). Still the most perceptive subjective portrait is Wilbur J. Cash, *The Mind of the South* (1941). To pick only the truly indispensable books in my reading on the South, I must mention John Dollard, *Caste and Class in a Southern Town*; V. O. Key, *Southern Politics in State and Nation*; and virtually all the writings of C. Vann Woodward, but especially his *The Strange Career of Jim Crow*.

CHAPTER 4

In a sense, obviously, all that I have read in twenty years of American politics, social science and even literature, and fourteen years of conversation on the same subjects, has been chopped up to make the raw material for the generalizations in this chapter. When I set out to try to analyze the assumptions that Americans took with them into the 1960s, though, I did distinguish to myself methodologically four kinds of sources. First, there was such evidence as could be found about the assumptions and beliefs of the American people as a whole. Reliable information, as opposed to impressions filtered through unknown biases and preconceptions, could be drawn only from survey data. I found two books based on survey research especially usefu¹: Hadley Cantril, *The Pattern of Human Concerns*; and Stuart Chase, *American Credos*. Albert H. Cantril, Hadley Cantril's son and himself a distinguished practitioner of the pollster's science, allowed me to use his collections of Gallup and Harris data. I soon came up against the comparability problem. It was not often possible to trace public opinion on any specific issue through a long series of responses to identical or even comparable questions. Given my limited resources of skill and time, I was driven to use poll data in an impressionistic way. Unsatisfactory as this must seem to social scientists trained to dismiss all but quantitatively verifiable propositions, the evidence did convince me of two broad and relevant propositions: 1. that the American people generally were in a mood of confidence about their own society and of trepidation about the Communist threat at the beginning of the 1960s, a mood that was to change dramatically in both its facets by the end of the decade; and 2. that the mood of the public at large was not widely out of tune with the ideas of the most influential elites at the time in these two crucial respects.

Secondly, I looked at the assumptions made by political leaders. It seemed to me that these assumptions were important for two reasons: First, successful politicians' assumptions have a self-verifying quality. If a President, for example, believes that public opinion will reward him for consistently tough stances toward Communist nations abroad and will not punish him for relatively neglecting social issues at home, then he is to some extent in a position to bring it about that those positions will for a time become orthodox opinion. More important, successful politicians are themselves sensitive estimators of public opinion. They read polls, including many that are not reported in the newspapers. But their whole life is spent in dipping their antennae into all the currents of opinion, informed and uninformed, general and elite. I read as much as I could find about the campaigns of the successful politicians of the 1950s—Eisenhower and Lyndon Johnson, Stevenson and Kefauver—but I concentrated on the two figures whose confrontation in 1960 dramatized what were seen as the important issues of the time and whose influence was to overshadow the ensuing decade. All the candidates' speeches in the 1960 campaign are to be found in a Congressional print: *Freedom of Communications*, published by the communications subcommittee of the Senate Commerce Committee, with the speeches of vice-presidential candidates Johnson and Lodge thrown in as a bonus in a third volume.

Thirdly, there were two extraordinary collective efforts to define the national assumptions. Their very existence tended to confirm the idea of a consensus, for their contributing authors came from a wide range of backgrounds: diplomats, industrialists, lawyers, academics; Republicans and Democrats; Easterners and Westerners and even a sprinkling of Southerners; old men and some representatives of the younger generation. The first was the reports funded by the Rockefeller Brothers Fund and published first as a set of five separate reports and then in one volume as *Prospect for America*: invaluable evidence of abandoned assumptions, and all the more so because the brief for the panels had been to look forward fifteen years; that is, to the very moment when I was beginning my research and finding the reports as dated as if they had been written in Hoover's administration. Second, there was the Eisenhower administration's official report, from a presidential Commission on National Goals, published as *Goals for Americans*. Rarely, if ever, have two such comprehensive attempts been made to codify the ideological and political beliefs of a nation's elite.

Finally, I tried to analyze the consensus of the intellectuals. I shall have to explain what I mean by that notoriously slippery word in this context. I looked not so much at the truly original theoretical thinkers of the period: in many disciplines I am hardly even qualified to know who they were; I drew my portrait—it will seem to some, perhaps, more a caricature—of the liberal ideology of the late 1950s and early 1960s with a particular handful of books in mind and at hand, all of which could be called works of the higher popularization. They were written, that is, by academics of the highest standing but for general audiences. These were the books that actually translated the ideas of the social science of the 1940s into the more or less unchallenged assumptions of educated Americans in the early 1960s.

What books specifically? There were, for example, four books that appeared in 1960 itself that cannot be ignored: Daniel Bell, *The End of Ideology*; Seymour Martin Lipset, *Political Man*; Richard E. Neustadt, *Presidential Power*; Walt W. Rostow, *The Stages of Economic Growth, a non-Communist Manifesto*. Two earlier books seemed to me symptomatic of the same cluster of ideas and at least as influential with the wider audience: David Riesman, *The Lonely Crowd* (1955); and John Kenneth Galbraith, *The Affluent Society* (1957). To make up the shortest of short lists, one would have to add the other works of those half dozen writers: Galbraith's *American Capitalism*, for example, published in 1952; and at the other end of the time scale of consensus, Lipset's *The First New Nation* (1963). Galbraith was in many respects far less typical of the economic thinking of consensus than many other New Economists. The most gifted expositor, popularizer, and journalist of the school was Paul Samuelson, who not only wrote the economics textbook for a generation of Americans as far back as 1948 but also commented on the interaction between events and ideas in *Newsweek* and elsewhere throughout the period I was looking at. I reread the essays and occasional pieces of historians such as the late Richard Hofstadter and Arthur M. Schlesinger, Jr., the latter especially a protean and prolific writer whose opinions on almost any political or cultural subject between 1948 and 1968 were a good starting point for the search when one was looking where liberal orthodoxy lay at the time. I foraged in the articles of such journalist-essayists as Irving Kristol, Richard H. Rovere, and Theodore H. White.

One of the first and most ambitious attempts to codify what became the ideology of consensus is to be found in the 1951 volume, by R. W. Davenport and the editors of Fortune, called *U.S.A., the Permanent Revolution*. Many of the ideas of the liberal consensus can be traced back to two even earlier works of popularization: Peter F. Drucker, *The New Society*; and Arthur M. Schlesinger, Jr., *The Vital Center*; both of which appeared in 1949. Although I have made no systematic attempt to trace the intellectual origins of the consensus, it is obvious that it owes substantial debts to John Maynard Keynes, to Joseph Schumpeter, and to Talcott Parsons, whose work I reread in this context.

Although the intellectual origins of consensus can be traced as far back as the late 1940s and beyond, I have followed Eric F. Goldman, *The Crucial Decade*, in dating the coming of political consensus 1954–55.

Professor Edward Shils's account of the 1955 Venice conference, first published in *Encounter*, was reprinted in *The End of Ideology Debate*, edited by Chaim Waxman, 1968, which also collects contributions on the subject from Bell, Lipset, Kristol, Michael Harrington and others. It is interesting that Lipset himself subsequently acknowledged that "the end of ideology" was itself an ideology of a kind: cf. *The Public Interest*, Fall 1968.

Gabriel Kolko's demonstration that income inequality has not been drastically diminished in the United States is to be found in *Wealth and Power in America*, 1962. The argument he made there, in its general lines, is now rather generally accepted: see, for example, the paper by Lester C. Thurow and Robert B. Lucas written for the Joint Economic Committee of Congress in 1972. The distinction between equality of opportunity and equality of condition is suggestively explored in Christopher Jencks, *Inequality*; and in John Rawls, *On Justice*.

On the history of the Left, I found John P. Diggins, *The American Left in the Twentieth Century*, a useful summary. For the extent to which liberalism was always directed against the Left, see especially Arthur M. Schlesinger, Jr., *The Vital Center*. See also an amusing, hurt passage in the introduction to the paperback edition of Lipset, *Political Man*. Lipset observes that many European writers have discovered a conservative bias in his work. Not so, he rejoins. Why, Talcott Parsons himself has certified him as a "nondogmatic Marxist." To clear things up, Lipset explains that when he calls himself a man of the Left, he does so in the sense in which he thinks of the United States "as a nation in which Leftist values predominate"!

The reference to Alvin Gouldner is to his *The Coming Crisis of Western Sociology*, which appeared in 1970. By that date, Gouldner was able to argue (overstating the case, in my opinion, yet plausibly) that an anti-Marxist bias is built into American social science and that in the case of Parsons and of some other leading figures, this bias was at least semiconscious.

## CHAPTER 5

The evolving doctrine of the presidency as at least first among equal branches of government can be traced in academic works, most of them mentioned in the text: Harold Laski, *The American Presidency* (1940); E. S. Corwin, *President, Office and Powers, 1787–1948* (1948); Sidney Hyman, *The American President* (1954); Clinton Rossiter, *The American Presidency* (1960); Richard E. Neustadt, *Presidential Power* (1960); Rexford G. Tugwell, *The Enlargement of the Presidency* (1960); Herman Finer, *The Presidency: Crisis and Regeneration* (1960); Ernest R. May, *The Ultimate Decision* (1960); Louis W. Koenig, *The Chief Executive* (1964).

The practice of the modern presidency can be studied in the presidential memoirs of Harry S Truman, Dwight D. Eisenhower, and Lyndon B. Johnson; in the books about the Kennedy presidency, such as Schlesinger, *A Thousand Days*, and Sorensen, *Kennedy*, and also in the syndicated columns of Evans and Novak, Joseph Kraft and Hugh Sidey. A short but interesting study written from the point of view of an extreme advocate of presidential predominance is Sorensen, *Decision-Making in the White House* (1963). A thorough account of one crucial episode is Elie Abel, *The Missile Crisis* (1966). The series of books by Theodore H. White on *The Making of the President*, dealing with the elections of 1960, 1964, 1968, and 1972, not only describe successive presidential campaigns in a readable way, but exemplify the high view of the Divine Right of Presidents. Textual study of the closing section of White's 1960 volume reveals how great his debt was, however, to Rossiter and Neustadt.

Two books by the columnists Rowland Evans and Robert Novak, *Lyndon B. Johnson: the Exercise of Power* and *Nixon in the White House: the Frustration of Power*, exemplify an interesting middle position. Without in any way dissenting from the conventional view, Evans and Novak, perhaps because they had spent too much time below stairs in the White House, were fascinated by the means and mechanics of the presidency, and especially its political manipulations.

David Halberstam, *The Best and the Brightest*, is the most comprehensive and one of the most sensitive of the many accounts of the presidencies of John Kennedy and Lyndon Johnson. Of the descriptions of the White House by insiders, Emmett John Hughes's account of the second Eisenhower term, *The Ordeal of Power*, if self-justifying, is a classic. Harry C. McPherson, *A Political Education*, if unduly indulgent, is an attractive picture of the Johnson White House.

The first widely noted revisionist critique of the overmighty presidency was by one of McPherson's colleagues, George E. Reedy, *The Twilight of the Presidency*, published in 1970. Arthur M. Schlesinger, Jr., *The Imperial Presidency*, is a thorough analysis of how the office came to be overmighty, especially noteworthy from a writer who had himself featured so prominently in the chorus praising FDR and John F. Kennedy for their "activism." The wheel comes full circle with a work, unpublished as of the time of writing, by Aaron Wildavsky and Nelson Polsby, which argues that while the presidency's power is no more likely to diminish than the state is likely to wither away, future Presidents are condemned to find themselves more and more unpopular with an electorate that no longer wants "a mighty lion" in the White House, but only a scapegoat.

*The American President,* edited by Sidney Warren, was a useful collection of the classic statements about the office. The quotation from Professor Marcus Cunliffe comes from an essay called "A Defective Institution?" which appeared in *Commentary* in February 1968.

### CHAPTER 6

Much of the material in this chapter was published in the quarterly *Foreign Policy,* Spring 1973.

The basic source material was the interviews I had in the fall of 1972 with a large number of men, some academics, some lawyers, bankers or businessmen, some still in government service, who had been, I considered, members of the foreign policy Establishment. Among them were George Ball, McGeorge Bundy, Clark Clifford, Chester Cooper, Lloyd Cutler, J. K. Galbraith, Stanley Hoffman, Richard Holbrooke, Townsend W. Hoopes, Thomas Hughes, Anthony Lake, Harry C. McPherson, Bayless Manning, Benjamin H. Read, Thomas Schelling, Richard Steadman, James C. Thomson, Cyrus Vance, Paul Warnke, and Frederick S. Wyle. The two *ur*-texts for Establishment studies are Henry Fairlie's article in the London *Spectator* in 1955 and Richard H. Rovere's *jeu d'esprit* in *The American Scholar* in 1961. In April 1964, Karl E. Meyer applied the Establishment concept to the Washington press corps in an amusing article for *Esquire. Life* magazine published, on June 9, 1967, an entirely admiring article by Theodore H. White called "In the Halls of Power," about what White called "the new priesthood . . . of American action-intellectuals." Although not all members of this "priesthood" were interested in foreign affairs, the article reveals the Establishment's assumptions with unconscious clarity. There were sequels in *Life* the following two weeks. J. Anthony Lukas wrote at length about the Council on Foreign Relations in the New York *Times Magazine,* November 21, 1971.

Three well-known books contain unfriendly assessments of the foreign policy elite's responsibility for Vietnam: Richard J. Barnet, *The Roots of War;* Noam Chomsky, *American Power and the New Mandarins;* David Halberstam, *The Best and the Brightest.*

Of the many books on the Pentagon, military policy and the political economy of defense, I found two particularly useful: Sidney Lens, *The Military-Industrial Complex,* and Adam Yarmolinsky, *The Military Establishment.* Samuel Huntington's distinction between the Establishment and the Fundamentalists is to be found in *Daedalus,* Fall 1963. Two excellent studies of the profession of arms in the United States are Huntington, *The Soldier and the State,* and Morris Janowitz, *The Professional Soldier.* Three articles from which I drew ideas or illustrations were Walter Adams, "The Military Industrial Complex and the New Industrial State," *American Economic Review,*

May 1968; H. L. Nieburg, "R & D and the Contract State," *Bulletin of the Atomic Scientists*, March 1966; David M. Shoup and James M. Donovan, "The New American Militarism," *Atlantic Monthly*, April 1969.

CHAPTER 7

My thesis—that successive phases in the mood of the country corresponded to phases in the internal history of the news media—is my own alone. I have found few people in journalism who are happy with it. But it was formed as a result of dozens of conversations, over more than ten years, with working journalists and as a result of reading and watching the finished product of their work for newspapers, magazines, and television. Of those whom I interviewed specifically for this book, there were some who were particularly useful, even if they, too, did not all accept my thesis: Elie Abel, dean of the Columbia School of Journalism; Eric Barnouw of Columbia; Edward Jay Epstein; the late Fred Freed of NBC; Fred W. Friendly, of the Ford Foundation and Columbia; the columnist Joseph Kraft; Robert MacNiel of National Public Television; Robert J. Northshield of NBC; Bill Small of CBS; Tom Wicker of the New York *Times*.

Two books were especially helpful for the history of television in the 1950s: Alexander Kendrick, *Prime Time*, with its detailed account of the quiz scandals and of the fortunes of Ed Murrow; and Eric Barnouw, *The Image Empire*, third volume of a history of broadcasting and a book that is too little known. Perhaps the most perceptive of the many other books about television I read was Robert MacNeil, *The People Machine*. I learned a good deal about the inside feel of the two big networks from a biography of Fred Freed, who worked for both CBS and NBC: David G. Yellin, *Special*. Two general works I found useful here as well as in the writing of a later chapter on the news media were Edward Jay Epstein, *News from Nowhere*, and Martin Mayer, *About Television*.

Much of the material on concentration in the newspaper industry was taken from the memorandum on press competition submitted by the International Typographical Union to hearings held by the Senate Judiciary Committee's subcommittee on antitrust and monopoly in connection with the Failing Newspaper Act, 1967.

The "responsible" journalism of the Cold War period was well evoked by Daniel Patrick Moynihan, *Commentary*, March 1971. The uncontextualized character of nightly network news was first pointed out, to my knowledge, by Lester Markel in the New York *Times Magazine*, March 12, 1967. Many writers have discussed the effect of TV news coverage of the Vietnam War, but none so intelligently as Michael J. Arlen, *The Living Room War*; both MacNeil and Epstein also have important things to say on this subject in their books, as did Robert J. Northshield and Wallace Westfeldt of NBC in interviews.

## CHAPTER 8

The basic source for my interpretation of the period of the assassination and the Johnson takeover is my own recollection, preserved in notes and in the weekly articles I wrote for my then employer, *The Observer* of London, supplemented and corrected by what I have subsequently read of the accounts of better-informed reporters than myself and by the participants themselves. The Kennedy administration was a paradise for energetic and enthusiastic reporters. It is perhaps invidious to select names out of so many kind and often indiscreet briefers: but I owe much of my general education in American politics, and specifically much of my knowledge of the plans and frustrations of the Kennedy administration, to the patience of such men as Lawrence O'Brien and McGeorge Bundy in the White House, Burke Marshall and Edwin O. Guthman in the Justice Department, and Robert Manning and Frederick G. Dutton in the State Department, who gave me more of their time than I had any right to.

Shortly before the assassination, it so happens that—irritated by an article someone had written entitled "Whatever Happened to Lyndon Johnson?"—I had started work on a full-dress profile of the Vice-President. I talked to a great many of his friends, staff and associates. Thanks to three of them—in particular, Horace Busby, Harry McPherson and Bill Moyers—I felt, when Johnson became President, that I had an insight into his personality that was better than that of many other reporters. The present chapter owes a good deal to those conversations in the fall of 1963, filtered, of course, through later reading and interviewing.

William Manchester, *The Death of a President*, is an indispensable source for the immediate period of the assassination, because of the author's industrious research, even if he seems at times obsessed with questions of status and punctilio. Michael Amrine, *This Awesome Challenge*, is a useful journalistic narrative of the first days of the Johnson administration. The central figure's own memoirs—Lyndon B. Johnson, *The Vantage Point*—obviously need to be taken with a judicious pinch of salt at times, but I found them an excellent source of presidential attitudes. Rowland Evans and Robert Novak, *Lyndon B. Johnson: the Exercise of Power*, is a workmanlike political biography that combines professional skepticism about Washington politics with a certain naïveté about the rest of the great wide world; unfortunately, it hurries over the crucial period of Johnson's succession too briefly. Tom Wicker, *JFK and LBJ*, is a brief but extremely perceptive essay. David Halberstam, *The Best and the Brightest*, is rich in Johnson anecdote, less rich in understanding of the man's political dilemma and his longer-term aims. Johnson is still an understudied as well as an underestimated figure, partly, it seems, because the sort of people who write political biographies and the sort of people who publish them in the United States simply didn't like the man.

My understanding of the way the mood of the civil-rights movement was shifting in 1963 owes much to the teaching of Harold Fleming, of the Potomac Institute; Bayard Rustin, of the A. Philip Randolph Institute; and many others whom I interviewed on this subject in 1962–66 as well as in 1972–73. I found several special issues of *Newsweek* rich quarries of poll data and well-chosen quotations, especially the issue on "The Negro in America," published on July 29, 1963.

My attention was drawn to the significance of the debate on segregation in the North at the NAACP's convention in 1963 by E. J. Golightly, president of the Detroit School Board, when I interviewed him in 1973.

My account of reactions to JFK's assassination, and in particular the comments of Bishop Mueller, Professor Commager, Senator Fulbright and Chief Justice Warren, were taken from the files of the New York *Times*.

Harry McPherson's account of his response to Dallas comes from his book *A Political Education*, and the anecdote about Liz Carpenter and Ladybird Johnson comes from *The Vantage Point*.

The description of the origins of the War on Poverty comes in part from interviews with some of the protagonists; also from D. P Moynihan, *Maximum Feasible Misunderstanding*; from a paper by Moynihan in *On Understanding Poverty*; from papers by James L. Sundquist and Adam Yarmolinsky in the companion volume, edited by Sundquist, *On Fighting Poverty*; from Robert A. Levine, *The Poor You Have Always with You*; and from Lyndon B. Johnson, *The Vantage Point*.

The account of LBJ's decision on Vietnam on first taking office comes from many sources, including: Chester L. Cooper, *The Lost Crusade*; Daniel Ellsberg, *Papers on the War*; Philip Geyelin, *Lyndon B. Johnson and the World*; Halberstam, *supra*; Lyndon B. Johnson, *supra*; the Pentagon Papers; Tom Wicker, *supra*. A fuller bibliographical note will be given in connection with a later chapter dealing more generally with the escalation of the Vietnam War.

I was myself present at Andrews Air Force Base on the evening of November 22, 1963.

CHAPTER 9

My interest in the southern civil rights movement dates back to Easter 1956, when, as a graduate student at the University of Pennsylvania, it so happened that I spent a few days staying with a black contemporary of mine from Oxford University who lived in Montgomery, Alabama. This was at the time of the bus strike, and it was then that I first met Martin Luther King, briefly.

Between 1962 and 1968 I spent a good deal of time traveling widely in the South, first covering the civil rights movement for the London *Observer*, then doing research for a projected book about southern history, and latterly making films for British television. I met and in most cases interviewed almost all the protagonists mentioned in this chapter: King, George Wallace, Stokely Carmichael, Ella Baker, Ezell Blair, Jr., Bayard Rustin, Julian Bond, Robert Parris Moses and many others. I have learned a great deal from long conversations with many others: in particular, Harold Fleming of the Potomac Institute in Washington; Pat Watters of the Southern Regional Council in Atlanta; Charles Morgan, Jr., first in Birmingham, then in Atlanta, and recently in Washington; Berl Bernhard and William Taylor, both formerly of the United States Civil Rights Commission; Vernon E. Jordan, of the Voter Registration Project; and Professor C. Vann Woodward, of Yale University.

The nearest there is to a general history of the civil rights movement is Benjamin Muse, *The American Negro Revolution*, written perhaps a little too close, for perspective, to the events it describes. Louis E. Lomax, *The Negro Revolt*, is useful on earlier events but was first published in 1962. *Portrait of a Decade*, edited by Anthony Lewis from the New York *Times*'s coverage from 1954 to 1964, is invaluable for reference. So are the reports of the U. S. Commission on Civil Rights for 1959, 1961 (five volumes) and 1963.

The best biography of Martin Luther King is David L. Lewis, *Martin Luther King: a Critical Biography*. Of King's own books, the most relevant are *Stride Toward Freedom: the Montgomery Story; Why We Can't Wait*; and *Where Do We Go from Here: Chaos or Community?* published, respectively, in 1958, 1964 and 1967. Lewis Chester, *Martin Luther King*, is a crisp biography with a good deal of ancillary material.

There are useful studies of individual civil rights organizations: Howard Zinn, *SNCC: the New Abolitionists*; August Meier and Elliott Rudwick, *CORE, a Study in the Civil Rights Movement 1942–1968*. Jack Newfield, *A Prophetic Minority*, has a good brief account of the origins and development of SNCC. James Forman, *The Making of Black Revolutionaries*, is an autobiographical narrative that contains invaluable material for the history of SNCC.

Of the many books I read for background understanding, a handful are worth special mention: Samuel Lubell, *White & Black*; Charles E. Silberman, *Crisis in Black and White*; Howard Zinn, *The Southern Mystique*.

Bayard Rustin, *Down the Line*, is a collection of essays, speeches and articles by one of the most thoughtful strategists of the movement. James Peck, *Freedom Ride*, is the best firsthand account of that episode.

For my account of the March on Washington, I found Jervis Anderson, *A. Philip Randolph: a Biographical Portrait*, helpful. I also interviewed many of the participants and organizers, including Dr. Eugene Carson Blake, John Lewis, Dr. Benjamin Mays, Joseph L. Rauh, Jr., Rustin, and Roy Wilkins. A fuller version of the account in this chapter was published by the Washington *Post*'s *Potomac Magazine* in 1973.

The files of *New South*, published by the Southern Regional Council, in Atlanta, were full of good things, as were those of *Freedomways*. Two special issues of magazines are worth mentioning: The April 1965 special supplement to *Harper's* on "The South Today" contains articles by Willie Morris, William Styron, C. Vann Woodward, D. W. Brogan, Louis E. Lomax, James J. Kilpatrick, Robert Coles, Walker Percy and others, many of them very fine. The Woodward article, in particular, "From the First Reconstruction to the Second," should be read in conjunction with a later article of Woodward's in *Harper's*, "What Happened to the Civil Rights Movement?" published in January 1967. The Fall 1965 edition of *Daedalus*, on "The Negro American," contains excellent papers by Rashi Fein, Harold Fleming, Thomas Pettigrew and others.

### CHAPTER 10

The most thoughtful book on Malcolm X is Archie Epps, *Malcolm X*. Alex Haley, *The Autobiography of Malcolm X*, is valuable, though it bears traces of Malcolm's wish to control his own legend. George Breitman, *The Last Year of Malcolm X*, is overeager to recruit Malcolm to the Trotskyites but otherwise interesting. Breitman edited the standard collection of Malcolm's speeches: *Malcolm X Speaks*. See also Louis E. Lomax, *The Negro Revolt*, one chapter of which contains perhaps the first account of Malcolm written for general readers. The standard work on the Black Muslims is C. Eric Lincoln, *The Black Muslims in America*.

I was present at the Freedom School in Oxford, Ohio, in 1964 and met Bob Moses there. The description of Moses hearing the news that the volunteers had disappeared is from my own memory, reinforced by the article I wrote for the London *Observer* at the time. I have discussed Moses' extraordinary personality and career with many of his friends, among whom Marcus G. Raskin of the Institute for Policy Studies and Stokely Carmichael were particularly helpful.

On the Mississippi murders, I used William Bradford Huie, *Three Lives for Mississippi*, and also Len Holt, *The Summer That Didn't End*, as well as newspaper files. Holt's book is the best account of the Freedom Summer project in Mississippi as a whole, and of the conflict over the seating of the Mississippi delegation at the Democratic National Convention in Atlantic City, which came directly out of it. There are many descriptions of the summer project by participants, among them Elizabeth Sutherland (editor), *Letters from Mississippi*; and Sally Belfrage, *Freedom Summer*. On the government's difficulty in protecting the volunteers, I interviewed Burke Marshall and John Doar, both then of the Justice Department.

The issue of nonviolence and the carrying of guns by SNCC volunteers was discussed by Stokely Carmichael in a long, tape-recorded interview, and is also touched on by James Forman, *The Making of Black Revolutionaries*.

I covered the Atlantic City convention myself and was able to use my own notes and the reports I filed, e.g., London *Observer*, August 29, 1964. Of those I interviewed for this book, Joseph L. Rauh, Jr., was conspicuously useful. I was also at Selma. The accounts of James Forman, *The Making of Black Revolutionaries*; David L. Lewis, *op. cit.*; and of Stokely Carmichael in an interview—all contributed to my understanding of the Selma episode. A sensitive report is Renata Adler, "Letter from Selma," *The New Yorker*, April 10, 1965.

I drew on similar sources for the closing section of the chapter, plus Meier and Rudwick, *CORE*; King, *Chaos and Community*, which contains King's version of the confrontation with Carmichael; interviews with Carmichael's ally Willie Ricks, said to have been the first to shout, "Black power!" and with Floyd McKissick. Paul Good, "The Meredith March," in *New South*, summer 1966, is first-rate firsthand reporting. I also viewed a great deal of film of the Meredith march and other civil rights activities of this period in connection with a documentary I made for British Independent Television, for whom I also interviewed Martin Luther King, Stokely Carmichael and others at this time.

### CHAPTER 11

The assessment of President Johnson's situation at the beginning of 1965 is based on my own observation at the time, which in turn was drawn from the President's own speeches, subsequently published in *The Public Papers of the Presidents*, and from press comment at the time. It is confirmed by Lyndon B. Johnson, *The Vantage Point*.

The basic source for the whole of the rest of the chapter was the *Pentagon Papers*. I worked with the four volumes of the Gravel edition, which was inconvenient because they have no index, but essential because this is far fuller than the New York *Times* edition.

I deliberately focused my attention on the critical decision to escalate to full-scale warfare, involving both an American expeditionary force of ground troops and bombing of North Vietnam, which was taken over, roughly, twelve months—from the late summer of 1964 to the fall of 1965. This approach omitted, for reasons of scope and space, the absorbing questions of how the United States became involved at all in Indochina from the beginning, and why this occurred. Those who wish to reanalyze these much-discussed questions will find, in a voluminous literature, certain reading indispensable. On the "Vietnam lobby" in the 1950s, Robert Scheer, *How the United States Got Involved in Vietnam*. On the French Indochina war and the carryover into the American commitment, Bernard Fall, *Street Without Joy*; Lucien Bodard, *The Quicksand War*; Frances Fitzgerald, *Fire in the Lake*; Robert Shaplen, *The Lost Revolution*; Edwin G. Lansdale, *In the Midst of Wars*.

They will have to read Halberstam, *The Best and the Brightest*, but they will also want to read his earlier book, *The Making of a Quagmire*, and they may agree with me that Halberstam's first interpretation is effectually demolished in Daniel Ellsberg, "The Quagmire Myth and the Stalemate Machine," published in Ellsberg, *Papers on the War*. Those who want to understand the American attitude to the French war will get the flavor as well as anywhere else in Graham Greene, *The Quiet American*, a fictional portrait of Edwin Lansdale.

Three close analyses of the process of involvement are Theodore Draper, *Abuse of Power*; Ralph G. Stavins, Richard J. Barnet, and Marcus G. Raskin, *Washington Plans and Aggressive War*; Franz Schurmann, Peter Dale Scott, and Reginald Zelnik, *The Politics of Escalation in Vietnam*. All but the Stavins-Barnet-Raskin volume were written without benefit of the Pentagon Papers, however, and some will find the tone of that book a little too denunciatory. Schurmann and his coauthors put forward the thesis that there was "a recurrent pattern . . ." whereby "movements towards a political settlement have been retarded or broken off by American interventions." Equally critical analyses are to be found in two volumes of essays by Noam Chomsky: *American Power and the New Mandarins* and *At War with Asia*.

Two troubled but less critical accounts, by former U.S. officials, have much to commend them as descriptions of what was going on inside the bureaucracy: Roger Hilsman, *To Move a Nation*; and Chester L. Cooper, *The Lost Crusade*. Unfortunately the publication of the Pentagon Papers has made both partially obsolete. Successive reports by Robert Shaplen, a journalist who originally sympathized with the objectives of American involvement but was realistic enough not to be deceived by false hopes of success, are brought together in Shaplen, *The Road from War*, which covers the period 1965–71. They originally appeared in *The New Yorker*. A collection of articles on Vietnam that appeared in *The Atlantic* between 1966 and 1969 was published as *Who We Are*, edited by Robert J. Manning and Michael Janeway. Two articles are particularly relevant to the question of the commitment of 1964–65: James C. Thomson, "How Could Vietnam Happen?" *The Atlantic*, April 1968; and an interview by Janeway with Bill Moyers, *The Atlantic*, July 1968.

The Pentagon Papers show that even a skeptical and skillful account of the Tonkin Gulf incident, Joseph C. Goulden, *Truth Is the First Casualty*, may have been too trusting. Even the incomparable I. F. Stone, whose writings in his *Weekly* and in *The New York Review of Books* were a constant illumination, suffers a little from this bathos: much that he suspected, was even attacked for suspecting, is there in the Pentagon Papers in black and white.

They remain an extraordinary source not only for the process whereby the United States became involved in Indochina, to so great a cost; not only, indeed, for the merciless light in which they reveal the preconceptions of the men who were responsible for that decision; but even more as an almost uniquely intimate and detailed documentation of a bureaucracy at work: rational, dedicated, blundering, and ultimately all but out of control of its masters.

I am indebted to Daniel Ellsberg for the observation that much of the language of the bureaucracy quoted in the Pentagon Papers is "the language of torturers"; or, rather, I am indebted to Patricia Ellsberg, his wife, for this phrase, according to his lecture in the Boston Community Church in April 1971, subsequently published in Ellsberg, *Papers on the War*.

## CHAPTER 12

This chapter assesses the economic costs of the decision to escalate the U.S. involvement in Vietnam in 1965. Specifically, it attempts to answer two questions: What, if any, was the causal relation between that decision and the steep increase in the rate of inflation that was recorded from late 1965 on? What was the relationship between the war and the U.S. balance of payments? Both questions took me into areas of specialization that were unfamiliar and demanded a good deal of reading.

On the performance of the economy year by year, the primary source is the annual Economic Report prepared by the Council of Economic Advisers for transmission to Congress. Two books written by former members of the Council of Economic Advisers give what might be called the New Economists' view: Arthur M. Okun, *The Political Economy of Prosperity*; and Walter W. Heller, *New Dimensions of Political Economy*. Two other good general introductions to the policies of the New Economists are Hobart Rowen, *The Free Enterprisers: Kennedy, Johnson and the Business Establishment*; and James L. Sundquist, *Politics and Policy: the Eisenhower, Kennedy and Johnson Years*. An excellent, if bitter and *ad hominem*, critique of the New Economists is Richard B. Du Boff and Edward S. Herman, "The New Economics: Handmaiden of Inspired Truth," in *The Review of Radical Political Economics*, August 1972.

After 1972 it became almost a cliché to attribute inflation to the war. One of the first to argue the case seriously was Edwin L. Dale, Jr., "The Inflation Goof," *The New Republic*, January 4, 1969.

A primary source for the whole question of the effect of the war on the economy is the U.S. Congress Joint Economic Committee hearings on the *Economic Effect of Vietnam Spending*, published in 1967.

A group of young radical economists published a thorough estimate of "The War and Its Impact on the Economy" in *The Review of Radical Political Economics* in August 1970. I have also had access to a dissertation proposal on "The Economic Consequences of the War in Indochina" by one of their number, Thomas A. Riddell, for the Economics Department of the American University in Washington. Many public-interest pressure groups and others have compiled material on the corporations profiting from the war. Some of the best of this material comes from the Council on Economic Priorities, for example a report published in April 1970 on the manufacturers of anti-personnel weapons.

The economist Robert Eisner made a study of the impact of war spending on the economy in general and inflation in particular. I found three of his papers useful: "War and Taxes: the Role of the Economist in Politics," *Bulletin of the Atomic Scientists*, June 1968; "Fiscal and Monetary Policy Reconsidered," *American Economic Review*, December 1969; and "What Went Wrong?" *Journal of Political Economy*, 1970. Indispensable reading for official or semiofficial views and estimates is the hearings on the "Impact of the War in Southeast Asia on the U.S. Economy," before the U.S. Senate Foreign Relations Committee, in 1970, especially the testimony of Charles L. Schultze, director of the Bureau of the Budget from 1965 to 1968.

On the balance of payments, Congressional hearings again provide much of the essential material, e.g., the Senate Committee on Banking and Currency, March 1965, "Background Information on U.S. Balance of Payments"; and hearings of a subcommittee of the U.S. Congress Joint Economic Committee, in 1971, which contains the classic remark of Chairman Henry Reuss (D.-Wis.) to a witness from the Federal Reserve: "We are trying to locate several billions of dollars. . . ."

Again, an indispensable source of statistical information was the U.S. Department of Commerce Survey of Current Business. On imports, there is a good summary in the *Federal Reserve Bulletin*, April 1971.

The person who first educated me in the workings of the U.S. balance of payments was Robert V. Roosa, then under-secretary of the U.S. Treasury and now a partner in Brown Brothers, Harriman & Co. Many of the ideas in this chapter are influenced by a long interview Mr. Roosa gave me in the spring of 1973 and by his speeches and writings over the years, of which three are particularly relevant: a speech to the Economic Club of Detroit, October 10, 1966; a contribution to a seminar reported in *Annals of the American Academy*, July 1969; and an article in *Euromoney*, June 1970.

A distinguished economist with whom I found myself less in agreement but whose work is nevertheless important to an understanding of balance-of-payments problems is C. Fred Bergsten. See, for example, his article in *Foreign Affairs*, January 1972, and his contribution to a book published by the National Planning Association, *A New Approach to New Realities*, November 1971. Another paper in the same book, by Robert E. Hunter, contained useful information on the decline of U.S. productivity between 1965 and 1970.

The size of the Eurodollar pool was estimated by Raymond F. Mikeshell, "Measuring the Size of the Eurodollar Market," *Euromoney*, October 1969, and by the Bank for International Settlements in Basel, Switzerland, whose higher estimate was cited in the Reuss hearings. A book edited by Bela Balassa, *Changing Patterns of Foreign Trade & Payments*, 1964, 1970, includes three particularly interesting papers: one by Judd Polk on production abroad by the affiliates of U.S. corporations; a second by Émile Desprès, Charles P. Kindleberger and Walter S. Salant arguing that the U.S. balance-of-payments deficit is not evidence of disequilibrium but of the U.S. role as a banker; and an attack by Edward M. Bernstein on "the Kindleberger thesis." Another book-length study, by the International Economic Policy Association, edited by N. R. Danielian, *The United States Balance of Payments*, provides an excellent chronological summary of measures taken to limit deficits and of their effect.

Two of many items on the different ways of measuring the U.S. deficit are Albert Kraus, *Euromoney*, February 1971; and Paul A. Volcker, speech to American Finance, Economic and Statistical Associations, Detroit, December

1970. The deficits, according to accepted measures, are tc be found in the IMF Balance of Payments Yearbook, volume 22, with seven pages of tables covering 1965–69.

## CHAPTER 13

The text of the Moynihan report is reproduced in facsimile ir *The Moynihan Report and the Politics of Controversy*, a most convenient volume, edited by Lee Rainwater and William Yancey, that also includes a well-sourced narrativε of the furore that resulted from the report's gradual publication, and the text of many responses to–for and against–"The Negro Family." I discussed the report, and the furore, with its author before, during, and after its curious publication.

Bayard Rustin, "From Protest to Politics," a brilliantly perceptive summing up of a situation that was changing at top speed, appeared in *Commentary*, February 1965. A fierce criticism from a New Left standpoint, arguing that Democratic politicians "co-opted the Negroes,' is Ronald Radosh, "From Protest to Black Power: the Failure of Coalition Politics' in *The Great Society Reader*, edited by Marvin E. Gettleman and David Mermelstein, an uneven collection that contains many interesting contributions to the debate over "the failure of liberalism," a phrase the editors took as their subtitle.

The books referred to as sources of some of Moynihan's thinking are E. Franklin Frazier, *The Negro Family in the United States*, and Kenneth B. Clark's report on youth in Harlem, the substance of which was included in his *Dark Ghetto*, which appeared at about the same time as the Moynihan report.

The account of the Howard speech is based on Rainwater and Yancey, op. cit., and on Johnson, *The Vantage Point*.

The quotation from "King's biographer" is a reference to David L. Lewis, *Martin Luther King: a Critical Biography*.

The Watts riot is narrated briefly in the "Kerner report" (Report of the National Advisory Commission on Civil Disorders), though this was more specifically concerned with the 1967 riots in New Jersey, Detroit and elsewhere. One sharp comment out of many journalistic responses was Bayard Rustin, *Commentary*, March 1966, itself a response to the "McCone report," *Violence in the City–an End or a Beginning?* produced by a commission appointed by Governor Edmund G. Brown of California and headed by John A. McCone, former director of central intelligence. The McCone commission is remorselessly exposed, and the preconditions of the Los Angeles riot well described, in Paul Jacobs, *Prelude to Riot*. The quotation from Lou Smith, the CORE worker from Los Angeles, comes from Meier and Rudwick, *CORE*. President Johnson's contrasting responses are taken from *Public Papers of the Presidents* and *The Vantage Point*.

The background to the White House conference was discussed in interviews by several of the organizers and participants, especially Harold Fleming and Harry C. McPherson, among the former. Fleming described to me the meeting to thank Heineman.

On the War on Poverty the following books were used: Daniel Patrick Moynihan, *Maximum Feasible Misunderstanding*; D. P. Moynihan (ed.), *On Understanding Poverty*; James L. Sundquist (ed.), *On Fighting Poverty*; Robert A. Levine, *The Poor You Have Always with You*; Walter Heller, *New Dimensions of Political Economy*. On the Mississippi Child Development Group, the best account known to me is Pat Watters, "CDGM: Who Really Won?" published simultaneously in *Dissent*, May 1967, and *New South*, Spring 1967.

## CHAPTER 14

The anecdote about Rusk's conversation with Soviet ambassador Dobrynin, and Rusk's language, are quoted from Lyndon B. Johnson, *The Vantage Point*.

The fact that draft cards were publicly destroyed as a gesture of protest as early as 1947, and much other material on the early history of American pacifism, came from Michael Ferber and Staughton Lynd, *The Resistance*. The files of *Liberation* gave me something of the feel of that movement. Among those I interviewed specifically for this chapter were David Dellinger, Staughton Lynd, Sanford Gottlieb of SANE, David McReynolds, Marcus Raskin, and Dr. Benjamin Spock.

An invaluable collection of material on the New Left generally, and SDS in particular, is edited by Massimo Teodori, *The New Left: a Documentary History*. This contains texts of many important documents, speeches, and articles, by Tom Hayden, Carl Oglesby, Todd Gitlin, Paul Potter and other early leaders of SDS, and by Dellinger, A. J. Muste and other pacifists, and indeed a wealth of material on all aspects of radicalism in the 1960s. It is also unusually well edited and provided with a bibliography I used extensively. Jack Newfield, *A Prophetic Minority*, contains a good but too brief account of the history of SDS. As a corrective to the New Left's view of itself, I worked through the clippings on SDS in the New York *Times* library, a resource I used, incidentally, on many other occasions. On SDS, it was perhaps the omissions that were most striking.

Hayden's own memoirs, published in *Rolling Stone* in 1972, are excellent autobiography, by a born writer. The details of SDS's position on the war and the draft are taken from Ferber and Lynd, op. cit. Michael Harrington's analysis of Schachtman and the Schachtmanites and their support for the war comes from an apologia published in *Dissent*, Spring 1973, to which my attention was drawn by Professor Ivar Oxaal, of the University of Hull.

I spent some time in the offices of the *Michigan Daily* in Ann Arbor, Michigan, where I found interesting material on the origins of the first sit-in. My colleague Eric Marsden of the London *Sunday Times* was kind enough to interview William Gamson on my behalf, as Gamson was living in Israel at the time.

Of the many recessional articles on the early days of the peace movement written in the early 1970s, one of the best was by Andrew Kopkind, *Ramparts*, February 1973.

<h2 style="text-align:center">CHAPTER 15</h2>

There is a good, objective history of student unrest in the early chapters of the *Report of the President's Commission on Campus Unrest*, the Scranton commission, set up by the Nixon administration after the killings at Kent State and Jackson State in the spring of 1970. For background on American universities in general, Jencks and Riesman, *The Academic Revolution*, can be contrasted with James Ridgway, *The Closed Corporation*, a denunciatory but perceptive book. The *Report on Higher Education*, funded by the Ford Foundation for the Department of Health, Education and Welfare, and published in March 1971, is a good guide to what official and semiofficial opinion regarded as the problems of the universities after seven years of what the report calls "disruptions."

I chose to tell the story of student upheaval through the microcosm of Berkeley partly because, though the effort of tracing the local differences in several hundred colleges would have been great, the essential pattern seemed to be the same everywhere as at Berkeley; partly because, thanks to the kindness of Dean Edwin Bayley, I had an opportunity to spend two months at the School of Journalism in Berkeley in the spring of 1973.

For those interested in the history of student dissent at other universities, there is an excellent bibliography in the Scranton commission's report. The best general discussion, from a largely unsympathetic viewpoint, is Daniel Bell and Irving Kristol (editors), *Confrontation: the Student Rebellion and Universities*.

On events at Columbia in 1968, the reader can choose between the "Cox Commission report," *Crisis at Columbia*; and the New York Civil Liberties Union's examination: Michael Baker and others, *Police on Campus*.

On the Harvard rioting of spring 1969, the best account is Steven Kelman, *Push Comes to Shove*.

John Searle, *The Campus War*, is a brilliant analysis by a Berkeley philosophy professor who began as a student radical, experienced the Berkeley upheaval as special assistant to the chancellor of the University of California for student affairs, and advised the Nixon administration on campus problems.

On Berkeley specifically, I read the Forbes Committee report (1965), *Report on the University of California*, by Jerome C. Byrne; a collection of articles, documents and statements edited by Seymour M. Lipset and Sheldon S. Wolin, *The Berkeley Student Revolt*; a collection of articles reprinted from *The New York Review of Books*, Sheldon S. Wolin and John Schaar, *The Berkeley Rebellion and Beyond*; and Hal Draper, *Berkeley: the New Student Revolt*, the latter written from a radical point of view. I also used the files of the *Daily Californian* and of the Berkeley *Barb*.

For the history of the University of California and a description of its triumphs and glories in and around the year 1960, I used the semiofficial history Verne A. Stadtman, *The University of California 1868–1968*. For the California background, I found valuable material in Richard G. Lillard, *Eden in Jeopardy*; Remi Nadeau, *California: the New Society*; and especially a remarkable book, Kevin Starr, *Americans and the California Dream*.

Among many people interviewed in Berkeley, I found talks with former President Clark Kerr, John Searle and Professor Neil J. Smelser, chairman of the Sociology Department, especially fertile of ideas and corrective of misconceptions.

CHAPTER 16

The counterculture, after all, is only part of the greater culture to which we all have access. It is a new selection, based on different principles and with different didactic aims, from the same infinite corpus of books, ideas, and traditions on which any other specific culture is free to draw. Some of the ideas and books that suddenly smote young people in California, in the middle 1960s, with the force of revelation, were already familiar. The ludicrous case is J. R. R. Tolkien. My mother used to read *The Hobbit* to me as a child in bed before World War II. *The Fellowship of the Ring*, admirable as it is, sprang from the comfortable, pedantic, old-fashioned society I grew up in. It was comic to think that this first cousin of William Morris' Victorian epic had become, for the rising generation in California, the myth of a new consciousness.

I tried to give myself at least an acquaintance with as many as possible of the oddly assorted traditions that went to make up the counterculture. It was fun. But there was never any danger that the books I was reading would fit together, as they seemed to do for my American contemporaries, into a unified gospel of emancipation. No doubt the reason was that my prison was in another place. In any case, I was rewarded in many ways, but not by a mystical experience. With pleasure, rather than with enlightenment, I rediscovered the Beat poets, and Aldous Huxley's later writings, and Hermann Hesse. Having poked my nose gingerly, guided by "Arthur Avalon," into the mysticism of the Tantra, I explored Zen Buddhism with the help of the Reverend Alan Watts and Mr. Justice Christmas Humphreys. I read the *I Ching* and the *Tibetan Book of the Dead*, though I cannot claim to have progressed far down any of these ancient paths to wisdom. I wandered a little aimlessly in the trackless pages of Marcuse, and allowed myself to be browbeaten, well this side of conversion, by Paul Goodman and Fritz Perls and R. D. Laing. I followed the surreal transformation of Dr. Richard Alpert into Baba Ram Dass, and I gained a superficial familiarity with the myth of Atlantis, with the metaphysical school of science fiction, with reinterpretations of the astrology of the Pharaonic pyramids, and with the ritual meaning of Stonehenge, a dozen miles from my former home.

A handful of books helped me to impose some order on this sprawling corpus of fashionable antirationality: William Braden, *The Age of Aquarius*; Theodore Roszak, *The Making of a Counter Culture*; Charles Reich, *The Greening of America*; William Irwin Thompson, *At the Edge of History*. Reich seemed to me sentimental and unreflecting but valuable for one or two conceptual ideas. Thompson's book affords the weird spectacle of a man with a first-class academic intellect progressively abandoning rationality as he writes. Yet both Reich and Thompson were for me illuminating. Roszak, the most accomplished of the four, achieves almost a pastiche of the academic pomposity of the liberal tradition whose antithesis he is describing: yet his is a fine book, strongly organized, and flecked with exciting writing. Braden, for me, is the best of the four. He draws on interviews thoughtfully and thoroughly conducted with two dozen of the most seminal, and not necessarily the best known, of the new sages. And he preserves from start to finish the modest tone of the seeker after truth who despises no fellow seeker, yet is not going to be talked into wasting precious days on a false track, just the same.

My debt to two earlier essays is explicit in the text: Norman Mailer, Part IV, "Hipsters," of *Advertisements for Myself*, and especially for the essay called *The White Negro*, which was written, astonishingly enough, in 1957. And Leslie Fiedler, "The New Mutants" (1965), in *Unfinished Business*.

The quotation from David Harris was taken from Michael Ferber and Staughton Lynd, *The Resistance*. Carl Oglesby's thoughts on Rennie Davis' recruitment to the Divine Light crew were published in the Boston *Phoenix* in the spring of 1973. The data on the attitudes of white and black people in Michigan come from the University of Michigan Survey Research Center, in particular a paper by Howard Schuman, "Two Sources of Antiwar Sentiment in America," *American Journal of Sociology*, November 1972, drawing on data collected in the 1971 Detroit Area Study, carried out in collaboration with Otis Dudley Duncan and others.

The Feiffer cartoon, I first found in John P. Diggins, *The American Left in the Twentieth Century*.

On Ginsberg and the Beats, I found the following especially useful for chronological sequence and for quotations: Bruce Cook, *The Beat Generation*; and Jane Kramer, *Allen Ginsberg in America*. For the early history of the counterculture, evolving out of the Beat companionship, I found valuable hints in Ralph Gleason, *The Jefferson Airplane*; Timothy Leary, *The Politics of Ecstasy*; Baba Ram Dass (alias/aka Richard Alpert), *Be Here Now*; and Tom Wolfe, *The Electric Kool-Aid Acid Test*.

## CHAPTER 17

The general background reading for this chapter overlaps with that for Chapter 16. A handful of specific books demand mention; they could equally have been mentioned in the context of the previous chapter: Erik Erikson, *Childhood and Society* and *Identity: Youth and Crisis*; Kenneth Keniston, *The Uncom-*

*mitted* and *Young Radicals*; R. D. Laing, *The Politics of Experience* and *Knots*; Herbert Marcuse, *Eros and Civilization* and the essay on "Repressive Tolerance" in Robert Paul Wolff, Barrington Moore, Jr., and Herbert Marcuse, *A Critique of Pure Tolerance*; Philip Slater, *The Pursuit of Loneliness*.

On marijuana: a good general introduction is the "Shafer Report," published by the Nixon administration in 1970, *Marijuana: a Signal of Misunderstanding*. See also, ten years earlier: D. Solomon (editor), *The Marijuana Papers*. The earliest advocacy of consciousness-expanding by drugs is in Aldous Huxley, *The Doors of Perception* (1954), though William Burroughs, *Junkie*, while not exactly advocacy, is even earlier: 1953. On the hallucinogens: Timothy Leary, Ralph Metzner and Richard Alpert, *The Psychedelic Experience*, came out in 1964; Solomon, *LSD: the Consciousness-Expanding Drug*, appeared in the same year; Leary, *The Politics of Ecstasy*, which includes his celebrated interview with Playboy, "She Comes in Colors," was published in 1968. The best general short introduction to the whole subject, in my opinion, is Harrison Pope, Jr., *Voices from the Drug Culture*.

The two descriptions of Esalen come from William Irwin Thompson, op. cit.; and Ed Sanders, *The Family*, from which I took the sinister picture of Charles Manson lurking around the edge of the campfire.

The figure for the number of heroin addicts comes from addict statistics reported by the Bureau of Narcotics and Dangerous Drugs for 1971. I also used Dorothy F. Berg, *Illicit Use of Dangerous Drugs*, a compilation of studies, surveys and polls, published by the bureau in September 1970, and other statistical data published by the bureau.

There are—or were in the high and palmy days of rock music—good critics writing in "straight" papers, such as Tom Zito in the Washington *Post*, and in profusion in underground papers of every kind. I dipped into these to get some idea of what I was supposed to think. The news magazines, from time to time, printed sententious essays trying to extrapolate some prophetic insight about the future of the world from the sales graphs of different bands and kinds of music. Most consistently, of course, *Rolling Stone* tells the devotee what he or she is supposed to think, and especially what she or he is supposed to buy. One critic at *Rolling Stone* has stood out for integrity and for genuine, as opposed to manufactured, insight into the relationship, real if subtle, between the trend of musical fashion and the mood of a generation: Jon Landau. He was helpful in giving me a sense of the shape of the historical development of the music in an interview, and some of his best writing is collected in Landau, *It's Too Late to Stop Now*.

There are plenty of other rock books, some of them indescribably obsequious in their adulation of their heroes. Those I found useful were Hunter Davies, *The Beatles*; Tom Wolfe, *The Electric Kool-Aid Acid Test*; Michael Lydon, *Rock Folk*; David Walley, *No Commercial Potential* (the story of Frank Zappa and the Mothers of Invention); two volumes of *The Age of Rock* edited by Jonathan Eisen; collections of magazine pieces from many, mainly underground, publications, edited by Jonathan Eisen. Most suffer from the monotonous hyperbole and hopeless imprecision of the genre. But some were well worth reading, notably T. Procter Lippincott, "The Culture Vultures," and Andrew Kopkind, "Woodstock Nation," both of which I quote from. I also drew heavily on a similar compendium devoted to a single musician: *Bob Dylan, a Retrospective*, edited by an Australian, Craig McGregor, which contains a mixture of the usual sycophancy and some much more interesting material, notably an interview with Dylan by Nat Hentoff. Some of my treatment of the commercial background to rock music is drawn from an interview with Bob Altschuler, of CBS Records. The whole section is heavily indebted to a learned historical memorandum written by my research assistant, Mark O'Neill.

I interviewed a number of editors specifically for the section on the underground press: Robert Silvers of *The New York Review of Books*; Jack Newfield of *The Village Voice*; Art Kunkin of the Los Angeles *Free Press*; Max Scherr of the Berkeley *Barb*; several of the editors at *Ramparts*.

Among the books dealing with the underground press in general, two are excellent: Robert J. Glessing, *The Underground Press in America*; and Michael L. Johnson, an especially patient researcher, *The New Journalism*. Ethel Grodzins Romm, *The Open Conspiracy*, is a somewhat naïvely excited pasan, which contrasts with an article written after the ball was over, Nat Hentoff, "Lifeline for the Underground," in [MORE] magazine. An early article for the general reader is Jacob Brackman, "The Underground Press," in *Playboy*. Two books by one of the creators of the Liberation News Service, Ray Mungo, are *Total Loss Farm*, steeped in gloom; and *Famous Long Ago*, which contains a notable defense of the underground's belief that "*facts* are less important than *truth*." Some interesting material on the economics of the underground newspaper came from an unpublished University of California thesis, Paul A. Slater, *The Fifth Estate*.

CHAPTER 18

On the Tet offensive and the reactions to it in Washington, I followed two books: Don Oberdorfer, *Tet!*, a superbly researched account of events both on the ground and in Washington; and Townsend W. Hoopes, *The Limits of Intervention*, the inside account of a high civilian Pentagon official who played a part himself in the dramatic turnabout of policy.

The quotation from McGeorge Bundy is taken from one of his off-the-record talks to the Council on Foreign Relations, of which I was fortunate enough to obtain a text from a participant. The talks were given in May 1971.

There is a vast literature on the conduct of the Vietnam War by the United States and on the question of atrocities, "war crimes," and the laws of war as they affect a modern guerrilla war. The full diapason of denunciation is to be found in *Against the Crime of Silence*, the proceedings of the Bertrand Russell International War Crimes Tribunal. Though much of the material is immoderate and motivated by blatantly prejudiced anti-Americanism, some of the factual material on torture, the effects of bombing, etc., appears to be valid and some of the contributors can hardly be accused of prejudice or anti-Americanism. A more measured and deadly case against U.S. conduct of the war, by a writer who supported it until 1965, is Telford Taylor, *Nuremberg and Vietnam, an American Tragedy*, with its powerful conclusion: "Few elsewhere do not now see our America as a sort of Steinbeckian Lennie, gigantic and powerful, but prone to shatter what we try to save." On the air war, reliable accounts are to be found in Frank Harvey, *Air War: Vietnam*, by a reporter who went to Indochina without doubts and returned horrified; and Ralph Littauer and Norman Uphoff (editors) *The Air War in Indochina*, a painstaking analysis of the cost, conduct, legality and effect of the bombing in Vietnam, Laos and Cambodia, published in 1972. On ground atrocities: Jonathan Schell, *The Military Half*; Seymour Hersh, *My Lai 4*. On the legality of the war, the standard collection of materials, which I cannot pretend to have more than glanced through, is the two volumes of Richard Falk, *The Vietnam War and International Law*. For the *Duffy* case, see Taylor, *Nuremberg and Vietnam*, pp. 150–53, and the New York *Times*, March 28 to April 5, 1970.

A detailed study of how the film of the shooting of a Viet Cong prisoner by Brigadier General Loan came to be shot and shown is to be found in *Journalism Quarterly*, Summer 1972, by George A. Bailey and Lawrence W. Lichty, "Rough Justice on a Saigon Street: a Gatekeeper Study of NBC's Tet Execution Film."

The account of the Wise Old Men's change of heart was pieced together by myself from interviews with many of the participants, including Clark Clifford, George Ball, Townsend W. Hoopes and McGeorge Bundy. A fuller version is to be found in my article "The Establishment," *Foreign Policy*, Spring 1973.

A fuller account of LBJ's decision to withdraw is to be found in Lewis Chester, Godfrey Hodgson and Bruce Page, *An American Melodrama*. See also Johnson, *The Vantage Point*.

The quotation from a rioting black on upper Fourteenth Street comes from *Ten Blocks from the White House*, by Ben W. Gilbert and the staff of the Washington *Post*.

The account of Mayor Lindsay's hesitation is taken from Daniel Bell, *The Public Interest*, Fall 1968.

The fact that Walter Heller, Joseph Pechman and others organized a campaign, which was endorsed by 320 signatures, to support President Johnson's tax surcharge without mentioning Vietnam, was taken from Du Boff and Herman, *Review of Radical Political Economics*, August 1972. The counterpetition, organized by Edwin Kuh, Wassily Leontieff, Kenneth Boulding, Robert Eisner and others, was reported in the *Bulletin of the Atomic Scientists*, June 1968.

The writer in the *Atlantic Monthly* was Bruce Jackson, "The Battle of the Pentagon," January 1968.

Professor Nathan Blumberg's thoughts were published in *Montana Journalism Review*, #12, 1969, "Chicago and the Press."

CHAPTER 19

Most of the sources referred to in the notes to Chapter 7 were also used here. In addition, I used a number of books and articles that did not deal with the earlier period. Among them were Ben H. Bagdikian, *The Effete Conspiracy*; Timothy Crouse, *The Boys on the Bus*; Robert Cirino, *Don't Blame the People*; James Reston, *The Artillery of the Press*; Sanford Unger, *The Papers and The Papers*; and the four volumes of the Columbia University Survey of Broadcast Journalism, *The Politics of Broadcasting*. Of a large number of articles read in journalism reviews and general magazines, two deserve special mention here: Fred W. Friendly, "TV at the Turning Point," *Columbia Journalism Review*, Winter 1970–71; and Robert MacNeil, "Electronic Schizophrenia: Does Television Alienate Voters?" *Politeia*, Summer 1972. As in Chapter 7, I owe a great deal to a large number of interviews and conversations, and especially to a seminar that was held at the Woodrow Wilson International Center for Scholars in early 1973 to discuss some of the specific ideas in this chapter. I must also mention, as a source of general ideas, the speech by Edwin R. Bayley, dean of the Graduate School of Journalism at the University of California, on April 17, 1971, an early and robust rebuttal of the Agnew thesis.

The anecdote about a CBS News vice-president comes from the recollection of a former employee with another network. The material on the Huntley-Brinkley budget comes from an article in *Fortune*, May 1, 1969, "The Rich, Risky Business of TV News"; see also Edward Jay Epstein, *News from Nowhere*; and cf. another *Fortune* article, March 1969, on the financial problems of ABC.

On the Chicago convention of 1968 see Nathan Blumberg, "Chicago and the Press," *Montana Journalism Review*, #12, 1969: and Chester, Hodgson and Page, *An American Melodrama*.

The material on press treatment of SANE marches comes from Sanford Gottlieb, director of SANE, who was good enough to give me access to his files, including files of press clippings.

I am heavily indebted to Epstein, op. cit., and also to conversations with Edward Jay Epstein, for material relating to the change of network policy on the war: I myself interviewed three of the key executives at NBC News, and two at CBS News, and also three or four well-placed people in public television. There was a thoughtful article by Byron Shafer and Richard Larson, "Did TV create the 'social issue'?" *Columbia Journalism Review*, September/October 1972.

For Buchanan's views, see, for example, an interview by Julius Duscha,

"The White House Watch over Press and TV," New York *Times Magazine,* August 20, 1972. And cf. the speech by Clay Whitehead, Nixon-appointed director of the Office of Telecommunications Policy, in Indianapolis on December 18, 1972, in which Whitehead criticized "ideological plugola" and "elitist gossip" in the media.

On the play given to the Pentagon Papers, see Unger, *The Papers and The Papers,* which goes into this in detail. For the coverage of Watergate before the end of 1972, Ben H. Bagdikian, "The Fruits of Agnewism," *Columbia Journalism Review,* January/February 1973.

The quotations from *TV Guide* and *Editor & Publisher* were found in James Aronson, *Deadline for the Media,* pp. 8–9.

## CHAPTER 20

The analysis in this chapter is extrapolated from data collected by Gallup, Harris and other polls, and especially by the Survey Research Center at the University of Michigan. I am grateful to Albert H. Cantril, Philip Converse, and Howard Schuman for giving me tutorials on the material and possible interpretations of it. Except where I have indicated that I am citing these experts, of course, the interpretations and any errors are my own.

The material is to be found in the following books and papers: Albert H. Cantril, "The American People, Vietnam and the Presidency," a paper given at the American Political Science Association, September 1970; Cantril and Charles W. Roll, Jr., *The Hopes and Fears of the American People* (1971); Milton J. Rosenberg, Sidney Verba and Philip E. Converse, *Vietnam and the Silent Majority;* Sidney Verba, Richard A. Brody, Edwin B. Parker, Norman H. Nie, Nelson W. Polsby, Paul Ekman, and Gordon S. Black, "Public Opinion and the War in Vietnam," *American Political Science Review,* June 1967; results of a survey by Daniel Yankelovich, Inc., published in *Fortune,* January 1969; Converse and Howard Schuman, "Silent Majorities and the Vietnam War," *Scientific American,* June 1970; and Schuman, "Two Sources of Antiwar Sentiment in America," *American Journal of Sociology,* November 1972.

## CHAPTER 21

This account of the environmental, consumer, women's, Chicano and American Indian movements does not claim to go into any of those fascinating subjects in any detail. It merely seeks to relate those movements to the general historical process that is the subject of this book.

The sources used, therefore, were largely journalistic. I depended heavily on coverage in the news magazines *Time* and *Newsweek,* and in the New York *Times* and the Washington *Post.*

My understanding of the environmental movement was greatly enhanced by my colleagues at the Woodrow Wilson Center, especially John P. Milton and Athelstan Spilhaus. I found the following books helpful: Rachel Carson, *Silent Spring*; Barry Commoner, *Science and Survival* and *The Closing Circle*; René Dubos, *Reason Awake*; Paul Ehrlich, *The Population Bomb* and *Population, Resources and Environment*; Frank Graham, Jr., *Since Silent Spring*; James Ridgeway, *The Politics of Ecology*. For robust skepticism about the pessimism of these writers, I found John Maddox, *The Doomsday Syndrome*, refreshing.

On the consumer movement: a series of articles on Ralph Nader in *Time* magazine; for critical views of him, *Newsweek*, "Spread Too Thin," April 14, 1972; an interview with Nader in the Washington *Post*, December 5, 1971; for biography, Charles McCarry, *Citizen Nader*; Robert F. Buckthorn, *Nader, the People's Lawyer*; for two good short assessments: Robert Hargreaves, *Superpower*; William Manchester, *The Glory and the Dream*. On Campaign GM: Emma Rothschild, *Paradise Lost*.

On the black movement in its later, separatist phase—the one imitated by radical feminists, Chicanos, etc.—I learned a great deal from Stokely Carmichael and Charles V. Hamilton, *Black Power*. See also, in a voluminous literature, Tom Milstein, "A Perspective on the Panthers," *Commentary Report*, 1970; Tom Wolfe, "Radical Chic," *New York*, June 8, 1970; Paul Feldman, "The Pathos of Black Power," *Dissent*, January–February 1967. Three pinnacles of black separatist rhetoric are Bobby Seale, *Seize the Time*; Eldridge Cleaver, *Soul on Ice*; and George Jackson, *Soledad Brother*. A sympathetic but perceptive journalistic account of the Black Panthers is Gilbert Moore, *A Special Rage*.

The classics of the women's movement, and it is very largely a movement grounded in literature, are Simone de Beauvoir, *The Second Sex*; Betty Friedan, *The Feminine Mystique*; Kate Millett, *Sexual Politics*; Germaine Greer, *The Female Eunuch*; Caroline Bird, *Born Female*. Two statements of the "radical feminist" position are Shulamith Firestone, *The Dialectic of Sex*; and Juliet Mitchell, *Woman's Estate*. Ella Levin and Judith Hole, *Rebirth of Feminism*, is a historical account, and two good magazine articles on the history of the movement are Martha Lear, "The Second Feminist Wave," New York *Times Magazine*, March 10, 1968, and Marlene Dixon, "The Rise of Women's Liberation," *Ramparts*, December 1969. Betty Friedan gave her own account of the origins of the National Organization for Women and other episodes in the history of the movement in "Up from the Kitchen Floor," New York *Times Magazine*, March 4, 1973. Convenient collections of materials are *Masculine/Feminine*, edited by Theodore and Betty Roszak; and *Woman in a Sexist Society*, edited by Vivian Gornick and Barbara L. Moran. An interesting skeptical view is that of Joan Didion, "The Women's Movement," New York *Times Book Review*, July 30, 1972.

I found an excellent collection of materials on the American Indian movement in *Red Power*, edited by Alvin M. Josephy, Jr. A masterly review of the literature on the Chicano movement is by John Womack, Jr., "The Chicanos," a special supplement to *The New York Review of Books*. On Reies Tijerina, I read Richard Gardner, *Grito: On Chavez*, Joan London and Henry Anderson Crowell, *So Shall Ye Reap*.

## CHAPTER 22

For the 1964 and 1968 election results, I relied on *Congressional Quarterly*. See also L. Chester, G. Hodgson and B. Page, *An American Melodrama*. The concept of the New Politics coalition was ably put forward in Frederick G. Dutton, *Changing Sources of Power*; see also Penn Kimball, *Robert Kennedy and the New Politics*; James M. Perry, *The New Politics* (which analyzes the new politics, however, far more in terms of the new technology of polling, etc.); and Jack Newfield and Jeff Greenfield, *A Populist Manifesto*. A harsh account of the reality of the Democratic Party's financial and business background is G. William Domhoff, *Fat Cats and Democrats*. John S. Saloma and Frederick H. Sontag, *Parties*, is an essentially optimistic account of the possibility of renovating the party system without fundamental realignment. David S. Broder, *The Party's Over*, is a sound but conventional account of the troubles of the existing party system. The Robert C. Wood speech was brought to my attention by Elizabeth Midgley of CBS, and a text was obtained from the Department of HEW.

On the Ocean Hill-Brownsville affair, I had some background, as I made a film in the neighborhood for British TV late in 1967. I found the volume *Confrontation at Ocean Hill-Brownsville*, edited by Maurice R. Berube and Marilyn Gittell, a great help. This contains the text of official and semiofficial reports, such as the Rivers, Niemeyer, Botein and Bundy reports, the texts of statements by the Board of Education and the union, etc., as well as articles by Nat Hentoff, Dwight Macdonald, Michael Harrington, Jason Epstein, and other writers, including the *Commentary* article, which I quoted, by Maurice J. Goldbloom.

An expanded version of the section on Gary appeared in the Washington *Post* as "Gary: Epitaph for a Model City," by Godfrey Hodgson and George Crile, on March 4, 1973. The article provoked an attack by James O. Gibson and Msgr. Geno Baroni, Washington *Post*, March 18, 1973, accusing us of "crisis rhetoric." In fact, however, the article was based squarely on the views of Mayor Hatcher and several key members of his administration, given to us in interviews. My research was greatly helped by Crile, who was familiar with the city, having worked for the local newspaper.

Besides the Reichley article in *Fortune* cited, an excellent analysis of Nixon's 1972 strategy is by Neal R. Peirce, *National Journal*, September 23, 1972. On Nixon's financial backing, see (for example) Morton Mintz, "Winners Still Get Money," Washington *Post*, February 4, 1973; and Ben Franklin, "Election Contributions Pose Awkward Questions for Nixon," New York *Times*, January 7, 1973. Just how awkward those questions became is well described in S. Aris, L. Chester, S. Fay and W. Shawcross, *Watergate*.

On Nixon as a "Tory man with liberal measures," I have talked to Daniel P. Moynihan. And see Evans and Novak, *Nixon in the White House*; Daniel P. Moynihan, *The Politics of a Guaranteed Income*; Leon Panetta and Peter Gall, *Bring Us Together*, as well as numerous columns, especially those by John Osborne in *The New Republic*.

The survey quoted on McGovern's performance was a private poll commissioned from Albert H. Cantril and Charles W. Roll by Jerry Wurf, president of the American Federation of State, County and Municipal Employees. The story of McGovern and "amnesty, abortion and pot" is told in Richard Dougherty, *Goodbye, Mr. Christian*, an attractive personal account of the McGovern campaign by the candidate's press secretary. The quotation from the 1968 Nixon campaign manual comes from an article by Richard Reeves for *New York* early in 1972, "Nixon's Secret Strategy." The analysis of the 1972 election returns was based on "The 1972 Special Election Report," *Congressional Quarterly*, October 7, 1972; Neal R. Peirce, "Building the 'New Majority' Bloc by Bloc," *National Journal*, November 11, 1972, which quoted the CBS News Voter Survey; and Michael Barone, "The Gains of Landslide Losers," Washington *Post*, April 1, 1973.

## CHAPTER 23

For the section on the Detroit riot of 1967, why it really happened, and why there had been no riot there since, I started with four basic sources; the *Report of the National Advisory Commission on Civil Disorders* ("the Kerner Report"), which deals largely with Detroit; the files of the Detroit newspapers, in particular those of the Detroit *News*, which I studied thoroughly; a best-selling book, John Hersey, *The Algiers Motel Incident*; and the script of NBC's documentary, made by Fred Freed with the help of Daniel Patrick Moynihan, "Summer '67: What We Learned," transmitted September 15, 1967, which deals with the Detroit riot.

Before going to Detroit I had long conversations with Dr. Edward C. Lurie at the University of Delaware, formerly of Wayne State University in Detroit, who not only helped me with a conceptual framework and with many introductions to Detroiters concerned with the questions that interested me, but also gave me access to his own research material, prepared for the Kerner Commission.

In Detroit I spent about a month in the spring of 1973 in intensive interviewing. Of the many people who helped me, I must single out, at the risk of being invidious, Peter Clarke and Paul Poorman, the publisher and editor, respectively, of the Detroit *News*; Norman Drachler, former school superintendent, and C. L. Golightly, president of the school board; the economist Karl Gregory; Leonard P. Doss, of New Detroit; Irving Rubin, at the Ford Motor Company; and Judge George W. Crockett. Two Detroit *News* publications were most helpful: a special report, "A Time of Tragedy," published August 11, 1967; and a series of articles that began on February 6, 1972, reprinted in booklet form as *The Voice of Detroit's Blacks*. My information on STRESS came from the files of the Detroit *News* and Detroit *Free Press*; on drugs and crime, from the same sources and also from the complaint filed by Judge Crockett in Recorder's Court on February 20, 1973.

On the question of black income: The article by Richard Scammon and Ben J. Wattenberg referred to was "Black Progress and Liberal Rhetoric" *Commentary*, April 1973. Cf. Wattenberg, *The Real America*. The Moynihan article mentioned was "The Schism in Black America," *The Public Interest*, July 1967, republished as "The Deepening Schism," in *Coping*. Herbert Hill's views were made known to me in two interviews in February and April 1973 and also in many of his published writings, notably a paper, "Racism and Organized Labor," in *New School Bulletin*, February 8, 1971. See also Julius Jacobson (ed.), *The Negro and the American Labor Movement*, which contains a good rundown of recent legal decisions affecting racial discrimination in employment by Robert L. Carter and Maria L. Marcus (recent, that is, at the time of publication, in 1968) and "two views" of organized labor's racial attitudes and practices by Hill and Gus Tyler. Census data were taken from Census Bureau publications, especially from *The Social and Economic Status of the Black Population in the United States* 1973.

The section on education and equality was based on research done for an article: Godfrey Hodgson, "Do Schools Make a Difference?" *Atlantic Monthly*, March 1973. For that article I interviewed a number of those involved in the controversy about education and equality, especially those in Cambridge, Massachusetts, including: Marshall S. Smith, Christopher Jencks, Daniel P. Moynihan, and Thomas F. Pettigrew. The findings of the Coleman report were summarized by Coleman himself in *The Public Interest*, Summer 1966, and Coleman discussed some implications in *The Public Interest*, Fall 1967. An early statement of Jencks's view is "What Color is IQ? Intelligence and Race," *The New Republic*, September 13, 1969. Richard Herrnstein summed up the state of work on IQ in "IQ," *Atlantic Monthly*, September 1971. The Armor paper on busing is David J. Armor, "The Evidence on Busing," *The Public Interest*, Summer 1972. The same issue contained another relevant paper, Lester C. Thurow, "Education and economic equality." Critiques of Armor's paper were contained in a letter from Professor Pettigrew to the New York *Times*, published August 5, 1972, and in a paper, "A Critique of 'The Evidence on Busing,'" by Pettigrew, Clarence Normand, Elizabeth L. Useem, and Marshall S. Smith, of which I have a copy of the typescript. Other papers used include: David K. Cohen, "Does IQ Matter?" *Commentary*, April 1972; Daniel P. Moynihan, "Equalizing education: in whose benefit?" *The Public Interest*, Fall 1972; Arthur Jensen, "How Can We Boost IQ and Scholastic Achievement?" *Harvard Educational Review*, Winter 1969; Noam Chomsky, review of B. F. Skinner, *Beyond Freedom and Dignity*, *The New York Review of Books*, December 30, 1971; Irwin Katz and Charles Greenbaum, "Effects of Anxiety, Threat and Racial Environment on Task Performance of Negro College Students," *Journal of Abnormal and Social Psychology*; Vol. 66, No. 6

(1963). I also had the help of a paper, then unpublished, by Professor Leon J. Kamin of Princeton, on "Heredity, Intelligence, Politics and Psychology." Three books, among them, contain much of the debate: Frederick Mosteller and Daniel P. Moynihan (editors), *On Equality of Educational Opportunity*; C. Jencks and others, *Inequality*; and Donald M. Levine and Mary Jo Bane (editors), *The "Inequality" Controversy: Schooling and Distributive Justice*.

On the broader implications of the theoretical debate for educators and politicians, I was put on several promising scents in interviews with J. Harold Flannery, of the Harvard Center for Law and Education; Louis Lucas, the Memphis attorney; Stanley Pottinger, of the Office of Civil Rights at HEW; Norman Drachler, former school superintendent of Detroit; and Congressman John Brademas (Dem.-Ind.).

The Nixon administration's position was defined in a statement issued by the White House on March 17, 1972. The position of the federal courts evolved through, among other decisions, those in *Swann* v. *Charlotte-Mecklenburg Board of Education et al.*; *Northcross* v. *Memphis*; *Monroe* v. *Jackson, Tenn.*; *Bradley* v. *Milliken* (Detroit); *San Antonio School District* v. *Rodriguez*; and others. Leading cases bearing on education and equality are brought together in convenient form in a compendium published by the Select Committee of the U. S. Senate on Equal Educational Opportunity, *Selected Court Decisions Relating to Equal Educational Opportunity*, 1972. Another convenient summary is *Education for a Nation*, published in 1972 by Congressional Quarterly, Inc. Two important articles, one giving an anti-, the other not so much a pro- as an anti-anti-busing view, are Nathan Glazer, "Is Busing Necessary?" *Commentary*, 1972; and I. F. Stone, "Moving the Constitution to the Back of the Bus," *The New York Review of Books*, April 20, 1972. The reports in the Washington *Post* were consistently useful both on public opinion and Administration policy, especially three reports on public reactions to busing, in Charlotte, North Carolina, Pontiac, Michigan, and Prince Georges County, Maryland, which appeared on November 20–22, 1972.

The article referred to is C. Vann Woodward, "What Happened to the Civil Rights Movement?" *Harper's Magazine*, January 1967.

CHAPTER 24

The quotation from Carl Kayzen comes from an article in *Life*, June 8, 1967, by Theodore H. White, "In the halls of power." The quotation from White himself comes from *The Making of the President 1972*. That from Tom Wolfe comes from *The Electric Kool-Aid Acid Test*.

The quotation about a "cure for death" comes from an interview with Jack Geiger, of SUNY, Stony Brook. On the "conquest" of disease, see my article in *Atlantic Monthly*, October 1973; Stephen P. Strickland, *Politics, Science, and Dread Disease*; Elizabeth B. Drew, "The Health Syndicate," *Atlantic Monthly*, December 1967.

The quotation from Leslie Fiedler comes from an essay written in 1952, "Our Country and Our Culture," which first appeared in *Partisan Review*, May–June 1952.

On the history of DDT, see Rachel Carson, *Silent Spring*; and Frank Graham, Jr., *After Silent Spring*.

Comparative figures for average wages in industrial countries are published by OECD. International wage comparisons are hazardous, not least because of shifting exchange rates. Cf. I. B. Kravis, Z. Kenessey, Alan Heston, and Robert Summers, *A System of International Comparisons for Gross Product and Purchasing Power*. Johns Hopkins University Press.

Riesman and Roosa, in interviews, both spontaneously raised the parallel between the pattern of the U.S. economy and that of the British economy in the late-nineteenth and early-twentieth century age of imperialism.

For the true rate of unemployment, see Andrew Levison, *The Working Class Majority*; and A. H. Raskin, "Unemployment—6% Is Only the Tip of the Iceberg," New York *Times*, June 25, 1972. The quotation from Peter F. Drucker comes from F. L. Allen, *The Big Change*.

For the history of the "Turner thesis," I found a convenient collection of materials in D. C. Heath's Problems in American Civilization series, *The Turner Thesis*. The history of the idea of a New Frontier is to be traced through the books cited; the Walter Prescott Webb article appeared in *Harper's Magazine*; "Ended: 400 Year Boom, Reflections on the Age of the Frontier," October 1951. The quotation of Otto Eckstein refers to remarks reported in the *Proceedings of a Symposium on Business-Government Relations* held by the American Bankers Association, 1966.

The remark of Dr. Arthur Burns about inflation was reported in the New York *Times*, August 1974. The Hudson Institute survey was published as *The Future of the Corporation*.

The section on the achievements and failures of the Great Society is obviously based on a long interview with Dr. Wilbur J. Cohen. Less obviously, it also draws on long interviews with Professors Irving Kristol, Daniel Patrick Moynihan, and David Riesman.

My ideas were also influenced by essays by Moynihan and Kristol, particularly those contained in Kristol, *On the Democratic Idea in America*; and Moynihan, *Coping*; and by numerous articles in *The Public Interest*, of which both Kristol and Moynihan are on the editorial board. See especially Lance Liebman, *The Public Interest*, Winter 1974; Aaron Wildavsky, "The Empty Head Blues," *The Public Interest*, Eli Ginzberg and Robert Solow, "The Great Society," *The Public Interest*, Winter 1974. See also Charles L. Schultze and others, *Setting National Priorities: the 1973 Budget*. The analysis of Medicare follows that in my article in the *Atlantic Monthly*, October 1973, "The Politics of American Health Care." The analogy with Positivism was suggested by a passage in Alvin W. Gouldner, *The Coming Crisis of Western Sociology*.

The analysis of the myth of the abolition of class was influenced by many, many conversations, especially with Marcus Raskin of the Institute for Policy

Studies; Msgr. Baroni of the Center for Urban Ethnic Studies; Christopher Jencks of Harvard University; Frank Wallich of the UAW; Jerry Wurf of AFSCME; and David Riesman. Long after I had started writing, the book cited above by Andrew Levison, *The Working Class Majority*, came into my hands, and I found in it detailed explanations of how several of the illusions that had so long baffled me had become so widespread. It is to that book that I owe the explanation of the statistical manipulation on which the myth of the middle-class majority is based.

The quotation from Daniel Bell comes from *The End of Ideology*. (Since I have been severe on some of the views held by Professor Bell in the 1950s, it is only fair to pay tribute to the brilliance of an essay in which he recants some of those views, "The End of American Exceptionalism," *The Public Interest*, Fall 1975.) The Hofstadter quotation is taken from *The Paranoid Style in American Politics*. The Walter Heller quotation comes from *New Dimensions of Political Economy*.

On Tom Watson, the classic book is C. Vann Woodward, *Tom Watson; Agrarian Rebel*. The books cited by Cash and Key are Wilbur J. Cash, *The Mind of the South*; and V. O. Key, Jr., *Southern Politics in State and Nation*. Michael Novak's remark was found in an essay, "New Ethnic Politics Versus Old Ethnic Politics," in Michael Wenk, S. M. Tomasi and Geno Baroni (editors), *Pieces of a Dream*.

George McGovern's bemusement at his working-class critics' attitude to inheritance taxation is quoted from Richard Dougherty, *Goodbye, Mr. Christian*.

**CHAPTER 25**

I owe the idea "American culture, . . . unlike the cultures of Europe, is essentially political" to a girl student, whose name I never discovered, in a seminar at the World Affairs Conference held by the University of Colorado in the spring of 1972. What she actually said, according to my notes, was: "Surely American national identity is defined by politics, where national identity in Europe is defined in cultural terms." The phrase "the religion of healthy-mindedness" is the title of a chapter in William James, *The Varieties of Religious Experience*. "The American, this new man," was a coining of Walt Whitman.

The account of the shoot-out in New Orleans, and of Louis Sirgo's speech, were both published in the Washington *Post*. So was the interview with Jeb Stuart Magruder, whose conversation with William Sloane Coffin was published in *Harper's Magazine*. Daniel Patrick Moynihan's talk at Andover Academy was published in the collection of his essays entitled *Coping*. Elliott Richardson's remarks were quoted in Tad Szulc, *Innocents at Home*. The Fiedler reference is to the same essay quoted above, "Our Country and Our Culture," *Partisan Review*, May–June 1951. The exact words of Thomas Jefferson, as so often, are worth quoting in full: "So we have gone on, and so we will go on, puzzled and prospering beyond example in the history of man." They are the last words of Daniel J. Boorstin, *The Lost World of Thomas Jefferson*, and were originally written to John Adams, January 21, 1812 (Jefferson, *Writings*, ed. A. A. Liscomb and Albert Ellery Bergh, XIII, p. 123).

# INDEX

Kennedy indicates John F. Kennedy

Pentagon, 132, 304, 363; lobby, 131; March on, 325

Pentagon Papers, 97, 125, 177, 237, 238, 242; media, 380–81

Percy, Charles, 69

Periodicals, 93, 94, 112, 127, 141, 172, 263, 265, 275, 285, 338, 363, 364, 388, 389, 401, 422, 469, 494. *See under* name

Perls, Dr. Fritz, 330

Peters, A. D., *xii*

Pettigrew, Thomas, 449–50, 455, 456

Philadelphia, 57

Philippines, 32

Phillips, Kevin, 422, 427; *The Emerging Republican Majority*, 414–15

Philosophy, 286, 287, 292, 300; of abundance, 51–52; of expectation, 34, 37–38, 39, 42, 463 ff.; New Deal, 402; political, 25, 51–52, 78, 379

Pickett, Clarence, 276

Pierce, Franklin, 104

Pinchot, Gifford, 402

Pittsburgh, 57

*Playboy*, 341

*Plessy* v. *Ferguson*, 461

Poets (poetry), 322, 323, 329, 344, 401

Poland, 26, 29

Police, 371 ff., 375, 495

Political economy (economists), 78. *See* Keynes

Political parties: campaigns: (1960), 68, 73–74, 153 (1968), 371; conventions: (1964), 213 ff., Democratic (1968), 370, 371, 426 (1972), 366, 489; Democratic Party, 46–47, 50, 88–89, 116, 201, 213, 412; elections: (1972), 380, 392, 423, 427, balance of power, 88, vote, 412, 427–28; Republican Party, 46, 116, 414; Socialist Party, 195

Political philosophy, 25, 51–52, 78, 379

Political science (scientists), 45, 80, 95, 97, 127, 301, 393

Politics, 51, 74, 87, 120, 122, 139, 164, 247, 379, 402, 407; class, 478 ff., 484; consensus, 385; Establishment: Fundamentalists, 127 ff., military, 132; international, 18, 24, 233; Left: defined, 89–90, tradition, 275 ff.; New Left: evolution, 278 ff., 301, manifesto, 278–80, 282; liberals, 89–90, 414, shift from (*see* New Majority); national morality, 368; "New," 363; New Majority, 411–28; peace issue, 277; polarization, 366, 484; political system, 490; populists, 415, 421, 422; post-affluence, 226 ff.; poverty, 275; presidential, 357 (*see* Presidency, the); press, 374; racial, 416; southern, 485–86; urban, 486–87

Pollution, 327, 402–3, 405, 408–9, 411, 471

Poole, Elijah, 202. *See* Muhammed, Elijah

Population, 259, 314, 406, 471; Commission on Growth, 403

Pornography, 348–49

Porter, Katherine Anne, 94

Positivists, 476–78

Potomac Associates, 455, 486

Potomac Institute, 194, 195

Potter, David: *People of Plenty*, 86

Potter, Paul, 281

Pound, Ezra, 45

Poverty, 55–56, 172–73, 181, 275, 363, 364, 497; "cycle," 173; politics, 275; War on, 172 ff., 270–72, 416, 474, planners, 263

Power, 102; balance of, 69, 88; Establishment (British), 112; of fashion, 329; frustrations, 75; moral basis, 276; Nietzsche, 309; patterns, 408; of private money, 417; road to, 115; romance, 359; structure, 298; of TV, 356, 378; vacuum, 120. *See under* Presidency

## About the Author

GODFREY HODGSON studied at Oxford in England, and at the University of Pennsylvania in the United States. He has been head of the Foreign Desk at the *London Sunday Times*, Washington Correspondent for the Sunday *Observer*, and a member of the Insight Team of the *Sunday Times*. He is well known as a TV reporter and commentator in Great Britain, where he now lives. Mr. Hodgson is co-author of *An American Melodrama* and of *Do You Sincerely Want to Be Rich?*